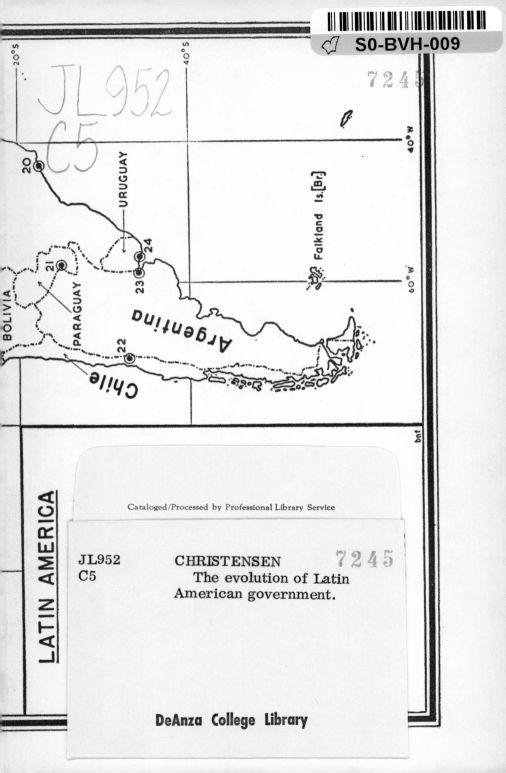

The Evolution of
Latin American Government

———————————— *The*

LATIN

Asher N. Christensen

Professor of Political Science
University of Minnesota

Henry Holt and Company

New York

Evolution of ——

AMERICAN GOVERN- MENT

A Book of Readings

To Allison:
Whose queries
initiated the work on this book

Preface

*T*HE North American who wishes to be informed on the political evolution and organization of Latin America now has access to many sources of information. Not only has there been a remarkable increase in the number of newspaper and magazine articles — several of them exceptionally well done — and a corresponding increase in radio and motion picture " documentaries," but we also have experienced a notable expansion of the number of good general reference and text books, and excellent monographic studies dealing with specific institutions or countries.

These latter studies, when they refer to government in Latin America, for the most part tend to be constitutional and institutional in their approach. Anyone familiar with the field at once perceives why his colleagues, when they write about the political institutions of Latin America, emphasize the constitutional nature of government rather than its political evolution, structure, and operation. Despite the great value of these studies they leave many questions unanswered.

It is well known that the actual operation of government in Latin America is often far removed from constitutional clauses and stipulations. That this is also true of the practice of politics and government in the United States is readily apparent. As an illustration one need only compare what our Constitution says about the election of the President with the manner in which we actually choose him. We in the United States know *why* the political practices have modified, or in some cases have completely altered, the meaning and intent of the written Constitution, and hence, to us, the gulf between the constitutional word and its political idiomatic usage is perfectly logical and sensible.

The facts or the crude data referring to government in Latin America are fairly well known. The entire area is characterized by the already-mentioned hiatus between the Constitution and governmental organization; by strong and in many cases continuing executives with correspondingly weak legislative and judicial departments; by a political turbulence unmatched elsewhere in the contemporary world; by revolutions that seem to effect little basic change in either the political or economic *status quo;* by federal systems that are in fact unitary; and by the absence of local self-rule.

Two principal objectives were constantly in mind in the planning and preparation of this book of materials on the problem and nature of government in Latin America. It was felt that a book of this kind should attempt to explain *why* governments in that area — be they those of Argentina or El Salvador, Brazil or Bolivia — all show these same common characteristics. What factors have conditioned Latin American political organization so that one encounters, almost everywhere, and at any time, strong executives, weak congresses and courts, and little or no local home-rule? In what ways have geography and climate, colonial history and institutions, and economic organization and problems set the mold? Are contemporary factors of any significance in changing the patterns outlined by the mold of the past?

A second goal might be indicated by this query: What are the directions in which government in present-day Latin America is traveling? Are the revolutions or political upheavals of the present time to be written off as " just another Latin American revolution " or do they presage really basic changes in the location, transfer, and use of political power? The editor of this book believes that fundamental and highly significant new trends are discernable, shifts which are evidenced by changes in the social content of the newer constitutions, by realignments in the political party pattern, by the broadening base of government even in the dictator countries, and, above all, by the rapidly expanding functions of government in Central and South America and in the Caribbean. The remarkable expansion of such activities as education and public health, and the interest of governments in economic diversification are trenchant with the potentiality of political change.

It is difficult, if not impossible, to secure the desired " balance " in a book of this type. Limitations of space preclude an equal consideration of each of the twenty republics; arbitrary decisions have to be made. In general, an attempt was made to select materials which have an America-wide application. If these could not be found, priority was given to articles that referred to countries whose political or economic significance made it imperative that they be dealt with. Above all, the decision as to the inclusion or exclusion of any essay or article was based on how well it explained the *why* of the institutions or political practices with which it was concerned. The reader will instantly note that none of the articles is taken from Latin American sources, although many of them were written by Latin Americans. The principal explanation of this is found in the fact that, up to now, the field of " political science " is almost undeveloped in Latin American universities. There are relatively few journals devoted to a scholarly examination of the nature of government or to an analysis of the political institutions of the area. When one turns to the semipopular magazines one finds that cold dispassionate objectivity is not one of their major virtues at least in so far as political writing is concerned.

It is not possible here to record, and consequently to thank, all those who have aided in the preparation of this book. Many influenced its content without realizing it. Dr. Josué Gollán, (h), former Rector of the *Universidad Nacional del Litoral,* greatly encouraged me by his discerning comments on the need for such a book. My students, at the University of Minnesota and at the Universities in Santa Fé and Caracas, shaped the final volume by their persistent, understanding, and shrewd observations and questions. Some of my co-workers and colleagues must be named. The advice and counsel of Professor William Anderson was always available and frequently used. Professor Emilio C. Le Fort listened patiently to the woes of an editor, and made many valuable criticisms and suggestions based upon his wide knowledge and understanding of both Americas. Professional co-workers in the Latin American field at other universities, among them J. Lloyd Mecham, Russell H. Fitzgibbon, and William S. Stokes, encouraged me by their interest in the project. A former student, Janet McCart Sigford, prepared an annotated preliminary list of periodical articles which proved to be of great assistance in the final assembling of the book. My wife not only initiated the whole venture by her continuing interest in why Latin American government differs so markedly from that of the United States, and kept it moving along when the pace tended to slacken, but she also prepared an enormous and extremely valuable bibliographical file. She also now more clearly appreciates the full meaning of the term " galley slave."

Finally, I wish to record my appreciation of the courtesy and co-operation that I have received from the publishers of the books and the editors of the journals and magazines from which the final selections for this book were taken, and to thank again the authors for allowing me to place their writings in this collection.

Despite all the help that I have received, I alone am responsible for the selection of materials that were finally chosen; any errors of omission or commission are mine. It is my sincere hope that even if the two goals of this book are not reached, or even approximated, the reader will more clearly see the enormous and complicated problems of government in Latin America.

Minneapolis, Minn.   A. N. C.
May 31, 1951

Contents

xi

PART ONE

The Heritage of the Past

CHAPTER 1

— The Gap — in Our Knowledge

No. 1 [Shortly after the close of World War I the late Doctor L. S. Rowe observed that " students of political science in the United States have usually taken it for granted that the methods of scientific investigation applicable to the highly developed political systems of England and continental Europe are inapplicable to the republics of Latin America. In fact, there seems to be a widespread belief that the term ' political system ' is applied to Latin America by courtesy but that a more exact designation would be dictatorship tempered by revolution."

In the quarter of a century that has elapsed since Doctor Rowe published his careful, discerning, and pioneering study, *The Federal System of the Argentine Republic,* and especially in the last ten years, American students of government have turned their attention to the problem of government in the vast regions that lie to the south of us. An examination of the bibliographies and professional journals reveals an increasing number of books, monographs, articles, and essays whose concern is the organization and operation of political institutions in Latin America. But, even after fifteen years of what may have been a too-much-emphasized and too-consciously-directed program of " know (and hence love) thy neighbors who live south of the Rio Grande," much of what Doctor Rowe wrote a generation ago still remains true.

Political science departments of colleges and universities in the United States annually graduate a large number of students who have been given some instruction in the governmental organization and political problems of the European states, large and small, the Asiatic nations, and the states of the Near East. These students are conversant with the governmental organizations of these areas and the problems with which those governments must deal. They can, and do, speak intelligently with reference to the factors which have caused the democratically organized states to function well here, indifferently there, or to fail completely elsewhere. However, if one questions them about analogous developments, trends, or conditioning factors in Argentina or Uruguay, Venezuela or Brazil, as I have frequently, one encounters a significant lack of basic knowledge.

The most common rejoinder seems to be that Latin America is an area marked by a high degree of political volatility — that bullets and not ballots determine succession to the places of power. It is certainly true that the Latin American states have exhibited, and still show, a marked tendency to change régimes (if and when they are changed) by recourse to violence. No area of the world has written — and abandoned — as many constitutions. Few, if any, regions have shown such a consistent tendency to rely upon the leader, the man on horseback.

Our knowledge of governmental processes is, it must be admitted, incomplete if it is limited to such observations as have just been noted. They, it might be argued, are but symptoms, and give us little insight into the state of health of the body politic. Unless we know *why* the area has been so constantly marked by violence and revolution; *why* legislatures are weak and distrusted; *why,* despite literally scores of constitutional clauses limiting the power of executives, the Latin American president is the center of political gravity in every republic; *why* idealistically conceived and beautifully written constitutions appear in an almost bewildering succession — we are uninformed on the government and politics of the area.

Students of government in the United States are partly responsible for the gap in our knowledge of the affairs of state in Latin America. Until recently the region has not interested them as it has the historian, the economist, the anthropologist, and the sociologist. Many reasons explain this indifference. Cultural dissimilarity, distance, language barriers, and lack of good communications have made it more difficult for them to use the same techniques of study and analysis in Latin America that they have applied to the study of European governments for well over a half century.

The Latin American scholars must also share in this responsibility. Political science, as a field of learning, is a discipline that has barely emerged in but a handful of Latin American universities, and it is still but an adjunct of training in the law. Monographs or studies in the field which we would label by the term " political science " are either for the most part evaluations of the political ideas of the pro-consuls, legalistic studies of the administrative organization of some major department of government (written principally for lawyers), or the all-too-numerous enthusiastic defenses of — or vitriolic attacks upon — the régime of some new " liberator " (or tyrant or usurper, as the case may be). *Personalismo* is not only a feature of Latin American politics; it also characterizes the study of government in the other American republics.

Owing to this lack of scientific and objective political studies, the American student who interests himself in the Latin American field can make a twofold contribution. He can, in the first place, enlarge the horizons of our information about the organization and work of *government* in an area in which we are, as yet, insufficiently informed. He can also influence the emergence and development of the whole study of politics in Latin America.

We lack not only formal training in the Latin American field, but in addition the primary media of mass communication — the press, radio, and the motion picture — usually neglect the region or, when they do turn their attention to it, frequently so emphasize the picturesque details as to distort the true picture. With reference to the press, Mr. H. B. Murkland, a practicing journalist, notes in the following article the results of this failure of the press to give Latin America its merited place in the news, and he suggests a program which might be followed. He, too, is much concerned over the gap in our knowledge.]

Editors' Blind Spot*

by HARRY B. MURKLAND

*F*OR years Latin Americans have complained about the way the United States press handles Latin American news. Why, they ask, is so little news of their countries published in North American newspapers? Why is the news that finds its way into print mostly about catastrophes, revolutions, and disorders while important political, economic, social, and cultural developments are ignored?

* Harry B. Murkland, "Editors' Blind Spot," *Américas* (May, 1949), Vol. 1, No. 3, pp. 12–14 ff. Reprinted by permission of *Américas,* a monthly magazine published by the Pan American Union in English, Spanish, and Portuguese.

There can be little argument about the justice of these complaints. Here are twenty sovereign nations, several of them larger than most European countries, one (Brazil) larger than the continental United States. They have a total population of about 140,000,000. Economically and strategically they are vitally important. Last year [1948], for example, Latin America bought 25.1 percent of United States exports and, with Canada, furnished 58 percent of United States imports. Yet, aside from the rumbas and revolutions, few North American newspaper readers have the faintest idea what is going on south of the border or understand the significance of the scraps of information that do filter through.

Brazil, for example, is one of the United States' most dependable friends in an undependable world. Because of its size, situation, and potential wealth, it is also one of the most valuable. In 1948 Brazil surpassed Great Britain in value of trade with the United States; it is now second only to Canada as a trading partner of Uncle Sam. Brazilian-United States trade is approximately twice that of the United States and France. Yet in the period June-July-August 1948, *The New York Times,* which probably has the most effective Latin American news coverage of any North American paper, gave only 125 column inches to news of Brazil, and most of this was odds and ends of trade information on the back business pages. In the same three months, the *New York Herald Tribune,* which also does better by Latin America than most United States dailies, had only 51 column inches to spare for Brazil.

Obviously, Latin American happenings will never be covered as closely as the life-and-death news of Europe and the Near and Far East. Certainly they deserve more and better attention than they are getting.

Assuming general agreement that Latin America is neglected in the news pages of the North American press, what is the reason? Is it because it is difficult to get constructive Latin American news? Or are United States readers just not interested in that part of the world?

There is no lack of Latin American news for the North American editor who wants it. Few newspapers can afford to maintain their own correspondents in Latin America. But the three major wire services are all busy there. The United Press has seventeen bureaus in Latin America, about four hundred full-time employees, and an even larger number of " stringers," who are paid according to the stories they write. The Associated Press has correspondents in every capital of the southern continent and stringers in many other cities. International News Service has about twenty-five correspondents scattered over South and Central America. Together, UP, AP, and INS send a minimum of approximately 15,000 words from Latin America to the United States every day: enough to fill two standard-size newspaper pages.

The news is available. Why, then, does most of it end up in the editor's wastebasket? The usual answer is lack of reader interest. It is pretty difficult to prove this, one way or the other. On the basis of my own experience, I believe there is a good deal more reader interest than most editors realize. But clearly there is no irresistible public demand for more news of Latin America.

The reasons for this go far back of the press. Historically, the foreign relations of the United States run east and west rather than south and north. Most of the people of this country are of European origin and such foreign ties as they have are with Europe. Our political and cultural roots are all in Europe. We were brought up on European history and English literature. Those of us who took any interest in languages started almost automatically with French. When there was a chance to travel, we tripped to London, Paris, Budapest, and Vienna. We have lived in a European world all our lives.

This means that, consciously or unconsciously, we have acquired a considerable background knowledge of Europe and European affairs. We know roughly what European peoples are like, how they live, how their governments operate. European names and places are at least vaguely familiar. Englishmen, Frenchmen, Germans, Italians, and North Americans, in a sense, speak and understand the same language.

North Americans and Latin Americans have no such common denominator. Except in the big cities and the borderlands of the Southwest, few United States citizens trace their origins to Latin America. It is only in recent years that Spanish has become popular with North American language students. Latin American studies are a comparatively new field in our colleges and universities, and, with rare exceptions, Latin America is still ignored in high schools. The result is abysmal ignorance.

George Gallup proved that two years ago. His pollsters gave thousands of persons from coast to coast an outline map of South America and asked them to identify eight countries: Ecuador, Colombia, Argentina, Peru, Brazil, Paraguay, Chile, and Bolivia. The college-trained person could identify four of the eight; the high school graduate found fewer than three. The average man scored 2.9, the average woman 2.6. Less than half could identify Argentina; only six out of ten recognized Brazil; and fewer than two out of ten knew Colombia and Ecuador when they saw them on the map. It is unlikely that people who don't know where a country is will know much about its institutions, politics, or leaders. To the average North American, Latin America is *terra incognita*. That, basically, is why he is not very much interested in it.

This, of course, is not the fault of the newspapers. Nor is it reasonable to expect them to make up for the accidents of history and the deficiencies of our educational systems. But by using a little editorial imagination they might adapt themselves to these accidents and deficiencies, and make Latin American news more interesting and more meaningful to their readers.

It seems to me that the basic reason for the paucity of serious Latin American news in our papers and for the lack of reader interest that is both the cause and the result of that paucity, is simply the presentation. The information is presented just like European news and that, under the circumstances, is wrong.

When the average North American newspaper reader reads a dispatch from Paris, for example, he puts behind it all he has learned about French politics in school, from the radio, from lectures, magazines, and general conversation, and he comes up with something of an idea of what it's all about. He probably knows that France has a multiplicity of political parties, and that, as a result, French governments are constantly changing. He knows what happened to France in the two world wars. He has the impression that France, nevertheless, is fundamentally sound. On the basis of this knowledge, he is able to evaluate the sometimes sensational happenings of the day.

Then he turns to a story from Bogotá. If he knows what country

Bogotá is in, there are only two chances in ten (see Mr. Gallup) that he knows where the country is. And there is practically no chance that he has ever studied its history and institutions or heard its politics discussed. So when he reads of some sensational happening in Colombia, being entirely without background information, he interprets it according to his preoccupations and fears of the moment. Which is to say he usually interprets it wrongly.

This was what happened during the unhappy outburst of April 1948. The name Gaitán was known to perhaps one in a thousand North Americans. Equally unfamiliar were the tense political situation and the economic problems underlying it. All the newspaper reader in the United States saw was a bloody uprising which, in the present state of North American nerves and the absence of any knowledge of the true background, became almost axiomatically a communist revolution. One piece of convincing evidence was the appearance of red flags on the streets — the red flags that were the banners of Colombia's Liberal party before anyone ever heard of communism!

Given United States ignorance of Latin American backgrounds, and given the way the North American press presents Latin American news, the result is bound to be confusion in the mind of the reader. And because he is confused, he is almost sure to be uninterested.

He will become interested only when he begins to understand. By changing their approach to Latin American news, the papers could quite easily — without taking on the job of the schools — help him to understand.

The way to do this would be to treat the Latin American news that comes into the newspaper office not as a finished product but as raw material. The copy desk would no longer slap a head on it and drop it into the paper as is. Instead, it would be handed over to an editor qualified by experience and knowledge to handle it. He would add the necessary background, identification, and interpretation, and only then would the story be printed.

For example: the wire services reported from Asunción on February 26 that General Raimundo Rolón, who had become President of Paraguay as the result of a *coup* only a month before, had just been ousted by another *coup*. It was reported as the sixth change of government within thirteen months. And this, apart from a few unimportant details, was the whole story. Some papers gave it front-page position. At least one in New York included a spot map to show where Paraguay is.

The map should be an almost automatic part of every Latin American story. Apart from this slight addition to his geographical knowledge, I wonder how much that story meant to the average reader, and just how interesting he found it. Not very, I suspect, on either count.

But it could have been made extremely interesting. No country in South America has a richer, more fascinating history than Paraguay. The country's troubles today are all deeply rooted in this history. If the relatively unimportant facts of the AP wire on Rolón's overthrow had been boiled down to one paragraph and the rest of the space given to this background, the reader would have learned not only that six Paraguayan governments have been overturned in thirteen months, but — what is far more important — the reason for so many changes. In the process of reading such a story, he would really have learned something about Paraguay. And I venture to guess that he would have found it very good reading.

A variation of this technique would be to save the odd scraps of Latin American news that come over the wire until they add up to something, fortify them with a little background, and serve as before. During March [1948], for example, there were frequent little stories reporting in a couple of lines that Panama and the United States were about to sign a civil aviation treaty. News of the signing was carried in due course. How much more informative and interesting this story would have been if it had been told, not five times in five lines, but once and at length, with all the tangled political, strategic, and technical background that make it much more important than the average U.S. newspaper reader would ever guess.

Latin American news treated in this way could not, perhaps, be printed as a straight news story. But it should be simple enough to work out some kind of column or box form to fill the purpose.

Not until some such experiment is tried will the press be able to arouse reader interest, which in turn will justify the printing of more — and better — news from Latin America.

CHAPTER 2

The
General
View

No. 2 [The present twenty Latin American republics exhibit perhaps as many geographic, ethnic and demographic, economic, historical, cultural, and political differences as any twenty sovereign states of Europe or Asia. The very term *Latin America* is a hazardous generalization if it connotes in the mind of the reader an area in which one encounters a high degree of political, social, and economic homogeneity.

These republics range in size from Haiti, with its 10,700 square miles, to Brazil whose 3,280,000 square miles make it considerably larger than the United States. The variations in population are equally large; Panama counts about 700,000 inhabitants, Brazil approximately 50,000,000. Some of the republics, like Bolivia or Honduras, are predominantly Indian, others are preponderantly white — as is the case with Argentina and Costa Rica — one is a Negro nation, and many reflect in their people a mixture and an amalgamation of the white, Indian, and Negro races.

In some, the indigenous people have had a deep and lasting effect upon the political and social scene; in others, few evidences of such a heritage are visible. In some, one finds that immigration has been as influential in determining the cultural pattern as it has in the United States; in others it has contributed almost nothing to the national life.

Although most of the states show common economic denominators, such as the dependence upon one or two products to maintain their foreign trade and bulwark the domestic economy, or the predominance of agriculture as the means of national livelihood, the variation in the kinds of economic activity, in the processes of industrialization, in per capita incomes, and in standards of living is as great as the variation in size or population.

It is equally difficult to generalize about their constitutional and political organization. Once again, it must be remembered that Latin America is comprised of twenty independent and sovereign states, each with all of the accoutrements of national statehood. Although eighteen of the twenty were once — and for over three centuries — parts of the Spanish colonial empire, even this common political origin did not result in eighteen contemporary republics whose political institutions show a high degree of uniformity.

Dr. Schurz, in the following discussion, notes the general constitutional character of the twenty nations, the political patterns and institutions that they have in common, and the governmental differences and variances that exist among them.]

Government *

by WILLIAM LYTLE SCHURZ

AFTER the attainment of independence, Latin America faced the problem of finding a workable system of government. In the solution of this problem its past offered little guidance for its future. Behind it stretched centuries of absolutist rule and habits of obedience to an authority imposed from above and directed from overseas. In this unfortunate heritage the only vestige of democratic tradition was the limited right of the colonials to participate in the government of their cities. Otherwise they were subjects of a vice-king, who ruled by proxy for an all-powerful king in Spain. Loyalty to the crown was so strong, in spite of the individual inadequacy of most of the monarchs since Philip II, that paradoxically enough the movement for

* Taken from *Latin America*, by William Lytle Schurz, published and copyright by E. P. Dutton & Co., Inc., New York, 1941 and 1949. The footnotes in the original version are omitted here.

independence actually originated in colonial protests against the treatment of the unworthy Ferdinand VII by the French conquerors of
Spain. The customary line of authority had been broken for the moment and the first impulse of the creoles was to demand that it be
restored to its familiar form. It was only because the reactionary
monarch failed to rise to the occasion by a display of gratitude and
appreciation and, instead, lectured his loyal subjects for their political initiative, that the bolder colonial leaders questioned the whole
system of government. But now that the kings and their viceroys had
been eliminated, those who took their place in the political scheme
had surprisingly little by which to go.

The great Bolívar, who lived long enough to observe the full trend
of events, toyed for a time with ideas of New World monarchy, in
which the Brazilians were to find refuge from the disorders that
afflicted their neighbors. But Spanish America was committed by
destiny and example to the republican form of government and to
the ideal of democracy. Free men, the Spanish Americans reasoned
from history, could live only under a republic; the United States
furnished an example from the present. The founders of the new
states ignored the circumstance that the French Revolution had
ended with Napoleon and the Bourbon Restoration, and that the
North American colonists had an active tradition of self-government
before they declared their independence. The Spanish Americans
believed that, by borrowing the original ideology of the French
Revolution and the machinery of American republicanism, they
could rationalize and implement their dream of democracy.

They took too little account of the realities of the situation wherein
they built an exotic framework of government. The stabilizing influence of a middle class was lacking. In most of the republics a large
and inert Indian population remained outside the political life of the
nation, and regarded all governments alike as potential oppressors,
to be given as wide a berth as possible. Thus, by a process of elimination an oligarchy of landowners and lawyer-politicians was inevitable. Oligarchy was tempered by pretorianism, for the veterans of
the wars of independence were a power to be reckoned with, and the
habits of violence bred by the long struggle with Spain created an
atmosphere that was favorable to the ambitions of the military. Those

who had the responsibility for rule lacked the knowledge of administrative organization and processes that might have enabled the governments to function with some degree of order and regularity in
spite of this incubus of the past. The only tried administrative capacity was in the hierarchy of the Church, but that powerful institution refused to reconcile itself to the new order and long remained
monarchical in its sympathies.

On the credit side were the nationalism born of the accomplished
fact of independence and a deep faith in the republican ideal. That is,
there were definite political sovereignties of their own making, to
which men could give their loyalties, and which might become real
democracies within their own qualified understanding of the term.

Yet, in the early republican period, the very nationalisms were ill-
defined and variable entities. Nations were in flux, and it was long
before the geographical limits of all the new sovereignties were fixed
with any approach to finality. By a process of division republics fell
apart to give birth to other states, as the young peoples sought some
common denominator of nationality and became conscious of the
differentia which distinguished them from their neighbors.

When the last Spanish force in the American continent surrendered to the patriots in January 1826, there were ten independent
nations in Latin America — Mexico, the United Provinces of Central
America, Great Colombia, Peru, Bolivia, Chile, the United Provinces
of the River Plate, Paraguay, Brazil, and Haiti. The Central American Federation had been a part of Mexico from 1822 to 1824, and was
to break up into its five component states in 1838. Bolívar's creation,
the Republic of Great Colombia, was dissolved in 1830 into the three
republics of New Granada, or Colombia, Venezuela, and Ecuador.
At the first revolutionary movement in Buenos Aires, in 1811, Paraguay set up an independent government and thereafter refused the
overtures of the Argentine patriots to join the United Provinces of
the River Plate. The present republic of Uruguay, then known as
the Banda Oriental, was part of Brazil, as the Cisplatine Province,
between 1821 and 1835. A confused struggle for independence, in
which a rude but valiant countryman named José Artigas distinguished himself, was unsuccessful, and Uruguay owed her freedom
as a nation to the rivalries of her larger neighbors. For a brief period

Uruguay was a part of the loose federation of provinces beyond the River Plate. At the end of a war between Argentina and Brazil both recognized the independence of the Banda Oriental in 1828. After a prolonged and cruel conflict, that had as much the character of a class struggle as of a war of independence, the Haitians attained their independence from France in 1803. From 1822 to 1844, the Spanish-speaking eastern end of the island was a part of the black republic of Haiti. In the latter year it gained its freedom as the Dominican Republic. Of the other states of present-day Latin America, the Cuban Republic dates from 1898 and the Republic of Panama from 1903.

History played an important part in determining the eventual scheme of Latin American nationalism. Mexico was the logical successor of the Viceroyalty of New Spain, as Colombia was of that of New Granada, Argentina, of the Viceroyalty of La Plata, and Peru of the second of the original viceroyalties. The more important of the outlying provinces of the viceroyalties also became republics under the new order. Sometimes the new states followed the lines of an old captaincy-general, as Chile and Venezuela did, and as Central America did until the dissolution of the Confederation. Others succeeded to the colonial *audiencias* or administrative courts. Among these, Ecuador was the republican heir to the former jurisdiction of the *Audiencia* of Quito, and Bolivia took over most of the territory that had been governed by the *Audiencia* of Charcas. Also, before the creation of the last two viceroyalties in the eighteenth century, there had been an *audiencia* in Bogotá and, for a short time, in Buenos Aires.

Other factors contributed to the influence of the past in deciding the course of nationality. By virtue of her Portuguese background and language, Brazil's right to nationhood was unquestioned. Similarly, Haitian nationality was founded on her distinctive race and speech. Sometimes a fundamental ethnic unity bound a people together as a nation. Perhaps it was a predominance of Spanish blood, as in Costa Rica and Argentina and Uruguay, or the unifying leaven may have been supplied by the aboriginal race, as the Maya-Quiché stock gave a certain unity to Guatemala, the Guaranís to Paraguay, and the virile Araucanian-Spanish mixture to the Chilean masses.

Uruguayan nationality has also been strengthened by the consciousness of the Oriental Republic's strategic and dangerous position as a buffer state between her two powerful neighbors.

Paraguay offers an interesting example of the development of nationality in Latin America. She possesses in unusual degree the basic elements of nationality. She is unified ethnically. The mass of her people are a mixture of Spaniard and Guaraní Indian. The Guaraní tongue, which is the idiom of the people, is another expression of this racial unity. The minorities within the country are too insignificant in numbers and influence to affect this essential oneness of the Paraguayan people. The Paraguayan race was also molded by the common experience of a series of remarkable mass disciplines, which were applied intermittently, but for long periods, over a period of three centuries. These were, by order of their appearance, the communal theocracy of the Jesuit " reductions," and the dictatorships of Francia and the López family. As the processes of history have made of Paraguay a true nation, so have the facts of geography. The real Paraguay, cohesive and integrated, is a natural fortress, with a wide, forest-lined moat on three sides, where the two great rivers almost encircle her. On the north the frontier follows the fosse of the Apa River and to the northeast the ramparts are constituted by the broken highlands of Ambaya and Mbaracajú.

Some of the other Latin American republics, like Bolivia and Ecuador, Honduras and Nicaragua, though in varying degree, still lack a real basis of nationality. They are afterthoughts of history, conceived with little regard to the factors that make of a country a nation. They have governments and flags and the other trappings of sovereignty. On occasion their populations manifest a rather bellicose patriotism. But all these do not make them nations. Only time and accumulated tradition, and common effort and wise leadership can evolve these amorphous states into organized peoples with a collective consciousness and personality. The fruition of that development will justify the privileges of independent existence, as it will fit them for its obligations. Until then, they will play, rather seriously at times, at nationhood.

Most of the Latin American constitutions are very new. The oldest is that of the Argentine republic, which has been in force, though with some important changes, since 1853. Nine countries have had new constitutions since 1944: Bolivia (1945), Brazil (1946), the Dominican Republic (1947), Ecuador (1945 and 1946), Haiti (1946), Nicaragua (1948), Panama (1946), and Venezuela (1947). Brazil has had three constitutions since 1933, one of which was promulgated in 1937 by President Vargas and promptly suspended by him. After a five years' trial, El Salvador abrogated the Constitution of 1939 and returned to an amended document of 1886. Chile, Cuba, and Paraguay promulgated new constitutions in 1940. The famous Mexican Constitution of 1917 has remained in force ever since. Sometimes a comprehensive series of amendments has radically altered the existing constitution, as happened in 1943 with the Costa Rican Constitution of 1871. Also the Colombian Constitution of 1886 underwent substantial alterations in 1944–45. The present constitutions of other countries were promulgated in the following years: Chile (1925), Honduras (1936), Peru (1933), and Uruguay (1934).

The constitutions of the Latin American nations have not only been relatively short-lived; they have certain other features which reflect the political restlessness of those peoples. A distrust of legislative processes has resulted in the incorporation in national constitutions of much that should normally be a matter for statutory enactment — a tendency that is by no means confined to Latin America. The lengthy Mexican Constitution of 1917 and the short-lived Brazilian Constitution of 1934 are cases in point. The former aimed to give definitive form to the fundamental ideals of the Mexican Revolution, which began with the overthrow of the Díaz régime, and the latter not only provided for recasting the framework of the Brazilian government, but contained the bases for a whole system of social reforms. Accordingly, the new constitutions are liable to express the prevailing political and economic philosophy of the moment, rather than such political ideas as may be deeply grounded in the nation's history. Also, realizing the fallibility of constitutional conventions and the excessive rigidity of constitutional checks in the face of political realities, provision is often made for the suspension of the constitution, or at least of the constitutional guarantees of the individual rights of the citizen, in the event of a political emergency. In such an event, the chief executive is the judge of what circumstances comprise a state of crisis or abnormal condition in the nation.

Conditions in several Latin American republics were favorable to a federal system of government. Strong local attachments and interests had grown up through the centuries about certain cities and their dependent territory. Centrifugal forces were fostered by geographical barriers and difficulties of communication. Remote and isolated cities, like Mérida, in Mexico, and the Venezuelan city of the same name, had little in common with the rest of the country. In spite of the centralized rule of Spain under the Hapsburgs and the Bourbons, the mother country had never been unified spiritually, and Spaniards had brought to the New World their traditions of separatism and provincial patriotism.

By reason of their very size, if by virtue of no other considerations, Argentina and Mexico were destined to federalism from the beginning. Yet it was only after long and bitter struggles between the partisans of a strong central government and of the federal principle that the latter triumphed. For a time the conflict between Buenos Aires and the Argentine provinces resulted in virtual anarchy and the disintegration of all national authority. The United Provinces of the River Plate was but a loose confederation, whose members went their separate ways and even waged war on one another. The dictatorship of Rosas was an interval of tyranny in this period of confusion and disunion. Meanwhile, several attempts to adopt a constitution on the general model of the United States were defeated by the opposition of the *Porteños,* as the citizens of Buenos Aires were known. A decisive step was finally taken in 1880 towards settling the long-contested issue between " the port " and the provinces by federalizing the municipal area of Buenos Aires and making it the capital of the nation.

When, after the end of Iturbide's short-lived empire, the question arose as to the permanent form of the Mexican government, Centralists and Federalists carried on an active controversy for the control of the new state. The constitution of 1824 represented a victory for the federal idea, but twelve years later another constitution, dictated by the famous Santa Anna, abolished the states and made Mexico a unitarian republic. The centralist interregnum ended in

1840, and in 1857 a federal system of government was definitely incorporated in the constitution under which Mexico was to live for another sixty years.

Long before the breakup of Bolívar's Republic of Gran Colombia in 1832 the issue between federalism and centralized government had developed in acute form. The first constitution of New Granada, as the independent republic of Colombia was known, provided for a centralized state in which the provincial governors were appointed from Bogotá. The process was reversed in 1857, when the new constitution of the Granadine Confederation left to the states all powers not expressly delegated to the confederate government. In practice the result was to render the central authority virtually impotent. In 1861 the name of the republic was changed to the United States of New Granada, and two years later, to the United States of Colombia. In the latter year the autonomy of the states was considerably curtailed, and in 1886 the present centralized republic was established under a constitution that was the basic law of the country for another half-century.

The first constitution of Venezuela represented a compromise on the basic issue which plagued the political life of her neighbor and former partner in the Bolivarian republic. However, the question arose again during the turbulent period which followed and led to armed conflict between Centralists and Federalists. In 1864 a new constitution established " the United States of Venezuela " as a confederation with large independent powers for the states. It was not until 1904 that the Venezuelan government received its present federal form in its entirety.

Central America presents an interesting example of the problem of coordinating the political life of neighboring peoples whose common heritage would appear to contain more elements of similarity than of divergence. The five original Central American republics — with British Honduras and the Mexican State of Chiapas — are heirs of the lands that comprised the old Captaincy-General of Guatemala. As an administrative appanage of the Viceroyalty of New Spain, it was for a brief period a part of Iturbide's Mexican empire. In 1824 a congress of representatives of the five provinces declared their joint independence as the United Provinces of Central America.

Discord early arose among the members of the Federation, which was, however, held together for a time by the ability and moderation of President Francisco Morazán. The union signed its own death warrant in 1838, when it agreed to permit any state to withdraw from the Federation. Nicaragua, Honduras, and Costa Rica were prompt to take advantage of the authorization and seceded from the union. A few years later El Salvador, Honduras, and Nicaragua set up the tri-partite " Central American Confederation," but the process of disintegration had already proceeded too far and the league shortly broke up with war between two of its members. Attempts to revive the persistent idea in 1849 and again in 1862 failed as completely. A fresh impetus was given to the movement for Central American federalism in 1876, when delegates of all five countries met at Guatemala City at the invitation of General Justo Rufino Barrios, President of Guatemala. Accumulated animosities and jealousies proved to be too strong to permit the re-establishment of the now long-defunct union. Other subsequent projects for voluntary federation had no better fate, nor did the efforts of President Zelaya, of Nicaragua, 1907, to bring about union by force.

In the same year all the states sent delegates to Washington to confer on plans for partial union. Several agreements were reached on subjects of common interest, but very little was accomplished towards the curtailment of national sovereignties in favor of a closer administrative union. In fact, the Central American Court of Justice, which sat until 1918, was the only tangible move in this direction. However, in spite of repeated setbacks, the idea of union still had so much vitality and made so strong an appeal to the imagination of Central Americans that three years later all the republics, except El Salvador, agreed on a union to be known as the Federation of Central America. The government of Costa Rica refused to ratify the pact and so condemned the move to failure. Meanwhile, the United States had given its encouragement to the general movement, but a second conference held at Washington in 1922 largely confined its deliberations to the international plane.

The obstacles to the consummation of the great design for a combination of the Central American states have grown with time. The independent republics have developed pronounced political personalities, and their ruling classes have a strong vested interest in national independence. There is general distrust of Guatemala as the largest member of the group, and Costa Rica is reluctant to compromise its superior political progress by a closer tie with her less-advanced neighbors. In the meantime, neither roads nor railroads have linked the five countries to overcome the physical barriers that separate them.

Of the other Latin American countries, Peru, broken up into a number of widely separated communities, had all the natural conditions that were propitious for a federal system. However, a tradition of government from Lima, set by centuries of viceregal rule, determined the unitarian pattern which Peru has followed from independence. Brazil, whom history and circumstances of geography predisposed to a federalist system, had to pass through a long period of unitary rule under the Empire before she realized her natural role as the United States of Brazil.

Certain states of the federal republics have manifested separatist tendencies at one period or another of their history. Disgusted with Santa Anna's arbitrary attempts to centralize all authority in his own person, the state of Yucatán attempted in 1839 to secede from Mexico, and for all practical purposes remained independent of the central government for several years. The Colombian province of Nariño long conducted its affairs as though it were a sovereign nation, and for a period even refused to honor the currency of the Bogotá government. The province of Panama, separated from the body of the country by the swamps and jungles of the Atrato region and conscious of its strategic position on the isthmus, showed an attitude of independence long before the fateful events of 1903. It revolted against Colombia in 1830, and during most of 1840–41 its name of the Free State of Isthmus was scarcely a misnomer. Throughout the various changes in the form of the national government, Panama retained a certain autonomous status that was conceded to no other part of the country.

In Brazil, the rich and progressive state of São Paulo has twice revolted against the federal government during the present century. The *Paulistas,* as the citizens of the state are called, complained that they carried an undue share of the country's cost of government.

Though the state occupied a privileged position in the federation, some of its leaders held the view that its interests would be better served by independence and seriously considered the possibility of secession. Meanwhile, the state had built up a large and well-equipped army that was more than a mere militia. The state flag was often displayed in the public schools above the emblem of the nation. The state government maintained quasi-diplomatic relations with foreign countries and sent its agents abroad to treat with foreign governments on matters pertaining to immigration and the all-important coffee trade. Civil war broke out in 1924 between São Paulo and the federal government. Again, in 1932, two years after a widespread revolt had overthrown the Washington Luís government, the state of São Paulo rose in arms against the dictatorship of Getulio Vargas and the new political régime which had been enforced on the proud state. The largest armies so far engaged in the history of the continent fought for several months, but the rebellion was finally crushed by the superior forces of the federal government, which was able to cut off the *Paulistas* from their outside sources of supply.

In view of the strong position of the executive in most Latin American governments, it was to be expected that ways would be found for controlling the members of a federal union of states. Thus, the president has become the instrument of counter-tendencies of centralization in the federal republics. Occasion for the assertion of the presidential or central authority against the government of a state may originate in any one of a number of circumstances. A state government may oppose certain fundamental federal policies to the point where its attitude constitutes incipient revolution, and so form a rallying point for discontent throughout the country, as happened in 1939 in the case of Governor Saturnino Cedillo, of the Mexican state of Aguas Calientes. A state governor may be so patently a candidate for the presidency that, unless he has the previous approval of the central administration, the realities of Latin American politics would not permit a president passively to accept the situation. A state government may make such commitments or contract such obligations abroad as would compromise the federal authority, if the state should fail to fulfill its agreements. The large borrowing powers which were left to the Colombian departments as a survival from the federal period of that nation's past were to create an embarrassing problem for the central government of Colombia, with the result that restraints were later placed on the fiscal independence of the departments. Due either to corruption, administrative inefficiency, or public disorders resulting from the struggles of political factions, a collapse of the regular processes of government within a state may require the central power to undertake extraordinary measures of control, temporarily restricting the sovereignty of the state.

A regular technique for meeting most of these situations exists within the constitutions of Argentina and Brazil. The federal government may *intervene* in the internal affairs of the state in question and supplant the ordinary machinery of administration until normal conditions are restored. During the interim of federal control the state is governed by a federal *interventor,* who is appointed by the president and responsible to him. This device has been resorted to several times in the history of both nations, but generally during periods of political crisis. Thus, in 1937, President Vargas of Brazil removed all state governors, except that of Minas Geraes, from office. Though some were reappointed as federal interventors in their states, others were replaced by special representatives of the president. As a phase of the same general overturn of the Brazilian federal system all state legislatures and municipal assemblies were dissolved.

In Mexico and Venezuela, the two other federal republics, other methods, usually extralegal, have been invoked in order to accomplish the same end. Porfirio Díaz and Juan Vicente Gómez, longtime dictators, effectively controlled the state governments of their respective countries by dictating the choice of governors. In Mexico, troublesome state governors have sometimes been intimidated into conformity by a display of federal force or have been removed from their local vantage point by appointment to some federal post of honor, usually in a foreign country.

Chile can be considered as typical of the centralized republics. She is geographically compact and unified to a high degree, since the ocean binds together the parts of the long, narrow country, and no serious natural obstacles separate the outlying parts of the republic from the capital and the important Central Valley. This natural unity has been further strengthened by the construction of a north-and-south railway, much of whose length serves a strategic, rather than commercial, purpose. In these respects she differs greatly from Bolivia, Ecuador, and Colombia, whose widely separated and distinctive regions have not been adequately linked together by railroads or other means of communication. Similarly, the authority of the central government is much more effective throughout a tightly knit country like El Salvador, which has a good network of internal transportation lines, than in the neighboring republic of Honduras, whose system of land communications is still very primitive.

The *intendentes* or administrative heads of the Chilean provinces are appointed by the president and hold office at his will. The *intendentes,* in turn, select the " governors " of the departments under their jurisdiction, and, in accordance with the descending order of appointive power, the governors name the local officials of the administrative subdivisions within their territory. In other countries, the names of the administrative divisions and titles of the various categories of the governing hierarchy differ one from another, but the basic pattern is everywhere similar, and, regardless of the variations of political nomenclature, the ultimate authority stems from the presidential palace in the capital of the republic. At the opposite end of the centralized administrative process, considerable influence is wielded by the *jefe político,* or " political chieftain," who, as the political " boss " of the community, is also ever-mindful of his position in the dominant party machine of the nation. Many of the worst abuses in Latin American government have been connected with the prevalence of *caciquismo,* as the rule of these petty political bosses is sometimes called, after a West Indian word for " chief."

Except in the national capitals or other large cities, whose mayors are generally appointees of the central government, there is liable to be more political independence and vitality in the municipal governments of Latin America than in the rural districts and in the field of provincial administration. There is not only a persistent tradition of city government from colonial times, but the urban citizenry is superior in respect to literacy and political education. It has a capacity for common action that is lacking in other groups of the national population, and which on occasion acts as a check on the more arbitrary exercise of power by superior authority. Sometimes this influence is wielded through the elective municipal councils; at other times it is exerted through an assertive public opinion, or even by more direct methods of protest.

The Latin American constitutions have frequently aimed to place restrictions on the great power of the presidency. As the president often dominates the deliberations of those who draft these charters of government, efforts are usually ineffectual. However, the re-election of a president for two consecutive terms is now prohibited in virtually all the republics. In Guatemala a president must wait twelve years before he can again become a candidate. This safeguard is partially counteracted by the circumstance that in almost half the republics the presidential term is six years. Sentiment in Mexico for this constitutional provision has been so strong that for a time every official communication of the Mexican government closed with the words: " Effective suffrage; no re-election."

Various devices have been found for defeating the purpose of this restriction on the presidential power. An ex-president may continue to control the actions of his successors, as Rafael Trujillo did during an interregnum in the Dominican Republic, though the attempt of General Calles to dominate Mexican politics after his retirement failed before the uncalculated independence of Lázaro Cárdenas. Also, while there were several interims in the long presidency of Juan Vicente Gómez in Venezuela, during which the dictator apparently retired to private life, the actual sequence of his absolute authority was unbroken by these hiatuses. The real seat of power continued to be the country estate of Gómez at Maracay and not the presidential palace in Caracas.

Several examples of arbitrary action will illustrate the methods by which ambitious presidents may circumvent the constitutional limitations on their terms of office. The late President Busch of Bolivia dissolved the national congress, declared the constitution nonoperative, and set up a totalitarian state, which was only terminated by his death and the restoration of the *status quo ante* by his provisional successor, President Quintanilla. President Vargas of Brazil ruled without a constitution for much of his dictatorship. In the case of President Ubico of Guatemala, who first took office in 1931, the constitutional ban on a second term was suspended by a "plebiscite" which continued the president's term until 1943, but General Ubico was not permitted to serve out his extended term. In Honduras, Dr. Tiburcio Carias Andino, elected President for the term 1933–37, was reappointed by the national congress for an additional six years, and still occupied the presidential palace in 1948. In the neighboring republic of El Salvador, the six-year term of General Maximiliano Hernández Martínez was extended by a constitutional convention from 1937 to 1943. General Anastasio Somoza, after serving as President of Nicaragua from 1936 to 1940, was re-elected under the new constitution of 1939 to serve a further eight-year term expiring in 1947. On the conclusion of his second term he removed his successor from office and reassumed the executive power.

The most radical step taken in any country to curtail the prerogatives of the presidency was embodied in the Uruguayan constitution of 1917. This constitution was largely inspired by the brilliant José Batlle y Ordoñez, President from 1903 to 1907, and again in 1911–15. It provided for a dual executive, whereby power was divided between the president and an administrative council of nine men. Under this plan the president appointed three ministers of the government and the administrative council appointed four. In the skilled hands of Baltasar Brum, president from 1919 to 1923, the scheme appeared workable, but the inevitable impasse in the executive gradually came to a head after his guiding influence was removed. Gabriel Terra, President from 1931 to 1935, resolved the problem by dismissing the congress and the administrative council, and starting thence with a clean slate. The constituent assembly which met at his call, prepared the constitution of 1934, which restored the presidency to substantially its former position in the government, while retaining the framework of the administrative council as an advisory body in matters of policy.

In most countries the president is elected by direct popular vote. Argentina has a system of electors on the American plan, and in Haiti, Uruguay, and Venezuela the president is chosen by the national congress.

There is nothing comparable to the American party convention, and candidates are generally selected by the leaders of the respective parties, sometimes acting as a party caucus in the national legislature. The president sometimes dictates the choice of his successor, in support of whose candidacy he then uses the existing machinery of government. In Brazil, it was long the custom to alternate the presidency between the two dominant states of Minas Geraes and São Paulo, with an occasional candidate from Rio Grande do Sul or the northern states of the republic. As the official candidate of the government, his election largely became a formality.

Though party politics are very active in Latin America, they have certain characteristics not found in the United States. Parties tend to depend on the personality of some prominent leader and are frequently known by his name. Thus, the *Irigoyenistas* in Argentina were partisans of Hipólyto Irigoyen, who was the Radical party's president during the period 1916–22 and again from 1928 to 1930, and the *Monttvaristas* in Chile represented the traditions of the Montt family and of Antonio Varas, a leader of the Montt faction. In these cases, the personal loyalties of the leader's followers are of more importance than any political issues. In Mexico the dominant political element is the National Revolutionary party, which represents the principles of the social revolution that began with the presidency of Francisco Madero.

Sometimes party names are truly indicative of real divisions of opinion on fundamental issues. Thus, the Conservative party usually represents the traditional vested interests of the country, such as the Catholic Church and the large landowners, while the Liberal party represents those who would institute certain reforms at the expense of those interests. Specific issues in the struggles between these parties may involve such matters as civil marriages, separation of Church and State, control of public education, extension of the suffrage, taxation of landed property and incomes, and social legislation. Such a division exists in Colombia, where it gives party lines a special significance seldom found elsewhere in Latin America. In Latin America political parties are generally known by the names *Democratic, Republican, Socialist,* or *Radical,* or by various combinations of the four. However, the names seldom give a clue to the special principles represented by the particular party, a practice by no means confined to Latin America.

Parties whose platforms embody more or less radical programs of legislation have become increasingly common in Latin America. One of the most interesting of these is the so-called *APRA*, or *Aprista* party, in Peru, which was founded by Raul Haya de la Torre, and whose name is an abbreviation of the significant words *Alianza Popular Revolucionaria Americana.* The conservative elements who have traditionally ruled the country long succeeded in keeping the party's candidates off the election ballots, or nullified its political influence by other methods. However, on the accession of the Bustamante Rivero government to power in 1945 the *Aprista* party was legalized and thereupon became an important factor in the political affairs of the republic.

The Communist party, sometimes disguised under another name, as in Costa Rica, has become a new and disturbing element in Latin American politics. It has been particularly active in Chile, where it had considerable strength in the national congress, and in Brazil, Cuba, and Uruguay. Very vocal Communist minorities also exist in Colombia and Venezuela. In 1948, the Brazilian government outlawed the Communist party, and in the same year, the Chilean government, under the leadership of President González Videla, purged its higher ranks of Communists.

In the early history of the Argentine republic the country was torn by violent conflicts between the advocates of a strong centralized state dominated by the capital and the province of Buenos Aires and those who favored a federal system of semi-autonomous provinces. This important issue long gave a meaning to political parties that overshadowed all other considerations. While partisan strife in Uruguay was even more prolonged and bitter than in Argentina, the division between the two dominant parties of the Oriental Republic early lost most of its original significance. The *Blancos,* or Whites, and *Colorados,* or Reds, first comprised the followers of Manuel Oribe and of Fructuoso Rivera, who carried pennons of those colors on their lances at the Battle of Carpintaria in 1836. For a time the *Blancos* were the party of traditionalism and were strongest in the country districts, while the *Colorados* were at least reputed to favor progressive measures of government and had their greatest strength in Montevideo and the other towns. As time went on, the two became only contestants in a chronic and meaningless civil war, with the *Colorados* holding the ascendency during the latter part of the century.

In contrast to the relatively simple partisan divisions of these countries is the complex party history of Chile. Party rivalries in that country originally followed the conventional formula of Conservatives and Liberals. The Conservative party represented the most powerful of the old landed families, and was strongly clerical in its policies. Under the able leadership of Diego Portales it incorporated its ideas of government in the constitution of 1833, which was the basic law of Chile for nearly a century. Except for a short Liberal interregnum, it dominated Chilean political life until the Balmaceda régime in the 1880's. Meanwhile, party lines had lost some of their clearness, as certain groups espoused varying degrees of liberalism or conservatism, or as strong personal followings displaced the normal party attachments. As a consequence, when the Chilean party system attained its ultimate complexity towards the end of the last century there were six well-defined party groups. In addition to the two classical parties, these consisted of the Radicals, who had strong anticlerical leanings, the Democrats, who championed the growing laboring class, the Nationalists, who represented the traditions of the Montt-Varas régime, and the Liberal Democrats, who were the political heirs of President Balmaceda. Due to the breakup of the old party system, congressional action became possible only by resort to blocs or combinations of parties, as in prewar France. This resulted in much logrolling and maneuvering at the expense of established political policies and principles, and set a lower tone for the parliamentarianism that was the outstanding feature of Chilean government during that period.

The United States system of ministerial responsibility to the executive is the rule among Latin American governments, in contrast to the European system of responsibility to the parliament. That is, the president appoints the members of his own cabinet and may remove them on his own volition. The former complex cabinet system of Chile, which was designed to hold the president in check, has been materially changed, but any cabinet member is still privileged to address the national congress in connection with the work of his department. There is considerable variety in the composition of Latin American cabinets. Except in the larger countries, responsibility for the national defense is usually concentrated in a single ministry. In Mexico, several heads of independent government agencies have full cabinet rank. The Minister of Interior, or "government," has an unusual position in the Latin American cabinet, as is customary in Europe. Except for serious disorders which may call for the use of the military, he is generally charged with the maintenance of order in the country, which may include surveillance of the political opposition. In addition to his police functions, he normally dispenses political patronage in the provinces, and through the *jefes políticos,* or political bosses, who often have the position of local governors, he controls the ruling party's political machine. Though the Minister of Foreign Affairs is usually the ranking member of the cabinet, in the Cuban and Peruvian systems the head of the cabinet has a status in some respects analogous to that of a European prime minister. A Minister of Economy, who is responsible for the execution of official policies designed to improve the economic life of the country or to regulate its economic activities is found in the cabinets of Bolivia, Colombia, Ecuador, Guatemala, and Mexico. An official with much the same functions has the title of Minister of *Fomento,* or development, in the Nicaraguan and Peruvian cabinets.

Executive councils, generally of an advisory nature, are increasingly common in Latin America. In Colombia a national economic council, composed of five representatives of banking, agriculture, and other industrial interests, advises the president on matters of economic policy. The Peruvian and Paraguayan constitutions provide for a similar body. The Nicaraguan president is authorized to form a council of state, to advise him on public contracts and other important questions. In Guatemala a council of state exercises a certain supervision over government concessions and contracts, and serves the president in an advisory capacity. Of its seven members, three are elected by the national assembly and four are chosen by the president, thus ensuring executive control of its actions.

A bicameral body, made up of a senate and a chamber of deputies, is the normal legislative pattern of Latin American governments, though most of the legislatures of the Central American republics are composed of a single chamber, commonly known as the National Assembly. The trend is now towards the popular election of the members of both houses, but Argentina still clings to the plan, which it borrowed from the United States, of selecting its senators by vote of the provincial legislatures. The term of office of members of the lower chamber is generally longer than in the United States. For example, a Chilean deputy holds office for four years, and a Mexican deputy for three years. On the other hand, the members of the unicameral legislature of El Salvador are reelected annually. At the other extreme, Chilean senators are elected for an eight-year term. An interesting feature of the Nicaraguan constitution makes all former presidents of the republic ex officio members of the national assembly for life.

Some of the republics, including Mexico, make provision for a Permanent Commission of the national legislature, which sits during the recesses between the regular sessions of the congress. This device not only gives continuity to the life of the legislative body, but serves as a check on the decree-making tendencies of the executive.

The idea of proportional representation has gained some ground in Latin American countries, notably in Chile and Uruguay. Important minorities are thereby given a place in the government in relation to their numerical strength, and share in the responsibility of rule, instead of harassing the current administration from the outside as an opposition party. For example, the important Uruguayan Council of Ministers is made up of nine members, selected in a ratio of six to three from the two political parties with the largest vote at the preceding elections.

Though the enforcement of electoral laws often leaves much to be desired, there is a growing tendency to surround elections with safeguards against the corruption or duress of voters or against the inertia of the voters themselves. Balloting is also secret in a number of the republics, where it is a strong influence for honest elections. It is customary to hold elections on Sunday, and, in order to reduce the chance of disorders at the polls, all places where strong liquor is dispensed are generally closed from the preceding evening until the votes are all in.

As a rule, the suffrage is limited to men over 21, who are able to read and write. The literacy qualification has the effect of disfranchising the majority of adult males in the countries where there is a large Indian population, as in Peru, and wherever the restriction is in force it materially reduces the size of the voting registers. In several countries the voting age is 18. In Mexico boys may vote at that age if they are the heads of families, but bachelors and those without an "honorable means of livelihood" are not eligible until they are 21. In Costa Rica, married males and school teachers may vote at 18, but bachelors are required to wait until they are 20.

Though sentiment is still strong and widespread against the participation of women in politics, female suffrage has made substantial gains in the newer constitutions. Women now have full voting rights in Brazil, Cuba, the Dominican Republic, Ecuador, Mexico, Panama, El Salvador, and Uruguay, and, if literate, in Guatemala. Chile, Peru, and Venezuela permit them to vote in municipal elections. Haitian women may hold office at 30, but do not have the vote.

Compulsory voting is in effect, at least theoretically, in Argentina, Brazil, Costa Rica, Guatemala, and Peru, but in Brazil voting is optional for unemployed women and for men over 65. In Guatemala, women and illiterate males may remain away from the polls if they desire.

Such was the scheme of government; its working was to prove very different. The plan — and much of its philosophy — was borrowed from the United States and France. It bore little relation to the experience of the peoples whose framework of rule it was to be. Realities quickly asserted themselves over constitutions and theories and ideals, and it is only in our own time that the two have anywhere approximated one another. Meanwhile, history, geography, and the state of society foredoomed the republics to a long period in which inexorable facts took precedence over forms.

It was in the nature of things that the republics should be monocracies and not democracies. The demos or sovereign people was still too backward and inchoate to rule. One-man government was the natural alternative, except in Chile, where the landed oligarchs held all power tightly within their class and ruled through the national congress. Therefore, the political history of Latin America has been largely a story of the cycle of dictatorship and revolution. Some of the countries have definitely freed themselves from the traditional formula; others have escaped for a time, only to relapse into the old ways.

Bolívar had foreseen the trend of events towards presidential autocracy, for the process took shape before his death. " My funerals," he predicted, " will be as bloody as those of Alexander." The South American counterparts of Ptolemy, Seleucus, and the rest of the Macedonian *diadochi* were the generals of the Liberator — Santander, Páez, Flores, and Santa Cruz — who ruled the lands which he had freed. They were the first *caudillos,* and set the basic pattern for an age in which absolutism alternated with anarchy.

The power of the president-dictators rested on a combination of conditions and methods. They represented the colonial tradition of personal rule — of obedience to a viceroy or a captain-general — which was the only system of government within the experience of their peoples, and so the only system whose elements the public understood. As such, their rule did not constitute a break in the political evolution of Latin America, but rather a logical stage in that development. Under new names and forms, they only embodied habits of action and ways of thinking that were deeply grounded in the custom of centuries. The peoples still mistrusted the efficacy of their own concerted endeavors, as they doubted the confused wisdom of legislatures, and preferred to trust their political fortunes to a strong and untrammelled individual who would satisfy their urge to get things done.

The national congress, which the constitutions designed to be a check on the executive, was only too often subservient to the dictator. Autocrats, like Díaz of Mexico, Estrada Cabrera of Guatemala, and Gómez of Venezuela, dominated their legislatures by manipulation or intimidation. The congress thus became a pliant instrument for giving legal validity to the arbitrary actions of the dictators, for the modern *caudillo* generally shared the colonial Spaniard's awe of the letter of the law.

A centralized scheme of public administration, with large appointive powers for the president, favored the position of the *caudillos*. It was particularly important to the dictator that he should control directly the treasury, the secret police, and the army. Only loyal henchmen could be trusted in charge of the customs houses, for import duties were usually the most substantial source of the government's revenues. It was the principal function of the national police to keep the president informed of the state of public opinion, especially among his enemies, so that revolts against his power might be forestalled and punishment meted out to conspirators.

Pretorianism was inseparable from *caudillismo*. Most of the early dictators were soldiers, many of whom had risen to power by barrack revolutions. In that event they carried with them to the presidential palace a nucleus of armed support. It was good policy to pamper the garrisons in the capital and in other key positions with good, or at least regular, pay and other favors, while keeping watch on the allegiance of their officers. One Haitian president is said to have locked up the national army in the palace courtyard every night, in order to prevent any rivals from tampering with its loyalty. Civilian presidents, though handicapped by the lack of military experience, often become, by their superior astuteness, as complete masters of the country's armed forces as any of the generals. While soldier-presidents have been the rule in some of the republics, like Mexico, Ecuador, and Guatemala, others, like Argentina, Chile, and Costa Rica, have drawn a majority of their chief executives from among the class of " doctors " or educated civilians. In the first half of 1948, only five of the twenty Latin American presidents were military men; of the others, two were physicians by profession and one was a well-known novelist. The only five who might be classified as dictators were generals.

The national courts have done little to restrain the activities of arbitrary and strong-willed presidents, but in matters which involved the prerogatives of the executive have usually been docile instruments of the current dictatorship, placing a judicial seal on his extra-legal or unconstitutional actions. Other sources of executive authority have been control of the electoral machinery and censorship of the press and of other agencies of public information. With the growing restiveness of the electorate in certain countries these devices have become important concerns of presidents who are desirous of perpetuating their power. Not only are editorial comment or news detrimental to the interests of the dictator banned from domestic circulation, but sensitiveness to foreign opinion may prevent news agencies or correspondents from sending out news unfavorable to the president or his policies. Foreign newspapermen who refuse to accept the official version of important events in their dispatches may be expelled from the country, as has occurred in Brazil and Mexico. Another source of control over the economic life of the country, which is sometimes utilized by the dictators, is through their participation in the direction of certain public monopolies of essential commodities or services. The notorious President Zelaya, of Nicaragua, resorted freely to this form of exploitation, and the famous Gómez, of Venezuela, took advantage of his position to indulge his stockman's instincts to the point where he controlled the cattle industry of the country.

There have been as many varieties of Latin American dictators as there were of their early prototypes, the Greek tyrants of Sicily and the despots of the Italian city-states. Some, usually the military *caudillos*, based their power on downright force, a certain elemental cunning, the appeal of soldierly bluffness, and the dramatization of their authority by pomp and ceremony calculated to impress the populace. These men represented dictatorship in its crudest form, and were as liable to be found among the early governors of the Argentine provinces as among the presidents of Central America or the Andean republics. Some of them were barbaric chieftains, like the second López of Paraguay, Carrera of Guatemala, Daza of Bolivia, and Melgarejo of the same country, who killed his predecessor and rival, General Belzú, with his own hand. These men were vain and capricious, often given to bizarre and fantastic display, and to sadistic cruelty, but sometimes had a dashing manner that commended them to the hero-worshipping masses. Of the same general type were such inept and bombastic leaders as Santa Anna, who bedevilled the political life of Mexico for a long period, and as Castro, of Venezuela, became in the latter years of his rule.

As opposed to the more violent breed of *caudillos*, there were dictators of a sinister type, who ruled by craft rather than by force.

Their power was based on a highly developed system of espionage and on terroristic methods that were more insidious and refined than those of their brutal fellows. Among their weapons were deception and intrigue, corruption and confiscation, secrecy and mystery.

Archetype of this more subtle category of autocrats was José Gaspar Rodríguez Francia, who was absolute lord of the Guaraní Republic of Paraguay almost from its inception until his death — in bed — in 1840. Dr. Francia, known to his subjects and to history as *El Supremo,* embodied in his own person practically all the attributes of government. He was a solitary figure, without ministers or confidants, of superior intellectual attainments, plain living and incorruptible, who gave the same meticulous attention to the details of administration as had Philip II of Spain, and as much later the dour and lonely Hipólyto Irigoyen was to give to the complex government of Argentina.

Francia cut his country off from the rest of the world and the disorders of the time, and personally supervised the very limited trading operations which were authorized at the few ports of entry. Within the closed frontiers he gave the country domestic peace and a degree of well-being consistent with its primitive standards of living. But the local aristocracy, from whose members opposition to his rule might arise, was kept in subjection by a peculiarly oppressive technique of terror designed to break down its consciousness and cohesion as a class. Similarly, he stripped the Church of its privileges and bound its weakened organization to himself in a humiliating dependence.

His younger contemporary, Juan Manuel de Rosas, master of Argentina from 1829 to 1852, though of a more active temperament, employed many of the principles of rule so effectively practiced by Francia in a smaller sphere of action. Rosas rose to power by way of the bloody civil wars between Federalists and Unitarians, which long divided the Argentine population into two irreconcilable factions. Though a wellborn *Porteño,* or native of Buenos Aires, he threw in his fortunes with the partisans of federalism against the metropolis. The richest Argentine of his day, an excellent horseman and experienced Indian fighter, he had qualities of leadership that won him complete ascendency over the wild and undisciplined Gaucho lancers of the pampa. Even Facundo Quiroga, half-savage chieftain of these centaurs of the plains, recognized his supremacy, as Páez, leader of the Venezuelan *llaneros,* had yielded to the mastery of Bolívar. As governor of the key province of Buenos Aires, Rosas, though champion of the federal cause, enforced on the divided nation its first unity. An able administrator, bold and enterprising in action, he was a ruthless autocrat, who would have no compromise with his opponents or, in fact, tolerate them within the bounds of the state. A secret group of his followers was the instrument of a terror that sent his most irreconcilable enemies to death or drove them into exile, while a proud people yielded him an obedience that bordered on servility. When his despotism was finally overthrown by General Urquiza, Rosas retired to England, where he lived as a country gentleman for another twenty-five years.

Some of the dictators were noted for their contributions to the material development of their countries. Their methods were no less arbitrary than those of the more destructive *caudillos* and their repression of democratic forces was as complete. But they had a sense of responsibility for the modernization of the nation's economy. They promoted the building of railroads and public works, the introduction of foreign capital for the development of the country's resources, the extension of foreign trade, and the financial stability and credit of the government. Among these " benevolent despots " of the Latin American republics were Montes, of Bolivia, Díaz, of Mexico, the brilliant Guzmán Blanco, of Venezuela, the pro-clerical García Moreno, of Ecuador, and Barrios, of Guatemala. In the balance against the infamies of the long dictatorship of Gómez in Venezuela were his liquidation of the foreign debt, his construction of an elaborate network of highways, and the impetus which he gave to the petroleum industry of Maracaibo. Some of these rulers were patrons of the arts, and Estrada Cabrera, who governed Guatemala with an iron hand for twenty-two years, was doubtless prouder of his ostentatious Temple of Minerva than of any of the other achievements of his autocracy.

By the middle of the century the conventional pattern of Latin American politics had noticeably altered. The age of dictatorships and the revolutions that alternated with them had by no means ended. Colombia was still to experience two long and sanguinary civil wars. In Uruguay the perennial armed struggles between *Blancos* and *Colorados* were to continue for many years, and, when President Latorre resigned from office in 1880 he declared that Uruguay, now one of the most orderly of Latin American republics, was " ungovernable." The first Uruguayan president who completed his term without armed opposition to his administration was Julio Herrera y Obes, who governed that country in the early nineties. Paraguay was to pass from the control of one ephemeral *caudillo* to another in rapid succession. The Andean republics were yet to sink to new lows of political disorder and arbitrary government. Our own generation was to witness a widespread reappearance of the familiar cycle.

Nevertheless, there were definite signs of progress towards a better order of things. New forces of stability, if not of immediate significance to the faltering struggle for democracy, rose in the republics wherever the bases of national life were essentially healthy. Though *caudillismo* persisted, its manifestations henceforth tended to take a less violent form and to assume, at least in the more advanced countries, more of the characteristics of political bossism in the United States. Meanwhile, the appearance of the noble Juárez was symptomatic of the possibilities of Mexican democracy, even though he was to be followed by the long interlude of the Díaz absolutism. Under the aegis of her governing aristocracy, Chile had attained a political peace that was only to be interrupted by the civil war between President Balmaceda and the partisans of congressional authority.

Advancement was most notable in Argentina. Though the after effects were to continue for some time, the long struggle between the provinces and the capital had ended with a compromise that was finally to bring internal peace to the long distracted country. Buenos Aires was made a Federal District, on the model of Washington, Rio de Janeiro, and Mexico City, while the seat of government of the province was removed to the nearby city of La Plata. The people were weary of the disorders and political repression that accompanied the old régime. As across the estuary in the Banda Oriental, there was a strong popular revulsion against the endless fighting and raiding, with their interruption of normal business and farming and with the killing of herds and flocks by the undisciplined bands of partisans. The country was on the eve of its extraordinary economic development, and the new industrial and financial interests exerted all their rising influence in favor of internal political peace and adherence to constitutional processes of government. The government and the national economy proved strong enough to weather, without political disturbances, a series of crises brought on by too rapid expansion. An extensive railway system was built, and the network of lines radiating from Buenos Aires sealed the union of the country and also enabled the federal government to deal more quickly and effectively with any incipient outbreak of rebellion in the provinces. Meanwhile, as elsewhere in Latin America, the first steps were taken to place the armed forces of the nation on a professional basis and to inculcate into the newly disciplined soldiery loyalty to the state, instead of to individual leaders.

Argentina was also fortunate in having, during this period of transition and development, a succession of able and public-spirited presidents, most of whom were civilians. By their superior intellectual qualifications and devotion to the public welfare, some of them represented a new type of Latin American statesmen. Bartolomé Mitre, who was President from 1862 to 1868, was an eminent publicist, author of a scholarly biography of San Martín, founder of *La Nación*, one of South America's great newspapers, and, on occasion, active commander of the national army. His successor, Domingo Faustino Sarmiento, was a voluminous writer, who was the author of *Facundo,* the classical novel of the Gaucho era. He enthusiastically promoted the cause of popular education, and on his return from a term as Minister in the United States, not only took back with him the pedagogical ideas of Horace Mann, but a company of American school teachers, who were to introduce progressive methods of instruction into the new public schools of the Republic. Nicolás Avellaneda, a leader of unusual intelligence and eloquence, had been Minister of Public Instruction in Sarmiento's cabinet before he became President of the federation in 1874. General Julio Roca, who followed him in the presidency, was not only a distinguished soldier of a new order, but by his political skill and administrative ability consolidated the gains made by his predecessors and set a high standard of public service for future governments. That such men could rise to the highest post in the state and govern it without interruption for twenty-four years was indicative of a momentous change in the life of the nation. Some of the later presidents failed to live up to the traditions of wise and moderate administration set by these remarkable men, and there were recurrent outcroppings of old political habits in the interior to plague the central government. But it was much that the precedents had been established, and, for the time being at least, the nation was to prove itself so sound economically and politically that it could survive these relapses without serious damage to its fundamental interest.

At the beginning of the fourth decade of this century an epidemic of political disturbances occurred all over Latin America, from whose incidence few governments escaped. At first sight, it appeared to foreign observers that the widespread nature of the overturn signified a general return to old political habits and the abandonment of most of the gains made towards more ordered government. Though a few of the dictatorial régimes set up at that time persisted until recently, in other countries the disturbances were relatively short in duration and represented only a violent attempt at the settlement of certain persistent political problems. Some were in the nature of revolts against dictatorships which had outlived the public acceptance of their rule. Thus, a common pattern was lacking as to the precise motives and methods of the revolutions. The ground was prepared by popular suffering and discontent resulting from the world depression which had seriously affected the national economies of all the republics by cutting down the foreign demand for their exports. It was this factor which was responsible for introducing into the revolutionary movements of 1930–31 a strong element of organized radicalism. The early 1930's were a period of more than customary disorder and political instability in Ecuador. In Bolivia, widespread distress due to the fall of tin prices, on which the country's economy largely depended, precipitated in 1930 the outbreak of popular unrest that forced President Siles from office. The same year the eleven-year-old dictatorship of President Leguia of Peru was ended by a military revolt headed by Colonel Sánchez Cerro, commander of the garrison at Arequipa. In 1931, General Carlos Ibáñez, " strong man " of Chile, resigned in the face of a popular demonstration.

On the east coast, the movement everywhere had serious repercussions, and left in its wake a number of fallen governments. In Argentina, the second term of President Hipólyto Irigoyen, who had been elected by a large majority of the voters, was brought to a close by a *coup d'état* directed by General Uriburu, a leader of the Conservative party. The aged president's peculiarly personal methods of rule, which involved his consideration of the minutiae of public administration, had led to a virtual stagnation of the national government before the opposition against him had crystallized into revolt. In protest against the political system whereby presidential elections were arranged by an understanding between the states of São Paulo and Minas Geraes, the government of the Paulista President of Brazil, Washington Luíz, was overthrown in 1930 by Getulio Vargas, governor of Rio Grande do Sul. At the same time Vargas laid the foundations of the dictatorship which endured for fifteen years. A year later Gabriel Terra assumed the virtually dictatorial powers, which he was to exercise in Uruguay until 1938.

In Central America there were political upsets in nearly all the republics. Uprisings took place against the government of President Mejia Colindres, of Honduras. The outbreak of the famous Sandino's guerrilla warfare against the American-supported rule of President Moncada of Nicaragua, dates from the same period. In Panama, President Harmodio Arosemena was ousted from office by a revolution led by Harmodio Arias. In El Salvador, Arturo Araujo lost the presidency to General Hernández Martínez. Even in Costa Rica, a rare armed demonstration took place against the government. In the Antilles, Rafael Leónidas Trujillo Molina began his long-lived Dominican dictatorship in 1932.

During most of this period the Brazilian empire presented a remarkable contrast to the disordered conditions of the seven Spanish American nations which adjoined her. For a few years after the separation from Portugal in 1822, there was a certain amount of confusion and turmoil, inevitable in a time of transition and adjustment to a new political order. However, the dislocations of normal life occasioned by the change were short-lived and unattended by the violence which accompanied the similar era in the former colonies of Spain. Much of the internal peace of Brazil was due to the relative mildness of the Portuguese character, which was naturally averse to sanguinary and extreme measures and disposed to believe in the efficacy of time and conciliation for the settlement of problems. The vast Oriental inertia of Brazil has always been a passive force for peace, and without resort to definite action the Brazilians have often talked themselves through what was apparently a serious crisis in their affairs. Also, the device of a constitutional monarchy offered a more gradual means of bridging the gap between the colonial status and eventual republican forms than was represented by the Spanish republics' abrupt break with the past. Thus, the processes of political evolution had an opportunity under the liberal empire to prepare the nation for self-government without undergoing the shock of revolution.

The first Emperor, Pedro I, exerted little influence on the trend of events during his short reign. A man of more than ordinary physical vitality and of a certain rough charm of personality, his natural impulses would have found a larger field in the cruder atmosphere of the colony. Frequently ill-advised by some of his Portuguese intimates, he tended to vacillate between a sincere desire to serve the best interests of the country and resentment at the limitations on his prerogative which were embodied in the Imperial Constitution of 1824. He especially resented the strong control of government affairs which was exercised at times by the Andrada brothers, particularly by the able José Bonifacio, who was leader of the Conservative faction. Meanwhile, the most important influence in the government of the empire was the opinions of the large planters, who were primarily concerned with a government that would give the maximum security to their interests. Widespread dissatisfaction with the conduct of certain military adventures in the River Plate region and with the Emperor's opposition to certain liberal measures and suspicion of his ambitions for a dual Portuguese-Brazilian monarchy forced the abdication of Pedro I in 1831.

He was succeeded by his five-year-old son, Pedro de Alcántara, who was to reign as Pedro II for fifty-eight years. In that time he gained such a deep hold on the affections of his subjects that aging Brazilians often express their *saudades* or nostalgia for the days of the good gray Emperor. Dom Pedro, as he is familiarly and reverently spoken of by the Brazilians of the republic, was a moderate and liberal ruler. His position was not only that of a moderator between opposing factions and forces in the country; he actively promoted its economic and cultural development. He foresaw the inevitability of republicanism and shrewdly avoided any move which might precipitate political rancor or conflict. In his personal life, he was a kindly man of scholarly instincts and democratic habits, and, unlike his rakish father, a model of the domestic virtues. No modern head of a state has been better fitted to meet the special needs of his time and his people.

During the Emperor's minority the stability of the country owed much to the strong hand of a priest, Diogo Antonio Feijó, who was for a time regent and Minister of Justice. Later the empire had the services of a group of able and public-spirited statesmen and publicists, like Saraiva and Nabuco de Araujo. In the sixties Brazil was drawn into a costly and long-drawn-out foreign war by the ambitions of the Paraguayan dictator, Francisco Solano López. The war strengthened the position of the military element in the state, with the result that the army increasingly became a disturbing factor in the politics of the empire. Republican sentiment, which had been slowly growing for some time, found support among the younger officers of the army. Meanwhile, considerable discontent had been aroused among the influential landholding class by the abolition of slavery in 1888. The Emperor's daughter, who had acted as regent during his absence abroad, and who held reactionary political and religious views, was held responsible for the act of emancipation and provided an object for the grievances of the opposition groups in the country. On the night of November 14, 1889, the empire was overthrown by a *coup d'état* headed by General Deodoro da Fonseca, who was to be first President of the Republic. Dom Pedro, against whose person no hostility was expressed, was nevertheless expelled from the country within two days, in order that the republic might start its existence unencumbered by the popularity of the Emperor.

The first years of the young republic were stormy. The administrations of General Fonseca and Marshal Floriano Peixoto were troubled by civil war and by the paralysis and corruption of public administration. The civilian presidents who followed the régime of the militarists had to contend not only with the problem of restoring political equilibrium but with grave economic questions involving the financial credit and industrial development of the nation. Whatever progress has been made in the meantime towards the solution of these problems has been due more to the private initiative of the people and the natural riches of the country than to the efforts of her leaders.

In spite of local setbacks, as in Brazil, democracy has made very substantial, though unequal, gains in Latin America. This progress has been the result of a variety of factors. The decline of illiteracy, due to extension of the public-school system, has widened the electoral base of democracy, since the ability to read and write is a common qualification for voting. The growth of literacy has also had the effect of producing a better informed public opinion, which is less responsive to the old appeals for its favor. The more public spirited newspapers have taken full advantage of this opportunity to extend their influence on the side of good government, and the independent members of the press have become increasingly a power to be reckoned with by the politicians. The introduction of the secret ballot in Argentina and a few other countries has removed the customary pressures from voters and made elections a more effective expression of the popular will. The rise of a middle class of citizens, consisting largely of members of the professions, small businessmen, and independent farmers, has formed a strong nucleus of democratic opinion in the more advanced republics. Similarly, wherever industrialization has proceeded on a considerable scale, factory workers and allied labor groups have become conscious of their political interests and assertive of their rights.

Though numerically small, one of the most active groups in support of the democratic movement is the body of university students. What they frequently lack in matured judgment and in patience with the evolutionary processes of political change the students make up in zeal and boldness of action. Their demonstrations against flagrant political abuses and violations of the constitutional order have several times precipitated crises of government, often at the cost of imprisonment or death for many of their numbers. The tradition of student liberalism, characterized though it has been by much imprudent knight-errantry, is one of the brightest phases of the long struggle for democracy in Latin America. The educated youth of the republics have at least been free from the cynicism and time-serving that have so often accounted for the inertia of their elders in the face of arbitrary government.

Certain countries have made much more progress than others towards the realization of the common democratic ideals of the Latin American peoples. Backsliding into the old ways is still possible in all these countries, but the chances of political retrogression grow steadily less and any relapses should be progressively shorter in duration. In Chile a period of instability, accompanied by considerable experimentation with new political formulae, including state socialism, followed the weakening of the old oligarchical régime which prevailed during most of the last century. During the Aguirre Cerda administration (1938–41) Chile was ruled by a popular front government, representing a combination of liberal and radical elements, which was committed to a program of advanced social legislation. Due to the extremes of wealth and poverty in Chile, and to the excessive fragmentation of parties that represent every level of opinion from communism to ultramontanism, political and social tensions are strong and debate is acrimonious. To have avoided the occasion of violence in an atmosphere so highly charged is no small tribute to the skill and moderation of those who have ruled Chile during most of her history.

Colombia has shown a remarkable growth in sound and orderly methods of government. Even during its long periods of disorder in the last century, the contending parties fought over issues rather than personalities, and the dictatorships so common in the neighboring republics were singularly lacking in Colombia. Under a succession of presidents after 1930, improved standards of public administration prevailed and government leaders displayed unusual political sense and moderation. Elections were free, the press uncensored, and the government more and more responsive to public opinion. However, Colombia's creditable record of political peace was suddenly and violently broken by an uprising which occurred in April, 1948. The occasion for the wave of violence which swept over the country at that time was the assassination of a leader of the Liberal party, but it was charged by the government that communist elements had quickly taken advantage of the initial confusion to obstruct the deliberations of the Pan American Conference then meeting in Bogotá.

The Central American republic of Costa Rica is one of the few genuinely democratic states of Latin America. Costa Rican democracy is based on the existence of a large body of small independent farmers of predominantly Spanish blood. Its civic life is not burdened with the incubus of a heavy population of economically dependent and politically inert Indians. It is relatively free from extremes of wealth and poverty, and its hard-headed citizens refuse to tolerate any curtailment of their political liberties by the government. Until the Second World War the national army was a small token force of a few hundred men and so conscious of its proper position in the state that pretorianism was impossible. In fact, it was a proud boast of the nation that it had more school teachers than soldiers. However, a dispute over the presidential succession in 1948 led to considerable armed disorder and a regrettable departure from the country's excellent record of political peace. Of the other Central American states, El Salvador possesses nearly all the elements necessary for a democratic system of government, but has been prevented from realizing its possibilities in that direction by the repressive influence of conservative army officers and large landholders. After a period of reaction which followed the overthrow of the Ubico dictatorship, a liberal régime was established in Guatemala, but since the large Indian majority of the population virtually live outside the nation's political system, democracy in Guatemala is only a relative term.

Basic conditions in Argentina would appear to be unusually favorable to the development of political democracy. It is peopled by a predominantly white race. It is free from the dead weight of a heavy Indian population, the too-mercurial influence of the Negro, and the disturbing leaven of mixed peoples, who move in an uncertain political and social world between the fixed status of the pure bloods. A large foreign-born element, who came late into the national life, have no part in the country's early traditions of revolution and *caudillismo* and are interested only in orderly and progressive government. A relatively high rate of literacy; an excellent press; an urban standard of living well above the average of Latin American cities; a sound economic order; considerable administrative capacity and experience for the conduct of public business; and an intense pride in the country's accomplishments and sensitiveness to its good name among nations — all these are sources of strength in Argentina's struggle for a political life in line with its constitutional design and the ideas of its political philosophers. These forces have to contend against the persistent incubus of personalism, that made possible Irigoyen's return to power, and against the sharp practices of the politicians, but the outlook appeared, nevertheless, to be fundamentally promising for a government at once ordered and democratic.

However, since the overthrow of the second Irigoyen régime in 1930 Argentina has passed through a period of serious, though non-violent, political disturbances that culminated in the dictatorship of President Juan Domingo Perón. It is significant of the political circumstances of this period that, of the eight presidents who held office for from two days to six years, only two, Ortíz and Castillo, were civilians. The uneasy years between 1942 and 1946 were characterized by the gradual rise to power of Colonel Perón, the outstanding member of a group of younger army officers who were discontented with current conditions in Argentine politics. As Vice President, War Minister, and Minister of Labor in the government of President Edelmiro J. Farrell, Perón early became the dominant figure in that administration. An extraordinarily shrewd politician, Perón used his position as Minister of Labor to build up the voting strength among the Argentine masses that was to sweep him into the presidency in the elections of February, 1946. As President, he initiated an ambitious program for the further industrialization of the country, the creation of a strong army, the regulation of the nation's cultural life, and for a political revolution that would transfer the traditional balance of power in Argentina from the landholding aristocracy to the lower classes of the population.

The circumstances which have determined the present direction of Uruguay's political life are similar to those in Argentina. The common denominators are a superior racial stock, a healthy economic base, which, however, lacks the variety of Argentina's more diversified resources, and a sound popular sense of political values; on the other side is a like heritage of long civil disorders that finally burned themselves out, leaving as a force for orderly processes of government a profound distaste for methods of violence. Though partisan feelings may run high in Uruguay, political manners are better than formerly. The principal points of divergence are a more compact and homogeneous physical setting, lesser extremes of wealth with a less conservative national society, a more independent and assertive electorate, and an urge for legislative experimentation in the social and economic field. As a democracy, Uruguay easily ranks in first place among South American countries.

The factors which have conditioned the present stage of democratic development in Mexico are peculiar to that country. Mexican democracy is a concomitant of a far-reaching social revolution, and its main features are colored by its relation to that movement. Its characteristics are also deeply impressed by the prevailing Indian motif of Mexico's politial life. Though the revolutionary movement is directed largely by men of white or mixed blood, its participants and beneficiaries are overwhelmingly Indian — as is the population of the country. In this sense it represents a democracy of the national proletariat, but none the less, a democracy. As a correlate phase of the class struggle inherent in the movement, it implies a corresponding abridgement of the position of the former privileged minority. Among the principal needs of Mexico in the present stage of her development are improved standards of public morality, a healthy opposition party, and a generally higher level of disagreement in political contests.

It is in these countries that Latin American democracy has made its most substantial, if unequal, gains. While other republics contain some of the indispensable elements of democratic government, they are still handicapped by certain local conditions which may delay the fuller fruition of the movement for some time to come. During the early period of the Second World War, the collapse of European democracies through their own internal weaknesses, when confronted with the threat or actuality of totalitarian force, tended to lower the prestige of democracy among its more half-hearted exponents in the New World. At the same time the appeal of personal government was correspondingly strengthened by the initial successes of the European dictatorships, and some of the current dictators indulged in the familiar verbiage and ideology of their Old World counterparts. This borrowing of alien concepts and devices in support of their rule is a radical departure from the customary practices of Latin American *caudillos,* whose autocracy in the past has, at least, been a highly indigenous product, unrelated to foreign dogmas of government. Notable among these presidents have been Vargas of Brazil and Perón of Argentina.

The young Cuban republic is an outstanding example of the countries whose democratic expectations have not been realized. Cuba has had an unfortunate political history. The best government she has had was in the administration of her first President, Tomás Estrada Palma, a famous patriot and one of the noblest figures in the history of Latin America. Except for brief interludes, her government has since been characterized by incompetence, scandalous political corruption, and, at least during the latter part of the Machado régime, by some of the worst features of tyranny. In a country where an army is a superfluous luxury, since it is protected from outside aggression by the self-interest of the United States, pretorianism has sometimes played a decisive part in Cuban politics. There have been at all times leaders and publicists of irreproachable character, like Enrique Varona and Manuel Despaigne, but their influence has not prevailed against the low standards of national politics. The majority of the Cuban people have so far shown a lack of the strong convictions and power of sustained indignation necessary to make an end to the political evils of their country.

After the first outbreak of popular vengeance, Venezuela's reaction from the death of President Gómez was to assert the pent-up aspirations of her people for self-government. The younger element in the population has shown great eagerness to undo in a few years the effects of political repression and stagnation during the long period of dictatorship. For a time, their natural enthusiasm was moderated and guided within feasible limits by the prudent government of

President López Contreras, who was sympathetic with the national desire for comprehensive reforms and was, at the same time, cognizant of the difficulties involved in a rapid transformation of the country's institutions. Impatient with the apparent caution with which the government was being democratized, a popular movement forced the next President, General Medina Angarita, out of office in 1945 and substituted an interim administration headed by Rómulo Betancourt, a prominent journalist. Free general elections, the first in many years, were held in 1948, and resulted in the election as President, of Rómulo Gallegos, Venezuela's foremost literary figure, who was committed to continue the liberal policies of the Betancourt provisional government. Among practical considerations in Venezuela's problem are a lack of administrative experience and technical knowledge in the governing personnel of the new political order, and deficient preparation of the masses for the civic responsibilities of democratic citizenship. In spite of the magnitude of the problem, there is much promise in the Venezuelan situation, but much depends on the intelligence and restraint that are to be applied to the task of political and economic adjustment.

Brazil's very size has accounted for some of the major defects of her political evolution. For lack of an adequate system of transportation the various parts of the vast union have never been effectively coordinated, either as a nation or as a democracy. Regionalism persists, fostered by geographical isolation, ethnic differences, and great economic inequalities as between the states. The federal government has not yet created an administrative system which could bind together all these divergent elements and direct for the common interest of the nation the latent loyalties and energies of the Brazilian people. The authority of the federation has been either too fitfully or too unworthily represented by its agents, or imposed by dictatorial fiat from Rio de Janiero, as it was under the long dictatorship of Getulio Vargas.

A masterly politician, if not a great political philosopher, Vargas attempted to revolutionize the whole political system of Brazil. He broke down the federal pattern of government by substituting his agents, or "interventors," for the elected governors of all but one of the states, though he was forced to suppress an armed revolt by the proud state of São Paulo. He disbanded state legislatures and the federal congress and ruled the newly centralized republic by decree, until the confusing mass of decree legislation became the despair of lawyers, litigants and judges. Through the special department known as D.A.S.P., he not only controlled the vast machinery of government of the *Novo Estado,* or New State, but improved its administrative personnel and procedures with a thoroughness which had never been known under the more easy-going régime that was so congenial to the political genius of the Brazilian people. When the Vargas rule was brought to an end by pressure from powerful influences in the nation, Brazil returned to her original federalism, but some of Vargas' administrative reforms have survived the end of his dictatorship.

In the early decades of the republic, the central government was cursed by barrack influences, but with the establishment of better discipline in the armed forces and a growing realization of its proper place in the state, the military has ceased to be a force for disorder. However, though it exerts its great potential influence with restraint, the high command of the army continues to be reckoned with in all important decisions that affect the political welfare of the state.

Much of the root of Brazil's political backwardness lies in the indifference of her cynical and fatalistic people, who refuse to take their civic rights and duties seriously enough, so long as their personal liberties are not appreciably curtailed. Where Brazilian democracy has failed, it was by default, and for a time it was in abeyance. The general acceptance of the suspension of normal political life by President Vargas was symptomatic of this deep-seated public apathy. However, in the past few years there have been widespread indications of a greater political consciousness in the Brazilian people that should augur well for the country's future.

Dictatorship still persists in Central America and the island republics, but its incidence has declined and the breaks are more frequent in the familiar political cycle of Middle America. In some countries the electorate is not yet ready for its responsibilities. Pretorianism is too frequently an established institution. And the material rewards of political power are too attractive, when compared with the returns from private enterprise in the poorer republics. But there are encouraging signs of improvement in Cuba and Guatemala and Haiti. The orderly fashion in which Haiti weathered a political crisis in 1946 was greatly to the credit of her leaders. Sometimes political strife is only rough and noisy, as it is liable to be in Panama. Born in intrigue and revolution, the bloodless turbulence of Panama's political history has many points of similarity with that of Cuba, though the sardonic humor of the Cubans would scarcely tolerate the tropical heroics of Panamanian politics.

Among other South American nations, Ecuador has an unexampled record of political disorder, and few capitals have witnessed so much street fighting between rivals for the presidency as has Quito. Some of her presidents and other political leaders have been excellent men, but they have seldom been allowed to remain in office long enough to impress their character on national affairs. In the three republics of the middle Andes, inability to integrate the large Indian population into their national life has seriously retarded their political evolution. In all these countries, but particularly in Bolivia, the Indians are as resistant to the incomprehensible *política* of their white and mestizo overlords as they are to the alien culture they represent, and in their present state of racial development are scarcely apt material for the exercise of conventional democracy.

CHAPTER 3

The Past
Shapes
The Present

No. 3

The Spanish American Colonial System

by ASHER N. CHRISTENSEN

A SYSTEMATIC study of the government of the United States almost
always begins with a consideration of the political and administrative
organization of the English colonies in North America, and with
their relationships, political and economic, to the mother country.
Much of contemporary American government — the federal system,
the principle of separation of powers, weak state and local executives,
local governmental organization, to mention but a few characteristics of that government — can be understood only if one knows and
understands what existed before July 4, 1776.

Similarly, a real understanding of contemporary government in
Latin America is in large measure dependent upon a knowledge
of the Spanish (and Portuguese) colonial system, and its operation.

It is not the purpose of this section to offer a full description and analysis of that system but rather to note its principal features and to emphasize the present-day influences of political institutions which have long since disappeared. Our concern is: To what extent are the contemporary political institutions of Latin America the products of the colonial systems of Spain and Portugal; in what ways did three centuries of colonial subjection and tutelage influence the structure and operation of the later independent governments?

Colonial government in Latin America was the end-product of a converging of many factors: the political institutions of the mother countries; the motives that lay behind the exploration and colonization; the indigenous inhabitants of Latin America and their social institutions; and the colonial policies that Spain and Portugal developed and attempted to enforce.

Although the government of England in the seventeenth century could hardly be described as democratic in the present-day connotation of the word, many of the roots of democratic political institutions were deeply embedded in English soil long before the landing on Plymouth Rock. Such institutions as representation in legislative bodies and policy decisions, local self-government, jury trial (which is so inextricably bound to the emergence of political democracy), and a limited monarch, and such basic concepts as the idea of civil rights and liberties were much more than statements of political ideals to be obtained at some future time.

Spain, on the other hand, at the time of the discovery, conquest, and colonization of its part of the Americas was an absolute monarchy. Although municipalities in Spain had once had a certain amount of self-government this had virtually disappeared by the sixteenth century. The Spanish crown was, in 1492, fully sovereign; Ferdinand and Isabella not only reigned but also governed. Freedom of speech and press, the right to be represented in a national legislature, political and administrative decentralization of power and authority virtually did not exist. One of the objectives of the North American colonists in their long struggle with the mother country was to " maintain the rights of Englishmen." None of the Spanish colonies in America, when their struggles for independence took place, had as their battle cry the preservation of the rights of Spaniards!

Almost all of the writers in speaking of the Spanish colonization of America refer to it as the *conquista* or conquest. The term is descriptive and apt. Spain indeed did *conquer* her part of America. The entire enterprise was a natural outgrowth of the reconquest of Spain from the infidel Moors; it contained within itself much of the flavor of a military enterprise, fortified by a religious zeal to convert the heathen. Although generalizations are hazardous and frequently misleading, the conquest of Spanish America was more directed toward the subjugation and conversion of the native inhabitants, and more concerned with the quick exploitation of the mineral riches that were supposed to exist — and frequently did — than it was with the establishment of settlements based upon the working of the soil. Argentina, now one of the most prosperous of all of the Latin American countries, was long neglected as a colony. Despite its name, no silver was found there! It is interesting, and important, to note that the English settlement of North America is seldom if ever referred to as a conquest.

This difference in basic objectives caused a difference in the character and nature of the first Europeans to arrive in America from Spain and from England. The *Mayflower* and most of the later vessels carried passengers who were mainly middle-class and lower middle-class Englishmen, intent upon founding a new home, finding an enlarged freedom, and establishing a new England in America. They almost immediately set themselves to the task of clearing the forest, breaking the soil, and claiming the small farms that became so much a part of our society and played so important a role in the development of our democratic political institutions. Although military men accompanied them, generals and captains were in a small minority and played a relatively insignificant part in the political life of the colonies.

In Spanish America, on the other hand, military men were the chief actors in the great drama of transplanting Spanish political and social institutions to the new world. To encourage them, and to reward them, the crown gave them staggeringly large grants of land. These grants included the rights to exploit the resources of the land and a control over the native inhabitants. The ultimate development of this latter control was the *encomienda* system, whereas the large land grants became the foundation of an economic problem that is of great consequence to this day: the large estate system. The military leaders — the *conquistadores* — were civil as well as military officers. The roster of Spain's high administrative officers in America resembles the roll of an army, or at least its higher echelons. Generals and captains abound.

The English who came to North America found a small number of Indians (which is one reason why military affairs were less important in English America than in Spanish), who were seminomadic and whose general cultural level was low. The Indian population of northeastern North America was so small as to offer little organized resistance to the settlement and expansion of New England, and there was little temptation to utilize the labor of the natives in the exploitation of the resources of the colony. There was slight possibility of a conflict between the laws, customs, and mores of the new arrivals and those of the original inhabitants, because the latter were numerically weak and culturally backward. The social and political institutions of the European — his life, personal or family — were almost untouched by the native American.

In Spanish and Portuguese America almost the reverse was true. The Indian population there was much larger than that of English America. Many of the Indian civilizations, such as the Mayan in Central America and that which is loosely called the Inca in South America, evidenced an amazingly high level of development. The large numbers of the Indians, plus the fact that in their own social organization the masses were bound to the service of the chiefs or *caciques,* offered a rich and immediately available supply of labor to undertake the arduous task of extracting the rich ores from the earth. The *encomienda* system was inevitable. Spanish laws and customs modified the Indian culture, but the latter, in turn, deeply influenced the ways of the European. And, partly due to the fact that the emigration to North America was a movement of families, while that to Central and South America was more a migration of soldiers and adventurers, the blood streams of the conquerors and the conquered were mixed in the one America and not in the other. This too had its influence upon later social, economic, and political development.

Church and State were closely linked in Spain and became so in

Spanish America. The Church, in the colonial period, was not only an ecclesiastical institution; it was also an economic power and a political force. In some of the areas which Spain controlled, the Church became the principal landholder, and remained so not only through the colonial period but also well on into the era of independence. High Church dignitaries frequently held high civil posts. The roots of the Church-State conflict, a conflict which has been so significant and so influential in shaping the organization and operation of government in Latin America, extend back into the colonial period. An analogous situation did not exist in England to the same extent, was not transplanted to English North America in the same form, and did not result in intra-national dissension and strife.

Spain followed the colonial policies that were prevalent in the sixteenth and seventeenth centuries. The theory of colonization and colonial administration at that time was based upon the fully accepted assumption that the colony existed for the benefit — the real, practical, commercial benefit — of the mother country. The colony was to produce the raw materials needed in the operation of the economy of the metropolitan area, buy its manufactured goods there, have its trade open only to merchants from the homeland, and was to be governed in the interests of the *home* government. Although Spanish and English colonial theory were similar, the practice was unlike. No other European nation had a colonial empire which rivalled that of Spain; none, perhaps, had the centralized and autocratic government, and few rivalled her in military or naval power. Spain, because she had the *power* and the instruments to lend sanction to a colonial policy based upon the theory of the time, carried this theory to its logical conclusion. She therefore regulated colonial affairs in her part of America much more closely, much more in detail, and much more harshly than England did in hers.

The volume of Spanish rules and regulations to govern almost every detail of colonial life is staggering, as the documents in the Archives of the Indies will attest. Prices of locally grown commodities in Paraguay, the planning of towns in Peru, the regulation of the professions in Chile, the conduct of local business enterprises in Mexico, the governmental organization of municipalities in Venezuela, all these and an almost unlimited number of other activities were the subject of minutely detailed regulations adopted and enforced by two agencies of colonial government in Spain: the Council of the Indies and the Board of Trade. The Spanish viceroys and other administrative officials in America were charged with the responsibility of enforcing these political and administrative regulations. If the laws or rules were unrealistic, if they were totally unadapted to the local situation in America — and this frequently occurred — or if they were completely at variance with local conditions, only two alternative procedures were open to those who wished to remedy the situation. The aggrieved merchant, the complaining lawyer, the dissatisfied farmer could initiate the interminably long and usually abortive negotiations to secure a change in the regulations by action of the home authorities. Or, he could attempt to influence the local administrator to wink at the regulation, or even to violate it. Spain was a great distance from America. The Spanish administrative officials were, without doubt, as honest and as concerned with the efficient conduct of public business as were their English counterparts. They became involved in bribery and corruption the more because the rules that they had to apply literally had to be suborned.

England, in theory, had the same power to effect minute and detailed regulations of colonial life in North America. In practice, however, she devolved much of this power upon the colonists themselves. Every student of American colonial government is deeply impressed by the amount of *self*-regulation and *self*-government England extended to her colonies. A highly significant number of the rules and regulations governing Englishmen in North America were the product of American legislative bodies, the town councils and the colonial legislatures.

These policy determining bodies, with authority to act and to give sanction to their actions, appeared very early in English America. For a century and a half before our independence from England, Americans were gaining a large as well as a rich experience in the art of self-government. They served as local officials, local councilmen, colonial administrative officers, colonial governors, judges, and even as officers of the English colonial system in America. Those who took part in the framing of our first and fundamental organic charters, the first state constitutions, the Articles of Confederation, and the Constitution, were, for the most part, men of wide experience in politics and public affairs. They brought to the task of writing a charter of government not only a knowledge of the political classics, but a knowledge of these classics tempered and refined by practical political experience.

The first constitutions of the newly independent Latin American states were drafted, in almost every instance, by theorists unschooled in the craft of politics. Almost every commentator on the constitutional development in Latin America notes the lack of an appreciation of the basic facts of political life evidenced in the original constitutions. The education of the men who wrote them compared favorably with that of the little group of Founding Fathers who wrote our Constitution; their experience, however, lagged far behind.

Spain followed the policy of appointing only Spaniards (*peninsulares*) to the high administrative posts in America; England appointed Americans. Almost no one in the Spanish colonies, at the time they secured their independence from Spain, had ever served in a legislative body, occupied an executive position, or filled an important administrative post. A very small number had obtained some political *expertisse* by their activities in the restricted and only form of self-government that Spain allowed her colonies: the municipal councils or *cabildos*. The newly independent republics of Latin America had to construct a new governmental edifice, and with untrained workers. In the United States, largely because of the nature of the English governmental system, the process was more of the continuation of a governmental structure, already well founded. The American Revolution retained more of English institutions than it discarded, and the new institutions were planned and built by master masons and carpenters.

Spain evolved an elaborate system of controls over the acts of her administrative representatives in America. Such institutions as the *audiencia,* the *residencia,* and the *visita* were parts of a complicated machinery of administrative control to enable the home government to maintain a constant check upon the fidelity with which its innumerable and highly detailed orders were carried out. Regardless of the motives that lay behind this intricate system of control, the results were apparent early in the colonial period. Spanish officers in America lived under the shadow of an investigation, announced or surprise, of all of their acts, and an apprehension of the consequences and penalties to be applied to any departure from the strict letter of the law or rule. The purposes of the system may be defended, the results were a stultification of administrative imagination, administrative zeal, and enterprise.

American travellers who have visited Latin America have undoubtedly grumbled over the vast amount of detailed paper work that accompanies even the simplest of transactions. Getting a registered letter, for example, out of the post office is frequently an enterprise that involves the expenditure of considerable time and effort. Impatience is frequently expressed over the failure to cut corners, to be practical. Perhaps few of these visitors see the problem in its proper perspective, few sense that excessive red-tape and bureaucracy may be an inheritance from a colonial system that obtained for over three hundred years. Similarly, and in a larger sense, such universal and contemporary characteristics of government in Latin America as the dominance of the executive, federal systems that are but faint shadows of a real federal organization of the state, the weakness — at times approaching servility — of the legislative and judicial arms of government, and the lack of any real local self-government likewise stem from a colonial system in which these same characteristics were, for the most part, totally absent. On the other hand, the presence, in our system of government, of separation of powers with strong legislative and judicial branches of government, a workable and working federal system, and a strong sense of the rights of municipalities to govern themselves are in part the natural expression and development of the political institutions of the mother country that controlled our destinies for well over two centuries.

Despite its inherent weaknesses, its unwise policies, its top-heavy bureaucracy, its penchant for regulating all things, great and small, from the homeland, the Spanish colonial system in practice did an amazing piece of work. As one writer has evaluated it, " not only to have conquered such an empire, but to have held it so long was an extraordinary achievement."

No. 4

The Wars of Independence and Their Effects

by ASHER N. CHRISTENSEN

ONE OF THE most important of the social and political phenomena of the nineteenth century was that general and continent-wide struggle which culminated in the independence of Spain's former American colonies. One unified colonial system was succeeded by originally ten and ultimately twenty independent and sovereign states. (Brazil never had to fight for its freedom from Portugal. Its separation from the mother country was peaceful and bloodless; it slowly transformed itself from a colony to an independent empire, and during the nineteenth century gradually moved towards its present form of political organization: an independent federal republic.)

The factors and events that initiated the open armed conflict between Spain and her American colonies, the chronology and history of the wars of independence, the brilliant campaigns and feats of arms that were planned and executed by such military geniuses as Bolívar, San Martín, Sucre (to mention but a few of the scores of patriotic and brilliant leaders), the sacrifices that were made by whites, Indians, and mestizos, all these constitute a significant chapter of the world's modern history. However, our concern is not with the causes of the wars, their conduct, and the ultimate victory. Far more important to the person concerned with the " why " of government in Latin America is how these wars, and their immediate aftermaths, affected the institutions of government. We are likewise interested in knowing if these effects were transitory or permanent.

These wars of independence left the Latin American states a number of legacies, most of which increased the difficulties normally encountered in the process of change from colony to independent state.

The wars were long and costly, exacting a heavy toll in men and in resources. Proclamations of " war to the death " were frequently made; they were not empty phrases or thoughtless expressions of

military bravado. In several areas the loss in manpower was so large
as to halt the progress of the area for years to come. The younger,
the more vigorous, and the politically better-trained elements of society were in some regions decimated; and in others they almost disappeared. In a few areas the independence struggles took on an almost racial character so that the white population was pitted against
the Indian or mestizo. The heritage of distrust, suspicion, and of
open animosity that exists between racial groups even today in a few
parts of Latin America has impeded the development of a feeling of
national unity, has retarded the process of working together for the
solution of common political and economic problems. Moreover, the
frequent contemporary alignment of landowners and the Church
(so common in Latin American political parties) against the larger
masses of the population is not an alignment that emerged *after* independence. It appeared *during* the course of the wars for freedom;
independence merely changed the form of the political battles between the groups, not the directions in which they were moving.

In most instances, the urban areas of the colonies were the focal
points of the independence movements. The cities, and particularly
the colonial capitals or sub-capitals, furnished the intellectual drive
and leadership, a large proportion of the sinews of war, and a significant part of the manpower. The councils or *cabildos* of these cities
were usually the first to sound the cry of freedom and to draft the
first declarations of independence. They then proceeded to act politically as though they represented the whole area, city and urban
hinterland, a procedure that was usually resented and frequently opposed by the rural regions. Visitors quickly sense the faint but persistent evidences of a basic conflict that exists in many, if not most,
of the Latin American republics between urban and rural regions.
The phrase that one hears so frequently in the interior provinces of
Argentina, " The head (Buenos Aires) is much too big for the body,"
refers not only to the great population and wealth of the capital city
but also to what the *provincianos* believe is its undeserved primacy
in the polity of the nation. The history of the attempts to establish
a national organization and a national government between 1810 and
1860 in the area that was once the viceroyalty of La Plata and later
became the Argentine republic can largely be written about the
struggle between the one urban center and its rural supporting and

dependent area. And this history can be duplicated in many of the other republics of Latin America.

Spanish colonial policy had discouraged the establishment of industrial and commercial enterprises in New Spain. The interests of manufacturing and commerce had been sacrificed to the quick exploitation and utilization of the mineral resources. Those small industrial and commercial undertakings that had been initiated and developed (either in violation of Spanish policy or, after the reforms of the late eighteenth century, in accordance with these changes) were either destroyed, damaged, or severely impeded in their operation by the course of the wars.

Contrast this situation with that of the United States in its post-independence war history. Manufacturing and commercial enterprises were remarkably well developed by the time we struck out on our own in political life. The progress of our war for freedom damaged our economic institutions it is true, but in no sense to the extent they were damaged or destroyed in New Spain. When the Treaty of Paris was agreed to in 1783, the founders of our republic could build the political edifice upon strong economic foundations. The progenitors of the Latin American republics had to construct new governmental structures on the flimsiest, underdeveloped, and most insecure of economic underpinnings. To complicate the economic problems, the institution of huge estates, with their soil-bound workers, was almost untouched by the wars. The vast bulk of the population, before and after independence, lived in a quasi-feudal society, bound to the soil and dependent upon the *patrón*. This in turn retarded the emergence of a middle class, which in most of the states did not appear until late in the nineteenth or early in the twentieth centuries. Political society in Latin America was for a half century or more without that stabilizing influence that we had from the beginning: the influence of a middle class.

Another unhappy result of the independence wars was the prominence which it gave to the military element in the society generally, or to local military leaders and chieftains specifically. The wars were waged not by national armies but by loose alliances between military chiefs who could count on the loyalty, the zealous devotion, of thousands of patriotic militiamen. Their loyalty however was not to such a vague concept or entity as the nation; it was to the visible personal leader. When the goal of independence was reached, these leaders were not content to lay down their arms, sheathe their swords, and return to the farm or estate. Pomp and glory were not to be found there but rather in the affairs of state. Consequently, the immediate post-independence period was characterized, in so many of the countries, by long and bitter civil wars in which one of the generals of the independence wars sought to continue on as the head of the state, but was opposed by another of his erstwhile companions at arms. A Peruvian writer once noted that the struggles between the lieutenants of Bolívar dominated the *political* life of South America (certainly its northern section) for at least a half century.

We in the United States escaped this result of a war for independence, but perhaps not by too wide a margin. Almost all are familiar with the dissatisfaction of the veterans of the Revolutionary War with the weak and vacillating government of the Articles of Confederation, and the appeal of a number of ex-army officers to Washington to be the man on horseback who should set civil affairs " straight." Had Washington heeded the call, had he been opposed to the point of armed conflict by some of the other generals, the political history of the United States might have shown some of the same features as that of Latin America evidences.

The new nations thus received a military tradition and heritage of far greater significance and future political import than that which we inherited. Our armed forces shrank almost to the vanishing point within five years after the signing of the Treaty of Paris. Standing armies, one might indeed say rival standing armies, of large size and representing the expenditure of a large proportion of the public funds were the rule in the new Latin American republics. The Latin American historian would mention here that their countries had a need for large armies, a need that did not exist in the United States. Our independence was recognized by several European states very early in our national life, and not too long after independence by the former mother country. Until the middle of the nineteenth century, a quarter of a century after the battle of Ayacucho, the Latin American nations lived under the constant fear that Spain would attempt to reassert its authority and control over its former colonies. Thus, military expenditures, though unduly large, were a necessity, and consequently, little of the public revenues could be devoted to the amelioration of the desperately weak economic bases of the new nations.

In summary, the heritage of the wars of independence greatly accentuated and complicated the general unpreparedness of the Latin American states to undertake the huge task of building a ship of state, launching it, and setting it forth upon its first trial runs.

No. 5 [In the previous selection reference was made to the fact that the wars of independence in Latin America greatly emphasized the role of military men in civil affairs. Dr. Charles E. Chapman, in the following article, examines the importance of these military leaders in the early life of the other American republics. Most students of Latin American history and government probably would agree with his observations that " *the* dominant fact in the political history of Hispanic America [and, it might be added, in the structure and operation of its government in the years following the attainment of independence] has been the existence of the institution of ' caudillism.' " The causes of the emergence of this unique and peculiarly Latin American institution, its characteristics, and its political and social effects are amply and understandingly discussed in " The Age of the Caudillos."]

The Age of the Caudillos: A Chapter in Hispanic American History*

by CHARLES E. CHAPMAN

A LITTLE over a century ago the Spanish and Portuguese colonies of the Western Hemisphere, except Cuba and Puerto Rico, broke away from the mother countries and set up independent governments of their own. Portuguese Brazil chose an imperial form of

* Charles E. Chapman, " The Age of the Caudillos: A Chapter in Hispanic American History," *Hispanic American Historical Review* (August 1932), Vol. 12, No. 3, pp. 281–300. Published and copyright by the Duke University Press. The footnotes in the original version are omitted here.

government, which continued until 1889, when a revolution established the republic. The Spanish colonies split up into a number of
countries, all of which have been self-styled "republics" from the
beginning of their independent life, and they were joined in 1903 by
Panama and in 1902 by Cuba, separated from Spain in 1898, in
which last-named year Puerto Rico was annexed to the United
States. One of the dominant facts — one might almost dare to say
the dominant fact — in the political history of Hispanic America in
this era has been the existence of the institution of "caudillism," based
on the rule of individuals commonly called *caudillos*. Somewhat
weaker terms occasionally employed to imply the same things are
the words "caciquism" and *caciques*. There is a vast literature on this
subject in the writings of Hispanic Americans, with whom it is a
favorite topic for study, especially on the part of some of the more
distinguished intellectual leaders in the southern republics. Yet,
strange to say, there is an almost complete lack of intelligent discussion of this factor in the books of Anglo-American writers —
hardly a word about it in the various textbooks and broad surveys
of Hispanic American history thus far published, except occasional
chapters in works of Hispanic American writers which have been
translated into English. The story, indeed, is worth at least a volume,
but for the present this outline must suffice.

It would seem that two preliminary questions might well be
asked. In the first place, just what are, or were, *caudillos?* And secondly, what are the dates for the era of their importance? The precise answer to each of these questions would have to be "I don't
know, and neither does anybody else." However, an attempt will be
made to give at least a hazy answer to the two questions just pro-
pounded.

One normally thinks of a *caudillo* as a military man, almost literally a man on horseback, who is at the same time the political boss
and absolute ruler of a country, or perhaps a district within a country, despite the democratic and republican provisions of constitutions and laws to the contrary. And yet there have been civilians in
power whose rule was of the same sort as that of the more numerous
soldier-*caudillos,* and they should not be excluded from the group —
Garciá Moreno of Ecuador is an example. Usually the word *caudillo*

carries with it some idea of opprobrium, since the great majority of *caudillos* were evil and violent men, little worthy of praise; but in some cases their merits far outweighed their defects, and a few were among the outstanding meritorious figures their countries have produced — as witness Artigas of Uruguay and the above-mentioned García Moreno and perhaps Porfirio Díaz of Mexico. Some of the *caudillos* were extraordinarily cruel and employed the element of terror as their principal method for maintaining themselves in power; while others, though brooking no opposition, joined hands with the capitalists and the Church in order to rule in an outwardly respectable and benevolent manner.

Generally, the more violent of the *caudillos* appeared in the early years of the republican era, while those of later years were somewhat less crude and barbarous. On a smaller scale, much the same sort of evolution manifested itself in the careers of individual *caudillos,* whose measures were much harsher during the years when they were insecure in their power than they were after they had established control. In other words, the *caudillos* changed, just as did the people whom they ruled, and tended to adapt themselves to public opinion in so far as it did not conflict with their own interests. They persistently vociferated their own alleged " patriotism," and conformed to the letter of the law and the constitution, or if some paragraph in the " fundamental document " interfered with their desires, despite their control over all branches of the government in fact, they simply wrote a new constitution and " obeyed " that. In any event, by whatever device, their rule was military and despotic, though often to the accompaniment of pomp and pageantry, display and etiquette, in order to produce the glamor as of royalty to impress the crowd.

Once in office, the *caudillos* ruled permanently, or until defeat overcame them. Periodical " elections " would be held, but as the henchmen of the *caudillos* made up the voting lists and counted the votes, these " manifestations of the popular will " were an overwhelming mandate in favor of the existing government, not infrequently to the extent of a nearly unanimous vote. In rare instances, a *caudillo* was able to pass on his power to a favorite of his own, but the usual route to retirement was through the rise of another *cau-*

dillo, who eventually took violent possession of the government. Such a successor might come from one of two classes. He might be one of a number of exiled opponents, several of whom aspired to take the place of the man in power. Often, however, the new *caudillo* was a one-time henchman of the old, who had gone over to the opposition in exchange for the assurance of succession to office. Such a man was Urquiza, who overthrew Rosas in Buenos Aires. The fact that Urquiza did not make selfish use of his opportunities does not prevent his case from being cited in order to show how a *caudillo* might be swept from power. Rosas had his Urquiza, but his nemesis might have been a Quiroga, a López, or a Reinafé.

These names call to mind another and very important point, namely, that in very disturbed times there might be *caudillos* in different regions of some one country, each of whom might be as despotic in his locality as were the greater *caudillos* who represented the nation. Many names of the greater *caudillos* are comparatively well known, but one must not forget the hundreds, perhaps thousands, of lesser lights out in the provinces. In comparatively recent times Mexico had its Pancho Villa. Hispanic America has known many a Pancho Villa.

Let this suffice for the moment for an answer to the question: What is a *caudillo?* And now, when were the *caudillos* in power? It is generally agreed that the *caudillos* were already in the field from the very moment of independence; indeed, it would be more accurate to say that the wars of independence against the mother country were contemporaneous with local conflicts among those who aspired to be *caudillos.* The strife of the Carreras and O'Higginses in Chile furnishes a perfect illustration of this point. Even Bolívar, San Martín, and the first Brazilian Emperor, Pedro I, were in a sense *caudillos,* although one dislikes to associate them with a status which has fallen into such general disrepute.

The determination of the duration of the era is not so easy. It is customary to date the emergence of Chile from the age of the *caudillos* with the appearance of Portales in 1830, and yet, for a generation thereafter, Chile was ruled by more or less autocratic presidents who, indeed, went out of office at the end of ten-year presidencies, but who nevertheless chose their own successors. In the case of

Argentina, some name 1852, the year when Rosas fell, and others, 1862, when Mitre ascended to power. Uruguay's emergence is dated from the 40's of the past century, but there has been a great deal of turbulence in Uruguay ever since. Colombia can hardly be said to have stepped into the clear until early in the present century. Cuba is not ordinarily considered to have entered the *caudillo* stage at all, but the governments of Gómez, Menocal, Zayas, and Machado have varied from those of some of the worst of the *caudillos* of Central and South America only in so far as they have been held in check by the threat of United States intervention. Costa Rica is often cited as an example differing from the *caudillo*-managed republics of the rest of Central America, but the claims of Costa Rica will not bear too close inspection; the difference is one of degree only.

The Andean countries of Peru, Bolivia, and Ecuador, and possibly Paraguay as well, had at least evolved out of the worst phases of caudillism by the close of the nineteenth century, but the presidents of these countries, if infinitely more decent than some of their predecessors and even devoted to some extent to constructive projects for national betterment, have exercised the power and employed some of the methods of the earlier *caudillos* in keeping themselves in office. What, for example, was Leguía of Peru, lately evicted from the presidency after some eleven years in office, if not a *caudillo?* As for Mexico, the Central American republics, the Dominican Republic, and its pseudo-French neighbor Haiti, not one of them has ever really graduated from the *caudillo* class. There may have been moments when they seemed on the point of doing so. With respect to Mexico, for example, the English writer Percy Martin once wrote a book in which he said that the institutions of Mexico were as sound and as little likely to upset through the medium of a revolution as those of the United States. His book was hardly off the press before the revolutions beginning in 1910 were under way. So it is not safe to count too much on a few years of comparative peace. Even in the best of the Hispanic American countries, one finds something of the shadow of the man on horseback. In 1930, there were successful revolutions or *coups d'états* in Peru, Bolivia, Argentina, and Brazil, and in 1931 another in Chile. In these same years, too, there have been a number of revolutions in Caribbean countries,

such as those in Guatemala, Panama, Cuba, the Dominican Republics and Salvador. Surely the generals are not dead. And each of these
revolutions represents at least the alleged illegal exercise of power
on the part of those in office, after the pattern of the old *caudillos*.

In the light of these facts who will dare to set the dates for the age
of the *caudillos?* At a venture, one might say that the earlier and
more violent forms of caudillism had passed away in Chile, Uruguay, Brazil, and Argentina, perhaps in that order, by 1862; that
they had spent the greater part of their force in the larger and more
important of the other countries by the close of the past century,
but continued in modified form from that time to the present, with
the possible exception of Colombia, which may deserve a better
rating; that Cuba probably belongs in this group; that all of the
other countries have advanced very little from old-fashioned caudillism, except as outside influence is brought to bear; and that over
all Hispanic American countries, without exception, there hovers a
possibility of a return to some phase or other of the institution of
caudillism.

So much for a brief definition. The rest of this paper will discuss
the question in greater detail and, perhaps, more convincingly. At
the outset a new query naturally arises: " Just why should this, to
us, strange institution have developed and taken such a strong grip
in Hispanic America? " The question is not easy to answer in a few
words. Many Hispanic Americans have written at great length in
an effort to explain its origins. At this time, only a few observations,
which can hardly be dignified by the title of a summary, can be
offered, but they may in some measure make clear the situation.

It is hardly necessary to say that caudillism grew naturally out of
conditions as they existed in Hispanic America; institutions do not
have the habit of springing full-blown and without warning into
life. One of the essential antecedents of caudillism is to be found in
the character of the Hispanic races which effected the conquest of
the Americas. Spaniards and Portuguese, then as now, were indi-
vidualists, at the same time that they were accustomed to absolutism
as a leading principle of political life. *" Del rey abajo ninguno "* is a
familiar Spanish refrain, which may be rendered freely " No person
below the king is any better than I am." It is precisely because of the

strength of this feeling that absolutism has become a necessary part of Hispanic practice, because usually only some form of strong dictatorship has been able to hold Hispanic peoples in check. Otherwise, in a truly democratic country of 10,000,000 Hispanic persons there would be 10,000,000 republics. Furthermore, it was the most adventurous and least conservative elements among the Spaniards and Portuguese who first came to America. Even some of their illustrious leaders were men of comparatively low origin in the mother country — men such as Pizarro, Almagro, Irala, and Garay, for example. In America, the conquerors were a dominant minority among inferior races, and their individualism was accentuated by the chances now afforded to do as they pleased amidst subjugated peoples. It must be remembered, too, that they did not bring their families, and in consequence not only was there an admixture of blood on a tremendous scale with the native Indians and even the Negroes, but also tendencies developed toward loose and turbulent habits beyond anything which was customary in the homeland. In other words, Hispanic society deteriorated in the Americas. To make matters worse, there were no compensating advantages in the way of political freedom, for the monarchy was successful in establishing its absolutist system in the colonies, a system which in practice was a corrupt, militaristic control, with scant interest in, or attention to, the needs of the people over whom it ruled. The Anglo-American colonies were settlements of *families* in search of new homes. They did not decline in quality, as there was no such association with the Indians as there was in Spanish America and Brazil. In Hispanic America, society was constituted on the basis of a union of white soldiery with Indian or Negro elements. It tended to become mestizo or mulatto, with a resulting loss of white culture and the native simplicity of life. Soon the half-castes far surpassed the whites in numbers, and, especially in the cases of the mestizos, added to the prevailing turbulence in their quest for the rights of white men. Even in the eighteenth century it was the custom in Buenos Aires for men to go about armed with swords and muskets, for the protection of both life and property depended more upon oneself than upon the law. As for the Indians and Negroes, they were usually submissive, but shared one feeling with castes and native-born whites — for, largely through the process of Mendelism, there was a native-born white class — that of abomination for the government. Most persons in colonial days knew no patriotism beyond that of the village or city in which they lived. For this, in keeping with the individualistic traits of their character, they came to have an exaggerated regard. Spending most of their lives in the one locality and shut off by the restrictive policies of the mother country from contacts with the outside world they looked upon the " cackle of their bourg as the murmur of the world."

In course of time, the " creoles," as the native-born whites were called, became more conservative and less turbulent in the towns, as they developed something of wealth and social prestige, even if on a lower plane than that of the " peninsulars," as the Hispanic political overlords were often called. They were ready, therefore, to place themselves on the side of authority against the disturbing elements, even on the side of the overseas Hispanic ruling class, until such time as they themselves could supplant them. One result of this social change was to push the adventurous characters into the rural districts, especially in the cattle countries. Thus, for example, there developed the Argentinian *gaucho,* or cowboy,

filled with violent pride, quick in reply, impulsive in aggression, exaggeratedly grand and gallant, with an Arabic passion for mad pursuits, for ballad singing, for trinkets and gems, with the conceit of the hidalgo and a Castilian disdain of work, taciturn and astute, malicious and reticent, with great nobility of manner and generosity of spirit, as of one who was not subject to the servility of daily tasks.

Even here, however, the creole master was a necessary factor in society, and he took advantage of his position to become the absolute lord of the district, at the same time that he descended in habits to the level of the *gauchos* upon whom he depended. Thus was created, for example, what Ayarragaray has called the *gauchocracia,* or " cowboyocracy," of Argentina, which produced Rosas and other far-famed *caudillos* of the Río de la Plata countries. To these forces in the colonial era must be added one more: that of hatred for anything foreign, with hatred for the peninsulars and their system taking first place among detested persons and practices. It was natural, therefore, that the overthrow of the rule of the mother countries would result in as great a departure as possible from the *form* of government of colonial days, especially in the Spanish American countries, because of the bitterness generated by the long and cruel wars of independence, but it was equally certain that the new régime would continue the essence of the old. Republics might be set up after the pattern of the then much admired United States, but there was no law or constitution which could save Hispanic Americans from themselves.

Without taking too much space for argument, a few words might be added in order to emphasize the existence of the factor of a favorable atmosphere in colonial days for the eventual development of caudillism. Indeed, the institution really existed throughout the pre-independence era. What were the *conquistadores* and *adelantados* and even the viceroys but absolute military and political bosses, except for the somewhat faintly exercised royal control? Not infrequently colonial officials continued to wield power despite higher orders to the contrary. An example of this, one out of many it would be possible to cite, was the case of Antequera in Paraguay, who held his position for ten years against royally named successors, claiming that the king's signature was a forgery. Among the aborigines, too, the chief had been accustomed to exercise absolute sway, until somebody else should surpass him in influence. For the latter, it was a natural transition from native *caciques* by way of Hispanic officialdom to the *caudillos* of the early republics. The social keynote was one of individualistic absolutism in all classes, instead of that love of, and subjection to, the law which were such marked characteristics of the Anglo-American colonists. In consequence, with the disappearance of the mother-country governments at the time of the revolutions, all authority fell with them, and there was no legal consciousness or political capacity ready at hand to cope with the turbulence which was to facilitate the emergence of the *caudillos*. When the citizens of Buenos Aires met together on May 25, 1810, to begin the movement for the overthrow of Spanish control, it was the first time that the people of that part of the Americas had exercised civic functions. Only the absolutism of the mother country had existed before, and in the bitter war period after 1810 it became a habit to denounce that dominance in exaggerated fashion as a tryranny of which the last vestige should be destroyed. There was no desire for a continuance of the institutions of the mother country such as there was in Anglo America. There was little in the way of political liberty worth preserving in either Spain or Portugal anyway. So institutions were adopted which were as far removed as possible from those of their former rulers, with the result that they did not fit the peoples of Hispanic America; in particular, an attempt was made to pass immediately from colonial absolutism to pure democracy. Naturally, the effort failed. It was possible to tear down the outward forms — one might say the nomenclature — of the old system, but its inner spirit remained, for it was ingrained in the habits of the people. As Alejandro Deústua, former rector of the University of San Marcos in Lima, once said to me: " There was no abrupt change from the colonial period with the winning of independence. The colonial period lived on." Indeed according to Deústua, to a marked degree it " still lives."

According to one of the Spanish viceroys, three centuries of Spanish rule had converted the inhabitants of the Indies " either into irreconcilable rebels or into men who were born to vegetate in obscurity or abject submission." That continued to be the case in the era of independence. The masses accepted their new rulers as easily as they had the viceroys, but the rebellious elements fought the new governments as they had the old. Indeed, it became, and has remained, a form of patriotism to inveigh against " the government," whatever it might happen to be. The wealthy creoles always favored those most likely to offer peace and security, and easily veered over to the winning side of any *caudillo* who might establish himself. Revolutions were fought in the name of various alleged principles, but only persons and ritual were overthrown; the social constitution remained the same, or changed but slowly. The wars against the mother country, in themselves, contributed to the development of caudillism. The reaction against the far-reaching centralism of the mother country inevitably drove the peoples of Hispanic America toward a localism which was in keeping with their individualistic character, but did not engender a patriotism as for a Virginia or a

Massachusetts as in Anglo America. In Hispanic America provincial divisions were mere administrative units, with boundaries which were not precisely fixed and in which few persons were interested. Thus, only a few years prior to the outbreak of the wars of independence in 1810, it was possible for the Spanish government to transfer the vast province of Cuyo from Chile to the viceroyalty of the Río de la Plata, without any thought of protest from anyone. With Cuyo, which includes a number of present-day Argentinian provinces, as a part of Chile, it would be Chile, not Argentina, which would be the most important country of southern South America today. But in independence times, the people rallied, not to an administrative division, but rather to a *leader* against the mother country — a leader who very easily evolved into a *caudillo*.

Ignorance, turbulence, and what proved to be their great ally, universal suffrage, combined to assure the rise and overlordship of the *caudillos*. The overwhelming majority of the people of Hispanic America were illiterate. Certainly, it would be a generous estimate to assert that as many as ten percent of the inhabitants could read and write. With this impossible background, democratic institutions were attempted. The meetings of the *cabildos* became demagogic tumults, with the masses sitting in the galleries and cheering the most radical and violent. It was on this account that new institutions were adopted by law which did not fit actual conditions, a prime cause of the failure of the early independence governments. The turbulence of the new alleged democracy could accept nothing less than universal suffrage, which of course was duly proclaimed. That meant the demagogue in the city. Much more important, it meant the *caudillo* in the rural districts, for the "sacred right of voting" became the principal legal basis of the power of the *caudillos*. Out of this there developed that curious phenomenon, the Hispanic American election. Elections were habitually fraudulent. The only question about them was whether the fraud should be tame or violent. If there were no resistance, various devices were employed to obtain the vote desired. But if there were opposition, the *caudillo* nevertheless won, but to the accompaniment of an orgy of blood. In the beginning the masses supported the demagogue of the city or the country *caudillo*. In these leaders, with their prating about the "rights of man," they found the vindication of their claims for political recognition. The conservative classes acquiesced. It was better to suffer the mob and grotesque usurpers than to lose one's life and property through any genuine participation in elections. All that remained for the *caudillos* to do was to conquer the demagogues. Then at last the work was complete. The cast-out and wandering spirit of Hispanic absolutism had found a new home in the personality of the *caudillos*. The "cowboyocracy" of the Río de la Plata and its parallels elsewhere in Hispanic America had established themselves in the seat of power.

The typical *caudillo* of the early independence era has been described in these terms:

Tenacious and astute, capable of converting himself into a dictator by means of his cynicism of temperament and his systematic cruelty, he was part cowboy, part actor, avaricious of omnipotence, manufacturer of the terror, without any uneasiness of conscience, and with an obstinate contempt for human nature.

Under the *caudillos* there was no hierarchy, no division of powers. They themselves were absolute. Their will was the law. Caudillism became the real constitution, despite imported "fundamental documents." The *caudillos* ruled on behalf of themselves and their following, and protected such others among the wealthy as made fitting arrangements with them. Their government was rudimentary and military. The chief of state and chief of the army were one and the same person. At times they permitted others to carry on the government in name, but the *caudillos* were the real power. Government was purely opportunist, the exercise of power for its own sake and the profits accruing therefrom. The most successful *caudillos* were those who combined audacity and an animal-like courage with the methods of the braggart and bully.

The violent *caudillos* of early days usually observed the forms of the constitution and the laws, but did not hesitate to override them if they proved annoying. As between acquiescence in the "sacred codes" to the accompaniment of delay on the one hand and usurpations and extortions on the other, they chose the latter. They employed fraud, terror, and corruption to reduce opponents to their control. The sword was never in the scabbard. The *caudillos* used it to get into power and to stay there. Those who resisted could expect no quarter, for cruelty was one of the fine arts of caudillism. Each of the *caudillos* might have his band of killers to assist him in his civic functions. Most notorious among such groups was the " Mazorca," or " Ear of Corn " — so called because of the cohesion of its members — of Rosas, an organized body of assassins. Naturally, all political jobs, all graft, and all the fruits of office generally were the sole perquisite of the friends of the *caudillo*. From president, down through members of congress to janitors and street-sweepers, all government was homogeneous.

Nevertheless, the *caudillos* did not forget the great outnumbering masses of the people. As already set forth, public opinion counted for something. So they made a practice of using the vocabulary of freedom and party principle. The documents of those days are filled to overflowing with terms like the following: the " liberator "; " restorer of liberty " — or " the constitution " — or " the laws "; the " pacificator "; " the only man capable of saving the country "; the " holy cause "; " the protector of the people from oppression "; " the deliverer of the people from chains "; " liberty "; " regeneration "; " restoration "; " purification "; " the voice of the people "; " the public interest "; " the honor of the country "; " the reign of public felicity "; and the opposites of these terms in such words as the following: " tyranny," which would certainly be " ominous " or " barbarous " or " funereal " or " execrable "; and the " monsters who dishonor humanity." Both sides shouted their party cries from the housetops at all hours — among others, " Federalism or death " or " Unitarism or death " — always nothing less than death! Rosas insisted that his adherents should display the party color, which was red, and so red bands and rosettes, red-painted interiors, everywhere something red, were the unfailing fashion in Buenos Aires. To wear blue, the Unitarist color, was to court disaster, even death itself. One even had to wear a mustache and by no means to have side-whiskers, the hirsute adornment of the Unitarists, to be a good Rosas Federalist. And denunciations of the opposition were in extreme form. Rosas once wrote to a subordinate always to use the word " savage " when referring to the Unitarists. " Repeat the word 'savage,'" he commanded; "repeat it to satiety, to boredom, to exhaustion." Thus did Rosas manifest his understanding of the psychological value of a phrase. And yet Federalist or Unitarist, or any party by whatever name, governed, once in power, in precisely the same fashion as the other party had done before it, in the absolute manner of the *caudillos*. The different leaders in no respect represented any real political or social conflict, but just different leaders. Government reduced itself to dominating and to resisting the efforts of others to dominate.

In point of fact this practice of exaggerated expression fitted in with the customs of the people. It was a Hispanic American habit to conceive of causes in the name of persons. There have been far more "Miguelistas" or "Porfiristas" in Hispanic America than "Progressives" or men of other party names, at least in popular parlance. The leader, which meant the *caudillo,* was party, flag, principle, and objective, all in his own person. If conditions were bad, it was because another leader was needed, and for that matter each group had its "liberator" or "savior" of the country. Indeed, hyperbole of civic phrase makes its appearance in all the documentation of Hispanic American history. All prominent men are national heroes or tyrants, according to whatever person happens to be writing. Thus Barrios of Guatemala is the god of Central American unity, or he is what might be called the very devil of a *caudillo*. It makes research in this field a matter requiring a great discrimination and critical appreciation, for hyperbole, I repeat, was and still is a Hispanic American disease. The following is a prose translation of a poem which illustrates this tendency:

No longer resound the terms Thermopylae and the plains of Marathon. Plataea and Salamis are as if they never were, and Leonidas and Themistocles are not now famous in the world. These illustrious names have been eclipsed by those of Alvear and Brown.

One Buenos Aires writer of the same period pronounced in favor of a government "under a system which should be free and at the same time heroic," and thought it would then be easy for the newborn nation to "surpass all others." Even a notable statesman like Rivadavia expected an immediate realization politically of all those benefits to which even France and England had not yet attained.

The *caudillos* did perform one real service for the regions over which they ruled, and that was to replace turbulence with order. They were the only curb as against the prevailing anarchy. In so much at least they fulfilled the desires of conservatives and ignorant mass alike. The price of peace was great, but perhaps not too high; for example, in Buenos Aires alone, there were twelve revolutions in the one year 1820. That is not to say there was no more fighting, for aspirants to the place of power schemed against the *caudillo* in office, and a neighboring *caudillo* might war against the *caudillo* in the next province. Insecurity was still a keynote of the times. One *caudillo* is said to have erected a scaffold before his quarters upon which he placed the inscription: " For them or for me." And, indeed, even at the height of their power, the *caudillos* were generally prepared for flight.

Eventually the age of the violent or " muscular " *caudillos,* as they are sometimes called, came to an end, although there was a Zelaya in Nicaragua and an Estrada Cabrera in Guatemala in the present century, and there would be others like them were it not for the influence, rather faintly exercised at times, of the United States. In most parts of Hispanic America there continued to be *caudillos,* but they were now of the " tame " and " semi-cultivated " variety. A few countries, notably Argentina, Chile, and Uruguay, banished the *caudillos* altogether, but their ghosts remained in the offing, ready to materialize in a political emergency. Several broad forces were back of the disappearance of the muscular *caudillo.* Chronologically first were the pronouncements of the great leaders in the wars of independence, Bolívar and San Martín. Both of these men believed in strong government and centralization, or unitarism, and in this respect did not differ from the *caudillos,* but they stood for great countries rather than sectionalism, and for at least a little something of political liberty, with the idea that the masses might in the future develop capacity to work free institutions. In a sense the political history of Hispanic America has been an evolution toward the ideals of Bolívar and San Martín, and these great heroes, rejected at first, came at length to be accepted for what they represented. This was in accord, too, with the influence effected by liberal movements in Europe in the middle and later years of the nineteenth century.

Within Hispanic America itself several other factors contributed to bring about the change. Wealth began to be more prominent and in some measure to rival or surpass the generals. Intellectual leaders were no longer despised, and almost to a man they cast in their lot against the violent *caudillos*. And the provincial *caudillos*, who at one time ruled little more than a district which could be encompassed by a hard day's ride on horseback, expanded their power until they controlled the destinies of a country. The railways and telegraphs and other developments in the field of communications were a great aid in bringing about this change. The local *caudillos* remained in existence, but they were now distinctly subordinates of the great *caudillo*, so long as they retained his favor, or until they might become strong enough to supplant him. To some extent, too, the masses were less easy to deceive than they had been before. Experience had taught, though none too thoroughly, that something more than a phrase, a ribbon, or a mustache was necessary for a good government and that the promised millennium never came.

So outwardly the *caudillo* changed. All legal forms were now carefully observed. If the constitution stood in the way, great pains were taken *to make a new constitution*, instead of an open departure from the old. The " tame " *caudillo* preferred intrigue to violence, or if violence were necessary sought to place the burden of guilt upon others. A José Miguel Gómez of Cuba could invite Pino Guerra for a friendly game of billiards at the presidential palace, and then have assassins await him as he took his departure, afterward denouncing the crime to high heaven — and making no attempt to apprehend the would-be killers (for Pino escaped), who were well-known henchmen of the president. Indeed, one of the outstanding traits of the tame *caudillos* was a certain feline duplicity. They were now afraid or ashamed of being thought to be *caudillos*. Nevertheless, *caudillos* they still were, with perhaps a little opposition tolerated now, though not always, but with the same absolutism as that of their violent predecessors, if in a new ambient. They no longer brandished the sword, but carried on organized pillage through the law courts.

Many of the *caudillos*, on the whole, deserve well in the verdict of history, even including some of the violent *caudillos*. Artigas, García Moreno, and Juárez are to this day great national heroes in

Uruguay, Ecuador, and Mexico respectively. And many of those who attained to the presidency of a republic, even when they are greatly disapproved, merit at least some praise. In this group might be included such names as Francia of Paraguay, Rosas of Argentina, Páez, Guzmán Blanco, and Gómez of Venezuela, Iturbide, Díaz, and Carranza of Mexico, Carrera and Barrios of Guatemala, Castilla of Peru, and Gómez and Menocal of Cuba. Santa Anna of Mexico, López of Paraguay, and the now " reigning " Machado of Cuba may belong on the border-line of at least a little decency and thoroughgoing badness. In Central America and Ecuador there have been many a Zelaya and Estrada Cabrera, and even in countries a grade higher there have been utterly bad *caudillos* such as Castro of Venezuela, Marroquín of Colombia, and Melgarejo of Bolivia — to mention only a few, for a complete list would take up considerable space. Still many more names would be required to make up the roll of provincial *caudillos,* among whom there would be found few muscular *caudillos* deserving of praise, and only a scant minority of the tame variety with any claims to virtue. Quiroga of Argentina, immortalized by the " Facundo " of Sarmiento, and Pancho Villa of Mexico are examples of this class. . . .

No. 6 [The scholars, political theorists, and philosophers played prominent parts in shaping the form and content of the first constitutions of the newly independent republics of Latin America. As noted earlier, Spain's colonial system was one which gave to the Spanish Americans no opportunity to learn and practice the art of self-government. All matters were regulated from Spain, and the directives were administered by Spaniards. Hence, in the early nineteenth century, there were but a few persons who were versed in the *practice* of politics. Large numbers, however, were familiar with the *study* of statecraft.

The timing of the independence wars accentuated the influence of the scholar upon political institutions. Coming so soon after the American and French revolutions, it was inevitable that these latter political and social upheavals would influence events in Spanish

America. Their history, their slogans, their charters, and the political thought upon which they were based profoundly motivated the intellectual leaders of fights for freedom in the colonies of Spain.

The Mexicans and the Argentines, and all of the national groups that lay between them, sought independence, liberty, the preservation of the rights of man and self-government. The United States and France had achieved these, so it was natural that the political charters of these two countries would have a profound repercussion in Latin America.

The list of scholar-constitution writers is a long one. The following selection, devoted to an analysis of the political thought of one of these intellectual leaders (who was also a military commander of the greatest significance), has been chosen for several reasons. It probes the thought of one of the two most influential men of the independence period; it traces the changes in his thought caused by changing events or a varying perception of events; and it comes from the pen of a distinguished Latin American scholar who has devoted a lifetime to the study of the person and the historical role of the Liberator.]

The Political Ideas of Bolívar*

by VICTOR ANDRES BELAUNDE

*I*N the already vast Bolivarian bibliography, studies dealing with the Liberator's political ideas occupy a place of prime importance. Nevertheless, it cannot be said that definitive conclusions upon the subject have yet been reached. Each author has interpreted Bolívar, the political thinker, in accordance with his own temperament or tendencies in matters of government. To this frequently unconscious or sentimental misinterpretation has been added that of the simplistic desire to integrate into a whole as perfect as a regular geometrical solid the extremely rich complexity of Bolívar's thought, itself a

* Víctor Andrés Belaúnde, " The Political Ideas of Bolívar," *Bulletin of the Pan American Union* (December, 1930), Vol. 64, No. 12, pp. 1368–1389. Reprinted by permission of the *Bulletin of the Pan American Union*. The footnotes in the original version are omitted here.

reflection of the varied and at times contradictory political conditions existing on the American Continent. We shall try in these pages to avoid both these pitfalls, presenting Bolívar's thought as objectively as possible.

At the close of the eighteenth century, the first manifestations of a political philosophy appeared in Spanish America. Two well-defined trends were evident, one progressive or reforming and the other revolutionary. The reforming trend presupposed the continuance of Hispanic unity by a monarchy or a federation of monarchies, and was closely linked with the intellectual movement of the time of Carlos III, as personified in Aranda, Campomanes, and, above all, Jovellanos. Their disciples were such American reformists as Baquijano, Villalva, San Miguel, Abad y Queipo, Salas, Arango, Belgrano, and Vidaurre. Revolutionary ideas, on the other hand, found their inspiration primarily in the independence of the United States and, later, in the French Revolution; this school of thought was, therefore, more directly connected with the political principles of the latter countries. Viscardo y Guzmán, Espejo, Nariño, and, especially, Miranda, represented the radical or revolutionary movement, or the desire for absolute independence. Their program was to break with Spain; its logical conclusion, to establish the republican form of government in separate nations. Miranda, however, proposed a monarchy including all Spanish South America. As for Bolívar, conditions in Venezuela, on the one hand, and circumstances of his life and education, on the other, placed him from an early age in direct contact with revolutionary or radical influences.

In a letter addressed to Santander in May, 1825, Bolívar refutes the statements of Mollien in regard to his education. After allusions to Rodríguez, Bello, and Padre Andújar, his first teachers, and to his studies in the Academia de San Fernando in Madrid, he says: " Certainly I am learned neither in the philosophy of Aristotle nor in the criminal code, but it may well be that M. Mollien has not studied as closely as I, Locke, Condillac, Buffon, D'Alembert, Helvetius, Montesquieu, Mably, Filangieri, Lalande, Rousseau, Voltaire, Rollin, Berthel. . . ." These words show that, in contradistinction to those who incorporated new ideas into traditional philosophy or harmonized the two, Bolívar, from early youth, was dominated by eighteenth-century thought, assimilated from original sources, and uncolored by the adaptations of Spanish reformists. Education and environment and, let us add, temperament were all contributing factors in Bolívar's radical and revolutionary attitude. His deep affection for his native land, with the tremendous influence of Humboldt and the feats and warlike program of Miranda, completed the work. All this explains the unique position of Bolívar from the time of the first insurrections, as compared with that of other American leaders who long had felt the weight of reforming or evolutionary theories. Little by little, at a rate which varied in the different countries, the reformists became radicals or revolutionists; in Bolívar the revolutionist was apparent from the first.

The 1810 uprising in Caracas revealed an intermingling of reformist ideas and revolutionary beliefs. To maintain that all the leaders, from the very beginning, were inspired by the ideal of absolute independence is to ignore the evidence. There was, in the insurrection of that famous year, a confused mixture of loyalty to Spain, sentiment in favor of autonomy, assertion of creole rights, and the spirit of reform; the revolutionary sentiment for national independence appeared only in embryo. Bolívar saw the absolute certainty of a break with Spain and the inevitability of the republic. Miranda's ideas, however, were affected by imitation of the English, or English influence, and his yearning, impossible of fulfilment, for South American unity. Bolívar, closer to his native land and more responsive to its spirit, reflected more accurately the nationalist and republican ideal. It is superfluous to cite as proof his inspired forgetfulness or violation, in his interview with Wellesley, of the instructions issued by the revolutionary junta of Caracas, or the climactic phrases of his famous speech before the patriotic society of that city. The impossibility of an imperial federation, the failure of the policy of reconciliation timidly advocated by the Spanish liberals, who were no less imperialistic than the reactionaries, and, finally, the absurd absolutist reaction, all went to prove advocacy of revolution to be not only the most perfect and most logical attitude theoretically, but the only one consonant with the needs of that historic hour.

Bolívar the revolutionist, Bolívar the nationalist, Bolívar the radical, Bolívar — let us not hesitate to say it — the demagogue, saw from the earliest days, by virtue of genius, what should be the true program for the independence of Spanish America.

But Bolívar's radicalism and revolutionary sympathies, necessary as they were to overthrow the old régime, were not merely destructive, nor did they cling to the formulas and practices of Jacobin utopianism. His talent as an organizer led him to realize that national cohesion, even liberty itself, required an authoritative and efficient government. The tragic experience of the First Republic of Venezuela and the horrors of civil war in New Granada were sufficient to give him this profound conviction. A mistaken application of the principle of sovereignty and the supremacy of the will of the people had produced maladministration and ruptures between the provinces.

In no part of America had the fall of Spanish rule caused greater anarchy and misgovernment than in New Granada and in Venezuela. While the situation in El Plata was one of anarchy in the seat of government (its consequence, provincial *caudillismo,* or armed petty chieftainship, only appeared later), in the countries forming Greater Colombia anarchy was universal and spontaneous. Confronting it, as when confronting the problem presented by the election of the earliest juntas, Bolívar found the right answer to the problem. This is the second stage of Bolivarian philosophy, the constructive stage. Against national disintegration, unity; instead of collective and transitory executives, a single permanent executive. Cohesion, continuity, efficiency, and, transcending the boundaries of the ancient divisions of the Spanish empire, continental solidarity — such was Bolívar's program, while the Jacobin aping of sovereign assemblies and artificial triumvirates, and the anonymous and irresponsible power of revolutionary clubs, as in El Plata, still afflicted the rest of South America.

The celebrated Manifesto of Cartagena was not simply a theoretical program. Bolívar carried it out in the famous campaign of 1813; and also after the fall of the Second Republic of Venezuela when, placing himself at the orders of the government of New Granada, he succeeded in modifying the articles of the old act of federation. Bolívar's thought and action, each perfectly balancing the other, were the embodiment of the unity and efficiency of a central government, the only means for triumphing over Spain.

In the year 1815, the taking of Cartagena by the Spaniards coincided with the victory of the reactionaries in Quito, Chile, and Charcas under the direction of Viceroy Abascal; independence seemed definitely lost. In El Plata, a compromise with Spain on the basis of a monarchy was unsuccessfully attempted; later, the Supreme Director, Alvear, could find no other solution than a protectorate by England. At the same time, monarchists and legitimists triumphed in Europe and the Holy Alliance was formed. At this juncture Bolívar, exiled in Jamaica, proclaimed his nationalist and republican faith. Independence, he prophesied, would be attained in the end, and the New World would consist not of a single nation, but of a constellation of fifteen or seventeen republics. With true genius Bolívar outlined the characteristics of these nations and their future. Concerning political questions, he reiterated the ideas contained in the Manifesto of Cartagena as to the necessity of a strong and stable executive power; he affirmed thus early the advisability of adapting the English constitution to actual conditions in the new countries, and hinted at the possibility that the chief executive should hold office for life, although the post should never, under any circumstances, be hereditary.

Upon the same occasion Bolívar grappled with the ethnological problem in America. The war of independence seemed at certain moments a civil war; many mestizos loyal to the king fought against the white aristocracy; in Peru, the indigenous population was turned by the Spanish generals against the creole aristocracy or mesocracy. But Bolívar was aware that this situation would pass, and that soon, in all the races, the desire for independence and nationality would assert itself. Here are his words: " We have, then, reason to believe that all sons of Spanish America, of whatever color, profess a fraternal affection for each other which no machination can alter. They will tell us that our civil wars prove the contrary. No! Internal conflicts in America have never arisen from differences in caste. They have sprung from divergences of political opinion and from the personal ambition of certain men, like all strife which has afflicted other nations. There is yet to be heard a cry of proscription against any color, estate, or condition, except against European Spaniards."

Years later, in a letter to San Martín, Bolívar was to see in the fusion of races the formation of a new stock — forecast of the cosmic race of Vasconcelos — the basis of the aggrandizement of the new nations. "Neither we nor the generation following us will see the glory of the republic which we are founding. There will be a new caste composed of an amalgamation of all races, which will produce a homogeneous people."

Bolívar, with that tenacity of genius admired even by his adversaries, pursued his program of absolute independence. Three years after writing the *Letter to a Gentleman of Jamaica,* when he had established his base of operations in Guiana, he had fresh opportunity to express his political ideas. Bolívar's constructive thought, first expounded in Cartagena and reiterated with greater fullness in the letter just mentioned, reached its apogee in Angostura. Bolívar represented the bases and then the whole draft of a constitution to replace the federal constitution of 1811. Until that time, the predominant influences in America had been the federalism of the United States, French Jacobinism, and the constitutional monarchism of Cadiz. Bolívar broke away from all these. His formula then, as in Jamaica, was the adaptation to America of the basic principles of the British government. It was not merely a sympathetic response to the only nation which had aided Spanish American independence; it expressed his fundamental agreement with the real and essential political conceptions behind those principles. Bolívar, a radical with respect to independence, was an evolutionary conservative as regards government. His realistic outlook explains the apparent contradiction between these two attitudes. In spite of their superficial logicality, at bottom the attitude of the Jacobin nationalists or the Hispanophile conservatives was illogical. Bolívar was a nationalist and a realist and, consequently, a nationalist, a conservative, and a centralist.

The essential element in the bases proposed for a constitution at Angostura is the distinction between the democratic or human ideal and the practical organization of government. With respect to the former, Bolívar reiterated his faith in and adhesion to the principles proclaimed in 1811 regarding sovereignty, nationality, and individual rights. But with respect to the political structure, his criterion was essentially definite and practical. " The most perfect system of government," he said, " is that which produces the greatest possible sum of happiness, the greatest sum of social security, the greatest sum of political stability." Such a government requires stability and force in the executive power, and independence and technical training in at least one branch of the legislative power. The central idea of Bolívar in the constitution of Angostura was the establishment of an institution not controlled by power, not controlled by public opinion. This institution was to be the senate. He found no other means of giving it the desired independence or specialized training than to make its membership hereditary. The Congress of Angostura, to our mind with better judgment, desired to make the senatorship only of life tenure. Political continuity could be obtained only by the executive holding office for life, or by the relative stability of one branch of the legislative power. Bolívar realized that life tenure of office was not advisable for the executive. In an earlier draft he proposed a presidential term of four years with the privilege, as in the Constitution of the United States, of re-election; but in the final form re-election was permitted only once. The Congress, however, fixed the term at six years without the possibility of immediate re-election. We insist upon these details in order to refute the belief that Bolívar was always a proponent of presidency for life.

In Angostura Bolívar did not propose a personal system of government and the supremacy of the executive power. The system which he advocated was institutional, based on a new political formula in which were combined the republican principle of government, the democratic election of the house of representatives, a professional senate, and a centralized and efficient executive power. From the democratic orientation of the revolution he took the essential foundation — a republican form of government and individual guarantees; and, while up to a certain point he was in sympathy with the conservative and centralist movement of El Plata, he nevertheless did not follow it so far as to favor a monarchy. From the machinery of democratic institutions he appropriated only popular election of the house of representatives, in reaction against the ideas and institutions of the first revolutionary period. He did not believe in the supreme and infallible character of the will of the people, and desired to avoid at any cost the pitfalls and dangers that lay therein. This provision for the expression of popular opinion was simply one element of the mechanism of government which he proposed along with the others — a strong and stable executive, and a senate which he desired to be independent and competent. The latter especially was the core of his system. We should not forget that he termed it the foundation, bond, and soul of the republic. It might be said, then, that the Bolivarian formula was the establishment of a conservative republic directed by a true intellectual and moral élite. Gil Fortoul says that Bolívar had no confidence in *absolute* democracy, but rather inclined by nature and by reflection to an intellectual oligarchy; and the same author agrees that such a system was the only one possible to effect the transition from colony to independence.

A golden mean that should embody the essential elements of Bolívar's idea was the inevitable basis on which, with individual variations, all political progress and all social stability in South America were to be established. Its essential parts were realized in one way or another, sooner or later, in all the countries of Spanish America; but when it was first proposed, it had to run counter to a Jacobin mysticism that was still very strong, especially in the countries which were to form Greater Colombia. On the other hand, those who opposed this tendency went to the other extreme. When the men directing the destinies of America forsook the sagacious influence of Bolívar, they wavered between two Utopias: That of the left, which was federalism; and that of the right, which was monarchy.

In Angostura, Bolívar put into effect the suggestion contained in the *Letter to a Gentleman of Jamaica* about the union of Venezuela and New Granada. Was the formation of this entity contrary to the ideas of nationalistic differentiation which were among the roots of revolutionary philosophy? At any rate, the formation of that nation was demanded by the exigencies of war; its permanence depended upon the outcome of the war and upon later experiences.

The congress which convened in Cúcuta after Bolívar's triumphs in New Granada discussed a new constitution. Unlike the Congress of Angostura, which accepted the essential points of Bolívar's proposal, the Congress of Cúcuta followed the Liberator only in the establishment of a centralized government; it differed from him not alone in confiding wholly to popular suffrage the designation of the two houses, which were differentiated only by the length of the respective term of office and by the respective electoral districts, but more particularly in giving congress definite authority over the executive power. The latter was made subject to the supervision of the legislative branch of government, with respect not only to the president and his ministers, but also to administrative officials of all ranks. The ultra-liberal character of the constitution itself was modified, notably by a provision granting the president exceptional powers in military zones. The Liberator felt that, according to democratic criteria, the members of congress who arrogated to themselves full sovereignty in the exercise of legislative powers were not genuinely representative of the Colombian people. In an admirable letter to Santander he tells us that the nation found its true expression not in congress but in the army, whose blood had won the liberty of America. But this statement, incidentally in conformity with historical fact, did not mean that Bolívar was even then thinking of establishing a personal and military régime; he was merely indicating the viciousness of the conventional congressional hegemony. Wedded to the idea of a strong government, he wished it to be at the same time liberal, legalized, and democratic. In a letter to O'Higgins he said: " Chile will do well indeed if she builds a government strong in structure and liberal in principles." After three years' trial of the Constitution of Cúcuta, under Santander's efficient and able administration, Bolívar said to him significantly:

The more I consider your government, the more I am confirmed in the idea that you are the hero of American administration. It is a prodigy of achievement that a new government be eminently free and eminently law-abiding and, moreover, eminently strong.

It may be asserted that until 1824 Bolívar preserved his faith in the possibility of this miracle, the union in one government of strength and efficiency with a true democracy. Bolívar could not but be aware that republican ideals and democratic liberal tendencies had shaped the revolution. We are not interested in ascertaining whether or not he believed sincerely in these principles or whether at heart, as Marius André and, to a certain extent, Gil Fortoul believe, Bolívar was antidemocratic; in either case, it is certain that his realistic vision led him to consider not only geographic, ethnological, and historical factors, but also the psychological elements, the intellectual environment, and the general ideas and aspirations which gave birth to the revolution.

Exceptional powers, granted either under the constitution or during its suspension to provide a more efficient dictatorship, could for Bolívar be only transitory, made necessary by war, and destined to end with it and be replaced by a strong but free government. The history of Bolívar's earliest activities in Peru shows his concept of dictatorship. And realizing the close connection between organized democracy and nationalism. Bolívar, at the same time that he asserted emphatically the necessity for institutions and laws, declared his respect for the principle of self-determination and organized each country with its own resources. There is no reason to question the sincerity of Bolívar's first declarations with regard to the national independence and institutions of Peru merely because, under the influence of later events, his attitude did not conform with his earlier declarations. The supposition that he was insincere — absurd with respect to such a man as Bolívar — should be superseded by one explaining the decided change wrought in the Liberator by his triumphant career, by the situation throughout the continent, and, above all, by the attitude of obsequiousness and absolute submission to him on the part of the liberated nations. It may be said that in the year 1824 the principles of well-organized nationalistic democracy were still uppermost in the Liberator's mind. His proclamations regarding the future congress in Peru which should establish such a democracy, and his invitation to the Congress at Panama, called to realize continental solidarity without hegemonies, were absolutely sincere.

The year 1825, however, marked a fundamental change in Bolívar's attitude. He began to lose his insight into actual conditions. Consumed by an urge toward heroic action, although independence had already been attained, his imagination soared at the prospect of intervention in Buenos Aires; and he saw imaginary dangers from Brazil and the Holy Alliance at the very time when England's attitude and the new policy of France augured an epoch of tranquillity and security. At times the dynamic dreams of Alexander or Napoleon passed through his mind; he longed to continue the epic; he himself felt that he had been born not for organization and peace, but for unending struggle. Sucre and Santander viewed matters from a different standpoint. With true impartiality they counseled him, particularly in order not to imperil the stability of the continent, against intervention in the Rio de la Plata, and urged the importance of not committing an act of aggression against Brazil, who was supported at the moment not only by the Holy Alliance but also by England. Santander summoned him to return to Colombia. Bolívar's dream at that time was to be the " arbiter and mediator of South America," as his letters to the vice-president of Colombia reveal. Frank revelations of genius! Nevertheless, he yielded to reason, renouncing intervention in Argentina and the dream of war against the Brazilian empire. Unfortunately, upon his return to Lima, the temptation to creative action took new form under the influence of his surroundings and the suggestion of sycophants and advisers. Bolívar might not be the arbiter and mediator of South America, but he could assume the leadership of a vast federation to include all the countries liberated by his sword from the Orinoco to the Potosí! This federation was not to be a monarchy but a republic headed, however, by a president holding office for life. Nothing could be more unjust than to judge this grandiose plan by the criterion which is applied to the schemes of mediocre political figures. The project embodied a vision inspired by genius, in keeping with the heroic stature of its author.

However, appreciation of the esthetic grandeur and the noble conception of that federation does not prevent our remarking its lack of accord with the sad reality of the moment. In the first place, the idea of so vast a nation was a contradiction of Bolívar's former ideas. He had said in the *Letter to a Gentleman of Jamaica:* " A state covering too great a territory, either in itself or through its dependencies, falls eventually into decadence and converts its free institutions into a tyranny, relaxes the principles which should preserve it, and ends in despotism. A great monarchy is difficult to consolidate; a great republic, impossible." That impossibility he would have attempted with this federation. Moreover, the project was incompatible with the real amphictyony which Bolívar outlined in the letter just mentioned, and for which he sent out the famous invitation in 1824. That Bolívar realized this is further proved by the fact that the project of the Federation of the Andes appears as a substitute for the Congress of Panama in a memorandum to Pando. The plan, moreover, was contrary to the strongly nationalistic sentiment of all sections of Spanish America. In view of the impossibility of achieving union by popular approval, the projected federation could survive only by maintaining a strong Colombian army in the Peruvian and Bolivian provinces. None of these objections nor obstacles deterred his partisan advisers. And Bolívar, who had magnanimously resisted the advances of Páez, Mosquera, and Flores when they suggested that he assume a crown, accepted in the main the plan of Pando and of Heres for establishing the Federation of the Andes.

The so-called Life-Term Constitution was the instrument for carrying out the federation. Bolívar offered it to Bolivia, but its essential points can be explained only by its possible application to the other nations liberated by the hero. In my detailed study of the Life-Term Constitution, I have attempted to prove that it was not the culmination of Bolivarian political philosophy, but rather, in a way, its rectification. Undoubtedly the Life-Term Constitution was based on the Napoleonic constitutions of 1808 and 1810, for it reflects the mental attitude of democratic imperialism. Its crux is the permanence in office of the executive, offset by the powers of the electoral bodies in political, administrative, and even ecclesiastical appointments.

Possible or impossible, sincere or insincere, the Bolivian project appeared to be, from the point of view of political thought, an attempt at conciliating incongruous principles, an endeavor to establish a mixed system. It must be frankly confessed that the juxtaposition of an extreme expression of the principles of authority (presidential permanence in office) and of democracy (popular participation in all nominations) resulted in an imperfect conglomeration rather than a harmonious whole.

It can be proved from Bolívar's own words that his purpose was to unite radically opposite principles. In recommending his plan to Páez, he said: " Herein are contained guaranties of permanence and liberty, of equality and order." Then he added these even more significant words: " The Constitution of Bolivia includes every extreme and every good point, since even the federalists find it meets most of their desires."

A truly composite government would have consisted in an adjustment between the two elements; authority or power in the hands of a minority, and democracy or majority rule, to create a coherent and logical organism. But Bolívar, instead of seeking such a formula, as he had done in Angostura, limited himself to combining, as he said, all extremes. From the principle of monarchy he took the element of stability, and from democracy, electoral power; from the unitarian system, absolute financial centralization; from the federal régime, popular participation in political nominations; from the oligarchy, the life tenure of the censors; and from the plebiscitary system, the right of petition and that of legalizing constitutional reforms. A genuine mixed system would have required not this duality of extremes, but the unity of a mean between the two. Such was the method Bolívar followed in Angostura. Between the extremes of an executive power permanent and hereditary, and one transitory and cameral, he there evolved the unipersonal presidency, elective and for a long term. Between pure oligarchy and the Jacobin régime with its single assembly, he established the middle course of the sage bicameral system, with an elective house and a senate, membership in which would be a profession. He wished membership in the senate to be hereditary, but the Congress of that time made it of life tenure; the senate might have evolved into a body similar to a corporation or guild. As a mean between the absolute centralism of the Napoleonic régime and the chaotic federalism of the first years of the revolution, he proposed a system of efficient political unity with respect for municipal autonomy. Accordingly, in the political constitution proposed at Angostura there were balanced against each other the minority and the majority, political power and public opinion, stability and provision for change, because no one element was carried to an extreme.

Such a combination was impossible in the constitution of 1826, which emphasized both the principle of authority and that of popular intervention. The Constitution of Angostura created a stable executive and a restricted suffrage; the Bolivian constitution, on the other hand, made the presidency of life duration, while amplifying the basis of suffrage. The heart of the Constitution of Angostura was the senate; that is, a permanent collective institution; the heart of the Life-Term Constitution was the presidency, or one person. The first was conducive to stable equilibrium; the second, to a hazardous situation, vacillating between despotism and chaos. There was, then, a radical difference between the two constitutions, the difference which lies between a conservative republic and a régime tending toward democratic imperialism. For this reason it is hard to conceive how so talented a commentator as Gil Fortoul can say that the Bolivian constitution was based on that of Angostura.

The best criticism which can be made of the former was written by Bolívar himself in an attempt to justify it:

In no covenant of any representative government do I see so much popular liberty, so much direct participation on the part of the citizens in the exercise of sovereignty, and so much strength in the executive power, as in this project. Herein are united all the attractions of federation, all the solidity of central government, all the stability of monarchical governments. All interests are interwoven and all guaranties established.

Bolívar wished to accomplish the miracle of uniting the advantages of all systems, and what he did in reality was to unite all their defects: the absolutism of life tenure, the demagogic agitation of electoral assemblies, the drawbacks of both centralism and federation.

But if the Life-Term Constitution presents the indisputable defects mentioned, Bolívar's exposition that accompanied it, inferior in certain respects to his address at Angostura, contains nevertheless admirable arguments concerning the impossibility and unsuitability of the monarchical form of government and the independence of the judicial power. " No power is so difficult to maintain as that of a new prince. If Napoleon could not maintain himself against the league of republicans and aristocrats, who in America will succeed

in founding monarchies upon this soil aflame with the bright fires
of liberty! . . . The true liberal constitution is known by its civil and
criminal codes; and the most terrible tyranny is that exercised by
the courts through the powerful instrument of law. The judicial
power contains the measure of the citizens' good or ill; and if there
be liberty, if there be justice in the republic, they are dealt by this
power."

The Life-Term Constitution was applied to Bolivia with modifications which diminished its defects; later it was imposed upon the
electoral colleges of Peru, disregarding the congress which those
colleges had elected and which Bolívar himself had convoked. The
application of the new charter to Colombia necessarily presented
greater difficulties, since the Constitution of Cúcuta had been in
force there since 1821. Although shaken by the insurrection of Páez,
the Colombian organization still manifested powerful vitality. The
historian must regretfully confess, in view of overwhelming documentary evidence, that Bolívar at first accepted the idea of a popular
vote (revolution from above), to extend the new constitution to his
native land.

The most interesting correspondence in the history of political
thought in America had preceded this movement. In the years 1825
and 1826, in letters which are documents of supreme importance,
Bolívar and Santander discussed the constitutional problem. Independence was won, Spain conquered and powerless, the Holy Alliance held in check by England; but how were strong and stable
governments to be established in America, convulsed by fifteen years
of a warfare which had destroyed economic foundations, overturned
the social structure, and almost annihilated a generation? The
Church had joined the movement late; property was half destroyed;
the middle class was as far as in the colonial epoch, or farther, from
free labor; and the fatal Iberian individualism had been intensified
by military enterprises and an environment of continuous heroism.
Bolívar thought that the Constitution of Cúcuta, and even more, the
Peruvian Constitution of 1823, providing for congresses elected by the
conventional popular suffrage and with interventionist or sovereign
tendencies, carried the seed of the perpetuation of anarchy; he
wished to replace this figment of constitutionality by the reality of a

strong and stable government based upon personal influence and inspired by a lofty ideal of political morality. Bolívar trusted in men; Santander in institutions. Bolívar desired free creative action, Santander, continuity and reform within the existing structure. Bolívar believed that legalistic structure was an obstacle to well-considered personal action; Santander held that personal prestige and initiative could consolidate and bring efficiency to established institutions. It must be confessed that in this discussion between Bolívar with his flashes of genius and the unquestionably talented Colombian vice-president, it was the latter who was right, and to such a degree that Bolívar had to yield before the evidence, and give up his plan for having a popular vote. Upon returning to Colombia, he did not assume the dictatorship offered him in the resolutions adopted at Guayaquil and Quito, but declared his allegiance to the constitution of 1821, only stating the necessity of reform and thus giving the Life-Term Constitution the status of a mere personal project or opinion. Bolívar not only changed his mind on this point; he also comprehended that the Federation of the Andes was out of the question, and in an admirable letter to Santa Cruz, which contains his confession of faith as a nationalist, he advises the latter to follow an exclusively Peruvian policy.

The national crisis produced by the revolt of Páez was settled, thanks to Bolívar's personal influence, by adopting a compromise which practically made Venezuela a political unit within Greater Colombia. The Constitution of Cúcuta, although somewhat battered, was still in force. The course proposed by Santander had triumphed, but he had lost his influence. Páez was in control of Venezuela, while Bolívar assumed the presidency in New Granada. Then political events took another interesting turn. The amendment of the constitution now was not to be demanded by Bolívar alone on account of the necessities of greater centralization and efficiency, but also by Santander himself who, in this ironic political game, sought amendment in the name of greater liberty and the federation of which he had been a sworn enemy all his life. The Constitution of Cúcuta was thus attacked from the right as well as from the left. Instead of the necessary cooperation, there appeared the most lamentable personal quarrels which were insincerely rationalized in opposing schools of thought, making impossible that patient labor of the adjusting and amending of existing institutions in which true political progress consists. But legality and institutionality were more real than had been believed. There was room in popular opinion only for the constitutional amendment almost unanimously desired. Ignoring the limit set by the Constitution of Cúcuta itself within which it might be amended, a special assembly to bring about the desired reform was convoked. Such was the Convention of Ocaña.

The principal problem confronting this assembly was more than a simple political reform, for it involved a more profound problem. At bottom, the constitutional crisis of Colombia was a conflict of nationalities; ever since his sojourn in Jamaica, Bolívar had seen with the clarity of genius that New Granada and Venezuela constituted distinct national individualities. Neither military cooperation, nor the prestige of Colombian arms, nor even the personality of the Liberator himself, had sufficed to surmount differences of a geographical and, to a certain extent, of a certain racial nature, and create the psychology of national unity. Sober judgment evidently brought Bolívar to accept the fact of the separation, which he had himself sanctioned by creating heads of government for Quito and Venezuela. But this rational and realistic solution was combated, on the right, by the centralism of the exaggeratedly Bolivarian faction and, on the left, by the federalism and radicalism of the Liberator's enemies. What was Bolívar's own attitude toward this problem? It is impossible to speak of a concrete Bolivarian solution to the problem for that period, as can be done for the years 1810, 1812, 1815, and 1819. It was the period of grievous vacillations on the part of the Liberator. The gravity of the political problem facing Spanish America presented itself in tragic guise to Bolívar's spirit. It might well be said that he was the new Kant of politics, discovering and pointing out alarming conflicts: between continental solidarity and the principle of nationalism; between the democratic ideal and that of a stable and progressive government; between the ideal of political and cultural equality and racial differences; between the cultural bond with utterly reactionary peoples such as France and Spain and the economic and political link with peoples of different culture and religion.

Did Bolívar at this tragic period find the solution to these problems? Did his spirit adhere to a given formula with his early firmness, faith, and resolution? Unquestionably, no. At bottom the Liberator's attitude was one of complete pessimism. Only in his doubts do we find anything constant — his consciousness of a mission to perform, his duty to attempt a solution, and the momentary revival of the heroic impulse to accomplish. We have numerous proofs in Bolívar's correspondence of his state of mind. The phrase which he repeated frequently, " Everything is bad and everything is worse," reflects the dilemma which he felt inherent in the problem facing Colombia. His sympathies inclined him to preserve the national unity by a strong and independent government, but he knew such a solution to be impossible. There remained only the peaceful separation of Venezuela and New Granada, which might be linked by a federative bond or the old federalist program of 1811. His work was destroyed in either case. From time to time his appreciation of facts reasserted itself, and he counseled his friends to support the separation of Venezuela and New Granada. But they resisted the idea, invoking the glory of the Liberator. Rather than accept a constitution which would not give Colombia the strong and independent executive which Bolívar advocated, his partisans preferred to withdraw from the convention, leaving it without a quorum. The semblance of constitutionality which had been successfully maintained was thereby broken, and Bolívar, heeding the summons of the people, assumed the dictatorship. This did not mean an arbitrary régime, nor that the situation would be permanent. Bolívar himself dictated a decree preparatory to making at the opportune moment that appeal to the will of the people which should decide the republic's destinies.

In spite of the attempt on his life in September, various abortive insurrections and, finally, the war with Peru, Bolívar did not change his plans, but decided to call a conference to decide the form of government, issuing a summons for the election of congress to meet in 1830. The proposal reveals the depth of Bolívar's conviction that the only way to decide upon the definitive form of government was in accordance with the will of the people. It is nevertheless evident that that proposal complicated and precipitated the political crisis which the dictatorship could not resolve and had barely been able to postpone. While Bolívar's partisans found no means of salvation other than the establishment of a monarchy to be headed by a European prince after the Liberator's death, the liberals revived with renewed intensity the federalist program, in conjunction with the separatist idea, or the division of New Granada and Venezuela.

Bolívar himself, convinced of the inevitable downfall of the dictatorship and the impossibility of a total consolidation of government, thought rescue lay in English support and an English protectorate. Colombia's death throes coincided with the waning of the Liberator's physical and moral strength and with the spiritual throes which preceded his end. His deep pessimism included not merely Colombia but the whole of South America. Beyond question, the Liberator's deepest desire was for voluntary exile and liberation from his impossible task. But he could neither flee from nor abandon his country. His remaining in Colombia can never be explained as motivated by vulgar ambition, for in that case it would have been accompanied by that substitution for the faith of genius which is the illusion of the mediocre. Bolívar was the conscious victim of an historic mission. While Rivadavia resigned the presidency in El Plata, and ceased to execute the constitution of 1826 in the hope of a reaction which never came, Bolívar, without hope, strove to the very end. It cannot be said that during this period Bolívar had a truly constructive philosophy; although maintaining his theoretical adherence to a strong centralized government, his words were rather criticisms of solutions proposed by his adversaries, the defects of the Constitution of Cúcuta, and the errors committed in its application.

The most important document of this period is undoubtedly his letter to O'Leary of October 13, 1829, which is the equivalent of a political testament. Here he reiterated with renewed energy his objections to the project for a monarchy, in which, as Samper has proved by the testimony of Minister Vergara himself, Bolívar had no part whatever; he refuted in its turn the unsuitability of the life-term presidency, foreseeing the chaos which would ensue upon his death; and, finally, he advised the friendly separation of Venezuela and New Granada, as he had suggested, notwithstanding the protest of his friends, during the Convention of Ocaña. Unfortunately, that suggestion came too late; it might perhaps have preserved, through a federal relationship, the existence of Greater Colombia.

When the congress of 1830 convened, Bolívar left the solution of the political problem entirely in its hands, and, for the first time during his long career, refrained from presenting a program of his own. To what was this negative attitude due? Did he respect the ability of that assembly, in which the first minds of the nation met, or did he completely lack faith in every solution? The only thing certain is that one definite deduction may be made from this attitude on Bolívar's part. In convoking an assembly elected with all freedom and good judgment, and in placing the destiny of the country absolutely in its hands, Bolívar showed that he had not lost his old criterion regarding the will of the nation.

Having examined the Liberator's ideas during the principal passages of his life, let us try to summarize them briefly. Unquestionably, one must clearly differentiate the following stages of Bolívar's political philosophy: First, that of the radical or demagogic propagandist whose program was the destruction of the old régime and a definite break with Spain; second, that of the revolutionary leader who advocated a strong and stable unitarian government to win the military conflict; third, that of the statesman who applied the same principles of unity, stability, and efficiency to the definitive political organization of a conservative republic, administered by an intellectual and moral élite; fourth, that of the victor in the struggle for independence, desirous of forming a vaster national entity from the different nations which he had called into being, a government based on a semifederal and semidemocratic imperialism, showing unquestionable Napoleonic influence; fifth, that of the statesman who, facing the complexities of the political problem and of the continued existence of Greater Colombia, hesitated between a conservative centralized republic under a vigorous executive, and the formation of separate governments in the respective historic national nuclei, which together would form a simple federation; sixth, that of the dictator who attempted to preserve national unity, and who, convinced of the transitoriness of this form of government, placed upon the will of the people the responsibility for deciding its destinies.

Enlightened and impartial analysis will reveal the fact that five of

these six stages have several characteristics in common, with differences of emphasis and circumstance: Nationalism; republicanism;
respect for the will of the people; unitarianism; a professional and
independent congress; administrative discipline, efficiency, and order;
independence of the judicial power; importance of cultural, ethical,
and religious factors; stability of institutions; and continental solidarity. Such is the essence of Bolívar's thought.

PART TWO

The

Basic Condi-
tioning Factors

CHAPTER 4

The
Influences of Land, People, and Social Organization

No. 7 [As was noted in the previous chapter, the Latin American constitution writers were deeply moved by the democratic political thought of the eighteenth century, and greatly influenced by the Constitution and constitutional system of the United States. For many reasons, however, they tended to give undue emphasis to democratic political mechanisms and machinery without fully considering how well these institutions which were the products of one environment would take root and flourish in another. The fact that our Constitution was the basis of a workable and working political society was sufficient evidence to them that its intricate machinery could be moved to Latin America.

The political charters of any nation are, of course, the constitutional expression of underlying geographical, social, ethnographic, and economic factors. Latin America copied the formal expression of these institutions — the Constitution — but it did not, nor could it, copy the social organization of England's colonies in America.

Dr. Crawford notes in the following article some of the social institutions of Latin America, such as illiteracy and the nature of the family and intra-family relations and loyalties that have shaped and molded the political machinery of those republics.]

The Pathology of Democracy in Latin America: A Sociologist's Point of View*

by W. REX CRAWFORD

THE only words in the title of this symposium which do not cause difficulty are " of " and " in," since even Latin America is a " nomer " that many protest is a " misnomer " for some parts of the region southeast of the U.S.A., and " pathology " and " democracy " can get into water as hot and deep as any that lies under the thin ice over which the social sciences skate. The very lumping together in our discussion of twenty republics varying as they do in Latin America is a procedure of doubtful accuracy, and one which at first encounter arouses the ire of any good nationalist in these countries. The term " pathological " suggests too strongly a complacent superior attitude on our own part that may befit the propagandist or the naïve and uninformed man on the street, but not the social scientist. The world does not fall so neatly into the patterns of perfect democracy and the outer darkness as Mr. Churchill has supposed. Can we not accept a certain relativity in these matters and remember the large-sized mote in our own eye?

With the struggle of almost innumerable thinkers to define the direction and goal, we are surely familiar. The writer has no intention of assembling all the definitions available, for if they were all assembled, sociologists might lay the emphasis not upon forms and constitutions so much as upon something broader that earlier theologians would have called men's will and men's love. Since the development of " Mr. Tylor's science," cultural anthropology, we would be more likely to say that the legal arrangements grow out of and express the culture; that back of them lies a slow secular growth

* W. Rex Crawford, " The Pathology of Democracy in Latin America: A Sociologist's Point of View," *The American Political Science Review* (March, 1950), Vol. XLIV, No. 1, pp. 143–147. Reprinted by permission of *The American Political Science Review*. The footnotes in the original version are omitted here.

of the idea that personality, the freedom and full development of the individual are ultimate values, not to be sacrificed to the state; that power may be necessary for survival, and that unity or consensus or conformity may be necessary to power, but that something like Albert Schweitzer's " reverence for life " is a deeper principle. These things are no sooner said than we realize that we often sin against the ideals we cherish and fear the freedom to which we give lip-service. The practice falls far short of the preaching.

The identification of democracies with constitutions, against which it is especially necessary to guard in the case of some Latin American countries, is only one of several tempting equivalencies. Men both individually and en masse seem to group together, as if they were related to each other, many things that have no more in common than being liked by the same people; and there are classes of hated objects, too, among which we do not stop to demonstrate logical connections.

A case in point is that democracy, because it is by definition good, means to most of us peace, progress, prosperity, and permanence, because they also are good. It should not need a Charles Maurras to sow the seed of skepticism here. We are writing about democracy in Latin America, not about the stability of government nor the standard of living, nor about backwardness, except in so far as they can be shown to have a relation to democracy.

A rephrasing of the topic that offers some advantages might abandon the analogy of health and disease and remain more irreproachably on the social science level by borrowing a hint from the Marxists, who are in the habit of referring to prerevolutionary situations and the necessity of recognizing them if one is to choose the right and hopeful moment for the intervention of a disciplined and instructed leadership. Or, for that matter, we might copy the educators who talk in these days of the reading-readiness of the child. We might make the enormous but congenial assumption that the paths of history lead inevitably to democracy, just as the people mentioned assume that reading will come sometime and that revolutions are ineluctable; this would lead us to ask what are the conditions that may help us to understand the varying patterns of life and government in Latin America.

The first thing to be noted is that most of the countries of Latin America contain large numbers of inhabitants who are not yet, as Sol Tax wrote in his excellent article on " Democracy in Middle America," " incorporated " in the social system; most of these countries have an extensive area claimed by the nation which is hardly effective national territory. The Indians of these areas scarcely think of themselves by the national name and have the vaguest idea of places beyond the reach of a day's walk. At best it can be said that they have democracy without its ideology, that in their internal arrangements life is simple, cooperative, and cannot be labelled fascist or totalitarian. However, it would probably be equally true to deny the description democratic. They simply live at a level of traditionalism and gerontocracy at which these modern tags we use are irrelevant, and the questions we raise are meaningless. Countries in which this situation is an important part of the picture might almost be better described by Ricardo Rojas' term " Eurindian," than as " Latin," for they are divided into two cultures, two ways of life, with, of course, some degree of crossing from one to the other. The crossing need not be biological; it is a matter of the language spoken, the clothes worn, the way money is earned and the degree of emancipation from pre-Columbian tribalism. This becomes a vivid reality when one hears the phrase, " When I was an Indian," being used.

It is only an act of realism on our part to recognize as the anthropologist does this element, unchanging and resistant, rather than dynamic and controlling, in the life of many Latin American republics.

Even in this part of the population, despite justified claims that some countries have more advanced labor legislation than we, or that others started national social security eleven years earlier than we and practice more social democracy, the common impression is that political democracy is more of a failure in Latin America than in some other parts of the world. There is something to discuss. And while refusing to admit that historians, political scientists, and sociologists are entirely distinct species of animals, we can agree that they may well emphasize different aspects of a problem such as the state of democracy in our sister (or half-sister) republics.

It is not mere prejudice on our part to believe that widespread illiteracy is under modern conditions a tremendous handicap in the attempt to operate representative government on a broad scale. It is nothing against either the goodness or the native intelligence of the analphabetic to recognize that access to information on national and international issues and the ability to use such information is a *sine qua non* of a tolerable democracy. Here again there is a variation that must be acknowledged, from highly literate Uruguay through a number of nations that are half unable to read and write to an extreme of approximately 80 percent illiteracy, largely due to the same Indian element in the population which has been stressed above in another connection. The number of university educated people who charm us by their wide-ranging conversation, and seem so superior to our half-barbarian alumni, is after all pitiably small, and the secondary school students, with the full ambitious program of their *liceo* years, are only a tiny fraction of our millions of high school teen-agers. Latin America has been slow to accept the idea of prolonged education for the masses and would find it economically difficult if it were accepted. She is trying still to be selective and aristocratic in education, in a day when both economics and politics demand the wide diffusion of skills and of literate political participation.

Obviously political literacy is more than a matter of years in school. In varying degrees the things that might be substitutes are also lacking. In the immense back country travel is slow and difficult, railroads do not penetrate, radio receiving sets are too expensive and movies are not seen. In spite of four hundred years of settlement and exploration, there is an isolation unknown to England and Scandinavia and the United States. A sparse population may lend itself to frontier democracy, but it certainly does not help the functioning of a centralized national type of democratic government.

We are in the habit of saying that another of the conditions propitious to the development of democracy is the attachment of high values to individual personality. The Latin Americans have an enthusiasm for individualism to the extent of denying to the Yankees in all their standardized mass production any possession of this admirable trait. They do not study personality as our psychologists do, but make it a goal and a movement: personalism. The paradox of all this is precisely the reason why, in the opinion of the outside world, democracy is sick much of the time in Latin America. The cult of the outstanding personality, the vote for the man rather than for the party or the platform, is a denial of the essence of the democratic process in which people as a whole control their government. The *caudillo*, from president on down to local politician, is a Latin American institution which offers disquieting suggestions of the divinity-genius-leader in some governments that seem to us anything but democratic.

In a related category is the overdevelopment, until it becomes a defect, of the virtue of family loyalty. Taking care of one's own (and they are likely to be numerous) leads to a lush growth of nepotism or *filhotismo*. It is most difficult for civil service ideals of competence and impartiality to make way against this deep-rooted tradition of giving practical expression of love and solidarity, in the case of one's kind. No reader of this journal is ignorant of the cases in our own country in which the pay roll of government or labor is loaded with relatives, but it is believed that the difference between the Anglo-Saxon tradition and the Latin one is real, nevertheless, and worthy of mention.

Equally natural, but perhaps less laudable, is a disposition to look after oneself while in a political position that makes it possible, and to line one's pockets with the money of others who need something badly and are in a position to pay. Americans attempting to do business in Latin America may be particularly conscious of the different form this practice takes in another culture, and forgetful of tribute they may have paid in one way or another for the supposedly free services of the police, municipal permits, lobbying and its expenses for entertainment, kickbacks to the party, and actual buying of votes. The poverty of Latin American countries and the impossibly low salaries they pay government officials and employees may serve as a partial explanation or excuse of practices of " squeeze " and graft. At the same time the low national income and the many urgent problems, that graft makes impossible of solution, mean that an amount of graft which we might feel we could afford without crippling ourselves bulks proportionally larger in Latin America. One cannot read Nathan Whetten's masterly exposure of the *mordida* in *Rural Mexico* without agreeing that here is the great challenge to the practice of efficient democracy in that and many other countries.

Even an idealist might argue that among these urgent problems confronting most of Latin America there are some that take precedence over the niceties of democratic procedure, and that it is more important to bring food to the malnourished and hospitals to the sick and dying by whatever methods than to worry about constitutional forms. Life comes first and politics second. When the general level of getting and spending has been built up to the level we think of as middle class, democratic institutions will follow of themselves.

This glorification of the middle class, an image of ourselves as we like to see us, is part of that tendency, already noted, to identify all the things that are ours and are good and to treat them as logically and causally related. It is not just a trick that our minds play upon us. There is justification as far back as Aristotle for the conviction that government works best when the middle class predominates or at least when it can be the determining factor in politics. It is hardly necessary to add the obvious caveat that even the middle class may be perverted, deceived, or fail to seek the good life along the right road. Amid all the uncertainties of definition of this class, and the inadequacy of statistics on the subject, can one not say that the middle class by the 1940's was as highly developed in Argentina as anywhere in Latin America? Do we approve of the results?

To guard against the possibility of the middle class becoming the victim of its own emotions and frustrations or of the politician's slogans and manipulations, it needs a long practice on the small scale of " give and take " and in the responsibilities and rights of representative government. In our own history we stress not only the middle class, but its experience of local self-government, its town meetings and school boards. In spite of what may be said for the *cabildo* this is a tradition that is lacking in Latin America. Repeated interference with parliamentary practices that have been set up has not helped matters.

The writer attended the first national meeting of the Brazilian Association of Writers just after censorship was eased. The only parliamentary order possible was secured by ringing a buzzer so loudly that no one could hear and thus silence would be forced momentarily so that the intolerable din of the buzzer would cease. Brazilian friends explained half in jest that in fifteen years of the Vargas régime they had forgotten how to conduct a parliamentary session.

Living in societies such as these and reflecting on their history have led some to apathy or cynicism about government. Neither indifference nor distrust of politics seems, however, to be the dominant impression. Freedom and democracy remain words to conjure with in Latin America. Few are those who dare to speak up in the literature and philosophy, that in Latin America are so close to politics, for any ideal other than the generous one of humanity and democracy. If countries are defined by the goals they set themselves, our neighbors are democrats. Students acquire their ideologies, and the action patterns that express them, along with their freshman textbooks or before. They are far more idealistic than our own youthful hedonists and are prepared for sacrifices of professional opportunities (when the universities are closed by authorities), of imprisonment (so common an item in the biography of the socially minded intellectual), and even of life. It would be less than just to men and women who suffer so freely for their ideals to leave the matter with the complacent statement that we have democracy, while they have the " pathology of democracy." Democracy in a world of human frailty is imperfect everywhere, but there is a restless striving toward it in Latin America, and men and women as intelligent, honest, and as devoted as anywhere in the world, are working unselfishly for an objective that unites good men everywhere — a people fit to govern themselves and a government of and by and for themselves.

No. 8 [Each of the twenty republics of Latin America has its own peculiar problems of geography and climate, of the location and nature of good arable land, and of the assimilation or " incorporation " of the original Americans into the social organization introduced by the Europeans. Dr. Gamio discusses, in the following essay, the specific nature of these factors and how they influenced the emergence and growth of the Mexican nation. One cannot, of course, generalize and hence extend to the other nineteen states the particular nature of these aspects of national life as they exist in Mexico. However, articles paralleling the following could and should be written for each of the other countries, for they too have been profoundly influenced by the geographic and social handicaps to which they must adjust their political life.]

Geographic and Social Handicaps*

by MANUEL GAMIO

To describe the development of the Mexican people authoritatively is difficult, especially if the problem is considered in relation to the geographical conditions under which they live. The scientific knowledge of the subject brought to light by the few and sporadic investigations of it that have so far been made is scanty and for the most part narrow in scope, since it is confined to a few of the many aspects of Mexican social development.

The deficiency of knowledge of this subject can be explained to some extent if one remembers how complex is the social structure of Mexico, how exceptionally adverse have been the conditions under which it has developed, and how extremely diverse are the regions that compose the national territory. Consequently, our knowledge both of the facts and also of the interrelations between them is fragmentary and incomplete. Correct generalizations are impossible, and what follows should be considered merely as an exploratory and provisional interpretation.

The reader will also note that the following pages are devoted not so much to the twice-told tale of the virtues of the Mexican people and the natural wealth of their country, as to pointing out the main geographical and social factors that have retarded their development. This task, far from being pessimistic, is in a very real sense constructive, since it permits one to appreciate at their true value the efforts and the sacrifices the Mexican people have made and are making to improve their conditions of life. It will also puncture the legend of the lazy Mexican who leans against a horn of plenty but will not even take the trouble to stretch out his hand for its fruits. We shall also make some contribution towards converting the heedless and ill-informed attitude of incorrigible optimists into one of careful attention to some of the most difficult of Mexico's national problems.

* Manuel Gamio, " Geographic and Social Handicaps," *The Annals of the American Academy of Political and Social Science* (March, 1940), Vol. 208, pp. 1–11. Reprinted by permission of *The Annals of the American Academy of Political and Social Science.* The footnotes in the original version are omitted here.

THE GEOGRAPHIC SETTING

In all the regions of the world that lie between the parallels 14° 30′ and 32° 42′, there is perhaps no other country that enjoys so privileged a geographical location as does Mexico. If the social and economic progress of its people is real and sustained, if the needs and aspirations of the Mexicans and the people of the United States are made to complement each other harmoniously and on an enduring basis, and if some day an interoceanic canal is built across the Isthmus of Tehuantepec or really cheap and rapid land transport is established there, this republic will become the most important highway of world commerce, the meeting place of great currents of race, culture, and wealth, and a huge factory which will work up the raw materials of half a continent.

Unfortunately this imposing prospect of what Mexico may become is confronted by a menacing question. During their colonial subjection the Mexican people had to contribute their energy and wealth to Spain. When they won their independence they thought they had freed themselves forever from foreign influence and exploitation; but they came to see that their new international situation was even more difficult and dangerous than before. Dependence upon Spain was ended forever, since it was out of the question for that nation to regain enough strength to make reconquests on this side of the Atlantic. On the other hand, the relations, contacts, and struggles between recently liberated Mexico and the United States were destined to last as long as the two countries were next-door neighbors — that is, forever.

THE UNITED STATES AS A NEIGHBOR

There was the sharpest contrast between these two peoples. On the one hand, the people of the United States were rich, powerful, and socially homogeneous. Except for the isolated minorities of Indians and Negroes, the great majority of the people belonged to the same type of civilization, the Western, and the same race, the Caucasian. Their population grew rapidly through heavy immigration and natural increase, and as they expanded they gravitated toward the south, the southwest, and the west. On the other hand, the Mexican people inhabited an enormous and thinly settled region. Racially they were extremely heterogeneous, for, while the majority of them were Indians in race, language, and culture, there was a large minority of mestizos (mixed Indian and white) who were culturally Indian, and there was also a very small number of whites of European origin whose culture was Western. Consequently, the thoughts, needs, and aspirations of these groups were divergent, with the result that the establishment of independence ushered in an almost uninterrupted series of revolutions in which were sought a better adjustment between these social groups and, above all, the establishment of a better distribution of wealth. All this resulted in the development of a poor, weak, divided nation.

After a quarter of a century of independent existence next door to such a neighbor as the United States, which was totally different in its historical background, race, culture, language, inclinations, and material power, the consequence for Mexico was the loss of more than half its territory, which was annexed by the United States. Since then, Mexico has not suffered any further loss of territory, for whether relations between the two countries have been cordial or strained, no situation has arisen which has not been susceptible of peaceful settlement on the basis of complete mutual understanding and agreement. The risks to which American investments in Mexico are exposed have frequently threatened to give rise to grave international incidents; but in recent years the friendly and intelligent Pan American policy of the Good Neighbor pursued by the Roosevelt administration gives reason to hope that controversies of this kind will no longer lead to international ill feeling and much less to armed conflict, as they did somewhat less than a century ago.

In happy contrast, geographical proximity to the United States has brought Mexico the following important advantages, especially since better means of communication were established between the two countries. A great deal of scientific and technical knowledge of many kinds has been imported into Mexico either by Mexican students at American universities or by American scholars and professional and business men who have come to Mexico either to give instruction and carry on scientific investigation or merely to develop business enterprises which had educational significance. Millions of Mexican laborers have suffered great hardships in emigrating to the United

States; and yet they have found that country a free university in which they have learned how to raise their standard of living considerably, to increase the small and rudimentary store of agricultural and industrial techniques that they possessed before they left Mexico, and to learn much else that they had not known before. The large investments of American capital that have been made in good faith and with respect for the laws of Mexico have contributed effectively to stimulate and hasten the progress of the country. Finally, a very important result of Mexico's geographical proximity to the United States is the influence exercised by the latter in the genesis of the revolution that began in Mexico in 1910.

CENTRAL AND SOUTH AMERICAN NEIGHBORS

Central America and Mexico not only are neighbors but they also form a geographic and social entity, whereas Mexico's South American kinsmen are socially isolated as well as geographically remote from it. To prove this assertion we need only compare the relatively large number of Central Americans living in Mexico and Mexicans living in Central America with the extremely small number of South Americans living in Mexico and vice versa. This isolation is due not only to geographical remoteness and the lack of cheap and easy means of communication but mainly to the following causes:

(1) Generally speaking, except for Argentina, Uruguay, and Chile, we and the other Latin American countries produce and export the same or similar raw materials and agricultural products, with the result that we cannot consume one another's products, but, on the contrary, compete with one another in the markets of Europe and the United States.

(2) The volume of production in our few and rudimentary manufacturing establishments is, generally speaking, so small that we not only have no surplus available for export, but are unable to satisfy even the very modest demands of our own people, who are obliged to import products and manufactured articles from Europe, North America, and Asia.

(3) In all the other Latin American countries, labor is generally cheap. Consequently, there has been no important emigration to them from Mexico, as there has been, for example, to the United

States, to which very large numbers of Mexican laborers have periodically gone in search of higher wages. How, then, could important material contacts develop between the people of Mexico and those of South America, when normally no commercial interchange exists to create, promote, and sustain them?

On the other hand, so numerous are the historical, racial, cultural, and spiritual bonds between Mexicans, Central Americans, and South Americans that in a more or less distant future they will probably form a great confederation which will share the American continents with the union already established by the Anglo-Saxon peoples of North America.

GEOGRAPHIC HANDICAPS

Geographical and social conditions in Mexico and the other Indo-Iberian countries have been less favorable to human development than those in other American nations, such as the United States and Argentina. This is shown partly by a comparison between the slow growth of population and the small volume of immigration in the former group of countries with the great increase in population and the very large immigration in the latter.

Confining our attention to Mexico, we see that if its territory had been habitable and agriculturally productive in proportion to its great extent (which is nearly two million square kilometers), its population would have been many times larger and much better developed than it is today, when it numbers nearly twenty million.

ADVERSE TERRAIN

The geographical factor which has proved a fundamental obstacle to social development and from which are derived the other factors that have affected it adversely, consists in the very rough and highly diversified character of the Mexican terrain. Mountains, cliffs, and gorges — that is to say, rugged land — constitute probably more than half the total area of the country, and in these regions farming and even the exploitation of raw materials is very difficult if not impossible. This topography has made it difficult to communicate and to carry on commercial and other kinds of interchange between the several regions of Mexico, many of which still remain in the same isolated situation in which they were centuries ago. The railroads and highways built in the last seventy-five years have improved the situation somewhat, but it has been impossible to provide all that were needed, because the cost of construction in such rugged terrain is very great in view of the limitations of the national budget. The disadvantages described above would have been compensated if the upheavals of remote geological epochs had raised the peaks of the mountains and volcanoes to a still greater elevation, for in that case many of them would be sufficiently covered with perpetual snow to form high, plentiful, and constant sources of irrigation; whereas actually these occur only on the Pico de Orizaba, Popocatepetl, and Iztaccihuatl.

These differences in altitude, combined with differences in latitude, temperature, hydrography, rainfall, and geological, mineralogical, and other factors, have helped to form many distinct climatic regions, different types of plant and animal life, and different biological characteristics in the inhabitants, especially in the Indians who have lived for thousands of years in this multiform environment.

In this synthetic article we cannot analyze and discuss in detail all the geographical factors which, taken together, indicate and explain the relative habitability and productivity of the soil. So, in the interest of brevity and clarity, we shall take as one of the most significant of these factors, that of the regional flora or vegetation — although we realize that in doing so we depart from established conventions and shall become involved in inevitable errors.

TROPICAL AREA

Generally speaking, the territory of Mexico consists of two grand divisions. In one of these the vegetation is tropical, and in the other it is nontropical. The regions in the first division cover an area much larger than is generally ascribed to the so-called hot country (*tierras calientes*), for they include all the coasts and slopes on which the vegetation is exclusively characteristic of a tropical climate, whether the plants are indigenous to Mexico or not. Since a long list of scientific terms would be out of place here, we shall give only the common names of a few of the most representative and best-known types of such vegetation, namely: banana, mango, coffee, cacao, rubber, chewing-gum tree, vanilla, coconut tree, and mahogany.

These regions generally present a sharp contrast between the potential and the actual. They are the richest and most fertile in the republic, and they ought not only to satisfy domestic needs but also to provide a large surplus for export; and yet for various reasons — mainly for reasons of health — their actual production is small. Living conditions in them are poor, and extraordinary energy and persistence are required to achieve what would be merely a normal program of work elsewhere. Human life is constantly menaced by tropical diseases such as malaria, which is endemic and widespread, and the states of physiological debility that result from it; the frequent amoebic dysentery, and the terrible onchocercosis, which is becoming increasingly common in southern Mexico. These adverse conditions, together with the high temperature and in some cases extreme humidity, have kept the density of population at a very low point, especially the population that is non-Indian, which has not become adapted to the environment, and consequently has not developed the Indian's relative immunity to some of these diseases.

NONTROPICAL AREA

In the region of nontropical vegetation, the most characteristic plants are wheat, oats, barley, alfalfa, vines, and such trees as the apple, walnut, peach, and pear. The bulk of the population of Mexico has been concentrated in this region from remotest antiquity, for here the diseases mentioned above are either unknown or else they are far less widespread and malignant. The climate is agreeable and much more salubrious, and labor is more efficient. Consequently living conditions and conditions affecting agricultural productivity are superior to those prevailing in the tropical regions. Absolutely, however, this productivity is very limited if one considers the great extent of this nontropical region. This apparent paradox is due to the following causes:

(1) The water supply is very deficient, since the rivers and springs in this region are few and yield only a small volume of water. In

fact, in the whole area of the republic, which is about 200,000,000 hectares, the cultivated land under irrigation amounted in 1930 to about 3,000,000 hectares, or 1.5 percent of the total. Since that date, artificial irrigation has made only an insignificant increase in the proportion. Moreover, most of the sources of irrigation, including the most important ones, are in the tropical region, and it is probable that in the nontropical region the area of lands under irrigation does not amount to as much as 0.5 percent of the total under cultivation.

(2) Next we must consider the dry-farming region (*tierras de temporal*). Here the success or failure of the crops depends exclusively upon the abundance or scarcity of rain and upon whether or not it comes at the right time. Under these conditions the rainfall is hardly adequate, as is shown by the following data, which may be regarded as typical of both of the two great regions or divisions that we have been discussing: In a rather restricted zone lying between the coast of the Gulf of Mexico and the southern slopes, the annual rainfall is exceptionally heavy, reaching 70 inches or more. It is much less abundant in the southern *Mesa,* where it varies from 20 to 40 inches. It is relatively light (from 20 to 30 inches) in the *Mesa Central,* which has always been the principal food-producing region of Mexico. Finally, in the great *Mesa del Norte* and a considerable part of the Pacific coast area, the annual rainfall does not reach 20 inches, and sometimes there are long cycles of drought unbroken even by a shower.

The total area of the dry-farming region, including both the tropical and nontropical divisions, amounts to 11,500,000 hectares, or 5.75 percent of all the land in Mexico.

To sum up, the Mexican people live mainly upon agricultural products which they can obtain only from the 14,500,000 hectares contained in the irrigated lands and dry-farming lands described above; and living conditions and productivity in these are subject to the uncertainties and disadvantages of a biological, climatic, topographic, and hydrographic character already mentioned. If we agree that the census to be taken in 1940 will show a population of nearly 20,000,000, as it probably will, each inhabitant of Mexico would theoretically be entitled to the agricultural production of seven tenths of a hectare (less than two acres) of these lands — such as they are.

SOCIAL HANDICAPS

The abnormality of the Mexican population remarked upon above consists in the fact that the number of its inhabitants has been very small at every stage of its development, as is shown in Table 1, although its birth rate (43 per 1000) is exceptionally high.

TABLE I

Year	Population
1794	4,483,569
1824	6,500,000
1854	7,853,395
1874	9,343,470
1900	13,545,462
1936	18,852,086

On the other hand, the population of Argentina grew from about 500,000 in 1818, to nearly 2,000,000 in 1870, 8,000,000 in 1914, and 12,500,000 in 1936; and that of the continental United States grew from 9,600,000 in 1820 to 38,500,000 in 1870 and 130,000,000 in 1937. In other words, since the establishment of Latin American independence (about 1820), the population has increased in the ratio of 25 to 1 in Argentina, 13.5 to 1 in the United States, and only 3 to 1 in Mexico.

The fundamental cause of the slow growth of population in Mexico has been the physical underdevelopment of the people. We showed above that unfavorable geographical conditions have made the volume of agricultural production inadequate to meet the needs of the people. Now we shall inquire into the low quality from which their diet has always suffered.

From the earliest times to our own day, the diet of the bulk of Mexican people has consisted basically of maize and chile, which lack certain important proteins, fats, and vitamins which are indispensable for the normal functioning of the human organism. This, together with the diseases mentioned above and the economic and cultural factors to be discussed below, is responsible for the fact that Mexico has the highest death rate in the world. Finally, add the fact that this country has never attracted many immigrants, and one can easily understand why the population of Mexico is so small notwithstanding the great extent of its territory.

We have frequently remarked on other occasions that excessive importance has been attached to Mexico's race problem and particularly to the question of mixed race (*mestizaje*). We agree that from the point of view of physical anthropology it would be well to continue investigations to determine what biological characteristics of the Indians, of those of mixed race, and of the whites are strictly racial or ethnic, so that we may then be able to classify them in typical groups according to their resemblances and differences. We have said "continue investigations," because neither in Mexico nor anywhere else has anyone yet succeeded in identifying and defining an ethnic group in scientific terms that permit us to state categorically what individuals belong to a so-called pure race. Still less are we able to state the proportions in which the racial characteristics of their ancestors are transmitted to persons of mixed race. Consequently we do not know, and we need not take the trouble to learn, which are the Indians and which the mixed breeds in Mexico, or how numerous they are; and as for the whites, all that can be said of them is that they are those who are known to be of exclusively foreign origin.

The race prejudice that causes dangerous conflicts in other countries does not exist in Mexico, where all careers are open to the Indians and the mestizos. We believe, therefore, that in studying the problem of race we ought first and foremost to consider its significance from an exclusively biological point of view. The Indian has been adapted to his environment by the process of natural selection over a period of thousands of years. He has thereby developed organic defenses, among which is his relative immunity to certain diseases — an immunity not enjoyed by foreigners and least of all by those who have recently arrived. Accordingly, the advantage of the crossing of whites and Indians consists in the fact that the mestizo offspring inherits, at least in part, the biological defenses of the Indian parent. In short, such ethnic-biological differences as may exist between the constituent elements of the Mexican people are only a minor factor in their development, but will always continue to exist in greater or less degree because in part they were produced and will continue to be produced by the great diversity of geographic and climatic conditions in the different regions of Mexico.

Among the most serious obstacles of a social character that have retarded the progress of the Mexican people at every stage of their development, the following should be mentioned: (1) an uneven distribution of wealth, one of the main results of which has been a low standard of living, both material and cultural, among the masses; (2) a sharply marked heterogeneity — cultural, psychological, and linguistic — among the social groups that form the population; and (3) the persistence of antiquated and ineffective cultural traits side by side with modern and effective cultural traits.

OPPRESSION OF THE MASSES

To the geographical conditions that have always limited the agricultural potentialities of Mexico were added in pre-Spanish times other factors unfavorable to production, which was much smaller then than in the colonial period, and infinitely smaller than it is today. In pre-Spanish times maize was the sole support of the whole population, and it was very badly cultivated. Plows, metal implements, cattle, and horses were all unknown, and planting was done by digging a hole in the ground with a stick and dropping the seed into the hole. Weeding the cornfield was a slow and painful process, for the weeds were pulled up by hand or cut with instruments not suited to the purpose; and sometimes no weeding was done. Consequently the crops were necessarily very small and the area under cultivation was proportionately large.

As long as the number of Indians living in the present territory of Mexico was limited, they were able to live without getting in each other's way; but when large numbers of other Indians entered the country, a struggle was begun for possession of the land. Thus the Mexican agrarian problem had its origin in remote antiquity. The most powerful groups — such as the Maya, Toltec, and Aztec — not only seized the best lands by fire and sword but also made tributaries of the weaker peoples, who eked out a wretched existence, since they were obliged either to work for their oppressors as well as for themselves or else to take refuge in isolated and barren regions. Even among the privileged groups, by no means everyone was able to live a normal life, for small theocratic minorities monopolized the largest and best part of the resources and production of the country, governed the masses, and forced them to live in poverty and to expend all their energy in farm labor, incessant warfare, and the construction of gigantic and beautiful religious monuments, such as those we admire today in Teotihuacán and Chichen Itzá.

During the Spanish conquest and the colonial period this unbalanced economy continued the same in almost every respect. The only difference was that power, wealth, and production were now monopolized by a small minority of European origin. The Indian nobles, priests, and chieftains of the old theocracy who had formerly enjoyed this monopoly were thrust down until they became mingled with the anonymous Indian masses; and the latter abjectly labored for their conquerors in mine and field, in the building of thousands of churches and cathedrals, or as auxiliaries in the conquest of groups of their kinsmen who had not yet been subjugated by the Spaniards. Although the latent protest and passive resistance of the oppressed elements were constant throughout the Spanish domination, no great armed rebellions occurred, because repression was bloody and thorough. The masses were deprived of the means of defending themselves, for they were not permitted to bear arms of any kind or to use horses. After the declaration of independence these restrictions were altered or relaxed.

During the colonial period the wealth was monopolized by a minority of Spanish origin which generally founded families in Mexico. Their capital and profits remained in Mexico; but later on a handful of absentee foreigners gradually extended their control over the means of production, until at last only a small fraction remained in the hands of Mexicans, and even the latter were a small and exclusive minority. In the nineteenth century the economic condition of the mass of the people was, therefore, in some respects worse than in the colonial period. As a result, the popular unrest that had been fermenting for three centuries broke out in frequent revolutions which often affected social development but did not in any perceptible degree improve the abnormal living conditions of the masses.

The revolution that uprooted the antiquated economic system of

Mexico and introduced the most effectual reforms is the one that began in 1910, has been going on ever since then, and has found its most radical expression in the past five years. In the latter period the Mexican masses have unquestionably bettered their economic condition. Unfortunately a still greater improvement has been prevented by the operation of certain long-familiar factors, mainly the geographic factor of which we have already spoken, and the cultural factor which we shall now discuss.

DIFFERENT CULTURES

Archaeologists have shown that before the Spanish conquest the people who inhabited Mexico were divided into different culture groups at different stages of evolution; but it is also believed that all these groups were fundamentally related to one another, all of them belonging to the pre-Columbian American type, and that they all sprang from a common though remote origin. The same may be said of the mental processes of these groups. On the other hand, there were profound differences between the languages they spoke.

From Cortés' conquest of Mexico in 1521 to the present day, two cultures, different both in type and in the stage of their development, have existed side by side in Mexico. One of these is the general culture of Indian type and pre-Spanish origin, which we discussed above and which embraces several subcultures — all of them now more or less degenerate or modified — such as the Maya, Tarascan, Aztec, and Zapotec. The other general culture is the Western or European, which has been adapted in greater or less degree to the new environment. In the colonial period this was represented in Mexico by only one of its subcultures, the Spanish. To this have subsequently been added the subcultures of France and the United States, and others of less importance.

PERSISTENCE OF INFERIOR TRAITS

The impact of the conquest, the burden of the Spanish colonial domination, and the civilizing influence of Europe and North America in the nineteenth century deprived the Indian culture of some of its main characteristics, such as its architecture, its picturesque mythology, its calendar, and its bloody human sacrifices. On the other hand, some of its least desirable elements have stubbornly persisted. Even today, primitive Indians predominate in some quarters and they are also found in considerable numbers among the mestizo rural classes. Some of their representative cultural survivals are as follows: a diet deficient in vegetables and consisting mainly of maize, chile, and kidney beans; unsanitary and uncomfortable dwellings; scanty clothing ill suited to the climate of the central plateau, which is where most of the population lives; and inadequate implements and tools for rural and urban workers, with a resultant low level of production and waste of energy. The mental operations of these people are not inspired or controlled by scientific concepts, but function spontaneously, instinctively, and arbitrarily, as in times past, with the result that the interpretations which, for example, they put upon the nature and origin of geographical, physical, and chemical phenomena and upon historical events are, generally speaking, erroneous, conventional, and often contradictory.

If these culture traits were inferior in practical value to the imported Spanish culture during the colonial period, today, when scientific knowledge and techniques of all kinds have made such great progress, they are not only inadequate to the needs of the masses but are a serious obstacle to their development. To be sure, not all these traits are antiquated; and among the exceptional ones that possess great value and ought to be preserved and encouraged are many forms of artistic and artistic-industrial expression and certain estimable qualities of a moral and social character.

FACTORS PERPETUATING INFERIOR TRAITS

Two powerful factors contribute in about the same degree to the maintenance of the inferior culture traits. The first of these is the lack of means on the part of the Indian and mestizo masses to provide themselves with the extensive material equipment and the abstract education that characterize Western culture. The second is that, having been accustomed for thousands of years to live within the pattern of their Indian culture, they are strongly opposed to abandoning its familiar ways. This has been demonstrated by a great many cases of individuals and groups who possess the necessary means and yet do not alter their outworn way of life. This attitude is probably strengthened by the fact that they have never discovered that they can live better than they do now if they satisfy their needs through agencies and instruments of modern Western culture.

Of course we do not believe that Western culture is above criticism or beneficial in every respect, or that it would be advisable to substitute it bodily for the Indian type of culture. At present Western culture in Mexico is the exclusive possession of a social minority which resides mainly in urban centers; and while it has brought with it many important advantages, it has also entailed some serious disadvantages. So the ideal solution of Mexico's cultural problem will be reached when we succeed in forming a composite national culture which harmoniously integrates the best traits of Western and Indian culture.

Until all the Mexican people can communicate with one another in Spanish, we shall not be able to say that Mexican nationality has really been founded; and since there are still a million Mexicans who speak only the Indian languages, and another million who speak those languages along with a faulty Spanish, it is imperative to " Castilianize " the whole Mexican people — that is, to teach them Spanish.

A HOPEFUL OUTLOOK

The historical, biological, economic, cultural, psychological, and linguistic heterogeneity which we have been discussing is directly responsible for the mutual differences, divergence, and antagonism displayed by the various social groups of Mexico in regard to their needs, desires, and ideals. And yet, if we consider that, despite the geographic and social handicaps which hinder the development of the Mexican people, they have raised their country to the point where it is one of the first in Latin America, we may reasonably hope that when its social structure has become more homogeneous, when a better distribution of wealth has been achieved, and when the handicaps of soil and climate have been more effectively counterbalanced, the Mexican republic will achieve a place of genuine importance in the family of nations.

No. 9 [Demographic factors have been, in the thinking of many students of the Latin American area, highly important determinants of political institutions and of public policy. Some of the questions in which these observers are interested are: In what ways has the distribution of population affected the political organization of the state? How has urbanization influenced the scope of governmental services and functions? Have internal population movements upset or changed the political equilibrium established by earlier constitutional arrangements?

A currently discussed topic is that relating to Latin America's ability and/or willingness to absorb peoples from the other areas of the world. Persons who feel that over-population is one of the basic causes of international unrest frequently express the opinion that Latin America could — and perhaps ought to — admit the excess populations of Europe and Asia. Mr. Davis, in his analysis of the suggestion, presents the facts directly bearing upon this proposition and, in so doing, also gives us essential information relating to population levels, trends and movements in the region as a whole.]

Latin America's Multiplying Peoples *

by KINGSLEY DAVIS

*I*N Latin America, as elsewhere, population trends are a significant clue to political, economic, and social developments. Indeed, in certain areas, population is regarded as *the* problem. Yet scarcely any other branch of Latin American study is exposed to so much careless handling — so much myth, fiction, and straight neglect — as this one.

There are two opposite views concerning the statistics of the region, both erroneous and both a priori. One holds that no reliable

* Kingsley Davis, " Latin America's Multiplying Peoples," *Foreign Affairs* (July, 1947), Vol. 25, No. 4, pp. 643–645. Reprinted by permission of *Foreign Affairs*. The footnotes in the original version are omitted here.

statistics on population can be obtained in the countries to the south, and that consequently nobody knows what is going on down there demographically. The other blithely assumes that all Latin American population figures appearing in print are correct, and draws its conclusions accordingly. The truth, of course, lies between the two. A number of the republics and dependencies have reliable figures on population, and a number of them do not. The question of validity cannot be decided for the region as a whole, nor can it be decided on an a priori basis. It requires a painstaking study of each country's statistics. Most countries are good on some kinds of figures but bad on other kinds. Even in a country where the data are not accurate, systematic analysis and correction may produce information of real value.

Like most other countries, including the United States, the Latin American nations generally have better censuses than vital statistics. Yet it often happens that the vital statistics can be checked against the censuses and thus corrected in some respects. The censuses themselves vary as to what they include and leave out, and as to what they do well or do poorly. Some countries (e.g., Brazil) get data on race, while others (e.g., Colombia) ignore this topic. Some have good returns on cities (Chile, Mexico), while others have poor returns on them (Guatemala, Jamaica). Some have taken many censuses (Chile, Cuba, Guatemala, Mexico, Venezuela), while others have taken few or none (Ecuador, Bolivia, Paraguay, Haiti). Argentina has good registration returns but has not taken a census since 1914. Chile and Puerto Rico have not only good censuses but also good vital statistics.

This wide variety of statistical achievement has a signal advantage. It enables one to find somewhere in Latin America fairly good figures on almost any demographic topic. Within each major region one or more countries can usually be found with figures reasonably reliable and roughly representative of the region as a whole. By critical analysis of sources, by due regard for regional patterns, by judicious use of corrections and estimates, it is possible to arrive at acceptable results. The margin of error can be reduced to the point where, in many instances, social and economic conclusions may be drawn with some confidence.

II

The opinion is sometimes held that the growth of population in South America is slowing down, if not approaching a decline. Olson and Hickman, in their *Pan American Economics,* say that "population increase in many of the areas is beginning to taper off." This view apparently comes, in most cases, from the writings of Alejandro Bunge on Argentina, but it represents a misinterpretation of what he said. Bunge, an able demographer and thoughtful patriot, repeatedly emphasized the decline of the birth rate with progressive urbanization in his country. He predicted that *if this trend continued,* the growth of the Argentine population would eventually stabilize itself, and (perhaps in order to arouse his government to action) he predicted that the point of stabilization might come as early as 1960, though possibly not until 1990. He did not deny, however, that at the time he was writing (in the early 1940's) the rate of natural increase of the Argentine population was quite high. Not only had the birth rate been declining, but the death rate had been doing the same, leaving still a substantial difference between the two. Today the Argentine population seems to be growing about as fast as that of any other country in South America. If this is true of the most advanced country in the Latin American region, we could not expect an immediate slowing down of population growth in the other countries.

As a matter of fact, the population of the entire region to the south of the United States is growing faster than that of any other major region in the world. It is growing at a phenomenal rate. During the 20 years from 1920 to 1940 it added approximately 40,000,000 or about 41 percent, to its number. In the same period the United States, starting with a larger population, added only 26,000,000, or roughly 25 percent. With a 1947 total of almost 150,000,000, Latin America now has about 8,000,000 more people than the United States. The present rate of increase in the region as a whole is more than double that of the world in general, although the world population itself is growing at the fastest pace in human history.

Rapid growth characterizes all regions of Latin America. The Caribbean, the Middle American, the Andean and the South Temperate areas all show a surprisingly uniform rate of increase. These regions may differ in other particulars, but not in this one. Even the crowded Caribbean islands, where one might hope for a slackening of human multiplication, are growing (as a whole) at as fast a pace as the rest. Puerto Rico, the Java of the Western Hemisphere, has a birth rate nearly three times its death rate. Mexico, second to Brazil in total numbers, adds almost half a million to its population every year.

How long will the Latin American area continue its extremely rapid population increase? The answer is difficult to give, because in the present condition of the statistics systematic projections such as those that have been made for Europe and the United States cannot be undertaken. Perhaps the continental census of 1950, a potential milestone in Latin American demography, will make possible such projections. In the meantime, certain things can be said. If, for example, the present rate of growth continues, the population of the entire region will be twice as large in 1987 as it is now, for it is doubling every 40 years; and by the year 2000 it will reach 373,000,-000. Such a total would not be impossible, because by the employment of today's technology, not to mention tomorrow's, the region is vast and rich enough to accommodate 400,000,000 people.

It is doubtful, however, that the current rate of growth will continue until the year 2000. Social and economic changes now occurring suggest that the peak rate will be passed within the next three or four decades, after which a trend toward a stationary population will commence. On the basis of a study of trends in mortality, fertility, and migration, the writer thinks that the break will not take place before 1970, but that it may occur shortly after that. He therefore believes that the population in 1970 will lie between 200,000,000 and 225,000,000, and that in the year 2000 it will lie between 300,000,-000 and 375,000,000. By way of comparison, one should note that the high and low estimates for the United States (much more systematically made) are: in 1970, between 150,000,000 and 170,000,000; in the year 2000, between 130,000,000 and 200,000,000. In little more than half a century, then, the Latin American population may be more than double our own. It should be emphasized, however, that the estimates for Latin America are hardly better than guesswork.

The prodigious growth rate in Latin America is not mysterious. Whenever an area has passed through the industrial evolution, it has manifested in the early stages a veritable crescendo of population increase, because industrial progress brings a drop in the death rate before it brings a drop in the birth rate. Later, as an urban-industrial milieu emerges, the birth rate begins to fall to the level of the lowered death rate and the population approaches again the same stationary condition it manifested before the great transition. The new balance, resting on both low mortality and low fertility, is much more efficient than the old, and its effects on human welfare are tremendous.

Western Europe, the United States and the British Dominions have already passed through the rapid growth phase of the industrial revolution. Their populations are now becoming stationary. The agricultural countries of Asia, on the other hand, are just entering the early phases of the cycle. Their populations, already abundant, have great and perhaps tragic potentialities for expansion in the future. The Latin American countries, in contrast to both these groups, find themselves in various intermediate stages of the industrial transition. Some have hardly begun the shift; others are far along. Everywhere in this region, however, we find urbanization accelerating, literacy increasing, health improving and communication expanding. It seems likely, then, that Latin America as a whole will make the transition from illiterate agriculturalism to literate industrialism in a few decades, and that her population growth will taper off as the change is completed.

There can be no doubt that death rates are falling in Latin America. In no country in the region can a long-run rise in the death rate be proven, whereas in every country having reasonably complete registration a downward trend is manifest. To be sure, the mortality is still discouragingly high, the crude rate in most countries being double or triple that in the United States. Yet the situation now is better than it used to be, and in the future it will doubtless be better still. The Latin Americans are taking an active interest in public health, and since new discoveries in the control of tropical diseases are being made, and financial aid and public education are being extended, a continued reduction in the death rate can be expected in the next decades.

Scattered evidence indicates that fertility is also declining, but not nearly so fast as mortality. Latin America still exhibits some of the world's highest birth rates — usually more than twice, sometimes thrice, what they are in the United States. With death rates likely to fall still further, future population growth will depend mainly on what happens to the birth rate. It seems likely that the rate will decline gradually, almost imperceptibly, for two or three decades, and more rapidly after that. In the most advanced countries, such as Argentina and Chile, fertility already shows a strong downward tendency. Throughout most of the entire region, as will appear later, social changes that normally produce a lowering of the birth rate, such as increasing literacy and urbanization, are spreading rapidly. The cities have a much lower fertility than the country regions, and as their influence spreads they should exert a strong downward pressure on the general birth rate. It is the probable decline of fertility that leads us to predict an eventual slowing down of population growth.

III

Mortality and fertility, of course, are not the only factors governing population growth in particular regions. There is also migration. One of the great myths about Latin America is that it contains huge open spaces that can easily absorb mass migration from a crowded world. This myth, believed by Latin Americans as by outsiders, apparently arises from the fact that the region has less than its share of the world's population. The region embraces 16 percent of the earth's inhabitable area, but only 6 percent of the earth's people. Asia, with a population of almost 1.2 billion, has an over-all density per square mile seven times that of Latin America. One recalls the empty Amazon valley, the vacant Patagonian plains, the unworked Chilean forests, the unexploited Guiana highlands. Then one imagines teeming populations in these huge areas and predicts that, in a crowded world, Latin America will provide a home for millions of immigrants. Immigration, however, is a political and economic question, as well as a demographic one.

Under certain conditions Latin America might absorb immigrants to the limit of her physical capacity, but it is not likely that these conditions will be realized. First of all, Latin American desires for a great influx of people conflict with the trend of the times. Immigration changed its character some time ago. Once it meant the pioneer settlement of new lands; now it is directed toward the centers of industry. Once a rural movement, it is now an urban movement. The Latin American nations refuse to recognize or conform to this great change. Though they enjoy a rising industry and might thus attract immigrants to their cities (bidding, however, against favored countries such as Canada and Australia) they turn their backs on this idea and think instead of attracting farmers and farm laborers.

Like peoples everywhere, they want somebody else to do what they themselves are loath to do — in this case, the grinding labor on the big pioneer-farming estates in the hinterland. They have deplored and tried to discourage the tendency of immigrants to settle in the cities. They know that historically, even in the heyday of immigration to their shores, the main attraction did not come from the open spaces. They know, or should know, that Europe itself has become heavily industrialized and urbanized, and therefore does not have a mass of peasants eager to become plantation peons or wilderness pioneers. Yet Latin Americans persist in assuming that somehow immigrants can be attracted to agriculture in the open spaces. These open spaces are, indeed, slowly and haltingly being settled, but more by the expansion of old settled areas than by the importation of aliens. The common notion that the hinterlands can be quickly filled by the simple process of bringing over masses of European immigrants is a myth that never was true and is certainly not true today.

Not only has Europe become urbanized, but its population growth has virtually ceased. No longer can it furnish millions of immigrants to the rest of the world without depleting its own human resources. As a consequence, many European nations refuse to permit large-scale emigration, and when they do permit it, other countries in Europe often bid for the migrants. There may be some distress migration on the part of displaced persons, but the estimated number of these is less than 1,000,000. There may be some emigration of Italians, but the Italian birth rate is declining steadily, and France offers a nearby outlet for surplus population. The prospect that Europe will supply a heavy migration to Latin America is not good.

But despite this fact the Latin American countries, like the rest of the world, want European — not Asiatic — immigrants. There are literally hundreds of millions of Asiatics who, under conditions far less favorable than the existing one, would be willing to settle new territories in Latin America, especially the tropical parts so hazardous for Europeans. But the oriental exclusion policy of the United States and Canada has now been adopted by the Latin American republics. Brazil stipulates that only " white " immigrants shall be admitted. Guatemala forbids persons of Mongolian race to enter. Other countries have similar restrictions. This resistance to Asiatic immigration is understandable in view of Japanese fifth-column activities and the difficulty of assimilation. But it is clear that the bars are being erected against the one kind of immigrants most likely to serve as laborers on the *estancias,* and pioneers in the topical frontiers.

The exclusion of orientals is but one aspect of a far-reaching change of immigration policy in Latin America. The old policy, extending from the wars of independence to the great depression of the 1930's, was one of laissez faire. The fledgling republics, feeling that they needed labor to replace the emancipated slaves, settlers to populate the vacant lands, capital to prime the economic pump, and ideas to overcome the colonial isolation, threw open their doors to immigration. They granted aliens the same rights as citizens, and sometimes even more favored treatment. The Argentine constitution of 1853, for example, inspired by Alberdi's famous dictum that " in South America to govern is to populate," placed the foreign born in a better position than the citizens, giving them all the advantages that the natives enjoyed and exempting them from certain obligations such as military service. In general, the immigrants were treated with respect and admiration, because they were in many ways more civilized than the erstwhile colonial population. The emphasis was not so much on assimilation of the stranger as on assimilation of the native. The immigrant often rose to the top of the economic ladder, frequently maintaining his connection with foreign interests.

The new immigration policy, beginning in 1930, reversed this century-old liberalism. It rests on a philosophy of protection and enhancement of the state as an integral unit, and of special privileges for citizens as against foreigners. Whereas the old law took rapid assimilation for granted, or else implied that the immigrants would assimilate the natives, the new legislation assumes that only certain races, ethnic groups or nationalities are capable of assimilation in Latin America. Peoples of Latin culture, especially those speaking the same language as the nation concerned, are likely to be favored, while others are discouraged. Certain occupations are also favored. The desire to bring in farmers or estate laborers leads to a prefer- ence for agriculturalists; but, once admitted, the aliens of this type are likely to suffer restraints not applied to the citizen. Such an alien may be forbidden to adopt certain occupations without express per- mission; he may be denied the privilege of employment in a govern- ment enterprise or public utility. As is well known, the Latin Amer- ican nations are trying to divest themselves of foreign control over their economic life. As a consequence, a high percentage of the posi- tions in foreign-owned businesses must, in many countries, be re- served for citizens. Latin America is no longer open territory.

Clearly, this new nationalism, this new self-sufficiency and resent- ment of foreigners have led to policies that discourage large-scale migration into Latin America. Yet this does not mean that immi- grants are not wanted. Nearly all South American and some Central American countries are looking for settlers and are ready to offer ac- tive inducements. The recent policies are not intended to curtail mi- gration, but simply to select and control it in the national interest. If the Latin American republics can get the kind of individuals they want, they are ready to absorb millions of strangers.

In fact, at the present moment, a new phase of immigration policy is emerging. Instead of emphasizing national interest through re- striction, as was done during the depression and the recent war, the republics are stressing national interest through the promotion of selected immigration. They are talking about immigration and mak- ing plans for it. There seems no likelihood, however, that they will return to the old laissez-faire policy, or that they will forget the ques- tions of assimilation, ethnic status, economic competition, foreign domination, and national security in choosing their immigrants. The latest phase of policy still places its emphasis on the immigration of farm workers and colonists, still looks to Europe as a source, and still leaves unsolved the thorny economic problems associated with European immigration in the modern world. Above all, it still undertakes to promote selected immigration and mass immigration at the same time, and still confuses the purpose of increasing the population with that of building the economy.

This inconsistency apparently rests in part upon the illusion to which we have already referred. The average Latin American contemplates the empty spaces of his country and jumps to the conclusion that, if they were populated, they would be economically exploited and his country would become rich. But such reasoning places the cart before the horse. The Latin American hinterlands are sparsely settled precisely because they have not been economically exploited. If the economic and social institutions of the original settlers had encouraged thrifty agriculture, a productive industry, and a low mortality, their natural increase and their power of attracting immigrants would long since have filled the favorable areas. But a régime of large estates, peon labor, nonproductive expenditure, and fixed social classes did not operate to produce the capital and enterprise necessary for adequate exploitation. The tendency was to rely on cheap labor to do what in other frontier regions was done by machinery and advanced technology. It follows that the remedy is not more people, but a new economic and social orientation. To acquire the people first would be to create problems rather than solve them; and, obviously, if people were all that were needed to fill Latin America's open spaces, they could be supplied from the region's great natural increase. Many Latin Americans, including experts, do not realize how fast the population is growing. Since Latin American fertility is bound to remain high for some time to come, the lowering of the death rate by only a point or two would create more population than any amount of encouragement of European immigration is likely to do; a reduction of just one point in the death rate would add approximately 150,000 to the annual population growth.

Doubtless there will be some immigration. With several Latin American countries actively seeking it, and with many people anxious to leave Europe, a certain amount of transfer is bound to take place. Furthermore, small migratory currents may prove highly useful. Any country, especially if trying to industrialize, can use persons above the average in training and capacity (though usually such persons do not want to migrate and, if they do, may be successfully wooed by competing countries). The real question concerns the long-run movement of masses of unskilled immigrants. Since the region cannot attract the kind of immigrants it wants, and does not want the kind it can attract; and since it does not need mass immigration anyway, it is a reasonable conclusion that Latin America will not receive mass immigration comparable to that of the past.

Moreover, it is easy to exaggerate the amount of land open to settlement in Latin America. Mexico, with some 22,000,000 people, is pressing hard, in terms of its economy, upon the available land, and is exerting strong migratory pressure on the United States border. Many of the Caribbean and Central American nations are also experiencing sharp pressure of population against land. There is no indication that wealth in Latin America increases as the density of population rises. If anything, the reverse is true. It seems odd, therefore, to expect mass immigration to enrich the nations to the south. The fundamental problem in Latin America is not lack of people, but lack of skills and capital.

IV

North Americans frequently hold the opinion that Latin America is virtually static economically and socially. The statistics prove otherwise. Two excellent indices of development — urbanization and literacy — both show a rapid advance in recent decades.

It may come as a surprise to some people to learn that Latin America is heavily urbanized in relation to its economic base, and at first this may not seem to be the case. The percentage of persons living in places of more than 5,000 inhabitants in the United States in 1940 was 53, and in Canada 43. In Latin America it was approximately 27. But in view of the very wide differential between the two regions in wealth and industrial output, the difference in the proportion urbanized seems small indeed. Argentina and Uruguay have as large a percentage of their people living in cities of 25,000 and more as does the United States, as the following table shows:

Uruguay	40	Germany	44
Argentina	40	United States	40
Chile	34	Canada	33
Cuba	29	France	30
Panama	25	Sweden	27
Mexico	17	Poland	16
Brazil	15	India	8

Latin America has five cities with more than 1,000,000 inhabitants, and four others with more than 500,000.

The growth of cities has been rapid, and it shows no sign of slowing down. In five countries with available data (Chile, Cuba, Mexico, Panama, and Puerto Rico), the population in places of 2,500 or more is growing about twice as fast as the rural population, on the average. And the larger the city the faster the growth. If there has been so much urbanization with a minimum of industrialization, it appears inevitable that future industrial development will enormously stimulate the already advanced urban growth.

The cities are growing primarily by virtue of migration from the rural areas. Their birth rates are much lower than those of the country regions, and their natural increase is consequently lower; but they are attracting people from the countryside. This does not mean that the rural areas are losing population; on the contrary, they have such a high natural increase that they can send a steady stream of people to the cities and still augment their own numbers. It does mean, however, that the growth of the urban population is relatively greater. Fragmentary figures suggest that well over 50 percent of the increase in urban numbers is due to rural migrants, but that this loss to the cities removes only about 20 percent of the natural increase of the rural areas. The Latin American population is truly growing on all fronts.

Although the cities are dependent on the countryside for their people, the countryside is dependent on the cities for its cultural advance. By almost any index one cares to use, the cities are in the van of social change. They show a higher percentage of literate as against illiterate persons, a higher percentage of legal marriages as against consensual unions, and a higher percentage of legitimate as against illegitimate births. It seems safe to assume that as the cities continue to grow, they will have an ever greater influence on the rest of the region and thus increase the tempo of modernization.

Already the influence of the cities on illiteracy can be seen. It is true that, for the region as a whole, more than half the population ten years of age and over is illiterate, but nevertheless the region is less illiterate than the world population in general. Furthermore, great strides have been made, and in the most urbanized countries illiteracy is now on the way out. In 1875 Chile's population (of all ages) was 77 percent illiterate; by 1930 that percentage was reduced to 44. In 1869 Argentina's population age 14 and above was 78 percent illiterate; by 1943, only 17 percent. The current figures on literacy by different age groups indicate that in the future the proportion of illiterates will be substantially reduced, and that in this respect the countryside will begin to catch up with the cities.

The fertility pattern of the cities also puts them in the van of progress. It is so low that only one conclusion is possible, namely, that their inhabitants are practising birth control. If this is true, and if the pattern of family limitation should spread with the continued growth of the cities, the rapid growth of the Latin American population will eventually wane. It is on this basis that an ultimately stationary population can be predicted. Fortunately, this stage will probably be reached before the region reaches the density of Asia. Already Puerto Rico, Haiti, Jamaica and some of the smaller Caribbean islands have fallen into a condition of chronic overpopulation, but the forces of modernization will doubtless exercise their moderating influence before the whole Latin American region reaches this sad state of affairs.

The countries of Latin America are not static. Social change is occurring there as elsewhere. We may summarize by saying that at present the region is in the midst of a cycle of rapid population growth, but the changes now under way will eventually alter this trend. So rapid is the population growth that mass immigration is not needed to fill the remaining open spaces, nor is such immigration likely to come, in view of the new nationalistic policy and the preoccupation with Europe as a source of rural labor. The need for capital and skills, more pressing than the need for people, can eventually be met by the capacity of the region itself. The immense human resources of the future, joined to a fuller and more equitable exploitation of the equally rich natural resources, offer the promise of a higher standard of living than the Latin Americans have enjoyed in the past.

No. 10 [One can easily imagine how difficult it would be for the economic advisers to the President of the United State to prepare an annual report and to indicate what specific legislative programs should be adopted if they had no way of determining such simple statistical data as the number of inhabitants of the United States, whether the population is increasing or decreasing, and the rate of urbanization. Their task would be an impossible one if they did not have ready access to information which can be obtained only by taking a national census.

A census is much more than a mere count of noses or heads. Without one, governmental planning is impossible and governmental action may be, and usually is, totally removed from the realities of the national life.

As indicated in the following article, many of the Latin American nations lack even an accurate population enumeration. The inter-American census, to which Dr. Compton turns his and our attention, is therefore a matter of real *political* importance. It also illustrates the potentialities of organized international action — how nations can and *do* cooperate in an attack upon and a solution of problems common to a geographical region and an international political community.]

How Many Americans?*

by GEORGE C. COMPTON

Do you know how many people live in Ecuador or Haiti? How much of Paraguay's population is rural? What percentage of Costa Rica's food is grown in family gardens? How birth rates compare in Bolivia and the United States? No? Well, don't be ashamed; neither does anyone else, accurately. But we will know a lot more about such things after the American nations finish the 1950 Census of the Americas.

  * George C. Compton, "How Many Americans?" *Américas* (July, 1949), Vol. 1, No. 5, pp. 3–6 ff. Reprinted by permission of *Américas,* a monthly magazine published by the Pan American Union in English, Spanish, and Portuguese.

This project, under which each country will conduct its own census but using common basic standards, came into being just because of our lack of real information and the difficulty of trying to compare data that are incomparable. And while a special committee set up by the Inter-American Statistical Institute works for uniformity in census questions and tabulations, United States government agencies are cooperating with the statistical services of other countries in a high-powered training and testing program to make sure this count means something. UN's Food and Agriculture Organization is helping to set the standards for the survey of agriculture, to fit in with the world-wide agricultural census it is sponsoring.

Here are a few examples of how little we know about ourselves: Ecuador has *never* managed to take a national census. The area was included in a roll call of Colombia in 1825, and a partial count was made in 1864. For three years in a row, from 1869 through 1871, executive decrees ordered immediate censuses, but somehow they never came off. The same occurred in 1906, except for the survey of Quito, the capital, and in 1929 and 1936. Seeing the impossibility of conducting a population census, the government tried to count at least the cattle in 1938, but insufficient funds cut off even this project. A census of the capital was carried out in 1947, sponsored by local civic groups with government approval.

Haiti has never had a real census either — only approximate estimates. In 1941 her vital statistics showed the impossibly low death rate of 3.1 per 1,000 (estimated population). Paraguay had a census of sorts in 1886, to determine the size of the legislature. But the authorities refused to accept the figures. That count gave the total population at 231,000. The official estimate in 1861 had been 1,300,-000; and not even the enormous losses in the war against Argentina, Brazil, and Uruguay (1865–70) could explain the difference. Partial or attempted censuses followed at various times. The last try was in 1936, when a revolution interrupted the tally.

The only Bolivian census ever published in full was taken in 1900. Lack of experience and difficulties of transportation and communication made it incomplete. No attempt was made to count the uncivilized jungle tribes. They were put down at a guess as 91,000. Subsequent estimates of Bolivian population have only been adjust-

ments of the inadequate 1900 count, assuming a fairly fixed geo-
metric rate of increase. Birth and death rates have been way off in
Bolivia, too, drawing almost exclusively on incomplete records of
baptisms and burial permits. Progressive little Uruguay has not had
a national population census since 1908.

More data are available on some of the other countries, and in
many of them specialized statistical agencies have been built up in
recent years. Chile has had pretty regular censuses ever since 1854,
and *Estadística Chilena* keeps up with vital statistics and current
figures. The preparatory work by Brazil's Institute of Geography and
Statistics made the 1940 count the best in Brazil's history. The Incas
had a remarkable system for keeping track of the number and nature of their population, counting by knots on brightly colored *quipu*
cords, but it was hard to estimate the number of modern Peru's inhabitants down to 1940. Training of enumerators and limiting of
questions to a few basic ones in rural areas made the Peruvian census of that year a good one, but they still had to depend on mission-
aries, traders, or soldiers for population estimates in the Amazonian
jungle areas.

Mexico's 1930 census was carefully planned and thoroughly discussed at a national statistical conference before the count was
taken. The extensive 1940 survey in Mexico included censuses of
population, agriculture, land, buildings, industry, business, and transportation. Colombia had her best census in 1938. Argentina's
1947 survey of population, housing, agriculture, transportation, business, and industry is still being compiled. Canada, which is joining
the OAS members in plans for the Census of the Americas, has had
regular tallies every ten years since 1851.

The census has a particularly exalted place in the United States,
which leads the participating countries in statistical techniques and
experience. There the count is required not just by law of decree, but
by the Constitution itself. Article I, Section 2, providing for the apportionment of representatives in the Congress, orders that " The
actual enumeration shall be made within three years after the first
meeting of the Congress of the United States, and within every subsequent term of ten years. . . ." The first, in 1790, was conducted by
United States marshals. In 1880, a trained force of enumerators re-

placed the marshals, and electrical tabulation made its appearance ten years later. The full-time Census Bureau dates from 1902. Coverage of subjects has grown more and more extensive until the Bureau's records now fill some nine million pages and a full mile of shelves.

The lack of a recent census in many countries not only produces a blind spot in the vision of educators and experts on social security, housing, health services, or food production; it also makes the next census more difficult. First, because of the lack of practical census-taking experience. Second, because of the people's unfamiliarity with the idea of a census and the resulting reluctance or even hostility toward the curious enumerator.

In the United States, householders' natural reluctance to reveal income or job information is almost always overcome by emphasizing the completely confidential nature of the inquiry. Answers to census questions cannot be used for taxation, police investigation, or any purpose other than preparation of the impersonal statistical tables. A United States law requires you to answer in the official census, but legal action has seldom been necessary to pry information from tight-lipped refusers.

But what about the other big reason for this drive — incomparability of data? Unless you agree on definitions, twenty census directors may mean twenty different things by " rural," " urban," " white," " mestizo," " literate," or even " married." So you may catch yourself talking about different things going by the same name in different countries. Or suppose you want to compare the proportion of children in the population in several countries. One prints the number in age groups one through five, six through ten, etc. A second gives those under five, five through nine, and so on. A third cites ten-year groups beginning with those " under ten." A fourth starts with " under five," then gives ten-year groups of five through fourteen, etc. How can you match them up? You can't.

That's a problem in tabulation and presentation of data. Another case involves variations both in definition and in tabulation. The 1930 census of Panama listed only 26,617 men and 25,528 women as married, with 7,286 widows and a few widowers and divorced or separated people, while over 97,000 men and an equal number of women were classed as single. Some 8,000 Indians were included in the table, unclassified as to marital status. But minors amounted to 200,474 or 42.89 percent of the population. If you try to get an idea of the fertility of married women on the basis of the table, you wind up with an unbelievable average.

The 1940 Panama tally cleared up the mystery by introducing the classification of *unión consensual* (common-law marriage). The earlier census had classed all who were not officially married as single. Then there were other improvements in the 1940 tables that made comparison with the earlier figures difficult. This time fifteen was the bottom age for marital status data, and percentages were figured without the children. Moreover, the figures were for the population under civil control of the government, disregarding the Indians living under tribal régimes. For the whole republic, 50 percent of the men and 42.1 percent of the women were listed as single; 26.8 percent of the men and 29.2 percent of the women as living in common-law marriage; and 20.8 percent of the men and 21.3 percent of the women as legally married.

Racial classification is a ticklish question, and one where it is difficult to agree on universally acceptable standards. Up to 1940, Panama distinguished between " white," " black," " yellow," " mestizo," " mulatto," and " Indian." In that year the " mulatto " classification was dropped as representing a vague and often highly subjective distinction. But Panama did not go so far as Puerto Rico, which in 1935 settled for just " white " and " colored." To the census officials, this simplification did not seem to fit the reality of the Panama situation or to be a suitable guide to immigration policy. Nor did they adopt the method Mexico had devised, abandoning the " racial " concept in favor of a classification based on a combination of cultural factors, such as language, use of shoes, customary diet — whether of wheat bread or corn tortillas — and sleeping habits — on the ground, in a hammock, bed, or what not. But when Panama dropped the " mulatto " group, the " mestizo " mass was extended to include more than the original colonial definition of the term as the product of white and Indian. The division into civil and tribal population established the real difference, much more important than the Indian ancestry of a villager.

There has been a considerable tendency everywhere to drop " racial " classifications because of the scientific inaccuracy of the concept of race and the presumption of discrimination in asking the question. But outright abandonment of the groupings may keep valuable information about the make-up and needs of the population from being known. For example, in the United States territory of Hawaii, the old classification as " Japanese," " Chinese," " Filipino," " Portuguese," " Hawaiian," " Part Hawaiian," " Other Caucasian," etc. was obviously arbitrary and somewhat misleading. But it did reveal many facts about the social and economic progress of the various groups that were introduced into the islands as contract laborers that cannot be found in the new-style tables of the 1940 census.

Specialists had been calling for census uniformity for many years. Back in 1897, the International Statistical Institute issued a call for a world census at its St. Petersburg meeting. The Pan American Scientific Congress in Santiago, Chile, in 1908 demanded uniform census questions. But it was Dr. Alberto Arca Parró of Peru who in 1943 really got the ball rolling for the Census of the Americas. As Peruvian National Director of Statistics and chairman of an IASI committee on population figures, he wrote to the statistical directors of all the countries proposing the hemisphere-wide survey. The First Inter-American Demographic Congress, meeting in Mexico City the same year, supported the idea and asked the Inter-American Statistical Institute in Washington, D.C., to take the lead in planning the joint enterprise.

The Institute, founded in 1940, is made up of both individual members — professional statisticians — and institutional ones — the Western Hemisphere governments and private organizations. It gets its funds from quotas assigned to the member governments, individual dues, and sponsoring business firms. Under an agreement with the OAS Council, the Institute will become a specialized OAS agency in July, 1950, with offices in the Pan American Union. The governments' share of its funds will then come out of the regular OAS quotas.

IASI named a special committee on the 1950 census, with most of the hemisphere's census directors on it, and proceeded to survey existing census data, census laws of the various countries, needs for mechanical equipment, and other problems of the project. The full committee met in Washington in September, 1947, and again in Rio de Janeiro last February [1949], to draw up minimum standards on topics to be included and tabulation methods. It will have a third session in Bogotá, Colombia, next November [1949], just before the Second Inter-American Statistical Congress convenes there.

As worked out at the first two sessions, the minimum program for population data covers total population, sex, age, marital status, place of birth, citizenship, language, education including literacy, fertility, economic characteristics, urban and rural population, and number and relation of household members. Additional optional items recommended are information on the dwelling place if there is no separate housing census, cultural characteristics, dependence on types of economic activity other than agriculture, and income from wages and salaries.

Not everyone counts in "total population": foreign diplomats and military personnel are out; but the country's forces abroad are included. Special mention must be made of any inaccessible groups known to exist but uncountable.

For marital status, the list should show single, married, widowed, and divorced. Division of the married group into common law and officially wed, or listing of *de facto* separations apart from legal partings, is optional. The minimum age set by law or custom should be used, but tabulation should show the figures for standard age groups in all countries.

On language, the countries are free to ask for mother tongue (language spoken in the home during early childhood), or language currently spoken, with recording of additional languages optional. Literacy is defined as the ability to read and write a simple message (not just your name) in *any* language. The census takers should also ask what school grade each person completed, may inquire into current school attendance if they like.

Fertility is to be calculated on the basis of population information, with a special question as to number of children born alive left optional.

Economic characteristics cover occupation (trade, profession, or type of work), industry in which employed, and industrial status or class of worker. Both the 1950 Committee and the UN have given detailed definitions of job classification.

Do you live in a ". . . place or agglomeration of population, which is identified by quantitative, socio-economic, and other objective criteria . . ."? Luckily, you won't have to decide that one yourself. Both the committee and the UN want the population of such places added up. Since a universal definition of " urban " and " rural " has not yet been adopted, each country should explain where it is drawing the line.

Recognition is given to the Mexican-Guatemalan program for checking on footwear and use of the national language in addition to the mother tongue among groups living out of contact with the rest of the people.

Housing questions should identify the type of dwelling unit, the number of rooms, occupancy status, and presence of running water. More details are called for if a full housing census is taken. It should cover such things as the material used in walls, roof, and floors, number of residents and sleeping rooms, toilet facilities, and optional questions on the kitchen, rent, and value of property.

Facts on agriculture are especially important to the American nations. The countries that take an agricultural census will coordinate their effort with the world survey FAO is sponsoring. The basic items on agriculture include size of farm, tenure, land and labor use, implements and mechanical power, number and kinds of livestock, volume of major products, and home processing of food. Farms producing wholly for home consumption should be counted. Data on farm population should be presented along with the agricultural information.

On the basis of its own experiment, the Inter-American Institute of Agricultural Sciences recommended combining population and agriculture in one household census schedule. Working with the Costa Rican government, the Institute staged a trial census of the area around its Turrialba headquarters. Basic agricultural production questions for small plots were listed right under the population spaces, with a separate agriculture query for larger farms printed on the back of the questionnaire. It found this system helpful in keeping track of the small family plots that account for a large share of total food production in many parts of Latin America. School teachers, including some extras from nearby districts, and students were given special training as enumerators. Local meetings to explain the purpose of the census to the people, posters, a loudspeaker truck contributed by a drug company, and other publicity won widespread cooperation. Only one family head out of 2,500 refused to answer. Many had information ready in advance or, if planning to be absent on census day, left written accounts of their crops and families.

The Rio de Janeiro committee session also outlined basic questions for those countries planning an industrial or business census. Basic standards were likewise set up for the tabulation of population data. They called for grouping the people in sex and age tables as under one year, one to four, and so on by five-year groups through eighty-four, with a final group of eighty-five and over. Age groups were also indicated for the marital status, nationality, and literacy reports. Other tabulation questions and problems of the economic censuses will be studied at the Committee's third session in Bogotá.

On the training front, work toward the 1950 Census of the Americas has been going on since 1942. By the end of this year something over one hundred officials from statistical bureaus in other countries will have taken special courses in census methods as part of the United States government's cultural cooperation program. The National Office of Vital Statistics, Bureau of Agricultural Economics, and Bureau of Labor Statistics have offered training and practice in their particular fields. But all trainees have gone through a four-month general census course at the Census Bureau.

This basic course, however, is not for beginners. All the students are experienced statisticans. Five days a week they take a bus out to the Bureau's office in Suitland, Maryland, some miles beyond the District of Columbia line. There they spend the whole day in lectures, discussions, laboratory work, or preparation of reports on special population problems. Much of the discussion and some of the lectures are in Spanish. Dr. Calvert L. Dedrick and his Census Bureau international statistics staff have used that language not only in the training program but also on frequent trips to Central and

South America to consult with census officials at first hand. The general course is to familiarize students with the mass handling of data in the enormous volume required by a census. Even for small countries, this means familiarity with mechanical card-punchers, counters, and tabulators if the job is to be done in a reasonable time. One of the little cards on which eighty or ninety columns of twelve rows of numbers are punched may be enough for an individual's record in the population census, but as many as thirteen may be needed for each farm in a detailed agricultural survey.

The Census Bureau's Dr. Herman Hollerith devised the first punched-card tabulating machine in the 1880's. He later went on in private life to found a company that became part of the giant International Business Machines. Another Census employee, James Power, invented the mechanical tabulator since developed by Remington Rand. The Bureau is especially proud of its Census Unit Tabulator, which counts items at the rate of 400 cards a minute. Moreover, it can be wired to reject impossible combinations such as " five-year-old father " or " three-year-old blacksmith." Special switches permit sampling anything from every second to every 110th card.

The commercial companies providing census machines show the students how they work. IBM invites the classes up to Endicott, N. Y., to go through the plant. Many manage to get in a side trip to Niagara Falls on this jaunt. The Remington Rand Institute in Washington offers special classes, in Spanish and English, for the trainees.

Advanced courses at the Bureau take up population theories and growth, preparing census data for publication, map making for census work, sampling methods, and other problems the 1950 head-counters will meet.

Practical field experience is gained through trial censuses. Last November the Census Bureau and Columbia University's Bureau of Applied Social Research organized a test census of a New York City area inhabited mainly by Puerto Ricans. The students went through the whole process of organizing the count, preparing maps and questionnaires, training enumerators, taking the actual count, editing the completed forms, and tabulating the results. Each was giving a specific job in the Little Census Bureau, and each served as an enumerator. The twenty students covered an area of eight Harlem blocks between Fifth and Park Avenues and 109th to 114th Streets, taking down the dope on 4,000 Spanish-speaking people.

The New York miniature census gave the students experience while it tested the questions and methods used. Deficiencies showed up in the employment questions, which led to confusion about the " inactive population." The need for care in recording and editing the data was graphically illustrated by a problem that came up in the card-punching. If the number assigned to a family was omitted in the report, everything else came out marked in the wrong column. The best training for enumerators, they found, was to interview each other. But for the Latin American officials the " Puerto Rican " census was not only a lesson in demography. It was also a revealing first-hand look at crowded living conditions in the world's biggest town.

Typical of the latest Census Bureau trainees are Alfredo Fernández Villamil of Uruguay, Manuel Mercado Montero of Bolivia, Ecuadorean Manuel Pérez Borja, and Dominican Domitila García Ramos. Señor Fernández, professor of mathematics and Director of the Statistical Institute in the University of Montevideo's Faculty of Economic Sciences, is making a special study of sampling theory and techniques. He is a member of Uruguay's census committee and will establish sample cross-sections to be asked additional questions about cattle and other things. Undaunted by United States pollsters' November 2 [1948] fiasco, he attributed their miscalculation of election results to use of unscientific population samples. The incident, he pointed out, did not impair the value of real sampling to census takers.

Both Señor Mercado and Señor Pérez got into statistical careers by the side door. Both held part-time jobs with their countries' statistical bureaus while studying at the university, then decided to make a career of it. Statistics is a new career in Bolivia, Sr. Mercado added. He is director of the technical department of Bolivia's statistical bureau. Amateur baseball player Pérez stressed the need for publicity to acquaint the people with the reason for the census. Ecuador, he pointed out, cannot carry out the hope of extending social security coverage to farm workers until she has real facts on farm wages, numbers and movements of the workers. In some regions of the country, he added, an interpreter must go along with the enumerator — or, better still, the enumerator should be one of the local people who won't stir up a flurry of resistance.

Señorita García was the first girl from the Dominican Republic to win a fellowship to study statistics abroad. After a year and a half at the information desk of the Dominican statistical bureau, she decided to take the exam for the Washington trip — and here she is. Statistics is something new for women in her country, though several have taken up such work with private companies. Señorita García loves baseball — the Dominican " national game " — and semiclassical music. After a year's course, she is about to return to her job on the Dominican Republic's 1950 population census.

" Alumni " of the training program hold top positions as directors of statistics and census heads in a long list of countries. And there has been a very low " casualty rate " among graduates in countries where governments have undergone rapid changes. In most cases, the technical staffs of statistical bureaus have not been affected by political instability. The importance of their nonpolitical work is winning recognition from all sides.

A special Census Training Center was held in Mexico City from September to December 1948, organized jointly by the Mexican government and FAO, with the cooperation of IASI, the UN statistical office, and the U.S. Census Bureau. Sixty students from sixteen Latin American countries took part in the courses, discussion, and census trials. Another Census Training Institute opened in Guatemala May 16, to run through June 24. All Central American and Caribbean countries were invited to take part, with the Guatemalan government offering six special fellowships. Guatemala's Bureau of Statistics, the University of San Carlos, and the U.S. Census Bureau all cooperated in planning this " census clinic." Fifteen professors and forty-five students discussed problems of population, agriculture, and housing tallies, then were to carry out practice censuses in both urban and rural areas. Still other regional training institutes may be held soon.

During the 1949–51 period allowed for the 1950 Census of the Americas, probably all the countries will hold a population census and most will make a separate survey of agriculture. Eight countries reported to the Rio meeting that they planned special housing inquiries. A few will tally industry, business, or transportation. Most extensive program is Mexico's, which calls for business, industrial, and transportation counts, and, for the first time, a census of localities, in 1949. Next year will see the population, agriculture, and *ejidal* censuses. Some questions on housing will be included in the population inquiry.

But much remains to be done. For example, Haiti, Honduras, Nicaragua, and Peru reported that authorizing legislation was not yet on the books. Congressional action was still pending in the United States on the projected housing census.

In the past, many censuses have been conducted without reference to maps. Maps are badly needed in Ecuador, Haiti, Paraguay, and other countries. Ecuador lacks equipment for the aerial survey necessary for some parts. There are still many unexplored places in Bolivia. Costa Rica's *Instituto Cartográfico* has been doing good work, but has about 60 percent of the territory still to cover. Brazil's Institute of Geography and Statistics has made splendid regional surveys, is directing the preparation of local maps. Guatemala has made good progress. The United States, whose Census Bureau has a collection of 6,000,000 maps, expects the new mapping to be completed by November.

Personnel and money are other big headaches for the census directors. In many countries, government workers and teachers have always been called on to take the census without extra pay or training. A trained staff of enumerators is the basic thing, and one of the hardest for Latin American census bureaus to secure. It is equally important for the governments to keep up their interest after the count has been taken, so that funds will be provided to complete the tabulation and publication.

This time, all twenty-two American countries mean to find out who and what they are. That's a whale of a job of self-analysis, but they know what they're in for.

No. 11 [One of the Latin American heritages from the past is the problem of Church-State relationships. In Spain, at the time of the conquest and colonization of America, Church and State were closely linked; this linkage was naturally transported to the New World. During the colonial period the Church continued to be a political and an economic force as well as an ecclesiastical institution. In some parts of Spanish America it even increased its economic power and enlarged its political influence. The attainment of independence did not, of course, solve any of the problems which flowed from the close alignment that had existed prior to the independence wars. The only change was that matters which were formerly settled in Spain now had to be discussed and resolved by the political arms of the independent republics.

In some of these nations the resolution of Church-State problems caused little or no political upheaval, in others much of their political difficulties stemmed from this source in the turbulent politics of the nineteenth century. In a few of the contemporary republics, conflicts, real or apparent, between the authority of civil society and the representatives of the Church have been a constant and continuing source of governmental and political difficulty.

Some years ago Dr. J. Lloyd Mecham published a study which reviewed the whole history of the Church-State relationship in Latin America, from the colonial period down to the early 1930's. The following selection is taken from the concluding chapter of his book *Church and State in Latin America.*]

Church and State in Latin America*

by J. LLOYD MECHAM

Tʜᴇ ecclesiastical policies of the various Latin American nations . . . present marked divergencies. In some countries, like Argentina, Colombia, and Peru, the old Church-State relationship that existed in the colonial period has been perpetuated, but with certain modifications. In other nations, such as Brazil, Chile, Cuba,

---

* J. Lloyd Mecham, *Church and State in Latin America* (Chapel Hill: The University of North Carolina Press, 1934), pp. 502–507. Reprinted by permission of the publisher. The footnotes in the original version are omitted here.

Panama, and Uruguay, the connection between Church and State has been dissolved, and a situation rather similar to that which exists in the United States obtains. In still other countries, of which Mexico is the best example, the Church has not only been disestablished, but has been put under strict State surveillance. That a predominantly Roman Catholic populace, which lived for centuries under a common politico-religious régime, should, after independent governments had been organized, apply such diverse remedies for the solution of the religious problem, is both interesting and perplexing.

When embarking upon their independent careers the nations of Latin America adhered for a time to uniformity in religious policy, i.e., Catholicism continued to be the State religion. Indeed, with the sole exception of Argentina (then called the United Provinces of La Plata) religious toleration to the extent of allowing the public exercise of dissident faiths was not among the guarantees of the first national constitutions. Thus, when the youthful nations of Latin America undertook the direction of their own destinies, they were faithful to the religious policy of the Motherland.

Yet, in a short time opposition to the favored cult appeared and it began to be shorn of its old-time privileges. In the decades of the 1820's and 1830's the Catholic Church was subjected to attack in many of the republics, particularly in Argentina, Chile, Mexico, and the Federation of Central America. What was the cause of this radical change in ecclesiastical policy?

The basis of this early opposition to the Roman Catholic organization — not the Roman Catholic religion — was largely political. The abolition of tithes, suppression of religious orders, confiscation of ecclesiastical property and like measures, were as a rule acts of vengeance wreaked upon the clergy by their political opponents. . . . The Spanish crown leaned heavily upon the members of the ecclesiastical organization for the governance of the Indies. Prelates and clerics held official positions high and low; they were a component part of the political organization. If it is not charitable to criticise too severely the failure of Latin Americans to govern successfully under representative political institutions, considering their tutelage for centuries under an absolute monarch, it is likewise unfair to expect the clergy to abandon immediately their ancient practice of participating in governmental affairs. It was inconceivable that this habit should be changed forthwith when independence was established. On the contrary, the ecclesiastics plunged into politics with greater zeal than before, for they felt, quite correctly, that their rights would be endangered in representative republics.

But those who engaged in Latin American politics, particularly as they were played in the early days of independence, ought to have been prepared for the consequences of defeat. The opposition, let it be known, was hardly ever "honorable," but was regarded as an enemy of the State and was generally meted the punishment of traitors. Since the clergy who adhered to colonial tradition and chose to take part in political questions were often so unfortunate as to be on the losing side, they frequently suffered the fate of the defeated opposition. Their rights and prerogatives were curtailed in order to nullify their ability to exercise political influence in the future.

These early anticlericals were not reformers in the proper sense of the term. Their opposition was not based on spiritual, social, or economic causes. The "Reformers," recruited almost exclusively from the creoles, had no complaint to find with Catholic dogmas and tenets; representatives of a privileged social class, they manifested little interest in the welfare of the lower classes; and if they regarded clerical wealth as an evil, it was because this wealth made the Church powerful politically. The pose of the anticlericals as champions of representative government, the rights of the masses, and purity of faith was often insincere and untrue. Usually their sole object was to acquire control of the government and make it impossible to oust them. It is conceded that there were sincere reformers like Gómez Farías, but such men were exceptional, and unfortunately they were impractical idealists who by unwise and precipitate action caused much more harm than good.

With the passing of the mid-nineteenth century, the position of the Catholic Church in Latin America became increasingly unstable. In Mexico, Colombia, Venezuela, Chile, Ecuador, and Central America, severe anticlerical laws were put into force, and in several of the republics Church and State were separated. The first republic to proclaim separation was Colombia in 1853. This status proved to be temporary, however. The first republic permanently to disestablish the Church was Mexico, but that state, as we have seen, was unwilling to release the Church and continued to exercise an oppressive supervision over it. Soon after Mexico, some of the Central American republics disestablished the Church, but intolerantly burdened it with strict State control. In 1890, in Brazil, the alliance of Church and State inherited by the Empire from Portugal was dissolved. In the twentieth century the trend toward separation has continued. Cuba and Panama, states which came into existence under the tutelage of the United States at the beginning of the century, provided in their constitutions for complete separation. In Ecuador only a quarter of a century after the most extreme clerical reaction in all the history of Latin America, ecclesiastical policy was carried to the other extreme and the official ties between the spiritual and temporal orders were severed. In 1917 Uruguay dissolved the old connection, formed in 1830. The most recent and one of the most serious losses sustained by the Pope was the separation of Church and State in Chile.

The revolutionary step of disestablishing the Church was accomplished peacefully in Brazil, Uruguay, and Chile. In these three important countries the Church was allowed to retain its property unconditionally, and to go its own way without governmental interference. Apparently the policy of releasing the Church properties and observing a minimum of surveillance contributed to the peaceful and seemingly successful transition. In Mexico, however, a contrary policy was adopted with most unfortunate consequences. Since the position occupied by the Catholic Church in that republic was not appreciably different than in other Latin American countries, it does not necessarily follow that the bestowal of complete independence upon the Mexican Church would have been followed by the same happy results. The activities of the clergy during the Maximilian period certainly proved that the time had not arrived to establish an independent Church. Since that time, however, the Mexican clergy have evidently learned their lesson, and at the present date it would probably be safe to allow the Catholic Church the same rights it enjoys in Brazil and Chile.

Citizens of the United States unacquainted with the facts have been too prone to regard Mexico as the only rebellious member of the

Catholic flock in Latin America. . . . In Venezuela, Colombia, Ecuador, and Chile, the Church was attacked, sometimes with considerable animosity. In several of the lesser countries too, like Guatemala, El Salvador, and Honduras, the same vicissitudes were suffered. Although the attacks in Mexico were more bitter and the results more disastrous, to say that the Mexican remedies were more severe because the abuses were more glaring would not be absolutely true. In other countries the Church was quite as wealthy, relatively speaking, and as much of a political factor.

A significant feature of the religious conflicts has been the uncompromising attitude of the opposing factions. The difficulty intrinsically is not insuperable, as is evidenced by its satisfactory settlement in several of the countries through the application of a policy of mutual respect and fair play. But in many of the nations of Central and South America the intolerance of clericals and anticlericals alike makes a solution well nigh impossible. Neither side is willing to concede any errors in its own program or virtues in that of the opposition. Consequently, as history reveals, there has been a constant ebb and flow of clerical and anticlerical oppression.

It would not be correct to contend that the anticlerical assault of the last three quarters of a century continued to be retaliatory vengeance for clerical political activities, although this is still one of the major causes. New classes and leaders primarily interested in social and economic reform began to emerge. They attacked the Church, a conservative institution always identified with privilege and vested interests, because it was regarded as an obstacle to social and economic progress. There was new appreciation that the ecclesiastical situation and Church-State relationships were antiquated, reactionary, and out of tune with modern conditions. Well-founded principles, and not merely partisan prejudice underlay the new anticlerical assault. Leaders like Juárez in Mexico, and Balmaceda in Chile formulated programs and inspired followings. In later days, therefore, anticlericalism in Latin America became, to a certain degree, a political philosophy and plan of action pointing the way to the modern world as the goal.

Americans are often puzzled to find the Church in admittedly Catholic countries subjected to more restrictive legislation than even in Protestant lands. The questions arise: Why is it necessary to hedge the Church by such restrictions? and, Why do the Catholics who constitute the majority tolerate such measures? The first question has already been answered. But, to repeat, the habit of the clergy of meddling in politics and assuming an inordinate supervision over the lives of their parishioners make restriction necessary. The clergy of Latin America are totally different from the priesthood in the United States. This fact must be borne in mind if the Latin American religious situation is to be understood.

As for the second question, it is indeed astonishing that an overwhelmingly Catholic populace should tolerate religious oppression. There were many prophecies in 1926, when the drastic anticlerical legislation was enforced in Mexico, that there would be a popular uprising. It is true that isolated revolts took place but a general uprising failed to materialize. One could reasonably expect that if the Latin Americans are as devoted to the faith as they are supposed to be, the antireligious laws would be impossible of enforcement. The writer takes no stock in the argument that the people do not revolt since they understand that the reforms are directed at the Church in its temporal aspects and not at the Church as a religion. Undeveloped intellects are incapable of appreciating such fine distinctions. The most loyal Catholics are to be numbered among the women and the members of the lowest classes — those least capable of offering opposition to the government's edicts. Most of the men of the higher classes are " nominal " Catholics, that is, they abstain from contact with the sacraments until the time for the ministration of extreme unction. These men would not fight to the death for the faith. It should be noted furthermore, that the lowest classes, principally Indians, entertain a profound respect for authority; obedience to superior will has been taught them for centuries, and therefore they would not be apt to oppose the will of the officials — particularly when they are backed by the power of the army. Thus it comes about that in Catholic countries the religion of the majority can be persecuted.

Several of the Latin American countries have, by adhering to wise and tolerant action, attained in separation a satisfactory solution of the vexing religious question. But in other nations the people are not prepared for the radical change, and therefore they must not be hurried. Their rulers must exercise restraint and make the transition as gradual as possible. On the other hand the Catholic Church should put no obstacle in the way of this change. It should recognize that the modern world is committed to the idea that the ideal ecclesiastical status is a free Church in a free State. Adherence to the old pretentions will lead to bitter disputes with inevitable anticlerical attacks and consequent weakening of the hold of the clergy upon the faithful. Recognition of the new order and accommodation to the changed world by a complete severance of Church-State relations, will lead to an active and prosperous Church, which can enjoy the confidence and love of its communicants.

CHAPTER 5

Economics and Politics

No. 12 [It is readily apparent that the economic organization of a society directly shapes its political institutions. Such factors as the nature and uses of property, the system of land tenure, what the people do to earn a living *and how much they earn,* the amount of foreign investments and in what enterprises this investment is made — to mention but a few — are influences upon the organization and work of government. It is doubtful that the town meeting, a political institution, would have developed in New England had not that society been built upon the solid base of the small farm. Slavery as an economic institution, and the manifold political problems that it gave to the United States, flowed from the basic economic organization of the South: the large plantation dedicated to the production of a commercial crop.

These and other economic factors not only shape the embryonic political institutions but also bring to the realm of government action some of the most difficult situations with which political organizations must cope. Professor Mosk, the author of the following selection, discusses the influences of general economic factors upon the political institutions of Latin America. He concludes by noting that " the most active economic agents of democracy in Latin America — land reform and industrialization — are clearly related developments, for a gain in the one is reflected in a better environment for the other."]

The Pathology of Democracy in Latin America: An Economist's Point of View*

by SANFORD A. MOSK

FOR the purpose of this paper, it is sufficient to make use of a broad and rough concept of democracy — namely, a political condition in which orderly channels are available to the people to transfer power from one government to another by peaceful means. In Latin America this condition typically has not existed. Instead, the functions of government have usually been carried out by a political oligarchy which continues in power until removed by revolutionary means.

It is not meant to suggest that developments of a democratic character have been entirely lacking in Latin America. In some countries, at times, they have gone far. For many years, Colombia and Costa Rica were cited as countries in which democracy had made great progress. Yet even in these two countries upheavals have taken place since the end of the war, and democratic institutions have received a setback from which they will not easily recover. Democracy is a delicate as well as a rare flower in Latin America.

Among the economic factors that bear on the failure of democracy in Latin America, the one which stands out from all the others is the system of land tenure. No other economic institution or condition can be put on the same plane. Indeed, the other economic forces militating against democracy have been largely derived from the system of land holdings, and depend upon it. These relations will be brought out in subsequent parts of this paper. First, however, we must examine the direct social and political influences of the land tenure system.

* Sanford A. Mosk, "The Pathology of Democracy in Latin America: An Economist's Point of View," *The American Political Science Review* (March, 1950), Vol. XLIV, No. 1, pp. 129–143. Reprinted by permission of *The American Political Science Review*.

The crucial feature of land ownership in Latin America has been, and is, the large estate — the *latifundio,* to use the general term commonly employed in Latin America for this institution. In most of Latin America, land ownership has been concentrated in comparatively few hands. Such a generalization is, of course, subject to qualifications of a regional nature, inasmuch as small, independent farms have been long established in parts of Colombia, Costa Rica, Haiti, and other areas. Other exceptions are often alluded to but these are apt to be more apparent than real because they relate to areas of sparse settlement. In such places, the ownership of land has been an academic question, and, it might be added, it is likely to continue to be an academic issue wherever difficult natural conditions of climate, vegetation, and soil make denser settlement impossible. We must fix our attention on the lands where agricultural and pastoral activities have been developed. On such lands, the large holding has been generally dominant.

Concentration of land ownership in Latin America is a development which dates from the early colonial period, although, as we shall see, the process was extended and refined in the national period. The point to be stressed at the moment is that the making of large land grants was basic to the colonial system of forced labor. It is true that a variety of other institutions and practices contributed to the same end. In the Spanish colonial system, for example, the *encomienda* and the *repartimiento* (to employ two of the broadest, most inclusive terms) were commonly used methods of coercing Indian labor. It is also true that the labor thus drafted was employed in mining and other occupations, as well as in agriculture. Nevertheless, it is difficult to see how the *encomienda, repartimiento,* and similar practices could have established themselves securely without a system of large landholdings, because they operated mostly for the benefit of the *latifundio.* It was the *latifundio* above all that called for compulsory services from native labor. Had it been absent, the system of drafting labor could not have become deeply rooted in colonial Latin America.

In some parts of the New World during colonial times, the operation of large agricultural holdings led to the introduction of Negro slavery. This was especially true of the sugar plantations in the

Caribbean area and in northern Brazil. From the standpoint of the subject of this paper, the difference between Negro slavery and forced Indian labor is not an important one. More important were two qualities which they had in common: (1) each was part of a rigid structure of social classes, and (2) each involved a lack of personal freedom for the bulk of the population.

The social structure which came to prevail in most of Latin America after European conquest can be described in a few words. Mainly an outgrowth of the land tenure system, it consisted of a small group at the top and a large group at the bottom, with hardly anyone between. The middle class was negligible in size. Those in the upper class were usually persons of European ancestry. This was not always true, for men with a mixture of white and Indian or Negro blood were also found among the colonial aristocracy. But in such cases a certificate of blood purification could be obtained from the crown or some other appropriate agency. This genial fiction, a source of much amusement to students of Latin American history, played its part in maintaining the wide gap between upper and lower classes. Not only was it an economic and social gap, but it was also thought of as a gap between whites and nonwhites.

The relations between the two classes, except where slavery existed, were feudal in character. Those in the lower class owed services to the landowners, mine operators, and others in the top ranks of society. The right to command such services was not an absolute one, for it was hedged in by numerous legal qualifications designed to prevent practices that were considered excessive in the exploitation of native labor. For the present purpose, the important fact is that the members of the lower class were tied to those of the upper class by personal bonds. In this sense their status was analogous to that of the medieval serf.

Thus, by means of slavery and the more common *repartimiento,* there was established early in colonial Latin America a condition in which the majority of the people lacked personal freedom.

In time, the *repartimiento* was supplemented, and to some extent replaced by, another method of forcing Indian labor — peonage. In this system, servile obligations as such were not owed to estate owners. In theory, the Indian was a hired laborer, working for cash wages. But this theoretical relation became subordinated to one based on a chain of debt in which the Indian was caught, and from which he could rarely escape. Such a debt relation often started when an Indian had to borrow cash to perform a ceremonial or religious function. Or, if he did not ask for a loan, the landowner might press one upon him at a time of festival. It was never difficult to arrange a loan, especially under the relaxing influence of alcohol.

Once in debt, the Indian was obliged to work for the landowner until the money was repaid, and, since he usually found it impossible to get out of debt entirely, his labor obligation tended to become a permanent one. In this way many Indians became permanently attached to their employers. They were free in a nominal sense, but not in any effective sense. The bond was a tight one, and, given the differences in education between the two classes as well as the habit of the one class to give orders and the habit of the other to obey them without question, the exploitation of native labor by means of peonage was probably more severe than that achieved by any other method.

What has been said above relates to the socio-economic structure of Latin America in the colonial period. The gaining of independence from European powers brought no significant change in the social structure of the former colonies. On the contrary, new trends of economic development which set in about the middle of the nineteenth century caused an extension and refinement of the basic elements found in the colonial period. These new trends were the outcome of a whole series of interrelated technical and institutional changes of world-wide scope. Certain aspects of these changes merit attention — namely, those relating to the nature and functioning of the world economy.

The great technological developments of the nineteenth century, such as those which occurred in the use of steam power and in the manufacture of steel, had revolutionary effects on transportation as well as on industry. The railroad and the steamship combined to provide cheap and regular transport services all around the world. The network of transportation thus created not only brought all parts of the world into closer contact with each other, but it also opened the way for new lines of economic expansion outside of

Europe. Many areas, including some of the continental interiors, which prior to the middle of the nineteenth century had had only slender connections with western Europe, now became effectively linked to the economy of that vital region, with profound effects upon the use of their soil, mineral, and timber resources. Resources formerly untouched were brought into exploitation, as new lines of production were undertaken and older lines of production were stimulated and extended.

The physical network of world transport was matched by institutional conditions which also made possible the functioning of a world economy from about 1850 to 1914. Three institutional conditions were especially important: (1) freedom for international trade, (2) freedom for the migration of people, and (3) a large flow of capital from the countries of western Europe to the less developed parts of the world. The first and second conditions were not, of course, absolute. The point to be stressed, however, is that these conditions strongly favored new paths of development in non-European countries, giving particular stimulus in such areas to the production of foodstuffs and raw materials for export to the industrialized nations.

As the new world economy took shape after the middle of the nineteenth century, economic activity in Latin America was quickened, stimulated, and changed in character. A strong impulse was given to commercialization of economic life — that is, production for markets instead of production for subsistence purposes. Not that commercial production became the more important. The total amount of labor time spent on raising subsistence crops continued to be much greater than that devoted to commercial output. But, even though subsistence production remained dominant, the gain in commercial production was large, and it had important repercussions of an economic and social character.

Once the stimulus of expanding foreign markets for Latin American agricultural and mineral products was felt, it was inevitable that some expansion would also take place in domestic markets within the Latin American countries. The transportation, handling, and, in some cases, the production of export products was carried out by persons who were divorced from subsistence farming. Employment increased in other service industries, such as communications and utilities, governments expanded their functions and personnel, and urbanization was encouraged. Thus, the growth of foreign markets was followed by a growth of internal markets, especially for food products.

As the foreign and domestic markets expanded, an extension of the system of large landholdings followed. In some cases, new large holdings were fashioned out of public domain, as lands which had not been worth exploiting under previous conditions, and which therefore had remained public property, became attractive to private owners. The typical procedure followed by Latin American governments in such cases was to grant or sell large tracts of public domain to a handful of individuals and companies in compensation for military services, or in payment for undertaking surveys of public lands, or for the purpose of promoting the settlement of sparsely-populated regions; such services were more often nominal than real.

Argentina and Mexico offer well-known illustrations of this method of creating new estates in the latter part of the nineteenth century. In Argentina, land grants were commonly given for service in the Indian wars. In addition, some extremely large grants were made to persons or companies for colonization purposes, under penalty of forfeiture or fine if a certain number of families were not brought in and settled. Apparently it was the honest intention of the government, at least during certain administrations, to promote settlement by this means. But between theory and practice there was a wide gap. In the majority of cases, nothing was done to colonize the lands with small farmers, and nothing was done to enforce the penalties. Even this program ended in land engrossment.

In Mexico the so-called colonization company also figured prominently in the disposal of public lands. A law of 1883 provided for generous land grants to companies that undertook to survey the public domain. In theory the lands thus received were to be sold in small tracts to settlers, but this aspect of the law was completely ignored by the government as well as by the companies. In 1894 even the pretext of colonization was dropped, and the large concessions made thereafter were openly rewards for supporters and favorites of the Díaz dictatorship. The size of some of the private holdings created out of public domain in Mexico after 1883 reached astonishing proportions, as the following figures illustrate: in the state of Chihuahua, seven concessionaries received a total of 35,000,000 acres; in the state of Durango, 5,000,000 acres were shared by two persons; in various parts of northern Mexico, a single company acquired more than 12,000,000 acres. These illustrations are extreme rather than typical, but there is no doubt that all grants made under the Díaz land laws after 1883 were large.

Public domain was not the only source from which new large holdings were fashioned after the middle of the nineteenth century. In some parts of Latin America estates were enlarged or newly created by depriving Indian villages of lands which they had possessed since before the Conquest, and to which their titles had been confirmed by the Spanish Crown. The most spectacular development of this kind took place in Mexico during the régime of Porfirio Díaz, when the Mexican government gave encouragement and assistance to the *hacendados* in stripping Indian villages of their lands. A variety of methods were used, ranging all the way from technically legal measures to outright robbery. The government was not slow to use military force in favor of the *hacendados* when Indian villages were stubborn and resistant about giving up their lands. It is not surprising that the ruthlessness shown in the destruction of Indian villages before 1910 should have been matched by bitterness and bloodiness in the civil strife of the first ten years of the Mexican Revolution.

In Bolivia, Indian communities have suffered a similar, if less striking, experience of losing their traditional holdings. A start was made in 1866 when President Melgarejo abolished the communities by decree, and some of the lands became the property of the Indians in severalty while others were confiscated by the state. Changes in this policy were made in 1871 after the overthrow of Melgarejo, and some of the transactions completed during his régime were declared void, but the granting of individual titles was continued, and this practice proved fatal, as it had in Mexico, to Indian ownership of lands that were considered valuable because of soil and location. Location became increasingly important as markets became more accessible through improvements in transportation. When George

McBride published his study on *The Agrarian Indian Communities of Highland Bolivia* in 1921, he pointed out that

Along the principal roads and railroads of today there have grown up also many large farms of recent creation composed of lands once held by community Indians but either bought or " acquired by other means " by men of white or mixed blood. It is in out-of-the-way corners of the country that community lands are still found: among the mountains where whites seldom penetrate, in secluded angles of the piedmont slopes, among the isolated peninsulas that border Lake Titicaca, on high inaccessible ridges, and out in semidesert wastes on the open *altiplano*.

Similar developments took place in Peru, and, to a lesser extent, in Ecuador. The common impulse for these changes was an extension of commercialized agriculture, but naturally other factors of a political, social, and geographic nature influenced the outcome in each case. In this connection, it should be pointed out that the sheer size of the holding cannot be taken as a criterion of " largeness." Large holdings in some of the Andean valleys must have seemed tiny when compared with the great *haciendas* of Mexico, but they were as large as topography allowed.

By encouraging the *latifundio,* the course of nineteenth-century economic development in Latin America tended to strengthen and solidify the economic power of the landed aristocracy. Inevitably, political oligarchy was also strengthened. This came about because those who governed were closely connected with the large land-owners. Most of the men who were influential in politics came from the landed class, even when the dictator who happened to be at the top was a man from the lower ranks of society. A *caudillo* who held power for any length of time usually became incorporated into the landowning class. In addition, the landed class was always well represented among the higher army officers. It is well known that control over the army in a Latin American country has been an essential means of maintaining control over the function of government. Because of these ties, the further concentration of economic power which took place in the nineteenth century was matched by a consolidation of political power.

Parallel to the extension of large landholdings in Latin America after the middle of the nineteenth century was a new trend in the development of peonage. The two changes went hand in hand. There are even grounds for believing that the encroachment on Indian community lands was sometimes motivated by a desire to get Indian labor rather than by a desire to get more land. Deprived of the lands which yielded them their sustenance, the Indians had no alternative but to become peons for a large landholder. Back of both developments — that is, the changes in land tenure and the changes in peonage — was the fundamental influence of the expanding market economy.

The bond which kept the peon subservient to the landowner was tightened, since his labor was now more necessary than ever for the operation of the *latifundio*. The average estate in Latin America did not become a rationalized organization in a technological sense after the middle of the nineteenth century, but it did become more rational in the use of its labor force, as the owners came to appreciate the satisfactions of enlarged cash incomes. The relation between the *patrón* and the peon was still a semifeudal one, but the feudal quality of mutual rights and obligations was clouded and distorted by the nominal wage paid to the peon. The payment of a wage made it plausible for the landowner to exact as much work as possible from his peons. The softening influence of the noncommercial environment of colonial times was now removed, wholly or in part. At the same time, the machinery for keeping the peon in debt was made more effective by setting up a store at which the peon was required to make all his purchases. The *tienda de raya* of the Mexican *hacienda* is the outstanding illustration of this kind of institution. In addition, control over the peon was strengthened by changes in the laws relating to employment, or by vigorous government action of an extralegal, and sometimes even of an unconstitutional, character.

To illustrate the changing nature of peonage, we may appeal to the experience of Guatemala. Peonage developed in Guatemala during the colonial period, chiefly in connection with the production of indigo, as a substitute for the *repartimiento,* or as a supplement to this older institution. In the latter part of the colonial period the production of dyestuffs for export markets dropped to low levels, and, since there were no other significant export commodities at that time, the economy of Guatemala retreated toward subsistence. There was a decline in the use of forced labor. Legally the Indians were still subject to labor draft, but the requirements for workers were small, and services were exacted with moderation. This condition continued for many years after independence. Forced labor existed, but it was not a severe burden on the Indian population.

After the middle of the nineteenth century the economy of Guatemala began to experience new vitality in the expansion of coffee production. The raising of coffee spread from the Antigua area to other parts of the country, many new plantations were established, and output expanded steadily. About 1880 the increase in coffee production attained striking proportions, as coffee became a commodity of more general consumption in Europe and the United States, and the plantation economy was stimulated and strengthened.

To assure themselves an adequate and steady supply of labor for raising coffee and preparing it for the market, the planters took advantage of all the various long-standing customs of forcing Indian labor in Guatemala. The favorite device, however, was peonage, since the others bore a more obvious resemblance to slavery. Peonage became practiced more commonly and applied more intensively.

The coffee planters were aided in getting labor by the Guatemalan government. In 1894 a national labor law was enacted to formalize relations between worker and employer. Contractual obligations to work were made enforceable. Responsibilities of the employer were defined and certain kinds of protection for the worker were established, but violations of the former were not made subject to penalties and violations of the latter were ignored by those who administered the law. As government authorities later admitted freely, the effect of the law of 1894 was to keep the Indian in a " status similar to slavery." To force Indians to enter into such contractual relations, vagrancy laws were enacted and vigorously enforced, and a number of other methods of exerting pressure were ingeniously contrived. Supplying labor for coffee plantations was for many years regarded a primary function of government in Guatemala.

It is obvious that the growth and intensification of peonage in Latin America in the late nineteenth century was a setback for democracy. In Europe, broadly speaking, commercialization of economic life in the nineteenth century helped to dissolve servile relations between peasants and landowners. In large part, remnants of a feudal society were replaced by relations of a contractual kind. It was thus a development which favored the advance of democratic institutions. The effect of commercialization in Latin America, as in many other parts of the world, was just the opposite. Servile bonds were tightened, personal freedom was restricted, and democratic tendencies were thwarted.

It should also be pointed out that the influence of commercialization in Latin American agriculture was felt in an expansion of tenancy as well as of peonage. Both developments took place side by side in some countries, and in some cases, tenancy has been simply a variant of a basic peonage condition. In purer form, tenancy became more common outside of the areas of Indian concentration than it did in such countries as Mexico, Guatemala, Ecuador, Peru, and Bolivia. Argentina is the principal example of a Latin American country where tenancy has flourished.

In the latter part of the nineteenth century the economy of Argentina underwent a remarkable transformation as expanding markets for grains and meat in western Europe were made accessible through improvements in transportation. The total acreage under cultivation was increased greatly as new lands were opened and cattle ranches were converted into grain farms. Since Argentina was sparsely populated, the need for more hands to till the soil was met by immigration. Some of the immigrants were seasonal workers, such as the *golondrinas* (swallows) who made an annual cycle of migration between Italy and Argentina, dovetailing their farming operations at home with the harvesting of flax, wheat, and corn in Argentina. But the majority of the Italians, Spaniards, and other Europeans who went to Argentina settled there permanently. However, because of the prevailing system of large landholdings, they became tenants rather than owners. In many cases they rented land on a sharecropping basis. Whatever the rental arrangement, the tenant, with minor exceptions, remained a tenant, and his sons also were tenants rather than owners. Tenancy in Argentina offered no path to ownership. Tenancy, like peonage, strengthened the existing social structure and the political power of the landed class. The tenant was no foundation for the building of democratic institutions.

Thus far we have dealt with the land tenure system and with the landowner-peasant relations that have arisen out of the concentration of holdings. Invariably the *latifundio* has been a powerful obstacle to democracy in Latin America. Other economic factors, although less important, have also played their part. Among these is " monoculture," as it is usually called in Latin America — meaning one-sided, or specialized, economic development.

As the world economy evolved after 1850, it fostered a high degree of regional and international specialization. Although this specialization was complex in detail, in a broad way it consisted of a division of labor between industrialized nations on the one hand, and nonindustrialized countries on the other. The latter, usually referred to as the " colonial economies," threw their main economic effort, apart from subsistence agriculture, into the production of foodstuffs and raw materials for export. Thus the countries of Latin America came to be but small consumers of their own commercial output. Most of what was produced in their fields, ranges, mines, and forests was shipped to export markets in the industrialized nations. In many Latin American countries an extreme degree of economic specialization was achieved, in the sense that a few commodities — or even a single commodity — came to account for most of the total value of exports. This has been the case with copper and nitrates in Chile, sugar in Cuba, tin in Bolivia, bananas in Panama, and coffee in El Salvador, to cite only a few examples.

At the same time, the Latin American republics became dependent upon sources of capital in the advanced industrialized nations for the investment needed to carry out their role as producers and exporters of primary products. It was largely foreign capital which developed mineral resources in Latin America, built the railways and improved the harbors, and provided the power, communication, and other utility services required for the expansion of their exports. In addition, substantial investments of foreign capital were made in agricultural production for export, as in the banana and sugar plantations of Middle America and the cattle ranches of Argentina. The proceeds of foreign investment, as well as their exports of primary goods, provided the Latin American countries with the means of payment to import commodities which they did not produce at home. Manufactured goods loomed large among these imports, but several of the Latin American nations also became dependent upon imports for a sizable fraction of their food consumption. Their ability to get vital imports depended on a flow of capital from the industrialized nations as well as on export markets in the same nations.

Prior to 1914, the dependence of Latin American countries upon export markets and foreign capital did not give rise to acute problems. The consumption of primary products by the manufacturing nations was not only expanding but it was little affected by cyclical disturbances in business conditions. The movement of capital to Latin America was steady, and the international economic order functioned smoothly. The First World War, however, brought an abrupt end to these conditions. The international economy was shaken loose from its foundations, and it proved impossible to reconstruct it in the uncertain political and economic environment of the 1920's. International capital movements became erratic. Policies of economic nationalism in European countries caused them to reduce their imports of foodstuffs and raw materials. Because of this and other developments, prices of foodstuffs and raw materials fell in relation to prices of manufactured goods, and all countries dependent upon exports of primary products were placed at a disadvantage.

Thus, in the first decade after World War I the Latin American countries found themselves in an uncertain, unstable economic world which greatly affected their internal economic stability. In some countries a state of semidepression became chronic, and producers wrestled with various kinds of " surplus " problems for major export products. In some cases they were assisted by governments (for example, coffee producers in Brazil), but even where no government program was developed, political conditions were strongly affected by the new economic conditions.

The economic dislocations and problems of the 1920's were multiplied many times over in the depression of the 1930's. What was left of the world economy broke down completely. World trade shrank to a fraction of its former volume. In Latin America, Chile and Bolivia experienced an 80 percent drop in exports between 1929 and 1932, and Cuba followed with a decline of 70 percent. The aggregate value of exports from all twenty republics in Latin America fell by approximately two thirds in the same period. At the same time, the inflow of foreign capital, which had been very important in financing imports, virtually came to a halt. The depression was keenly felt in Latin America. To point this out is not to imply that the depression was more severe in Latin America than in the industrialized nations. It was severe everywhere. The point to be stressed is that the one-sided, specialized nature of their economies made it more difficult for Latin American countries to combat deflationary pressures coming from abroad, and also made it more difficult for them to adopt recovery measures. Furthermore, as bilateral and other new trade agreements were negotiated during the 1930's, each Latin American country found that it was at a great disadvantage in bargaining with the major industrialized nations — a disadvantage which arose out of: (1) its extreme dependence on one or two export products, and (2) its relatively small position as a buyer of the exports of any industrialized nation. It cannot be denied that Latin America suffered from a peculiarly grave kind of economic instability during the 1930's.

To appreciate fully the bearing of this instability upon democracy in Latin America, it must be realized that the governments of Latin America have typically derived a large fraction of their revenues from taxes on export products. These levies are collected in the form of export duties, or perhaps in the form of royalties on mineral production. Whatever the form, the amount of such revenues is closely related to the volume of exports. The drying up of foreign markets, therefore, has immediate and severe repercussions on government finances. Moreover, duties on imports are another important source of government revenue, and they also drop off as importation is curtailed by the decline in exports and in capital inflow. The financial position of the Latin American government is thus extremely vulnerable to a decline in foreign trade. A severe depression is obviously a threat to political stability anywhere. It is all the more so where, as in Latin America, a government suffers a drastic and rapid loss of revenues.

Political conditions in Latin America, unstable at best, have therefore been deeply affected by the vulnerability of their economies to unfavorable changes in exports and in the flow of foreign capital. Economic conditions in the 1920's, and even more in the 1930's, must be held responsible for much of the political tension experienced in Latin America. In 1930 there began a wave of revolutions that affected more than half of the republics of Latin America by 1933. Some of the progress that had been made in the development of constitutional government was lost during these revolutionary upheavals, and much of what was lost has not yet been recovered. Even in countries where no revolution occurred, mounting tensions led to a tightening of dictatorial powers. There can be no question that monoculture in Latin America has encouraged political control by *caudillos,* and that it has been a handicap to the development of democratic institutions.

We must also consider the effect of low standards of living on political institutions in Latin America, bearing in mind the fact that these standards have been basically determined by the system of landholdings. Once established, the distribution of property in the form of land fostered a high degree of inequality in the distribution of income. Typically a large fraction of the national income in a Latin American country has gone to a handful of persons, while the average income for the bulk of the people has been very low, and thus average standards of living have also been low. It must be granted that other causes have contributed to the same end. Deficiencies in natural resources and other physical conditions such as a difficult climate for work, by restricting total productivity, have also reacted on standards of living. Giving full weight to such conditions, however, it is certain that a different pattern of income distribution would have yielded higher average standards of living in all Latin American countries, and very much higher standards in some.

Low standards of living tend to foster and perpetuate political oligarchy. Deep poverty, and its twin, illiteracy, make it possible to continue a situation in which political power in a nation is concentrated in the hands of a few. But if the average person in such a country attains a greater satisfaction of his material wants, and a certain amount of leisure time in which to acquire literacy, new avenues are apt to be opened in his thinking. The influence is a subtle one. Higher standards of living create a feeling of responsibility, a willingness to take responsibility, and a desire to share the responsibility of government. What a person accepted before without question may no longer seem just or reasonable to him. Thus the position of any privileged minority becomes questionable and it may soon become untenable. Even if this last reaction takes place very slowly, it is clear that a rise in average standards of living favors the development of democratic institutions.

We may readily believe, therefore, that the political oligarchies of Latin America are fundamentally opposed to measures which bring about a rise in standards of living for the bulk of the population, no matter what they may say for public consumption. They realize that such measures imply a threat to their position. To point this out is not to suggest that the oligarchs reach this conclusion by sociological analysis. Reasoning is unnecessary. As though by intuition, they inevitably come to the conclusion that the mass of the people are happy living in poverty rather than in plenty.

The existence of large foreign investments in Latin American countries must also be recognized as an economic factor which has tended to weaken rather than strengthen democratic institutions in Latin America. Big foreign concerns have at times intervened in local politics, giving financial and other aid to dictators who could supply the kind of stability that was favorable to business operations. The evidence is difficult to evaluate. Some writers on " economic imperialism " have treated this question in an exaggerated and overly dramatic manner, discovering plots and conspiracies on every page of the history of foreign investment in Latin America. Such interpretations can be readily dismissed without denying that the influence of foreign corporations has been found often on the side of dictatorship rather than that of democracy.

More important than direct intervention in politics is the fact that most foreign investment of the past has fitted in with the interests of the landed aristocracy. Foreign enterprises engaged in agricultural production in Latin America have sometimes behaved exactly like native landowners in relation to their workers, taking full advantage of peonage and other means of getting forced labor. Much foreign capital has gone into the construction of railroads and the improvement of harbor facilities. By stimulating exports, these developments have strengthened the economic position of the large landowners. In mineral production, the foreign companies have had less direct economic ties with the landholding class, but they have shared a common point of view on many basic questions. The foreign company engaged in mining or petroleum production in a Latin American country has not been interested in the domestic market, since all or most of its output has been shipped to export markets. It has had little or no concern with average purchasing power within the country, or with standards of living. The technical and managerial personnel in charge of operations has usually been quick to adopt the attitude of the aristocracy toward the bulk of the population. Moreover, they have been wont to believe that their companies bear an unduly large proportion of the tax burden, and thus they have been typically opposed to increasing government expenditures for education. Whatever the intention, the effect of this action has been to impede the development of democratic institutions.

The preceding discussion has brought out what we consider to be the main economic forces that militate against democracy in Latin America: (1) the system of land tenure, and its major corollary, peonage; (2) one-sided economic development; (3) low standards of living; and (4) the nature of foreign investment. The objective of this paper has been to analyze these economic conditions in relation to the problem of democracy in Latin America. We can hardly leave the subject, however, without setting forth briefly a few propositions of a positive nature about economic changes favorable to the development of democratic institutions in Latin America. Although these propositions have been implied in what has gone before, they now need to be clarified and examined in relation to each other.

The emphasis given in this paper to the system of landholdings naturally suggests a similar emphasis on land reform as a corrective. Land reform itself will not insure democratic institutions. It is well known that Mexico, the one country in Latin America where a major program to redistribute land ownership has been carried out, is far from being a democracy. Before democracy can prevail in Mexico in any meaningful sense of the term, many other changes will have to occur. They will take place slowly, because the heritage of the past cannot be written off easily. Nevertheless, Mexico has started on the road to democracy. As long as peonage held sway there was no hope at all for democracy in Mexico. At least that great obstacle to democratic development has been removed. Land reform, however imperfect, has achieved personal freedom for the bulk of Mexico's rural people, and has paved the way for the spread of education. If democracy in Mexico is not yet a reality, at least it is a possibility.

To stress the political importance of land reform in Mexico is not to suggest that other countries in Latin America will have to undergo an experience similar to that of the Mexican Revolution, or that they will have to follow the Mexican model in their land programs. The nature and scope of land reform will vary substantially from country to country. But as to the basic need for it, wherever peonage exists, there can be no question. It is difficult to imagine how peonage can be eradicated without a redistribution of land ownership.

In the light of what was said in a preceding section of this paper regarding monoculture, or one-sided economic development, it is evident that economic diversification has a political as well as an economic meaning for Latin America. Diversification is no absolute guarantee against economic instability, but it is a means of reducing the kind of instability from which the Latin American countries have suffered through a collapse of exports and of foreign investment. In diversifying their economies they lessen their dependence upon business decisions made abroad — such business decisions are naturally made with reference to conditions in foreign countries. Diversification, too, puts them in a better position to combat deflationary pressures originating abroad, and makes it easier to put into effect recovery policies in a time of depression. Again, diversification supplies new sources of government revenue, and thereby lessens the chance of a crisis in government finances whenever exports and capital movements fall off sharply. In all these ways, economic diversification lessens the threat of economic instability, and, therefore, of political instability.

Moreover, diversification in Latin America invariably means an increase in manufacturing. The degree may vary from country to country, but industrialization is a necessary component of building a more diversified economy. Industrialization is never solely a technical and economic development. It is a social and cultural process as well, and in underdeveloped countries nowadays it is also likely to have profound political repercussions. Manufacturing development creates a new class of businessmen, with an interest in an expanding internal market. Higher average standards of living make sense to them. In the absence of a rising standard of living for the people as a whole, they cannot hope to realize their plans and ambitions for industrial development. Purchasing power for industrial products has to be created among the agricultural people, since this group forms a large percentage of the total population. The peon is no customer for manufactured goods. Thus the new industrialist class quickly appreciates the need for measures to improve the lot of the peasant farmer, including among such measures, land reform. Their business interests lead them to favor economic and social changes which establish a better base for democratic institutions.

In a broader sense, it can be said that the growth of industry is favorable to democracy because it creates new blocs of economic power, thus lessening the concentration of political power in the hands of one group. The industrialists make up one new bloc of this character. The trade union movement, which is also encouraged by industrialization, is another. Neither the one nor the other *insures* the full development of democratic institutions. That is not the question. The point is that in the prevailing economic, social, and political structure of Latin America they are both bound to be forces of a pro-democratic character.

It should be observed, too, that in recent years there has been a growing tendency for foreign capital to invest in manufacturing in Latin America, producing goods for domestic rather than export markets. The amounts involved are relatively small, but the trend promises to continue. To the extent that foreign concerns become interested in the domestic market, they also can be expected to throw their weight behind measures to raise average standards of living.

The most active economic agents of democracy in Latin America — land reform and industrialization — are clearly related developments, for a gain in the one is reflected in a better environment for the other. The foreign policy of the United States government is avowedly directed toward promoting the spread of democracy in the Western Hemisphere, as elsewhere. It must, therefore, encourage both land reform and industrialization in Latin America. Obviously, it is difficult for the United States government to promote land reform in another country by direct measures. This end must be achieved through promoting industrialization, inasmuch as industrial development will facilitate land reform as well as strengthen democracy in its own right. Thus the Point Four Program, now in the process of being worked out, is a crucial element in United States political policy, as well as an essential component of its economic policy, toward Latin America.

No. 13   [The preceding selection was a discussion of the general economic pattern that is found in Latin America, and of the interaction that exists between the economy and the organization and conduct of government. Professor Mosk noted, among the several broad economic characteristics of Latin America, its peculiar system of land tenure.

The authors of the following article concentrate their attention on the place of agriculture in the national life. They discuss not only the *latifundio* base of land tenure but also the uses to which the land is put, the characteristics of the process of land use and exploitation, and how these affect the economic and social, and hence political, life of the various Latin American nations.]

*Geographical, Cultural, and Land Problems**

by GEORGE SOULE, DAVID EFRON, AND NORMAN T. NESS

. . . I<small>F</small> anything useful is to be done about this situation [the *latifundio*], however, it is necessary first to know more about the causes that lie behind it. We also must inquire concerning the unused potentialities for improvement. We therefore turn now to the fundamental conditions which have perpetuated the low levels [of income] and the resources that are available for development in order to produce a better result. Is the lack of human satisfactions consequent on any poverty of natural fertility in the land, or lack of mineral resources or of anything else that cannot be supplied? What is the system of exploitation of land and natural resources, and what are its effects on production and distribution? What is the framework of Latin American economy?

. . . We have been unable to deal in detail with some factors that may be considered important. One is the great diversity that exists between various parts of a great continent — diversity in natural

* From *Latin America in the Future World*, by George Soule, David Efron and Norman T. Ness. Copyright, 1945, by the National Planning Association, and reprinted by permission of Rinehart & Company, Inc., Publishers. The footnotes in the original version are omitted here.

riches, climate, population, and customs. It must be understood that because of such diversity, nothing that may be said can be applied to all sections or to all sections in equal measure. Nevertheless there are certain generalizations useful for our present purposes that may be made at least as a basis for further testing.

A large omission is that of a population study in ethnographical and general cultural terms. Historians, geographers, and travelers often remark on the significance of facts in this realm. It is, for instance, important that the early European settlers in Latin America came for the most part as conquerors, seeking to exploit natural wealth and native labor for their own benefit and that of the mother countries, rather than to set up a new civilization with their own toil. It is significant that the Indians, instead of being continually pushed back into smaller and smaller areas and becoming a small fraction of the population as in North America, remained as a subject or working class in many regions. It is significant that racial intermixture occurred on a large scale. Such considerations must not be overlooked, yet they do not decrease the influence of the economic and other factors which are here discussed.

One cultural fact at least requires brief treatment. It is often pointed out that those Latin Americans of European blood, many of them descendants of the *conquistadores* and inheritors of their traditions, do not regard highly the traits necessary for a progressive industrial society. They have rather the point of view of a landed aristocracy, which measures wealth and distinction by the ownership of great estates, which looks down upon those who work with their hands or those who make money in " trade," and which is a bulwark of hereditary privileges. On this account, it is said, an energetic middle class, necessary for enterprise in business and for management in industry, is lacking. There is undoubtedly much truth in this observation. Yet to argue that because of this tradition it is impossible to begin or to develop a technically efficient industrial civilization would ignore the facts of history elsewhere. A dominant landed aristocracy has not been lacking anywhere in the world where industrialism has sprung up. It certainly was not lacking in England in the eighteenth and early nineteenth centuries, or in France before and even after the French Revolution, or in Germany, or in Japan.

Even the United States was at the beginning an agrarian country, with agrarian traditions and many large landholders; and this fact created difficulties for the birth of modern industry. Yet in all such cases, the obvious advantages of mechanical industry led to its eventual development.

Likewise it cannot be argued that the abject condition of a working class, undernourished, sick, and lacking in experience with machinery, is an insuperable obstacle to the introduction of more modern methods and higher productivity, whether in industry or agriculture. Such conditions were not lacking in any of the feudal societies where modern technology has already taken hold. The development of skilled and productive workers accompanies, and cannot precede, the development of a productive machine technology.

Finally it should again be emphasized that our point of view, in portraying both the living conditions of Latin American populations and the factors that lie behind them, is not the offensive one of philanthropy or reform from outside. We attempt merely an analysis of a situation which is equally important to the nations of Latin America and to the United States, engaged as they are in a common cause and subscribing to a common set of purposes. It is a part of inquiry as to how all parties concerned may in the common interest best help themselves.

THE LAND

In Latin America, perhaps more than in any other area of the world, the life of the people depends directly on agricultural and pastoral pursuits. Though statistics are not exactly comparable, certain indications seem usable in a broad sense. The United States in 1930 had less than a fourth of its gainfully occupied people working in agriculture, forestry, and fishing. In Western European countries the portion so engaged ranged from a sixth in Belgium to perhaps half in Italy. In India it might have been two thirds. But in Mexico and Venezuela it was three fourths. (Chile, apparently with only 57 percent, must be a highly exceptional case.) Probably the populations of Eastern Europe and China are the only ones comparable to Latin Americans in direct dependence on the soil. It is likely that by studying land use we can go far in accounting for the low levels of living previously described.

What, then, are the distinguishing features of Latin America's agricultural economy?

There appears to be a tendency among United States students of the subject to keep the discussion chiefly on a geological and technical level. From the bulk of the writings one gets an impression that the agricultural problems facing the Southern Good Neighbors are primarily those of indifference to soil-conservation needs, inadequate use of fertilizers, lack of modern machinery, poor marketing facilities, and the like. Surely these problems exist, and a program for improving Latin American agriculture must include measures to change such conditions. But in our view they cannot be the starting point. They are symptoms of a deeper trouble.

Remedies cannot really be worked out unless the forces which perpetuate inadequate techniques in the face of available science are known and recognized. What are the controls which operate with such a stifling effect? That is the question to which analysis must address itself first. These seem to be the important problems:

1. The prevailing organization of agriculture in Latin America is feudal or semifeudal. Except in Haiti, in the northern part of the Dominican Republic, and in parts of Mexico, Costa Rica, and El Salvador, most of the productive soil and the livestock, and a considerable part of commercially used forests, are owned or controlled by a relatively small number of absentee landlords — native gentry or foreign corporations. Monopolization of land has been and still is both the source and the technique of political power in Latin America.

2. The distribution as well as the production of agricultural commodities is largely controlled by an handful of monopolistic grain, livestock, fruit, and railroad corporations, whose headquarters in many cases are in Europe or the United States. Frequently these companies have an international character through interlocking directorates. Many of the big landlords and cattle barons in Latin America function merely as their intermediaries.

3. The overwhelming majority of the rural population lives and labors under trying conditions of peonage, share cropping, or tenancy with oppressive stipulations.

4. In several countries (Peru, Ecuador, Bolivia, Paraguay, Central America, Mexico) the problem of land control is essentially correla-

tive with the so-called Indian problem. Historically, usurpation of land by feudal *conquistadores* and their successors involved economic, social, and political subjugation — and even actual ownership — of the autochthonous population. Only where some measure of agrarian reform has been achieved, or where capitalist industrial agriculture has been developed, have medieval forms of labor exploitation been replaced by the wage system.

5. Protective legislation for rural workers in general, and especially for Indian peons, is largely nonexistent or remains a *de jure* concession neither complied with by owners nor adequately enforced by public officers.

6. Land use in Latin America has traditionally been characterized by search for quick profits through production of single cash crops or grazing or speculative land buying. Typical both of landholding families and of modern foreign corporations, this attitude has also filtered down into some of the small-merchant and farmer groups. It is reflected in soil-mining practices, in narrow range of products, and in hoarded land (kept idle with an eye to increased demand or of shift from one product to another).

7. Frequently prestige is an even stronger motive than quick profits among the landed gentry, mere ownership of vast tracts being considered a more distinctive sign of class superiority than commercial wealth. This also makes for idle land; and even when the soil is put to agricultural use, the existence of the landholding class as rentiers, or unproductive consumers, burdens the productive community with a land levy not subject to the fluctuations of agricultural production and prices.

8. Landholders, through the great political power springing from their control of resources, have succeeded in keeping rural property relatively free from taxation. Besides bolstering their control, this limits public revenues, holding back the provision of badly needed social services. Together with the fact that both rural and urban workers' incomes are so low that they cannot be taxed, it necessitates dependence for revenues on export and import duties — a highly unstable source. . . . The rural population suffers through unfair distribution of what funds there are.

9. Landholders have depended on peonage and low wages rather than on increased productivity to yield the desired profits. Machinery,

fertilizers, and other modern tools and organizational techniques are little used.

10. Agricultural production being keyed to foreign demands, large sectors of the rural population are frequently exposed to sharp economic crises resulting from fluctuations in the demands, and are highly vulnerable to war interruptions of shipping and trade. The development of intensive subsistence agriculture, badly needed to supply domestic requirements and reduce the effects of sudden crises, has been inhibited.

11. Transportation facilities serve chiefly the big landowners and the grain- and cattle-exporting companies. Underdeveloped transport hinders the building up of agricultural production for domestic needs.

12. In most countries rural electrification is almost completely absent.

13. Agricultural credit facilities, except in a few countries, are inadequate. The situation looks much better on paper than it is in reality. True, state funds have in some cases actually been set up; but, owing to the absence of workable programs for developing domestic production on holdings by independent farmers, these funds have often been used to bolster the large estates.

14. Generally in some countries (such as Ecuador and Peru) and here and there in others, the soil is not fertile enough to permit successful independent farming on very small holdings, at least under existing technical and economic conditions; and even considerable improvement of the latter will not do away with the problem entirely. Several limited experiments in parcelling land from large estates to develop independent small farms have failed because attention was not paid to these geographic, technical, and economic factors.

15. Although growing in some countries, the agricultural cooperative movement is still largely undeveloped. This is another instance where progressive measures have been " enacted " but hardly acted upon.

Before enlarging upon this analysis of present problems, it will be illuminating to review briefly the historical background as it relates to them.

THE ALIENATION OF PUBLIC DOMAIN

Historically, the economic and social matrix of the system of land monopoly in Latin America is to be found, of course, in the feudal structure of the Spanish and Portuguese conquests and " colonization." These conquests, though encouraged by the Crown, were not state-managed to insure rational development of the newly discovered areas, but had rather the character of a " private business " entrusted to the conquerors and their descendants. The Crown's chief interest in its colonies was their value as a steady source of raw materials and of easy revenue derived from land grants and concessions, particularly in mining areas. The Spanish and Portuguese " colonists " were not pioneers in any sense of the word, but adventurers interested solely in the accumulation of gold and other riches as a source of prestige and power within the mercantilist structure of empire. In the achievement of this goal they exhibited a ruthlessness and a disregard for human values naturally associated with such practices. Humanistic attempts on the part of progressive elements in the Catholic clergy and in local administrations (such as Father Las Casas and the Viceroy Toledo) to stop the abuses of the conquerors were thwarted by force, legal cunning, and the " antiheathen " zeal of the more fanatic representatives of the Spanish hierarchy. The protective legislation wrung from Philip II in 1592 (" Laws of the Indies "), purportedly guaranteeing the inalienability of Indian communal properties, forbidding the system of " personal services " (labor servitude) and instituting minimum nutritional allotments to the Indian mine and *hacienda* workers, was only occasionally complied with and proved to be a merely formal concession. In the name of " King, Country, and God," the immense riches of the Latin American continent were systematically ransacked and its aboriginal populations decimated by torture, undernourishment, and illness in the mining camps and plantations of their alleged protectors. The policies and practices of the *conquistadores* pointedly illustrate the essential difference between *colonialization* (usurpation of the labor power and the means of subsistence of a people) and *colonization* (creative release and development of untapped human and natural resources for the benefit of the people concerned).

The chief methods of land and labor usurpation used by the Iberian imperialists in Latin America were the *capitanias* or *repartimientos* (grants of huge extensions of land, with their Indian inhabitants, to court favorites and military leaders), *caballerias* (special allotments to mounted troops), and at a later period the famous *encomiendas* or " trusteeships " of public domain and of its native occupants. In addition, there were the *reducciones,* or Indian communities supervised by the Church for purposes of evangelization, and in some areas the communal system of the *ejidos* (common land). Theoretically, the *encomienda* lands were revertible to the Crown if kept unused by the grantees (or, if exploited, after an occupancy of two generations). Actually, this principle of reappropriation of public domain by the metropolitan government was seldom enacted, the grants finally becoming *de facto* possessions of the trustees. Through speculation, barter, and further usurpation of the Indian communal properties, most of the soil later became concentrated in the hands of a small group of aristocratic and military families. Similarly, the trusteeship of the native populations was turned into outright ownership, with an uncontested right on the part of the landowners to the labor and lives of the Indian workers, their women, and their children. Thus developed the system of the *mitas* (mine slave-gangs) and *obrajes* (textile workshops). As Solórzano, the famous and respected analyst of colonial institutions living in that very period, has put it, " In their urge for economic profit the *encomenderos* showed an utter disregard for the temporal and spiritual welfare of the Indians, working them harder than beasts of burden." This, incidentally, ought to serve as a grim historical reminder of what might lie in store for the Latin American countries should the Axis-inspired program of " Hispanicism " — the revival of the Spanish empire — be successful.

Two examples will illustrate the feudal pattern of land usurpation by Spanish and Portuguese conquerors. In Brazil, all the conquered territory was divided into fifteen " chieftainships " and allotted to only twelve Portuguese courtiers, with the right to make subgrants to whom they saw fit. All the occupied land in Chile was divided by Valdivia, in 1544, into sixty portions given to an equal number of families. Two years later, owing to a growing scarcity of Indian labor, the number of these concessions was reduced to thirty-two, some of the grantees "falling heir to whole valleys, extending from the sea to the cordillera, with their corresponding Indians. . . . The system remained as established and served as the foundation for the acquisition of property rights in Chile."

By a technically different process, ecclesiastical organizations also gradually became the recipients of vast tracts of Indian land — particularly through "inheritance" of the properties of the deceased members of the communities under their supervision, and through the imposition of levies upon the surviving ones. In the words of a prominent Catholic historian of Ecuador, "All the regular members of the clergy, especially the Jesuits, accumulated *haciendas* and riches. In an evil hour, a worldly ambition overtook the fathers of the Jesuit Order, not only in the ancient kingdom of Quito but in the whole of Spanish America." Thus developed the institution of mortmain — uncultivated, tax exempt land, owned and speculatively used by convents, monasteries, and individual members of the clergy. The amount of such church property increased steadily as time went on, through state land grants for the maintenance of religious institutions and through individual bequests to priests in return for masses to be said for the repose of the donors' souls. In the course of three centuries, the Church became the greatest landowner in Latin America. It has been estimated that at one stage more than half of the total property in each Latin American country belonged to the clergy. Thus, according to the celebrated German scientist Humboldt, who traveled through the Spanish colonies early in the nineteenth century, four fifths of Mexican land was then owned by religious organizations and individual members of the clergy. The situation, it is important to note, greatly enhances rather than detracts from the democratic role played by a number of Catholic leaders in movements for national independence. It was, indeed, a member of the Catholic clergy — the Mexican Father Hidalgo — who kindled the first spark of Latin American revolt against the Spanish Empire.

While land monopoly began with Spanish colonization, actual consolidation of the feudal apparatus of landownership below the Rio Grande took place not during the colonial period but — paradoxical as it may seem — in three different stages of the republican era: (1) the civil wars in the first half of the nineteenth century, followed by (2) the "Indian wars," and (3) foreign-capital influx during the last two decades of the nineteenth century and the first two of the twentieth. Fully as much public domain and Indian communal land was alienated into the hands of a few aristocratic families, military officers and foreign companies and individuals between 1830 and 1920 as during the three centuries of Spanish domination.

The wars of independence in Latin America are generally thought of as a people's revolt against foreign oppression. Popular aspirations were indeed stirred, but their fulfillment was seriously checked by the fact that these wars were at the same time a contest of the native creole merchants and planters against their Spanish rulers for the control of the colonies' trade with the outer world. The creole leaders' need to enlist, in their economic struggle against the Spanish monopolists, the Indian mestizo and mulatto populations was continuously counteracted by their apprehensions about the amount of economic and political control they would have to relinquish were these groups to gain strength and cohesion in fighting for their democratic right to an equitable share in the products of their labor. Hence the creole entrepreneurs relied on the financial and military help of foreign powers more readily than on the aspirations of their own peoples. They even joined forces on occasion with the Spanish armies themselves to subdue revolutionary uprisings having a truly popular base, such as the one led in 1810 by Father Hidalgo. They were more interested in maintaining the economic inferiority of autochthonous populations than in attaining economic equality with the Spaniards for themselves. They opposed relentlessly, for example, and succeeded in emasculating Bolívar's early attempts to restore and guarantee to Indian communities the lands that had been taken away from them.

It is important to evaluate unromantically the role played by the creole *hacienda* and merchant classes in the Latin American wars of independence, if we are to understand the perpetuation of feudalistic landownership and its effects into the present. The history of republican Latin America is full of all kinds of legal and military confiscations of Indian properties for the advantage of the native ruling groups and of foreign corporate investment. The technique most commonly used was that of declaring such lands public domain and, shortly after, distributing them free of charge among the military " in payment for services rendered "; auctioning them off at giveaway prices to influential families or individuals; or leasing them as long-term concessions to already powerful landlords, or to English, German, and American companies. As a rule, the purpose of these land sales, gifts, and concessions was ostensibly to foster the establishment of European or native colonists on a small-property basis, the grantees or lessees being committed by law or decree to finance and carry out their respective colonization projects within a specified period. However, except for a few halfhearted attempts, these commitments were never fulfilled. Most of the " colonizers " eventually became full-fledged owners of these state lands, either by means of government-tolerated legal stratagems or by purchase at extremely low prices.

With the coming of railroads and the development of foreign agriculture and livestock markets, the process of land concentration gained momentum: speculation was stimulated as well as, in some cases, even further expropriation of peasant-owned properties or of lands still held communally by Indians. This time the usurpation was facilitated by legalistic " revisions " of the traditionally ill-defined system of title deeds to farm lands, particularly in the frontier areas of the larger countries. Through further speculation, and in less than twenty-five years, a very sizable part of the agricultural and livestock resources of the Latin American continent thus fell into the hands of a relatively small group of native families and foreign corporate enterprises. By the end of the nineteenth century there was hardly any public domain left in several of the most important countries below the Rio Grande. Today, more than a century after the liberation of the Latin American colonies from the Spanish yoke, the institution of the *latifundio,* with its quasi-feudal forms of labor exploitation, is as entrenched in Latin America as it was in the times of the *encomiendas.*

PRESENT PROPERTY STRUCTURE

In Latin America, in general, methods of utilizing the soil and its resources are basically determined by private monopolistic land control in the interest of commercial monoculture and grazing for foreign markets, or of rent revenues and speculative gain; and the forms of control cannot be understood apart from their political aspect. In some of the countries (particularly in the Caribbean area), the pattern of this control is preponderantly of a foreign corporate nature; in others, it is more of the traditional native family type; in others still (probably the majority), the two forms coexist side by side.

Although differing occasionally in their economic structure (the former exhibiting sometimes a more pronounced trend toward industrialized production), these two forms of land concentration are basically alike in their opposition to the diversification of agriculture and the development of a domestic market. This opposition presents two fundamental characteristics: (1) a tendency to keep in idle reserve vast areas of potentially productive land on account of hoped-for increases in demand for products now exported; and (2) a reluctance to enter into any kind of contractual agreement with tenant farmers that might interfere with the landlord's freedom to adjust quickly to a shrinkage or qualitative shift in foreign demand.

The first characteristic (hoarding of land) is illustrated by the well-known practices of American oil, sugar, and fruit companies in Venezuela, Cuba, and Central America, respectively. . . .

The second characteristic is strikingly illustrated by the eviction of cash-crop tenant farmers which since the outbreak of the present war has been taking place in several parts of Argentina. Instead of facilitating agricultural diversification as a way out of the problem of cumulative stockpiling of unmarketable money crops, the Argentine landowners have chosen to replace their wheat- and corn-growing tenants with smaller numbers of alfalfa-raising or cattle-breeding peons, thus substituting for a relatively perishable stock of agricultural commodities (if we may be pardoned a pun) a *live*stock pile which can wait " on the hoof " for an eventual resumption of international trade. The fact that such a policy strands the evicted farmers, further depresses rural levels of living, and dislocates the country's economy is considered secondary to preserving the speculative basis of the *latifundio* and its role as an ever-ready source of raw materials for the export market. How characteristic such dislocations are, and how extensive they have been from time to time, is suggested in the following table.

SHIFTS IN PERCENTAGE OF PRODUCTION FROM STOCK RAISING
AND FROM CROPS IN ARGENTINA

Year	Stock Raising	Agriculture
1897	73.2	23
1900	46.1	50.1
1913	38.7	58.1
1918	68.3	21.39

Note the wartime cattle boom of 1918. Even such a conservative Argentine economist as the late Alejandro E. Bunge (himself a member of a powerful landowning family) was unable to repress his criticism of this " crudely commercial conception " of agriculture. " Land conceived as a merchandise," he repeatedly pointed out, " is an obstacle to the rational utilization of our natural resources, to the increase of our population, and even to the stability of our institutions." He was not reticent in calling the landowners' attention to the bad effects of their " mystico-pastoral mentality " which conspires against the stabilization of the Argentine peasantry " on a small family-property basis."

A quantitative analysis of landownership controls in several Latin American countries will provide a concrete measure of the basic obstacle besetting the balanced and rational development of agricultural resources below the Rio Grande for the benefit of the local populations.

No. 14   [The instability and precarious nature of the Latin American economy is the result of other economic forces and institutions than the *latifundio* system, and its consequent shaping of the whole agricultural pattern. Two highly important additional influences are the so-called one-sided nature of the economy, and the absence of a well-balanced and well-coordinated program of industrial development. These are discussed in the following article.

Much has been said and written in recent years about the rapid " industrialization " of Latin America, and to many this portends a brighter economic and political future. It is therefore important that one understands what *kind* of industrialization is taking place.

The authors note that as yet one cannot describe the process as " industrialization " in our sense of the word; the establishment of small processing plants rather than large manufacturing firms constitutes the major change. The economy of Latin America is still susceptible to severe economic dislocations, and even collapse. Economic crises frequently bring with them political upheavals. The latter, as the experience of the past two decades has shown in Europe, Asia, and the Americas, makes it easier for the man on horseback to ride to political power.]

The Pattern of Economic Activity*

by GEORGE SOULE, DAVID EFRON, AND NORMAN T. NESS

" ONE-SIDEDNESS " OF THE ECONOMIES

*W*HAT is the economic pattern which underlies the poverty, the ill-health, and the social conditions heretofore described? If we can identify it and discover its flaws, it may be possible to discover what fundamental remedies are available.

It is often stated that the Latin American economies are " one-sided," and the statement is true. It is not true, however, as often believed, that these nations are mere mining camps deriving their whole sustenance from the export of raw materials.

Actually a great part of the population of Latin American countries is engaged in production for domestic consumption. Statistics showing the occupational distributions of the several countries of the Caribbean and South America are in no case wholly adequate and in most cases lacking altogether, but something can be gleaned from those which are available. Thus, the 1930 census for Mexico (whose exports consist largely of minerals) showed that 77.2 percent

* From *Latin America in the Future World,* by George Soule, David Efron and Norman T. Ness. Copyright, 1945, by the National Planning Association, and reprinted by permission of Rinehart & Company, Inc., Publishers. The footnotes in the original version are omitted here.

of all employed workers were engaged in "agricultural and other rural industries" and that only 6.3 percent were in the "mineral and manufacturing industries." In Chile — another "mining camp" — the same year's census revealed agriculture to be the most important field of employment, with manufacturing second in rank. Clearly, in these two countries the great part of the populations' economic activities is domestically oriented. A similar situation prevails in the others. The Royal Institute of International Affairs has estimated that 65 percent of South America's population is dependent upon agriculture. Of course not all of the products of agriculture are used domestically. As a matter of fact, such goods enter largely into the exports of some countries; but even in the extreme case of Argentina (whose exports consist almost wholly of the products of field and pasture) domestic consumption far outranks exportation, as far as foods ready for human consumption are concerned. The case of Guatemala is particularly revealing. Together, coffee and bananas account for about 90 percent of that country's total exports, but the acreage devoted to the principal crops is as follows: corn, 866,000; coffee, 276,000; beans, 169,000; bananas, 83,000.

Of course it does not follow that because a large part of the product of a nation is domestically consumed, that product is sufficient, or of the right kind to sustain health or a high standard of living. That is a matter of the efficiency of production, its quality and variety. It is in these respects that the one-sidedness of Latin American economies appears most clearly.

It might be argued that Latin American republics, though individually one-sided, would prove to be complementary to each other if trade were developed. The data we employ come to us on a country-by-country basis, and we may fall into the error of attributing to the whole what is really true only of its parts. If, for example, one has been impressed by how largely staple foodstuffs enter into the imports of many Latin American countries, it proves a surprise that "rice is one of the few main agricultural products of daily use in which the continent [of South America] as a whole is not self-sufficient."

Nevertheless it is impossible to speak of a "Latin American economy," since trade among the several nations is not sufficiently active.

LACK OF INDUSTRIAL DEVELOPMENT

Any given economy is presumably *not* one-sided if its broader branches — agriculture, mining, industry, and the like — are balanced one with another. The economy need not be completely self-sufficient, but if the branches be roundly developed rather than directed to one or a few specialized products, the economy possesses a measure of resiliency and independence. To be sure, it cannot stand entirely undisturbed in times of stress, but it can rely upon itself with fair success.

Latin America cannot be said to measure up to this test. One at least of the broad branches has never been developed to the point where it stands in anything like balance with the others. That branch is manufacturing industry. This conclusion is strengthened when attention is given to the structure of such industry as does exist.

Only in a few countries — particularly in Argentina, Brazil, Chile, and Mexico — has manufacturing taken anything like a firm hold. Unfortunately, statistical sources are inadequate, but some generalizations are possible. Thus, from a study of the best available data George Wythe estimates, in his *Industry and Nationalism in Latin America,* that " the value added by manufacturing in Argentina and Brazil . . . amounts to about 30 percent of the total value of production in each country." This figure is not insignificant; but in the United States a comparable proportion is accounted for by the metalworking trades alone. Similarly authoritative estimates are not available for Chile and Mexico, but some inferences are possible. In Chile in 1930 some 296,201 persons (in a total population of 4,288,000) were classified as employed in manufacturing industries. In Mexico's census of 1930 but 6.3 percent of the employed population was put in the class of " mineral and manufacturing industries."

Statistics such as these must be treated with caution. What, after all, does one mean by " industry "? Alejandro Bunge, in his *Una nueva Argentina,* used the method employed by the official census of 1914 to estimate that 2,136,000 were engaged in " industria " in 1933, but the census of 1935 (now employing different categories) found only 544,000. There is good reason to suppose that most official estimates grossly exaggerate the degree of industrialism in Latin

America. An extreme instance is supplied by the estimate of the Costa Rica *Secretaría de Trabajo* that there were some 2,916 industrial establishments in that small country. Indeed, it is questionable whether one should apply the terminology of highly developed economies to those Latin American countries in which the hand of feudalism still lies heavily upon economic activity. In the course of a discussion of the " Industrial Development in Mexico," Preston E. James remarks:

As in most of the countries that have been discussed, there are many small-scale manufacturing plants scattered throughout the territory. Each of these industries employs a few workmen, makes use of local products, and sells to a market which is well protected from outside competition by the high costs of the transportation. *These small industries are really part of the feudal pattern — they do not indicate the presence of the urban-industrial way of living.* . . .

The Bolivian census of 1900 (the only one in that country's history) disclosed a not-inconsiderable " industrial " population, but more significant than this finding was the fact that the subclasses under the general heading of " industria " all bore craft names.

" Industry " appears, then, to range from the one extreme at which some Latin American countries have attained a considerable measure of industrialism (but cannot yet be classed as industrial) to that other extreme in which " industry " consists of the essentially handicraft operations of quasi-feudal societies.

The implications of this situation emerge clearly when attention is given to the structure of Latin American industry. In a study to which reference has already been made, George Wythe observes that such industry as does exist falls into three classes:

1. that which engages itself with the *processing* of local raw materials destined for export, e.g., meat packing, metal refining, and the like;
2. that group of essentially *local* undertakings, " like power, foundries, and construction, which provide services for immediate use "; and
3. the " finished manufactures, primarily for domestic consumption, chiefly consumers' goods but also some capital goods."

This classification is hardly a description of a developed, rounded industry. The first class is what we would call " semimanufactures."

It includes a surprising proportion of what is sometimes designated as the industry of Latin America. Witness, for example, the role of meat packing and refrigerating in the industrial life of Argentina. It is, however, to the third class that attention is most often drawn when the development of Latin American manufactures is in question. " The leading industries in Latin America are those which produce articles of a kind and quality suitable for popular consumption, such as textiles and foodstuffs. In Mexico and Brazil, almost exactly one third of the total number of factory workers are in textile mills." If the economic history of Great Britain, the United States, and similar nations may be taken as a guide, this situation is symptomatic of an early stage of industrialism.

Further evidence of deficient industrial development is afforded by the statistics of Latin American foreign trade. In no case does the class of " manufactures " loom significantly among exports (unless it consists largely of what, as already pointed out, are really " semi-manufactures "). On the other hand, such goods occupy a prominent place in the list of imports in all countries. It is impossible, given the variation of customs nomenclature from country to country, to rank the several classes of imports into Latin America as a whole, but even a casual perusal of the United States Tariff Commission's studies of the different countries will reveal the extent to which the more highly fabricated machine products dominate purchases abroad. In Argentina, for example, the leading classes of imports are (in the order of their importance in 1938): textiles and (their) manufactures; machinery; combustibles and lubricants; iron and (its) manufactures. In Brazil the order (in the same year) was as follows: machinery, apparatus, utensils, and tools; iron and steel; vehicles and accessories. The record for Chile and Mexico (other leading industrial countries) was much the same.

It must be borne in mind that these remarks about the backwardness of industrial development in Latin America apply to the continent as a whole much more than to the more advanced economies such as those of Argentina, Chile, and Brazil, and that in these cases there is no implication that great progress has not been made. The situation is rather that the full possibilities of development have not been realized, as compared with an economy like that of the United

States, or as judged by the needs of the Latin American populations. During the war, and since the studies on which this section is based, there has been a considerable industrial development. . . . There is a question, however, how permanently valuable the installations for the production of strategic materials will be.

NARROWNESS OF THE ECONOMIC BASE

If Latin America exhibits an underdevelopment of the industrial branch of its economy, a somewhat different order of one-sidedness is found in the several countries within it. Latin America, so far from being a single economic area, is really a compound of twenty separate national economies. *It functions chiefly in terms of these largely independent compartments.* The one-sidedness appears also in the narrowness of the typical economic base. Thus, the displacement of natural by synthetic nitrates bore not upon Latin America but upon Chile, and no small part of the dislocation which ensued may be attributed to the plight of a national treasury which, like the country it served, was dependent upon a single export product.

Latin American countries lean heavily upon their export markets and tend to a marked degree to specialize on a few products. There is, unfortunately, no way of measuring accurately what proportion of Latin American national incomes are derived from foreign trade, for income statistics are in most cases nonexistent and those for exports are notoriously inaccurate. Some estimates are, however, available. The calculations of Alejandro Bunge indicate that in Argentina as much as one third of the national production goes into the foreign market, and a comparable proportion has been attributed to Chile. One may set the Brazilian Ministry of Foreign Affairs' estimate of national production in 1938 (25,646,310 contos) against that year's exports (5,096,890 contos) to arrive at the conclusion that a fifth was exported. There is good reason to suppose that Cuba and Mexico would find their place alongside these countries in any ranking of Latin American nations in order of dependence on exports. If in some of the countries the proportion is lower, this is — in particular cases at least — for a reason which does not invalidate the general conclusion, a not-inconsiderable proportion of the population being outside that world of commercial dealings out of which foreign trade arises. In Bolivia, for example, a large part of the population lives and works apart from the market nexus, and its contribution to the national income ought not to be reckoned by calculating the proportion of exports to national production.

In a world in which trade seems almost characterized by disruptions of one sort or another, large dependence on foreign markets certainly implies vulnerability. Equally significant, however, is the narrowness of the foreign trade of individual Latin American countries. The exports of these countries consist of but a few individual products. . . . In nine of the twenty countries, a single product contributed half or more of the total value of exports. In eighteen of them, three exports accounted for 50 percent or more of all goods sold abroad.

Not only do Latin American countries tend individually to concentrate upon a few export items but furthermore they exhibit, as a group, a rather remarkable tendency to select the same items. . . . A list of twenty-four products includes the three leading export items of all twenty countries. What is more, six of these twenty-four items — chicle, corn, hides, canned meat, tobacco, and tungsten — make their appearance only in the third rank for some country or other. Each of these nations has but few eggs in its export basket, and each chooses eggs like those in its neighbors' baskets.

This lack of diversity in the products Latin America sells abroad renders it generally vulnerable to shifts of demand and to competition from other continents. The danger is greatly magnified by the nature of this restricted list of export products. Almost all are of a kind peculiarly sensitive to cyclical variations. It is by now a commonplace that industrial raw materials and agricultural foodstuffs suffer especially from business depressions. The prices of goods such as these fall sharply when recession sets in. The United States Tariff Commission, in the course of its country-by-country studies of *The Foreign Trade of Latin America,* gives evidence on this score. In the study made of each country a sharp decline of exports after 1928 is noted, and in the course of explanation this sentence almost always appears: " The decline in the value of exports between 1928 and 1933 was due principally to the fall in prices of goods exported."

Latin American economy, then, is in several respects one-sided. In the first place, the whole area has less than a balanced development of industry. As a result, it must depend upon sources abroad for most of its supply of fabricated products. In the second place, much of its productive energy is directed to exportation. More is here involved than the need to balance a large volume of imports. A country which buys abroad must also sell there, but (as will appear shortly) in countries like those of Latin America exports ramify through the whole of business activity — domestic as well as foreign — and generally determine its tempo. It is this fact which lends peculiar significance to Latin America's marked tendency to concentrate its export efforts upon relatively few products, and those of the class which are highly sensitive to cyclical variations.

ROLE OF EXPORTS

That exports play an important role in Latin American economic life is not often denied. Indeed, exaggeration is more often encountered than is its contrary. An instance may be cited:

[The mountains], barriers though they have been to transportation and communication, have provided much of the wealth upon which Bolivian economy has been built. Tin, of course, is the chief source of this wealth. So large does it loom in the nation's exports (68 percent) that the metal and the country have become almost synonymous.

What makes this assertion the more remarkable is its appearance in a journal whose writers, having dedicated themselves to *Agriculture in the Americas,* undoubtedly know that in Bolivia an overwhelming proportion of the population derives its livelihood not from mining but from agriculture. Wealth is not primarily derived from exportation but from productive activity.

If the internal production of a country like Bolivia could be improved in quality and quantity, the population would benefit more than by any conceivable increase in exports. This point is clearly seen by those who ridicule mercantilist economic conceptions. They make a mistake, however, when they point out that when the price of tin falls, or demand for it declines, nothing more is involved than a temporary inability to pay interest on foreign investments or to buy automobiles or machinery abroad. For the fortunes of foreign trade, in a nation largely dependent on it, affect seriously what happens in the domestic sector of the economy, as well as the ability to purchase imports.

Every modern economy has within it a crucial sector upon which the efficient functioning of the whole depends. In their analysis of cyclical fluctuations in the United States and Great Britain, for example, economists have agreed that investment is uniquely significant. In these countries a low proportion of income is devoted to consumption. Standards of living are high, relative to those of other countries generally, because the income is large, but a considerable fraction of current income is nevertheless saved. Now the act of saving abstracts buying power from the income stream, and it is essential if saved funds are to find their way back into it, that there be an equivalent amount of current investment. What the savers take out, the investors, by their outlay of saved funds, must put back; otherwise total demand will have fallen and a drop in productive activity will result.

The effects of a slump in investment are not confined to producers in the heavy industries. The failure to restore income-flow has repercussions through the whole economic system. When investment falls, a steel worker, for example, is unable to buy as freely as before in the consumption-goods market, and the consequences bear upon the merchant and the farmer. Contrariwise, the growth or upsurge of investment spreads buying power through all trades and occupations. Investment, it is urged, is " income-creating."

On the face of things, quite as much can be said for any kind of economic activity. All expenditures ramify widely. In countries like Great Britain and the United States, however, two circumstances operate to set investment apart as crucial. It is, in the first place, distinguished from other expenditure by its high variability. Building, plant construction, renovating — all these have been found, in experience, to fluctuate sharply from year to year. The second (and more fundamental) distinguishing circumstance is that investment must take place in great volume if it is fully to offset the enormous savings. Where the amount of saving is large, investment dominates all else; lacking it, the economy bogs down.

The countries of Latin America do not save a considerable proportion of their income. Individual incomes are smaller than in Great Britain and the United States, and little is left when the necessities of life have been bought and paid for. These nations' savings are small, both in absolute amount and relative to their total national incomes. Failure to invest can, accordingly, occasion but little disturbance of the economic system. The savings-investment logic holds, but investment ceases in these circumstances to be crucial.

There is, however, another segment of the economy which, for the Latin Americas, exercises a similarly dominating influence. It is interesting to consider the conclusion, reported in *The Economic Journal* by Colin Clark, reached in his joint study with J. G. Crawford of the *National Income in Australia*. Though unlike Latin America in many respects, Australia does resemble it in dependence on exports of raw materials:

In our analysis of the Australian statistics, Mr. Crawford and I adopted the definition of putting changes in value of exports on exactly the same footing as changes in the level of investment. Both generate income without increasing the supply of consumption goods and both may be regarded as original stimuli. . . . We have included therefore both exports and investment in the category of [income] determinants. . . .

A Chilean exporter, for example, sells copper in the United States and is paid in dollars. These he exchanges at the *Banco Central* for the pesos he needs in the course of his business. The pesos, whether drawn from the reserves of the *Banco* or "credit-created," add to the income stream of the country. Going through the hands of wage-recipients or of material-suppliers, they ramify through all of the economy. In this respect their effect is not different from that of the dollars paid out by an investor in Great Britain or the United States. What distinguishes them is the fact that *in the circumstances of Chilean economy*, export-pesos play a more important role than do investment-pesos. Exports bulk largely in the total of economic activity while saving-investment takes subsidiary place.

A considerable part of the Latin American economy is adapted to export outlets. When circumstances arise which restrict such sales, an appreciable part of production must be closed down and the people involved suffer unemployment and restriction of income. The matter does not end there, for the consequent stoppage of expenditure affects all other employments adversely. Farmers, for example, lose a part of their market. The entire business economy suffers decline. It is this sequence which lends special significance to the high variability of Latin American export values. The sensitivity to cyclical fluctuations may be emphasized by observing that between 1929 and 1932 the dollar value of the exports of the twenty republics fell 64.3 percent. Like a comparable decline in building and construction activity in the United States, this was enough to spread depression through all the business economy.

In this kind of influence, then, is found the role of exports in Latin American life. They do pay for imports and (along with all other productive activity) they yield wealth, but their rise and fall go even farther to set the tempo of economic activity. It is in exportation, given the present constitution of economy there, that one finds Latin America's " crucial sector."

The implications of this circumstance are both striking and disturbing. If in the United States it is investment which sets the pace of economic activity, there is at least the comfort that the decisions which determine the volume of that investment are " made in America." It is otherwise with Latin America. To a very considerable extent the forces which fix the value of its exports operate not within its own borders but abroad. The decisions which determine the productive capacity for Latin American exports are, of course, largely made at home, but those which bear upon demand for them, and hence upon prices, are foreign. And, as has already been indicated, these latter are peculiarly important.

Perhaps the most dramatic evidence of Latin America's essentially passive position is afforded by the sequence of events during a typical business cycle. High prosperity in such countries as Great Britain and the United States calls for more imported industrial raw materials and foodstuffs. With recession and depression, however, such demands decline, and in consequence the prices (and with them the total values) of Latin American exports drop sharply. The activating force behind this round of events resides in the world's more highly industrialized countries. There is no evidence to indicate that depression in the great industrial countries arises from a decline in demand for their manufactured goods on the part of the raw-material exporting countries. On the contrary, demand for manufactured goods comes mainly from the highly industrialized regions themselves, and when this demand declines, the raw-material sellers suffer as a consequence. This fact would be generally admitted by all who consult the statistics of trade and production, whether or not they subscribe to the theory that fluctuations in new investment cause the changes in economic activity. The generally restrictive effect upon Latin America of the United States' failure fully to recover during the 1930's is now generally recognized. Indeed, the prompt response in Latin America and elsewhere to this country's abortive 1935–1937 expansion illustrates positively (as the subsequent decline does negatively) the consequences of the less-advanced nations' passive position in world economy.

These cyclical fluctuations bear upon the whole of Latin America. This is not the outcome of any integration of the several national economies, for of this there is but little. It arises, rather, from the uniformity of Latin American export products. If recession affects one of those products, it affects almost all.

Another important factor which creates difficulties for Latin America is the long-run tendency of prices of agricultural products to lag below those of manufactured products — a tendency illustrated by the " price disparity " which has played so large a role in agricultural relief in the United States.

Political or administrative disruptions of trade and of markets have been on the whole less generally disturbing than the unplanned fluctuations of demand. Even the wave of trade restrictions (tariffs, quotas, and the like) which set in during the late 1920's and " snow-balled " during the 1930's did not affect all countries with equal severity. Most deeply affected were the countries which, like Argentina and Uruguay, ran afoul of Europe's quest for self-sufficiency in foodstuffs. None, of course, escaped wholly the consequences of bilateralism and trade controls, but those which sold their chief export products in relatively free markets almost succeeded in doing so. The republics of the Caribbean, for example, have not, on the whole, had to bear the combined weight of depression *and* trade restrictions which has been the lot of their less fortunate neighbors to the south and west.

One type of disturbance has characteristically affected single countries only, namely, shifts of demand or the appearance of a new and competitive source of supply. Instances have appeared all too frequently in Latin American economic history, and the list of products affected is a long one indeed: rubber, nitrates, quinine, silver, cacao, cane sugar, among others. Because of the tendency of Latin American nations to specialize on a few export products, the loss of an outlet for any one bears heavily upon one or a few countries rather than upon Latin America as a whole. If its economy were well integrated, the region might " average out " the losses to which it seems by nature destined, but a single country cannot.

Speaking generally, then, Latin America appears to be almost uniquely vulnerable to the hazards inherent in international economic intercourse. The basic uniformity of its products subjects a large part of the whole area's productive mechanism to the full impact of cyclical fluctuations. What is more, the exporting sector of its economy goes far to set the pace for the whole. Finally, because of each nation's specialization upon a few export products, the consequences of structural change are highly localized. A shift of tariffs, the establishment of quotas, the appearance of substitutes or of alternative sources of supply — all such changes bear with full weight upon particular countries. Latin America tends to live dangerously, and, as already has been shown, it hasn't the compensation of living well.

PART THREE

The Constitutional Bases of Government

CHAPTER 6

Democratic Constitutions—and Undemocratic Governments?

No. 15 [Government in Latin America is based, in theory at least, upon written constitutions. For many and diverse reasons, the political leaders of the several republics, at the time that independence was secured, believed it advisable to draft *written* charters of government. Earlier chapters of this book have indicated and discussed the milieu in which these constitutions were written, the social and economic forces which influenced their shaping, and the political ideas and experience of the men who wrote them.

A survey of the constitutional development of the twenty republics is an enormous undertaking, accentuated and complicated by the political fact that Latin America has given birth to more written constitutions, in little more than a century, than any other region in the world. Bolivia, for example, has written and promulgated fourteen constitutions since it became an independent state in the early nineteenth century.

If we can secure an over-all view which enables us to see the spiritual and actual sources of these constitutions, the unique traits and habits of constitution-writing they exhibit, and the trends that can be isolated and subjected to analysis, our understanding of the government of the area is broadened. Such a synthesis of constitutional growth is offered in the following essay.]

Constitutional Development in Latin America: A Synthesis*

by RUSSELL H. FITZGIBBON

" Do not give to a people institutions for which it is unripe in the simple faith that the tool will give skill to the workman's hand. Respect Facts. Man is in each country not what we may wish him to be, but what Nature and History have made him." Bryce, *Modern Democracies*, I, 206.

W ITH minor exceptions, the panorama of constitutional growth in the Western Hemisphere reveals two main streams. The United States Constitution, the British North America Act of 1867 (which is the Canadian fundamental law), and the organic laws of the various New World British possessions of today all stem, obviously, from English constitutional and institutional ancestry. The constitutions of the twenty Latin American states, on the other hand, all reflect in varying degree the experience and institutions of their three mother countries. These modern constitutions are, it is true, influenced by alien examples at one point or another, but the core is indubitably Latin. More narrowly, the inspiration is Hispanic; and still more narrowly, Spanish.

It is not easy to explain in detail the degree of similarity between French political institutions and those of the Iberian peninsula in the centuries between the emergence of the several national states and the political revolutions in Latin America. At least, the French belonged to a not unrelated family. A much closer relationship is easily discernible among the political institutions of the three main Iberian entities that ultimately became the national states of Spain and Portugal, viz., Castile, Aragon, and Portugal. It is often forgotten that for many generations no political or constitutional " Spain " existed, that Aragon and Castile were as distinct from each

* Russell H. Fitzgibbon, " Constitutional Development in Latin America: A Synthesis," *The American Political Science Review* (June, 1945), Vol. XXXIX, No. 3, pp. 511–522. Reprinted by permission of *The American Political Science Review*. The footnotes in the original version are omitted here.

other in most ways as either of them was from Portugal, that an easily possible union of the ruling houses of Castile and Portugal — supplanting the marriage of Isabella and Ferdinand — might have changed the whole subsequent course of history.

Complete amalgamation of Castilian and Aragonese institutions was difficult — indeed, it has scarcely yet taken place, nearly five centuries after that famous wedding of 1469. It is well known that by far the major activity in Spanish exploration and colonization was that of Castile, and that Aragonese influence on the shaping of the New World empire was incidental at best. Hence, though such an Aragonese office as that of the viceroy was early borrowed for both Spanish and Portuguese colonial development, and the *diputación general* finds a modern counterpart of sorts in the *comisión permanente,* most of the stream that watered later Latin American constitutionalism was of Castilian origin.

The cisatlantic shaping of the contemporary and recent political institutions of the Latin American states began at least as early as the first decades of the colonial period. Although it is easy to exaggerate the difference in motives, course, and consequences between Spanish (and, for that matter, Portuguese) and English colonization, important variations did exist. In so far as factors influencing political development were concerned, it is worth while to recall that much of English colonization was undertaken in a conscious or unconscious framework of revolt — not revolt in a formal or political sense, but rebellion against the religious, social, or economic constraints that prevailed in England. English governmental neglect was also a factor in explaining weaker colonial institutions. Spanish colonization, on the other hand, was from the beginning strictly controlled, even regimented, by royal mandate that quickly developed into all the institutional formalism represented by the Council of the Indies. This tendency, and especially the attitude of mind it suggested, had an inevitable effect upon the political institutions of the Spanish colonies, which they transmitted to the independent states succeeding them.

It would be unfair and unsafe to generalize by concluding simply that constitutional development in Spanish colonies represented rigidity while in the English it was characterized by flexibility. The

Spanish institutions were in many cases the result of adaptation, of conformity to environment or circumstantial influence. On the whole, however, the degree of variation represented by, say, the three general types of colonial government along the narrow North Atlantic seaboard (the corporate, proprietary, and royal) was almost unknown in all the broad extent of Spanish America.

In view of this general uniformity of pattern throughout the other America, it is not surprising that one of the strongest conditioning elements in the whole picture — through thousands of miles of space and hundreds of years of time — has been the seemingly eternal conflict between the centripetal and the centrifugal, between the forces of centralization and those of decentralization. This is age-old. It is by no means limited in the New World to Latin America: the great variety of reflections of the "states' rights question" in the United States through a century and a half is eloquent testimony to its prevalence here. In Europe, it has been the problem of devolution in Great Britain, the pathetic struggle of the German Länder to maintain their position, the question of regional or departmental autonomy in France.

In Latin America, this conflict has been one of the most persistently present of all factors. When the Emperor Charles V decreed in 1530 that " without our command, it is not our intention or will that the cities and towns of the Indies meet in convention," he was but taking cognizance of this already crystallized problem. When a " decentralization congress " of disaffected Colombian local delegates met at Cartagena in July, 1944, it was reflecting exactly the same problem. Speaking generally, the centralists have had the better of the argument — or at least have usually carried the day — in both the colonial and independent epochs; but the problem is as lasting and basic as the need for government itself.

In the Spanish colonial government, the king and his agents personified the forces of centralization; the *municipalidades* were the bulwark, such as it was, of local autonomy. It is unnecessary to recount all of the geographic, social, and economic contributions to one or the other tendency. Suffice it to remember that during the greater part of the colonial period municipal government languished — that it never attained the splendid vigor it had enjoyed briefly in

Castile a few generations before Columbus. The instruments of national unity, such as the uniformity of administration, legislation, and justice, the strong concentration of authority in the royal officials and agencies, and the sustaining hand of the Church, all operated, as long as circumstances remained at all normal, to submerge the localist influences.

The thing that introduced abnormality into the situation was the complex combination of factors that focussed the movement for independence. In the intervening generations, as is well known, the *cabildos* and *ayuntamientos* had become the governmental haven and almost the only political forum of the creoles. That they represented the shadow of authority without its substance would subsequently be of great significance. The early revolutions were in effect movements for municipal autonomy; their development into campaigns for national independence was in some respects only incidental. With Spanish authority expelled, it became certain that a renewed competition between the two tendencies would ensue. Municipal leaders had in many instances taken the initiative in the politico-military resistance of the second decade of the nineteenth century, and their political stage was largely local. On the other hand, the horizon of the average *caudillo* was bounded only by the limitations of his power.

The narrow political training and experience from which most of those in authority after the winning of independence suffered was one element in the initial incapacity and confusion that characterized the independent governments. Another element was the fact that no native political institutions had been borrowed on the higher levels by the Spanish or were, at the time of the revolutions, available for borrowing. Hence, those in control had to look abroad and rely on their own judgment in seeking models on which to base their governments.

The search for those models was largely academic and artificial. It was the political philosophers, now having a holiday of constitution-making, who were concerned. As Miss Williams aptly puts it, " What the amateur politicians really attempted was the impossible feat of leaping from political medievalism to modern democracy." The *caudillos* were much more interested in sheer power. The imitative tendency of the early *constituyentes* became a habit that persisted for a century. It is generally accepted that the United States and France were the sources of constitutional inspiration for the fledgling Latin American states. That is true — but it needs to be qualified. Many governmental agencies, especially on the lower levels, were carried over intact from the colonial era. In numerous constitutions, the French influence was funneled through intervening Spanish connections, specifically the liberal constitutions of 1812 and 1820. A recent study has shown, for example, that much of the source for the constitution-making of Central America in the 1820's was not the United States, as has generally been supposed, but rather the Spanish Constitution of 1820.

The United States was in a peculiarly favored position to exert an influence. It, like the Latin American states, had a colonial origin. Its frontier position and other factors resembled those of Latin America. Henry Clay and a few others had aroused a fraternal response through the length of the continents. The prestige and the more than four decades of successful operation of a revolution-born government made it inevitable that the Latin American states should look to their northern neighbor in establishing their own governments. Good examples of this imitation are found in the Venezuelan Constitution of 1811, the Mexican of 1824, the Argentinian of 1853, and the Brazilian of 1891 (especially the third of these); piecemeal borrowing is present in very many others.

It is not coincidence that the four states just named represent the outstanding examples of Latin American federations. After all, the great contribution that the United States had to make to the organization of members of the modern community of states was the federal principle. Theoretically, it fitted the needs of those of the Latin American states that were larger in area or were poorly knit by reason of difficulties of topography or transportation. On the whole, however, federalism has not been notably successful in Latin America. It is arguable that, other things being equal, the federal type is more difficult to carry on than either the confederate or the centralized. In the third of those named, the national authority need pay only such deference to the component units as graciousness and a sense of fair play dictate: there are no basic constitutional or legal restraints upon its freedom of action. In the confederacy, at the opposite end of the scale, the subdivisions may be as cavalier as they wish toward the central government. Neither type calls for any fundamental attitude of adjustment or compromise. Of course, it can also be argued that from the point of view of practical operation the confederacy is the most difficult to preserve, as witness the experience of the United States between 1781 and 1789.

Federations find it extremely difficult to maintain the *status quo* of any given time. The trend, as suggested previously, is usually toward centralization. The only significant difference in this respect between Latin America and Anglo-America is that in the former the movement has suffered less retardation by the tradition of local self-government. In Brazil, for example, the process has undergone such acceleration and formalization in recent years that it is now a fair question as to whether federalism still prevails in that republic. The process has not been uniform: Colombia and some other states have oscillated. But in most federations the principle itself has suffered — the Latin American examples almost appear to furnish support to those who maintain that federalism is, after all, only a transitional form of government. Thus, one of the great constitutional principles of the United States, imitated in several of her Latin American sister states, has been largely modified in all, practically abandoned in one.

The separation and coordination of powers is another of the deeply rooted principles of the constitutional system of the United States. In part, it was due to colonial experience, in part, it found its inspiration in Montesquieu's *L'Esprit des lois*. The early Latin American constitutional architects looked upon it and found it good. It was regarded in the United States as a great guarantee against tyranny, and this was considered commendable in Latin America. People in that area had had more experience with arbitrary and tyrannical government than those in the British colonies. That the principle, in addition, had a French theoretic foundation was no discredit. It was all but universally adopted in the scores of Latin American constitutions of all generations. This principle, too, and the system of checks and balances by which it has been implemented, have been profoundly modified in their application in Latin American constitutional systems. "Executive dominance" is an even more common phenomenon in those states than times of crisis have shown it to be in the United States.

It is in order to cite one further constitutional principle that can be said to be borrowed in part from United States practice and precept. It is that of the protection of private rights. The foundation of United States documentary development of this principle was, of course, the English Bill of Rights of 1689, a great parliamentary milestone in the constitutional history of the mother country. The French Declaration of the Rights of Man and of the Citizen was also a pillar of fire in this regard. Thus, the United States can by no means claim exclusive credit for the inspiration of the Latin American constitutions at this point, although in many of them a definite phraseological similarity is apparent.

The principal borrowing of Latin American constitutionalism from French sources was in the intangible realm of philosophy. Not only in regard to the specific philosophical foundations of one constitution or another were the Latin Americans indebted to the French, but also for the broader egalitarian and republican thought of various eighteenth-century French intellectuals. It is difficult for people in the United States to realize the extent and depth of attraction that the Gallic mind has for generations possessed for Latin Americans. This is as true in the field of constitution-making as in other areas. It was more true, indeed, a hundred years ago than it has been in recent times because of the greater restriction of Latin intellectual horizons in the early period. Rousseau, Voltaire, and Montesquieu were more familiar to and more influential upon early Latin American leaders than were Jefferson, Paine, Locke, and other United States and English thinkers. The finely developed logic of early French constitutions and the artistic symmetry of their political institutions had a strong effect as the Latin Americans essayed their first steps in these directions.

But there are concrete points, as well, that show the French influence on Latin American constitutions. The Council of State, found in several Latin American systems at one time or another, owes more to the French than to any other alien model. Parliamentary interpellation, as some Latin American states work it out, resembles the prewar French practice probably more than the British. The requirement of ministerial signatures to authenticate acts of the presidents is a borrowing from the French. The whole pattern of " decree legislation " is similar to what prevailed in France rather than elsewhere. The scheme of courts of administrative litigation (*tribunales de lo contencioso administrativo*) resembles the former French system of administrative courts. The *ministro de gobernación* is much more akin to the former French minister of the interior than to any British or United States official. Police organization, the development of municipal administration, the device of proportional representation, and the structure of law codes are other specific instances of French influence. The multi-party systems of some Latin American states have much less in common with the biparty pattern of the United States or Great Britain than with the former French party system, although at this point it must be admitted that the resemblance is more accidental than intentional.

The influence of English sources upon Latin American constitution-making was considerably less than that of United States or French models, except, of course, as the United States system was itself molded by its English inheritance. At the formative stage of Latin American constitutional development, contacts with Britain (other than commercial) were comparatively unimportant. If it is assumed that parliamentary or cabinet government is an English contribution to the world's constitutional evolution — and certainly that country furnished the prototype — then the few Latin American states that have experimented with it might be said to be indebted to England at that point. But parliamentary government has encountered particularly rough weather in Latin American latitudes. Neither Brazil under Dom Pedro, Chile from 1890 to 1920, nor Cuba since 1940 furnishes a complete or satisfactory example of the operation of genuine parliamentary government. The inspiration for ministerial participation in congressional debate is perhaps as much British as French. Habeas corpus and jury trial are devices of English origin but the latter, in particular, has never taken deep root in Latin America.

In a few instances, the authors of Latin American constitutions, dissatisfied with what the United States and France had to offer, turned to ancient Greece and Rome for inspiration, usually with bizarre and impractical results. The classic example is the famous Bolivian Constitution of 1826, the best documentary embodiment of Bolívar's own ideas of the desirable organization of a state.

Just as the early leaders' lack of practical experience with the hard realities of politics pointed toward ill-considered imitation of foreign models, the latter in its turn made almost certain the artificiality and naïveté that were so characteristic of many of the early basic laws. Moral precepts, endless philosophizing, fantastic rhetoric, elaborately impractical governmental machinery, were common in the first constitutions. The early constituent assemblies were devoted to symbol words — the French trinity of liberty, equality, and fraternity, of course, and federalism, democracy, unity, and others — and these were clothed with an almost sacramental virtue; in other words, the approach was ritualistic. Gradually the appearance of callowness and immaturity was sloughed off in successive documents, but there long prevailed the unconscious feeling that a written constitution was the panacea for all political ills, and that if one proved unsatisfactory all that needed to be done was to draft another. That attitude explains in part the passion for constitution-making as a means of regularizing a revolutionary régime: a new fundamental law of his own drafting (though perhaps little changed from its predecessor) gave a president who came into office by a *coup* or a revolution a feeling of greater legal security and solidity.

The passing decades of the nineteenth century gave the Latin American states various opportunities to shake off the dead hand of tradition from their successive constitutions. Despite piecemeal experimentation now and then, no nineteenth-century constitution made a successful break with the past. The closest approach was in the Mexican Constitution of 1857. That document was born of profoundly disturbed conditions, and it did, indeed, reflect contemporary revolutionary thought in its anticlerical and other provisions. Had the constitution of 1857 had a fair chance to prove itself, it might have attained the stature of its successor as an innovator. But the early succession of the Maximilianic interlude and the long grip of *Porfirismo* effectively prevented any honest attempt to apply the spirit of that constitution — it was consistently honored in the breach rather than the observance. Another important constitution of the century, the Brazilian of 1891, again reverted to that of the United States for its inspiration. The quick recognition that the United States had extended to the new-born republic, the traditional Brazilian friendship for its North American sister state, and the prestige that the United States then enjoyed as a prototype of republicanism, made such imitation virtually inevitable.

The year 1917 is probably the most significant date in the whole panorama of Latin American constitutionalism. It was the year of the adoption of the new Mexican basic law at Querétaro. This document, like its predecessor, was the product of deep disturbances. But the difficulties that in the mid-1850's had been chiefly religio-economic had now broadened and reflected social facets, too. Politics at either time was but the outward manifestation of the other forms of cleavage. The constitutions, in turn, were only the crystallization of the political thought of the moment.

The broader matrix in which the new Mexican Constitution was set was also significantly different from that of three-score years earlier. It is true that at the earlier time Mexico's northern neighbor was rapidly plunging toward an abyss, but it was a local crisis. Latin American conditions and the general world scene were placidly Victorian. Hence, the waves of influence that would have spread out from the constitution of 1857 — even assuming that they were not to be dammed by the French intervention — might easily have fallen on unresponsive shores. In 1917, the situation was radically changed. The World War had been rocking preconceived notions for almost three years. Military collapse was full upon Russia as the Mexican convention was ending its work, and the social and economic earthquake soon to come in eastern Europe was already rumbling. Though the Latin American area was but casually involved in the war, it could not escape the impact of the conflict. Closer at home, the changed relationship of the United States to Latin America since the turn of the century was raising questions that were disturbing — the answers to which the states of the south could not yet give.

New constitutional currents would soon make their appearance in Russia, in the Baltic and Austro-Hungarian succession states, in the Weimar document in Germany, and later in the Spanish republican constitution and elsewhere. The new departure in Mexico antedated all of these, however, and hence, in a narrow sense, it may be described as the product of a strictly national situation. Viewed more broadly, it mirrored a situation that was well-nigh world-wide and certain to come into focus. It was simply Mexico's fate to have the changes crystallize there at an earlier date than elsewhere. Had it not been Mexico, some other Latin American state would soon have won the distinction, at least as within Latin America.

That the changed direction and emphasis were certain does not, however, lessen the significance of the Mexican Constitution. Its principles and provisions have been borrowed in varying degree by almost every Latin American constitution subsequently drafted. The Querétaro law provided a formal expression of the political thought of a new generation. The World War had closed the door on what may be called the period of imitation, and the Latin American states were now ready, a century after independence had been won, to write constitutions that would be more inherently national than any that had gone before. Latin American constitution-making had come of age. In the respect that the Querétaro constitution introduced this new era, it may be regarded as symbolically Latin American rather than narrowly Mexican.

The dominant note in the Mexican Constitution is its strong and conscious nationalism, both political and economic. Latin American basic laws had regularly prescribed sovereignty and independence, but the Mexican document goes far beyond perfunctory requirements in that direction. This heightened consciousness of nationalism is one of the significantly outstanding political phenomena of contemporary Latin America; and one of the first places where it found formal expression was the Mexican Constitution of 1917.

Another of the basic innovations of the new constitutionalism — again illustrated by Mexico — is that " private " property is a social function and that individual rights relating to it can and must be subordinated to the social welfare. The Mexican Constitution does not declare this principle as forcefully as some of the others, but its famous Article 27 set the pace for later statements. The Mexicans, because of the long controversies over petroleum and land, were particularly concerned with problems of ownership and expropriation. It was an outstanding illustration of economic nationalism. A consequence was the related trend toward constitutionalizing the "Calvo clause," the provision that an alien should be estopped from ordinary appeal to his country's diplomatic representatives in support of claims. The whole attitude at such points was distinctly at variance with the nineteenth-century tendency to emphasize the doctrines of the natural rights of man and of economic individualism.

It was not alone in the economic seas that new courses were being charted. The same was true of social waters. Mexico's equally famous Article 123 has been called Latin American labor's Magna Carta — an over-rhetorical characterization, no doubt, but still a suggestion of the degree of departure from earlier constitutional channels. Virtually statutory detail concerning all aspects of labor regulation, prohibition of monopolies, restriction of the competition of foreign labor, social security, and provision for the educational and cultural advancement of the working classes are typical of the bold imagination shown by Latin American constitution-makers in these socioeconomic fields in the past quarter-century.

Both in recognition of groups — the family, the trade union, cultural organizations — and in emphasis on individual and group obligations as well as rights, the new Latin American constitutions are at one with their postwar European counterparts. It is society that is stressed, rather than the individuals who make up society. It is a further illustration of a distinctly twentieth-century attitude rather than that of the eigheenth century, when modern constitutions first began to be written.

In its strictures on religious organization and activity, the Mexican Constitution is less typical. Here, again, the provisions must be set in perspective. "The conflict between the civil power and the clergy" (to borrow the title of a semiofficial government apologia of several years ago) had been carved in higher relief in Mexico than anywhere else in Latin America. It was only natural, consequently, that in other Latin American states the religious and ecclesiastical provisions of the constitutions should be couched in more moderate terms, even moving in some instances toward an advanced degree of religious toleration, though at the same time illustrating a tendency toward separation of church and government.

Greater Latin American willingness to experiment has been reflected also in innovations in the structure of governmental machinery and organization. It was no new sort of move when Chile in 1925 formally abandoned the parliamentary system with which it had been struggling for a third of a century; return to the presidential pattern was simply a reversion to type. But when Cuba fifteen years later and Guatemala in 1945 adopted a semiparliamentary scheme, that did represent more of a novel step. Peru in 1920 made guarded gestures toward constitutionalizing a species of political regionalism (without going the full distance toward federalism), but the plan was never fully implemented. Uruguay in 1919 began a not altogether happy experiment of a decade and a half with a bifurcated executive branch. Two or three states have taken tentative steps in the direction of functional legislative representation. Cuba has made provision for optional forms of municipal government.

Possibly the most important, though certainly not the most spectacular, experiments of this kind are the provisions in several constitutions, notably that of Brazil of 1937, for technical advances in public administration. In some cases such provisions are perhaps nothing more than imitative gestures, but in others they doubtless possess genuine substance. Traditional executive dominance may thus come to be supplemented by a professionally trained bureaucracy. Whether this means reinforcement or restriction for an arbitrary president depends upon the bent given this evolution in years to come, a question it is yet too early to answer. It is worth while to point out, however, that a development of this sort could conceivably exercise a democratic and leavening influence.

It has long been customary for commentators to point out the divergence between constitutional prescription and governmental practice in Latin America. Another way of putting it is to say that the basic laws have often served as symbols rather than as instruments. Such comments have usually been made in conscious or unconscious disparagement. It seems in order to suggest, however, as scientifically as may be, that to the extent that such characterizations are true, it is because for so many decades Latin American constitutions failed to be the creatures of their own environment; they were simply alien adoptions and adaptations. In the last two or three decades, that condition has been much less true. Social forces such as education, trade union activity, and others now have an increasing impact. It hence seems logical to conclude that with the gradual accretion of experience along these new lines the divergence between governmental fact and constitutional theory will decrease, that most fundamental laws will ultimately come to be instruments as well as symbols. The Mexican Constitution has gained prestige — if not a halo or perhaps even a " tradition " — from more than a quarter of a century of operation. Chile's basic law is now two decades old. Colombia's and Costa Rica's are venerable by comparison. And in Argentina the ninety-two-year-old constitution, though temporarily sidetracked, is by no means the less a tradition and force in the popular mind. On the other hand, of course, many constitutions have been replaced in the last decade (often with little change), and the period since mid-1944 has seen four abrogated. In general, however, there is a wholesome and increasing tendency to regard a Latin American constitution as something not to be cavalierly brushed aside if its observance becomes inconvenient. The inclination to give weight to Viscount Bryce's dictum, with which this discussion begins, gains ground.

A qualification or two must be added. It is still a typical Latin American approach to make new constitutions the product of reason, to base them upon what ideally ought to be. Hence, in some respects, they are anticipatory, and particular provisions may, for many years, lack supporting legislation or even the popular approval to make them effective. In the United States, on the contrary, constitutional changes customarily represent long-debated and finally crystallized public opinion; it is, natural that the latter approach should give the appearance of a more practical and enforceable document. As Dr. Gil Borges once put it, the United States attitude is realistic, the Latin American logical. Then, too, the informal growth of constitutions differs importantly as between Anglo-America and Latin America. In the former, " convention " and custom play a larger role. The development and influence of judicial review also differ in the two areas.

Until the hemisphere and the world see the end of a period comparable in significance to that which closed with the second decade of this century, we may expect to see present basic trends in Latin American constitution-making continue. No one can tell what may happen in a succeeding epoch.

No. 16 [Every person interested in the study of government, ancient or modern, American or European, knows that the written constitution of a nation gives, at best, an imperfect and an incomplete picture of the actual organization of the political institutions. The enormous importance of judicial review in our government would be but faintly perceived by one who has read only the written constitution. Even when these documents cover a point in some detail there may be a gulf, small or vast, between the constitutional strictures and the political reality. We do not, for example, elect our presidents in the manner indicated by the Constitution. In many, if not most, written constitutions there are also clauses that are the more observed in the breach than in the compliance. A reading of Section II of the Fourteenth Amendment illustrates this point in so far as the Constitution of the United States is concerned.

Mention is made of these matters because the Latin American republics are so often dismissed by the casual observer as countries in which the constitutions are meaningless; in which the governmental organization may or may not — usually the latter — follow the constitutional outline. It is perhaps true that disparities and divergences between the constitutional provisions and the operating political mechanisms are greater in Latin America than in any other region. Hence it is important to understand the causes of this political ambivalence.]

Political Ambivalence in Latin America*

by KINGSLEY DAVIS

*E*VERY political system attempts to solve an essentially insoluble and perennial problem — namely, how to guarantee that those who represent the group, who protect it and enforce its laws, will use their power for common rather than private ends. Democracy cannot lay

* Kingsley Davis, " Political Ambivalence in Latin America," *Journal of Legal and Political Sociology* (October, 1942), Vol. 1, Nos. 1–2, pp. 127–150. Reprinted by permission of the *Journal of Legal and Political Sociology*. The footnotes in the original version are omitted here.

sole claim to having seen or tackled this problem, but simply to having offered one type of solution. Whereas autocracy utilizes the sentimental acceptance of a social hierarchy to fuse the common and private ends of the rulers, democracy distinguishes and attempts to
insulate these ends one from the other. The former regards the rulers
as a special class whose every act carries a superior authorization,
while the latter regards them as private citizens whose special function, for the time being, is governmental. Which form is " right "
depends upon the value adopted, but which one will *work* depends
upon the society.

According to our thesis, the democratic form of government, like
any other political form, constitutes merely a part and, in the main,
a resultant of the total institutional structure. This proposition,
though often forgotten, would be banal if it were without application, and it is our intention to apply it to the Latin American republics. Sociologically neglected, these republics, with their similarities, differences, and kaleidoscopic changes, afford almost a laboratory
for the study of government and society. Furthermore, they look
at first sight like glaring exceptions of our general thesis, because
they embody democratic forms of government in a social order in
many ways undemocratic. While this paradox is more apparent than
real, it nevertheless suggests a fundamental difficulty of the republics, and raises the question of how they came into such an ambivalent situation. Finally, the very contrast between the kind of government and the kind of society the Latin Americans possess brings
out, as nowhere else, the difference between political and social
democracy, the dependence of one upon the other, and the perversion of one in the absence of the other.

POLITICAL DEMOCRACY

An outstanding trait of Latin American political life is its fascination for the machinery of democratic government. Such machinery
can be viewed as the political technology by which the people's ends
are made known to and mandatory upon the governing officials. In
nondemocratic systems the sovereign, being an exalted person, is
often presumed to know these ends intuitively, even better than the
people themselves. Sometimes there is a means for bringing the

people's wishes to his attention — e.g., by " petitions " and " prayers," as if otherwise he would not deign to hear. In less autocratic régimes the wishes are presented as " demands " on the government, which must accede or take the consequences. In a democracy, for example, the machinery for expressing the people's views, for instituting and replacing governments, is highly elaborate. It includes constitutions, party primaries, secret ballots, parliaments, checks and balances, judicial reviews, vetos, limited terms of office, recalls, referendums, etc.

It is this democratic machinery which the Latin Americans, since achieving their independence, have found especially fascinating. They have constantly tinkered with it, added to it, and thought about it. They have been inveterate constitution-makers, setting forth each time the elaborate political devices which would, until the next constitution, be followed. They have tried to solve one problem after another by manipulating the apparatus. For instance, the tendency of presidents to prolong themselves in office has been dealt with by a practically universal prohibition upon the re-election of a president for two consecutive terms. In several countries, notably Argentina, Costa Rica, and Peru, an attempt has been made to overcome the lethargy of the voters by compelling them to vote. Also it has generally become customary to hold elections on Sundays, and against the chance of disorders occurring at the polls, to close all dispensaries of strong liquor from the preceding evening until the votes are all in the next day. Not all the manipulation of democratic techniques has been in the direction of democracy, but the general drift has represented a persistent effort to give greater reality to the democratic ideal.

This preoccupation with the technical forms of democracy suggests that the republics are trying to accomplish something by mechanical means which requires a deeper readjustment. They resemble the neurotic patient who manages to cure one symptom after another, only to find that the underlying neurosis still remains. The trouble is that in Latin America political democracy did not grow up gradually as a result of social evolution, but came suddenly as a result of cultural diffusion. The social order was, and in many ways still is, inimical to political democracy; it, rather than the oft-cited circumstances of settlement in the new world, is the primary obstacle to such democracy. The fascination of Latin Americans for political democracy therefore arises partly from natural curiosity concerning something new, and partly from the faith that by somehow altering the instrument the necessary conditions for its use will appear.

Unfortunately, social democracy cannot be produced merely by formal political machinery. It is more likely to create than to be created by this machinery. The latter can manufacture social democracy only to the extent that it works well, and it works well only to the extent that social democracy already prevails. In order to see this, and to understand Latin America better, it will be necessary to review briefly the principal characteristics of a democratic social order — the kind of order which, according to our thesis, is essential to the effective operation of the democratic machinery.

CHARACTERISTICS OF SOCIAL DEMOCRACY

Ethical Equality. In its ultimate religious and moral evaluation, the democratic society has traditionally held all individuals to be intrinsically equal. It has regarded their extrinsic differences, however great, as accidental merits and demerits less ultimate than the supreme merit of being a human individual. One may argue that in any society the members possess worth simply as members and therefore equality in an ultimate sense, and that in democratic societies the alleged ethical equality is obscure and ineffectual in actual social organization. But there is evidence that the notion of ethical equality places some limit upon actual inequality — as against slavery and suffering — and that, translated into political terms, it rationalizes the view that each citizen, regardless of social position, should have one vote, basic issues being settled on the basis of the largest accumulation (the majority) of such votes.

Opportunity to Advance. The traditional democratic society has also been an " open " one, in which individuals could advance according to their merit. This characteristic reveals why the notion of equality is kept mainly on an ethical plane, because the " merit " which gives rise to social advancement is a differential rather than an equal merit. The only way to prevent the equality notion from interfering is to translate it merely as equal opportunity. Thus, pushed to its logical extreme, a democratic régime is one in which all individuals have an equal chance to advance in the social scale. Such a statement means nothing, however, until we have defined "equal chance." Strictly defined, it would mean that all *significant* differences are equalized at the start. But this would render any subsequent differences a complete mystery, or assign them purely to differences of (free) will power. What is meant, rather, is that the differences at the start shall not be due to social factors extraneous to the individual's will, but rather to biological qualities which, with appropriate effort, the individual can transmute into social advancement. Thus the inheritance of wealth is extraneous, because the individual did not earn it. True, he did not earn his high I.Q. either, but this is something over which society has no control, and consequently the kind of difference which, with will power, has in an open society a chance of expressing itself in meritorious conduct.

Even in this modified sense equal opportunity is never provided by, and is not indispensable to, a democratic régime. It is impossible to eliminate all involuntary social advantages at the start. The only requirement of a democratic system is that there be *some* opportunity to advance. Everybody knows that the son of a minister and the son of a farmer do not have an equal opportunity to become governors, but nobody can deny that they both have some chance. To a degree, the presence of differential social opportunity, just like the presence of differential biological quality, puts a premium upon will power and effort. The farmer's son, if he exerts enough effort, may overcome his initial handicap and beat out the minister's son. The less the opportunity, the greater the merit of success. The son of the rich man is therefore to be pitied, because he begins life with such an advantage that his winning the race is no proof of merit, no proof that the virtues of thrift, abstinence, and hard work have been exercised.

Opportunity to advance has still another implication — namely, that the advance be in terms of true merit, i.e., achievements *relevant* to the duties of office. The *caudillo* who moves into power with machine guns rattling has achieved his office, but he has not proved his fitness for the function of lawful government. Likewise the person who buys his way into office has proved a capacity for shrewd bargaining but not for ruling. The irrelevant achievement of office or status, just as much as the ascription of status through birth, is contrary to the democratic ideal.

The connection between opportunity to advance and technical democracy is now easy to see. Political positions can be occupied by only a small percentage of the population. If these positions were ascribed, especially on the basis of birth, they would change hands only once per generation and the rest of the population would have no hope of occupying them. Unless other positions in the society were also ascribed, such political ascription would be out of joint with the structure. Therefore, in a democratic society provision is made for the achievement of political office through the competition for votes. Limited terms of office and periodic elections assure a considerable turnover in the governing personnel. If the principle were absent in society generally, it would be absent politically.

Public Education. In a régime of achieved status it is axiomatic that the educational system be open to everyone. Since the schools form a primary channel of training and sifting, any denial of access to them automatically relegates the individual to a low status.

Moreover, if decisions on important matters are to come from the people themselves, the necessary knowledge must derive from extensive public education. While it is possible to overstress this point and fall into the error of the rational society, it remains true that universal literacy, political awareness, and appreciation of the democratic way of life are essential in a liberal-democratic system.

Laissez-faire Economy. A second channel of vertical mobility is a fluid economic system. The open market provides a catalytic field in which each person, within broad rules, can fend for himself and advance by thrift, wit, and work. True, it tends inevitably to produce differential advantages so great as to become monopolistic, and to displace democracy with plutocracy. But monopoly, while it may result from laissez faire, is not identical with it. Antitrust legislation, for example, represents a very democratic, if drastic, effort to avoid the undemocratic consequences of democratic laissez faire.

Laissez faire has, however, another connection with democracy. Whether communist or fascist, the totalitarian state controls too much of life. Liberal-democratic régimes reserve something from the government and thus guarantee spheres of action to the individual which the state can touch only remotely. These nonpolitical spheres provide a balance or hedge against the government, whereas if the State is everything there is no source for independent criticism and resistance to its power. A dilemma of modern democracy is the necessity of limiting private enterprise without at the same time creating a totalitarian state.

Tolerance. If all citizens are ethically equal, any differences between them become secondary and may be tolerated. Liberal-democracies thus exhibit relatively high tolerance, as exemplified in two great freedoms — the freedom of worship and the freedom of speech.

The difficulty with religion is that it has in its dogmatic and ritualistic aspects an ultimate and absolute nature, and therefore is not conducive to tolerance. Hence the democratic nation achieves religious tolerance only by a certain amount of secularization. Differences in religion are tolerated either because they are trivial (as among the Protestant denominations) or because they are removed from the real affairs of life.

With reference to opinion, the principle of majority rule has two implications: first, that there is a minority which has been allowed to express its opinion, and second, that the rulers, who are always a minority, do not restrain the judgment of the majority — namely, the ruled. A free press is essential, because it is the primary organ for stating and defending the conflicting points of view, as well as for keeping the public informed of the actions of its officials. The cleavages of opinion, as with religion, had best not be fundamental. If general over-all agreement prevails, the specific issues can refer to means rather than to ends, and tolerance will come easily. Opportunity to advance helps by reducing sharp class cleavages and marshalling sentiment behind the general ends of the entire society. Public education helps by providing standard indoctrination.

The various democratic freedoms mutually limit each other. Free speech is limited, for example, by religious and other forms of tolerance, because an acute form of intolerance consists precisely in defamatory statements about other creeds, races, and classes. Unless the freedoms thus limit each other, the democratic system falls into a weakness which may be described as too much tolerance — tolerance for the enemies of the democratic system itself.

THE COMING OF POLITICAL DEMOCRACY TO LATIN AMERICA

Presently we shall maintain that if these are the essential principles of social democracy, the Latin American countries on the whole possess them only imperfectly, and that this lack makes the operation of political democracy difficult. But first let us return to political democracy itself and raise the question as to why, if social democracy did not prevail, the Latin Americans ever adopted democratic government in the first place.

The republics began with an orgy of constitution-making, as if by paper magic they could find the formula which would give them genuine rather than spurious democracy. Within a hundred years Venezuela had fifteen constitutions, Ecuador thirteen, and Bolivia ten; and since 1810 the total for all countries has been about one hundred and thirty. There has been a tendency to alternate extremely liberal or downright utopian constitutions with absolutistic régimes. Each new dictator has felt an urge to clothe his power with a new basic law. The procession of new constitutions has lasted until the present time [1942], with fourteen new ones since 1925, six of them less than six years old. Some of the documents have called for a decentralized federation, others for a highly centralized government; some have called for an alliance between Church and State, others for a complete separation or a subordination of Church to State; some have made the executive a supreme ruler, others have made him a nonentity. But while in nearly all countries constitutions of varying types have followed each other with notable frequency, there has run a thread, a persistent attempt to find some formula that will produce democracy.

The chief source of this persistent attempt at political democracy has lain in cultural diffusion. The nineteenth century was the golden age of democracy, and its doctrines permeated the intellectual atmosphere. The new South American nations, looking around for models to follow, found ready at hand the philosophies of the French and American Revolutions.

But if Latin American society was unpropitious for the borrowing of democratic techniques, why, in spite of the intellectual atmosphere, were they borrowed? Anthropologists and sociologists generally maintain that diffusion is as much a function of the receiving as the giving culture, and that the new trait is not received unless it is somehow compatible, or can be made compatible, with the existing culture.

The solution of this paradoxical question can be found only by reference to the class structure of the South American peoples. The revolt against Spanish rule was not a revolt in the sense of the French and American Revolutions. It was not a revolt of the masses or a people's war. The masses had been kept far too ignorant, poor, scattered, and isolated by the Inquisition, the Index, the *hacienda,* insufficient education, and colonial taxation to participate in a revolution for democratic ideals. So far as the masses were concerned, the colonies were astonishingly loyal. No matter how carefully the contemporary historians may whitewash the black legend, the cruelty of the Spanish administration shows through as the equal of anything known in ancient or modern history. Despite the good intentions of the capable Council of the Indies, murder, torture, treachery, rapacity, bribery, and secrecy were everyday tools of local officials for keeping down even the possibility of revolt. Yet the people, with rare exceptions, remained loyal, like faithful wives who expect to be beaten frequently by their prodigal husbands.

The incentive to revolution came from a class treated much better than the masses — from the creole class. The creoles were placed in that typical anomalous position which breeds rebellion: they were identified in race and culture with the ruling group, and yet were not allowed to rule. They constituted a small élite, educated, capable, wealthy, and familiar with conditions in their own land, yet not a governing élite. Their position made them ripe for revolt. And their education, which was mainly foreign, gave them the democratic ideals current at the time. The Chilean conspiracy of 1781, for example, was led by two Frenchmen (Gramuset and Berney) and a creole (José Antonia Rojas) who had lived in Europe and acquired the spirit of French social philosophy. Miranda, the visionary creole revolutionary, spent more time in Europe and the United States than in South America. Bolívar traveled extensively in Europe as a young man and met Miranda in England rather than in Venezuela. The revolutionary Coimbra Club was made up of young intellectuals impressed by the success of the American Revolution, corresponding with Thomas Jefferson, and expecting aid from the new republic to the north. The conspiracy of Minas Geraes in 1789 was led by Tiradentes, who had read widely in French literature and was associated with men who had been in France. San Martín, the outstanding military genius of the revolutionary period, had received his initial experience in Europe.

The creoles were a typical upper caste in a colonial situation where Indians, slaves, and freedmen were at the bottom, they themselves in the middle, and the foreign administrators at the top. They were marginal men. Whereas the mass had little to gain by a change of rulers, the creoles stood to gain everything, for they would then be the rulers. It was to them, therefore, that the revolutionary ideas were diffused. Yet, even so, it is doubtful if they would have rebelled (at least at the time) if it had not been for the utter collapse of Spain at the hands of Napoleon. And it is certain that, in spite of their ideological borrowing, they did not have in mind the creation of a complete social democracy.

LATIN AMERICAN SOCIAL ORGANIZATION

The circumstances under which political democracy was borrowed gave no assurance that it would thrive in the social order of the new territory. In fact, what might have seemed a natural period of uncertainty and confusion immediately after the revolution tended to prolong itself until the suspicion arose that somehow democracy was not well adapted to the situation. The only country which did not immediately establish a republic, Brazil, had a less turbulent history than the others — presumably because it continued the monarchical tradition to which the people were accustomed. Whatever else may have contributed to the thwarting of democratic government, it seems certain that the main factor was a legacy which the new republics could not repudiate — namely, the Iberian-Catholic social organization. An examination of this organization will reveal why.

Ethical Equality. As Christians the Latin Americans believe in the ethical equality of all individuals, but as Catholics they participate in the medieval form of Christianity which, despite the doctrine of equality, permits great and relatively fixed eternal differences. Church traditions suggest a patriarchal view of the State, where unequal sufferings represent punishment for original sin and where clergy, gentry, and rulers, as God's lieutenants, protect the lower orders. Men are expected to accept their lot, and if they cannot accept it, to escape into the monastic life. The other way out, open revolt against earthly inequalities, is condemned and persecuted as heresy. Precisely because all share alike in God, where more or less is inconceivable, material differences lose their importance.

Yet slavery was abolished at an early date in the republics, Negroes and Indians were Christianized from the first in the colonies, the Indians were protected as far as possible by the Church, race prejudice was always less than in the United States, and a strictly caste order never developed. It is difficult to believe that the doctrine of ethical equality had nothing to do with these results, despite the limitations which the temporal organization of the Church placed upon it. The doctrine is, if anything, the strongest democratic element in the cultural tradition.

Class Structure. If it was the peculiar class position of the creoles which brought political democracy to Latin America, it was the total class structure, and indeed the new position of the creole class itself, which contributed largely to the frustration of democracy.

In colonial days the attitudes and sentiments of class had been the same as those on the Peninsula. In fact, since the medieval order of Iberia had already started to crumble at the time of the conquest, the colonial system became in many respects more archaic than its predecessor across the ocean. But the strata were differently constituted and newly aligned. At the top the *conquistadores* had been given control over lands, mines, appointments, taxes, and Indians. The last, in a land of abundant resources but little manpower, had been the most valuable of all, and the *encomienda,* a sort of feudal suzerainty over Indian serfs, had laid the first foundation of the New World aristocracy — a landed aristocracy. In addition, in spite of herself, the mother country had been forced to create a colonial bureaucracy, which opened lucrative positions to the younger sons of a proud but declining peninsular nobility. This class, along with lawyers and men of letters, protected and maintained the rights of the original *conquistadores*. Below them had come the small proprietors and village artisans, neither of which made much headway against the landed nobility. And below these had come the Indians. Soon at the top the distinction between *peninsular* and creole grew up, cutting across economic lines, and at the bottom mulattoes, mestizos, and Negro slaves were added. The creoles were discriminated against because of their birthplace, the colored groups because of their race.

The Spaniards and Portuguese brought to South America their notions of large landholdings, of familial inheritance, and of leisured munificence. The new lands were not for the common man, but for the aristocracy. The lower classes, whether of the same or different race, were subject classes, born to serve their masters. Their standard of living was not to be raised above subsistence, nor their intellect above childishness. They were to live on large estates under the patriarchal care and protection of the owner or overseer. The upper classes were to have as little connection with the means of livelihood as possible. If they could, they were to return to Spain after becoming rich. If not, they could at least move to a city — preferably the political capital, where their wealth could be displayed to advantage and they could participate in governmental intrigue. For them the ideal condition, then as now, was absentee ownership.

The size of the landholdings was naturally huge, because the invaders spread themselves over tremendous continental areas and secured enormous grants for themselves and their followers. With control of large areas, and with the *encomienda* and *mita* systems, the traditions of aristocracy found a firm footing; for the élite were definitely set apart from the mass. Under the *hacienda* and *estancia* system the same was true; and the coming of slavery did not improve the plight of the free laborer, whether black, brown, or white. In some areas, as in Peru, race lines long remained fairly distinct, while in others, as in Chile, the population became almost homogeneous; but in every case the whites who did not own land and did not acquire a profession tended to sink into the degraded laboring class.

Economic Consequences of the Class Structure. The concentration of land ownership in huge estates has in many of the republics persisted until today. In the rich central valley of Chile, for example, 98 percent of the farm land is included in 3 percent of the properties. The census of 1925 listed 375 properties of more than 12,350 acres each. These, which constituted only 0.45 percent of the total number of properties, accounted for 25 percent of all the privately owned land. The largest estate comprised about 618 square miles, giving it an area half the size of Rhode Island. The owners of these *haciendas*, constituting but a handful of the Chilean population, form a close-knit plutocracy which has always managed to control the political destiny of the country. The laborers (*inquilinos*) on the *haciendas*, constituting a sizeable portion of the population, are politically voiceless and inert. They are free by law but actually attached to the soil, and their standard of living remains close to the subsistence level. For decades the large estates were held together by a system of entail (*mayorazgo*); this privilege was not abolished until 1857, and even since then the custom of keeping family holdings together has persisted. The situation varies in detail from country to country, but everywhere the *latifundio* constitutes the dominant economic institution. Though in some areas they have declined, in others they have increased in size and influence, at least until very recently. In Mexico, during the Díaz régime, landownership became increasingly concentrated, single estates (such as those of Terrazas and Creel) comprising millions of acres. In Durango, ten owners held over 4,700,000 acres in 1905, and in Michoacán another ten held 1,229,000 acres. No wonder 97 percent of all rural families in some Mexican states were landless. In very few areas (notably Costa Rica and Antioquia) do holdings take the form of small farms. The independent small proprietors generally subsist on marginal land squeezed between the large estates, and count for little either economically or politically.

Since the economy of Latin America is primarily agricultural and extractive, the ownership of land means private control over the major instrument of production. And concentration of this ownership in the hands of the few produces as much inequality as does concentration of private industrial ownership in the United States or Britain. But the social pattern connected with the *latifundio* is basically different from that connected with industrial capitalism.

The aim of the *hacienda* or *estancia* is to yield a profit for the owner, and this can be accomplished only by the cultivation and sale of a commercial crop. Such a crop cannot be sold in the agricultural region itself, but must be shipped to other areas — usually to urban-industrial centers in foreign countries. The profits filter down to the workers only slightly, because the workers receive their chief remuneration in the form of subsistence from the plantation itself. Therefore, no reserve of purchasing power is built up in the general population. Without this purchasing power, there is little business. The owner does not invest his money in business, because he finds little opportunity in the locale for business expansion, because he is not a businessman (that being left to Jews, Syrians, Germans, and Yankees), and because he wants his sons to enter honorable occupations such as the army, clergy, or gentry. The owner, or *patrón,* therefore puts his money either into enlarging the estate or into spending it on consumption. His consumption, again, is mainly outside the local area — in the form of education for the children, travel for the family, or residence in the city. Whole regions thus come to be characterized by the abundant production of one or two crops sold in foreign countries, and we may speak of some of the Latin American nations as virtually " one crop nations."

So long as the foreign market keeps expanding, the élite may grow wealthy, the peons slightly better fed, and the government more solvent. Railroads, utilities, highways, and processing establishments may be built. The equipment and technical labor for these developments, however, must be purchased from foreign lands and paid for by the commercial crop.

But foreign markets for agricultural and mining products are highly unstable, the competition always keen. Success tends to be followed by failure, population increase by decrease, wealth by ruin. No internal market has been created which can sustain the economy when the foreign market disappears. No diversification of products has been achieved to cushion the disaster. No capital reserve has been accumulated in the hands of the people. No extensive middle class has been developed by commerce and industry. When failure comes, therefore, whole areas, specialized for the production of a commercial crop for a foreign market, are depressed. The life of the peon changes relatively little, but the élite is hard hit.

Local capital being unobtainable to meet the crisis, resort must be had to foreign capital, which exacerbates the economic problem by draining off the profits from an already exhausted local situation. With foreign capital comes foreign ownership, so that mines, oil wells, telegraph and telephone systems, railroad and airplane communications, manufacturing establishments, meat packing plants, textile plants, and merchandising establishments are in foreign hands. The profits from these enterprises, being drained off, further prevent capital accumulation, and salaries are likely to go mainly to foreigners who are only temporarily resident in Latin America or who are working secretly as political agents. The foreign capital is often secured by means of concessions, sometimes monopolistic in character. The import and export business tends to fall into foreign hands, and the business of the nation becomes controlled by foreign interests, whose investments are aimed at the quickest exploitation of the local resources at the lowest cost. In some cases foreign companies enter into agriculture itself and, as in the case of sugar and bananas, become large landowners — thus accommodating themselves to the Latin American pattern. By virtue of this foreign control of their economies the republics, but shortly emancipated from the colonial status, fall back once more into a colonial dependency — this time to imperialistic capitalism which assumes no political responsibility. The new dependency makes the practice of self-government all the more difficult.

The *latifundio* system leads to technological as well as economic stultification. The owner, doing no labor and paying subsistence wages, being often away and thinking about other matters, takes little interest in labor-saving machinery. The *mayordomo* lacks the incentive for such interest. And the laborer, ignorant, isolated, and traditionalized, lacks the ability.

In short, the economic system of Latin America, so productive of uncertainty and poverty, has as its primary cause the original class structure and social institutions of the Peninsula. Had these been different, the economy would have been different. As it is, the plantation economy, dominated by foreign capitalism, finds difficulty in lifting itself by its own bootstraps into something else. Neither the class structure nor the economy gives the ordinary individual an opportunity to advance; neither approximates the condition of laissez faire.

Class and Education. The Ibero-American class organization never fostered more than a meager education for the bulk of the population. The traditional labor of the *hacienda* could be learned by the apprentice method. The traditional attitudes of reverence and obedience could be learned at church. Hence, for ordinary individuals, whose problems were settled by priest and *patrón,* whose social position was fixed, and whose minds were closed, no book knowledge was necessary. Learning was reserved for members of the clerical, legal, literary, and owning professions, and was scholarly or artistic rather than scientific.

Illiteracy figures are not highly reliable, and the situation varies greatly from one country to another, but it is safe to say that over half of all Latin Americans cannot read and write, that in some countries less than a fifth of them can do so, and that in no country can more than four fifths of them do so.

Educationally, the republics have had to struggle with two major problems: first, how to reduce the Church control of schools, and second, how to overcome the class obstacles to universal schooling. The Church's frequent role as an opposition party and its anachronistic methods make it unsuitable as the instrument of universal education. The class difference between élite and mass has influenced the very structure of the schools.

In many areas the children of the rural proletariat are lucky if they get two years in an elementary school, doubly lucky if they go into town for two more years in a sort of elementary " finishing school." In an attempt to provide for these children, *patróns* have sometimes been compelled to establish schools on their *haciendas*. In an effort to promote democracy in town schools, pupils in many republics have been required to wear uniforms — making less obvious the distinction between rich and poor.

Liberal governments have frequently attempted to utilize the schools as an instrument for creating greater social democracy. They have enacted compulsory attendance laws, have tried out new systems of instruction, and have employed foreign educators. Such governments undoubtedly are on the right track, but the obstacles are many and the process slow. Not only is it hard to get support for the schools, but if the educational system progresses too fast the graduates will be drugs on a local market which cannot absorb them. Public education, therefore, cannot get too far ahead of other social changes, and vice versa, and yet it remains the chief instrument by which political democracy tries to create around itself a supporting social democracy.

The anomalous status of the lower-class youth in a higher educational institution helps explain one striking Latin American phenomenon — the extreme political activity of students. But several other factors — all connected with popular education in this type of society — also help explain it. Since university students are predominantly from the governing class, politics is their game, their means of survival. At the same time, studying the theories diffused by the democratic nations, and finding these theories compatible with the ideals but not always with the practices of their own government, they wish to right the discrepancy. Since many of the ultra-élite youth are away in foreign universities, the students are more receptive of radical ideas than would otherwise be the case. In addition, the students are in a position to compare their own governments with those in other lands. It is also true that Latin Americans generally place a higher value on political than on scientific activity. The scientist has neither the elegance of the artist nor the prestige of the lawyer, and few would choose eminence in chemistry as against eminence in politics. Moreover, university and political life are closely interrelated by location (both usually being in the capital) and by political intrigue (the university often being a political football). Finally, the organization of university life is loose. Students sometimes dictate university policies, and make the mistakes which their inexperience would suggest.

Church-State Conflict. While a state church is not irreconcilable with democracy, as Sweden and Norway illustrate, a Catholic state church does tend to be so. Catholicism attempts to control so many aspects of life, to encourage so much fixity of status and submission to authority, and to remain so independent of secular authority that it inevitably clashes with the liberalism, individualism, freedom, mobility, and sovereignty of the democratic nation. Whereas in a democracy each citizen settles public opinion for himself and votes in the light of his own reason, Catholicism prefers to settle his issues for him. The Jesuits, for example, have been accused of making automatons of the Indians whom they sheltered with such zeal. They did not cultivate in the Indians any creative faculty, will to action, or sense of self-reliance. They taught them by a process of mechanical apprenticeship rather than genuine education. The same accusation, to lesser degree, can be made of the Church's tutelage of the people generally.

The Church had by no means evaded conflict with the Spanish Crown before the revolution, because the Crown was disconcerted by the tremendous mortmain wealth of the colonial Church, which in some colonies (e.g., New Spain) aggregated over half the productive real estate. Nevertheless, the relationship was so close between the two that the one enforced the other's laws, and some of the highest offices in the two organizations were held by one and the same person. When the revolution came, the higher ecclesiastic officials therefore sided with the Crown, while the lower orders of the clergy generally followed the revolution. Since the revolution was in no sense a revolt against religion, the new republics universally made Catholicism the sole and exclusive religion of the State. In a short time, however, opposition to the favored cult developed. The chief reason was that the Church, accustomed to being a component part of the colonial government, plunged into the politics of the republics with great zeal, because it felt a danger to its rights in representative government. Joining in partisan fights, the clergymen found themselves as often on the losing as on the winning side, and hence suffered the usual fate of the political opposition.

The position of the Church became increasingly unstable after the mid-nineteenth century. Mexico, Colombia, Venezuela, Chile, Ecuador, and Central America passed severe anticlerical laws. Colombia was the first to proclaim the separation of Church and State in 1853, but by no means the last. At times the Church question has been the main issue, with both sides taking a completely uncompromising stand and resorting to the bloodiest of armed conflicts. In Colombia, for example, priests led rebellious armies against an anticlerical government. Of late, however, anticlericalism has taken a somewhat different turn. As disestablishment has forced the Church out of partisan politics, opposition has developed on the ground that the Church, a conservative institution identified with privileged interests, is an obstacle to social progress. Anticlericalism has become " a political philosophy and plan of action pointing the way to the modern world as the goal." The success of the anticlerical governments in countries which are overwhelmingly and devoutly Catholic is attributed by Mecham to the fact that the most loyal Catholics are women and poor people, who are politically unimportant, and that the Church has so thoroughly inculcated the duty of obedience to authority that rebellion does not occur to them. In addition, it seems hardly probable that the alignment of the Church with vested interests, or the connection between anticlericalism and certain benefits, totally escapes the eye of the common man.

Each can claim that it represents the people — the Church that it gives them what they, as devout believers, actually want; the government that it gives them what, as human beings and equal citizens, they really need. To bear out its claim, the democratic government must teach the people new wants — wants which the Church cannot satisfy. The Church must set itself against these new wants. Each must lean more heavily upon the vested interests than upon the common people, yet the emancipation of the common people favors the government and threatens the Church; consequently, the government is more willing to make concessions of a social and economic sort. The conflict will not be settled soon and will long remain an unstable influence, but to the extent that the republics become democratic the Church must continue to lose.

CONDITIONS OF THE NEW WORLD

Had the social order of the invaders been different, the conditions of the New World would not have counted for much. But under the circumstances they added their bit against the orderly development of political democracy.

Isolation and Underpopulation. With 19 percent of the world's area and only 6 percent of the world's population, Latin America suffers today, as always, from an insufficiency of people. " Only two countries in mainland Latin America make effective use of all parts of their national territories — these are little Salvador and Uruguay. Vast stretches of the South American continent have almost no human inhabitants."

This condition is aggravated by the fact that because of the topography the population, small anyway, is not distributed evenly but is arranged in isolated clusters — clusters separated by empty spaces across which transportation and communication are difficult. Most of the national boundaries fortunately run through these empty spaces and international conflict is thus reduced, but the isolated clusters within nations possess strong separatist tendencies and make national unity difficult. Extreme localism, in fact, made the establishment of centralized republics almost impossible in the first place, and has inspired many revolutionary movements ever since.

Economic problems also arise from isolation, because without transportation otherwise profitable areas remain unproductive. Attempts to build railroads to inaccessible areas have in many instances been economically unsuccessful; the high cost of construction required excessive capitalization and prohibitive rates — with the result that, railroads or no railroads, goods continue to trickle over the same mountain trails on the backs of the same mules and llamas.

Such isolation seems explicable in terms of geographical conditions — high altitudes, steep grades, deserts, tropical rain forests, etc. But it is also explicable in terms of sparse population. Were the population greater, most of these difficulties would be overcome. The sparse population can hardly be attributed to the geography itself, but rather to the Spanish-Catholic culture which permits an extremely high mortality. The conservatism, poverty, ignorance, and general neglect which this culture permits in the bulk of the population cause a high mortality. The infant mortality rate of 230 per 1000 births in Chile, one of the world's highest rates, is not unconnected with the *hacienda* system of that country.

Racial Diversity. The colonial class structure rested partly on race, but the laxity with reference to interracial marriage and concubinage soon produced such mixture as to render racial castes impossible. In some countries terms such as *Negro, indio,* and *mestizo* still have class connotations, but nowhere is the line between first and second class, between élite and mass, a strictly racial line. Thus the Latin Americans escape the most antidemocratic feature of American society — a caste-like distinction between races.

North and South Americans alike fall into the error that race mixture has somehow affected the civilization of the republics. Wilgus says, for example, that in Brazil " the result was a hybrid class that often inherited the worst characteristics of both races." In another place he implies that the native element in the population is inherently indolent, improvident, unambitious, and distrustful. But since a socio-cultural explanation of Latin American history seems adequate, it is unnecessary to call upon biological determinism.

Cultural Diversity. Latin America has had its share of cultural divergencies. The greatest cleavage is that between Indians and Europeans; the next greatest that between the various immigrant groups; and the third greatest, now almost gone, that between Africans and non-Africans.

Of all the European subcultures, that of Spain was probably most compatible with Indian cultures. The Catholic religion blended with Aztec, Mayan, and Incan religion; the stable agricultural system fitted with the similar system of the sedentary Indians; and the authoritarian type of government suited many of the tribes. Yet despite all this the Spanish culture, being European, was fundamentally incompatible with the Indian culture.

The Indian way of life does not use wealth as a basis of status in the manner that Europeans do. Its aim is subsistence, and all members of the community are satisfied with a traditional mode of gaining subsistence from the land. For the Indian, therefore, property is a means of life and is, generally speaking, communally owned. For the Spaniard, at least the upper class one, it is a means for profit. In the Indian's way of life economic rationality is only slightly developed, his bartering and trading at local fairs being as much a social as an economic pursuit. For the Spaniard, however, economic rationality is an independent aspect of life, and he pushes it as far as he can in order to gain power and prestige. It follows that the Indian communities remain local and static in a way that Spanish communities do not. The Spaniard, in order to gain profit, must raise a cash crop and sell it on a distant market. He must have transportation and communication with the outside world. He must have means of bookkeeping, management, and improvement. He is a competitor and must constantly struggle to gain an advantage. His whole life, his whole outlook, is thus fundamentally more dynamic and individualistic than that of the Indian. True, these traits characterize the élite more than the peasants, and that is why the Latin American peasant is closer than most European culture types to the Indian's static way of life — why, in fact, he often is an Indian today. The guidance of Latin American society, however, is not in the hands of the peasants but in the hands of the élite; and to them the communities which have preserved the speech, attitudes, and customs of the Incas are static elements in the life of the republics, impeding the lively intercommunication and movement upon which a democratic nation depends.

Buenos Aires has more Italians than Rome, and there are more Argentines of Italian ancestry than of any other nationality. In the Brazilian state of São Paulo, there are hundreds of thousands of Italians. In addition, each of these countries has numerous other types of immigrants. São Paulo received 177,551 Japanese immigrants between 1827 and 1936, 413,161 Portuguese, and 386,613 Spanish.

Whereas the United States, with an even greater immigration, has fairly well assimiliated its newcomers, Latin America has not. It has generally assimilated the Italians, for they are also Latin, but it has not always assimilated the Germans, because it finds it difficult to combat the German drive to retain a Germanic mode of life and a strong bond with the homeland. The Germans, more than any other nationality, have developed a new type of immigration — political immigration, on the principle that German descent, not birthplace or residence, determines citizenship. It is not new with them, but dates from the period prior to World War I. Even in the 1890's German thinkers, both in Germany and the United States, were expressing the view that millions of Germans should settle in Latin America as an extension of the German state. Schools in Germany long ago began to emphasize Spanish and Portuguese and systematically taught colonization in tropical countries. In Latin America closed German agricultural colonies, German-language schools, German clubs, German business firms, and German newspapers have extended their influence. This " peaceful " penetration, a part of the Axis struggle against all democracy, has been something the Monroe Doctrine could not touch, and which the Americans, with their continental insularity, could not match.

THE STRENGTH OF LATIN AMERICAN DEMOCRACY

It should now be clear that the democratic philosophy borrowed by the creole class found the Latin American environment unpropitious. The outstanding characteristics of this environment were twofold: first, the Spanish-Catholic social organization, involving a class structure based on birth and land ownership, a plantation economy based on fixed labor and the cash crop, and an intrenched religion based on authority and a celibate clergy; and second, certain conditions of the New World, including underpopulation, isolation, and cultural diversity.

If our discussion of these unfavorable conditions has seemed to stress the weakness of Latin American political democracy, such should not be the final impression. On the contrary, if the conditions have been so difficult, the attainment of a substantial measure of political democracy, as has been the case in Latin America, demonstrates the strength of the democratic idea. Whence comes that strength?

In the first place, the diffusion of democratic philosophy to Latin America did not take place all at once and then stop. It has been a continuous diffusion — from France, England, the United States, and many parts of the world. Throughout the nineteenth century most of the foreign ideas which bombarded the Latin American countries were democratic ideas.

In the second place, in spite of conservative forces, the social order of Latin America has gradually changed in the direction of industrial and commercial modernism. Recent European immigration, constant world trade, sporadic acquisition of wealth, the high cost of foreign manufactured goods, the gradual growth of population, the slow improvement of transportation and communication — all have quickened Latin American life until today the conditions for democracy are in many countries turning the scales on the favorable side.

In the third place, the formal political machinery, though more of a result than a cause, has nevertheless acted to some extent as an independent variable. The government's position vis-à-vis the landed élite and the clergy on the one hand, and the people on the other, has often found its advantage in strengthening the hand of the people. It has not always been a democratic government which has thus advanced social democracy. Some of the most progressive changes have been instituted by dictatorial régimes. But with each step in the general direction of social democracy the government has strengthened the hand of the people and has thus imposed on itself the necessity of taking still another step.

It is thus understandable why, in spite of contrary conditions, political democracy in Latin America has not been merely an empty form. Often enough it has been; but also often enough, and more often now, it has not been. The thesis that social democracy and political democracy are mutually dependent receives a clear, though complex and ambivalent, illustration in the case of Latin America.

No. 17   [Another explanation of the distinctions that exist in Latin America between what the constitutions *say* and what the government *is,* and of the paradoxical situation presented by vehemently democratic constitutions in countries with openly dictatorial régimes is advanced by the author of the following selection. It may be true that the failure of democratic constitutions to result in democratically based and operated governments is, in large measure, due to the fact that ideas of what democracy is and how it is to be attained have varied so greatly in Latin America during the past century. Contemporary political thought of the region gives additional evidence of the deep and widening rift between what Professor Whitaker calls radical and conservative democracy.]

The Pathology of Democracy in Latin America: A Historian's Point of View*

by ARTHUR P. WHITAKER

S OME years ago, Harold J. Laski sketched the modern evolution of the democratic idea in terms which are still valid today for Latin America, as well as for other parts of the world. The three main points which were developed by Laski were, first, that while the essence of the democratic idea is equality, nineteenth-century democrats made liberty their first goal on the assumption that equality would follow, once liberty was achieved; second, that when experience proved this to be a mistaken assumption, the twentieth century shifted the emphasis back to equality and sought to achieve it even at the expense of liberty; and third, that this shift was accompanied by a broadening of the democratic idea, which ceased to be essentially political and became economic and social as well. Laski's generalizations provide a good framework for the history of democratic thought in Latin America. Their validity for this purpose is indicated by the fact that the details of his historical sketch, which he drew almost exclusively from the history of Europe, might have been drawn equally well from the history of Latin America.

The continuity of foreign influence upon political thought in Latin America should be stressed, for it is too often forgotten or ignored. The common impression is that, after being held incommunicado for three centuries in the darkness of their colonial dungeon, the Latin Americans suddenly emerged into the noonday glare of the revolutionary thought of France, England, and the United States, and were blinded by it; that almost immediately they were again cut off from the outside world and plunged back into darkness

---

* Arthur P. Whitaker, "The Pathology of Democracy in Latin America: A Historian's Point of View," *The American Political Science Review* (March, 1950), Vol. XLIV, No. 1, pp. 101–118. Reprinted by permission of *The American Political Science Review*. The footnotes in the original version are omitted here.

by the outbreak of alternating despotism and anarchy which afflicted most of the new states as soon as their independence was assured; and that only in the present century have they renewed contact with the outside world on a large scale and begun to catch up with liberal thought in the more advanced countries.

Actually, as Silvio Zavala has demonstrated, even in the colonial period Spanish America maintained a strong liberal tradition, which was mainly Spanish but also more broadly European and which provided one of the foundations for the democratic movement since independence. As others have shown, the European revolutions of 1848, particularly the French, had profound repercussions throughout Latin America. In the latter half of that century, as we shall see, positivism played an important part in reorienting Latin American thought about the problems of democracy. And it is general knowledge that the United States, too, continued to influence the political thought of Latin America during the supposedly dark age between the end of the wars of independence and the close of the nineteenth century — witness the large-scale borrowings from this country in the Argentine constitution of 1853 and in the Brazilian constitution of 1891.

To be sure, there was never an absolute identity between democratic thought in Latin America, on the one hand, and the United States or Europe, on the other. Thus, de Tocqueville, who made a strong impact upon the thought of his time in the United States and Europe, was almost completely ignored in Latin America, whereas his contemporary and rival, Lamartine, enjoyed a vogue in Latin America that had no faintest counterpart in the United States. Again, when James Bryce visited South America early in the present century, he was pained to learn that " the European books most popular among the few who approach abstract subjects are those of Mr. Herbert Spencer " and that " those few are unwilling to believe that he is not deemed in his own country to be a great philosopher."

Yet the fact remains that in its thought on political subjects, including democracy, Latin America has always followed the major trends in Europe and the United States. The only exceptions of any note have been occasional romantic essays in Indianism, which have not produced any major alterations in the political thinking of a single country. These facts have been understood by the observers who have at various times written about what we are calling the pathology of democracy in Latin America. The concept of pathology presupposes a norm, and Latin Americans took as their norm the democratic ideals and performances of western Europe and the United States. As both norms and diagnosis changed with the passage of time, it may help to review some of the principal stages in their development.

II

Let us begin with that eminent pathologist Simón Bolívar. His testimony is important because he was for two decades an eminent practitioner of politics in several South American countries; because of the broad social range of his diagnosis, which led García Calderón to call him " the first sociologist of these romantic [Latin American] democracies "; and because of the vogue his ideas still enjoy in certain circles.

Bolívar's diagnosis was pessimistic in the extreme. His belief that his fellow Latin Americans were unfit for self-government amounted to an obsession. Over a period of twenty years he examined every nook and cranny of the social structure for proof that he was right; and he found it everywhere. " For centuries we were political ciphers [under Spain's rule]; our condition was even lower than slavery," he asserted in his famous Jamaica letter of 1815. " That is why it is so hard for us to rise to the enjoyment of freedom. In everything that concerned public affairs, we were left in perpetual infancy. . . . Events have already shown that completely representative institutions are not suited to our present character, habits, and education [conocimientos]. . . . As long as our fellow citizens do not acquire the talents and virtues which distinguish our brothers to the north [i.e., in the United States], a system of government by the masses, far from being good for us, will bring ruin upon us. Unfortunately, we seem to be far from possessing these traits. . . . We are ruled by the vices which are inevitably formed under the rule of nation like Spain, which has always been noted for its fierceness, ambition, vengefulness, and greed." He saw still other bars to democracy — such as racial heterogeneity, poverty, and personalism — but

most of these, too, he regarded as bitter fruits of the heritage from
Spain.

This gloomy view was based upon the first five years of the Spanish American effort at self-government, and Bolívar recognized
that it was still too early to speak with certainty. But subsequent
experience confirmed and deepened his pessimism, and twelve years
later he recorded the conviction that the people of Latin America
were unfit, not only for republican government, but for constitutional government of any kind.

If Bolívar's diagnosis is suspect on the ground that he was rational-
izing his Napoleonic lust for power, consider the one offered by the
great Argentine statesman and schoolteacher-president, Domingo
Faustino Sarmiento, whose devotion to democracy is not open to
suspicion. Generalizing from the experience of his own country,
which accepted for two decades the domination of the tyrant Rosas,
he declared that " an ignorant people will always elect a Rosas."
Ignorance, which he equated with illiteracy, was therefore in his
mind the chief obstacle to democracy in Spanish America; but there
were two other formidable obstacles which were closely related to it,
namely, the low standard of living and what he called the Spanish
" racial " heritage. His diagnosis thus resembled Bolívar's in some
important respects. Sarmiento was, however, far more hopeful of
effecting a cure, though he recognized that this would be a long and
painful process, since his diagnosis meant that Spanish America
would have to be revolutionized culturally, economically, and socially before democracy could thrive.

Recognition of this fact led some of Sarmiento's less sanguine con-
temporaries, such as Alberdi, the so-called Edmund Burke of Latin
America, and the " burgeois socialist " Echeverría, to the conclusion
that the ills of democracy in Latin America were due not only to the
character of its people, but also to the faulty definition and technique of democracy which Latin American liberals of the first generation had accepted on faith from their doctrinaire European men-
tors. The greatest mistake, said Echeverría, had been in " giving
votes and arms to the common man, thus putting the destiny of the
whole country at the mercy of the masses." " So long as you let the
populace decide," said Alberdi, " the populace will always elect

children who mouth pretty phrases." This restatement of the problem in terms of conservative democracy involved the rejection of one set of European authorities, the doctrinaire liberals of the eighteenth and early nineteenth centuries; but it was carried out with the aid of newer European authorities, mainly French (Saint Simon, Leroux, Lammenais, Lerminier), but also German (Hegel and Savigny) and English (Bentham).

The result was the development of a new criterion for measuring the health of democracy in Latin America, namely, its ability to develop an élite capable of making conservative democracy function successfully. The conservative revision of democratic ideas in the 1830's and 1840's found notable expression in many other countries besides Argentina. For example, in 1848 the Peruvian Bartolomé Herrera, described by another prominent Peruvian writer of the present day, Víctor Andrés Belaúnde, as "the most clear-sighted of our political philosophers," published a book which made a frontal attack on the whole conception of popular sovereignty and majority rule.

At the same time, diagnosticians clung to the popular conception of democracy, which was greatly strengthened by the enthusiastic response of many Latin American liberals to the European revolutions of 1848 and particularly to Lamartine's ideal of an equalitarian republic. In short, professed democrats in Latin America were sharply divided by the mid-nineteenth century over the interrelated questions of definition and ways and means. The difference between the two wings, radical and conservative, may be described as one between being and becoming, between immediacy and gradualism. A rough analogy may be drawn with the Marxist schism of communists versus socialists in the twentieth century.

The schism was widened by the coming of positivism, which, according to its leading historian, Leopoldo Zea, held as dominant a position in Latin American thought from the mid-nineteenth to the early twentieth century as scholasticism had held there during the colonial period. By no means did all Latin American positivists support the conservative redefinition of democracy. Only one of its two main wings, the one inspired by Auguste Comte, did so, whereas the other, with Herbert Spencer as its patron saint, contained many followers, particularly in Argentina, who bent their effort toward giving democracy a still wider definition and applying its principles more vigorously.

The bifurcation between conservative democracy and radical democracy became definitive in the third quarter of the nineteenth century; and the two branches together have continued to dominate Latin American political thought. On the one hand, early in this period the fading cause of monarchy was at bottom the cause of conservative democracy — it was in this sense that the Argentine, Alberdi, for example, was a monarchist. In our own times, authoritarian régimes, which have been branded as fascist and totalitarian by their critics, have been described by their champions in the long familiar terms of conservative democracy. Thus the Brazilian, Benjamín Vargas, used Auguste Comte's own term, " sociocracy," in justifying his brother Getulio's régime.

At the other extreme, even among the so-called communists of present-day Latin America, there are many who are not communists at all (in any sense of the term that would be acceptable to Stalin or even to Tito), but radical democrats; and, in any case, the total number of Latin American communists, whether deviationist or simon-pure, is probably very small. Whatever their numbers, they, too, use the democratic label and claim that their package contains the only genuine article. For the past three quarters of a century practically all Latin Americans have been in favor of democracy, but they have thus been split into two radically different groups on the question of what constitutes democracy. This split has led them to give widely divergent answers to the question, What is wrong with democracy in Latin America?

The problem is further complicated by the fact that since the split became definitive, each wing has been not only strengthened but also modified in some important respects. Conservative democracy gained an important accretion of strength from the racist doctrines, associated with the names of Count Gobineau and H. S. Chamberlain, which swept over to the Atlantic world in the latter half of the nineteenth century. The central doctrine of Frankish or Germanic or Teutonic or Anglo-Saxon supremacy brought no grist to Latin American mills; but it was quite otherwise with another tenet of the racist faith. This was the belief that in the whole hierarchy of races the lowest of all were the mixed races, the " mongrel breeds," for these combined all the vices of the " pure " races without any of their virtues.

How this idea was applied to Latin America is shown by the Argentine, Lucas Ayarragaray, in his book on anarchy and *caudillismo* in Argentina, first published in 1904. " Our political backwardness," he wrote, " is and always has been simply a phenomenon of the psychology of race: a hybrid mind has been the source of creole, i.e., hybrid, anarchy. The mestizo element has been the cause of the most fundamental defects in our [national] character." Since the inferiority of " pure " Indians and Negroes had always been taken for granted, the pseudo-scientific discovery that the great mass of mixed races (mulatto and zambo as well as mestizo) were likewise irretrievably condemned to inferiority fortified the social élite, who were mainly of " pure " European origin, in the belief that they were also a natural élite and therefore the only proper custodians of political power in their respective countries. The result was to strengthen the morale of oligarchies, for they were now more sure than ever that their rule provided Latin America with as large a measure of democracy as the racial composition of its masses permitted. Thus they were able to use with a clear conscience that vocabulary of democracy which had now become the only viable vocabulary of politics in Latin America. The time has long since passed when any creed but the democratic can be professed there with any hope of success. Dictatorial and oligarchic régimes have continued to flourish in superabundance; but not one of them has failed, or now fails, to do lipservice to democracy. Even attacks on existing democracies have been made on the ground that they were " decadent," " plutocratic," or otherwise perverted, and have contained the promise that truer democracies would be set up in their place.

Meanwhile, on the other wing radical democracy has also been stimulated by developments of the past two or three generations. Most of these developments have been related to the impact of modern capitalism and technology upon the various Latin American countries at successive periods since about 1870; increasing urbanization and increasing contacts with economically more advanced and politically more liberal countries; the formation of a more or less rudimentary middle class, an industrial proletariat and organized labor; the rise of a new plutocracy — commercial, financial, industrial — which has sometimes reinforced the older oligarchy of great landowners, but has more frequently weakened it. These developments have varied from country to country, generally in proportion to the intensity of the foreign impact; and their effects, while scarcely noticeable in some countries, such as Haiti and Paraguay, have been quite considerable in those countries that contain the bulk of the aggregate population of Latin America, namely, Argentina, Brazil, Chile, Colombia, Cuba, Mexico, Peru, Uruguay, and Venezuela.

III

The past seventy-five years have seen not only the strengthening of these two brands of democracy, but their modification as well. In both cases the modification has consisted mainly in the injection of an economic content into an ideal which was originally political. Generally speaking, conservative democracy has become identified with free economic enterprise, and radical democracy with state intervention in the name of economic democracy. So far as the former was concerned, the pattern had already taken shape in Mexico in the early days of the Díaz régime. There the celebrated *Científicos*, followers of the Comtian school of positivism, had by 1886 adopted the formula under which they were to administer Mexico, though not to control it (for Díaz kept the control in his own hands) for the next quarter century. The formula was: in politics, limited democracy, with political functions concentrated in an élite; in economics, free competition, no government interference, survival of the fittest. This was their version of economic democracy.

This version was at first shared by many democrats of the opposite wing until in Latin America, as elsewhere, unbridled laissez faire began to produce some rather appalling results in the widening gap between wealth and poverty, with all the dire implications for the future of political democracy (according to any definition of the term that radicals could accept). The chief justification of conservative democracy had been by its promise that the temporory restriction of political power to the élite would be the quickest means of assuring the ultimate establishment of full democracy by raising the general standard of living and culture and gradually training the masses for self-government. Instead, the rich got richer, the poor got poorer, and entrenched privilege prostituted democratic forms to its own ends and suborned or suppressed those who sought to carry out the promised broadening of the democratic base.

The reaction of radical democracy to this situation is best illustrated by the case of Argentina, as described by José Luis Romero. There it was expressed in two different ways by the Radical party of Leandro Alem and Hipólito Irigoyen and the Socialist party of Juan B. Justo and Alfredo Palacios. Starting out about 1890 with a conception of democracy that was almost exclusively political, the Radical party laid increasing emphasis upon both economic nationalism in relations with foreign countries and also state intervention in the domestic economy of Argentina. These economic policies might have been carried out in such a way as to justify the party's claim that it voiced the democratic aspirations of the whole nation had not two other developments taken place simultaneously in the party. In the first place, its leaders lost effective contact with the masses. In the early years its leadership was largely middle-class, but as time wore on the leaders of this class rose to higher and more comfortable positions in the social scale and the party also recruited a new type of leader from the more liberal element among the wealthy landowning class. In the second place, the Radical party failed to live up to its own principles, and its downright abuse of power, such as the use of fraud and intimidation in elections, was strongly reminiscent of the wicked old régime that it had set out to reform. In the end, the Radical party did not serve either political or economic democracy; it was just another political organization that existed for the purpose of getting, keeping, and enjoying office.

These developments had been foreseen back in the 1890's and had been one of the main reasons for the formation of Argentina's Socialist party, which fought its first political campaign in 1896. The Radical and Conservative parties alike, declared its manifesto in this campaign, are representatives of the wealthy and bourgeois classes and of a capitalist system that oppresses and exploits the masses.

Unlike both of them, the Socialist party does not make the hypocritical claim that it represents everybody's interests; it represents only the interests of the working masses of Argentina, which everybody else has betrayed.

Romero does not carry his analysis into the *Peronista* régime (in fact his book, published in 1946, was written before that régime was firmly established). However, even Perón has at least paid lip-service to democracy and has carried on the modern trend, illustrated by Argentina's Radical party and still more by its Socialist party, towards shifting the emphasis from political to economic democracy.

Simultaneously, conservative democracy in Latin America was moving further to the right. The whole process was summed up in the personal history of that able Peruvian diplomat, publicist, and historian, Víctor Andrés Belaúnde. Although Belaúnde believed that the Peruvian masses were not yet prepared for self-government, he nevertheless looked forward in 1914 with confidence and approval to the time when they would share political power with the upper and middle classes. By 1940, however, he was apologizing for what he had written at that time " in an atmosphere of classic liberalism." Since then, he said, "the intellectual climate . . . has changed completely," thanks to the new light shed by such works as José Ortega y Gasset's *La rebelión de las masas* and Charles Maurras' pitiless exposure of the myths of Jacobin democracy. So Belaúnde kept up with the times by revising his own ideas about democracy.

The title of the essay in which he set forth the results was " The New Concept of the State "; but the most important part of this essay consisted of nothing newer than what Belaúnde himself called a " return to Bolívar," that is, to the authoritarian ideas proposed by Simón Bolívar more than a century earlier. Belaúnde's " return to Bolívar " suggests one of the main reasons why the Bolívar cult has spread so rapidly in upper-class Latin American circles in the past generation. Its spread betokens not so much growing gratitude to the hero of independence, the liberator, as an increasing use of his prestige for political purposes: the Bolívar cult is largely an expression of the conservative reaction in Latin America. It is one of the chief obstacles to democracy in those parts in which Bolívar's name carries weight.

This sketch of certain developments in Latin American thought about the problems of democracy brings out three points: (1) that ideas about what democracy is and how to achieve it have varied so greatly from time to time and from place to place that, if Latin American thought on the subject is to be our guide, we have no norm by which to determine the pathology of Latin American democracy in the national period as a whole; (2) that the one clear trend to emerge from this welter of change is the widening rift between radical and conservative democracy — a rift which has proceeded so far that the extreme fringes of the two now represent respectively socialism and authoritarianism, though both continue to use the democratic label; and (3) that while Latin American thought has reflected foreign, and particularly European thought in all this period, it has also been characterized since the 1830's by an effort to adapt the rather plastic idea of democracy to the needs and capacities of Latin America.

The trend of the radical wing in that area can be explained in terms of the inner contradictions of the democratic idea itself. If the idea is expressed in the well-worn motto, " liberty, equality, fraternity," every schoolboy knows that the teamwork of this triad has always left much to be desired. Fraternity has never given much trouble — that patient draft animal will serve almost any system; but the other two are high spirited steeds which have never been able to work in harness together. Liberty breeds inequality; equality can be attained only by sacrificing liberty.

Two ways of escape from this dilemma are open. One is to give up all pretense of absolutism, recognize that complete liberty and perfect equality are unattainable, and settle for whatever degree of each will be acceptable. That seems eminently sensible; but it is by this process that many Latin Americans have justified régimes that we call dictatorships or oligarchies.

The other alternative is to convince oneself (as Harold Laski convinced himself) that, no matter what the sages of the past or present may have said on the subject, the essential core of the democratic idea is equality — more particularly economic equality. Once this is done, there will be no qualms about what happens to liberty; it will not be excluded from the democratic feast, but will have to be content

with the left-overs after equality has been served. This step takes
care of fraternity, too, for it is now made consubstantial with equality. It is toward the equalitarian version that the newer developments in the radical democratic thought of Latin America have been
tending.

IV

The problem of Latin American democracy as we know it today
was beginning to take shape by the eve of the First World War.
Some insight into the problem may be gained by examining the reports prepared at that time by two talented diagnosticians, one a
Latin American, Francisco García Calderón, the other an Englishman, James Bryce.

Though a diplomat, García Calderón was also a man of letters and
his diagnosis was presented in his now classic *Latin America: Its
Rise and Progress.* Completed in 1911, this book was based upon
first-hand knowledge as well as on wide reading, though it was
written in Paris, dedicated to Emile Boutroux and prefaced with an
introduction by Raymond Poincaré.

For all its shortcomings, Bryce's diagnosis has the great merit of
considering the problem of democracy in Latin America both as a
historical phenomenon and as a problem in comparative government. As a historian of parts and a leading authority on democratic
governments of his day, he was well qualified for the task, and he
performed it remarkably well, considering his limited firsthand
knowledge of Latin America. By combining the outsider's report
of Bryce with the insider's report written by García Calderón, we
have a fair sample of the best thinking of the period just before the
First World War.

In important respects both García Calderón's diagnosis and prognosis resembled those of Bolívar, whom he admired greatly; but
there were also important differences. Although he too thought that
the obstacles to democracy in Latin America were so numerous and
deep-rooted in the colonial age as to make its future dark, he attributed the difficulties to the Indian and to Spanish heritage, and to
Catholicism as well, and he noted democratizing influences that had
appeared since Bolívar's time.

" All the history of America, and the inheritance of the Spaniard and the Indian," he wrote, " has ended in the exaltation of the *caudillo*. Government by *caciques,* absolute masters, like the *caudillos* themselves, is very ancient in Spain. . . . The [pre-Conquest] American Indians [too] obeyed *caciques;*" and this original pattern was strengthened by the physical environment, for " the desert is monotheistic; over its arid uniformity one imposing God reigns supreme . . . Páez and Quiroga were divinities of such regions . . . [Latin] American revolutions are like the Moorish wars directed by mystic Kaids." Escape from this pattern of political absolutism is made difficult by the prevalent Catholic pattern of religious absolutism, which breeds among the various parties and groups an " aggressive intolerance " that makes orderly political life well-nigh impossible. Hence the incessant revolutions, which are " a necessary form of political activity," for " It is only by violence that the [opposition] parties can emerge from the condition of ostracism in which they are held by the faction in power, and it is by violence that they return to that condition."

The passage of time, he continues, has not greatly changed this pattern. " Even when the social classes were organized and the economic interests defined, the rivalry of the leaders continued, and politics remained personal." The main difference has consisted in a lowering of the degree of intensity and a tendency towards the substitution of fraud for force. " The drama has replaced the epic; the conflict of passions and interests succeeds to the battles of semidivine personages. . . . Men buy votes; electoral committees falsify the suffrage, as in the United States, by force of money," and *caudillo*-presidents make legislatures pliant by filling them with bureaucrats.

A conservative democrat, García Calderón believed that the only immediate hope of amendment lay in a return to the system proposed nearly a century earlier by Bolívar: infrequent elections and the concentration of power in the hands of a president checked only by the " moderative power " entrusted to a unicameral assembly similar to Bolívar's " life-Senate " — " a serene assembly untroubled by democratic cravings . . . [or] by the anonymous or Jacobin will of the multitude." He cites with approval the Venezuelan Machado Hernández's thesis that " the best form of government for [Latin]

America is that which reinforces the attributions of the executive and establishes a dictatorship " — a thesis further developed by another Venezuelan, Vallenilla Lanz, in terms of " democratic Caesarism." García Calderón made it even stronger; to him, autocracy seemed not only the best but the only practical means of government in Latin America.

But he did not entirely despair: he saw some signs of improvement in Argentina, Uruguay, Brazil, and Chile, which he attributed to the fact that the economic life of these nations had become more " intense " under the impact of foreign capital and business enterprise. Following the Argentine writer, José Ingenieros, he expected that conflicts of economic interest would replace personal and clan rivalries as the basis of politics in these countries and would lead to the development of a two-party system similar to that of England. This process would in time spread to other Latin American countries and the results would be salutary in many ways. But such a foreign impact contained a threat as well as a promise, and the people must be on their guard lest the " mandarin " bureaucracies which, as Justo Sierra pointed out, now ruled these countries, let control slip into the hands of " the victorious foreigners who are making themselves masters of the soil." " The great political transformations of the future," he concluded, " will be due to the development of the common wealth; new parties will appear and the bureaucracy will have to be diminished."

Simultaneously with the original French edition of García Calderón's book and some twenty years after the publication of his own great study of democracy in the United States, James Bryce followed up a brief visit to part of Latin America with a book in which he discussed the pathology of democracy in the whole of it. The first thing to be noted is that he conceived of democracy in political terms ("representative," "responsible," "constitutional," are his key terms) and, in contrast to García Calderón, he mentioned economic considerations only as a conditioning factor, with a half apology for mentioning them at all. Next in importance is the fact that he took an even gloomier view of the present condition of Latin American democracy than García Calderón, but was more generous in extenuating its shortcomings and somewhat more hopeful of its improvement. Otherwise there are close similarities between the two diagnoses, though they were apparently written quite independently of each other; neither mentions the other even in later editions or printings (e.g., García Calderón, 1919, and Bryce, 1923).

To begin with, Bryce sets Chile and Argentina in a class apart, as the only bona fide republics in Latin America. The other republics he divides into two groups: those countries in which democracy has been a mere farce (e.g., Haiti), and those including the Mexico of Porfirio Díaz, which maintained an autocracy under legal forms — to the great benefit of Mexico, adds Bryce. His distinction between the two groups is unimportant for our purpose, however, for he lumps together all the countries in both groups in the statement that "these states never have been democracies in any real sense of the word." But he hastens to defend them against censures and criticisms on this account. They "could not be real democracies," he avers, because of their racial composition, their sparse population spread over a vast area, and their lack of training in self-government. The liberal experiments of the early days of independence therefore only made existing matters worse; the constitutions of these states did not suit the facts and only produced a vicious circle of fraud and force.

As to the best means of breaking this circle, Bryce was in substantial agreement with García Calderón so far as some of the Spanish American communities were concerned. "The best thing for them," said Bryce, probably with Porfirio Díaz in mind, "is the strong rule of an able ruler," perhaps a monarch, though he also preferred "honest" oligarchy, "i.e., one professing to be what it really is," to a "sham democracy." Bryce regarded Chile out of all the Latin American states as "the one which best answers to European or North American notions of a free constitutional commonwealth." He admitted that the governing power in Chile was practically monopolized by a small landed aristocracy and a few lawyers; but government and the party game were carried on in much the same way as in eighteenth-century England; peace and order were the rule; national policy was stable; and the level of capacity, eloquence, and national spirit was high.

Argentina, like Chile, was now a constitutional republic from which that "flavor of militarism which was so strong in former years has now virtually disappeared," partly as a result of railroad construction, an influx of Spanish and Italian immigrants, the growth of cities, and a general prosperity which created " a growing sense of the value of order and peace." Foreign merchants contributed to the process by " making the native men of substance feel that frequent revolutions were retarding the development of their properties." The case of Argentina, he believed, was an indication of the process by which other Latin American states might " advance toward a more settled and legal government," for " the more property there is and the more industry there is in a country, the smaller is the proportion of those who join in a revolution either from a love of fighting or in the hope of bettering their fortunes." Also, a more prosperous country can do more for public instruction, which is " one of the most urgent needs of these nations," because " education, if it does not make men good citizens, makes it at least easier for them to become so."

Admitting that this linking of increasing wealth with political progress might sound strange to Europeans and North Americans familiar with the corrupting influence of money power upon free institutions, Bryce maintained that there are stages in a nation's history when "whatever makes for security makes for progress " — implying that all the Latin American countries were now in that stage. Some of them were already making progress and their example would encourage the rest. In conclusion, he advised European liberals who were critical of Latin America to look in the mirror. " Since 1859," he said, " power has in many countries [of Europe] passed from the hands of the few into the hands of the many, but no millennium of virtue and peace has yet followed . . . every sensible man feels that the problems of government are far more difficult than our grandfathers had perceived. . . . These things being so, ought not the judgment passed on the Spanish Americans to be more lenient? Their difficulties were greater than any European people had to face, and there is no need to be despondent for their future."

Despite two world wars and the many upheavals affecting Latin America, the ills of democracy there are still diagnosed in long-familiar terms: the colonial heritage, Indian and Negro as well as Iberian; the continuing racial heterogeneity; the old landlordism with its *latifundio,* and the new plutocracy with its slums; illiteracy and poverty; personalism and militarism; and so on. But there have been modifications of various kinds: new lists of the " truly " democratic countries; some mitigation of the charges against the Spanish part of the heritage; more concern with the definition of democracy and less agreement on any definition; a more explicit development of the economic implications of the term; a much stronger stress on the importance of the middle class as the pillar of democracy; and some fresh analyses of particular problems of democracy.

V

Let us consider the case histories of those countries which represent Latin American democracy at its best. García Calderón listed four: Argentina, Brazil, Chile, and Uruguay; whereas, Bryce's highly selective list named two of these, Argentina and Chile. By the close of the present decade most experts had dropped Argentina and Brazil and had added Colombia and Costa Rica. Thus in 1946, Robin A. Humphreys (Britain) and in 1949, Austin MacDonald (United States) mentioned the same four: Chile, Colombia, Costa Rica, and Uruguay. In 1944 the Colombian, Eduardo Caballero Calderón, answered both " yes " and " no " to the question whether democracy exists in Latin America, and the two countries in which he thought the best case could be made for its existence are both in the Humphreys and MacDonald lists: Chile and Colombia. While individual writers might include other countries, the weight of opinion seems to be that over any considerable period of time the countries which have approximated most closely to the democratic ideal have been the six mentioned above: Argentina, Brazil, Chile, Colombia, Costa Rica, and Uruguay.

To what extent do the case histories of these six comparatively healthy countries bear out the commonly accepted explanations of the weakness of democracy in Latin America at large? Since we cannot examine all the supposed factors making for weakness or strength, we have chosen for analysis four of the factors which seem to be widely regarded as of crucial importance, namely, literacy, urbanization, the middle class, and party organization.

1. **Literacy.** In the present century the literacy average of the six countries in this group has been above the general Latin American average. Argentina and Costa Rica have the highest literacy rate in all Latin America of around 85 percent. Brazil and Colombia have a low rate of not over 50 percent. Moreover, of the two countries where the rate is highest, Argentina has been dropped from the list for several years, and it may be seriously questioned whether Costa Rica should remain on in the light of events leading up to and following the revolution in 1948. Since a still more recent crisis has raised the same question about Colombia, the list of Latin American democracies is at the present writing [1950] reduced to two, Chile and Uruguay; and in both of these the literacy rate is only about 65 percent, which is far below the rate in undemocratic Argentina and dubiously democratic Costa Rica. If democratic citizens are the best citizens, we may suspect that even the temperate James Bryce was over-optimistic when, with special reference to Latin America, he wrote that "education, if it does not make men good citizens, makes it at least easier for them to become so."

2. **Urbanization.** In general, commentators on democracy in Latin America have shared the belief expressed by Laski that "organized democracy is the product of urban life." For a long time this proposition seemed to be borne out by the history of democracy in a considerable part of Latin America; but recent events have raised serious doubts about its validity. The greatest center of urban life in Latin America, the metropolitan area of Buenos Aires, is a case in point. This area was formerly the chief source of support of the two democratic parties of Argentina, the Radicals and the Socialists; but in the present decade it has played a decisive part in establishing and maintaining the Perón régime, whose existence constitutes the main reason for Argentina's exclusion from current lists of Latin American democracies. Moreover, in so far as communism is a threat to these democracies, the threat comes from the cities, and the most united opposition to it comes from outside the cities. In the latter connection, it should be noted that Laski's proposition has never been true

of Costa Rica, which in the quarter century before 1947 came to be regarded as perhaps the soundest of all the Latin American democracies. Costa Rica has no large cities; it is an overwhelmingly rural country, and in its heyday its democracy was of the Jeffersonian small-farmer type.

3. Middle Class. Largely by implication in the nineteenth century, but explicitly and more frequently in the past generation, diagnosticians have attributed the ills of democracy in Latin America to the lack of a middle class, and conversely have explained the growth of democracy in a few of its countries to their rare good fortune in possessing such a class. This correlation of democratic health with middle-class strength finds considerable support in the history of several Latin American countries, but recent developments have shown that it would be a great mistake to assume that the Latin American middle classes can be counted upon as the champions of democracy under all circumstances.

As far back as 1914, Belaúnde pointed out that the middle class in Peru, Chile, and Argentina, small though it was, had become an effective engine of oppression by letting itself become " bureaucratized " under the control of strong executives; the resultant system he dubbed "bureaucratic Caesarism." At the present time, as indicated in a book published in 1948, one of the chief dangers in Latin America is that the middle classes, caught in the economic squeeze between price inflation and frozen incomes, and the political squeeze between the communism of Russia and what they regard as the pluto-democracy of the United States, may adopt the alternative of " creole fascism " of Spanish American Falangism on the model of Franco Spain. In support of this opinion, an editorial published in the Colombian newspaper, *El Liberal*, in July, 1946, was quoted; and the opinion expressed therein has been endorsed by a noted Peruvian intellectual and former cabinet minister, Jorge Basadre. This point of view has also found considerable basis in subsequent events in Peru, Venezuela, and Colombia, and perhaps Costa Rica as well.

It is misleading to answer that there is no fascism in Latin America, that its present authoritarian or other antidemocratic movements are merely a continuation of its age-old patterns of oligarchy and dictatorship. So far as the past is concerned, there is a large element of truth in this answer; but it is not wholly correct even with regard to the past and it fails to take account of present tendencies which are likely to make it quite inaccurate in the near future. The measure of truth in it is indicated in the recent analysis of problems of democracy in Latin America by the able young Colombian socialist, Antonio García. According to García, the Latin American fascists of a few years ago did nothing to give effect to the totalitarian and corporative systems of Mussolini and Hitler, of Franco and Oliveira Salazar, which they pretended to admire. Instead of establishing a new order, they merely used the new ideas and catchwords of fascism to bolster up the old Latin American order of class privilege and oligarchy.

Yet García's book itself is evidence that a situation is developing in Latin America which favors the growth of fascism — not the imported variety of a few years ago, but a native growth, or to use *El Liberal's* phrase again, "creole fascism." This situation arises from the spread in Latin American parties of both the right and the left of statism, which can hardly fail to produce a long, bitter fight for control of the state in most of Latin America, where economic and social differences are wide and where the stakes are correspondingly high. Statism is not new in Latin America. It has roots in the Iberian tradition; it survived even in the laissez-faire atmosphere of the nineteenth century; and there have been many evidences of its growth in the past thirty years — witness the Mexican Constitution of 1917, the Uruguayan social legislation of the 1920's and subsequently the popularity of national planning in the depression decade of the 1930's, the numerous *fomento* corporations of the recent war period, and Brazil's recent *SALTE* plan.

What this trend will mean to the middle and upper classes if the masses gain control is indicated by the current redefinition of democracy in economic terms. To put the matter plainly, as it has been put by Antonio García and his fallen chieftain, the late Jorge Eliécer Gaitán, it will mean a redistribution of wealth for the benefit of the masses. As usual, the pinch will be felt first by the middle class, and, to quote Laski's phrase again, fascism is at bottom " a defense of the middle class against the onslaught of the masses." There is no reason to expect that the oft-mentioned individualism of the Latin Americans will stem this tide. Their individualism has been much exaggerated and in Latin America, as elsewhere, the trend of the modern age is the other way.

4. **Party Organization.** Made at the height of the nineteenth-century emphasis on the mechanics of democracy, Bagehot's apothegm, " Party organization is the vital principle of democracy," set a pattern of thought which is still strong in diagnoses of the ills of Latin American democracy. That the Latin Americans generally have been highly deficient in political organization, and that this deficiency has been a handicap to democracy there, will have to be admitted; but in line with the present inquiry, we are now concerned with, not the worst, but the best that Latin America has to offer.

The palm for political organization goes to Colombia in the generation before 1945. The country then had not only well-organized political parties under able civilian leadership, with no taint of military interference, but also freedom of speech, comparatively orderly campaigns, and honest elections. It also had the classic two-party system, the quintessence of good political organization á la Bagehot. Yet this model Latin American party system has been in serious trouble for years past, and in the past few months [1950] it has broken down completely. The Colombian presidential campaign just closed reproduced all the familiar features of Latin American political life at its worst — widespread violence and heavy loss of life; declaration of a state of siege, with consequent suspension of all personal rights, including freedom of speech and assembly; the president's intervention in favor of his own party; and abstention of the other party from voting. The president-elect, Laureano Gómez, is not a conservative; he is a reactionary. He has been called a Falangist sympathizer, but denies that. His election has been described by some commentators as setting back the cause of democracy in Colombia a whole generation.

In the long prelude to this Colombian tragedy, the much-admired two-party system was publicly abjured as far back as 1946 by no less a person than the brilliant young Liberal leader and then President of the republic, Alberto Lleras, whose devotion to democracy no one can question. Theoretically, he said, the two-party system was the best form of political organization and actually it was working well in Britain and the United States; but in Colombia it was completely unworkable because it placed excessive power in the hands of the majority party under a unitary, presidential system of government which did not contain either of the checks on power that enabled the two-party system to function successfully in the other two countries — in Britain, the check of cabinet responsibility to Parliament; in the United States, the check of the federal system, with its division of power between the central government and the states.

The case of Uruguay raises doubts about the soundness of Lleras' reasoning. In that country there is a unitary government and a great concentration of power in the hands of the president, and while he and his cabinet are nominally responsible to the congress, that responsibility has never been effective. The arrangement has not produced the dire consequences feared by Lleras. On the contrary, Uruguay is today one of the two most democratic countries in Latin America. At the same time, the alternative preferred by Lleras, a kind of coalition government of the two parties, was adopted and adhered to in Colombia for two troubled years until it broke down completely.

VI

There is a slightly brighter side to the story of Latin American democracy in recent years which has not been discussed. Mexico would be one of its highlights. But there the story would have to deal more with democratic promise than fulfillment, and even this promise is qualified by the fact that, although nearly forty years have passed since the dictator Porfirio Díaz was overthrown, the country is still governed under a one-party system. As practiced in our southern states, that kind of system has not been generally regarded by the rest of the country as a very close approximation to democracy.

In Latin America at large, the state of democracy's health does not seem as good as it did a decade or two ago. Nor does it seem that we have made much progress in the diagnosis of its ills. It is not that the " causes " which have been assigned are wrong, still less that there are not enough of them, for the main trouble with them is that they are too numerous. They tell both too little and too much. When applied to any particular country, they are like a charge of buckshot fired at a silver dollar at fifty yards: three or four shots may hit the mark, but the rest will miss it.

A clue to a better answer than we have yet had can be found in the fact that, while diversity characterizes the twenty countries of Latin America, uniformity of failure to maintain orderly and stable democratic governments over a long period of time also characterizes all of them, even the two present-day " bests," Chile and Uruguay. Does not this suggest that there must have been some important factor, or explanation, which was common to all these heterogeneous countries?

Looking back over the history of their democratic thought and action in the past 140 years, we find only one such factor or explanation. This consists in the fact that the efforts to introduce and foster democracy in Latin America during these years have been accompanied throughout by changing conceptions of that which was to be introduced. These changing concepts have consequently been the subject of widespread and often violent disagreement among professed democrats. If it is indeed true that democratic government can function successfully only in countries where there is general agreement on " basic principles " and " significant issues," we need hardly wonder that democracy has developed so imperfectly and haltingly in Latin America.

No. 18   [In the following article Professor Fitzgibbon addresses himself to an examination of the present status of political democracy in Latin America. If it is true that despite democratic constitutions nondemocratic political societies characterize the area, what is the evidence that supports the contention? What specific indictments can be made? What is the outlook for future political development? Are the forces and factors that have made democracy weak so deep and pervading that the likelihood of really basic directional changes is a remote one?]

The Pathology of Democracy in Latin America: A Political Scientist's Point of View*

by RUSSELL H. FITZGIBBON

LORD BRYCE, in one of his well-known works, once defined democracy as "that form of government in which the ruling power of a State is legally vested . . . in the members of the community as a whole." This definition of democracy will serve as a point of departure in this paper.

Whether or not they agree with Bryce, most Latin Americans who have been at any time in an influential political position have invariably held aloft a democratic banner. Even that dubious democrat, Juan Domingo Perón, has written that " I [speak] in defense of democratic ideals, because my country is democratic and the constitution I have sworn to observe is also democratic." This democratic ideal has been espoused ever since the revolutions for Latin American independence. In the contemporary period, Vargas of Brazil has been one of a very few Latin Americans openly to call into question the desirability of democracy as a governmental objective and form. More typical of the Latin American point of view is the statement of a recent president of Panama who said at the opening of the first Foreign Ministers' conference in his own capital city in 1939 that " American dictatorships have never been imperialistic or totalitarian. They have been the expression of an incipient patriarchal state or the logical product of the incapacity of the governing classes to handle the machinery of democracy. In not a few cases they have been founded on the desire to accelerate artificially the slow process of the education of the people for the same democracy that they in reality have harmed."

* Russell H. Fitzgibbon, " The Pathology of Democracy in Latin America: A Political Scientist's Point of View," *The American Political Science Review* (March, 1950), Vol. XLIV, No. 1, pp. 118–129. Reprinted by permission of *The American Political Science Review*. The footnotes in the original version are omitted here.

This banner of democracy, it must be confessed, has often been lifted unreasoningly and in blind imitation of what appeared to be politically fashionable in the hemisphere. Too often, especially in the early days of independence, was there unthinking confusion between a republican form of government on the one hand and the democratic base (including private rights) for that form on the other. García Calderón, a profound *pensador* of an earlier generation, has commented penetratingly on the conflict between the trilogy of liberalism, federalism, and democracy and that of conservatism, oligarchy, and unitarism. " Militarism, revolutions, and the warfare of the *caudillos*," he says, " were in part explained by the profound differences between the champions of tradition and the soldiers of liberty."

Many writers have blamed Latin American difficulties in the application of democratic government on the lack of apprenticeship in self-government during the colonial period. Bryce, for example, joins this group. This is an easy assumption and, as far as it goes, a valid one. It errs, however, in assuming that the pathology of democracy yields to a political diagnosis alone. It does not. A problem as complex as this must necessarily involve the diagnostic efforts of the sociologist and the economist, the anthropologist and, of course, the historian. Especially in connection with an analysis of democracy is it essential to look to the past, both for the nature of the institutions and the difficulties confronting them.

Even a superficial survey of Latin America's past reveals the strong thread of individualism running through the pattern. It is an individualism inherited from the Spanish and Portuguese and, in so far as the Indian contributed to an assimilated contemporary culture pattern, from him also. The creole leaders of the revolutionary period looked largely to France for their intellectual stimulus and in eighteenth-century France they found an atomistic conception of democracy which emphasized the narrowing of the authority of the formal sovereign and the expansion, almost the exaltation, of the rights of the individual. That which was French was almost automatically popular in creole circles in Latin American cities of the revolutionary period. This French emphasis on " the rights of man and of the citizen " operated, unconsciously if not consciously, to reinforce the individualism normally inherent in Latin American political thinking.

The *caudillismo* of the revolutionary and later periods was a normal and almost an inevitable successor to the *caciquismo* of an earlier era and represented individualism carried to an extreme. The early independent governments were sometimes rudimentary, and, maintains García Calderón, " the excessive simplicity of the political system [allowed] opinion . . . no other means of expression than the tyranny of oligarchies on the one hand and the rebellion of the vanquished on the other. . . ."

Wherever " democracy " is actually individualism in this disguise its logical endpoint can easily be anarchy. That result was unfortunately attained in various parts of Latin America in the early days of independence, too often under the guise of allowing " democracy " to have its own way and learn by its own mistakes. Bolívar was one leader who realized the perils of an unrestrained democracy. " Knowing history, Bolívar was forced to admit," Belaúnde describes his reasoning, " that monarchies and aristocracies had set up strong and enduring régimes. And he is also aware of the weakness, or better, the fragility of the republican [or democratic] régime, especially in countries of complicated structure." Belaúnde then quotes Bolívar as arriving at the conclusion that " the most perfect form of government is that which produces the greatest degree of social security, the greatest amount of political stability."

II

That Bolívar came to favor British political institutions as best avoiding the dangers inherent in an unrecognized but destructive conflict between liberty and authority is beside the point. What is more important at this moment is the question as to what was the lack in the political milieu or mentality of Latin America at the time of the revolutions and subsequently — a lack which removed the checks on the new-found democracy so that in consequence it often destroyed itself by its excesses. The answer in one word would seem to be integration.

Democracy is, of course, a luxury type of government and political process. It is occasionally more expensive than other forms of political control, it is sometimes less efficient, it is often slower to function. But it is based on the assumption of the ability and the right of the average man — the citizen — to participate in the political process, and hence rejects the concept of an élite group which must monopolize that process. The phenomena that are possible symptoms of a pathological condition of democracy in Latin America — dictatorships, revolutions, overemphasis on the military, political inarticulateness of masses of people, farcical elections, obstacles in the path of free communication of ideas — all need to be examined critically in the light of what we expect democracy to be and to do.

Again we come back to the effect of the lack of integration in the national life of Latin America on the whole problem of democracy. It should be obvious that in a discussion of factors contributing to and subtracting from a unifying process, attention cannot be devoted exclusively to *political* integration. There are also necessarily involved the economic, the social and cultural, the religious, the ethnic, and doubtless other aspects of the problem. What occurs in the political sphere is inevitably a product and a projection of developments along other lines.

The Catholic faith has been the greatest single unifying or integrating element in the Latin American scene. It has penetrated more widely than the Spanish language and, in any event, is a positive force making for oneness that the linguistic common denominator could, in its very nature, never be. We often do not realize what a tremendous influence the Catholic faith and ecclesiastical organization have had in inducing a like-minded outlook in matters social and political, and even economic.

But, though life has been viewed almost universally in Latin America from a Catholic angle, this has not made for that socio-political fusion in which democracy could best flourish. It is not simply that the Catholic Church is an authoritarian organization or that it has almost always been allied with conservative groups, movements, and individuals in Latin America. The indirect but more pervasive effect of the great influence of Catholicism has been to transfer a tendency toward acceptance of authority into other fields than the spiritual and ecclesiastical, especially into the field of politics. Thus, there is developed less of the sturdy attitude of questioning constituted political authority than would provide the most fertile soil in which to plant democracy. This sort of response is especially characteristic of considerable numbers of the illiterate and the lower social classes generally and is almost universally true of the women of Latin America.

Another integrating element which writers have been fond of citing is the " soul," or " ethos," or " spirit," or " Geist " of the Latin or, at least, of the Latin American peoples. Rodó is the classic spokesman of Latin America in this wise and the indictment his *Ariel* makes against the Calibanistic culture of the United States is well known. Rodó and other writers with his leanings were, for one thing, describing the attitudes and feelings of an intellectual minority who are certainly not now, if indeed they ever were, the expression of the political life and spirit of Latin America. To assert this is not to deny the affinity of " poets, politics, and polemics," to borrow a chapter title which Mrs. Romoli uses in her discerning volume on Colombia. The most that could possibly be said for the political implications of Rodó's analysis of the Latin American scene would be that he thought in terms of a society based on the Greek concept of democracy — and even if the Greek idea might have been somewhat applicable a century ago it surely is not pertinent now in the middle of the twentieth century. The integrating influence of a common upper-level culture becomes, particularly when projected into the political field, so tenuous as to be almost without significance.

Much more impressive is the evidence indicating lack of integration in Latin American life. The evidence falls into several categories. One of them is the geographical. Latin America is not a geographical unit. It is not even twenty units, corresponding to the twenty states. Localism is still, after four and a half centuries, so overwhelming a fact in Latin America that it underlies much of the political behavior of even the best-knit states. Within a state like Ecuador, furthermore, the local, or at least the regional, division is so strong that the country becomes, in Professor Whitaker's aptly borrowed phrase, " a tale of two cities." Latin America, which occupies an area three times as large as the United States, has railway and highway mileages roughly comparable to those of this country. Had the larger area proportionate lengths of railways and highways those arteries would provide a degree of integration that would inevitably be reflected in politics.

Though it is not the province of this paper to discuss those facets in detail, the economic and social picture is much the same. " Social life in the Spanish American colonies was always based on the principle of inequality," writes Miss Fisher in the opening sentence of a study of the Mexican struggle for independence. That principle of social inequality, resulting in lack of integration, has in large part been transmitted to the contemporary scene. The Chilean *hacendado* and his *inquilino* are widely separated from each other, though their dwellings may be only a hundred yards apart. The gulf between the Goajiro Indian and the cultured member of the Colombian Academy of History at Bogotá is at least as great as that between a sharecropper and a Union League stalwart.

It is inevitable that in a land thus divided in so many directions and on so many planes democracy would find flimsy foundations. Democracy presupposes a tough-minded and tenacious acceptance of the nation as deserving a continuing loyalty which transcends loyalty to class. Democracy assumes that the proper adjustments and accommodations among classes, probably accompanied by vigorous debate and pulling and hauling, will be made peacefully within the framework provided. If loyalty to a class, whether a proletariat in the professional sense or an élite group, supersedes the common loyalty then democracy suffers correspondingly.

III

This political pattern is largely a relic of the days of Latin American revolutions a century and a quarter ago. The phenomena of that period were in turn traceable to the circumstances of the colonial era. *Caudillismo* is inherently antithetic to democracy. The color of *caudillismo* has long remained a part of the Latin American picture. A stereotype of the earlier and more extreme sort of *caudillo* would require the use of such adjectives as ruthless, pretorian, intolerant, cynical. They are not adjectives with which we would describe a democrat. Later in the nineteenth century certain developments began to have their inevitable, if slow, political consequences. They were such developments as the less localistic view which peoples and rulers took, the impact of mid-nineteenth century liberalism, the integrating effects of railway, telegraph, and telephone building, the pacifying and restraining consequences of wealth in the form of trade, investment, and rudimentary industry. The general effect of these developments was to produce a *caudillo* less given to violence and more to intrigue and duplicity. And in proportion as respect for the intellectual and the businessman increased, doubt about the utility and the inevitability of the *caudillo* also grew.

In the first twenty or twenty-five years of the present century a new and not altogether creditable or palatable factor came to play a part. It was in those years that the impact of newly burgeoning United States foreign policy fell most directly and (the Latin Americans often say) oppressively on the sister states to the south. The crystallization of canal politics in 1900–01 pointed inescapably — even if heavy earlier investments in and trade with Mexico and Cuba would not necessarily have done so — toward a general interest in and concern with Latin America, especially the Middle American region. The rather sudden advent of the United States as at least an embryonic world power was characterized by a certain amateurishness in conduct of international affairs, and nowhere was that novice's approach felt more quickly or more unfavorably than in Middle America. The manifestations of it were the " Big Stick," the " Caribbean Policeman," the era of protectorates, the " I-took-the-Canal-Zone " attitude.

The effect on the actual or potential development of Latin American democracy was harmful. The United States government quite understandably wanted to see order and stability maintained in Latin America, especially in those Middle American countries where disorder and instability might threaten our newly established strategic interests in Panama. But too often the technique used by the State Department was to uphold the heavy hands of those Middle American régimes which, with or without benefit of democratic support, showed a will and an ability to maintain order. Too often the United States took the easy way out by extending aid and comfort to whatever represented the *status quo,* and almost always the *status quo* was inconsistent with the cause of Latin American democracy. Such democrats as Haya de la Torre, for example, often became dedicated and sometimes bitter yankee-phobes. Thus the struggling democratic forces in one or another Latin American state found that they had to combat not only the persistent native *caudillo* but also, in effect, the Colossus of the North in whose shadow he took refuge.

The United States acquired more finesse in the conduct of its Latin American relations after the middle 1920's, especially after 1933, when it removed some of the undesirable consequences of its earlier policy. Nevertheless, the early twentieth-century responsibility of this country in providing an unfavorable setting for Latin American democracy was considerable.

IV

What are some of the specific factors which indicate that democracy in Latin America may not be in an altogether healthy state today? For one thing, the population of countries such as Guatemala, Peru, Ecuador, and Bolivia is overwhelmingly Indian. Other countries have an Indian population only relatively less important. In practically all of those countries or parts of countries the Indian, after four and a half centuries, still is not "a part of the national life." Politics in the occidental sense remains a monopoly of the white or very-near-white segments of the population. The Indian's contacts with the white man's government are usually with the police official, the recruiting officer, or the tax collector. None of those persons is the best possible salesman of democracy. It is no coincidence that the Latin American states which we usually assume to be most democratic (with our Europeanized concept and definition of the term) are those with the largest percentages of European population: Uruguay, Costa Rica, Chile, and Argentina. The dominant whites of many areas are reluctant to share political power even with the mestizos. Hence, this latter population fraction constitutes, as William L. Schurz well puts it, a "disturbing leaven of mixed peoples, who move in an uncertain political and social world between the fixed status of the pure bloods."

If the state of the ethnic man has a distinct relation to the condition of democracy in Latin America, so do the needs of the physical man. A factor of very real importance is the continued low standard of living and the presence of endemic diseases in large parts of Latin America. We take for granted the fragile state of democracy in certain parts of Europe when the daily food intake of many persons has been reduced to 1,000 calories or less. We assume that merely the stark struggle to keep stomachs reasonably full precludes much concern for such a luxury as democracy with its civic demands on the individual. Prevalence of tuberculosis and rickets and typhus does not give the best environment in which Central European democratic experiments can be undertaken. But we often forget that malnutrition and disease are fully as characteristic of large areas of Latin America as they are of devastated Europe.

To the ethnic and physical man must be added the cultural man. Despite the most optimistic statistics of ministries of education, Latin America is still an area of widespread illiteracy. Many Latin American governments make " culture " and " education " almost synonymous, and too many are content merely to translate " education " into " literacy." Some of the more advanced educational programs in Latin America are now putting the stress on agricultural or vocational training. It still remains true, however, that the ability to read and write is almost a *sine qua non* for progress toward any educational objective. And, traditionally, that ability — literacy — has been a prerequisite for the individual to make much impact on the governing and political processes simply because without literacy those processes had almost no substance, meaning, or vitality for the individual. The significance of this limitation is reduced somewhat through the growth of political education by use of the radio. This means of communication gives the skillful candidate access to a vastly larger audience than he could ever have through the printed word. Its development has great pregnancy for the future of democracy in Latin America. Television will, of course, enrich the political appeal which the radio allows. But until radio and television facilities are more widely used in the political life in Latin America the low level of literacy will necessarily be a retarding factor in the development of democracy.

To complete the picture of the various selves presented by the Latin American, final mention should be made of the political man. For the best condition of democracy it is necessary that the individual, in large numbers, think of himself, as the Costa Ricans and Uruguayans do, as a political unit rather than a political cipher. To personal dignity, which most Latin Americans have perhaps in overabundance, must be added political dignity. To many Latin Americans the *politicos* are a caste apart, somehow tainted and tarred. The defeated party in an election too frequently assumes, with all the automatic response we attribute to a Dodger baseball fan, that " they was robbed." Costa Rica's most eminent international lawyer once told the writer that he would never run for political office because of all the mud-slinging involved in a campaign. People of intellectual attainments and those in business and the professions thus often shun political participation. This view obviously does not point to the growth of a democratic attitude or form of government.

When staunch journalistic defenders of democracy such as *La Prensa* and *La Nación* in Buenos Aires are "intervened" by the government, the results on the condition and potential progress of democracy are necessarily harmful. The same effect is suffered when a Vargas institutes a radio censorship or a Trujillo sends policemen to break up opposition political meetings. Democracy is necessarily predicated on free and untrammeled access to and transmission of information, ideas, opinions. Hence, anything that interferes with that access and transmission inevitably injures democracy. So close and so ancient is the relationship between democracy and a free press and free speech that the point as it applies in Latin America needs no demonstration at all.

Another unhealthy symptom revealed by the Latin American body politic is the condition of its political parties. In a few of the states the parties, either on a biparty or a multiparty basis, have vigor, organization, continuity, respect, forthrightness, and influence. Under other circumstances and in other places, a *Partido Domincano* is the only party legally permitted, or there is a favored machine under a Carías or an Ubico. Or again, there are countries in which parties seemingly flourish but in which the whole weight of tradition plus various pressures combine to produce a complete dominance by one party. Mexico's *P.R.I.* is a case in point; it operates to make that country effectively a one-party state. We look in vain in Latin America to find a party which assumes in any respect the role of His Majesty's loyal opposition. The idea of paying an extra stipend to the legislative leader of the opposition party, solely for that service which he thus performs, would leave Latin Americans completely bewildered.

The nature of elections in a given Latin American state is also revealing of the status of democracy. We are entitled to ask if the campaigning is free and substantial, if the balloting is orderly, if the votes are honestly counted. When an opposition candidate is admitted to have won in a free and fair election the particular state has taken a long and democratic step forward. Thus it was with Irigoyen (for his first election) in Argentina, Alessandri (also for his first), and Aguirre Cerda in Chile, Olaya Herrera and Ospina Pérez in Colombia, Bustamante in Peru, Grau San Martín in Cuba. The nature of the election laws also provides a test. If, for example, they allow the polls to be organized and controlled by the representatives of the first party to arrive there on election morning (in effect, the fantastic situation which has prevailed under the election laws of Mexico), we may be justifiably skeptical about the democratic character of these laws.

All of the Latin American constitutions have elaborate bills of rights. It is apparent that the courts of these states are faced with heavy responsibilities in interpreting and applying the law as it relates to civil rights, especially if the constitutional statement of such rights remains couched in nineteenth-century terms. For the most effective functioning of the courts in these matters, two or three considerations are probably fundamental: The judges must have a conviction of their own broad responsibility, the affected public must be conscious of the role of the judiciary, the courts must establish a satisfactory *rapport* with the other branches of the government, and mutual tolerance and respect must exist among the several branches. It surely must be apparent that these basic conditions do not exist in certain Latin American states, and to the extent that they are absent democracy is thereby harmed or retarded.

Another factor of importance is the attitude toward and the status of social legislation in a given country. President Perón, whatever his motives, doubtless had some justification when he wrote not too long ago that "this situation [i.e., disregard of the rights of the working classes] did not exist only in Argentina or America; a very similar state of affairs existed at the peak of the democratic era in those countries that boasted more of their democracy. It may be said that the systems of liberty and democracy have not been incompatible with the exploitation of man by man." Those Latin American states which have kept themselves cognizant of and responsive to the changing socio-economic situation as indicated by the social legislation have experienced fewer changes in government such as occurred in Argentina after 1943.

Still another element in the Latin American problem is the relationship of the military and civilian arms of the government. If a given country was nurtured on militarism in the days of its revolution for independence and if its people have not since raised serious questions about the naturalness or inevitability of *caudillos*, it is unnecessary to cite supporting evidence as to the sickness of democracy in that state. The military dialectic can sometimes contort itself into a democratic appearance but, at least in Latin America, we are probably always justified in questioning the sincerity of that transformation. It is somewhat heartening to realize that in such a country as Colombia, despite all its recent political vicissitudes, the army has apparently remained largely in the background and has kept itself subject to supreme civilian control. That Mexico's latest presidential election presented a situation in which both major rivals for the office were civilians is a fact worth passing mention. But, by and large, the odds are still long in favor of the *caudillo*. Technology is on the side of the dictator; machetes are inadequate against machine guns and street barricades against tanks.

Here, then, are some eight or ten of the most important factors which have a direct bearing on the condition of democracy in Latin America. All of them are closely interrelated and their features and characteristics determine in large degree the status of democracy in Latin America.

V

What does the mirror of the recent past reveal about democracy's condition? Some of the revelations are, it must be admitted, disturbing, at least in a short-range view. The reversion of Argentina is familiar. It was a lapse from democracy which was legalized in February of 1946, and constitutionalized in March of 1949. Peru and Venezuela, within two months during the latter part of 1948, saw their respective promising experiments in democracy collapse. Costa

Rica has lately experienced a long and unaccustomed period of electoral turbulence not unmixed with military activity. Chile has become less politically tolerant than before. The *Herrerista* movement in Uruguay continues to be ominous. Paraguay within a recent thirteen-month period suffered six *coups*. A Liberal boycott of the late Colombian election and the general nature of the campaigning in that contest are distressing in view of Colombia's long record of democratic progress. The tragicomic kaleidoscope of Panamanian politics has brought to the presidency a man of very questionable democratic sentiments. Perhaps these several set-backs are to be explained in large part as war-born distortions. But the short view is discouraging.

VI

Finally, a prognosis may be in order. The long view is admittedly better than the immediate one. Just as certain forces operated in the nineteenth century to remove the rawness of the political process and slowly paved the way for democracy, so there are other deep-lying forces operating in the mid-twentieth century. They are for the most part nonpolitical forces. Perhaps first in importance among these forces is the inevitable economic growth of the area. Economic maturity — expressed in terms of trade, industry, large-scale agricultural and mineral exploitation — demands political stability and abhors the mercurial sort of political process which Latin America has so often known in the past. And stability, despite the sometimes cynical identification of it with dictatorship, probably contributes in the long run to democratic development.

Industrialization necessarily means the development of an urban working class. This group is at once far more politically conscious than its rural counterpart and, furthermore, it lends itself much more quickly to organization. The political potency of large labor organizations is universally recognized and they have long played a part in Latin American politics out of all proportion to the stage of growth of industrialization. There is no reason to think that the political effectiveness of Latin American labor will be less in the future.

Another force is cultural or, more narrowly, educational. The education of a people, even if it involves nothing more than the spread of literacy, operates powerfully to integrate them " into the national life." Social reforms, a prerequisite of democracy, are made more intelligible and desirable to a literate than to an illiterate people. Then, too, mass living standards are gradually being raised with the resulting incorporation of more persons in the national life. A " middle class," which we long have considered a cornerstone of democracy, is thus born.

This trend toward democracy must be indigenous. It cannot be imposed by the United States. It is scarcely contagious from one Latin American country to another. Duncan Aikman, an observing and penetrating correspondent, put it well when he wrote that "Democracy, in a word, does not 'spread' from one republic to its neighbors like a disease or a fashion in wall paper. Where it appears at all, it grows from roots which can take hold of something tangible in the social situation and draw nourishment from its surroundings." Although the spread of democracy is thus socially vertical rather than geographically horizontal, it is likely that the persons and groups which deplore democracy in one country will take courage to uproot or retard it because of successful attacks on it elsewhere in the hemisphere. Hence, the entire problem does show an interrelationship for the whole of Latin America.

We cannot expect to attain in this century ideal democratic conditions in all of Latin America. The problem is too vast and too intricate for such rapid improvement. Nevertheless, the long view is promising.

CHAPTER 7

Change by Revolution?

No. 19 [It is quite evident that constitutions in Latin America have been changed more by revolutions and by revolutionary governments than by what we would call the normal processes of constitutional amendment and revision. Likewise, it is true that changes in political administration have been frequently made by recourse to bullets and not by the techniques provided by the ballot box. In a few of the republics violent upsets have more characterized the transfer of power from one political group to another than changes of office by election.

Our knowledge of the fundamental operations of *government,* in Latin America or elsewhere, is not sufficient if we can do nothing more than to note that governmental changes are likely to be accompanied by turbulence and violence. It is essential that we go behind the symptoms and try, at least, to comprehend the basic causes, trends, and directions of these revolutions.

The revolutions of Latin America are not in a special class or category. They are, as elsewhere in the world, the result of basic economic and political maladjustments. The fact that *more* revolutions occur in Latin America is but a reflection of the existence of more unresolved fundamental problems and conflicts.

The following article is written by Dr. Germán Arciniegas, an outstanding contemporary American man of letters, and a person who has been active in the political life of his own country, Colombia. He presents what he believes to be the basic explanation of the frequent and many revolutions in Latin America.]

Revolutions*

by GERMAN ARCINIEGAS

*W*HEN United States newspapers mention one of the Latin American republics, it is usually in connection with an attempted or successful revolution. Is there something in the complicated racial make-up of those peoples or in their geography that inevitably leads to disorder and revolt?

From the very first day of independence, Latin America's political life was an unstable one. The civil wars of the last century established what is very nearly a tradition of anarchy. But why was this the pattern in the south, while north of the Rio Grande problems were settled with the success that has made the United States first among the world powers?

Students of this fact often place too much emphasis on the racial combinations which make up the Latin American countries, or on whether the population lived in the Andes, on the seacoast, or in the jungles. This ignores the historical process, which is fundamental. The fact is that the two peoples, north and south, came into being and developed under the same democratic love of liberty. But from the very first they moved in opposite directions.

In Latin America, conquest came first. In a matter of thirty years — from 1513, when Balboa discovered the Pacific Ocean, to 1548, when Alonzo de Mendoza founded La Paz on the highest plateau of the Andes — Spaniards and Portuguese overran three quarters of the American world. Next came the colonial period, which lasted more than two and a half centuries. Then the Wars of Independence, in which victory created for the victors the problems of self-government.

In the United States, things happened in reverse order. Here the colonial period came first, and the inhabitants governed themselves almost from the beginning. There were little more than one hundred fifty years of colonial life — the *Mayflower* anchored in Plymouth

* Germán Arciniegas, " Revolutions," *Américas* (March, 1949), Vol. 1, No. 1, pp. 22–24 ff. Reprinted by permission of *Américas*, a monthly magazine published by the Pan American Union in English, Spanish, and Portuguese.

harbor in 1620 and the Declaration of Independence was signed in 1776. Once the colonies were separated from England, they put into operation on their own, principles of government they had been practicing for some time. The conquest was put off, to be accomplished a hundred years later.

The three hundred years between the Spanish conquest and the winning of the West by the North Americans gave the Pilgrims and their descendants time to establish a civilization in the thirteen English colonies. This fact affected the whole historical process in the North. The Spanish conquest resembles a medieval museum piece. It was accomplished with lances, swords, and bucklers, with coats of mail and heavy armor, with greater trust in St. James the Apostle than in arms. To keep the advantage horses gave them over the awestruck Indians, the Spaniards had to lift the struggling animals in rattan baskets up the precipices of the Andes. One of the most effective arms — decisive in the conquest of Darién and in many other places — was dogs, which bit the Indians to death. These are pictures from the fifteenth and sixteenth centuries, which seem more like cartoons for Gobelin tapestries than stills from a motion picture.

The Pacific coast was explored, and the *conquistadores* proceeded to the conquest of Peru in vessels made by carpenters who knew nothing of shipbuilding. These were built in shipyards improvised in the wilderness, on the banks of rivers. They made sails from scraps of shirts, ironwork and cordage from heaven knows what.

By contrast, the conquest in the North, postponed until the middle of the nineteenth century, had the help of the steam engine and several other modern inventions. The gold rush to California started thirteen years after Samuel Colt had invented the pistol that made his name famous. To get to California or to Montana, people went on wheels. Instead of struggling over the nearly impassable Andes, the emigrants' covered wagons stampeded across the plains west of the Mississippi. Even before those who went by prairie schooner could get there, California's new El Dorado was reached by those who embarked in New Orleans in steamboats, crossed the Isthmus of Panama by land, and took passage on the first line of steamers to ply the Pacific coast.

Washington, in all his warfare, never reached the right bank of the Mississippi. Bolívar and San Martín, on the other hand, had to play their roles on a stage that, from Atlantic to Pacific, from the Caribbean to the southern tip of South America, extended over both sides of the Andes. In winning the independence of Spanish America, as in its conquest, everything was done on an unprecedented scale. In North America during the colonial period as well as in the winning of the West, there was a central, compact core from which mass migration set out, leaving no vacuum behind. It was the frontier that moved: not the bridgeheads, not the lance tips. In Spanish or Portuguese America, the first ambitious strides in each historic period were born of extraordinary enthusiasm stimulated by such words as " honor " and " glory." The soldier of the Conquest dragged himself over mountain passes that he knew would lead to death, because he was not going to have any one questioning his honor. In the same way, the liberator in the war of independence cherished his glory.

The speed of the Spanish and Portuguese Conquest changed, first of all, the color of the family. The family — except perhaps in the case of gypsies or nomadic tribes, which have attained no higher culture than can be produced under canvas — is the fruit of repose. The Pilgrims of the *Mayflower* sailed from Plymouth — and they were the prototype of all who followed — without cutting family ties. Of the hundred who came on that ship, twenty-eight were children. During the voyage two more were born. They crossed the Atlantic to found a colony, not to undertake a conquest. And women's skirts were no hindrance whatever to the development of the program. Today North American writers note with unconcealed surprise how those families begot dozens of children, as many as were biologically possible.

For a Quesada, a Cortés, a Valdivia, an Irala, a Ponce de Léon, an Hernando de Soto, it was unthinkable to set out except at the front of masculine armies. Occasionally a bold woman accompanied the captain, sometimes one of those Indian women who for love opened the way among peoples of alien tongue. She was just one more soldier. None of the warriors brought his wife from Spain to these enterprises. And when the armies halted in Mexico or in Cuzco, or wherever else, love, obeying the simple laws of nature, went on joining white and red.

In the north, the Danes, the English, or the Germans of the thirteen colonies had no reason for having anything to do with native women. As their settlements grew, they pushed the Indians farther west until the red man's back was against the wall. There has been much talk of Spanish cruelty, and there has been too much ado about the extermination of the native races by the *conquistadores,* taking the theme from the impassioned plea by Fray Bartolomé de las Casas. That cruelty is undeniable, but it should be considered not so much Spanish, as the legacy of an epoch: the Middle Ages. But the final fact is that in Spanish America many millions of Indians remained alive, as is plainly evident now. The extension of the conquest from Mexico to Chile would have been impossible without the collaboration of the aborigines. In the thirteen colonies in the North the opposite occurred, and only a few native specimens survived to be anthropological studies or to satisfy tourist curiosity.

In a book on the development of the United States I read recently: " In a century and a half, the Americans colonized effectively an area of about 200,000 square miles, more than twice the size of Great Britain." The author underlines this as a remarkable fact, which indeed it is. But it is a fact that impresses the Latin American reader as a drop in the bucket. Chile alone, which is one of the smallest nations of Latin America, has 286,000 square miles. In thirty years during the sixteenth century, Spaniards and Portuguese raised the flags of their kings over lands three times as large as all the Old World.

Bernal Díaz del Castillo described Hernán Cortés in a phrase that might be applied to all the *conquistadores*: " He had a heart that did not rest." Prescott's judgment of him was similar: " He was," he said, " a knight errant." But what word, then, should we use for Hernando de Soto, who after taking part in the entire conquest of Peru, came to the banks of the Mississippi to meet his death? Or for Alvear Núñez Cabeza de Vaca, who after a ten-year odyssey from Florida to Mexico, leaving his bloody footprints on the vast amphitheater of territory that overlooks the Gulf, returned to Spain to be made the governor of Paraguay and the Río de la Plata, beginning anew the story of his misfortunes? Or for Jiménez de Quesada, who at eighty, after he had founded in his middle age the New Kingdom of Granada, still led his armies, though he had to be carried on the backs of Indians because he no longer had the strength to mount a horse? Or for the fighting friar Don Bartolomé de las Casas, who crossed the ocean fourteen times, and at ninety still fought spiritual battles and wrote volumes in defense of his humanitarian principles?

During those thirty years the *conquistadores* explored rivers that are among the greatest in the world, the Amazon, the Orinoco, the Magdalena, the Plata, and a good part of the Mississippi. They discovered the Pacific Ocean. They founded the capital cities of Mexico, Panama, Guatemala, La Paz, Lima, Quito, Buenos Aires, Bogotá, Asunción del Paraguay, Santiago de Chile — some on the Atlantic, others on the Pacific, some at sea level, others at altitudes up to twelve thousand feet. They subdued native empires and savage tribes. They bore the image of Christ first across an uncharted ocean and later through lands of a world several times greater than the one that fifteen centuries before had been traversed by the most ardent of Christ's apostles.

Even the cities traveled; they moved from one site to another; they were born and reborn. The kings issued grants to pacify adventurers, to re-establish families, to keep the genealogical trees uncontaminated, to maintain the prestige of white or blue blood. On the human side of the New World experiment, all that was of no avail. The soldiers rose against their captains, and with their wind-whipped banners of rebellion cried: " Long live the King! " The friars fought against the enslavement of the Indians, but the *conquistadores* divided them among themselves, and castes of servants and masters were formed.

The process was less violent in Brazil, and this was duly reflected in its history. Penetration into the interior was postponed until the eighteenth century, but from 1535, when Olinda was established, until the founding of Rio de Janeiro twenty years later, there was a series of conquests indicative of the destiny of the future colony. Portugal was more of a seafaring nation than Spain. The Portuguese took pleasure in founding ports. Bahia, Santos, Vitória, and Recife rose during those twenty years, and there, too, the family and the social strata followed the same course as in the Spanish conquest.

By contrast, the master-and-servant set-up had little chance to develop in North America. The thirteen original colonies of the North had an all-white population, and there was a leveling into a single social category. Those who came as servants sold their services for a few years. Later, when their contracts were fulfilled and if they were still alive, they were considered the equals of the rest, had the same opportunities, became owners of the same lands. As a matter of fact, from the very first day, everyone seized his axe and cut wood, washed kettles, made beds, baited fishhooks, hunted wild animals. Equality was accentuated even more as the frontier moved west and the new settlers created their own fortunes.

In Spanish America, as in the southern United States — where political control was for a long time in the hands of Spaniards or Frenchmen — the social classes were gradually stratified. From the wealthy plantation owner or the commissionaire to the servant or the slave there was a rigid scale of distinctions, which later became an acute problem from the point of view of democracy.

Latin America suffered from the faults of the monarchical idea. The monarchy based everything on favor. The king graciously distributed lands and men, elevated protegés, bestowed titles, imposed taxes, put upon the humble the weight of daily labors. This formed habits of idleness and adulation, ideas of privilege, superiority complexes in certain families, which eventually cost time and bloodshed to abolish. In other European countries where the industrial revolution took place earlier, those medieval institutions were not so enduring as in sixteenth- and seventeenth-century Spain. It is curious that much of what the Latin Americans are most bitterly censured for is a strictly European product. On the other hand the settlers of the thirteen North American colonies came from the Hanseatic League cities and from nations imbued with the mercantile, industrial spirit, the middle-class spirit which reacted against hierarchies of the nobility.

In our America to the south, those who succeeded in making their fortunes surrounded themselves with slaves, peons, servants. In today's Latin American speech there is an astonishing variety of colorful words to describe the precise status of those who do the work for the rest.

I was born in a middle-class family in Bogotá — a city where there were no Negro slaves because the climate is too cold for them — and I remember that there never were fewer than four servants in my house, as well as the many peons who cared for the animals and did the chores in the fields. The peons called my father " my master " and they greeted me as " my little master." The women called my mother, and still do, " your grace." My home was typical.

Thus when the countries of Spanish and Portuguese America became independent, many aspects of life had to be revolutionized before they could reach the democratic level that came easily in the thirteen colonies of the North. To create democracy where there have been no differences in color or social position is child's play.

These minor matters have gradually disappeared in Europe as a result of wars or revolutions, but Latin America has had to face them since the Wars of Independence. In 1775 the United States fought a war of independence, and nothing more. The revolutionary aspects of that war were reduced to more definite expression of principles, for even the colonies had been quite free. In Latin America, once independence from Spain had been won with the victory at Ayacucho, the revolution continued. That revolution must transform our social customs to achieve the democratic level that is indeed the unswerving ideal of all our nations.

It is very possible that our revolution is not yet over, that it still has a long road to travel. That explains at least part of Latin America's political instability.

No. 20 [Revolutions in Latin America are also the subject of Mr. Dozer's essay which follows. In his discussion of this widespread phenomenon he is primarily concerned with the causes of the violent changes of the last ten years, the actions of the revolutionary juntas, once they secured control of the government, and the factors which explain why these new governments, despite their sincerely expressed programs of reform, have been able to effect so few really basic changes.

He clarifies the picture, however, by his careful analysis of the two types of revolutionary movements in Latin America, the political and the social, and indicates that many of the revolutionary governments have initiated and carried through basic reforms, reforms which we would label " democratic."]

Roots of Revolution in Latin America*

by DONALD MARQUAND DOZER

Dᴜʀɪɴɢ World War II revolutions in Latin America resulted in the overthrow of governments in Argentina, Bolivia, Ecuador, El Salvador, Guatemala, and Panama. Compared with earlier periods the number of revolutions was relatively small. Since the close of the war, however, the revolutionary tendency has reappeared with such vigor as to suggest that it may no longer be following the usual Latin American pattern. Recent events have excited apprehension in some quarters as to possible revolutionary developments in the entire area. Let us try to determine, then, what the Latin American pattern of revolution is; whether recent outbreaks do in fact conform to or deviate from it; and what the prospects are of continued revolutionary activity in the future.

Factors making for a violent change in the status quo exist in many parts of Latin America. Almost everywhere opulent minorities flaunt their riches before a " melancholy sea of illiterates." The wealthy few, who maintain estates of thousands of hectares, derive lucrative fees and commissions from foreign business firms, and drive about in expensive American limousines, have little in common with the miserably underprivileged masses of the people, whose role throughout life is to serve as beasts of burden, shine the shoes of the upper class in the town plaza, or sell lottery tickets. It is difficult to name other areas of the world in which so few have so much and so many have so little. With the possible exception of Argentina, Chile, Mexico, and Uruguay, the Latin American countries contain only an infinitesimally small middle class. The social ladder has only two rungs — the lowest and the highest. The low is very low, and the high is very high. The gap is so wide that those on the lowest rung can almost never reach the one above. However passionately Lazarus may desire to become Dives, his chances of doing so by orderly processes are, except in rare cases, nil.

* Donald Marquand Dozer, " Roots of Revolution in Latin America," *Foreign Affairs* (January, 1949), Vol. 27, No. 2, pp. 274–288. Reprinted by permission of *Foreign Affairs*. The footnotes in the original version are omitted here.

This basic class cleavage can be illustrated by a few figures. Approximately 90 percent of the national wealth of Colombia is controlled by 3 percent of the population. In Argentina, 15 families own one tenth of the entire land area of Buenos Aires province, the wealthiest area in the country; and the same families have landholdings throughout the nation amounting to 7,000,000 acres. In Chile, 0.3 percent of the total number of landed proprietors own more than 52 percent of all the farm land of the nation. In Venezuela, fewer than 3 percent of the landed proprietors own more than 70 percent of the land. In Mexico, a similar concentration of landownership, under which in 1910 only 1 percent of the Mexican people owned 70 percent of the country's arable land, was a powerful factor in causing the epochal revolution which broke out in that year.

The overwhelming majority of agricultural laborers in the 20 countries of Latin America, all of them agricultural, live under oppressive conditions of peonage, sharecropping, and in some cases even unconditional slavery. As the Secretary-General of the Organization of American States, Dr. Alberto Lleras Camargo, said recently: " There are millions of inhabitants without a home or an organized family life, without schools, without land, without even personal belongings. Their only risk in joining a revolutionary movement is the loss of the following day's wages." The people live constantly on the verge of starvation and in the shadow of death from disease. It was calculated in 1942 that whereas wage earners in the United States had to spend less than 38 percent of their income for food, those in Brazil had to spend 48 percent, in Mexico 56 percent, in Argentina 60 percent, in Colombia almost 66 percent, and in Chile as high as 80 percent. Today these percentages are higher. As a result it is estimated that two thirds of Latin America's approximately 145,000,000 people are physically undernourished and one half of them suffer from either deficiency or infectious disease. Life expectancy ranges from a high of 47 years in a few areas to a low of less than 32 in Peru, compared with almost 63 years in the United States.

Since the end of World War II the basic social and economic maladjustments in Latin America have been seriously aggravated by cost-of-living developments. Of 13 Latin American countries for which even fairly reliable statistics are available, only one — Uruguay — showed in June 1948 a cost-of-living index figure — 175 — which was comparable to that of the United States — 169 — both calculated upon a 1937 base. In the other 12, living costs ranged upward to almost four and one half times the prewar level, reaching 334 in Peru, 364 in Mexico, and 437 in Chile. To meet these rising costs the normally marginal and submarginal groups who in most cases derived no benefits from wartime prosperity have received either no wage increases or increases which have not been commensurate with rising prices. At the time of the revolution against President Elie Lescot of Haiti, in January 1946, groups of workingmen were striking for an increase in their basic wage of six cents an hour. Many similar groups throughout Latin America, remembering the wartime promises of a more abundant life, and struggling with their present difficult living conditions, are resolving to live no longer in the shadows on the husks.

The complete rationale of revolution in Latin America is not simple. Unsatisfying, for example, is the explanation of F. García-Calderón that "both the Indian and the Spanish races which settled America were warriors, and their spirit explains the disorders in these republics." Equally unsatisfying is the jaundiced view expressed 30 years ago by the Argentine scholar, Carlos Octavio Bunge, that revolutions in Latin America "result from the habitual inactivity of the people, who do nothing but accumulate bile." Bunge compared their periodic uprisings to epileptic fits. To him it seemed that throughout the nineteenth century Argentina had to experience an internal upheaval every ten years. In Bolivia between 1825 and the end of the century more than 60 revolts occurred and six presidents were assassinated. Venezuela had 52 important revolutions in a century. Revolutionary movements may thus be said to have become part and parcel of the Latin American way of life, and must be explained in terms of the entire Latin American *ambiente.*

What are the reasons for this frequent resort to revolution in Latin America? Certain secondary factors such as historical tradition, official defalcation and malfeasance, personal ambition, and inflexible constitutional and political practices contribute to it. In general, revolutions may be said to result primarily from social pressures which have been building up for generations and which finally find an outlet in violent change. A popular leader in Colombia, the late Senator Jorge Eliécer Gaitán, has been quoted as saying, "When pain becomes despair it breaks all the dikes." The Latin Americans have often found that they could attain the basic "goods" in life only by direct and forcible resistance to the status quo. That the methods which they employ are illegal tends to impeach the law rather than their methods.

II

Maldistribution of wealth and income has been a characteristic of Latin American economy and society ever since the days of Spanish and Portuguese rule. Revolt has therefore been latent there at all times. The vast majority of Latin Americans, resentful of lifelong exploitation and frustration and despairing of any improvement in their levels of living by orderly methods, are chronically ripe for revolution. From this situation of underlying and widespread dissatisfaction with the social and economic status quo a dashing leader has often emerged to start a revolutionary movement. A century ago a vigorous and picturesque Argentine *caudillo,* Facundo Quiroga, his eyes flashing, was reported to have said to a companion: "Look you, if I should go into the street, and say to the first man I met, 'Follow me,' he would follow me! " This magnetic influence over men's minds and actions has impelled many a *caudillo,* whether lured on by unabashed greed for power or by zeal for the common good, to attempt a *coup d'état* which would overthrow his country's administration and install him in the presidency. Once established in office, he may try, either for personal or group ends, to enlist popular support by redressing social grievances and effecting constitutional reforms. As long as he can gratify the public demand for reform in this way he can gain and retain a popular following. Very often, however, because his leadership is intensely personal, his commendable social impulses are frustrated and his reform program defeated by the greed of the palace clique who surround him and who feel no comparable obligation to the masses of the people. So it is that attempts to redress social grievances usually result only in exploitation of the people by a new group of officeholders, and attempts at constitutional reform usually take the form of amendments confirming the *caudillo* in power. *Plus ça change, plus c'est la même chose.* Such a revolution produces a change only in the chief of the government and the bureaucracy surrounding him; the perplexing problems of the basic political and social system continue. Such were the revolutions that made Getulio Vargas president of Brazil in 1930 and that brought the army, led by its own *caudillos,* to power in Argentina in 1943.

The experience of *caudillo* governments, whether or not they are of revolutionary origin, demonstrates that the problem of social stresses and strains in Latin America cannot be solved effectively by personalist and paternalistic methods. For if revolution is latent in Latin America, so also is democracy. Revolution is very often the price which a Latin American country is forced to pay in order to realize the democracy which would otherwise remain dormant or suppressed. It has been the common purpose of such revolutions to accomplish, in the words of a perspicacious Colombian publicist, Gregorio Sánchez Gómez, " the overthrow of systems which were considered outworn or anachronistic or contrary to the common interests and wishes in order to put in their place institutions better suited to the fulfilment of a people's destiny." New groups have arisen clamoring for a revision of basic economic, social, and political processes and agitating for radical constitutional reform. In many of the revolutionary movements above the level of the palace *coup d'état,* the primary motivation has often been an urge for a more democratic type of government, to be achieved mainly through the rewriting of constitutions.

The constitutions of the Latin American countries, usually drafted either by dictators or by conventions representing the privileged classes, and modeled along nominally republican and oligarchical lines, have been numerous and ephemeral. They have been changed so often largely because they were unsuited to the needs of their peoples. They did not satisfy the often inarticulate requirements of politically unsophisticated communities. Simón Bolívar's first constitution for Bolivia, for example, set up a grotesquely complicated machinery of government including a president with life tenure and a tricameral congress made up of censors, senators, and a house of tribunes. Furthermore, the absence of a firm heritage of judicial review of legislative acts — a heritage which can be regarded as peculiarly Anglo-Saxon and North American — has rendered it difficult for national courts in the Latin American countries to interpret constitutions in such a way as to keep them in harmony with changed conditions. Small wonder that these organic documents are usually soon set aside by popular action or by the fiat of a dictator and come to serve only as curious historical exhibits!

Revolutionary reforms of constitutions have been frequent occurrences in all the Latin American countries. They have called attention to the difficulty if not the impossibility of revising basic constitutional forms by legal procedures and have represented in many cases a violent protest against the continued imposition or maintenance of a rigid political strait jacket on a society which was beginning to generate new dynamic elements. The constitutions of both El Salvador and Guatemala recognize " the right of insurrection " under certain circumstances. This type of revolutionary outburst was exemplified in the successful revolt against the Argentine dictator Juan Manuel Rosas by Justo José de Urquiza in 1852. This resulted in the Argentine constitution of 1853. Other examples were the overthrow of the Brazilian monarchy of Pedro II in 1889, which culminated in the Brazilian Constitution of 1891, and the successful movement against President José Manuel Balmaceda of Chile in 1891. Today, fifteen of the twenty Latin American countries are governed by constitutions adopted since 1933, and nine of these by constitutions adopted since 1945. This rapid supersession of constitutions obviously has not tended to create a veneration for existing constitutional forms, although it has not derogated from the generally recognized importance of constitutional arrangements.

More specifically, many revolutions have sought to broaden the basis of government when the existing governmental machinery was cumbersome, inflexible, and unresponsive to the political desires of the people. The presidential system, taken over from the United States Constitution and providing for a fixed tenure of office for the chief magistrate, forces the opposition to wait for scheduled elections. But in these countries the mercurial temper of opposition parties, of those who mold public opinion in newspaper, press, and radio, of exploited and underprivileged groups often changes too rapidly to make delay practicable. An administration which at the time of its election may admirably accord with the general will may in the course of a few months, or sometime before the expiration of its constitutional term of office, commit such egregious errors or fail so completely to fulfil popular expectations that the people rise in fury against it. If a president who symbolizes the shortcomings of such an administration insists upon serving out his legal term of office he can generally be ousted only by revolutionary means. It may be suggested that the long experience of the presidential system during the last century and a quarter has conditioned Latin Americans to the necessity of revolution, which provides them with a substitute for a needed but unscheduled election. Often it represents an effort by the nation's loyal opposition to make its influence felt upon the governing group. If their effort fails they are almost never denounced as traitors by the triumphant administration but, under the *noblesse oblige* of the system, are allowed to retire quietly into exile.

III

Several recent revolutions have demonstrated not only the seriousness of the social maladjustments which exist in Latin America but also the unsuitability of existing political systems to meet the problems which those maladjustments create. The revolutionary movement which resulted in the election of Juan Domingo Perón as president of Argentina in February 1946 was originally launched for the expressed purpose (among others) of overthrowing oligarchic control and effecting social and economic reforms. As suggested above, it followed the normal twentieth-century pattern of *caudillo* revolution, of which perhaps the best recent example was that of Getulio Vargas in Brazil. Just as Vargas, after seizing power by force in 1930, proceeded to introduce reforms by fiat and thus to build up powerful labor support for his régime, so Perón has sought to carry out a program of social and economic justice and has thus consolidated his position of leadership with the laboring and other underprivileged classes in Argentina. In executing this program he has been criticized for employing paternalistic and dictatorial methods which have denied political democracy and deprived even his followers of the means of complaint. Many Argentines fear that in the long run this policy will not create conditions of permanent political stability but rather will build up a revolutionary potential.

The revolution which overthrew President Isaías Medina Angarita of Venezuela in October 1945 came as the culmination of a movement for wider popular participation in government which had been growing ever since Juan Vicente Gómez's death in 1935. If the electoral base in Venezuela had been broader and a parliamentary system had been a part of the country's political pattern, Medina's government probably would have been retired from office peacefully some time before it was finally ousted by violence. Presidential elections were scheduled for April 1946. As they approached, the construction work on Medina's new palatial home in a Caracas suburb gave rise to rumors of personal graft. At the same time the hope for political reform and the amelioration of obviously worsening social and economic conditions evaporated. The president's popularity therefore declined to a low point. The constitution enabled only some 250,000 in a total population of more than 4,000,000 to vote even for municipal officials, and it contained no provision for direct popular voting for president. Medina had done little to broaden the voting base and nothing to prevent members of the national congress, which would elect the new president, from serving in his bureaucracy. Indeed, early in October 1945 he singled out an unusually large number of senators and deputies for appointment to lucrative posts in his administration. According to the leftist opposition, the result was a " patriarchal autocracy " of a personalist character constituting a " palpably fictitious democracy."

Inasmuch as the Venezuelan constitution prohibited the immediate re-election of a president, Medina selected as his successor his relatively little-known Minister of Agriculture, Angel Biaggini. This was interpreted as evidence of Medina's policy of *continuismo,* which violated the spirit of the constitution and was unpalatable to the opposition. The rightists immediately responded by nominating ex-President Eleázar López Contreras, who in the popular mind was identified closely with the remnants of the hated old dictatorial régime of Juan Vicente Gómez. Certain leftist opposition leaders, confronted by what they regarded as only a choice of evils and possessing no means of influencing the outcome of the election in the national congress, readied themselves for revolutionary change.

The revolution was spearheaded by a tightly organized group of disaffected young army, navy, and air force officers, but its political base rested in the small, efficient, socialistic, noncommunist opposition party, *Acción Democrática*. These two groups concerted their plans for the overthrow of the administration. After the revolution started, the young officers' group invaded the presidential palace, seized Medina and López Contreras, formed a revolutionary governing junta with a civilian, Rómulo Betancourt, as chairman, and eventually forced the two ex-presidents into exile. During the revolution, riots broke out in Caracas, many shops were looted, and the homes of Medina's cabinet members and of other leaders of his party were singled out for ransacking by the mob. Similar uprisings occurred in other Venezuelan cities, where, although *Acción Democrática* was notoriously weak, dissatisfaction with the Medina administration was sufficiently strong to incite them. By October 22 order was restored and the new régime was receiving testimonials of support. It then proceeded immediately to make arrangements for a new constituent assembly elected by universal suffrage and to inaugurate certain popularly supported economic and social reforms. These reforms were incorporated in the new progressive constitution which was adopted in 1947. By these means the new forces which have been dominant in Venezuelan political life since 1945 expect to enable Venezuela to become politically stabilized.

Other postwar revolutions in Latin America have resulted either in the adoption of new constitutions embodying similar democratic reforms or in the return to constitutional practices of a democratic nature which had been violated or ignored by the overthrown government. In Brazil, the fifteen-year-old dictatorship of President Vargas tried to recoup its declining prestige early in 1945 by announcing plans to democratize the country. Among his avowed aims were a free press, freedom of political organization, amnesty for political prisoners, and the promulgation of election laws. But then in October 1945 Vargas appointed as chief of police his brother, who was the leader of the forces urging the continuation of the dictatorship. The Brazilian army and people thereupon rose against him and brought the régime to an end. A provisional government headed by the chief justice of the supreme court took control and held free elections on December 2, which resulted in the inauguration of a constitutional administration with General Eurico Gaspar Dutra as President. Soon afterward a new constitution was adopted.

Another example occurred in Haiti in January 1946 when student demonstrations broke out against the government of President Lescot. The demonstrators demanded abolition of the state of siege, liberation of political prisoners, granting of freedom of speech and press, and holding of normal elections. Lescot was taken prisoner and the homes of members of his administration were looted. A military cabinet of three officers then assumed charge of the government and proceeded to hold free elections. These brought to power a civilian, Dumersais Estimé, as constitutional President in August 1946 and resulted in the promulgation of a new constitution.

A revolution in Bolivia in July 1946 caused the overthrow and murder of President Gualberto Villarroel. It was provoked by a succession of unpopular acts by the administration, including fraudulent elections on the previous May 5, the subsequent declaration of a state of siege throughout Bolivia, the assumption of absolute control over the Bolivian press, and a bloody assault upon students demonstrating against the government. The provisional régime which supplanted Villarroel announced that it would govern the country in accordance with existing constitutional laws pending a free election, which was subsequently held.

Constitutions alone cannot solve the social problems which beset the Latin American governments. It nevertheless is noteworthy that the new constitutions contain whole chapters dealing with public health, education, the rights of labor, and social security. Even if they are regarded only as piously hypocritical pronouncements which are not intended to be carried into effect, they at least show that deference must be paid to the new social forces in the politics of these countries.

It also is noteworthy that a few Latin American governments are tending to follow the example of Cuba, which since 1940 has had a cabinet responsible to congress. The presidents of these countries are constrained by political exigencies, even if not by constitutional mandate, to govern through cabinets whose members are in effect responsible to a congressional majority. This *de facto* parliamentary system does not guarantee that administrations will be free from oligarchic control, or that political corruption will be eliminated; but it broadens the base of government representation, exerts a democratizing influence, and is undoubtedly a deterrent to revolutions of the political type.

IV

Some of the above revolutions, though primarily political in character, showed overtones of the second general revolutionary type, the social. In this latter type, according to the Colombian publicist quoted above, " the very structure of human society . . . finds itself menaced by the presence of new and dark elements of dissolution and at times even of death. . . . Age-long injustices or tremendous tensions in human living conditions motivate and justify them." Such inversions of the social order have occurred in Latin America, but they have been rare. Domingo Faustino Sarmiento, describing one phase of Argentina's revolutionary war against Spain, wrote that " in less than twenty-four hours a fiddler had become a general, a lame cobbler was making laws, and a clown deciding the fate of a country." A better example is furnished by the successful War of the Reform in Mexico, fought to vindicate the socially revolutionary constitution of 1857 and led by Benito Juárez, a full-blooded Indian. Another is the Mexican Revolution which began in 1910 and which was associated with the names of Francisco Madero, Emiliano Zapata, Venustiano Carranza, Alvaro Obregón, and Lázaro Cárdenas. Of the revolutions which occurred in the depression year 1930 in Bolivia, Peru, Argentina, and Brazil, however, Professor Clarence H. Haring observed: " In no case were elements of a social revolution involved, although . . . the word 'Communist' was frequently bandied about by the vested interests to disparage the violence of their adversaries."

No event since World War II has so dramatically highlighted the factors making for revolution in this hemisphere or so vividly revealed the revolutionary potential that exists among our neighbors to the south as the abortive revolution in Colombia on April 9 last,

[1948]. Analysis of this incident will bring to a focus the generalizations made above, for, like a microcosm, it disclosed all the elements of Latin American revolution.

The movement within the Colombian Liberal party headed by Jorge Eliécer Gaitán represented a protest against the record and program of both the right wing of the Liberal party and the entire Conservative party. To the *Gaitanistas* neither the old-line Liberals nor the Conservatives seemed to offer any hope of redressing grievances or improving living standards. The reforms accomplished by the Liberal party while it controlled the presidency from 1930 to 1946 were considered the mildest of palliatives for the social sickness afflicting the mass of Colombians. The protest became articulate and importunate in Gaitán's unsuccessful campaign for the presidency in 1946. But though that campaign demonstrated the almost idolatrous fervor and surprisingly large strength of his popular following, it split the Liberal party and made possible the election of the Conservative candidate, Mariano Ospina Pérez.

The new president adopted a policy of national union against the determined opposition of the right wing of his own party. Recognizing the weakness of his own political position and the consequent necessity of deferring to the Liberal congress, he appointed and maintained a cabinet equally divided between members of the Liberal and of his own Conservative party. In the administration of the national government he thus in effect tempered the presidential system of Colombia with the parliamentary system by attempting to rule with a political coalition. The result, however, was neither the one system nor the other. The responsibility for government was not definitely fixed upon either the Conservative or the Liberal party. The cabinet did not truly reflect the congressional majority, since Ospina Pérez assigned the key positions in it to members of his own party and gave only the less important posts to the Liberals. On January 28, 1948, Senator Gaitán, chief of the Liberal party, was joined by members of the Advisory Board of the party in presenting a memorandum to Ospina Pérez charging that the president's policy of national union, with which they were in accord, was being violated by some of the president's closest collaborators. These, said the Liberals, were taking advantage of their positions to impose a reactionary pro-clerical educational system, to persecute organized labor, to perpetrate electoral frauds, and to instigate violence against Liberal party members.

Meanwhile the worsening economic plight of the masses of the Colombian people, aggravated by war and postwar dislocations, was exacerbating already serious social tensions and increasing popular dissatisfaction with the national administration. During 1947 the cost-of-living index in the captial, Bogotá, rose more than 30 points to a new high of 254.2 (calculated on a base of February 1937). These rises continued in 1948. During the single month of March 1948 the cost-of-living index for an average Colombian workingman's family rose by 17.3 points to a new high of 283.8 (calculated on the same base). In the capital, where preparations for the forthcoming Ninth International Conference of American States had an inflationary effect, the cost of living rose 20.6 points for the same period, reflected principally in sharp increases in the prices of bread, butter, milk, potatoes, fresh vegetables, and meat. Prices for shirts rose 25 percent. It became obvious that the Colombian Office of Price Control was powerless to curb speculation and prevent price inflation. Moreover, efforts of organized workers to secure wage increases commensurate with these increases in the cost of living appeared in several cases to be thwarted by government action.

As long as the government of national union continued, the Liberal party had to share the blame for these acts of omission and commission by the administration. On February 29, therefore, the party decided to withdraw its members from all positions in the national administration and thus to terminate the hybrid arrangement on the grounds that it no longer was satisfactory to the party or consonant with the Colombian constitutional system. " Our position is based on two postulates," explained Liberal leader Darío Echandía in a letter to the editor of *El Tiempo,* " that this is a democratic country and that it is a country with a presidential régime. As a democratic country, its government must adapt itself to the laws, that is, to the administrative norms or directives dictated by Congress; as a country with a presidential régime, the political composition of its government is independent of its Congress." He thus stated succinctly the fundamental dilemma between the concept of "a democratic country" on the one hand and the constitutional requirement "of a presidential régime" on the other.

Thenceforth Ospina Pérez, a minority president, exercised power only because the opposition respected his constitutional position under the presidential system. He was to find this a weak reed on which to lean. He was at once confronted with the alternatives of appointing either a cabinet dominated by Liberals — a decision which all factions of the Liberal party would undoubtedly have applauded — or an all-Conservative cabinet, which would obviously represent a stark return to the presidential system and which would consolidate control of the minority Conservative party over the executive branch of the government. He chose the latter course, and in constituting his all-Conservative cabinet brought into it as Minister of Foreign Affairs the titular chief of the party, Laureano Gómez, who through a long political career had fought the Liberal party, in season and out, as the party of radicalism, communism and anti-Christ. To the Liberals of every faction, therefore, Gómez was a hateful figure symbolizing aristocracy, reaction, and clericalism.

The assassination of Gaitán by an obscure taxi-driver ignited this combustible situation. The grief of rank-and-file Colombians over the death of their political champion soon gave way to rage, and rage to violent action against the government. The building housing *El Siglo*, Laureano Gomez' newspaper, was burned to the ground; with one or two exceptions every building used by the government was either gutted or burned; and even churches, closely interlocked in the public mind with the Conservative oligarchy, were sacked and in some cases burned. In other parts of Colombia, mobs which formed soon after the news of Gaitán's assassination was received descended upon Conservative newspapers and the homes and offices of Conservative officials. A general strike of all workers throughout Colombia was proclaimed by the Confederation of Colombian Workers, representing approximately 109,000 of the 165,000 organized workingmen in Colombia.

In the face of this appalling demonstration of mass opposition, as clearly revolutionary in spirit as in deed, Ospina Pérez declared a state of siege and later martial law, imposed strict censorship, and issued a statement charging that "professional agitators with express orders from Moscow" were responsible for the revolt. Finally on April 10 he announced the formation of a new cabinet which included six Liberal ministers. His solution to the problem of revolution in Colombia, therefore, was to return to the quasi-parliamentary system represented by his policy of national union. It remains to be seen whether the old formula of equal representation of Liberals and Conservatives in the cabinet will provide the democratic government and social justice which the Colombian masses obviously desire and which seem needed if the national tensions are to be relaxed.

V

Latin America is demanding democratic government and social justice. New leaders both of the right and of the left are making strong appeals to aggrieved individuals and frustrated social classes. In Argentina, President Perón, one of the first beneficiaries of the ferment of the *descamisados,* offers them material benefits which though satisfying to some seem to others to be purchased at the high cost of democracy. In Venezuela, *Acción Democrática,* and in Peru, *Apra,* or the People's party, offer programs of social reform within the framework of capitalism. Further to the left, in Colombia, Gaitán's program contains many elements of state socialism, such as communal ownership of property by indigenous groups, obligatory use of land near towns for the production of prime necessities, the establishment of state cooperatives, national and municipal ownership of public services, worker participation in company profits in certain fields, and close government control over the professions to insure equitable geographical distribution. To Gaitán's followers, liberty has come to mean the right of each man to the opportunity to work, equality has become economic and social democracy, and fraternity means the cooperation of men in production. The Communists, too, with a still more radical program, are making strong bids for leadership in many parts of Latin America and, while generally disdaining the "social scum" or *Lumpenproletariat* of Marx, are consolidating their position in leftist labor organizations. But, as the Liberal party leadership in Colombia declared in a recent statement rejecting the overtures of the Conservative party for the formation of an anticommunist front, "No responsible individual can accept the infantile opinion that the communist hand is at work in every demand for social justice."

Political leaders in Latin America often resort to revolution as a desperate means — sometimes, indeed, the only means — to achieve democratic government and social justice. The demand for these "goods" may be expected to grow in scope and intensity as the governmental machinery through which they should be achieved falters, as political leaders show ineptitude or apathy in promoting them, and as controlling minorities refuse to relax their stranglehold on the prevailing political and economic system. Just as protests against an oligarchic political system often result in a revolutionary overturn of government, so protests against an oligarchic social and economic system by the increasingly self-conscious and restive masses in Latin America may, under the influence of appropriate leaders, take the form of a struggle between classes and social overturn.

It is the tragedy of Latin America that, in the existing socio-political milieu, the process of transferring power from one *caudillo* to another, from one ruling clique to another, or from the few to the many (this last-named operation being essentially a democratic one) has so frequently been accomplished by revolutionary means because, in the judgment of the political opposition, it could not be accomplished otherwise. It is an equal tragedy that once revolutions fall into the hands of totalitarians they may develop in a direction inimical to the interests of the masses and in this way may defeat the basic objectives for which they were organized. To the extent that this occurs, in Latin America or elsewhere, such revolutions may be considered to run counter to the interests of the democratic peoples of the world.

No. 21 [One of the many political characteristics of Latin America which puzzles the North American is the relative ease with which a military or political clique displaces the government in power. Although many of the revolutions have been long, bitter, and sanguinary conflicts, rivaling our own Civil War in proportional cost, the majority have been changes effected by a small group acting in the national capital. Loss of life is small, there is little of the barricades and fighting in the streets, the life of the nation goes on almost undisturbed, and within a few days the new government appears to be firmly entrenched.

To one who is interested in the large problem of government and, consequently, in the manner through which changes in political power are brought about, the technique of the *coup d'état* is highly important. It is the more so in a region where it has been, and perhaps still is, the most important of the mechanisms for political change.]

The Technique of the Coup d'Etat in Latin America*

by KURT CONRAD ARNADE

*I*T would be absurd to suppose that some police chief or general heading a contingent of some twenty-five soldiers could walk into the Capitol, in Washington, declare himself and his friends the new " Board of Government," and follow his proclamation with the dissolution of Congress and promise of a new election. Such an action in the United States would be tantamount to lunacy. Why then is it possible in the capitals of South and Central America?

What, we ask ourselves, is the solution to the enigma which underlies the succession of political upheavals, plots, and counterplots which has characterized our good neighbors? We find no hint of political naïveté or intractability in our friends, the statesmen from these countries. On the contrary; in them we observe a finely drawn culture and a type of social philosophy which would seem to derive from stable and mature governments. Nor is there any hint of in-

* Kurt Conrad Arnade, " The Technique of the *Coup d'Etat* in Latin America," *United Nations World* (February, 1950), Vol. 4, No. 2, pp. 21–25. Reprinted by permission of *United Nations World*.

stability in the agreements and treaties of these countries, documents drafted with such sagacity and refinement of detail as to dim the thought that internal violence in these countries was even a remote possibility.

Why then do the perennial Latin American *coups d'état* meet with such docile acceptance? What becomes of the high-ranking officers and police officials who have sworn fealty to the constitution of the country? What is the role on such occasions of the members of Parliament and of the Supreme Court?

There are a number of answers to these questions, but all hinge on the cardinal fact that Latin American countries today, with the exception of Uruguay and Chile, are nominal but not actual democracies. It would be more in the line of reality to speak of them as oligarchies — in the classical Greek sense of the word. Their democracy is essentially a democracy of the upper classes. Rule is essentially centered in a circle of large landowners, influential families, and militarists. This circle controls the press and radio, molds public opinion, and dictates political policy.

The so-called revolutions are for the most part intestine affairs, not involving issues outside the circle. Motives for political violence in these countries are usually found in such transient factors as injured vanity, personal insults, competition between personalities or business interests within the group. The conflicts are virtually never concerned with broad or significant national issues; they seldom reflect the antagonism between left and right, labor and management, or socialism and capitalism.

The recent revolution in Panama [1949] is a case in point. Dr. Chanis, the legally elected president, and Colonel Remon, the chief of police, had long been personal enemies. The Panamanian Supreme Court had handed down a decision disbanding certain monopolies, including the one affecting slaughtering. According to charges later made by Dr. Chanis and others, Colonel Remon was himself a large stockholder in these enterprises. But whether or not this is true, Colonel Remon refused to enforce the court's order. He responded, instead, with a *coup d'état.*

In Cochabamba, Bolivia, I was once witness to a revolt instigated by Colonel Peño y Lillo, commander of an influential officers' training school. The revolt was entirely without political significance.

The motivating factor was a personal one. Colonel Peño y Lillo had served in the Chaco war against Paraguay. His record was that of an efficient officer, competent organizer, and a gentleman. But since his organizing ability had been utilized almost exclusively for supply rather than combat activities, rumors — in my opinion completely unjustified — were circulated to the effect that he was a coward.

It was Colonel Peño y Lillo's belief that his commanding officer, General Quintanilla, was responsible for the rumors. When, after the war, General Quintanilla became President of Bolivia, Colonel Peño y Lillo sought revenge. The revolt was the expression of his sense of personal injury.

The oligarchic nature of Latin American governments is abetted by the fact that large segments of the population take no interest in politics.

The majority of the inhabitants of these countries live in remote and often scarcely accessible areas. To reach the polls, long journeys are often necessary, sometimes through jungles, across bridgeless rivers, and along roads impassable during bad weather. Why go to all that trouble? And for what? Most of the citizens of Latin American countries have learned through experience that elections are a tweedledum-tweedledee affair, and that a change in government means only a change of the men in power — not of conditions affecting their daily living.

This is not to say that there is not in Latin America a large liberal and politically-mature group to which the corruption and social incompetence of such governmental opportunism is abhorrent. This group, however, perhaps because of its importance in the face of intransigent realties, has acquired an ivory tower attitude, and for the most part takes refuge in professional work or travel abroad.

REVOLUTIONS REPLACE WARS

The number of wars in Latin America, in contradistinction to the number of revolutions, has in the course of several centuries been small — especially when considered in the frame of reference provided by Europe and Asia. The long period of peaceful training embellished only with tactical maneuvers and occasional parades does not satisfy the urge for activity of ambitious and energetic officers.

These men look for additional outlets for what in the military sphere would correspond to the artist's " creative urge."

One of the most intelligent officers I have known was the Bolivian Major Armejo, who in the course of his long career had been obliged to spend most of his time with small garrisons in such remote places as Charana, on the Chilean frontier, high in the Cordilleras, and Choretti, an outpost in the steaming, disease-ridden jungle.

During his years of service with these isolated garrisons, the radio and books were his only bridge to the outside world. Lack of contact with society and with a cosmopolitan spread of ideas made him, as well as his fellow officers, susceptible to the new doctrines being voiced by Hitler and Mussolini. To them radical political activity of any sort spelled escape from their tedious life of inaction, isolation, and seclusion.

As a result of this isolation and pent-up desire for activity, Major Armejo eagerly welcomed every opportunity to become involved in *coups d'état* and revolutions. He usually was given a mild punishment and sent back to a post even more remote where he plotted and planned anew until the next political upheaval came into view.

So far we have considered the role of high-ranking officers in the periodic uprisings. But what of the subordinate officers and the rank-and-file soldiers, all of whom have taken oaths to support the constitution? What of the civilian officials? Why do they not oppose the breach of constitutional procedure and violation of the oath to which they are committed?

To this there is a simple answer. The subordinate military personnel and government officials are voiceless pawns in the major operation, and they know well what it will mean to them to be on the lists of the losing party. For military men in the lower ranks, an unlucky affiliation means transfer to a back-country garrison and loss of promotion; for higher ranking officers and civilian officials it means discharge and loss of pension. It follows that alignment with the winning group is a matter of paramount importance in terms of position and security. Where revolts have only a slight chance of success, military subordinates affiliate themselves with their commanders, and put faith in the device so often utilized by Nazi underlings: " Orders are orders, and it is a soldier's duty not to question but obey."

Another form of opportunism is employed by military personnel and civil servants in communities remote from the scene of action. During uprisings it is usually the policy of hinterland officials to ignore government orders and notices. Everyone, in fact, is quite happy when regular communications are interrupted by the revolutionaries. At such moments, no news is good news, and permits officialdom to adopt a safe Fabian policy. Many functionaries so isolated declare themselves neutral, in order to be " on the side of the people " no matter which faction wins.

A TYPICAL POLICE CHIEF

I once had an opportunity to observe such diplomatic tactics at close range. News had come to the small Bolivian town in which I was stationed that a revolt led by young officers had developed in the capital. I asked the police captain in my precinct if he had enough arms and ammunition to maintain order throughout our area.

" Colonel," he replied, " as you know, I am a loyal police officer and will always carry out my orders. But first, I am sorry to say, I don't know anything about the revolution. Second, about the ammunition: I sent yesterday most of our firearms to Headquarters for cleaning and repair — because they were in bad shape. If Headquarters doesn't send them back, there is nothing I can do."

When we compare the cyclic revolutions which occur south of the Rio Grande with revolutions in other parts of the world, we can distinguish a special design stamped, perhaps, with the words, " Made in Latin America." About 85 percent of the Latin American revolutions are relatively bloodless and of short duration because they lack the interest and active participation of the masses. When, however, the people's interests are involved, as in Bolivia's *Revolución Libertadora* of 1946, which was a struggle to overthrow a cruel and oppressive régime, the upsurge assumes the turbulent form which characterizes all struggles of liberation, the classical examples of which are the French and Russian Revolutions. But even in such revolutions, the aftermath of terror and bloodshed ends more quickly.

THE GRAND STRATEGY OF THE JUNTA

The strategy of most Latin American revolutions follows a formal and almost standardized pattern. The new government, or more properly, "*Junta de Gobierno*," is formed well in advance of the actual uprising. Key men are selected for all strategic offices. Other supporters, usually former diplomats, are planted in the capitals of other countries to negotiate a speedy recognition of the new "democratic" government, once the *coup* has been accomplished. Lines of retreat to countries friendly to the plotters are also established, making a swift exit possible should plans miscarry. In today's revolution it is also fashionable to import from the United States trained air force "mercenaries," who can double in civilian air transport capacities, once the revolution has been effected.

Preparatory techniques usually include use of the old Roman principle of *Columnare audactor, semper aliquid haered,* that is, "Always slander, something sticks." Stories attacking the government in power are invented and given wide circulation. Time-tried themes are the corruption of the officials, privileges accorded favored business interests, and treaties entered into by the government which run contrary to the sovereignty, economic welfare, or democratic traditions of the country. Small details are exaggerated and distorted until they appear as major crimes. The junta strikes before the slanders can be neutralized by counter-propaganda.

The following is an illustration of this technique: Some years ago Bolivia's dictatorial President Busch confiscated certain oil lands which had been leased legally to the Standard Oil Company. Extensive litigation was the consequence. A later government, under President Peñaranda, ended the protracted and embarrassing litigation with a gentlemen's agreement acceptable to both sides.

President Peñaranda's enemies at once made capital of what was actually a masterful act of commercial diplomacy. He was accused openly of treasonable sale of national rights, and a story — an outright fabrication — was circulated to the effect that Peñaranda and his Secretary of Foreign Affairs were direct personal beneficiaries of the settlement.

A few weeks later a serious strike developed in one of the mines. The local police were not equipped to maintain order in the mine area and consequently were reinforced with a battalion of infantry. It is customary for troops in such situations to use only blank cartridges when called on to fire, the sound of the fire being sufficient to restore order without bloodshed. In this instance, however, Major

Villaroel, chief of the operations section of the general staff and a secret conspirator, saw to it that blank cartridges were replaced by live ammunition. When the troops were ordered to fire on the strikers a considerable loss of life resulted. The conspirators, including Villaroel, then accused the president of " wanton murder."

Revolutions are scheduled almost invariably for holiday or Sunday afternoons. At such times official offices are empty, and the president and department chiefs out of communication with one another.

I once received an invitation to attend a party at the house of a high government official. On entering the house I discovered that the junta had originated the invitation, and, after assembling the entire government in one reception room, locked the doors and assumed power.

On another occasion, I went to an airfield to meet a president returning from a state visit abroad. As I was waiting, together with a police official, word arrived that armed revolutionary officers in civil dress had surrounded the field and were waiting to take the president prisoner. A message was radioed the president to continue his flight. No action could be taken against the officers because no overt action had taken place.

CAN REVOLUTIONS BE STOPPED?

Illustrations of this nature can be cited by the hundreds. But what conclusions do they lead to? How can the United Nations or friends outside Latin America aid in establishing political stability and guarantees of constitutional democratic procedures in the countries to the south?

There are no easy answers. Latin American political factors are derivative of other internal factors, including problems of economy, communication, education, population groups, and terrain. External diplomatic or economic pressures can in no way alter the internal structure of these countries.

I would like to cite an example of a typical Latin American revolution. On December 20, 1943, a small group of young Bolivian officers, stimulated by the examples of Hitler and Mussolini, formed a secret *loggia* with some seventy members. The announced aims of the *loggia* were (1) eliminating corruption from government, (2) extension of communications, (3) construction of new railroads,

(4) universal education, (5) absorption of Indians in national life and abolition of discriminations, (6) land reforms.

An inner circle consisting of fifteen officers — the future *Junta de Gobierno* — had been formed, and this was charged with establishing a program for dictatorship, directing a campaign against democratic political parties, and effecting cooperation with extreme rightist elements.

PLOTS, AGENTS, EMERGENCIES

A campaign of slander had been launched against the government some weeks previously, and the government, observing the traditions of free speech and a free press, had taken no steps to offset it. Finally, when it became obvious to the government that foreign agents were implicated in these activities, a state of emergency was declared. This was taken by the conspirators as a signal for revolt.

On the afternoon of Sunday, December 20th, at exactly five o'clock, the central communications building in the capital was seized by a small group of technicians especially trained for this task by Major Ponce, leader of the conspirators. Regular telephone and telegraph services were permitted as usual, but all communications with offices of the government, city, and police were interrupted. Within fifteen minutes all police stations in the city, operating as they were with diminished holiday personnel, were taken over by the revolutionists. A squad of officers then entered the relatively unprotected presidential palace and placed the president under arrest. Other members of the government were arrested at their homes or at points to which they had been summoned by various ruses.

The same procedures were followed in the provincial towns of Oruro, Cochabamba, and Santa Cruz. Here the conspirators were merely waiting for word from the capital to the effect that operations had succeeded according to plan. In Cochabamba, where I lived, the city and government officials were confined in the building of the war academy, and youngsters who the day before had been students and subordinates, suddenly found themselves the jailers of their teachers and superiors. The revolution was completed in seven hours. Not a single shot was fired.

I personally escaped imprisonment by a stratagem. For some days I had been suffering from a cold. When the officers came to arrest me I suggested that they keep some distance away from me inasmuch as I probably had a diphtherial throat infection. The heroes at once backed out of the room, promising to send an army doctor the following day.

WHAT PRICE LOYALTY?

When the doctor finally was announced, I put an open wallet containing two hundred pesos on my night table. The doctor observed the pesos and immediately declared me dangerously ill and not able to withstand transportation. When he departed the two hundred pesos left with him.

An hour later I heard over the radio an announcement that the new government — the one which the army doctor had diplomatically praised during his visit — would now definitely suppress all corruption.

I was satisfied.

No. 22 [An earlier essay in this chapter indicated that many of the revolutions in Latin America, initiated, led, and carried to a successful termination by a small group or *junta* had, as their primary objective, the displacing of a dictatorial régime. Others were caused by the desire to overthrow an administration which was threatening vested interests by its social and political reforms, an administration which we would say was " democratic." Unfortunately, many of the revolutions of the first category resulted in little more than the substitution of one dictator for another, and those of the second type had, as their primary objective, the establishment of a less democratic political society. Latin American revolutions seem to result in either setting up new dictatorships or continuing old ones. One writer has characterized government in Latin America as " dictatorship tempered by revolution."

Mr. Humphreys, in his contribution to this book, " Democracy and Dictatorship," wisely warns us that the conventional distinction between democracy and dictatorship cannot be applied to this area of the world. He counsels that we examine not so much the form of the government but rather the kind of authority it exercises, and in whose interests power is used.]

Democracy and Dictatorship*

by R. A. HUMPHREYS

FROM the revolutionary wars the Spanish American states emerged weak and exhausted. Their peoples had passed from tutelage to independence. But they had yet to comprehend and organize the freedom they had won. They had achieved statehood but not nationhood, and for self-government they were ill equipped. " We are still too little elevated from servitude," wrote Bolívar, " to rise easily to the proper enjoyment of liberty." The masses, oppressed by poverty and ignorance, were indolent, docile and savage by turns, and almost entirely illiterate, and for them independence meant a change of masters, not of systems. The new ruling minority, the creole aristocracy of landowners and lawyers, was undisciplined and untrained; it was, as Bolívar observed, " without practice in public affairs." There was no organized public opinion and no middle class to give stability to politics. For fifteen years the exercise of authority had been fitful and violent; and the wars of independence had encouraged the military, not the political virtues. The new states, moreover, or many of them, were huge, and the problems of their administration complex. Their centers of population were remote from one another and the means of communication slow and hazardous. Regional rivalries divided them. Local chieftains competed for power. The brave new world which idealists wished to build was contradicted by the facts of the political and social order. Nations cannot be founded on political theory.

Yet political theory ruled. The machinery of constitutional government has always exercised a peculiar fascination in Latin America. Nowhere are constitutions more elaborate — or less observed; and the founders of the Spanish American republics attempted to establish a pattern of freedom in charters which combined the Declaration of the Rights of Man with the machinery of the Constitution of the United States. The American Constitution was the great

* R. A. Humphreys, *The Evolution of Modern Latin America* (New York: Oxford University Press, 1946), pp. 69–86. Reprinted by permission of the publisher. The footnotes in the original version are omitted here.

exemplar of liberty. But it was the letter and the form of the Constitution rather than its spirit which so strongly appealed to its Latin American imitators. In the United States the fathers of the Constitution were concerned not to make America safe for democracy but to make democracy safe for America. Power was limited and divided, checked and balanced. The controlling principle was the rule of law; and the Constitution was itself the expression of a great moral and legal tradition, deeply rooted in seventeenth-century political thought and eighteenth-century colonial experience. These roots were lacking in Spanish America. The Spaniards are a highly individualistic people. The dignity of the individual is with them a passionate belief. This sense of personal dignity was as true of the Spaniard in America as of the Spaniard in Spain; but it was combined with the traditions in government of a paternal autocracy and a centralized absolutism; and the absolutism which Spanish constitutional theory predicated of the Crown, French revolutionary doctrine predicated of the people. While, therefore, the form of the American Constitution was in any event ill adapted to the needs of the new states, except perhaps in Argentina, and to the capacities of their peoples, French revolutionary thought triumphed over American Constitutional theory. The Latin American dictator was the natural and inevitable product.

The contrast between form and reality, between logic and life, between theory and experience, could hardly have been more complete. " The codes consulted by our law-givers," wrote Bolívar in 1812, " were not such as could instruct them in the practical science of government, but rather the inventions of well-meaning visionaries, who, thinking in terms of ideal republics, sought to attain political perfection on the supposition of the perfectibility of the human race." " Until our compatriots," he observed, in his famous Jamaica letter in 1815, " acquire the political talents and virtues which distinguish our brothers of the north, entirely popular systems, far from being beneficial, will, I very much fear, come to be our ruin." " Is it conceivable," he asked, " that a people but recently freed from its chains can ascend into the sphere of liberty without melting its wings like Icarus and plunging into the abyss? " The states of Spanish America, he believed, were not yet suited to " perfectly representative institutions "; they needed " the kindly guardianship of paternal governments " which would heal " the sores and wounds of despotism and war."

There can be no question but that Bolívar was right. History and experience alike supported him, and, like John Adams and Alexander Hamilton, Bolívar perceived that democracy is not necessarily synonymous with liberty. Of the unfettered exercise of the popular will he entertained a profound distrust. It is, he affirmed in 1820, in words which John Adams himself might have written, " a recognized principle in politics that a completely democratic government is as tyrannical as a despot. Thus, only a tempered government can be free." This was the explanation of his ardent and freely expressed admiration for English institutions and practice, and of his feeling, which San Martín also shared, for the principle of the rule of law. The judicial power, he remarked, in drafting his constitution for Bolivia in 1826, " is the measure of the welfare of the citizens; if there is liberty, if there is justice, they are made effective by this power. At times, the political organization has little importance, provided that the civil organization is perfect, if the laws are rigidly enforced and considered as inexorable as destiny."

San Martín's solution of this political problem was monarchy; and it may well be argued that the survival of the monarchy in Brazil was at least in part the explanation of Brazil's peaceful constitutional evolution in the nineteenth century. There was no abrupt break with the colonial past, no long struggle for the control of the instruments of government, no " anarchistic equalitarianism." The constitution of 1824, which survived for sixty-five years, recognized facts, if it ignored ideals — some ideals. But Brazil was a fortunate exception. There the monarchy was of native growth. It was consolidated without long and bitter wars. It possessed, from the first, trained administrators, and it was peculiarly happy in the character of the second emperor, Dom Pedro. But, as Bolívar realized, what was possible in Brazil was not feasible elsewhere. The argument against the establishment of monarchical régimes was not that they would have meant " a hierarchy of churchmen, landlords, mine owners, and wealthy merchants, with a following of lawyers, physicians, army officers, and the like." For this, in point of fact, is very much what nineteenth-century society in most of the Latin American countries tended to be. Nor was it that there were no possible candidates who might have been tempted to aspire to New World thrones. But a monarch imported from abroad, or a monarch elevated at home, could not have survived. Maximilian of Mexico was to be the tragic example of the first, Iturbide of the second. Haiti is the only other Latin American country to have established monarchs, but their fate can hardly be called happy, or their example inspiring.

Monarchy, then, was rejected, though it had many adherents and there were long and intricate negotiations now with this scion of a royal house and now with that. But rejected also were Bolívar's elaborate attempts to secure what was in fact a constitutional monarchy in disguise; and with anguish and despair the greatest of the Latin American dictators, nearing his tragic end, watched the spectre of anarchy rising from the ruins of empire. "There is no faith in America," he wrote in 1829, "neither between men nor between nations. Treaties are only papers; constitutions, books; elections, combats; liberty, anarchy; and life, a torment."

In parts of Latin America, indeed, society itself seemed on the point of dissolution. In Argentina, in the 1820's, the national government disappeared. In 1820, the "year of anarchy," the province of Buenos Aires alone had at the least twenty-four governors. Local government fell into the hands of local *caudillos,* the *gauchos,* whom it took a *gaucho,* Rosas, to subdue. The nineteenth and the twelfth centuries, wrote Sarmiento, dwelt side by side, one inside the cities, the other outside them.

All interests, all ideas, all passions, met together to create agitation and tumult. Here was a chief who would have nought to do with the rest of the Republic; there, a community whose only desire was to emerge from its isolation; yonder, a government engaged in bringing Europe over to America; elsewhere, another to which the very name of civilization was odious; the Holy Tribunal of the Inquisition was reviving in some places; in others, liberty of conscience was proclaimed the first of human rights; the cry of one party was for confederation; of others for a central government; while each different combination was backed by strong and unconquerable passions.

Buenos Aires alone retained a certain degree of stability, which it owed principally to Rivadavia, and promised in 1824, to form the nucleus of an ordered state; but not only did Argentina make war against Brazil, the provinces made war against Buenos Aires and one another; and the natural and inevitable opposition between Buenos Aires and the provinces — the one the proud city dominating the life and commerce of the republic, the others, jealous of its power and scornful of its manners, and strongly imbued with the sense of local independence — was long to give meaning and form to Argentine history.

Across the River Plate, conditions in the Banda Oriental of Uruguay, long coveted both by Argentina and Brazil, were equally chaotic. If ever a state was born of war and international rivalries, that state was Uruguay; and of its life after independence was achieved the Uruguayan historian, Zum Felde, has remarked: " The leaders could readily agree on a general principle and declare: Nothing must separate us. And promptly they would be separated." Chile, it is true, attained to relative order by 1830, after having lived under five constitutions in twelve years, and Paraguay, under the iron despotism of Dr. Francia, enjoyed peace, if little else, for more than a quarter of a century of almost complete isolation from the outside world. But Bolivia, after an attempt to subjugate Peru, was engulfed in anarchy, and the political heirs of Great Colombia seemed set on a course to justify Bolívar's despairing words: " I believe all lost for ever and the country and my friends submerged in a tempest of calamities." Nor in Mexico and Central America was the prospect much brighter. As constitutions followed constitutions and presidents followed presidents in bewildering succession, the Spanish American states, rent by factional and regional strife, seemed destined to move, in monotonous rhythm, from an excess of anarchy to an excess of despotism.

Dictatorship was inevitable, even necessary. The conditions of life, physical and economic, the essentially hierarchic structure of society, its racial composition, its traditions, were alike inimical to the working of representative institutions. Three centuries of colonial experience were not to be obliterated by twenty-five years of revolutionary dogmatism. From one point of view, indeed, the dictators who so early arose were as much the expression of the Spanish American revolutions as Napoleon was an expression of the French Revolution. From another, dictatorship represented the triumph of experience over theory. It was the tradition of personal rule that survived, reinforced by that pretorianism which was the inevitable legacy of the revolutionary wars. The army was the immediate, if not the ultimate, support of the ruling faction of the governing oligarchy or of the dictator which replaced it; and though it is, apparently, colonels and majors, rather than generals, who now make revolutions, the tradition of barrack-room intervention in politics dies hard. Nor was it difficult to legalize despotism. Even where constitutional forms were observed, the constitution tended to make the president strong, and circumstances to make him stronger. Where, as in most Spanish American countries, dictators, at one time or another, assumed the " sum of power," it needed only a little manipulation to establish their legal authority or a plausible and easily found excuse to pose, with Messianic fervor, as the restorers of the laws and the constitution.

All the Spanish American states, without exception, have experienced periods of violence and tyranny, some of prolonged violence and prolonged tyranny. Rosas ruled Argentina for twenty-three years before he was overthrown to die in exile near Southampton. Francia's " reign of terror " in Paraguay endured for twenty-six years. Gómez was the master of Venezuela for twenty-seven years and Díaz of Mexico for thirty-four. It would be folly to assume that these absolutisms were wholly unpopular. Rosas, the greatest and the worst of the Argentine tyrants, ruled by terror, but he ruled also with the support of the rural masses. Francia's despotism was founded on the determination of the creoles of Asunción to preserve their independence against Buenos Aires and on the veneration which he inspired among the Guaraní and mestizo peasantry. Díaz enjoyed the support of the landowners, the Church, and the army, as well as a distinguished reputation abroad. Even Francisco Solano López, who, whatever interpretation may be placed upon the origins of the Paraguayan war, bears a fearful responsibility for that struggle, and led his people along a road of serfdom, blood, and tears, retained their loyalty to the hideous end, and is not now without honor in his own country.

There were autocrats who waded through blood to presidential thrones, ignorant adventurers who perpetrated unspeakable crimes. But not all dictators were tyrants, for though, as Lord Acton has remarked, " absolute power corrupts absolutely," there were relatively good as well as wholly bad dictators, and some, even among the worst, by breaking and molding lesser despots to their will, helped to substitute a larger conception of the state as a nation for the agglomeration of personal and local loyalties which hindered its action and restrained its growth. Nor is it possible to dismiss the history of a continent during a long period merely as the history of dictatorship tempered by assassination and revolution, to believe that all the protagonists in this drama were actuated " by no other motive than a desire for self-aggrandizement, and their respective supporters by nothing save a desire for booty," or to brush contemptuously aside the efforts of the Spanish American peoples to establish their liberties by written constitutions as *palabras y nada más.*

For the Spanish Americans cherish their freedom. In Latin America persons have always mattered more than programs, and parties were, and are, as much the expression of personal loyalties as of political principles. The dictators themselves were personal rulers; there was not, and could not be, that regimentation which has been the foundation of the modern totalitarian state. It was an excess of individualism which, in the guise of a conflict between Centralists and Federalists, Clericals and Anticlericals, Conservatives and Liberals, gave such bitterness to party strife and sundered the rivers of the republics' life. And beneath this turbulence, life followed its old customary pattern. Politics was a way of life and of making a living remote from the control and interests of the masses. The majority were, and were content to be, spectators of events, indifferent to the form of government, provided government did not too arrogantly trespass on the affairs of the governed. Even revolutions, those established extralegal habits of replacing one régime by another, were often parochial affairs.

It is [wrote W. H. Hudson, in 1885, of one of the then most chaotic of Latin America countries, Uruguay] the perfect republic: the sense of emancipation experienced in it by the wanderer from the Old World is indescribably sweet and novel . . . the knot of ambitious rulers all striving to pluck each other down have no power to make the people miserable. The unwritten constitution, mightier than the written one, is in the heart of every man to make him still a republican and free with a freedom it would be hard to match anywhere else on the globe.

These general conditions obtained at one time or another in all the Spanish American republics, and in some the conventional patterns of politics is still little changed. Intentions may be good; but the forces of inertia are too strong, the struggle for power is too ardent, and the problem of administrative efficiency too great. Hence oligarchy gives place to dictatorship and dictatorship to revolution. But the differences in the political evolution of the Latin American states are at least as great as the resemblances, and far more significant. The basis of their future national differentiation already existed during the colonial period, in race, in custom, and in administration; and the Bourbon reforms in the eighteenth century themselves stimulated a regional self-consciousness and a local nationalism. Paradoxically, the territorial definition of the new states was already vaguely fixed before the wars of independence began. But the transition from statehood to nationhood, and all that that implies, was a longer and far more complex process than that from colony to republic; dictatorship was, apparently, and may still be, an essential element in it; but it followed different lines in different countries; it is still imperfectly understood; and it is not yet by any means complete. The so-called "nationalist movements" in Latin America are born not of the assurance of national unity but of the absence of assurance.

In South America three states early established for themselves a position of marked superiority. Brazil, under the rule of her scholar-emperor, Pedro II, was, in her imperial form, her "peculiar institution" of slavery, her generally peaceful internal evolution, *sui generis,* until, in 1889, a bloodless revolution deposed the emperor and prepared the way for the establishment of the federal republic. In Chile the reign of the *caudillos* virtually ceased with the adoption of the constitution of 1833, and under the dominance of a landed, but not always enlightened, aristocracy, Chile evolved a relatively stable political order and a remarkable quasi-parliamentary system. Argentina's institutional organization was confirmed when, in 1861, the battle of Pavón, fought between the army of Buenos Aires and the forces of the Argentine Confederation, established in 1853, resulted in "the definitive union of all the Argentine provinces"; it was finally consummated by the federalization of the city of Buenos Aires itself in 1880. In each of these countries the immigrant and immigrant capital were, in lesser or greater degree, transforming influences; in each, economic progress was accompanied by a widening of the basis of society and of politics, the rise of new social forces, a new industrial aristocracy, a middle class, and organized labor; and what wheat and meat were to Argentina, cotton and then coffee were to Brazil and nitrates and copper to Chile. Yet, in the face of the world economic crisis, each returned to violence as well as fraud in politics. Chile's political life was plunged into confusion. Brazil, which had abandoned monarchy for republic in 1889, abandoned constitutionalism for dictatorship in 1930. Argentina, whose politics had undergone a progressive liberalization since 1890, retrod a well-worn path in the 1930's and finally, in 1943, frankly exchanged the ballot box for the barrack room.

Three other countries, Colombia, Costa Rica, and Uruguay, emerged at the end of the nineteenth century from conditions of instability or dictatorship to develop democratic or quasi-democratic institutions, though only in Colombia has there been no interruption in this peaceful constitutional evolution. Here a devastating civil war, from 1899 to 1902, caused "incalculable losses. On the battlefields 100,000 men or more perished; thousands were maimed for life; commerce was ruined." Colombia then, in 1903, suffered the loss of Panama. Yet these were the last disasters to overtake the republic, and thenceforth its history was "happily, not spectacular and only conspicuous for those qualities which need no record." [The picture was abruptly changed in 1948.] On the whole, since the fall of the last dictator, who retired into voluntary exile in 1909, elections have been genuinely fought and peacefully won, and have resolved themselves into contests between Clerical Conservatives and mildly Anti-Clerical Liberals, who, though much given to divisions between themselves, have held power since 1930, have served the Church from the State, and have pursued a policy of moderate social reform; and, more, perhaps, than in most Latin American countries, the conflict of political parties represents a genuine conflict of political principles.

Costa Rica, with the advantages of a comparatively homogeneous population, a high degree of literacy, and a considerable number of small landowners, has also succeeded since 1902 (with a brief interval between 1917 and 1919) in solving its problems by constitutional methods, in notable contrast to its Central American neighbors. Indeed, so vigorous is political debate in this small nation-state that it may be argued that the average Costa Rican is, if anything, too politically minded. Finally, Uruguay, like Colombia and Costa Rica, dates its peaceful democratic development from the turn of the century. Of the twenty-five governments which ruled, or failed to rule, Uruguay between 1830 and 1903, " nine were forced out of power, two were liquidated by assassination and one by grave injury, ten resisted successfully one or more revolutions, and three were free of serious disturbance." But since the first term of its great President, José Batlle y Ordóñez (1903–07), the republic has undergone a remarkable transformation. From one of the most backward of the South American countries it became, with a few years, one of the most vigorous and most progressive. As the state entered into business and industry, and embarked on a program of state socialism and advanced labor legislation, Uruguay offered to the world the example of the first " New Deal " in the Americas.

Uruguay's constitutional evolution, however, like that of Argentina, was interrupted in the 1930's, when President Terra, in 1933, dissolved congress, carried out a *coup d'état,* convoked a constituent assembly, and secured a new constitution. President Terra's excuse for this procedure was the need for decisive action in meeting the world economic depression, which struck Uruguay with great severity, and the inability, as he alleged, of the somewhat cumbersome constitutional machinery then existing to provide such action. But its result was deeply to divide Uruguay's two traditional political parties against themselves; and an arrangement in the new constitution, which entitled the largest minority party not only to representation in the senate but also in the cabinet, placed a premium on political obstruction and in turn led to further extraconstitutional action in 1942 and fresh constitutional revision. To the observer from outside, Uruguayan politics are apt to exhibit a scene of extraordinary confusion, heightened by the polemics so freely indulged in by the press. But there can be no question of the attachment of the Uruguayan people to the processes of democratic government.

Chile, Colombia, Costa Rica, and Uruguay are the countries of Latin America which most nearly approach to the true type of representative democracy; and to this type Argentina until recently also conformed. They enjoy vigorous political debate; elections are something more than a formality; and the press is free. All four have attained to a relatively high degree of social coherence, and in them the transition from statehood to nationhood has definitely been achieved. Yet only Chile and Uruguay have benefited to any considerable extent by immigration, and only Costa Rica and Uruguay are predominantly peopled by a pure white strain. Geography as well as history has imposed a certain unity upon Chile, and Uruguay and Costa Rica are small and compact. But Colombia is one of the larger Latin American states and it is still underpopulated. In Costa Rica the system of landholding has been favorable to the evolution of political democracy, but this is certainly not true of Chile; and while in Uruguay and Costa Rica there is a high degree of literacy, it is far less high in Chile and Colombia. Those who seek a common factor to explain a similar movement of civilization in different countries at the same time may, perhaps, find it in the growth, through economic diversification and industrialization, of a middle class; yet the economy of all of these countries, even including Chile, is still primarily an agrarian economy, and in none has diversification proceeded far.

The remaining states of Latin America all profess a common democratic faith; but this is the substance of things hoped for rather than the evidence of things already seen; and for some of the republics democracy, as a form of government, means little more than republicanism. Some, such as the Dominican Republic, El Salvador, Nicaragua, Honduras, and Guatemala, are dictatorships undisguised, or only lightly camouflaged, though in Guatemala, General Ubico, the dread and envy of his neighbors, who had ruled his country with an iron hand since 1931 and ruled it not unwell, was overthrown in 1944 by a " democratic " movement. General Ubico described himself as a " Liberal Progressive," and certainly had some claim — not shared by all his Central American colleagues — to the latter epithet. But the limits set by the social and economic structure of these countries, and by the low educational and cultural level of the politically inert masses, themselves define the form and quality of their governments. Even in Central America, however, dictators now prefer to prolong their power by " constitutional " means, if possible, through amendments to the constitutions or by the staging of plebiscites.

Elsewhere in Latin America the outward forms of political democracy are somewhat more scrupulously preserved. Mexico, like Brazil, is in a class apart. The machinery of representative and responsible government there exists and to some extent functions, and political democracy in Mexico, limited and halting as it is, is not a meaningless phrase. Cuba, which held unprecedentedly free elections in 1944, operates, somewhat precariously, a semiparliamentary system, and Venezuela, which endured, till the death of Gómez in 1935, one of the most oppressive dictatorships in Latin American history, has moved from absolute tyranny to relative freedom. Peru is to outward appearance a democracy, but the party with the greatest popular appeal, the *Alianza Popular Revolucionaria Americana,* was . . . banned from formal participation in politics, and the traditions of the ruling class are inimical as much to the theory of democratic government as to its practice.

Politics, indeed, in the Andean republics of Peru, Ecuador, and Bolivia, where the Indian masses are inert and apathetic and the bulk of the population is illiterate, are still the monopoly of a privileged minority; and behind the political disorder which has characterized Bolivia, Paraguay, and Ecuador, lie the solid facts of ignorance and poverty and of social and economic incoherence. Paraguay has barely recovered from her devastating war (1865–70) with Brazil, Uruguay, and Argentina, in which two thirds of her people perished, and still less from her conflict with Bolivia (1932–35); and the tragic sequence of politics in Bolivia is heightened by the sense of bitterness and national frustration of a country which lost in one war its Pacific coastline to Chile and failed in a second to secure an outlet to the Atlantic from Paraguay.

There is no sealed pattern of democracy. If democracy means merely a particular form of representative government, then, in Latin America as a whole, it is an aspiration rather than a fact, and not everywhere an aspiration. But the conventional distinction between a democracy and a dictatorship is no sufficient criterion by which to judge the working of government in the Latin American states. Democratic governments as well as dictatorial governments may be tyrannical; and a dictator, no less than a parliamentary assembly, may claim to voice the will of the people. The real question which should be asked is not whether the form of the government is democratic in the conventional sense, but whether the authority it exercises is absolute and arbitrary or whether it recognizes the existence of limits to that authority and is characterized by a fundamental respect for the rights of the individual; and in this sense democracy in Latin America is not meaningless. The Latin American countries have been subjected to arbitrary rule, but the demands which the rulers have made upon the ruled have rarely been total. Dictatorship has been formless rather than systematic. There is, indeed, a broad tolerance of life which has so far prohibited the organization in the New World of the totalitarian structures of the Old. The temperament of the Latin American peoples does not easily lend itself to regimentation, and in a very real sense democracy in Latin America has been, if not a form of government, at least a habit of mind and a climate of opinion.

Yet it remains true that the social structure of the majority of the Latin American states is profoundly undemocratic, and there can be no political democracy without a measure of social democracy. The patriarchal organization of colonial society has shown, indeed, an astonishing capacity for survival. The economy of all the Latin American countries is primarily an agrarian economy in which landownership means control of the major instrument of production. The dominance of the *hacienda,* the great landed estate, has not only fostered the stratification of society; it has tended to perpetuate a concentration of political power in the hands of small minorities. Not only, moreover, in the Indian and mestizo countries do the Indians themselves form a society within a society, and a society whose conduct is governed by a pattern of life and a scale of values fundamentally different from those of the surrounding civilizations, but throughout Latin America the educational and cultural level of the masses of the people and the general standards of public health are extraordinarily low. The average *per capita* income in Latin America is probably less than $100 a year, and in the cities as in the rural areas, except in a few favored regions and industries, the standard of living of the urban and rural workers is often far below that required for the maintenance of a decent level of subsistence.

These are not the conditions favorable to the growth of political democracy. The challenge to the traditional pattern of Latin American society, however, has been made, and the age-old struggle between town and country is being transformed into a clash between a new commercial and industrial civilization and an old agrarian way of life. The dominance of the *hacienda* has been directly challenged in Mexico; it is indirectly challenged elsewhere by the changing pattern of economic life and the rise of new social forces. It is true that the middle class in all the Latin American countries is still relatively small. It is true also that the number of Latin American workers who are effectively organized is by no means large, though the trade union movement, under the guidance of the Confederation of Latin American Workers, now transcends state boundaries and is a force increasingly to be reckoned with. But the effect of these newer social forces is illustrated not merely by the enactment of labor codes, social insurance legislation, and national planning and development schemes, but by the rise of new political parties; and it is significant that the twentieth-century constitutions of Latin America all reflect, in more or less degree, a preoccupation with social problems as well as with political, and that labor legislation, partly no doubt for nationalistic reasons as well as social ones, preceded rather than followed trade union organization.

But the path of social reform, as experience has too tragically shown, may be the road to serfdom as well as freedom. It was a new and ominous element in Latin American life when some of the Latin American dictators, like the late President Busch of Bolivia, imported the language of National-Socialist doctrines; and the theory that bad elections and good government are preferable to good elections and bad government is a dangerous one. Though, moreover, there has been evident an increasing approximation between constitutional aspirations and political practice, and a greater adaptation of political theory to social needs, the tendency in all the Latin American states is toward the concentration and centralization of power. The constitutions reflect indeed the fear of presidential dictatorship; but the fact of presidential power is everywhere apparent, and even in the federal republics, though federalism is a theory, centralization is a fact. Finally, the problem of administrative efficiency, a problem which has long perplexed the Latin American countries in the absence, in most, of a highly trained, disinterested civil service, is more easily resolved, in the short run, by authority imposed from above rather than by that arising from below.

It is primarily to the operation of economic forces and to the rise of the new industrial aristocracy and the new middle class that such fusion as has been attained between the feudal and democratic traditions in the political fabric of Latin America has been due. On the capacity and honesty of these classes and of organized labor depends the extent to which that fusion can become complete. But it is foolish to assume that higher standards of living, bathrooms, refrigerators, and electric light automatically make for democratic habits; and meanwhile it would obviously be unwise to ignore the danger to the stability of existing institutions or to the future of representative government arising from the " extremist fringe " of politics, on the left and on the right, and in that zone where left and right mingle, and exemplified in particular in so-called " nationalist " groups, which draw their support from army leaders, old-fashioned conservatives, current ideological doctrines, and idealistic or disillusioned youth.

It is in any event certain that nationalism, both political and economic, will be one of the forces molding the future, and socialism another. But what direction these and other forces now at work in Latin American society will take it is impossible to foresee. Their manifestation is not uniform. It may be that the experience of Mexico will be repeated in some at least of the other republics and that suppressed social discontents will burst into conflagration. The forces of nationalism and socialism could be harnessed together in the service of the totalitarian state. It is possible also — and the experience of the past affords some hope for the future — that democratic development may follow the lines of traditional liberalism. The Latin American states are now a laboratory of political, social, and racial experiment, and the transformation which is in progress is only in its beginnings. Future developments depend not only on changing conditions in Latin America but on the conditions of world change. But the issue is no longer the simple issue of democracy or dictatorship; it is the larger issue of freedom or servitude.

PART FOUR

The

Organization
and Institutions
of Government

CHAPTER 8

Federal or Unitary Governments?

No. 23 [When the newly independent Latin American states began to chart their own governmental organization and political course one of the problems that received most attention and discussion referred to the basic distribution of political authority. Should the new states be organized on a unitary basis, with all power to act lodged in one central government, or should the example of the United States be followed and a federal system established? Many Latin American students of government have maintained that this is the most basic and most important aspect of government in their countries. Some have asserted that the cause of the failure of early governments to maintain order was due to the exaggerated federalism that was ordained by the original constitutions. Provincial *caudillos* could, and did, constitutionally resist the policies and programs of the central authorities. Others have asserted that the failure to establish federal systems ran so counter to local or regional feelings that separatism was encouraged, *caudillos* shrewdly built their power on this local resentment, and that the " age of the *caudillos* " is largely explained by the existence of unitary governments. It cannot be denied that the whole question of " federalism " is one that is basic in an understanding of the problem of government in Latin America.

Inasmuch as geographic, demographic, economic, and social factors have emphasized separatism in many of the Latin American states, and because of the fact that these states in their colonial organization and experience were all highly unitary, the problems of federalism in Latin America are in many aspects unique. Some of the republics originally established federal systems of government and have clung to them. Others have shifted back and forth between unitary and federal political organization. Still others have maintained unitary governments since the dates of their independence.

The following discussion lays the groundwork for the sections which follow. Why *did* some of the republics originally adopt the federal form of organization? What is the general picture of the place of federalism in Latin America?]

Federalism in Latin America*

by C. H. HARING

THERE are four so-called federal republics in Latin America: Argentina, Brazil, Mexico, and Venezuela. . . . [One of them] Brazil, is represented as coming by a federal organization legitimately; the other, Mexico, as an artificial creation. Between the other two republics, Argentina and Venezuela, the same distinction may be drawn. Argentina has been genuinely, perhaps inevitably, federalistic; in Venezuela, since the middle of the nineteenth century, federalism has been imposed by doctrinaire thinkers, political theorists, who considered federalism the ideally perfect form of democracy; their country therefore must have it, at least on paper.

Federalism was also tried for short periods of time in several other republics: in Colombia for about thirty years before 1886; in Chile for a few years in the first decade of its independent history; in Central America immediately after independence, when the provinces of the former captaincy general of Guatemala tried to hang together

* C. H. Haring, " Federalism in Latin America." Reprinted from *The Constitution Reconsidered*. Edited for the American Historical Association by Conyers Read. Copyright 1938 by Columbia University Press.

under a federalist régime, provinces which have dreamed ever since of recovering their former unity. In Peru, under President Leguia's constitution of 1919, a step toward federalism was taken in the establishment of three regional legislatures with limited powers. But as these three regions were not considered to be sovereign entities, perhaps we should not call this federalism. In one country, Bolivia, because of the strength of local, particularist sentiment and jealousies, and the wide separation of centers of population, one might have expected to find an outcropping of federalism. But such, as a matter of fact, possibly for a variety of reasons, has not been the case.

One might surmise that in the four present-day federal republics, this form of government would be most effective in the nations in which the development was a natural one — and this seems to be borne out by the observations of history. Federalism has been more effective in Argentina and Brazil than in Venezuela and Mexico. In both of these latter countries presidential autocracy, more or less disguised, has been the rule. Constitutional forms have generally been used, or misused, merely to maintain in office, whether in the national or state governments, a small political clique dominated by some great *caudillo.*

None of the Latin American nations was prepared for a federal organization when the day of independence arrived. They had always lived under a highly centralized régime, under viceroys or captains general appointed by and responsible alone to a despotic sovereign in Europe. And at the end of the colonial epoch, with the administrative reforms introduced by the Spanish Bourbons, especially the system of *intendentes,* this centralization was greater than ever before. The contrast between the situation in the Latin American communities and that in Anglo-Saxon America was patent enough, and has often been stressed by historians. Yet the example of the new federal republic in North America — and, interestingly enough, of Mexico in the 1820's — was very powerful, in spite of the counterattractions of the highly centralized, bureaucratic organization which Napoleon· had devised for France, and with which some of the early Latin American political thinkers were familiar. And as every patriot wanted the very best for his own country, regardless of any consideration of its appropriateness to the social, material, and geographic conditions prevailing in that country, it was probably inevitable that in some places the federal experiment should be made — as happened even in Chile in the years 1826–28. Federalism and liberalism were considered by many as virtually synonymous; centralism and conservatism were the cause of all evils.

[Another part of this chapter discusses the factors which made federalism inappropriate in Mexico.] . . . Some of them prevail still in some areas of Latin America. They still constitute obstacles to the federal union of the Central American republics. And in Colombia two generations ago they led to disaster — almost to the political dissolution of the republic.

One disqualification could be pleaded more easily a hundred years ago than it can today: that is, the utter and complete lack of political experience among those who devised the first constitutions — inexperience in formulating the terms of the constitutional document, and inexperience in administering the institutions which that document provided for. There was an abysmal ignorance of political science, and a fatal attraction of words and phrases in place of genuine political principles. Words and phrases still play an unmerited role in all societies, whether Latin or Anglo-Saxon. But the educated classes of Latin America have now a century of experience behind them — often a bitter one — and that experience is reflected, not only in the increasing stability of Latin American governments (taking a long view of their history) but also in the greater realism reflected in recent constitutional changes — as in Uruguay, Chile, and Colombia during the past two decades. A century ago, however, men of political experience and administrative ability were rare. There were too few to provide the personnel for a centralized administration, let alone for the more scattered and complex machinery involved in the government of a group of federalized states.

Brazil today [1938] seems to be at the crossroads. She has just passed through — or entered upon — a crisis in her political history. Highly decentralized in spirit and organization during the three centuries of colonial rule, on achieving independence from Portugal she happily retained a monarchical form of government under a prince of the Portuguese royal house. But it was a centralized monarchy, and one of its weaknesses was the stress and strain caused by the persistence of provincial sentiments and ambitions. When the monarchy was overthrown in 1889, the republic which took its place, as was to be expected, was a federal republic, with a constitution fashioned after that of the United States. Yet provincial jealousies persisted, an equilibrium between the states was not attained; and this is the basic explanation of the revolution of 1930 which put Getulio Vargas in the presidency.

After four years as chief of a provisional government under which federalism was practically nullified, and over three as president under a revised federal constitution, Vargas chose in November, 1937, to declare himself dictator, for reasons best known to himself. Although a hastily written temporary constitution imposed by presidential decree declares Brazil to be " a Federal State constituted by the indissoluble union of the [existing] States, Federal District and Territories," the opportunities for presidential interference and control are unlimited, and in Brazil today federalism is virtually nonexistent. What the future will bring forth no one can tell. At least I have no aspirations to the role of prophet. And the censor in Brazil takes good care to keep from us any information concerning the actual state of public opinion in that country at this moment. The Brazilians are a liberty-loving people, and the republic till now has been a loose federation of autonomous states jealous of their rights. Whether President Vargas can maintain a centralized, dictatorial government sufficiently strong to overcome the historic particularism of Brazil is a major question — and I have my doubts.

The Latin American republic in which federalism is presumed to have functioned most successfully is Argentina. The Rio de la Plata region in colonial days, it is true, was no more decentralized in government than was any other part of the Spanish American empire. But certain circumstances made for the existence in 1810 of a strong local, particularist sentiment: the scant population of the country, and the separation of the various centers of population by great open spaces dominated by hostile nomad Indians; the very recent promotion of Buenos Aires to be the political capital, residence of a viceroy; its ambition to dominate the interior provinces, which till then had been more closely allied with Chile on the one hand and with Upper Peru on the other; its ambition also to dominate the up-river provinces, which till then had enjoyed equal contacts with the outside world, so as to force them into economic dependence upon the one great seaport; the consequent absorption by Buenos Aires of the financial and commercial activities of the country, causing the interior provinces to experience a notable decay; also the monarchism of the Porteño leaders, the success of whose plans would have sealed the hegemony of the capital on the Rio de la Plata. Buenos Aires as the symbol of a traditional loyalty the other provinces had at least endured; they saw no reason why the inhabitants of Buenos Aires should constitute themselves the sole heirs of the monarchy.

It was pre-eminently these circumstances which made possible the rules of the provincial *caudillos,* and the anarchy that prevailed during the years immediately preceding Rosas and during most of the time that he dominated the country. The educated urban class was inclined toward unitary principles of government, but the country at large remained steadfastly federalist. When the constituent assembly, dominated by Buenos Aires, in 1819 produced a centralized constitution, most of the provinces repudiated it. In 1826 followed another constitution which provided for a limited amount of decentralization through the deliberations of provincial assemblies. The governors, however, were to be appointed by the national executive, and there was no pretense of sovereign states' rights. Again it was repudiated, and upon the ruins of a civil war Juan Manuel de Rosas imposed a dictatorship extending over the entire country. Yet he always considered himself to be a federalist — most of the members of the unitary party he killed or drove into exile. He believed that his stern rule, by destroying the disruptive, centrifugal forces represented by the provincial *caudillos,* was a necessary preliminary to a national federalist organization. Meantime the *Pacto Federal,* a treaty drawn up and subscribed to by the provinces of Buenos Aires, Santa Fé, and Entre Rios in 1831, remained the sole legal evidence of national union.

Thus the federalistic provinces, outmaneuvered in the constituent congresses of 1819 and 1826, awaited only the elimination of the greatest of the *caudillos,* Rosas, to organize the country definitely on a federal basis in 1853. All parties, *Porteño* or *Arribeño,* in this respect at least were of one mind. Or perhaps it would be more accurate to say that the educated classes, relieved of the incubus of Rosas, took refuge in federalism as the only formula by which the country could be united other than by a dictatorship. And the constitution they devised, under the inspiration and leadership of Juan Bautista Alberdi, reflected more closely that of the United States than has the constitution of any other South American nation. It happens also to be the oldest surviving constitution south of the Rio Grande.

One observes today in Argentina the same course of development as in the other two effectively federalist states of America, the United States and Brazil: that is, the tendency of the federal government to increase its authority and influence at the expense of " states' rights." In Argentina it has been more marked than in this country. It is due in part to the poverty and social backwardness of many of the autonomous provinces, and to the concentration of the wealth and intelligence of the nation in the great city of Buenos Aires. There has been a marked inclination of all the provinces, rich and poor, to lean more and more heavily upon the national treasury. The federal government has for years made grants to the less-favored provinces for internal improvements, such as irrigation works in the country and sanitary systems in the towns. During the past thirty years it has participated more and more in the support and control of primary and normal schools, a responsibility which under the constitution should belong to the provincial governments; so that educational progress in the country at large is due almost entirely to the initiative and activity of the government in Buenos Aires. Very recently, in 1934, when the system of taxation was remodeled and simplified, the federal government assumed entire responsibility for collecting most of the internal taxes formerly belonging to the provinces. The proceeds are now distributed to the provinces on a quota basis, adjustable every ten years. This radical innovation has resulted in more efficient administration and in largely increased revenues. The provinces have profited greatly. Yet it only emphasizes the propensity to federal encroachment upon provincial autonomy. And it has the effect of giving to the national administration an undue, if not overwhelming, influence in the politics of many of the provincial governments.

I said that in most of the Latin American states after independence political experience and administrative ability were too uncommon to provide for the effective management of a decentralized, federalist type of government. The remark applies also to Argentina. The economic and social stagnation, the lack of population and resources, of many of the provinces carry their inevitable corollary of political disorders. Domination by selfish and corrupt political bosses or cliques, with consequent graft, bribery, intimidation, or open violence, are only too common. They are the signs of a raw and incipient democracy.

And this has given excuse for frequent interventions by the federal government — in Argentina as in Mexico and Brazil — intervention permitted by the Argentine constitution (as by our own) to maintain a republican form of government in the several states. In recent times in Argentina it has been used chiefly for ulterior purposes: to displace provincial governors and the members of provincial legislatures unfriendly to the national administration, and to put the province under the rule of a federal *interventor*, who in the succeeding elections will see to it that individuals acceptable to the national government are chosen. Owing to the vagaries of provincial politics, pretexts are generally not difficult to find. The device was used in a wholesale manner by President Irigoyen after the Radical party for the first time came into power in 1916 — twenty interventions during the six years of his first administration. But it has been used in equally scandalous fashion by the Conservative minority which ruled the republic before 1916 and which has been in control again since the revolution of 1930. The most recent and one of the most notorious instances has been the federal intervention in the important province of Santa Fé, from October of 1935 to the middle of 1937. It prepared for, and helped to make easier, the Conservative victory in the national elections of . . . September [1937]. Federal intervention is one of the abuses of Argentine political practice which makes impossible that equilibrium between the federal and provincial governments which was anticipated by the members of the constituent congress eighty-five years ago.

Whether the federal form of national organization was the most desirable for Argentina in 1853, and since, may easily be questioned. That it was the necessary basis of any common agreement among the politically conscious elements in the nation at that time, it would be difficult to dispute. But the whole course of Argentine political evolution — at least since 1880, when Julio Roca became president — has been in the direction of centralization, of a unitary type of government; or perhaps, one might better say, of that mixed type which, stopping short of provincial sovereignty, combines centralized control with decentralized administration, and which was the ideal striven for by Bernardino Rivadavia and his unitary allies in 1826.

As Dr. Rodolfo Rivarola wrote, as early as 1908, in the preface of his volume *Del régimen federativo al unitario,* "La palabra *federación* ha perdido ya su acepción etimológica; solamente la *unidad* expresa a la vez el orden, la fuerza, y la justicia." ["The word *federation* has now lost its etymological acceptance; only *unity* expresses at once order, strength, and justice."]

No. 24 [Reasons of size, population, diversity of economic activity, and internal political tensions seem to indicate that Brazil is one Latin American republic in which a federal organization furnishes a logical answer to the query: How should the nation be organized?

Professor Martin, in the following essay, describes the genesis and evolution of the federal idea in Brazil and analyzes its constitutional expression in the constitutions of 1891 and 1937. The emphasis is given to those factors which have made it difficult to apply the theory and the practice of federalism to that republic. Although his article was written eight years before the adoption of the 1946 constitution it is by no means dated. All of the factors which he discusses were re-examined in the constituent assembly which met at Rio de Janeiro a few years ago. Article 7 of Chapter I of the current constitution, as well as many other chapters and articles, indicates the great importance of federal-state relations in Brazil and the persistence of the conflict between federal and state authority. The new constitution is but another effort to achieve a working and workable harmony between the central government and the twenty states which comprise the nation.]

Federalism in Brazil*

by PERCY ALVIN MARTIN

Federalism occupies a place of major importance in our political history. It has been the constant, unswerving objective of our political evolution for four centuries. It is the dominant preoccupation of the country. Despite delays, dissimulations, attempts at suppression, it has finally emerged triumphant. It is the necessary solution of our political organization. It is the salvation of our national unity. It is the guarantee of our national progress.

THUS wrote in 1914 Dr. Levi Carneiro, one of the foremost writers on constitutional law in Brazil, a member of the Brazilian Academy of Letters and of the Brazilian Historical Institute. If federalism plays in the evolution of Brazil anything like the role assigned it by Dr. Carneiro, a brief survey of its historical development is surely worth making. In the following paper, the writer will examine the genesis of Brazilian federalism in the colonial period, trace its development through the stormy days of independence, note the manner in which it was modified under the empire, and consider its emergence for good or ill under the republic. Finally, an attempt will be made to consider its place in the new Constitution of 1937. Throughout, allusions will be made to the influence of the United States and its Constitution.

There are not lacking authorities who allege that the first organization of Brazil, that of the hereditary feudal captaincies, contained the germs of federalism. Something is to be said for this contention if we consider decentralization and particularism elements of federalism. Of much greater importance, however, is the fact that in the majority of cases these captaincies were identical in their boundaries with the later provinces and the states in the federation today. The significance of this situation will be emphasized later. Had the system of hereditary captaincies succeeded, Brazil might eventually

* Percy Alvin Martin, "Federalism in Brazil," *The Hispanic American Historical Review* (May, 1938), Vol. XVIII, No. 2, pp. 143–163. Reprinted by permission of *The Hispanic American Historical Review*. Published and copyright by the Duke University Press. The footnotes in the original version are omitted here.

have split up into a number of independent units even as happened in Spanish America. But as early as 1548 a royal decree created the office of governor general, and all of Brazil was brought directly under the control of the metropolis. From then on the royal administration became increasingly centralized.

For reasons which we cannot take up here, something like a national consciousness began to appear in Brazil well before the end of the colonial period. Many of the Brazilians — as we may call them now — found the complete subordination of the colony to the capital increasingly irksome. The first attempt to break away from the leading strings of Portugal was the so-called conspiracy of Tiradentes which took place in the captaincy of Minas Geraes in 1789. Its importance for us lies in the fact that the example of the United States was prepotent among the conspirators, who were well acquainted with the labors of the Constituent Convention of Philadelphia. The plot was crushed with quite needless severity. While we may sympathize with the conspirators, we may rejoice at the outcome. Federation, had it been applied at this time, would have spelled the breakup of Brazil, whose inhabitants at the cost of enormous sacrifice had laid the foundations of national unity.

The advent of Dom João and the Portuguese court to Brazil in 1808, though it brought no immediate change in the status of the captaincies or provinces, powerfully reinforced the idea of unity and eventually made possible the formation of a great empire. But this same unity — the achievement and maintenance of which may be regarded as the greatest accomplishment in the whole history of Brazil — was threatened from an unexpected quarter. In 1820, a revolutionary movement broke out in Portugal. The Côrtes of Lisbon, though loud in its protests of liberalism, wished to reduce Brazil to its former status of colonial dependence. It set about to suppress such autonomy as existed in Brazil and, on the Roman theory of divide and rule, endeavored to make the various captaincies directly dependent on the mother country. Under such conditions nothing short of complete separation from Portugal could have saved Brazilian unity and the liberties which the Brazilians had enjoyed since the coming of Dom João VI. Accordingly, in 1822, the young Dom Pedro, the son of Dom João VI, formally proclaimed the independence of Brazil.

The new ruler, known as Dom Pedro I, possessed sufficient political acumen to realize that a full return to the absolutism of the eighteenth century was impossible. Throughout most of America and in parts of Europe constitutions were regarded as the great panacea to the political ills then afflicting the world, and Brazil could not escape the contagion. A constituent congress was elected in 1823 and in a few months produced a constitution providing for a limited monarchy. Although the term federalism was nowhere mentioned in this document, the subject had been discussed during the sessions of the congress. Federalism had its fervent defenders, men who had read widely and in some instances had traveled abroad; many of them were familiar with the Constitution of the United States. But it was the opinion of the great majority that in these critical times the chief *desiderata* were unity and independence, and that for these boons the firmest guarantees were to be found in a centralized monarchy.

Dom Pedro, whose conversion to liberalism was only skin deep, soon found himself at odds with the constituent assembly. The tension reached such a point that he dismissed this body in November, 1823, and the constitution, the fruits of its labors, was destroyed. Realizing, however, that the setting up of an absolutist régime might mean the loss of his throne, he ordered his Council of State to prepare an instrument "twice as liberal" as the one he had rejected. As a matter of fact, the Constitution of 1824, under which, with certain modifications, the empire was governed until 1889, contained most of the liberal features of its predecessor. Nowhere in the document is the term federalism mentioned.

The dissolution of the constituent assembly and the rejection of the constitution of 1823 were ill received throughout large parts of the empire. Especially was this true in Pernambuco, where seven years earlier a rebellion had flared up against the arbitrary government of Dom João VI. The conviction was general that a constitution should be not the gift of the ruler but the expression of the popular will. The new Constitution, that of 1824, was therefore unacceptable. The leaders frankly avowed themselves federalists. A so-called "Confederation of the Equator" was launched in Pernambuco, and the various provinces in northern Brazil were asked to join. Singularly enough the juridical basis for the confederation was supplied by the constitution of Colombia and not that of the United States. For a number of reasons, into which we cannot enter, the rebellion was short-lived. Had the movement succeeded, large parts of Brazil would have been organized on the basis of a federal republic with the consequent break-up of the unity of the empire. It may be noted in passing that federalism was apt to be associated with the revolutionary movements in Brazil whenever their purpose was the establishment of a republic.

As this paper is concerned only incidentally with the narrative history of Brazil we shall pass over in silence most of the events of the reign of Dom Pedro I (1822–31). The Emperor's increasing despotism, his dissolute life, and the ill-success which attended his war with Buenos Aires caused him to lose favor with his subjects. It is interesting to note that the strength of federalism grew in proportion to the decline of the popularity of Dom Pedro. As the reign was approaching its twilight, the Emperor undertook a journey up into Minas Geraes to bolster up his cause. In the capital, Ouro Preto, he issued a blunt proclamation in which he characterized federalism (*federação*) as a crime against the constitution and a violation of the oath which the Brazilians had taken to defend it. But the appeal fell upon deaf ears. On his return to Rio he found that his unpopularity had reached such proportions that he determined to abdicate in favor of his young son, the future Dom Pedro II, an act which was consummated on April 7, 1831.

For the next nine years Brazil was governed by a regency. As may readily be imagined, it was a period of intense political activity both within and without the national assembly. Three parties appeared in the arena of combat: the *Partido Restaurador,* which desired the return of Dom Pedro I to the throne; the *Partido Republicano,* which came out squarely for the overthrow of the monarchy; and the *Partido Liberal.* This last party was in favor of the monarchy but insisted on the need of a number of reforms to the Constitution of 1824. The liberals soon split into two sections: the *Moderados* and the *Exaltados.* It is the latter group with whom we are particularly concerned as they were the sponsors of a federative monarchy.

Did time permit, a fascinating study could be made of the debates which took place in the chamber of deputies at this period on the subject of federalism. The discussion centered about the grant of a larger degree of autonomy to the provinces. The debate in the session of September 9, 1831, is especially illuminating. Carneiro da Cunha refused to be frightened by the idea of a federal type of government, declaring that " federalism already exists, though more or less concealed." Carneiro Leão emitted the opinion that if the federal system were adopted it should be accompanied by a new division of the provinces, thus removing the disadvantages growing out of their enormous disparity in size and resources. The idea was freighted with possibilities; the later history of Brazil was to show that, had this project been adopted, some of the country's worst political ills might have been exorcised. Deputy Hollanda declared that the unity of Brazil was bound up with federalism, and that the Constitution of 1824 was in effect federal in principle. He added that " whoever is not a federalist is not a constitutionalist." The debate continued throughout the better part of 1832. Finally, the assembly (chamber and senate) passed a law on October 12 granting future legislatures the right of amending the constitution in the sense that the provincial councils might be converted into provincial assemblies.

In the bill as finally passed the expression " federative monarchy," which had been employed in the debates, was carefully avoided. The famous Marquez de Barbacena, speaking in the senate on this point, declared:

The word *federativo,* which is not even Portuguese, will be the apple of discord among us. The friends of constitutional monarchy shudder whenever they hear it; the friends of a federal republic conceive false hopes; the enemies of Brazil take advantage of the opportunity to promote intrigue and disunion to our detriment.

But the idea of federalism would not down. For this the United States was in part to blame. The example of the North American republic, strong, prosperous, the component parts united by a federal bond, exercised on many Brazilian writers and public men an enormous fascination. To such an extent was this true that in the legislature of 1834 the deputies Cornelio, Antonio, and Ernesto Ferreira Franco introduced a bill providing for the creation of a federal union between Brazil and the United States. Two or three articles of this legislative curiosity are worth quoting:

Article 1. Brazil and the United States will be federated (*federados*) for the purpose of mutually defending themselves against foreign pretensions and will aid each other in the development of the internal wealth (*propriedade interna*) of both nations. . . .

Article 3. Each one of the nations shall be represented in the national assembly of the other.

Article 4. The products of each nation shall be received in the other in the same manner as its own, free from all imposts.

As was to be expected this fantastic project died a-borning and never came to a vote.

The most important step ever taken in Brazil in the direction of federalism prior to the establishment of the republic was the adoption of the so-called *Acto Addicional* of 1834. Though containing a number of important provisions, this important amendment to the Constitution of 1824 is chiefly of interest to us through the fact that it provided for an increased grant of autonomy to the provinces. In place of the general councils, which up to that time had been simply consultative in character, there were set up in each province legislative assemblies with a large sphere of action in provincial matters. The assemblies were to be unicameral, with members elected for a term of two years. The most populous provinces were to have thirty-six members; the remainder from twenty-eight to thirty. The creation of these assemblies was undoubtedly a step toward decentralization and was thoroughly in line with the aspirations of the federalists. But when the out-and-out federalists proposed that the presidents of the provinces should be elected instead of being appointed by the Emperor, the act was rejected by the national legislature.

There can be little doubt that at this period the agitation for federalism constituted a disintegrating force in Brazil. Under the regency and during the first decade of the rule of Dom Pedro II, the hard-won unity of the empire stood in jeopardy. The most striking proof of this contention is revealed in the long revolution which, from 1836 to 1846, devastated the rich province of Rio Grande do Sul. This revolution of the so-called *Farrapos* has been the object of an immense amount of investigation, especially in 1935, the centenary of the outbreak of the struggle. There is no complete unanimity among Brazilian writers as to the purposes of the leaders of the revolt, the most serious internal menace which the empire ever had to face. A number allege that the rebellion was aimed at the complete severance of the province from the empire, and they point to the establishment of the republic of Piratiní as the proof. But the burden of opinion is that the rebellion had as its goal federation rather than separation, and that even the sponsors of the so-called republic really aimed at forcing the imperial government to grant a larger amount of autonomy to the province. It is significant that, when peace was finally made in 1845, the most impelling motive was the need of a united front against the machinations of Rosas, the dictator of the Argentine Confederation.

As has already been intimated, the *Acto Addicional* represented the greatest triumph obtained by federalism under the monarchical régime. The consequences of this measure in the political life of Brazil were profound. By granting the provinces legislative power, even in a restricted field, it afforded them a means of voicing their aspiration and of solving many of their most pressing local problems. It was in the provincial assemblies that many of the most noted statesmen of the empire — particularly deputies and senators — made their debut in political life. The establishment of this equilibrium between the provinces and the central government helped to make possible, decade after decade, the smooth functioning of the imperial machine.

Following the winding up in 1845 of the great civil war in Rio Grande do Sul, federalism ceased for over two decades to be a vital issue in Brazilian political life, and the subject was rarely raised in parliament. This was owing partly to the fact that aspirations for provincial autonomy were in part satisfied, partly to the absorption of the interest of the Brazilians in other fields. The writer, Agenor de Roure, remarks in this connection that federalism did as a matter of fact exist in practice though the term was carefully avoided. He characterized the system as one of limited federalism (*federação limitada*).

In 1868, the question of federalism once more came to the fore, partly as the result of discord within the so-called Progressive party which had been governing Brazil since 1868. From this schism arose what might be called the new Liberal party, which, under this traditional name, was to last until the fall of the empire. The leaders of this party had had as one of their objects the curtailment of what they regarded as the arbitrary and despotic power of the Emperor which they wrongly supposed the source of political corruption throughout Brazil. One means to this end was the further increase of local autonomy "to free," as one writer put it, "as rapidly as possible the local centers and provinces from the intolerable pressure of the power of the crown," which "like a new Briareus was extending its hundred arms over the entire nation."

At this point we see the first clear evidence since the 1830's and 1840's that federalist propaganda was taking on a decidedly antimonarchist tinge. There was a considerable group, especially of the younger writers, who considered the expression "federative monarchy" a contradiction in terms. The majority of the leaders of public opinion still saw nothing anomalous in the development of a full-fledged federal system within the confines of a liberal empire. In 1868 was launched the program of the Liberal party; it included a long list of demands among which were freedom of instruction, curtailment of the faculties of the Emperor through the abolition of the moderative power, the extinction of slavery, election of police in the municipalities, and what for our purpose is most important, the election of the presidents of the provinces. Many of these demands harked back to the early 1830's; as we shall presently see, some of the most important were to be revived in the 1880's.

Presently a new constellation rose above the political horizon. In 1871 appeared the Republican party which had as its avowed aim the overthrow of the monarchy. In its manifesto, issued in December of the same year, much attention is, as we should expect, devoted to federalism. One paragraph is worth quoting:

Long before the idea of democracy arose in Brazil nature charged herself with the establishment of the federative principle. The topography of our territory, the different zones into which it is divided, the variations in climate and productions . . . indicate the direction which administration and local government should follow. The divisions created by nature and imposed by the immense extension of our territory should be respected.

The Republican party never rose to a position of major importance under the empire. None the less, its influence was considerable. Though the number of its adherents was small, they included some of the ablest writers and thinkers of the time, many of whom occupied high posts after the overthrow of the monarchy. At all times and in all places it placed federalism in the forefront of its propaganda. For example, one of the most active of the Republican leaders in Rio Grande do Sul, Venancio Ayres, launched a newspaper with the title of *Federação*. Each number played up the caption " Federation spells unity; centralization, dismemberment." Running true to form these propagandists held up as a model the Constitution of the United States.

During the decade 1878–88 federalist agitation suffered a temporary eclipse. The reason was a simple one. These were the years when the campaign for the abolition of slavery reached its maximum intensity, culminating, as is well known, in complete emancipation in 1888. But after the passage of the *lei aurea* on May 13 of this year, federalism once more leaped to the fore. Among the champions of the movement two stand out head and shoulders above the rest. The famous Joaquim Nabuco, orator, parliamentarian, and above all abolitionist, threw himself heart and soul into the campaign. With equal zeal the cause was espoused by Ruy Barbosa, a brilliant journalist and later recognized as one of the greatest jurisconsults ever produced by Hispanic America.

Nabuco was a monarchist and at the same time a liberal. He acknowledged no inconsistency in the idea of a federal empire. " The truth of the matter is," he wrote in *O Paiz* at the time, " that today there is only one reform which can forestall the coming of the republic and this is autonomy of the provinces." Years later, when speaking of the last days of the monarchy, he declared: " I counseled the acceptance of federalism, and had the crown accepted my advice it might have been saved." It was his conviction — an erroneous one as events fell out — that with the satisfaction of popular demand through the abolition of slavery and the implanting of federalism the monarchy would be strengthened.

As for Ruy Barbosa, his conversion to federalism was of long standing. As editor of the *Diario de Noticias* he wrote impassioned articles on the subject during the spring and summer of 1889. He refused a portfolio in the cabinet because the government declined to commit itself on what he called a *federação franca*. With increasing fervor he stressed the alternative: " either the federation or the republic." And as a matter of fact in the last days of the monarchy he went over bag and baggage to the Republicans.

On June 7, 1889, came into office the last cabinet of the empire. It was recruited from the Liberal party and was presided over by Affonso Celso de Assis Figueiredo, Visconde de Ouro Preto. The new prime minister was a man of ripe experience in public affairs. As a close student of political and economic problems he realized that the maladies from which the monarchy was suffering were amenable only to the most drastic and thoroughgoing remedies. The program which he submitted to parliament embodied the most comprehensive series of reforms ever sponsored by any of Dom Pedro's ministers. These reforms included extension of the suffrage, abolition of the life tenure of senators, reorganization of the Council of State, and what is important for our purpose, full autonomy of the provinces and municipalities, and election of the presidents of the provinces by indirect vote instead of their appointment by the Emperor. Could the program have been carried out in its entirety, these various reforms would have gone a long way toward neutralizing the propaganda of the Republicans by showing that the monarchy was quite capable of meeting the demands of the Brazilian people for a fuller participation in public affairs.

When submitted to the chamber of deputies on June 11, 1889, the program of Ouro Preto met with a frigid reception. It fully satisfied neither monarchists, federalists, nor republicans. Nabuco found the diluted form of federalism unsatisfactory. The scenes in the chamber were highly dramatic. Deputy Padre João Manoel caused a tremendous scandal by shouting " viva a republica "; Dom Antonio, bishop of Pará, declared that he was attending a session of the French Convention and added that the " days of the monarchy are numbered." The veteran parliamentarian Saraïva advised Dom Pedro to return to the nation the crown which had been presented to him in 1831. It was evident, however, that as a whole the chamber was much less liberal than the prime minister. By a vote of seventy-nine to twenty it expressed its lack of confidence in the government, whose program was characterized as frankly liberal, reforming, and almost revolutionary. The body was dissolved and never reassembled.

The immediate occasion of the advent of the republic on November 15, 1889, was a barrack-room conspiracy engineered by some of the higher officers in the army, but the ultimate causes reached far back into the history of the monarchy. While it will not do to stress the point unduly, certainly one of the contributing factors to the debacle was the inability of the statesmen to find a formula which would reconcile the apparently mutually hostile principles of federalism and monarchy.

The civilian leaders of the revolt had long been propagandists for federalism and republicanism. It was natural and fitting, therefore, that the first decree of the provisional government should establish " a federative republic as the form of government of the Brazilian nation." The history of federalism under the republic is a story too long to be rehearsed here, nor is it possible to analyze in any detail the three constitutions under which Brazil has been governed since 1891. Rather, in the brief time remaining, an attempt will be made to point out how federalism, the official form of government to which Brazil has been committed, worked out in practice.

A constituent assembly met in 1890 and formally promulgated a new constitution on February 24, 1891. In taking this step the assembly did little more than make minor revisions of a draft drawn up by Ruy Barbosa, who in turn drew his inspiration chiefly from the Constitution of the United States.

The Constitution of 1891 remained in force something over forty years. Even its most enthusiastic supporters would be willing to admit that it was not without its defects. Two of the most striking of these shortcomings have been the blameworthy intervention of the executive power in the states for the purpose of forcing upon them the rule of factions favored by the authorities in Rio de Janeiro, and the toleration of flagrantly unconstitutional acts by state governments enjoying the favor of the national executive. A complaint also frequently voiced is that the president, by one means or another, has built up a new kind of centralization of power, infinitely greater than anything existing under the empire. Through suspension of constitutional guarantees and other means, the chief magistrate has been able for relatively long periods to arrogate to himself virtually dictatorial power. As a remedy for this situation there has been proposed at various times the introduction of a parliamentary system such as existed under the empire. It would seem, however, that no considerable number of Brazilians have rallied to this view. But perhaps the most serious charge which can be brought against federalism as established in the Constitution of 1891 has been the failure satisfactorily to adjust the relation of the states to the federal government. The magnitude of this problem will perhaps become more obvious when we consider for a moment the Constitution of 1934 and the one put into effect on November 10, 1937.

The earlier of these two instruments was adopted, it will be remembered, after the revolution of 1930 and the establishment of the dictatorship of Dr. Getulio Vargas. Perhaps the chief innovations were the more careful definition of the powers of the executive, the changes in the method of electing the president, and the articles dealing with social and economic welfare. There are also evident a strong tendency toward greater nationalism. When we come, however, to a consideration of the second document, we find a number of innovations which profoundly alter the organization of the state.

The entire world was startled when on November 10, 1937, President Vargas staged a *coup d'état* by the assumption of dictatorial power. Congress was dissolved, the state governors (with a few exceptions) were deposed, and a new constitution written by Dr. Francisco Campos, the Minister of Justice, was promulgated.

As is well known, these events have been interpreted by many as signalizing the entry of Brazil into the group of fascist or near fascist states. For reasons impossible to enumerate here the writer does not accept this view. He will merely recall the substance of a statement submitted by Dr. Vargas to foreign newspaper correspondents in which he pointed out that Brazil had not ceased to be a democracy, and that it was neither fascist nor integralist, but Brazilian, working out its own problem in its own way. The country, added Dr. Vargas, is still solidly pro-Pan American and will not look to Europe for advice or example. He added that his country thoroughly approved the Good Neighbor policy of President Roosevelt, whom Brazilians consider one of the great statesmen of today.

It is obviously too early to attempt anything like a final appraisal of the new Constitution. Some of the articles are obscure. Others are doubtless provisional in character and will be modified as occasion dictates. But this much is certain: federalism as it had existed under the Constitution of 1891 or even that of 1934 has suffered very considerable modifications. To be sure, Article 3 of the new instrument states:

Brazil is a federal state made up of the indissoluble union of the states, the federal district and the territories. The present political and territorial division is maintained.

A study of the document will show, however, that Brazil has moved, in practice, a long direction [sic] toward a unitary state. The powers of the president are enormously increased, in many instances at the expense of the states. For example, the faculties of the president for intervention in the states have been considerably expanded; a case in point is the right, *without* the authorization of the chamber of deputies,

to administer the state when for any reason whatever one of its powers shall be prevented from functioning.

Upon agreement with the federal government

the states may delegate to the functionaries of the Union the power to execute the laws, services, acts, or decisions of their government.

In fiscal matters the faculties of the states are further abridged. They may not contract external loans without the previous authorization of the federal council (which takes the place of the senate); they are forbidden to levy an export tax higher than 10 percent *ad valorem*. The control of primary and secondary education, hitherto within the incumbency of the states, is apparently to be taken away from them.

The foregoing provisions of the constitution will probably fall most heavily on the large states; such as São Paulo, Minas Geraes, and even Rio Grande do Sul, which on occasion have chafed at federal control and have in effect regarded themselves as *imperia in imperio*. An ingeniously organized electoral college, plus limited faculties accorded the president to nominate his own successor, should in practice strike a blow at the quasi monopoly which these powerful states have hitherto enjoyed in alternating in the selection of president.

The smaller, weaker, or less populated states have constituted a problem of a somewhat different order. It has long been the contention of many Brazilians that a number of these states, especially those in the north, have lacked such bases for existence as diversity of products and resources, and differences of climate. Some of these states as at present geographically constituted have lost all reality as economic units. Even as rough boundaries of cultural unity and traditional loyalties few of them possess a great amount of vitality. And the opinion is widespread that these states have frequently constituted obstacles to the efficient functioning of the federal system. Though they enjoyed in the federal senate a representation equal to that of their larger brothers, they have at times been under the control of local machines or even single families. Brazilians have frequently described them as " feudal states." At one time it was perhaps not too fantastic to compare them to the rotten boroughs in England prior to the Reform Bill of 1832. The new Constitution frankly considers the possibility of uniting these smaller states into larger units or even converting them into national territories. Article 5 provides machinery whereby the states may unite to form new states; Article 6 empowers the union to create federal territories out of the dismembered parts of the states in the interest of national defense; Article 8 provides that any state which for three consecutive years cannot raise sufficient funds to maintain the services for its own particular needs will be transformed into a territory; and Article 9, letter *e,* authorizes the federal government to reorganize the finances of a state which for more than two consecutive years shall suspend the servicing of its funded debt. In other words, an offending state may meet the same fate as recently befell Newfoundland, when the British government assumed entire control of its fiscal system.

The power of the states in the federal congress has also been curtailed in various ways. The chamber of deputies, whose members are hereafter to be chosen by indirect election, shares its legislative functions with the president, who enjoys extensive faculties of the issuing of so-called " decree-laws " (*decretos-leis*). In place of the old senate is a federal council whose members are to be elected by the state legislatures, plus ten members appointed by the president. Its competency is almost exclusively confined to matters relating to the federal district, the territories, and Brazil's foreign relations.

The constitution says nothing in regard to the manner in which the governors of the states are to be chosen, but presumably they will be selected by the president of the republic. At the present moment, the states are under the control of *interventors* appointed by the executive.

The powers of the central government extend to fields unrecognized by the Constitutions of 1824 and 1891 and only adumbrated in the Constitution of 1934. A national economic council, representing the various branches of the national production, is to be set up. This body bears considerable resemblance to the corporative parliament of fascist Italy. Many of its activities still remain to be determined by legislation, but it seems reasonably clear that it is designed to further a system of planned economy and rationalization of industry, as well as to banish all labor conflicts through the creation of syndicates.

An analysis of the remaining features of this interesting constitution is less germane to our purpose and will be omitted.

During the course of this paper we have followed the development of federalism from its beginning in colonial days, through its partial acclimation under the empire, to its definite enthronement under the republic. We have seen that at no time has it been able to adapt itself with complete success to the conditions as they exist in Brazil. The chief difficulties with which it has had to contend we have considered at some length. In general, they have had to do with a more satisfactory definition of the powers of the executive and the relations of the provinces, and later states, to the central government. To these maladjustments, inherent perhaps in a nation like Brazil where, with the exception of an intellectual élite, the civic consciousness is still undeveloped, and where the disparity among the component parts is so great, might be added other problems which have become especially noticeable in the last few decades. As early as 1908 Professor Leacock pointed out that many of the defects of federalism are the results of the growing complexity of economic and industrial conditions which demand uniformity of regulation. In other words, to the partial breakdown which federalism has shown in its political aspects, are to be added weaknesses on its economic side. With the growing industrialization of Brazil, accompanied by a heightened tension between capital and labor, it would seem that the federal

form of government should of necessity have to make way for a
more centralized type of government, capable of regulating, and if
necessary, even taking control of the economic activities of the nation. The new constitution is pre-eminently designed to meet such
ends. How successful it will work out in practice only the future
can tell.

No. 25 [The republic of Mexico has a written constitution that
clearly indicates the desire, at least, to establish a federal organization of government. Professor Mecham, in the following essay, examines this question: Does Mexico have a federal system in *fact?*

In his answer he notes how certain factors, such as the broadly
stated delegated powers of the central government, the powers of the
executive, the influence of the military in civil affairs, the party system, and many others, have modified the federal system so that one
may really ask if federalism in Mexico is fact or fiction.]

*Mexican Federalism — Fact or Fiction?**

by J. LLOYD MECHAM

FEDERALISM was introduced into Mexico with republicanism. After
the overthrow of Emperor Agustín I, the Congress, on June 12, 1823,
declared in favor of a federal republic, and issued a call for a constituent congress. The federalists, under the leadership of Miguel Ramos

* J. Lloyd Mecham, " Mexican Federalism — Fact or Fiction? " *The Annals of the
American Academy of Political and Social Science* (March, 1940), Vol. 208, pp. 23–
38. Reprinted by permission of *The Annals of the American Academy of Political and
Social Science*. The footnotes in the original version are omitted here.

Arizpe, were in the majority in the Constituent Congress which met on November 7, 1823. Despite the opposition and able arguments of Father Servando Mier, leader of the centralistic minority, who decried the logic of disuniting Mexico in order to unite her, the Congress, on January 31, 1824, approved the *Acta Constitutiva* which provided for a " popular, representative, federal, republican form of government."

ADOPTION OF FEDERALISM

The adoption of federalism was unfortunate, yet understandable. It was unfortunate because it was unnecessary; Mexico was a unity, and had no need of federation, but rather a strongly integrated national state capable of holding together unruly elements. Moreover, federalism, " the most complicated and delicate governmental mechanism ever devised by man," called for a political maturity and experience unknown in newly liberated Mexico. In the light of this political immaturity, federalism could not but result in a reign of disorder and anarchy. The consequence has been as Father Mier warned — control asserted from the center in disregard of constitutional law.

Yet, the reasons for the adoption of federalism are clear. Centralism, because of colonial experience, was identified with autocracy and despotism. The great, outstanding, and unique example of republicanism at the time was the federal republic of the United States. It followed, therefore, that federalism was essential to the operation of republicanism. With little comprehension of the real nature of the American state, the Mexican constituents regarded federalism as a guarantor of local and individual rights. It meant freedom from the oppression and inequalities of the old order. As opposed to centralism, which meant reaction and a transitional step to the restoration of monarchy, federalism meant liberalism, the security of newly won liberties; in short, it was the essence of the democratic republic.

The adoption of federalism, in 1824, did not prove to be definitive; on the contrary, for the next quarter of a century the political pendulum swung several times between the extremes of federalism and centralism. It reacted to the ebb and flow of the struggle between the forces of progress and reaction. Federalism was abandoned in

1835, and a highly centralistic form of government was established under the Constitution of 1836, the so-called *Siete Leyes*. Following the *Siete Leyes* came, in 1843, the *Bases Orgánicas,* an even more centralistic constitution. During the turmoils of the Mexican war, federalism and the Constitution of 1824 were restored. After a brief relapse into centralism, in 1853, when Santa Anna enjoyed his final term of power, there was a return to federalism under the Constitution of 1857. The adoption of that constitution, which reflected the ideology of Mexican liberalism, presented the issue of liberalism-federalism versus conservatism-centralism more clearly than it had ever been presented before. Consequently, the Liberal victory over the Conservatives in the Wars of the Reform permanently and definitively disposed of the problem of centralism as an issue in Mexican politics. From that day to the present, no serious proposal has ever been made that Mexico should return to centralism. In the constituent congress of Querétaro, which drafted the contemporary Mexican Constitution of 1917, not a word was uttered in favor of centralism.

THE MEANING OF FEDERALISM

According to the able Mexican publicist Miguel Lanz Duret, the first constituent congress was free to choose between federalism and centralism. This freedom of choice, however, was not enjoyed by the Congress of 1857, and least of all by the Congress of 1917, for by that time the Mexican people had become thoroughly attached to the liberal tradition which had become identified with the magic name "federalism." It is a significant fact that the novel interpretation of the federalistic principle which dictated its adoption in Mexico in 1824 continues to be the Mexican's understanding of federalism, and stiffens his determination to preserve it; this, despite the fact that federalism, as we in the United States understand it, has never existed in fact in Mexico. One might well ask whether the actual functioning of government in Mexico would have been any different under constitutional centralism. In all likelihood not; yet by adopting the only kind of constitution which had a chance of being observed, certainly there would have resulted a greater respect for the law.

How is it that in Mexico, with a constitution modeled after that of the United States, a degree of centralization is accomplished which far exceeds the aspirations of the most extreme New Deal zealots in the United States? There is a general impression in the United States that a concentration of authority is effected in Mexico City by coercion, fraud, and a willful disregard of the constitution. To some extent this is true; yet the constitution itself affords ample means for the subordination of the states to the will of the center. To understand the true nature of federalism in Mexico, it is necessary, therefore, to take into account not only the exceptional grants of power to the federal government, which are considerably greater than in the United States, but also those expedients, legal and extralegal, which are used to accomplish an actual centralism.

Like the United States Constitution, the Mexican Constitution of 1917 delegates powers to the national government, reserving to the states those powers not expressly vested by the constitution in the federal authorities. Although the Mexican states were artificially created, and thus were not the original possessors of independent powers, this does not alter the fact that by act of the Mexican people they have been endowed with residuary powers. Therefore, although there was an original difference concerning the source of state powers in Mexico, as to be contrasted with the United States, there is now no difference as concerns the principle of a division of powers — but with this exception, that the extent of the powers vested in the Mexican federal government is considerably greater than in the United States. Moreover, the limitations and prohibitions on the Mexican states are likewise greater, thereby more narrowly limiting their sphere of action. These departures from the example of the American Union will now be discussed.

EXCEPTIONAL LEGISLATIVE GRANTS

We consider first the more extensive legislative grant. The national congress has been given the power to legislate on all matters relating to mining, the cinema industry, commerce, institutions of credit, and the electrical industry, and to create a sole bank of issue.

The whole domain of public health, with extensive police powers, is assigned to the federal government under a constitutional grant to the congress to legislate " in regard to the general health of the

Republic." The result is that the states are deprived of their principal powers of sovereignty in matters of public health, and a federal dictatorship of sanitation is created. The sanitary authority is declared to be executive, and its orders must be obeyed by the administrative authorities of the nation. Thus since the jurisdiction of the federal agency embraces all general conditions of hygiene, leaving to the state and municipal authorities those sanitary matters which appear to be merely local, very little in reality is left to the states.

The Mexican federal government is also given a control over education which is not enjoyed by the United States federal authorities. Express, although not exclusive, power is delegated " to establish, organize, and support in all the Republic " schools of all classes and grades, and to make laws designed to " distribute conveniently between the Federation and the states and municipalities, the exercise of the educative function, and the economic apportionment due each public service, with the object of unifying and co-ordinating education in the whole Republic." Although the control over education is understood to be a concurrent power, in fact, since the adoption of a constitutional amendment in 1934, the possibilities of federal supremacy in the field of education are unlimited. To date, however, the federal government has confined its energies very largely to the support of rural education.

Jurisdiction " in matters of religious worship and outward ecclesiastical forms " is also vested exclusively in the national government (Art. 130). Beyond the right to determine the maximum number of ministers of religious creeds according to the needs of each locality, the states exercise very little control over religious cults. Moreover, all property which formerly belonged to the Church, and all buildings which are used for ecclesiastical purposes, have been nationalized. In short, the control of religious cults in Mexico is almost exclusively a federal matter.

Constitutional Article 27, which embodies new concepts of property rights, and Article 123, which seeks to emancipate the laborer, convey new and exceptional powers to the federal government, particularly to the president. Since these grants epitomize the philosophy and vital objectives of the revolution, it is readily understandable why their control and enforcement has been intrusted to the central authorities. There is little need here to do more than briefly indicate the extension of federal control under these articles.

Article 27 makes the basic declaration that in the nation is vested direct and inalienable ownership of all subsoil resources, which can be exploited only by means of concessions granted by the federal government. Here is the constitutional basis of Mexico's far-reaching nationalization program, which has been the cause of so much international friction. Article 27 also provides for a redistribution of lands — a power enjoyed by both the federal and state governments. In practice, however, the prosecution of the agrarian program, particularly as concerns the restoration of the *ejidos,* has been assumed by the federal government. . . .

[With reference to the broad powers of the central government in the field of labor legislation] suffice it to indicate at this point that the Constitution of 1917 originally authorized the congress and also the state legislatures to issue labor laws based on the necessities of the regions and without contravening the enabling article itself. This was altered, however, on August 31, 1929, when the federal congress was given exclusive jurisdiction concerning workers and workers' contracts. The reason for this was to harmonize and unify labor legislation throughout the republic.

INTERVENTIONIST POWERS

Perhaps of even greater importance than the more extensive powers of legislation granted to the Mexican federal government when compared with those of the United States central government, is the larger measure of control vested in the national authorities over the state governments in Mexico. As if it were the manifest purpose of the framers of the constitution to nullify their efforts in creating a federal state, they granted the federal authorities exceptional interventionist powers in state affairs. The most important of these are found in Article 76. Express power is given to the Senate

to declare, when all the constitutional powers of any state have disappeared, that the occasion has arisen to give to the said state a provisional governor, who shall call for elections to be held according to the constitution and the law of the said state. The appointment of such a governor shall be made by the Senate with the approval of two-thirds of its members present or during recess by the Permanent Committee by the same two-thirds majority from among three names (*terna*) proposed by the President.

Moreover, the Senate is empowered " to adjust all political questions arising between the powers of a state whenever one of them shall appeal to the Senate or whenever by virtue of such differences a clash of arms has arisen to interrupt the constitutional order." Most of the federal interventions, as will be shown later, have occurred under the authorization of Article 76. It is to be noted that only in cases of *political* controversies within the states can the senate intervene.

On the other hand, if there is a conflict between the powers of a state concerning the *constitutionality* of their acts, this is a question to be decided by the Federal Supreme Court. According to Article 105, " the Supreme Court of Justice shall have exclusive jurisdiction in all controversies . . . between the powers of government of any state as to the constitutionality of their acts." Here is a grant of jurisdiction to the federal judiciary unknown to the United States Constitution.

Closely coupled with the foregoing, in a listing of interventionist powers, is Article 122, which orders the federal powers, in cases of insurrection or internal disturbance within a state, to give it the necessary protection, provided the legislature of the state, or the executive thereof if the legislature is not in session, shall so request. In the event that the federal authorities are not petitioned for assistance by the state authorities, the President, by virtue of powers conferred on him by Article 89, can dispose the federal forces for the domestic safety and the defense of the union. Moreover, since the constitution prescribes for the states a popular, representative, republican form of government, and since it requires that state governments be based on the principle of popular sovereignty, the President, under his oath to defend and enforce the constitution, enjoys both a mandate and a sanction to enforce upon the states his own interpretation of representative and republican governments.

Such are the principal constitutional clauses which facilitate federal intervention in Mexico. We now turn to a consideration of their practical application.

INTERVENTION IN PRACTICE

The agency created by congress to assist the President in keeping informed on state affairs is the *Secretaría de Gobernación*. To one of the bureaus of the *Secretaría* is assigned supervision over subjects known as *relaciones interiores,* the most important of these being " elections and conflicts between state authorities." To it are sent reports, petitions, and complaints from local officials, political parties, candidates, and private citizens. This information is usually supplemented by reports of *Gobernación* agents sent to investigate local situations. On the basis of these findings the *Secretaría de Gobernación* tries to settle intrastate controversies by recommending a solution. In the great majority of cases the recommendation of *Gobernación* is sufficient to settle the controversy. For example, in March 1925 a political conflict in Tlaxcala arising out of the existence of two legislatures, one made up of members of the Socialist party and the other of members of the Agrarian and *Laborista* parties, was solved by *Gobernación* in granting recognition to the legislature installed in the official legislative hall. Since recognition of the legality of a state government is a requisite for the maintenance of relations with the federal government, this is a powerful sanction enjoyed by *Gobernación* to impose its will upon the state governments.

An important function of the state legislatures is to tabulate and announce the vote for governor. Since this function is performed in a highly partisan fashion, and not necessarily in harmony with the popular poll, the usual aftermath of a gubernatorial election is the meeting of two or more legislatures each claiming to be the legal body, and each announcing the election of its favorite candidate as governor. Since it is all-important that the recognition of *Gobernación* be secured, the federal government is afforded an ideal opportunity, and seemingly a legal one, to recognize the state administration which is most to its liking. Need one wonder, then, that the local authorities are subservient to the will of Mexico City?

However, on occasion the dictum of *Gobernación* is rejected by the contending local factions. Since the *Secretaría* has no authority to enforce its proposed solutions, it then will refer the matter, with all pertinent information, to the senate. The arbitrariness and partiality of senatorial intervention will be apparent in the following cases.

SENATORIAL INTERVENTION

In 1925 there was political conflict between Governor Elizalde of Aguascalientes on the one hand and the state legislature and judiciary on the other. The federal Senate, having been appealed to by the legislature, requested the President to afford guarantees to the legislative and judicial powers of Aguascalientes. This the President did by lending the support of the federal troops to the removal of the governor by the legislature.

When a state election has not proceeded according to the wishes of the center, the Senate, acting on the advice of the President, will refuse to recognize the legality of the election and will declare the disappearance of constitutional powers. This calls for the appointment of a provisional governor and the holding of another election under his auspices. Thus, in Chiapas in 1924, the regular state election resulted in the establishment of rival legislatures, both appealing to *Gobernación* for recognition. *Gobernación*, after making an investigation, reported to the President that the elections were fraudulent, and advised another election. The Senate, acting on the advice of the President, declared that a state of anarchy existed in Chiapas. Then, from a list of names submitted to it by the President, the Senate appointed a provisional governor under whose auspices another election was held. To insure the correct electoral results, the commander of the federal troops in Chiapas, the so-called *jefe de operaciones,* was ordered to cooperate.

From the foregoing illustration it will be noted that the federal authorities assume the right to decide local elections. President Calles declared that it was the privilege of the executive to discover whether the state legislatures were truly the rightfully elected representatives of the people, before establishing relations with them. In 1927 the Supreme Court mustered up courage to declare that " no Federal authority may arrogate to itself the power to decide local elections of a state, nor even to place in question the decisions of the representative electoral colleges." Needless to say, this opinion has not served as a deterrent to federal interventions in local elections.

DISAPPEARANCE OF CONSTITUTIONAL POWERS

The Senate declares the disappearance of constitutional powers when in fact not all, or perhaps not any, have actually disappeared.

This is regarded as the greatest abuse of the interventionist powers. In spite of the fact that it was clearly understood in the Convention of Querétaro that the existence of only the judicial power would render intervention impossible, in practice this is completely ignored. In 1927, President Calles commented that "the existence of solely the Judicial Power signifies nothing, for if it is certain that it remains as the nucleus of local sovereignty, it is also certain that it remains isolated and powerless to reconstruct the other powers." A grave abuse of the Senate's power was the removal, in December 1935, of *Callista* governors in the states of Sonora, Sinaloa, Guanajuato, and Durango. After the break between Cárdenas and Calles, the former succeeded in getting rid of pro-Calles governors by ordering the Senate to declare a disappearance of the powers because of seditious activities.

All too often it is charged by the Senate that a situation is violative of a state constitution and consequently it declares a disappearance of all constitutional order. It would appear that such a case would call for judicial settlement; but the President, with the acquiescence of the Senate, arrogates to himself the judicial power to interpret state constitutions. Experience shows that it would be quite futile to appeal to the courts, for they inevitably reject jurisdiction on the ground that the question is political. For example, in 1926 the three deposed powers in Nuevo León appealed to the Supreme Court from the act of the Senate in according recognition to an independent legislature. The appellants held that the granting or withholding of recognition was not within the competence of the Senate, and therefore the Supreme Court should grant them *amparo*. The Court, however, ruled that recognition was a political act, and consequently it had no jurisdiction. Because of the timidity of the courts (or should we say, because of their dependence on the executive?) the political departments of the federal government are left to interpret their interventionist powers very much as they see fit.

LIMITATIONS ON STATE AND LOCAL GOVERNMENT

Detailed provisions in the federal constitution determining the organization of state governments still further restrict their sphere of autonomous action. Article 115 requires that state governors, members of state legislatures, and municipal presidents and councilors shall be directly elected and shall not be eligible for re-election in the succeeding term. These limitations imposed on elected state and local officers were the literal, if not practical, application, down to the very grass roots, of the revolutionary slogan, " Effective suffrage, no re-election."

Article 115 also provides that governors shall be native-born Mexican citizens, and natives of the states, or residents thereof for at least five years immediately preceding election. The federal authorities have intervened to effect observance of this requirement.

The minimum number of representatives in the state legislatures is also fixed by constitutional mandate. Federal enforcement of this requirement is illustrated by the case of Hidalgo. In 1928 the federal constitution was amended reducing from fifteen to seven the minimum number of representatives who were to compose the state legislatures. The state of Hidalgo reduced the number of its representatives without going through the formality of amending the state constitution. The *Secretaría de Gobernación* warned the governer of Hidalgo that until the state constitution was amended the federal government would " not enter into official relations with the elected legislature." The constitution of Hidalgo was hastily amended. *Gobernación* sent a similar warning to the governors of other states calling their attention to the necessity of amending their state constitutions before proceeding to a reform of their electoral laws. On this incident, one of the leading Mexico City newspapers editorialized as follows:

The Federal Constitution which established in a definite manner the political relations that should exist between the center and the local authorities, obliges the Federal Executive to sustain a critical intolerance of all that is contrary to the spirit of the Constitution. When one of the governments of the states violates any of these fundamental dispositions, the indifference of the Federal Executive Power can be interpreted as sympathy with the acts of that government, and as such will establish a dangerous precedent for the political harmony of the nation.

State officials are bound to publish and enforce the federal laws, and they are liable to impeachment by the Senate on charges brought by the deputies for violation or nonenforcement of the constitution and the federal laws. Since interference with the free exercise of the franchise in state and federal elections is considered to be violative of the federal constitution, the ease with which state officials can be set aside by the impeachment procedure can be readily appreciated.

VIOLATION OF MUNICIPAL FREEDOM

The federal constitution is also specific concerning the organization of municipal government and the guarantees of municipal freedom. One of the most important reforms accomplished by the Convention of Querétaro was the abolition of the notorious *jefe político,* a local centralizing agent of the federal and state executives, who, under the Constitution of 1857 and during the Díaz régime, completely submerged municipal liberties. In a further effort to guarantee municipal liberty, Article 115 provides that each municipality shall be administered by a council (*ayuntamiento*) chosen by direct vote of the people; that municipalities shall enjoy juridic personality; and that they shall freely administer their own revenues which shall be derived from taxes fixed by the state legislatures.

It should not be implied from the constitutional guarantees that municipal freedom has been established in Mexico. To the contrary, the charge is freely made that the old-time powers and practices of the *jefes políticos* have been assumed by the state governors, who continue to manipulate municipal elections and impose municipal officials to suit their fancy. Superficially, the violation of municipal liberties by state authorities would not seem to be a matter falling under the jurisdiction of a federal government. However, since the federal constitution of Mexico guarantees the autonomous municipality, the federal government has seen fit to act as a watchdog over municipal liberties.

In spite of the federal guarantee of the free municipality, several of the state constitutions provide that the state legislatures shall decide contested municipal elections and withhold recognition from, or depose, local *ayuntamientos.* When a municipal council is deposed, the governor appoints a provisional government called a *junta de administración civil.* The practice of deposing *ayuntamien-*

tos became so abusive that the federal authorities intervened. On September 3, 1935, the *Secretaría de Gobernación* warned:

Federal Government cannot consent that the local authorities should impede the municipalities in the exercise of their functions. This would be a subversion of the constitutional order which the Federal Government is obliged to maintain in all the Union.

Consequently the federal forces were ordered to give *ayuntamientos* "complete guarantees necessary for the performance of their institutional mission."

On June 14, 1938, the Supreme Court came to the support of the free municipality. An *amparo* had been granted to the municipal officials of Ixtlaltepec, Oaxaca, against the acts of the governor of the state, who, because of the alleged inability of the *ayuntamiento* to elect a municipal president, had deposed it and appointed a *junta de administración civil*. The Supreme Court held that in such a case the municipal ordinance should rule, and that there was no occasion for gubernatorial intervention.

But in spite of the foregoing, municipal liberties continue to be violated by the state authorities, often, it is alleged, in conspiracy with the national administration. This can be implied from a campaign speech, on November 12, 1939, by presidential candidate General Juan Andreu Almazán, who pledged himself to the restoration of "*ayuntamientos* whose existence does not depend on the governor or the legislatures, but solely on a vigilant citizenry who alone have the right to revoke their mandate when their representatives have failed in their duty."

THE AMPARO A SUPPORT OF FEDERAL SUPREMACY

We now proceed to a consideration of the important role of the judiciary as a support of federal supremacy. Under Article 103 the federal tribunals are given jurisdiction over "all controversies arising out of laws or acts of authorities when the latter infringe any individual rights, also "all controversies arising out of laws or acts of state authorities which invade the sphere of the federal authorities." This grant operates, by recourse to the *ley amparo*, to protect the individual in his individual rights as enumerated in the first twenty-nine articles of the federal constitution. In Mexico the federal bill of rights is a limitation upon both federal and state authorities.

The *ley amparo* is a peculiar recourse in Mexican jurisprudence combining the essential features of the common law writs of *habeas corpus, certiorari,* and *mandamus.* It is necessary to establish a judicial process to prevent invasions into respective powers and attempts against individual rights. To secure this end, Mexico has instituted the *Juicio Constitucional* or *Amparo.*

Since the federal tribunals are given jurisdiction over all cases involving a violation of individual rights, and since *amparo* has been established as the brake to restrain the abuse of these rights, it follows that *amparo* is an exclusively federal writ. Another characteristic of *amparo* is that it seeks to grant relief to the individual against the abuse of authority, it affords protection to the citizen against the unconstitutional acts of officials, federal, state, and local — and *only* against the acts of officials. Thus, when the congress exceeds its powers and deprives someone of his rights without due process, or infringes the reserved powers of the state, then the Supreme Court, by means of a writ of *amparo,* grants relief to the individual or the local officials against the acts of the federal authorities.

It is by means of the *amparo,* and only within the limits of the use of *amparo,* that the Mexican Supreme Court can hold an act of the Mexican congress to be unconstitutional, in the sense that it grants relief against the enforcement of the law in special cases. But it is to be noted that the *amparo,* as a judicial process to prevent the illegal invasion of the respective powers of the federal and state governments, usually operates, since the courts are politically controlled, as a restraint upon the local governments alone. Very few are the instances in which the Supreme Court has granted *amparo* in restraint of the federal authorities.

According to Lic. [*Licenciado,* i.e., Doctor] Salvador Urbina, the able and well-known commentator on Mexican constitutional law, there does not exist in Mexico a judicial power as a sovereign entity. He calls it "the semi-sovereign judicial power." He asserts that in controversies between two or more states, or between the powers of one state, the action of the Supreme Court is not independent, because of its control by the executive. The real judicial power is reduced to controversies between individuals. As concerns questions affecting the sovereignty of the people, such as legislation concerning property, labor, social welfare, or taxes, "the Executive is the absolute master, and the judiciary enjoys only an illusory and tardy interference by means of the *amparo.*" To illustrate his point Urbina cites the unique power given the executive by Article 27 to declare null and void the thousands of contracts and concessions granted or concluded from 1876 to 1917 respecting lands, waters, and natural resources. This signifies, he says, "the exclusion of the judicial power whose intervention should be most necessary in any constitution which is based on a republican system of the separation of the powers.

Also, with respect to the agrarian program, the function of administering justice is given to the executive, to the absolute exclusion of the judicial power, including the use of *amparo.* This amounts, in fact, as far as the agrarian laws are concerned, to a perpetual suspension of the guarantees. But the omnipotence of the executive over the judiciary is not all, as a brief description of the predominant position of the executive in the Mexican government will show.

EXECUTIVE DICTATORSHIP

Lic. Salvador Azuela, a professor of law in the University of Mexico and an outstanding authority on constitutional law, says, "In Mexico, in reality, we live in a régime of absolutism — of the Executive Power." Lic. Gabino Fraga, another constitutional authority, denominates the Mexican government, because of the predominance of the executive, the "presidential type."

It is the Mexican President's *facultades extraordinarias,* or extraordinary powers, that enable him to become a dictator within the framework of the constitution. The source of these powers is in Articles 29 and 49. According to the first,

in cases of invasion, grave disturbance of the public peace, or any other emergency which may place society in grave danger of conflict, the President . . . with the concurrence of the Council of Ministers, and with the approval of Congress, or of the Permanent Committee in case Congress is not in session, shall have power to suspend throughout the whole of the Republic, or in any portion thereof, such guarantees as shall be a hindrance in meeting this situation promptly and readily.

Article 49 provides for a division of the powers into the legislative, executive, and judicial, and prohibits the union of two or more of these powers in the same authority, " nor shall the legislative power be vested in one individual except in the case of extraordinary powers granted to the Executive, in accordance with the provisions of Article 29."

Article 29 does not mention a delegation of legislative powers or of extraordinary powers, but provides merely that the President shall apply certain norms or laws, or suspend others, in determined cases, without making this authorization in any sense a delegation of legislative power. Yet, Article 49 clearly implies that when an occasion arises which calls for a suspension of the guarantees, an exception is to be made to the constitutional mandate that the executive and legislative powers are to be kept separate. This has been the practical interpretation of extraordinary powers by the political departments of the government, and the judiciary has obediently acquiesced.

In the very week that the constitution of 1917 was promulgated, President Carranza was vested with extraordinary powers to legislate concerning the oil industry, the situation being declared a national emergency. The decrees issued by the executive under its extraordinary powers were claimed by the affected companies to have emanated from incompetent authority, and so they sought *amparo* in the courts. The Supreme Court, in denying *amparo,* held the *facultades extraordinarias* to be constitutional. Since all the attributes of the legislative power were not surrendered to the executive, this did not represent a union of the two powers. Furthermore, the Court said, " this does not amount to a delegation of legislative power to the Executive, but is rather the cooperation or aid which one power gives another."

Although there has been a great deal of argument in Mexico concerning the constitutionality of extraordinary powers, the fact remains that the President has many times been delegated the legislative function, and often in normal times. In response to demands that the extraordinary powers be limited to the exceptional cases mentioned in Article 29, a constitutional amendment was adopted in 1938 which provided that " only in cases indicated in Article 29 does the Executive enjoy the extraordinary power to legislate." This amendment has accomplished little, since it is stated in such vague terms.

One of the delegates in the convention of Querétaro, 1917 said:

Although the Constitution of 1857 did not expressly concede extraordinary powers to the Executive, this was annulled [by the practices of Juárez, Lerdo, and Díaz]; now that they are expressly conceded what will the result be? Clearly, it will make for dictatorship!

This warning was correct, for a government of extraordinary powers is the negation of all constitutional systems, since the initiative, the personality, the ambition of one man are all, and law counts for nothing. "This provision," says Ramón Beteta, "permits the President to tax the country without asking the consent of Congress, to put people in jail without a trial, and to be, in short, a veritable tyrant."

In view of these extraordinary powers, Beteta continues,

we are now in a position to understand why it is so very difficult to be a good president in Mexico. We place in the hands of a single man almost omnipotent power. We charge him to be good, to be honest, to be true, and at the same time not to profit personally by the privileged position which we permit him to occupy. It is more than human nature can bear!

Other legal and extralegal powers enjoyed by the President, which contribute to the exaltation of the *poder executivo,* can only be enumerated. The President has at his command the material force of the state: the army, the public treasury, and the bureaucracy. He is the supreme dispenser of favors; he appoints public officials. Moreover,

the Executive, by virtue of his position as a *caudillo,* exercises personal powers stronger than his legal powers. The "man on horseback" derives his power not so much from his official position, as from the fact that he is a popular hero. It is because of these extralegal powers that the President of Mexico can rule Congress and put under his foot the Supreme Court of Justice.

THE FUNCTION OF THE ARMY

A discussion of Mexican centralization without remarking on the role of the army would be sadly deficient. The Mexican army of more than 50,000 troops is under the control of the President, acting through the ministry of national defense. Mexico is divided into military zones, each under the command of a zone commandant or *Jefe de Operaciones Militares*. In most of the state capitals are located zone military headquarters and the federal barracks. The *Jefes de Operaciones* are perhaps the most important centralizing agents of the central government, for they are always ready at a moment's notice to execute on state administrations the will of Mexico City. When it comes to actual authority in local affairs, the *Jefe* usually overshadows the governor. By virtue of the President's power " to use the forces for domestic safety," the *Jefes* are constantly employed to coerce or remove recalcitrant state authorities, to impose decisions of the central government, and to " preserve order " during elections. Although prohibited by law from doing so, the *Jefe de Operaciones* actively participates in state political issues, and, needless to say, his " preservation of order " during elections usually insures results satisfactory to the national régime.

It is a well-established fact that no presidential candidate can be successful unless he has the army at his back. The army is still an acute necessity in Mexican politics, and there will not be much democracy until it is replaced by a nonpolitical constabulary or militia. The Mexican army is a political instrumentality; it is not designed for national defense against a foreign invader, but rather to preserve internal order and support the régime. According to a well-known authority on Mexico, " the sole function of the Mexican army as at present constituted is to kill Mexicans for the sake of the preservation of the central authority."

THE PARTY SYSTEM

There is a phrase attributed to Benito Juárez to the effect that if the Mexican government does not make the elections, the elections will not take place. From this we can infer that if the Mexican people were politically capable, their electoral function would not be confined to the ratification of results already determined by the national régime. We have already commented on the interference by the central authorities in local elections, but there remains to be discussed the party system and how completely it is subordinated to presidential control. Here, without doubt, is the principal extralegal instrumentality at the disposal of the executive to effect a personal dictatorship.

In Mexico there have never been (at least prior to 1929) political parties. The so-called parties have been personalistic followings. From 1917 to 1928 the Mexican dictators supported a system of a plurality of such parties, among which were usually distributed supporters of the régime. These parties launched their candidates, engaged in electoral campaigns, and after the balloting the *expedientes* would be sent to the dictator, who, "actuated by the impulses and resorts of an autocrat, would arbitrarily distribute among the parties, the triumphs and defeats."

Then in 1928, imitating the example of contemporary states organized under the system of a dictatorship of a single party, General Calles abolished the plural party system and founded the *Partido Nacional Revolucionario* in order better to control all adherents of the régime. General Calles explained the need for the party on the ground that the death of Obregón had deprived Mexico of a *caudillo,* and that the time had arrived to change electoral methods to convince the people that they enjoyed a free vote, and that impositions were a thing of the past. This of course was not true, for Calles was himself the new *caudillo,* the strong man of the revolution.

When the *Partido Nacional Revolucionario* was organized, other parties were not outlawed; but the *P.N.R.* was made the official party, and it was given such a tie-up with the government that it became the *one* party. For example, all public employees were required to belong to the party. On January 25, 1930, President Portes Gil ordered a discount, in favor of the *P.N.R.,* on all salaries of government employees equal to one day's pay for each month with thirty-one days. This act was severely criticized, since it denied to employees the liberty of belonging to a party of their choice. Since the Portes Gil order was patently a denial of individual liberty, it was revoked, to be continued, however, as an " understanding " which is fully comprehended by public employees.

Theoretically, the *Partido Nacional Revolucionario,* like its successor the *Partido de la Revolución Mexicana,* was a party with municipal, state, and national conventions to devise political programs and nominate candidates. In fact, it was an organ of the state, dependent on the President, whose orders were received by the national executive committee, which in turn transmitted them to inferior organs of the hierarchy. The acts of local conventions were constantly revised by order of the president. Since nomination by the *P.N.R.*, like a Democratic nomination in the South, meant an assured election, the interventions of the national executive committee so effectively controlled municipal, state, and federal elections that with good reason it was called "the Ministry of Impositions."

THE P.R.M. SUPPLANTS THE P.N.R.

In March 1938 the *P.N.R.* convoked a national constituent convention to organize a new party. The initiative for the convention, be it noted, came from the President alone, who was desirous of having the party reflect the existence of the class struggle. In the words of Barba González, former president of the *P.N.R.*, "it was felt necessary that there be a union of all sectors against the aggressive manifestations of capitalism." The preamble of the constitution of the *P.R.M.* reads:

The Party proposes, in a strict revolutionary sense, to serve loyally the cause of the emancipation of the proletariat, the supreme aspiration being the triumph of social justice. It considers that a firm class consciousness is the effective base for the unity of wage earners.

In accord with the presidential plan, the new party was declared to be the party of the various "sectors": workers, agrarians, soldiers, government employees, and the middle class. Representatives of each sector were given the right to participate in the determination of party policy and in the nomination of candidates. The designation of the delegates of the "unorganized sectors" is managed by the governors of the states and by local politicians following traditional methods. The delegates of the labor organizations are designated by their executive committees; and those of the army — nobody knows.

The granting of representation to the army caused no little comment and protest. *Excelsior* commented: "For the first time in the history of our country, the army will intervene officially in national politics." However, said *La Prensa,* "there will be less danger of a *cuartelazo* when the army participates in politics. It represents itself. Its political participation signalizes a fortifying of the revolutionary régime." When it was argued in the federal senate that participation of the military in the new party violated the military ordinance, a member pointed out that this ordinance was habitually violated. He called attention to the fact that a number of the military were in the senate and the chamber; that eighteen governors and various chiefs of departments and ministries were military men. Since this was a fact, it was best to recognize it.

Although the new party adopted certain changes concerning membership and objectives, it is generally agreed that its tactics continue to be about the same as those of its predecessor, and that it merits the name given to the former party — the *Ministerio de las Imposiciones.* When the *P.N.R.* was supplanted by the *P.R.M., Excelsior* editorialized as follows:

The *P.N.R.* was the *only* party; there is no record of its ever having lost an election. Its enemies were on occasion the victims of persecution. The *P.N.R.,* in a word, was the gravedigger of effective suffrage.

To date, the history of the *P.R.M.* has been no different. It remains to be seen if the outcome of the present [1940] presidential campaign adheres to historical precedent. [The name of the party was changed in 1946 to *Partido Revolucionario Institucional; P.R.I.*]

THE SIX-YEAR PLAN

Having provided for the perpetuation of the revolutionary régime by the creation of an official party, the next step, also in emulation of European dictatorships, was to employ this unified and highly personalistic party control for the social and economic unification of the country. Thus, the *P.N.R.,* under the influence of the highly publicized Russian five-year plans, announced its own six-year plan.

First mention of such a plan came in May 1933, when General Calles said that the hour had come to " formulate a detailed program of action for the period covered by the next six-year presidential term." This proposal is supposed to have represented a move " on the part of the Calles right-wing leaders . . . to appease by promises the demands of the left-wing elements for further reform." In December 1933, such a program, or party platform, was drafted by the convention of the *P.N.R.,* and on January 1, 1934, it was formally inaugurated as official governmental policy.

The plan was represented as a " program that shall be a pledge to the Nation that a social, economic, and administrative policy shall be followed, through which the principles proclaimed when armed strife prevailed are to materialize." It reaffirmed the principles of the revolution with the purpose of revivifying waning revolutionary spirits. Although influenced by the " political vogue in other countries of a tendency toward planned economy," the Mexican plan bears but slight resemblance to the Russian and Italian plans, because of the absence of carefully calculated schedules for the progressive attainment of future economic and social goals. On the other hand, because of certain crude schedules relating to a few subjects like education and communications, it departs from the ordinary party platform. The six-year plan is neither fish nor fowl, but is as indigenously Mexican as is Mexican " Socialism."

Examination of the plan, therefore, reveals a unique instrument designed to " step up " the revolutionary pace during the Cárdenas administration, and to act as a propaganda vehicle to set forth the thesis of current Mexican revolutionary philosophy. This thesis, the plan's most important feature, is that " the Mexican State assume and maintain a policy regulatory of the economic activities of the Nation." The *coup de grâce* was to be administered to prostrate states' rights.

With this keynote expressed, the plan deals with the following subjects: agriculture, labor, national economy, communications and public works, public health, education, government, army, foreign relations, finances, and community promotion. " The whole document is an enunciation of the policies announced in the beginning of the Revolution by the Constitution of 1917." It contains little that is new, and, as has been remarked, it is deficient in statistical schedules to measure progress. Therefore, to evaluate the success of the plan is equivalent to testing the adherence of the Cárdenas administration to the basic revolutionary program.

ACCOMPLISHMENTS OF THE PLAN

By 1939 a considerable road-building enterprise had been completed, and in southern Mexico the railway system had been extended. Certain ports had been improved. A number of great irrigation projects had been completed, thereby reclaiming lands for new distribution. Education, looking toward the incorporation of the Indian population in the nation, had been speeded up. Illiteracy had been greatly reduced. The labor movement, which had previously suffered serious reverses, had been revived by the sympathetic support of a labor-minded government. Following the beacon of economic nationalism as found in Article 27, the Cárdenas government expropriated the oil industry, and limited and restricted foreign capital. But it was in connection with the agrarian program that the greatest progress was made. More land was expropriated and given to the *peones* than in all the preceding administrations combined. Moreover, a credit system was worked out to facilitate the progress of agrarian reform. In short, it can be said for the Cárdenas administration that not one of the revolutionary aims was neglected. This is to be contrasted with the fact that shortly before Cárdenas assumed power, the revolution had been pronounced dead. Today there can be no doubt of its virility.

But the enforcement of the revolutionary program has met with bitter criticism. A food shortage and higher commodity prices, disturbing conflicts resulting from the adoption of " socialistic " education, paralyzing strike epidemics, and a general business depression have all been laid at the door of a planned economy. In spite of increasing criticism, the régime has not lost faith in the thesis of state intervention in social and economic affairs. Its only comment is that the six-year plan did not go far enough. That defect was remedied by the convention of the *P.R.M.* in November 1939. A second six-year plan was adopted, and was indorsed by General Avila Camacho, the party's presidential candidate. It is in the main a continuation of the first plan, but with more emphasis on the new state role of regulator.

Different from the first plan, the second six-year plan will face what appears to be a true test in the coming [1940] presidential election. It has been made the focal point of attack by those who disagree with the party's program. General Almazán, opposition candidate for president, assails the second plan as communistic. A group of independent parties charge that it sounds the death knell of the small proprietor, seeks the destruction of national institutions, destroys municipal liberty, and creates a socialistic state. An editorial in *El Universal* comments on the plan as follows: " If the First Six-Year Plan has scarcely left us our shirts, the Second will leave us practically nude."

Whatever the outcome of planned economy in Mexico, it still will be true that an executive dictatorship will persist, because of, and in violation of, the federal constitution. Personalism will continue to be the determining factor in Mexican politics.

No. 26   [The introductory essay of this chapter noted that Argentina is the Latin American republic in which a federal system is presumed to have functioned most successfully. The written constitution of that nation, especially when it refers to federal organization and to federal-provincial relations (a province in Argentina occupies theoretically the same place in that country as a state in ours), reads much like the Constitution of the United States. Some of the sections are, in fact, little more than translations of the analogous parts of our organic charter. In both constitutions one finds that the central government is endowed with powers which enable it to guarantee to the states or provinces a republican form of government.

When the editor of this book was teaching a course in " Comparative American Government " in an Argentine university eight years ago the questions most frequently raised by his students were: Why has Argentine constitutional and political practice, under similar guarantees of a republican form of government, diverged so widely from that of the United States? Why has not a strong " states' rights " sentiment acted as a brake or block to federal intervention in provincial matters in Argentina as it has in the United States? Why has not the central government of the United States sought and used every excuse, constitutional, political, or imaginary, to control the state governments?

Professor Gomez in the following essay concentrates his attention on the technique of intervention in Argentina, and on the number and kinds of interventions that were ordered by the central government between 1860 and 1930. His concern is the *what* and not the *why* of intervention. The latter is partially discussed in the other sections of this chapter and also in the chapters that precede it.]

Intervention in Argentina, 1860–1930*

by ROSENDO A. GOMEZ

THE defeat of Juan Manuel Rosas at the hands of the governor of the province of Entre Ríos, Justo José Urquiza, opened a new chapter in the long and often bloody history of Argentina's political organization. It paved the way toward the ultimate unification of the country under a truly national government. In fact, the constitution of 1852–53 and the reforms of the Buenos Aires convention of 1860 formally established a federal system of government, honoring thus the fundamental provisions of the Federal Pact of 1831 and the *Acuerdo de San Nicolás* of 1852.

The victory of federalism, as subsequent developments demonstrated, was to a considerable extent formal. The tendency toward a strong central government latent in Argentina since before the revolution of 1810 was far from annihilated by the constituent assembly of Paraná. On the contrary, the constitution of 1852–53, though federalist in tone and intent, has provided the national government with a most effective instrument of control and suppression of provincial autonomy. The instrument in question is the right of the federal government to intervene in the internal affairs of the provinces, under conditions specified in Articles 5 and 6 of the constitution.

The power of intervention is not a principle peculiar to the Argen-

* Rosendo A. Gomez, "Intervention in Argentina, 1860–1930," *Inter-American Economic Affairs* (December, 1947), Vol. I, No. 3, pp. 55–73. Reprinted by permission of *Inter-American Economic Affairs*.

tine constitution. Other constitutions, notably those of the United States and Switzerland, contain analogous provisions. In fact, the principle of intervention is an essential element of any system of federalist organization. What is perhaps unique in the case of Argentina is the frequency and manner in which intervention has been invoked and applied by the federal government. Both are eloquent testimonials to the persistent and on the whole successful efforts on the part of the national government to circumvent the spirit, if not the letter, of the federalist principles of the constitution. Indeed, it may well be argued on the basis of past experience that in spite of the constitution federalism in Argentina never became a living reality, but, on the contrary, has consistently given way to the centralizing tendencies of the national government.

The purpose of the present paper is twofold. First, it is proposed to examine the nature and development of the concept of intervention in Argentina. Second, an attempt is made to present a quantitative analysis of the frequency and manner in which the right of intervention was invoked by the central government during the period between the Buenos Aires convention of 1860 and the revolution of 1930.

II

When the Argentine constituent congress at Paraná came to define the power of the central government to intervene in the internal affairs of the provinces, it had two outstanding examples to draw upon. These were the constitutions of the Swiss confederation and of the United States.

The Swiss Constitution of 1848 contained seven separate articles bearing upon the power of intervention. Article 5 guaranteed " to the provinces their territory, their sovereignty, with the limits fixed by Article 3 [the sovereignty of the cantons is limited by the federal constitution], their constitutions, the liberty and rights of the people, the constitutional rights of citizens, and the rights and powers which the people have conferred on those in authority." By Article 6 the confederation guaranteed the cantonal constitutions provided that the cantons safeguarded the exercise of political rights, " according to republican forms, representative or democratic."

Other relevant provisions of the constitution deal with protection in case of foreign invasion, internal disturbances, and inter-cantonal disputes. In the case of internal disturbance, or if danger is threatened by another canton, the authorities of the threatened canton are to give notice to the federal executive. The Federal Council is empowered to act on its own up to the limit of employing two thousand troops, subject to the additional condition that the troops are in action no more than two weeks. Otherwise, the Council must call a session of the assembly. Under certain conditions intervention may take place in the absence of a request from the cantons.

The provisions of the Constitution of the United States are simpler. In Article IV, section 4, the power of intervention was defined in the following terms:

> The United States shall guarantee to every State in this Union a republican form of goverment, and shall protect each of them against invasion; and on the application of the Legislature, or of the Executive, when the legislature cannot be convened, against domestic violence.

Besides the examples of the Swiss and North American Constitutions, the congressmen at Paraná had before them the agreements of 1831 and 1852 and the suggestions of Alberdi. The tri-partite treaty of 1831 between Buenos Aires, Santa Fé, and Entre Ríos provided, among other things, for mutual assistance in case of aggression against any of the signatory provinces. The agreement of San Nicolás entrusted to General Urquiza the organization of the provisional government pending the convocation of the constituent congress. Neither of these precedents offered much in the way of experience.

Alberdi's draft of a proposed constitution for the Argentine confederation contained three articles which outlined the power of intervention. They were as follows:

Article 4. The Confederation guarantees to the Provinces the republican system, the integrity of their territory, their interior peace.

Article 6. . . . The Confederation intervenes without requisition in their territory for the sole object of re-establishing order disturbed by sedition.

Article 7. The Confederation guarantees the stability of the provincial constitutions, so that they are not contrary to the general Constitution, for which reason they will be revised by the Congress before their sanction.

Alberdi's idea, it will be noted, was based on the principle of prior sanction of the provincial constitutions by the national congress. In a note to Article 7, Alberdi declared that his proposal was preferable to the provisions of the Constitution of the United States, since it required that provincial constitutions be patterned upon the national constitution. By requiring sanction of the national constitution the form of government in the provinces was assured.

The power of intervention was formulated by the congress of Paraná in Articles 5 and 6 of the constitution of 1853. The text of these articles is as follows:

Article 5. Each confederated Province shall draw up for itself a Constitution under the representative-republican system, in accordance with the principles, declarations, and guaranties of the national Constitution, by which is assured the administration of justice, its municipal régime and free primary education. The provincial constitutions will be revised by the Congress before promulgation. Under these conditions the federal government guarantees to each Province the enjoyment and exercise of its institutions.

Article 6. The federal government intervenes, with the requisition of the provincial legislatures or governors or without it, in the territory of any of the Provinces for the sole object of re-establishing the public order disturbed by sedition or of assuring the national security menaced by a foreign attack or peril.

It may be noted that Article 5 drew heavily upon the Swiss model whereas Article 6 introduces the American feature having to do with the legislatures and governors being specified as authorities. The provision that intervention is permissible without requisition was of Swiss and Argentine origin, and was strongly advocated by Alberdi.

Articles 5 and 6 were accepted without debate, a fact which was much regretted by many. During the interval between the 1853 Constitution and the Buenos Aires convention of 1860, two schools of interpretation arose. One school led by Alberdi adhered to the letter of the intervention clause and held that intervention could be exercised without request from provincial governments. The other school was of Buenos Aires motivation whose chief spokesman was

D. F. Sarmiento. This latter group, fearful of the central government in the event Buenos Aires joined the Confederation, maintained that intervention must not be invoked except at the request of the provincial legislature and governor, unless, of course, such a request was not possible. The Alberdi theory was accepted by Presidents Urquiza and Derquí, who invoked the intervention clause about twenty times in the period between 1853 and 1860.

Articles 5 and 6 of the Constitution of 1853 were modified in 1860 largely at the insistence of Buenos Aires. Little need be said about Article 5, in which two changes were made. Firstly, the requirement of "free primary education" was changed to the simpler "primary education," and secondly the requirement of prior sanction of provincial constitutions was altogether deleted. Article 6, on the other hand, brought forth a prolonged discussion. It was the procedure of invoking intervention with which Buenos Aires was concerned most. Three different formulae were considered. One advocated by Sarmiento was that used in Article IV, section 4, of the Constitution of the United States. The second formula was a rather lengthy provision which called for legislative and gubernatorial request in cases of sedition but which permitted intervention without request in cases where the authorities of the province had been overthrown or in cases of foreign peril or difficulties involving more than one province. The third proposal, the one finally adopted, is a mixture of the United States provision and Alberdi-Swiss ideas. In their final form Articles 5 and 6 in the Constitution read as follows:

Article 5. Each province shall adopt its own constitution, which shall provide for the administration of justice in its own territory, its municipal system, and primary instruction, such constitution to be framed upon the republican representative plan, in harmony with the principles, declarations, and guarantees of the national constitution. Upon these conditions, the federal government shall guarantee to each province the enjoyment and exercise of its institutions.

Article 6. The federal government shall have the right to intervene in the territory of the provinces in order to guarantee the republican form of government or to repel foreign invasions; and when requested by the constituted authorities, to maintain them in power, or to re-establish them if they shall have been deposed by sedition or by invasion from another province.

It may be well at this point to ascertain the meaning of certain terms of Article 6 of the Constitution as modified by the convention of 1860. To begin with, the convention failed to define more closely the term "federal government." Sarmiento would have liked to define the term in such a way as to eliminate the executive branch. The interventions from 1853 to 1860 had been significantly of executive manipulation and Sarmiento, along with many others, deplored the summary action of the executive in some of these interventions. The sinister events of the intervention in San Juan in 1857 were still fresh in the minds of the Buenos Aires delegates. However, precedents favored the broader interpretation, which included both the executive and legislative branches in the term "federal government." No definitive answer has been found and practice of the moment dictates the procedure.

Secondly, why was the phrase "to guarantee the republican form of government" used? It was known that in the Constitution of the United States the phrase referred to historical possibilities of the rise of aristocracy or monarchy. Alberdi argued that the phrase had no such application for Argentina since there were no political parties which advocated a monarchical or aristocratic form of government. At the convention, however, Sarmiento felt that the phrase could be interpreted to cover the threat to republican form of government inherent in *caudillismo*. Although the thought was not openly expressed at the convention, it is probable that the dictatorship of Rosas and the fear of General Urquiza induced the men of Buenos Aires to insist upon a safeguard against the emergence of dictatorial régimes in the provinces.

Thirdly, the term "requested" was not fully clarified, nor was it clear whether compliance of the federal government was optional or obligatory. The convention itself was divided on this point. General Bartolomé Mitre felt that the federal government was obliged to act upon the request of a province. Vélez Sarsfield, on the other hand, argued that the federal government was not obliged to heed such requests, since otherwise the armed forces of the government would in effect be at the beck and call of the provinces.

Fourthly, what was understood by the phrase "constituted authorities"? The committee which studied the constitution of 1853 and then drew up proposals for the convention of Buenos Aires had used the phrase " legitimate authorities." But ultimately this was changed to " constituted authorities." It was felt that by this change the area of requests was widened. There was also the desire to leave room for requests by *de facto* authorities, as well as those elected according to the law. The phrase " constituted authorities " has given rise to some interesting debates on the legitimacy of requests for intervention. The convention was somewhat obscure as to the scope of the term " authority." Sarmiento would confine the term to the legislature and the governor, whereas General Mitre was indefinite on the point. One thing was clear, the term was not intended to extend down to minor official positions. Dr. Basilio Salas remarked at the convention that the phrase as established could conceivably extend even to justices of the peace, but General Mitre threw this likelihood out with a statement which is now famous in Argentine writings on the subject: " It is one thing to say constituted in authority and another to say constituted authority."

Article 6 of the 1853 Constitution authorized intervention for the sole object of re-establishing public order disturbed by sedition. What was the significance of the change to the phrase " to sustain them or re-establish them if they have been deposed by sedition "? Sarmiento objected to the wording of the Constitution of 1853. He felt that in many instances of public disturbance the provinces needed no assistance from the national government. Intervention of this type, therefore, was made to hinge upon actual overthrow by sedition. In order to guard against possible removal of officials as a result of intervention, an attempt was made to give only two alternatives — either sustaining or re-establishing authority. Practice has shorn this phraseology of all the original intentions.

A glance at Article 6, as formulated by the convention of 1860, seems clear enough to the " outsider." Simply stated, the federal government can intervene without request to guarantee the republican form of government or to repel foreign invasions. When there is a case of sedition in a province which threatens the authorities in office, the federal government, upon request from the authorities of the province, will intervene in order to safeguard the status quo. If as a result of provincial sedition authorities are deposed, the federal government, again upon request, steps in to re-establish the deposed government.

III

During the seventy years following the convention of 1860, there were 101 officially ordered interventions into the provinces. Their distribution in time was rather uneven. In years of political stress interventions were more numerous and also more frequent, while in periods of stability they occurred infrequently or not at all. During Irigoyen's first administration (1916–22), when the *Unión Cívica Radical* was sweeping the provinces clean of the old conservative officeholders, there were as many as 9 provinces intervened at the same time in 1917 and 1918. On the other hand, there were periods when only one province was intervened or when no province was under the control of the central government. The longest lapse during which there were no interventions was a period of 3 years and 9 months from the spring of 1873 to early 1877 — a period when the intervention into Entre Ríos by Sarmiento's administration ended and early 1877 when Jujuy was intervened under President Avellaneda.

As for duration, the average intervention lasted from 5 to 6 months. The one of longest duration, 3 years, 6 months, and 2 days, was that in San Luis begun in May 1919; the shortest, 10 days, that in Mendoza, January 1889. La Rioja is second on the list of longest interventions — 2 years, 3 months, and 7 days; Buenos Aires, Catamarca, Corrientes, Entre Ríos, Mendoza, San Juan, Santa Fé, and Tucumán all endured interventions which lasted more than 12 months; thus, together with San Luis and La Rioja, 10 out of the 14 provinces had this experience. All of the provinces had short interventions ranging from 2 months and 8 days in Tucumán to 10 days in Mendoza, with 8 of the 14 provinces having interventions of less than a month's duration. (See Table I, opposite.)

It is interesting to inquire into the total duration of interventions in each province as compared with their frequency. The province of Corrientes had 11 interventions, followed by Catamarca and San Juan with 10 each, to rank as the highest; in the lowest category are Entre Ríos with 4 and Salta with 3. The number of interventions in

TABLE I. INTERVENTIONS IN THE PROVINCES — NUMBER, DURATION, AND FREQUENCY, BY PROVINCE

(October 1860 to September 1930)

Province	Number	Total time intervened	Percent of time intervened	Intervention of longest duration	Intervention of shortest duration	Longest period no intervention
Buenos Aires	7	3 yrs.	4.3	1 yr., 6 dys.	1 mo., 5 dys.	19 yrs.
Catamarca	10	4 yrs., 7 mos.	6.6	1 yr., 8 mos., 4 dys.	17 dys.	17½ yrs.
Córdoba	5	10 mos.	1.2	3 mos.	1 mo., 6 dys.	42 yrs.
Corrientes	11	5 yrs., 11 mos.	8.5	8 mos., 18 dys.	28 dys.	14 yrs.
Entre Ríos	4	2 yrs., 2 mos.	3.0	1 yr., 29 dys.	19 dys.	27 yrs.
Jujuy	7	2 yrs.	2.8	5 mos., 16 dys.	20 dys.	33 yrs.
La Rioja	9	6 yrs., 8 mos.	9.6	2 yrs., 3 mos., 7 dys.	1 mo., 4 dys.	14½ yrs.
Mendoza	8	6 yrs., 2 mos.	8.8	1 yr., 5 mos., 2 dys.	10 dys.	25½ yrs.
Salta	3	1 yr., 4 mos.	1.9	8 mos., 11 dys.	12 dys.	58½ yrs.
San Juan	10	4 yrs., 4 mos.	6.2	1 yr., 11 mos.	1 mo., 15 dys.	34 yrs.
San Luis	7	4 yrs., 11 mos.	7.0	3 yrs., 6 mos., 2 dys.	14 dys.	34 yrs.
Santa Fé	5	3 yrs., 5 mos.	5.0	1 yr., 4 mos., 17 dys.	2 mo., 6 dys.	25½ yrs.
Santiago del Estero	9	2 yrs., 8 mos.	3.8	8 mos., 15 dys.	12 dys.	22 yrs.
Tucumán	6	3 yrs., 8 mos.	5.2	1 yr., 2 mos., 7 dys.	2 mo., 8 dys.	27 yrs.
Total	101					

the other 9 provinces varied between these extremes. There seems to be no correlation between the number of interventions and the total duration. La Rioja was intervened for a total of 6 years and 8 months but ranked fourth in the number of interventions (9); Mendoza was intervened 8 times for a total of 6 years and 2 months; Corrientes, with 11 interventions, ranked third in total intervention time — 5 years and 11 months. In Córdoba 5 interventions lasted only 10 months; yet in Salta, the total time of its 3 interventions was 16 months.

As shown in Table I, no province was intervened for as much as 10 percent of the period under review. La Rioja was intervened for 9.6 percent of the period; Mendoza, for 8.8 percent of the period; Corrientes, 8.5 percent. At the other end of the scale Córdoba was intervened for 1.2 percent of the period and Salta for 1.9 percent. Each province enjoyed long periods without interventions — from Salta and Córdoba with respites of 58½ and 42 years, respectively, to La Rioja and Corrientes with lapses of 14½ and 14 years, respectively. Salta was not intervened until April 1918.

San Luis, the province with the longest intervention on record, had 7 interventions in all, but the long single intervention of over 3 years took up practically all of the total intervention time, leaving to the other 6 interventions a total of a little over one year.

In no province were there 2 consecutive interventions, although in some instances the interval between interventions was short. Generally speaking, the interval between interventions in any province was at least 6 months.

There does not appear to be any correlation between sizes, wealth, political make-up, or other physical and social characteristics, and the number of interventions in any province. Wealthy and poor provinces are found scattered through the list; large and small follow the same pattern; nor does there seem to be any special significance in geographical location.

During the period with which this study is concerned there were 18 presidents of the Argentine republic. Of these, 5 succeeded to the presidency from vice-presidential posts. Only one of the 18 presidents had no intervention connected with his administration — Pedernera, who as vice-president succeeded Derquí after the latter's resignation, and who served for only one month in the last days of 1861. During the administrations of all the other 17 presidents there was at least one intervention, either by presidential decree or congressional statute. Irigoyen led all the others with a grand total of 24 interventions during his 2 terms (1916–22 and 1928–30). As already intimated, Irigoyen was the first Radical President and he therefore undertook to place the Radical party in the ascendancy in all the provinces. Not a single province escaped intervention during Irigoyen's 2 terms, and Mendoza and San Juan were intervened 4 times each. The next most intervention-conscious President was Alvear, who followed Irigoyen's first administration and who continued the Radical policies (1922–28). In Alvear's administration there were 10 interventions in 8 provinces (2 each in La Rioja and Santiago del Estero). Four presidents had 8 each to their credit — Santiago Derquí, Bartolomé Mitre, Julio A. Roca, and Luis Sáenz Peña. The least intervention-conscious President, excepting Pedernera, was Quintana (1904–06), during whose administration there was but one intervention — and that one was ordered by congressional statute. Quintana did not serve a full six-year term, however, and his successor, Alcorta (1906–10), who rounded out the term was involved in 7 interventions.

The number of interventions in the administrations of the 5 presidents when well over half of the interventions occurred can be accounted for by reference to the pattern of political developments. Mention has already been made of Irigoyen and Alvear, leaders of the victorious Radical party. The two Radical presidents were involved in 34 interventions. Derquí and Mitre, the first 2 presidents to hold office after the 1860 constitutional reform, were involved in 16 interventions. These can be explained, generally speaking, by the fact that the republic was in the throes of the old unitary-versus-federalism controversy, and was faced with the problem of the all-powerful *caudillo* régimes in the provinces. The question of Buenos Aires' shaky allegiance to the confederation was also a significant factor. General Urquiza, the republic's first President, was still alive and was an important factor in the 2 administrations. Luis Sáenz

Peña, during whose administration there were 8 interventions, was faced with the problem of putting down, in the provinces, revolutions stirred by the newly formed Radical party silently and strongly led by Irigoyen. Six of Luis Sáenz Peña's interventions were caused directly or indirectly by these revolutions.

Of the 101 interventions, 64 were initiated by presidential decrees, 6 of which were later sanctioned by congress; 37 interventions were initiated in the first instance by congress.

As was the case with the total number of interventions in certain administrations, the number of interventions by decree under specific administrations was conditioned by political developments. Irigoyen and Alvear, the Radical presidents, accounted for 22 decrees — over one third of the total 64. So, too, Derquí and Mitre, busy with the affairs of the *caudillos* and federalist tendencies in the interior, relied on presidential decrees to effect their policies to the extent of 14 decrees between them. President Sarmiento enters the picture at this point with 6 decrees (two of which were sanctioned by congress) which were the result of Sarmiento's unyielding stand on the authority of the president to initiate interventions in the interest of speed and effective action. Sarmiento also was immersed in the *caudillo* question and, with a deep hatred of *caudillismo,* took action to wipe out the last vestiges of its power in the interior.

Most of the presidents decreed at least as many interventions as the congress ordered by statute, with a substantial number of presidents decreeing considerably more. The congress held its own in ordering interventions during the period from 1880 to 1910 — a period comparatively uneventful as far as political upheavals are concerned, with the exception of the Radical revolution of 1893. The Radical revolution resulted in interventions which were largely the result of congressional acts. Luis Sáenz Peña, the President at the time, was never strongly convinced as to the presidential right to initiate intervention, and, furthermore, the Radical uprisings were of such nature that the congress felt itself endangered. Added to this was the fact that the uprisings occurred during the session of the national congress. Uriburu, the vice-president who succeeded Sáenz Peña, also made little use of the decree and the congress ordered 5 interventions during his administration. Luis Sáenz Peña and Uriburu were elected as compromise candidates and during this administration the congress definitely held the upper hand.

There is no doubt that there was a tendency on the part of the executive to invoke intervention when congress was not in session. Of the 64 interventions ordered by presidential decree, 51 were ordered when congress was in recess and the remaining 13 while congress was in session. Since 6 of the 13 decrees while congress was in session were later sanctioned by congressional acts, only 7 intervention decrees were without congressional approval. Irigoyen and Alvear again led all the other presidents in decrees ordering intervention during congressional recess, Irigoyen accounting for 15 and Alvear for 7 intervention decrees. The first 4 presidents, excluding Pedernera, accounted for the bulk of the remainder — Derquí with 2, Mitre 4, Sarmiento 4, and Avellaneda 3. All the presidents decreed intervention during the recess of congress except Pedernera, Roca (in his first term), and Quintana, and these 3 did not resort to the decree in any form. It should be noted that intervention by decree during congressional session went out of fashion after Avellaneda except for the lone example of Roca in his second term — and this was one which the congress later sanctioned. Thus, it was not until the 1880's that the congress was respected while in session and the expedient of decreeing intervention during recess became fashionable. It is true that intervention by decree was not unknown during the early administrations, but it was not until after 1880 that this form of intervention became generally accepted. The period represented by the early presidents was really a formative one when the decree was resorted to at any time the president felt so inclined.

Classification of interventions into the reconstructive or executive types is not easily accomplished, principally because the decrees and statutes often make no specific mention of the constitutional articles invoked or even the nature of the constitutional authorization. Thus recourse must be had to the circumstances giving rise to the intervention and these are not always sufficiently unequivocal to permit a clear-cut classification. Furthermore, reconstructive intervention is the broadest sort of intervention and might well be based upon facts which by themselves could be considered as leading to executive intervention. Many Argentine interventions initiated merely for the purpose of sustaining or re-establishing authorities were eventually broadened into the reconstructive type on the grounds that the republican form of government was threatened.

Taking the specific references to constitutional authorizations and considering the circumstances surrounding interventions, the reconstructive type appears the most frequently invoked. There were approximately 65 cases of reconstructive intervention, 24 executive interventions, and 12 which were authorized by the justifiable right of the central government to put down rebellion and to enforce the national laws. It is well to bear in mind that many of these are classified on the basis of superficial motivations and do not take into account the machinations of the central government in manufacturing conditions requiring intervention. The great bulk of the reconstructive interventions — about 55 out of 65 — were concerned with the organization of the provincial government after revolutions or deadlocks between the executive and judicial branches. In such cases the " organization of the powers " fell under the guarantee of the republican form of government or the exercise and enjoyment of provincial institutions. The other reconstructive interventions were concerned with foreign attack and states of anarchy resulting from various causes.

Executive interventions involved deposed authorities which requested assistance (although the request was at times merely implied). In some cases all the authorities were deposed; in others, a single power or pair of powers may have suffered. The deposing of the authorities was usually caused by revolutions and uprisings of various kinds in the provinces. A few of the executive interventions were invoked as a result of invasions of one province by another.

Decrees and statutes for intervention are likely to omit mention of the requesting authority just as the omission of constitutional authorization was often omitted. Of the 101 interventions, 46 appear to have been requested, another 18 were imposed without request, 5 were based on information from a special investigator sent into the province by the president, and the remainder are doubtful (it is likely that many of the doubtful ones really involved requests).

Requests for intervention originated in all branches of the provincial government, although some were more active in this respect than others. As already stated, at least 46 interventions involved positive requests from the provincial authorities. The governor was the most active of the authorities in requesting intervention. In 18 cases, a deposed governor requested intervention in order to restore himself or, if sedition threatened to depose him, to sustain himself. In at least 7 others, the governor requested intervention along with the legislature; and in at least 2 cases, the interim or provisional governor made such request; the defeated candidate for governor requested intervention in at least one case; and the governor was represented in 5 other requests which were issued in the name of the " powers " of the province. The next most frequent petitioner was the legislature acting alone (10 such requests), usually because the governor thwarted it in some way. The legislature, in the 7 cases mentioned above, was a partner to requests with the governor and in 5 cases it was one of the " powers " requesting intervention. In a few cases the legislative request was made by the president of the legislature. In at least one case one of two elected legislatures requested intervention. The provincial judiciary was not a significant factor in requests for intervention. In the 5 cases where the " powers " made the request, it was a party to the proceedings. The judiciary did attempt to bring about intervention on its own account but without success. In one case the electoral college made a successful request. In 2 cases, requests appear to have been made by obscure individuals or groups of individuals with no official standing.

Of the 101 interventions, 41 were the direct result of the inability of the governor and the legislature to cooperate. A large share of these were involved in impeachment proceedings; another major cause was conflict in the selection of national senators. Another 11 interventions were ordered to " organize the powers "; these point to the desire to reorganize the provincial governments which are generally ineffective or simply inimical to the dominant party. In 12 cases rebellion against the central government brought intervention. Ranking high in frequency also are the 26 cases involving the actual or threatened deposition of authorities by revolutionists — 11 of these involving the governor, 3 the governor and the legislature, 6 involving all the powers, one involving the deposition of provincial senators, and 5 involving the threat to one or more powers.

Among the less frequent causes of intervention were anarchy (3), foreign attack (2), and to conduct long-overdue gubernatorial elections.

As has been intimated, the president often had a hand in creating conditions that would justify intervention on constitutional grounds. There is sufficient evidence to show that in many instances the provinces could very well have ironed out their difficulties without the benefit of intervention. With the weight of the central government known to be sympathetic to a faction out of power in the province, it was not difficult to inspire uprising to effect a change; and, on the other hand, it was an easy remedy for the provincial authorities who enjoyed the favor of the president to call for intervention for the purpose of settling conditions without the inconvenience of making concessions.

The usual method of action in case of intervention was to conduct elections and to turn over the government to the victorious candidates. This meant either the legal re-establishment of the same authorities, the legal support for authorities set up by sedition or revolution, or the election of new authorities altogether. Out of the 101 interventions, 72 resulted in elections of the legislature, the electoral college, the governor, and others, or some one of them, or in various combinations. In 20 other cases there were no elections — the authorities either being sustained or re-established or a mere pacification enforced. The result in the 9 remaining interventions is not clear, although most of these probably involved election to some degree.

Complete statistics on the result of the elections are not available. In his *Historia de las Intervenciones,* Sommariva sets forth the results of elections in 62 interventions for the period from 1860 to 1910. In these interventions, 14 favored the governor or his group, 4 favored parties of neither side, 6 amounted to nothing except local disturbances, and 38 favored the opposing faction. On this basis it is probably safe to state that of the 72 interventions up to the September revolution of 1930 which resulted in elections, well over half, and probably two thirds, favored the candidates of the factions that opposed the provincial administration.

TABLE II. INTERVENTIONS — DECREES AND STATUTES,
BY PRESIDENTIAL ADMINISTRATION

(October 1860 to September 1930)

President	Years	Number of interventions	Decrees	Statutes	Decrees followed by statutory sanction
Derquí.........	1860–61	8	7	I	0
Pedernera *....	1861 (Nov.–Dec.)	0			
Mitre..........	1862–68	8	7	I	I
Sarmiento......	1868–74	6	6	0	2
Avellaneda.....	1874–80	6	5	I	2
Roca..........	1880–86	2	0	2	0
Juárez Celman..	1886–90	2	I	I	0
Pellegrini *.....	1890–92	3	2	I	0
L. Sáenz Peña..	1892–95	8	I	7	0
Uriburu *......	1895–98	6	I	5	0
Roca.	1898–1904	6	3	3	I
Quintana.......	1904–06	I	0	I	0
Alcorta *.......	1906–10	7	4	3	0
R. Sáenz Peña..	1910–14	2	2	0	0
V. de la Plaza *.	1914–16	2	I	I	0
Irigoyen.......	1916–22	20	15	5	0
Alvear.........	1922–28	10	7	3	0
Irigoyen.......	1928–30	4	2	2	0
		101	64	37	6

* Vice-presidents succeeding to the presidency.

TABLE III. INTERVENTIONS BY DECREE, DURING THE
RECESS AND SESSION OF CONGRESS, BY PRESIDENTS

(October 1860 to September 1930)

President	Years	Decrees during recess	Decrees during sessions	Sanctioned by statute
Derquí.........	1860–61	2	5	0
Pedernera *....	1861 (Nov.–Dec.)	0	0	
Mitre..........	1862–68	4	3	1
Sarmiento......	1868–74	4	2	2
Avellaneda.....	1874–80	3	1	2
Roca..........	1880–86	0	0	
Juárez Celman..	1886–90	1	0	0
Pellegrini *.....	1890–92	2	0	0
L. Sáenz Peña..	1892–95	1	0	0
Uriburu *......	1895–98	1	0	0
Roca..........	1898–1904	2	1	1
Quintana......	1904–06	0	0	
Alcorta *.......	1906–10	4	0	0
R. Sáenz Peña..	1910–14	2	0	0
V. de la Plaza *.	1914–16	1	0	0
Irigoyen......	1916–22	15	0	0
Alvear.........	1922–28	7	9	0
Irigoyen.......	1928–30	2	0	0
		15	13	6

* Vice-presidents succeeding to the presidency.

CHAPTER 9

Presidents or Dictators?

No. 27 [With but few exceptions the Latin American republics have established presidential systems of government which are based, as is our own, upon the theory of separation of political powers. The parliamentary or cabinet system, founded upon a fusion of executive and legislative authority, has not been attractive to the architects of government south of the Canadian border.

The constitutional and political expressions of the theory of separation of powers in the United States are seen in the establishment of three great government departments: the legislative, the executive, and the judicial. This is the order of their mention in the Constitution of the United States. Each of these departments is relatively independent *of* the other two, each has some check or control *over* the others. American political literature reserves a large proportion of its pages to a discussion of the question: "Which of the three major departments is really supreme?" Or, to use Woodrow Wilson's phrase, in which of them will one encounter the real center of political gravity? The quantity of the writing and the very divergent points of view it presents indicate that in a general sense the answer is not clear. While one may clearly see, at any given time in our constitutional and political history, that the President, Congress *or* the Supreme Court seemed to be the final arbiter of political action it is virtually impossible to generalize for the whole sweep of American political history. This indicates that we have the practice as well as the theory of separation of powers.

If Dr. Gallup were to poll Latin Americans on the question: " Where, in *your* system of government, does the real power lie? " the answer would be an almost unanimous one. The constitution makes the president of the republic the officer who initiates policy, largely controls its formulation or adoption, and who has few checks upon his authority in the executive-administrative field. It is not without significance that Latin American constitutions almost always mention first the executive power.

Professor Fitzgibbon's article refers to what he calls the " over-development " of executive power in Central America. He indicates what the constitutional bases for this over-development are, and how these constitutional factors influence, and in turn are influenced by, the party system and the actual operation of government. Although he restricts his study to the Central American states, the nature and trends of executive power he finds there are, in fact, characteristic of almost all of the republics of Latin America.

Presidents in Argentina or Bolivia, Uruguay or Venezuela, and most of those in between have a constitutional executive authority that makes the power of the President of the United States seem weak by comparison. In these countries, too, the broad constitutional power is augmented and enhanced by the chief executive's political controls.

We in the United States have had several " strong " Presidents, but even they have not been able completely to dominate the other branches of government during their administrations. Usually we have reverted to Congressional control of our political machine when our " strong " Presidents have retired from office. Latin American executives, with but few exceptions, fall into the category of " strong " presidents.]

Executive Power in Central America *

by RUSSELL H. FITZGIBBON

*T*HE predominant factor in the governments of the Central American states is force. This does not, of course, make them unique among the Latin American republics. Nor can it be said that this *leitmotif* is uniform throughout the five countries under review. If

* Russell H. Fitzgibbon, " Executive Power in Central America," *The Journal of Politics* (August, 1941), Vol. 3, No. 3, pp. 297–307. Reprinted by permission of *The Journal of Politics*. The footnotes in the original version are omitted here.

there be value in generalization, however, this common element of force as the mainspring of governmental action may be said to characterize the area. Force is present as extensively as it is because of a wide variety of elements. The situation may be summed up by saying that many of those factors which make for the good life and the full life of peoples are lacking or only inadequately developed in the isthmian area and, hence, in the absence of the controls which such factors produce, sheer physico-military power moves in to regulate the governmental and political mechanism. One could better say that force *remains* in, since in the evolution of many governments it is the original controlling influence — the more enlightened controls develop only with the social growth of the population.

It is difficult to say whether *caudillismo* is a thing of the past in the Central American republics. The difficulty flows from the fluid definition and the uncertain boundaries of the term itself. Certainly *caudillismo* in time tends to become refined in technique and constitutionalized, though perhaps none the less dependent on the military for support. As executive maturity thus subtly comes, perhaps we should drop the term *caudillismo,* with all its connotations of political immaturity, and substitute " strong presidential government." Even the threadbare term *dictatorship,* with all of its lack of precision in definition, is in some ways preferable to *caudillismo.* In practice the various terms may represent a distinction without a difference. They do vary in implications, however. At any rate, the continued dominance in four of the five countries of governments put and kept in office because of their reliance upon armed forces is result as well as cause.

It is the result of a relatively low standard of living which has made considerable masses of the population so intent upon gaining a subsistence that by default they have allowed political control to gravitate into the hands of those who were willing and even eager to assure that control by resort to force. It is the result of an appallingly high percentage of illiteracy, well over 50 percent in four of the five states, which has prevented that dissemination of ideas and information which in time introduce a slow leaven operating toward political consciousness, articulateness, and control. It is the result of an inadequate network of railroads and highways which has intensified and prolonged that isolation and localism which permit control by the one who can surmount such barriers with armored trucks, machine guns, and military airplanes. It is the result of an economic base traditionally so narrow that the successive governments have simply lacked the financial resources that would enable them to forego arbitrariness and oppression. The many parts of the jigsaw picture fit intricately into one another and the pattern of military dominance is the product of the whole picture when completed. In such circumstances the electoral process becomes in greater or less degree a farce. Bullets or the threat of bullets must inevitably take precedence over ballots. Revolution becomes a customary and indispensable political tool. Revolution breeds and feeds on itself; and, hence, the vicious circle is completed and the sordid system perpetuated.

Such is the general picture. Like all general views, however, it is necessarily compounded of more specific and tangible elements, and it therefore becomes important to examine some of them. We may start with the general premise that if the executive power in any or all of the Central American republics is overdeveloped in accordance with some yardstick to be adopted from the "typical" and "standard" democracies of the world — whichever ones they may be — it is *prima facie* evidence that certain other elements in the public political life of the isthmian area either have atrophied or have not yet developed adequately. Among these elements may be included the legislative and judicial branches of the several governments, political parties, and the more amorphous public opinion. It becomes necessary, then, (a) to look to the constitutions of the various countries to see what light they can shed on the position and role of the executive, (b) to examine the actual operation of government so that we may detect any divergences between it and the constitutional norms which the basic laws set up, with especial reference to the relations between the executive and the other branches of the government, and (c) to survey the party scene, public opinion, and other such factors.

It is well known, of course, that Latin American statesmen have often written their utopias into their countries' constitutions and that these basic laws have frequently embodied more the hopes, ideals, and aspirations of their authors than the crystallized and accepted convictions of the mass of the people for whom the authors presumably spoke. The pathetic futility of blind and naïve reliance on constitutional forms, even good forms, is excellently illustrated in various experiences that some of the Central American states have had. Granted that some of these constitutions seem to have been written almost *in vacuo* and that they often reflect a lack of realism, it is still important to see what they contain at certain points since they at least serve as points of departure for the actual practice of government.

The customary organization of the national governments into legislative, executive, and judicial " powers " (*poderes*) or branches, in that order, is naturally a violation of logical arrangement because of the pre-eminence of the presidency in all of the states with the possible exception of Costa Rica. All five republics maintain the fiction of a freely elected presidency although in the four northern states recent amendments or new fundamental laws — changes which have been popularly labeled " *continuismo* " — have produced thinly disguised constitutional dictatorships.

The various constitutions naturally specify presidential qualifications, both positively and negatively. Among the latter are the debarment of those who are closely related to the incumbent chief of state, those who have participated in revolutions or *coups d'état,* generals, ministers of state, and others. These negative qualifications are reminiscent in part of some of the provisions of the Washington treaties of 1907 and 1923, but in greater degree are typical of the customarily useless Latin American attempts to keep presidential domination within proper limits by constitutional fiat. The ineffectiveness of such provisions, it may be remarked parenthetically, is illustrated by the current [1941] situation in Central America. President Somoza of Nicaragua was doubly ineligible on constitutional grounds for the office he maneuvered himself into; General Martínez of El Salvador attained the presidential chair by a *coup d'état* and hence was nominally disqualified although he was constitutionally in line for the presidency, and the legality of Carías' accession to the Honduran presidency might, by any sort of rigorous interpretation, be seriously questioned.

All of the Central American constitutions except the Honduran establish presidential responsibility. The statements of it vary widely, and from the language employed there is little to indicate that it might not mean political as well as legal responsibility. The entire absence through all Central American political history, however, of any suggestion of cabinet government would definitely preclude any assumption that other than legal responsibility is intended, and in any case the actual development of the Central American governments makes any constitutional statement of executive responsibility chiefly rhetorical.

Each of the constitutions provides, of course, for a cabinet or ministry, and in all cases the appropriate minister is required to attest the acts of the president with his countersignature before they can become effective. Almost the whole implication of the various constitutions is, though, that the ministers are subordinated to the president: not only are their original choice and their continuance in office matters of their chief's pleasure, but their entire political responsibility is to the head of the government. No constitution even requires their appointment to be submitted to legislative confirmation, and impeachment is as awkward and rare as it is in the United States.

But executive powers and duties are, after all, more important than the structure of the executive office. The five constitutions are very similar in their description of presidential powers, although in a few instances particular references suggest, subtly and perhaps unconsciously, individual political problems or situations peculiar to the respective countries. Thus, some of the Honduran president's powers are reminiscent of the old fear of invasion or foreign political intervention; in Costa Rica the description of presidential duties and responsibilities emphasizes, indirectly at least, the importance of individual rights in that democratic little republic. The grant of powers in Nicaragua involves the longest step toward constitutionally established presidential dominance.

The very general powers and responsibilities — defense of the territorial integrity and independence of the nation, enforcement of compliance with the constitution and the laws, and others — are stated much more broadly in most Central American constitutions than anything we find in the basic law of the United States. We are familiar, of course, with the casually imposed — or at least casually developed — military role of the President of the United States as commander in chief of the army and navy, but in the various Central American constitutions the grant of military power is not only much more detailed, but it also carries the impression of much more reality and importance than the simple statement in Article II, section 2, of the United States Constitution. Central American development illustrates the tremendous advantage possessed by the man with epaulets, especially if he can be at the same time a man on horseback, and such a stacking of the political cards finds some constitutional reflection. The Salvadorian fundamental law, for example, prohibits (as is common) political activity to members of the military, but, as an exception, makes them eligible for the presidency.

The constitutions commonly specify the president's powers over the legislative process. Each of the chiefs of state may formally introduce bills (*proyectos de ley*) in the congress. All of the constitutions except the Nicaraguan provide for the issuance of presidential regulations for the execution of the laws passed. In addition, the president in one or another of the countries has various other controls over legislative activity. Many miscellaneous functions — economic, social, cultural, religious — are constitutionally laid on various presidential desks.

In the domain of local government the average Central American president has great *de jure* as well as actual power. The whole constitutional implication is that the territorial departments are simply political and administrative subdivisions of the respective central governments. The president in each country appoints the governor (*jefe político*) of each department, and in Nicaragua the national executive appoints all municipal officials as well. It is a recognized fact, even if not always stated in constitutional black and white, that the provincial governors are, first of all, the political agents of the national president. The municipalities, too, even with their greater tradition of autonomy, are largely subject to this same presidential dominance. In Guatemala the president is authorized to fix the municipal excise taxes and to modify (or provide if necessary) town ordinances. In Nicaragua the chief executive has supervision over all functions of the municipality; all local laws are subject to his approval.

Were the constitutions of the Central American states less easily changed, both in theory and practice, one would expect more divergence between them and the governmental forms and relationships they describe. As it is, the basic laws reflect with fair faithfulness the actual forms and relationships encountered, since their amendment is little more than a matter of presidential will. There is a great deal of political flesh to be added to the several constitutional skeletons, however.

It is one thing to say, after reading the constitutions, that the ministers are the dignified heads of separate executive departments and that their signatures are prerequisite to the validity of the president's acts. The fact remains that in all of the countries — an exception is scarcely to be made of Costa Rica — the ministers are the political allies and very definitely the subordinates of the respective presidents. It is too belittling a phrase to call them glorified errand boys, but if a willful and capable person occupies the presidential palace, even a strong and ambitious minister is likely to pale into unimportance beside him.

It is one thing to say that all presidents, including the Central American, are apt to have some constitutional grant of military power, but it is quite a different thing in fact when one realizes that with the exception of President Calderón Guardia of Costa Rica the incumbent presidents represent lifelong military backgrounds and that in the same four cases the figurative avenue to the presidential office was lined with bayonets.

It is one thing to suggest that the Central American presidents have certain carefully prescribed legislative functions but the facts go much beyond the unilluminating constitutional verbiage. In the four Central American dictatorships a large fraction of the ultimate legislation is that enacted by decree rather than by the normal legislative process. The president's ordinance power is such that he can ordinarily alter the spirit as well as the form of congressional enactments by means of the regulations by which he puts them into operation. In the four northern republics it is not necessary to resort to indirection; the president simply exerts his influence upon the legislature itself and the amenable members pass bills in the desired form. Even in Costa Rica presidential influence is felt. What customarily happens there is that in the regular sessions of congress, where the agenda is unrestricted, the very lively wrangling by the congressmen and the large-scale introduction of their own measures prevent much progress in the realization of a constructive legislation program. It is consequently necessary for the president to call frequent and prolonged special sessions, in which the legislature may consider only those matters presidentially referred to it. Two results are that the legislature is frequently in session during a large part of the year and that the bulk of important legislation is passed during special sessions.

So far as the judiciary is concerned, it is usually free from interference in the lower levels and in routine matters because presidential domination is not a matter of importance. The upper reaches of the court systems of all of the states except Costa Rica, however, are very much subject to executive influence for political purposes. Judicial independence becomes a fiction and public opinion, while perhaps not sympathizing with this situation of subordination, does not demand that it be otherwise.

Local government lacks vigor and personality in Central America. Exceptions are to be made to this generalization, especially in the case of Guatemala and to a lesser degree of El Salvador and Costa Rica. The general situation, though, throws this natural school for political training into the hands of the respective president, and he customarily exploits it almost as a matter of vested interest.

We normally look to political parties for the canalizing of sentiment pointing toward control of a government. Political parties are a natural and inevitable accompaniment of democratic government. They have flourished like the green bay tree in the Central American states even though currently in Guatemala and Honduras one finds at least a *de facto* approach to the monopoly of the party scene by an " official " party as in Germany, Italy, or Russia. Parties are fluid things — nowhere more so than in the average Central American state. But unless that fluidity thins out into a watery insubstantiality (as is unfortunately frequently the case with the isthmian groups), we can cite it as a positive advantage; it permits adaptation to changing political circumstances, issues, and problems, which keeps the party a vital and energetic control over government.

Several factors in the evolution of Central American parties are worthy of brief note. It was a natural and easy, perhaps almost an inevitable, tendency for the politically articulate Central American population of the immediate post-revolutionary period to gravitate into the two groups receiving the names *Liberal* and *Conservative.* The impetus of this isthmus-wide organization of parties carried over after the disintegration of the Central American Federation in 1838. Parties then became international in character: each of the five independent states had its Conservative and its Liberal party, continuing, with a certain evaporation, their distinctness of policy and composition. This situation prevailed for a long generation and was kept the longer, no doubt, because of the practice of party adherents in one republic sympathizing with and aiding those bearing the same political label in the other states.

In the 1870's, because of a complex of political and social factors, the feudal character of party politics in Central America began to disappear. With it gradually passed the habit of interference in the political affairs of neighboring states. The result was that politics in Central America became less international in character and, by the same token, more confined in its form and manifestations within the limits of each state. Contemporaneous with this subtle change the earlier distinctions between the Liberals and Conservatives began to fade, both as to policies and composition. *Liberal* and *Conservative,* although the impetus and prestige of the names carried on for a long time (in some cases to the present), became mere party labels and not true descriptions.

The next gradual step in this evolution of parties was the manifestation of a tendency toward fractionation. It was a logical step in view of the personalism inherent in Central American politics. Each republic's Conservative and Liberal parties began almost unconsciously to split into " splinter parties " following this or that Conservative or Liberal leader. This inevitably meant a greater degree of impermanence in party organization and a continued decline in political conviction as the basis for party adherence. A further trend, suggested before, and illustrated in those states in which democracy has most languished, has been toward the outlawing of all parties except that supporting the dictator in power. This has led to the grim jest that each of the more strongly governed states has two parties —

the one in power and the one in jail. Party opponents of the administration in power in the more dictatorially ruled countries must, in effect, keep their baggage packed for a hasty exodus depending on the turns of the political wheel of fortune. The result has been the gathering of colonies of political exiles from the four northern states, chiefly in Mexico City and San José de Costa Rica, although Los Angeles and San Diego have their quotas, too.

The net result of this involved course of party growth has been the perversion of parties from their normal and desirable functions as demonstrated in countries of longer party development. There is in no Central American state anything even remotely approaching " His Majesty's loyal opposition " or even faintly akin to that intelligent and constructive watchfulness which Mr. Willkie bespoke for the Republican party as its role. Parties in Central American public life have become converted almost solely into instruments for realizing personal political ambitions. Aside from the venality which one might find in the party functioning of any country, there is a degree of accommodation and *sub rosa* cooperation to be found in the party life of certain Central American states which augurs poorly for any early growth of political vitality or control over the presidents and the processes of government.

That tenuous thing we know as public opinion is particularly mercurial in the Central American area. It is, of course, only in recent years that we have begun anything like a scientific study of this subject in the United States, and much yet remains to be done in the way of devising measurements, definitions, and controls. How much less capable of test-tube analysis must public opinion be in Central America!

In Costa Rica public opinion may be said to exist, but it is highly volatile, certainly. Its expressions and reflections become so volcanic, especially on the occasions of the quadrennial presidential campaigns, that an intelligent and internationally known figure like Señor Luis Anderson refuses to take part in conventional politics because of the amount of mud-slinging involved — and the mud there is very, very black and sticky.

Public opinion in El Salvador, expressed primarily through commercial and professional organizations, had developed to a point

where many people hoped that it might soon become an effective
control against presidential arbitrariness. Yet the insubstantial nature
of such a control even in that tight little republic was easily demonstrated by the facility and unconcern with which President Martínez flouted the unquestioned sentiment of large segments of the
population in 1939 and engineered his own re-election to the presidency by the channel of constitutional distortion.

In the other three republics public opinion is, for all practical purposes, nonexistent. The Indian population of Guatemala and the
bulk of the mestizo population of Honduras and Nicaragua is so politically inarticulate and even unconscious that trial balloons need
form no part of the arsenal of presidential techniques.

In the comments that have preceded this there has no doubt been
reflected a considerable overtone of criticism. That is perhaps only
natural when one surveys the Central American political scene from
what we fondly consider to be the Olympian superiority of democratic achievement in the United States. Yet something is to be said,
in view of circumstances, for the type of rule found in the northern
Central American states. Call it what we will — strong presidential
government, dictatorship, a modified *caudillismo* — it is perhaps de-
fensible in some ways. As I had occasion to write elsewhere, one
school of thought argues, " What is needed is not illusory popular
participation in the business of government but rather the peace and
order which will make possible the material and cultural progress
that will ultimately lead to a genuine democracy. A large fraction of the population of such countries no doubt honestly prefers the
stability and calm of a dictatorship, especially if a reasonably constructive one, to the uncertainty and confusion of ' democracy.' "

This demonstration of strong executive power is in varying degree
an ever-present fact in Central America today. The government of
Guatemala is in all likelihood the most dynamic and constructive. It,
as is normally true of Latin American dictatorships, is but the lengthened shadow of a man, and it so happens that in General Ubico the
republic possesses a dictator who combines firmness with energy,
some vision, and a considerable concern for the welfare of his country. His interesting " reforms " — he himself might scorn that word
— may well in some measure outlast the man himself and become a
national habit in Guatemala. President Martínez of El Salvador has

in general patterned his administration after the Ubican régime, but it has on the whole lacked the positive character and accomplishment of the other. The dictators of Nicaragua and Honduras offer still less in the way of capacity, achievement, and promise than do those of Guatemala and El Salvador; in both cases they speak only the language of a microcosmic *Machtpolitik*. Most Costa Rican presidents have been able to exercise a considerable influence over their government; but in that country, government falls far short of approximating the one-man institution which exists for all practical purposes in the other four states.

The prospects of government and politics in the isthmian republics are not by any means hopeless. Dictatorships seem firmly in the saddle in four of the states, but the type of dictatorship is becoming stabilized and clothed in a garb of constitutionalism. The net effect of the changes has been to discourage the " insurrectionary habit," as Theodore Roosevelt labeled it, because the current rulers have had such firm hold on the reins. The same end is served by the balance wheel furnished by the growing economic interests (both domestic and foreign) of the several countries, interests which correctly see in successive revolutions only a disturbing and disrupting situation — revolutions are not " good for business."

It is the exceptional dictator who does not strive for material accomplishment during his period of power. The amount of constructive gain will quite likely be measured in terms of the dictator's own capacity, but the desire is almost always present even if for no other reason than adornment of the niche he is to occupy in history. This achievement means in concrete language the improvement of communications, the building of roads, the construction of ports, the distribution of lands, the passage of labor legislation which may ultimately gain some real force, in time even campaigns against endemic disease, illiteracy, maldistribution of wealth, and other such intangible problems.

These accomplishments must inevitably result in a gradual social maturing and this in turn in a certain amount of political education. With the growth of the latter, particularly as re-enforced by the stabilizing influences of a developing economy, dictatorship in Central America may well face the handwriting on the wall. Costa Rica has pointed the way. In the meantime it regards the troubled strivings of the other republics with a certain aloofness and detachment, but in some future of unpredictable date there is no reason why some or all of the other states should not align themselves alongside Costa Rica.

No. 28   [The nature and characteristics of presidential control over the machinery and actions of government in one of the major Latin American countries is the subject of Professor Tannenbaum's essay. In his detailed examination of what so many Latin American writers have labeled *personalismo* he notes those factors which have combined to make government in Mexico *presidential* government. These include the constitutional grants of power and their interpretation and application, the important role which the army plays in civil affairs, the tax system which gives to the central government the bulk of the public revenues, and the nature and organization of the controlling political party.

In evaluating presidential control over government in Mexico he comments on the influence of organizations of workingmen and farmers and expresses the opinion that the personal nature of government is being given a broader mass base through these groups. It is his conclusion that the executive must be strong in Mexico or Mexico will face revolution.]

Personal Government in Mexico *

by FRANK TANNENBAUM

FOR a half a century up to 1876, the one political certainty in Mexico was that any government, regardless of party or announced purpose — good, bad, or indifferent — would be overthrown. Only two governments in all this time lasted through their allotted periods, and even these only because they had the good luck to defeat numerous efforts to overthrow them. Almost every part of Mexico at one time

* Reprinted from *Mexico: The Struggle for Peace and Bread* by Frank Tannenbaum, by permission of Alfred A. Knopf, Inc. Copyright 1950 by Frank Tannenbaum. (The article " Personal Government in Mexico " originally appeared in *Foreign Affairs* [October, 1948], Vol. 27, No. 1, pp. 44–57. Reprinted by permission of *Foreign Affairs*.)

or another threatened to set up a separate government, and the miracle is that only Texas carried the threat to fruition. Entire regions were independent of the federal government for years at a time.

The Díaz régime produced the great political miracle in modern Mexico — stability. It is probably true that the Díaz régime was no more just or free from violence than the previous improvised administrations. But it did keep order. At least everyone knew where the power rested — in the person of General Díaz. By controlling the army he controlled the country. It was under this régime that Mexico became a nation with a sense of destiny and coherence. An extensive program of development of railroads, ports, telegraphs, and so on was possible, and this in turn contributed to political consolidation.

The revolution of 1910 returned the nation to chaos. Between 1910 and 1930, the country was either torn by revolution or in active preparation for revolution. The local *caudillo* reappeared and the federal government did not dare challenge him for fear that he and his friends — or he and the government's numerous enemies — would prove stronger than itself. The governments lived upon sufferance. All the astute ruthlessness of Obregón and Calles, with the deliberate killings of leaders of any uprising, was required to give the political situation a semblance of stability.

Even under Cárdenas there was a revolution, and that was as late as 1938 — a revolution by a man who may be said to have been the last of the revolutionary *caudillos,* Saturnino Cedillo. He was a semi-literate man who had risen to power in local fighting, unillumined by any political doctrine except a greed for personal aggrandizement. At one time, during the Cristero rebellion, he had control of more than 8,000 men who belonged to him, and whom he had armed and brought into the field. He had a certain kind of loyalty to his own, but was completely ruthless. He traveled, even on horseback, with armed guards with sawed-off machine guns right behind him, and his automobile, in which I once rode, was crowded with arms, machine guns, and ammunition — a fort on wheels. I heard him say one day to a man who had some grievance, " I ought to have you strung up." In the state of San Luis Potosí his will was the law, the rule, and the way. There was no authority to which an appeal could be addressed, for even the federal government, unless it wished to stir up a rebellion, preferred not to interfere too much. The governor of the state, a nondescript little man in black, with a squeak in his voice, once said when I asked him who he was, when he made an unexpected visit to the home of Cedillo, " Who, me? I am the governor of the state. It is a job the old man gave me." Such a situation made rebellion inevitable, and revolution the natural beginnings of any election. As it turned out in this case, Cedillo rose in rebellion and was finally killed in the mountains.

In the election of 1940, when General Avila Camacho succeeded to the presidency, there was active talk of an uprising, and only the strength of General Cárdenas and the well-known policy of the United States government to give implicit support to the government in power prevented a revolution. This violence evidenced the narrow basis upon which Mexican government rested. The relative peace of the last twenty years may be taken to mean that the purpose of the constitution of 1917 to strengthen the government has succeeded. It brought into being the agrarian and labor organizations upon which the government could fall back in time of crisis.

II

But it is still true that the army is the chief source of the government's power. As President Cárdenas once expressed it, " When the land belongs to the villages, the government will also belong to them, but now the government depends upon the army." That day may come, but it has not yet; and it has not because the very machinery of the government is self-defeating. The government of Mexico is the president. There is no other way of expressing it. If the president is not strong enough to be the government, then he is overthrown, as was Ortiz Rubio. Or if he is not strong enough to be the president, then the real power is some *caudillo* — the great man who can and does control the government. In recent history, that was Calles. He did not wish to be a *caudillo* in the beginning, but was forced into the position of dictator to prevent the recurrence of chaos. The leaders accepted his will because he could enforce it, and that settled the matter.

I recall meeting a general in charge of troops in one of the northern states one day in a train. We were on the way to Tehuacan, where Calles, long after he had retired from the presidency, was recovering from an illness. I asked him where he was going, and he replied, " Well, yesterday I saw the president in the City of Mexico, but now I am going to see *el mero jefe*" — " the real chief." And that was that. To prove that he was in control, Cárdenas found it necessary to put Calles on a plane and ship him out of the country.

The president is the government, and all discussion of Mexican politics must assume that fact. It is possible to discern other trends, and the day may come when this will no longer be true. But for the time being, the president has in his hands the military, political, administrative, legislative, and judicial power. The legislature takes its policies and its laws from the president, and there is and can be no effective opposition in the congress. The judiciary takes its views from the administration. All one has to do is to read the decisions of the courts under the Carranza, Obregón, Calles, and Cárdenas administrations in matters of land and labor to be convinced that the court reflects, as a matter of course, the political predilections of the head of the state. He is the effective chief of the administration, and the members of the cabinet are simple instruments of his will; and if he is an energetic and hardworking man, he keeps track of even the minutest details of their labor. He is also the active head of the army, and it is he who decides where and at what post this or that general is to be placed. The total pattern is such that nothing within the political or governmental realm escapes his control, and all decisions, even of minor importance, are made by him.

In a subtle sense, the mass of the rural population, Indian or mestizo, illiterate or schooled, expects the president of the country to play the part of the great father. There is an implicit submissiveness, a bending of the head, which unconsciously forces upon the president the exercise of arbitrary power. Only the president can make a final decision. No other power is final, no other authority is absolute. He who would govern must also rule, or he will not be able to govern. Like every father, he must rule personally, in detail, and cannot delegate his authority. If he does, he will risk losing it. Men,

big and little, will sit for weeks in the antechamber to be heard over
a detail that any clerk might have disposed of. But the clerk is a
poor shadow of the great father, and so is the member of the cabinet.
The personality of the president must be part of every minor trans-
action between the rural folk and their government — time matters
not at all. Years may be spent in securing an audience just so as to
have the judgment come from the only source where authority is
not only political, but also moral. It is this situation that administration breaks down.

Like a good father, the president cannot say no, and if he does, the
no is not final. Surely the father's heart can be mellowed, his kind-
ness reawakened, his true virtues as the father of his children
brought to bear upon the issues in hand. These issues are so small,
so unimportant, and the president is so great and so all-powerful,
that only bad advisers stand in the way of his doing the justice the
people ask for. And if he refuses, then he is no true father, he is no
true leader, he governs arbitrarily and without moral authority. He
is a stepfather, a tyrant, a usurper, a villain, or he has no power,
being a tool of unfriendly and inimical forces. It becomes essential
to drive him from office. There is no alternative between personal
government and revolution. Inefficiency, corruption, cruelty — if
personal — are all acceptable. What is not acceptable is the cold, impersonal, efficient government. Compliance is not important, the
promise is. The people will wait, if they are not denied.

Traditionally speaking, the president of Mexico must be able to
do everything he wants to, or he will be unable to do anything he
wants to. He either has all power or no power; there is no middle
ground. The constitutional formula for a division of powers among
the legislative, judicial, and executive is merely a formula. And this
is so because, outside of the army, there is really no effective body
politic that the government can rest upon.

The administration — that is, the president — must be its own
architect of political security. The government is unstable except
in so far as the president can stabilize it, and all of his efforts are
bent toward giving it permanence by surrounding it with friends in
every office, every post, every organization, every significant grouping. Those that he cannot control are enemies. If he cannot control

his friends, they too become enemies. In effect, he manages all of the political life of the country. The charge that Díaz had puppets in the state governments was true enough. This has always been the case, but it is now easier, legally, than ever before for the central government to determine who can be elected, who can stay in office if elected, and who is to be removed if it becomes desirable that he should be removed. The cause can always be provided, the machinery to eject the undesirable official is permanently available, and the fiction of state sovereignty remains a fiction as always. The constitution of 1917 has made it simpler for the president to be a dictator than it used to be. It has always been necessary.

III

The organization of the *P.N.R.* (*Partido Nacional Revolucionario*) by Calles in 1928 merely facilitated what was already a sanctioned if not a sanctified practice. Under the Constitution, the Senate has the duty of deciding upon the legality of a state government, or of breaking off all federal relations with the state; and the Senate, therefore, ultimately decides who has been elected governor. But the Senate, like the governor of a state, is also a creature of the President, and the Permanent Committee of the Senate, which acts when that body is not in session, is hand-picked by the President. It is he who finally decides who has been elected governor of the state. The question of the legality of the state government comes before the federal government in many ways. Most frequently the question comes before the federal government because two and sometimes three governors, each with his own legislature, claim to have been elected by a huge majority. As the local legislature must decide who has been elected and then must have the count accepted by the federal government, it always follows that each candidate for state governor has his own legislature elected with him. After the election, two or three state legislatures each announce that their candidates have been elected, establish themselves as near the state capitol building as possible, organize a government, and bombard the President, the Secretary of the Interior, and the Senate with telegrams announcing their candidate's election. It is a little difficult to believe that three candidates have all been elected for the office of governor at the same time. It therefore falls upon the Permanent Committee acting for the Senate to make the decision as to who was really elected. But the Permanent Committee is the arm of the President, and the President, therefore, really makes the final decision. Once the issue has been settled the local military chieftain is instructed to see to it that the properly certified governor is permitted to take office, and to enter the state capitol building. The President has to make the decision. If he did not, there would be civil war in the state.

I recall one instance in Aguascalientes, after an election for governor, when the President happened to arrive there. He was met by a large crowd in an organized parade, armed with banners, demanding that its candidate be recognized, insisting that he had been elected. There was much shouting and yelling, and the President heard many strong words and speeches on his way to the state capitol building. Finally, after settling down in the state capitol for a while, he came out on the balcony and made a statement to the people in the square below. He said that the central government had no interest in the local election except that a good man be elevated to the office of governor. Two men could not both occupy the governor's chair at the same time, and if the candidate the crowd was clamoring for had really been elected by a majority, he would see to it that he was put in office in spite of the fact that the other man had already been declared legally elected. But if the man they were opposing was really the properly chosen official, *he would take the responsibility of keeping him in office.* To keep the peace, the federal government must choose the local governor, and be prepared to enforce its decision, as there is no other authority which could enforce its will, or even the will of the majority, without a test of arms.

There have been many instances when within one year the federal government removed a number of governors. Thus in 1935 the senate removed the governors of Sonora, Sinaloa, Guanajuato, and Durango. President Alemán has removed six governors in the last two years. The governors, in spite of the federal system established by the constitution, are the instruments of the President. And it is further clear that this is so because it is the only way of minimizing the prospect of rebellion.

The continuous fence-building so essential to the preservation of the president's political power takes another form. The President controls the election of the members to the Congress and the Senate. No one can be elected to either without his consent and approval. I have seen a man who thought himself elected senator, and whom everyone else thought to have been elected, arriving in Mexico City, flushed with victory, living in the best hotel, spending money freely. Then suddenly I saw him crestfallen, moving out of the hotel, counting his pennies. "What has happened?" I asked. "The old man thinks I was not elected." "What are you going to do?" "The old man has given me a good *chamba*. He has made me collector of customs in Matamoros. He really is a good person and knows what is best."

The technique is a simple one. The Senate and Congress each pass on the credentials of their own newly elected members, and they seat the right persons. The Senate and the Congress have to be hand-picked. They are an essential tool in the effective political control of the country. If the members of Congress were not controlled by the President, it would be impossible to govern in Mexico, except by sheer and unattenuated dictatorship. This way there is some semblance and, in effect, some measure of democratic politics even inside so highly centralized a government.

The same course occurs with members of the House of Congress. A friend of mine in Mexico, a young and devoted attendant of the President, told me one day that he wanted to be a member of Congress. I asked him if he had talked with the president. "Oh, yes," he replied. Two months later I learned that he had been elected. "Tell me exactly what happened. I want to know how you were elected." "Well, it was this way. We had an election but my opponents stole all my ballots." "What did you do?" I queried. "Well, you can't go before the committee without ballots so my friends and I sat down and made up the ballots. We knew everyone had voted for me." "And you were elected?" "Yes, unanimously." Two years later he had been elected senator. I said to him, "I hear you have been elected senator." "Yes," he replied, "unanimously." This is a verbatim report. He could only be elected at the will of the President, as was everyone else.

It is not that there is no electoral machinery. There is. Nor is its greatest shortcoming the cumbersome manner in which it is administered. The difficulty lies in something else. It lies in the absence of an effective independent political conscience and organization upon which a government can rest. The government, to survive in peace, must devise its own party, its own governors, its own members of Congress. The alternative is chaos and rebellion. It is not necessarily true that this system in the hands of a good man is less representative of the interests of the people. It may be in a sense democratic, but it does not rest upon effective suffrage. It is no one leader's fault. It is not even the fault of any one historical period. Nor is it suddenly and easily remediable.

It will not be easy for the reader to understand the significance of these controls unless he recognizes them as part of the technique for passing on the administration from one president who can complete his term to the next incumbent in office. If the machinery were to break down, the next election would be settled by violence and civil war. It is really an instrumentality for the maintenance of internal peace. I am not sure that the Mexicans themselves appreciate this fact. The behavior is automatic and determined by tradition, and it operates upon a kind of political " instinct " or intuition. But that is the function it serves. The most important decision that the President has to make, and that fairly early in his own administration, is who is to be his successor. Someone has to make that decision, and he who can make it becomes the effective head of the government. If the President cannot or will not do it, then he will either be faced with a revolution or become a mere puppet of the group surrounding the new candidate.

I am not even sure that the decision has to be formalized until fairly late, but there arises a kind of implicit commitment which everyone " in the know " understands. Watching Mexican politics closely, one begins to discern the drift of the new alignment by noting changes in the cabinet, and asking: Whose friends are they? What is true of members of Congress and the cabinet is true of the army. Who has been promoted, or retired? Who has been shifted in command from one post to another? All are evidences of political manoeuvring. An unreliable general is suddenly shifted to another state in which the President feels absolutely sure of the lower officers. The general knows it and his hands are tied. It used to be customary for the general to move with his own troops. He had raised them and trained them, and they were his people. It took three unsuccessful revolutions after 1920 and the purging of hundreds of army officers before the principle could be established that the troops a general commanded did not belong to him, and that he could be moved without them. It was one of the essential conditions to the peaceful succession of power.

IV

The election campaigns, speeches, and propaganda are part of the play for the alignment of the popular opinion for or against the prospective candidate; and, at the same time, they tend to strengthen the conviction that the right candidate has been chosen. A political campaign in Mexico is in the nature of make-believe. The candidate who has official approval is certain of election. Tradition and popular expectation ask for a campaign and for General Cárdenas, for example, the period of the campaign was an opportunity to travel into every corner of the country and visit the humblest villages in the mountain regions. But the election itself is never in doubt. The opposition candidates have, in spite of an active campaign, no expectation of being elected. They know that their people will probably not be permitted to vote; that if they do vote their vote will not be counted; that, if counted, and sent into the final test in the national Congress, it will be disregarded; and finally, that if elected by some strange accident, they could not govern. An opposition candidate, elected to the presidency, could not if he took power even name his own private secretary. In fact, the election is decided before the voting takes place. It is decided by those who are going to count the votes officially, and their count was determined before they were entrusted with the privilege of going through the motions.

What, then, is the purpose of the opposition candidates, parties, and campaigns? The answer, I think, is clear: it is to build up moral justification for a revolution. No one is fooled by the process. No one expects the opposition to win. No government has ever lost an election unless it was first driven from office by force. What the opposition does expect is that it can so work on the popular discontent, so stir up political passions, so confuse public opinion that it can win the allegiance of large masses of people to its side, and especially that of the army. There is always some hope that parts of the army can be won over — sometimes the whole army, or nearly the whole army, as in the electoral campaign of Obregón against Bonilla in 1920. If the army can be won over, or if a part of the army can be won over, then the electoral campaign may have helped to provide the moral environment within which the rebellion can be successful.

Luis Cabrera has suggested that there have been more than a thousand *pronunciamientos* between 1812 and 1921, but only three revolutions. The distinction is important. The military uprising is an electoral device, a way of changing the authorities in power, of driving out one government and replacing it with another. A peaceful election is frequently regarded as an evidence of imposition. When the government is strong enough to assure the election of the official candidate without violence, as in the case of the long Díaz régime, it is a sure sign of tyranny. A rebellion has, therefore, the respectable dress of an attempt to give the opposition a chance to secure office. The fact that, if successful, it will play the same preponderant role as the actual government in electing the next preferred candidate, is beside the point. If there had been no rebellion, the government in office would have perpetuated itself by imposing a chosen candidate. Rebellion, therefore, is an accepted instrumentality in an electoral campaign. If it does not occur, it is sometimes due to the fear that the United States will take sides with the government in power. That was certainly the case in the election when Almazán was defeated for the presidency.

But while rebellion is an electoral device, revolution is an accepted instrument of social and economic change. This kind of revolution may have the approval even of the conservative elements in Mexico. An illegal revolution, which ultimately becomes legal because it succeeds in imposing its desires upon the nation by force and rewriting the law to fit its program, is considered necessary " in such countries as ours." The political philosophy of Mexico is saturated with the belief in violence, both for electoral purposes and for social change.

The official government party, regardless of the various names which have been given it by the different governments, is in effect the recognized electoral machinery of the administration. Although other parties are in existence, free speech is unrestricted, and political activities and organizations go on, the effective electoral control is organized by the government through this new instrumentality, and it has tended to reduce violence in political elections. If there were no official party, the elections would no more reflect popular suffrage than they do now. But they would be less free from local violence. The party in power — that is, the group that made the revolution in 1910 and retains its hold in office — has found a medium to carry on the government without having to fight a new revolution over every presidential election and face civil strife in every state at every local election.

The political outcome of the revolution has, clearly enough, greatly strengthened the power of the central government and of the president. The one single government-party system is merely additional evidence of the fact. It has given the presidency an officially sponsored agency to deal with Mexican politics. The older Díaz tradition of control by disregard of the law — for it has been truly said that the Constitution of 1857 was forgotten in his personal administration — has been replaced by a constitutional mandate to control the state governments. The creation of an officially sponsored party has facilitated the control of Mexican politics.

To some extent, the difference between the old system of Díaz and the present one is the difference between open and secret control. Both the constitutional provisions and the government party system tend to make the centralized control of the political life of the country matters of greater public knowledge, and to that extent tend to make them a more conscious part of the life of the nation. Their very legality and publicity tend to have a restraining influence upon the too arbitrary use of the powers at the president's disposal. With all of their shortcomings, these changes must be recognized as, on the whole, a stabilizing and democratizing influence in Mexican political life.

V

The Mexican complex is such that the alternative to highly centralized power is anarchy; and, for the time being, anyway, the revolution has tended in the direction of centralized temporary power.

The one clear gain, politically, is the principle of no re-election. Obregón tried for re-election but was assassinated, and that, perhaps, was the last attempt in that direction for a long time. The president can, within limits, perpetuate his policies by throwing his influence toward the election of his successor; in fact, as we have noted, he must do so. But he cannot succeed himself or, as things stand, be a candidate again at any time.

This change has not eliminated the army from politics, but it has to some extent changed the character of the army's participation. The individual general probably can no longer impose himself upon the nation because he happens to have a group of friends who will follow him in battle. But as long as the central government has to use the army for its own political purposes in controlling the states, the army is bound to possess great political influence, and no man could come to the office of the presidency against its will.

But a significant new influence has come into being, politically speaking, in the form of the organized labor unions and the agrarian communities. These have given the government a wider base in the populace, and this change is especially important for its latent implications. In a crisis, as was shown at the time of the De la Huerta and Escobar rebellions, the labor unions and the agrarian communities, especially the latter, proved of very real military value to the government. The rebels found that they could hold only the land they physically occupied, for the agrarian communities were hostile to them and actively supported the government. These two new institutions are, however, bound hand and foot by the government.

It is hard to see how the agrarian communities can emancipate themselves. The government's participation, especially in the large cooperative *ejidos,* is such that it has, in a measure, replaced the old plantation owner. The *Banco Ejidal* extends credit to these communities between the crops. It does not pay wages. The credit is a weekly allowance to be repaid out of the crop. The profit is divided between the members of the *ejido.* But the bank must, for its own safety, have a degree of supervision which makes the federal government an integral part of their every activity. Presumably, in time — but not at any visible time — these communities will accumulate enough savings to become their own credit agency. They could then become an independent influence in politics. For the time being, they are part of the governmental machine, but nonetheless they have given the government a wider base than it had before.

Something of the same is true of organized labor. There is no independent trade union movement of any consequence in Mexico. There are a few unions that have outlived government opposition, but they are not strong or numerous. The great movements in labor were not self-sustaining — in the time of Calles the *C.R.O.M.* (*Confederación Regional Obrera Mexicana*) was a child of the Obregón and Calles governments, and the *C.T.M.* (*Confederación de Trabajadores Mexicanos*) was a creature of the later administrations. The government has financed, protected, and nurtured the trade union movement as a stick to lean upon, or to be used against its political enemies in and out of the country. But the stick is only as strong as the arm that wields it. The trade union movement may, in time, become politically independent. Today it is important chiefly as the vehicle of the politics of the administration, that is, the policies of the president. The unions and the *ejidos* serve one important function; they give the president a seeming, and in a measure a real, support in the populace. That has political significance for the future.

But with the widened base for the government, there has come an increase in the range of its responsibilities. The federal government has both by constitutional mandate and by legislative provisions assumed a supervising interest over all mining, the moving picture industry, commerce, banking, the electrical industry, public health, public education, labor, land distribution, and agricultural credit through the *ejidal* bank. In addition, there are other activities which are now largely in the hands of the federal government, such as road building, aviation, the railroads, the oil industry, coastwise transportation, the tourist industry, telegraphs, and through the control of labor or credit, textiles, sugar, and cotton.

That is, the centralized government has assumed the burden of managing the greater part of the economy of the nation. The president has become the arbiter of the economic activities of the people. The burden of governing is infinitely greater than it was when the revolution began, and the political instrumentality has not grown to equal the new burdens. The idea of a directed economy has taken increased hold of the government, while the character of the political machinery has changed but little in comparison to the new administrative responsibilities. Nor has the efficiency of government nor the integrity of the bureaucracy kept pace with the increased powers of the government over the national economy. There is even some reason to assume that the older habits of petty graft have increased with the newer opportunities. It is no accident that the prevailing political mood in Mexico is cynicism. Graft had a kind of traditional sanction when most of the economy of the nation was in foreign hands, when government officials shared through special favors some of the profits of private concerns. But when the government itself is the major entrepreneur, through direct or indirect control, the problem is different. The growth of that kind of selfless public service which the situation demands is not in sight.

The political disequilibrium in Mexico lies in part in the nature of the tax system. Most of the tax collected goes to the federal government. The states receive a pittance and the municipalities even less. It thus turns out that all other political units in the government are dependent upon the federal government for favors. I have seen towns build their schools with their own hands, and then sit around for years waiting for the state or federal government to give them the money to buy the windows or doors which they could not make, or even send a delegation a hundred miles to see the governor or even the president in Mexico City for the same purpose. What is true of the school is true of a bridge, of a pipe for a water system, of an engine to turn a mill. There is really no prospect of Mexico possessing a vigorous democratic government resting upon a broad popular base unless the flow in income from taxes is redirected so that the towns, the municipalities, and the states can enjoy financial independence. This is probably the change most essential to Mexico's welfare, but it is the one least likely to occur.

This analysis should not be thought to be an unfriendly comment on the presidential powers. The executive must be strong in Mexico, or Mexico will face revolution. The alternative to a strong president is rebellion. The alternative to political decisions made in detail and enforced by the president is decisions which no one can enforce. The fact of the matter is that the president must decide because no one else's decision will be accepted. The older tradition that the king rules has survived in modern dress: the president rules. He rules rather than governs, and must do so if he is to survive in office or if he is to keep the country at peace. The issue, in political terms, is the absence of effective political opposition. All opposition presumes eventual revolution. If and when there develops in Mexico the tradition of " His Majesty's loyal opposition," loyal to the government, even if opposed to its policies, then it may come about that party government rather than personal government will become the rule. But that day is still a long way off.

No. 29 [*Continuismo* is a word that is constantly encountered in the political writing of Latin America. Its meaning and the origins and application of the process it describes are discussed in the following selection.

Although the area subjected to scrutiny is but a part of the entire Latin American region, the political characteristic is not so geographically limited. *Continuismo* is a political factor of considerable importance in many of the South American nations. The devices used by President Vargas to continue his power were, as the author notes, another variant of the fine art of continuing in authority a constitutionally terminated régime. Professor Fitzgibbon's observation that other South American nations might try the technique were born out within a decade by Argentina. The constitution of that country was but recently amended so as to permit the re-election of the chief executive!

Furthermore, *continuismo* has frequently taken on another form of expression in South America. Instead of perpetuating themselves in power, the presidents of some of the republics have been able to continue their policies and programs by the controls they were able to exert over the nomination and election of their successors. This more subtle form of the attempt to avoid constitutional closure of an administration has apparently achieved as satisfactory results to its practitioners as its more blunt and direct counterpart in Central America and the Caribbean area.]

Continuismo *in Central America and the Caribbean**

by RUSSELL H. FITZGIBBON

THE republic of Nicaragua promulgated a new constitution on March 23, 1939, an interesting and significant, but not unique, feature of which was the prolongation of the term of the incumbent president for eight years. As late as December 16, 1939, the constituted authorities in Honduras took action by which the régime of the president of that country is to be constitutionally extended until January 1, 1949. Since the beginning of 1940 the same technique has been frequently — if unofficially — suggested in Mexico.

Thereupon hangs a tale of considerable political significance. The first two republics mentioned completed, in brief, a list of seven sovereign states in the Central American and Caribbean area to experiment with the new constitutional technique now popularly known in Latin America as *continuismo.* The political friends of the régimes which have thus amended their countries' constitutions are prone to deny, indeed, the existence of any such thing as *continuismo.* The dictionary supports them: it does not include any such word, admittedly synthetic. *Continuismo* is one of those verbal coinages with which the Spanish Americans, with their Latin facility for turning ideas into crystalline words and phrases, have happily enriched their language.

A definition is in order. *Continuismo,* we may say, is the practice of continuing the administration in power in a Latin American country by the process of a constitutional amendment, or a provision in a new constitution, exempting the president in office, and perhaps other elective officials, from the historic and frequent prohibition against two consecutive terms in office. The precise form of the consti-

* Russell H. Fitzgibbon, " 'Continuismo' in Central America and the Caribbean," *The Inter-American Quarterly* (July, 1940), Vol. 2, No. 3, pp. 56–74. Reprinted by permission of the author. The footnotes in the original version are omitted here.

tutional change may vary — the general pattern is simple and uniform.

Cuba was easily the dean of experimenters with the device. General Gerardo Machado y Morales was elected president of Cuba in the balloting of 1924, to take office May 20, 1925, under a campaign pledge limiting him to one term in office. Machado, who had resigned a cabinet position years before in protest against the re-electionist plans of his then chief, José Miguel Gómez, declared in his election manifesto in September 1924 that " a Liberal President cannot be re-elected. This is now a noble tradition — the most noble of this party." The General seemingly slammed the door shut, locked it, and threw away the key when he declared in July 1927 that " a man whose lips had never been defiled by a lie, would lower his dignity, and dishonor himself, if after a political labor of twenty-five years during which he opposed the principle of re-election with the word and the sword in two revolutions, he should now accept the principle for himself."

If Machado had locked the door upon himself he proved a skillful locksmith, however, and soon found a way of opening it. The Machado-dominated Cuban congress in the spring and summer of 1927 passed a set of resolutions aimed at a comprehensive amendment of the constitution. Among other changes, the presidential term was to be fixed at a single six-year period and Machado's own term was to be lengthened two years. All went legally until May 9, 1928. The congress submitted the series of amendments, as was required of it, to a special convention on May 9, 1928 which, the same day, adopted a resolution asserting that

the Constituent Assembly does not vacillate in reaffirming that General Gerardo Machado y Morales, because of the obligation he has contracted and because of his role as founder of the Republic, is unavoidably bound to accept a new presidential period.

The convention concluded its simple task two days later but with the omission, inadvertent or otherwise, of the provision regarding the prolongation of Machado's term for two additional years. It specified instead that the single, six-year term provision should become operative with the first subsequent election. The changes became effective as part of the constitution on publication in the *Gaceta,* May 11, 1928.

With the way constitutionally cleared Machado became the candidate of all three political parties in the 1928 elections, held on November 2, and was chosen without opposition to succeed himself, " ignoble," " undignified," and " dishonorable " though it was! The first of the recent attempts at *continuismo* thus became history.

The contagion of *continuismo* spread first in the Caribbean. The Dominican Republic next fell victim to the malady, although it did not furnish as good a case study as some of the later instances. A symptom of what was to come had manifested itself in the Dominican Republic even before the Cuban changes of 1928. Horacio Vásquez had assumed the presidency in Santo Domingo (as the capital was then named) on July 12, 1924, under a constitution of June 13, 1924, which established a four-year term for the chief executive with ineligibility for an immediately successive term. The fruits of office apparently tasted sweet, for in 1927 a constituent convention revised the basic law to provide, among other changes, a two-year extension of the terms of the president, vice-president, and members of the congress. This change, effective June 16, 1927, legally continued Vásquez in power from 1928 to 1930. Presidential provisions in the constitution again were juggled in 1929 when an additional amendment on June 20 restored the four-year term for the head of the state and at the same time removed the prohibition on re-election. A further political insurance policy for the ruling régime was the revision of the electoral law of 1924 in a manner which convinced the opposition parties that an attempt to win through election was impossible.

With these changes on the statute books, President Vásquez announced in 1929 that he would be a candidate for re-election in May 1930. Political tension increased throughout 1929 and came to a head early in 1930.

Vásquez' refusal to meet the demand for minority representation on the local election boards was the clue for revolution, which broke out in the north on February 23, 1930, and was carried through to success five days later by the ousting of the régime in power. Chief factor in the success of the insurgents was the defection of General Rafael Leónidas Trujillo Molina, commander of the government forces and an erstwhile private in the United States Marine Corps during its occupation of the island republic. A provisional president,

General Estrella Ureña, set presidential elections for May 16, 1930, and himself became the candidate for vice-president on the "government ticket" headed by Trujillo. The withdrawal of the opposition nominees two days before the election permitted the choice of the favored candidates without a contest.

On August 16, 1931, the first anniversary of his inauguration, General Trujillo organized the *Partido Dominicano,* including all members of the government and many state employees and private citizens. This was followed by the scrapping of the bi-party system and the liquidation of all opposition parties, perhaps the first New World example of the adoption of this fundamental characteristic of political totalitarianism. The Dominican party in 1933 and the early months of 1934 organized so-called "civic reviews" throughout the republic, mass demonstrations designed to voice support of the Trujillo régime. Based on the alleged expression of popular support for the administration as reflected by the civic reviews, Dr. José E. Aybar, a strongly pro-Trujillo dentist of the capital city, proposed a symposium in March 1933 by asking 150 leading citizens for an expression of opinion as to whether it would not be proper, as an economy measure, for the *junta central electoral* to declare Trujillo chosen for a new term without the expense of a formal election.

This trial balloon, if such it were, was abandoned as a procedure and elections were duly held on May 16, 1934, with Trujillo and Dr. Jacinto B. Peynado, formerly a cabinet member, as the candidates for first and second places on the only ticket presented. Potential opposition had been removed in advance by the exiling of many political opponents during the tightening military dictatorship. The election resulted in the necessarily unanimous choice of Trujillo and Peynado, with 256,423 votes out of a total registration of 286,937. The same election saw the choice of thirty-three members of an *Asamblea Revisora de la Constitución* to draft a new fundamental law for the country. The revising assembly quickly completed its work, on the basis of a previously prepared draft constitution, and the new law was declared in effect June 9, 1934.

The iron hand of Trujillo's dictatorship continued firmly in control during his second term in office. He might, presumably, have remained in the presidency indefinitely, but occasioned some surprise by announcing in a radio broadcast on January 8, 1938, that he would not be a candidate for re-election in the balloting of that year. Trujillo announced as " my candidates " Vice-President Peynado for first place on the Dominican party ticket and Dr. Manuel de Jesús Troncoso de la Concha, rector of the national university, for his running mate. The two candidates were duly nominated and elected with no opposition, Trujillo having stated a month before the balloting that he considered them already elected.

The changes in the Dominican Republic did not give an entirely orthodox illustration of *continuismo*. The spirit of the changes, however, was so much that of the same development in the other countries that the trend and results in the island republic cannot well be omitted from any such account.

Caribbean experimentation with *continuismo* was completed by Haitian efforts in that direction in 1935. Important changes in the presidential tenure in Haiti had been made in 1928. The constitution of June 12, 1918, had provided for a four-year term of office with re-election permissible. The most outstanding of a series of thirteen amendments submitted to a popular vote on January 10, 1928, provided that Article 72 be amended to the effect that the president should serve a six-year term and should be ineligible immediately to succeed himself. The amendments were all given overwhelming approval by the electorate.

President Louis Borno was peacefully supplanted in the spring of 1930 by a provisional president who was pledged to call popular elections for a national assembly to succeed the *de facto* legislative agency, the council of state. The elections were held as scheduled, on October 14, 1930, and the assembly thus chosen proceeded on November 18 to elect Sténio Vincent, an antioccupationist newspaper editor, as constitutional president of the republic.

A new constitution, effective July 21, 1932, omitted the absolute two-term limit prescribed for the presidency by the amendments of 1928 but retained the provision that a president could not immediately succeed himself. The six-year tenure was similarly kept intact. With President Vincent's term of office due to expire on May 15, 1936, and faced by a twice confirmed prohibition on immediate re-election, it was necessary for the administration to take steps. The result was the drafting of a new constitution by a special commission of the national legislature during the late spring of 1935. After having been signed by nearly all of the members of both houses, the draft constitution was submitted to a plebiscitary vote on June 2 and received an overwhelming approval. The new law became effective on its publication in the *Moniteur* on June 17, 1935.

The constitution of 1935 provided the most clear-cut illustration of *continuismo* yet offered by any Caribbean or Central American republic. The presidential term was, indeed, shortened from six to five years but it was provided that a president might be immediately re-elected, although with an absolute limit of two terms in office (Article 34). More to the point was the inclusion of Title XIV which provided that

Citizen Sténio Vincent, now President of the Republic, having deserved well of his Country . . . and the majority of the Country having publicly expressed the desire that there should be no interruption in the work undertaken by the present President, Citizen Sténio Vincent is appointed for a new term of Five Years to begin May 15, 1936.

It was not surprising that with these repeated and presumably successful demonstrations of the efficacy of *continuismo* in the Caribbean republics, the contagion should spread to the neighboring mainland governments of Central America. The first to undertake such experimentation was Guatemala, the efforts of which were, indeed, practically concurrent with those of Haiti. Guatemala had had a long unenlightened political history, alternating between despotism and virtual anarchy. After kaleidoscopic changes in the control of the executive branch late in 1930, General Jorge Ubico came to the presidential palace on February 14, 1931, through elections held February 6–8. The constitution promulgated January 1, 1928, established a six-year term for the president and prohibited re-election during the twelve years following the expiration of the term. The whole emphasis of the relevant articles in the 1928 constitution was on the prevention of indefinite continuance in office, nepotism, and allied problems.

Ubico moved quickly to consolidate his position in the presidency. The *Partido Liberal Progresista,* the candidate of which Ubico had been in his campaign for the presidency, soon became a well-knit personal following. Taking time by the forelock, the president on

May 5, 1935, won for his Liberal Progressive party, by methods which may be guessed at if not documented, a majority of the seats in an *Asamblea Nacional Constituyente,* created to consider revision of the basic law. The constitutional assembly, which held only seventeen sessions, worked from the basis of a draft constitution submitted to the *Junta Preparatoria* and by the latter to the full assembly. While Ubico's message to the first plenary session of the assembly contained no reference to the possibility of his own re-election to the presidency, it was a foregone conclusion that with the proceedings under full executive control some provision pointing in that direction would be an easy and logical way out.

The constitution retained the 1928 provision (Article 66) that twelve years must elapse from the expiration of an initial term before a president could again occupy the office. The assembly then provided for the holding of a national plebiscite on the question of continuing Ubico's term of office. This step — convenient substitute for a regular presidential election — was consummated on June 22–24, 1935, and resulted in an officially announced vote of 884,703 to 1,144 in favor of the continuance of General Ubico in the presidency until 1943. Following this overwhelming popular mandate the constituent assembly duly decreed certain transitory provisions under date of July 11, 1935, the first of which provided that

The Constitutional Presidency of General Jorge Ubico shall end on March 15, 1943, and with such an object the purpose of Article 66 of the Constitution remains in suspense until that date.

A theoretically complicating factor in the case of Guatemala and the other Central American republics was the nominal continuance in force of the General Treaty of Peace and Amity signed by representatives of all of the Central American governments at Washington on February 7, 1923, and subsequently ratified by the five signatory governments. Article V of the treaty provided that

The Contracting Parties obligate themselves to maintain in their respective Constitutions the principle of non-reelection to the office of President and Vice President of the Republic; and those of the Contracting Parties whose Constitutions permit such reelection, obligate themselves to introduce a constitutional reform to this effect in their next legislative session after the ratification of the present Treaty.

This inclusion, seemingly clear enough in its design, had been popularly lost sight of to a considerable degree in the face of the greater attention bestowed on Article II of the same treaty, dealing with mutual nonrecognition of revolutionary governments. The unofficial *coup de grâce* was given to the 1923 treaty in January 1934 by the general recognition of the revolutionary government of Martínez in El Salvador. Article V of the treaty presumably collapsed along with other portions, although as late as 1936 opponents of the dictatorial régimes in Guatemala, Nicaragua, and Honduras were endeavoring to bolster their position by invoking the principle of the article.

The Guatemalan nucleus of *continuismo* spread fan-wise in Central America, first to Honduras, successively to El Salvador and Nicaragua. The Honduran constitution of September 10, 1924, provided for a president who would hold office for four years and be ineligible immediately to succeed himself. Following a turbulent campaign in 1932, liberally mixed with revolutionary activity, General Tiburcio Carías Andino was elected president of Honduras, with government support, on October 30, 1932. The campaign was over but the insurrectionary movements continued until early in 1933. Carías assumed office, however, on February 1, 1933.

Although the term was not due to expire constitutionally until early in 1937, political unrest became rife in Honduras late in 1935 because of the obvious plan of Carías to perpetuate himself in power. Opposition arose even within Carías' own Nationalist party and was repressed by methods which allegedly were unequalled in their severity in any of the other Central American or Caribbean dictatorships. Although Carías publicly denied any intention of continuing in office, he formerly requested congressional action early in 1936 to amend the constitution to permit consecutive presidential terms. The submissive congress complied by passing legislation for the election of an *Asamblea Nacional Constituyente* on January 26, 1936. The election was held as scheduled, and fifty-nine pro-Carías delegates were chosen for the assembly, which first met on March 8. Carías in an opening message emphasized the need for constitutional reform, and the assembly then proceeded on the basis of a previously prepared draft. With this preliminary " spade work " conveniently out of the way, the assembly was able to complete its work within twenty days and announce a new constitution to go into effect April 15, 1936.

The new Honduran basic law lengthened the presidential term from four to six years and changed the date of inauguration from February 1 to January 1. More important, however, was the special provision in Article 202 which stated in simple terms with no rhetorical attempt at rationalization that

The Constitutional Presidency and Vice Presidency of the Republic held, respectively, by Don Tiburcio Carías Andino, Doctor and General, and Don Abraham Williams Calderón, Engineer and General, shall terminate January 1, 1943; and for this reason the effects of Article 116, 117, 118 of the Constitution [dealing with the election and tenure of the executive offices] shall be suspended until that date.

The Honduran assembly played fast and loose with established procedure in adopting the new document. In addition to its disregard of the provision in the 1924 constitution that amendments to the basic law could be made only by the action of a two-thirds majority in two successive legislatures, the assembly provided that it should itself automatically become the regular Legislative Congress, with its members continuing in office until December 4, 1942. A logical aftermath came in the above-mentioned action of December 16, 1939, by which the presidential term of Carías was extended for a total of ten years, thus bringing it to an end — as now specified — on January 1, 1949.

After the completion of the Honduran experiment, the fourth one in three years, more than three and a half years were to elapse before the next chapter in the history of *continuismo* materialized — in El Salvador. A revolution on December 3, 1931, at San Salvador had forced President Arturo Araujo to flee. He was succeeded the following day by Vice-President Maximiliano Hernández Martínez whose early failure to obtain diplomatic recognition from the Central American countries and especially from the United States, because of the provisions of the Washington treaty of 1923, made his hold upon the presidency precarious. His tenure was domestically solidified and regularized by the action of the Salvadorian congress on February 5, 1932, in declaring him constitutional president and confirming him in office for a four-year term, although almost two years' time was to elapse before the coveted recognition by the United States was gained.

The Salvadorian constitution of August 13, 1886, provided a four-year presidential term and prohibited immediate re-election. To give the continuation of his administration some appearance of constitutionality, General Martínez requested, and on August 25, 1934, was given, permission to retire from the presidential office and turn it over to the First Designate. The change in office was made on August 29 and Martínez was then constitutionally free to pursue his announced intention of seeking the presidency in the elections of January 13–15, 1935. So consolidated had the régime become that Martínez was unopposed in the January elections and was inaugurated for a new four-year term on March 1, 1935.

First steps toward constitutional revision were taken in 1935 with the appointment by the congress of a commission to study reforms. The process was further advanced with the approval by the national legislative assembly on December 21, 1936, of a decree for the calling of a constitutional convention. The elections of January 10–12, 1937, resulted favorably to government-supported candidates. The constituent congress met on February 1 and by early June had completed constitutional amendments intended to facilitate the re-election of Martínez in 1939. The way seemed cleared for a perpetuation of the administration, but during 1938 a vigorous if uncrystallized movement of opposition to its continuation arose in the capital city. Public opinion, expressed chiefly through commercial and professional rather than party channels, has more volume, weight, and effect in El Salvador than in any other Central American country except Costa Rica, and in the summer of 1938 a favorite and animated topic of discussion was that of whether President Martínez would continue his efforts to succeed himself. The government felt called upon to counter with a systematic propaganda campaign.

The government attempted a new tack when the congress on September 26, 1938, passed a law authorizing the municipalities to issue a call on October 16 for elections to be held October 23–25 for the choice of delegates to an *Asamblea Nacional Constituyente* to meet in November. A single slate of government-endorsed candidates was duly elected (without opposition, of course). The regular session of the National Legislative Assembly adjourned November 14 after providing, as its final important act, for presidential elections to be held January 8–10, 1939. Three days later the constitutional assembly was installed. The assembly worked from a draft constitution prepared before it met, but the exigencies of the current situation would not permit it to proceed in a political vacuum. Various straws in the wind indicated a continued opposition to the perpetuation of the régime, and in answer the constituent assembly on December 7 suspended the presidential elections scheduled for January 1939.

The assembly proceeded rapidly with its primary work of constitution making and by January 4, 1939, had approved the important item pointing toward the legalizing of a continuation of the régime. A threat of revolt — easily subdued — characterized the closing days of the convention, the work of which in final form was published on January 20. The new document established a six-year presidential term and provided as one of the paragraphs of Article 91 that

Exceptionally, and in order to safeguard the national interests, the citizen who shall exercise the Presidency of the Republic from March 1 of the current year [1939] to January 1, 1945, according to this Constitution, shall be elected by the Deputies to the National Constituent Assembly, and the disqualifications referred to in Article 94 [chiefly a prohibition on immediate reelection] are set aside on this sole occasion.

The constituent assembly, acting on the convenient ground that the time for regular congressional elections had passed, reconstituted itself (Article 194) as the ordinary legislative assembly, thus taking a leaf out of the book of Honduran experience. With the constitution disposed of, the assembly dutifully proceeded, on January 21, to choose Martínez as president for the term ending January 1, 1945. An interesting by-product of these developments was the resignation of several high governmental officials in protest against the course that the president was taking.

The last country — to date — to attempt *continuismo* was Nicaragua. The prelude was the political campaign by which General Anastasio Somoza, head of the *Guardia Nacional*, became president in 1937. He had in 1934 announced his entry in the 1936 campaign,

although he was doubly barred on constitutional grounds by the fact
that he was a nephew by marriage of the incumbent president, Dr.
Juan Bautista Sacasa, and by his headship of the national guard.
The political situation was further complicated by the alleged com-
plicity of General Somoza in the assassination by national guard
members of General Augusto Sandino, long an opponent of United
States marine occupation of Nicaragua, on February 21, 1934. Somoza more formally entered the presidential race with a statement
published in September 1935 in *El Cronista* at León, traditional
Liberal stronghold, promising that he would " eliminate all other
candidates who bar my path " to the presidency. The political situation tightened as the 1936 elections approached, and on June 6 of
that year Somoza forced his uncle out of office. A Somoza partisan
became provisional president, and on June 15 the Liberal party gave
the national guard chieftain its nomination. The elections on December 8, 1936, were farcical: Somoza received approximately 117,000
votes against 1,100 given his exiled coalition opponent.

Continuismo flowered in Nicaragua with less than half of Somoza's term gone. Dr. Carlos A. Morales, a Liberal justice of the
Supreme Court, suggested in an article in *La Prensa* at Managua,
the capital, on May 14, 1938, that steps be taken for the revision of the
constitution. The congress in August passed the necessary legislation
for elections to an *Asamblea Constituyente* to convene on December
15. The elections, held on November 6, resulted in the choice of
twenty-seven Liberals, eleven Conservative Nationalists (the pro-
Somoza wing of the Conservative party), and seven Conservatives.
The president on December 8 issued detailed " provisional regulations " for the government of the constituent assembly, and the
plenary sessions opened on December 16. The main work of the
assembly got under way early in February 1939 when it began consideration of an 18,000-word draft constitution. This task was completed some seven weeks later with publication of the document in
the *Gaceta*.

The 1939 constitution contained several provisions bearing on the
presidency. In the first place, after specifying a six-year presidential
term, it provided flatly (Article 204) that " the immediate re-election
of the President is forbidden." Other seemingly rigorous restrictions
upon eligibility and succession were included. A " joker " appeared

in Article 350, though, in the statement that

The amendment of the provision which prohibits the re-election of the President of the Republic and those concerning the duration of the presidential term . . . cannot be decreed except for future need, in order that the amendment may not be a detriment or a help to the officials in service at the time of its promulgation.

In the first of several transitory provisions, the constituent assembly arrogated to itself the function of electing " a citizen who is to exercise the Presidency of the Republic during a term . . . from March 30 of the current year [1939] to May 1, 1947." In the article immediately following, the constituent assembly, with the model of its two northern neighbors before it, transformed itself for an eight-year period into the ordinary legislative congress. In compliance with its self-imposed mandate to choose a president for the ensuing term, the assembly voted on March 24, 1939, the prize going to Somoza with forty-six votes as against seven for Fernando Guzmán, a prominent Conservative party leader. In his inaugural address on March 30 Somoza declared that " One of my greatest ambitions was reformation of the Constitution to represent the will of the people "!

The technique of *continuismo* has been limited in its modern manifestations to the Caribbean and Central American area. Only Brazil in South America has undertaken anything like the same step, and the famous Vargas *coup* of November 1937 with its attendant new constitution did not represent an orthodox example of *continuismo*. Certain political elements in Panama toyed with the idea at one time. A draft constitution proposed in 1938 for the isthmian republic included two innovations dealing with the presidency, one permitting immediate re-election of the chief executive, the other lengthening his term from four to six years. It has been suggested on various occasions that Lázaro Cárdenas' supporters might seek a second term for him in the presidency of Mexico, especially if Roosevelt were nominated in 1940 for a third term in the United States. The plan would have required a Mexican adaptation of *continuismo*, since the constitution forbids immediate re-election, but so far Cárdenas himself has given no indication of any such leanings.

There are South American countries which might logically try the technique and it may well spread to them. Whether it may be abandoned in any of the Middle American countries remains to be seen. On the other hand, of course, its easy adoption in them to date may induce its repetition. *Continuismo* has thus far given the color of legality to dictatorships of considerable length, presumably a total of sixteen years in the case of Carías. What is to prevent a virtually life-long tenure by such methods?

One should be extremely cautious in drawing conclusions and moral judgments about *continuismo*. Especially is this true for an *Estadounidense* (to borrow a Spanish American coinage for the impossible " United Statesian "), who lives in a largely different political atmosphere and stems from an entirely different constitutional background. It is in order, however, to raise a few questions and, perhaps, to venture highly tentative answers.

Why has the practice under discussion been so localized? What conditions in the body politic favor the entrance of such an infection? How incompatible is it with what we define as " democracy "? It may even be proper to ask if it is a disease, i.e., an undesirable manifestation. Two explanations may be suggested as possible and partial answers to the first question. The simple fact of geographic nearness encourages an imitation of political trends and techniques which neighbors have adopted. A certain vague common denominator underlies the countries of " the American Mediterranean," variant though their ethnic compositions, their economic interests, their social structures, and other factors are. In the second place, the location of the countries concerned within the sometime international political orbit of the United States induced a certain lip service to constitutional forms as such. This found its most specific exemplification in the ready Central American acceptance of the artificial restrictions of the Washington 1923 treaty. The United States on more than one occasion — in Mexico in 1913, Nicaragua in 1926, Cuba in 1933, for example — demonstrated a tenderness for the constitutional letter, assuming, evidently, that the spirit would care for itself. The average Latin American constitution has been more symbol than instrument, however, and it is understandable why, with any external examples of this sort seemingly stressing form, the Central American and Caribbean governments should be concerned with such an aspect. The anomaly appears in the willingness and casualness with which on more than one occasion the régimes endeavoring to preserve the appearance of legality have departed from the prescribed legal methods of effecting new constitutions or constitutional amendments. Viewing the whole picture, the question of sheer constitutionalism becomes artificial and dogmatic.

Continuismo has been favored in middle America by just those conditions which nurture dictatorship — and to just the same extent. A high degree of illiteracy, of political inarticulateness and even unconsciousness, of governmental concentration, all make for those expressions of exaggerated personalism of which this legalized perpetuation of control is a form. Dictatorship has been a normal rather than unusual type of executive development in most of the countries under consideration, and *continuismo* is but a natural result of a dictatorship which wishes to give the color of legality, either for domestic or foreign eyes, to its continuance. Costa Rica is a country of greater literacy, more general popular participation in political processes, more widespread landholdings, greater freedom of political expression and consciousness of governmental problems; these factors have a very pertinent relationship to the entire absence of any suggestion of the adoption of *continuismo* in that country.

The practice seems to be in direct and immediate contradiction to political democracy as we know the term. It is naïve, of course, to assume that in any of the countries the constitutional perversion has been accomplished in other than the harshest and most arbitrary sort of manner. The exiled opponents of the various régimes have been loud and persistent in their charges of constitutional perversion and violated democracy. Such charges are naturally to be discounted because of the personal elements entering in, but they certainly contain a strong half-truth.

If we can divest the condition and progress of democracy in Latin America from all the personal and emotional factors involved, it develops that there has as yet been precious little of it except upon a local scale. A Central American commentator, writing in defense of certain constitutional changes, has aptly if somewhat exaggeratedly said that

neither Liberty nor Democracy has ever existed or been practiced . . . in the Latin American countries. . . . It is for this reason that there can be seen despotisms, dictatorships, the Government of groups, of castes, of family, and it follows, consequently, that the masses are not first prepared for the conscientious, intelligent, and sincere exercise of such principles. To speak of Democracy, of Liberty, is an irony and a bloody and disgraceful irony.

A question as to the pathology of *continuismo* is perhaps the most difficult of all to answer. It at once involves a consideration of the entire problem of dictatorship and of the possibility of democratic progress in relation to the fundamental needs of the particular country. It is easy, and somewhat fashionable, to decry dictatorship in Latin America. The term itself is a " devil word " in the United States, the more so since the advent of the practice in certain major European states. The case for or against dictatorship in Latin America cannot be dismissed lightly, however. Many sociological, psychological, and economic elements enter in to complicate the picture, and these elements demand consideration. The prosecution charges that dictatorship represents a reversion to the *caudillismo* of the early period of independence, that it displays the worst and most selfish side of politics in the particular country, that it retards if it does not stifle democratic growth and experience among the electorate. The defense counters that in the present state of maturity of the average Latin American country, what is needed is not an illusory popular participation in the business of government but rather the peace and order which will make possible the material and cultural progress that will ultimately lead to a genuine democracy.

There is certainly something to be said for the introduction first of a measure of social and economic equality before the superimposition of political democracy is attempted. A large fraction of the population of such countries no doubt honestly prefers the stability and calm of a dictatorship, especially if a reasonably constructive one, to the uncertainty and confusion of " democracy." On the other hand, the leaven of education seems almost inevitably to encourage a demand for the sharing of political control. Until we find more accurate ways of measuring the public opinion of these republics, until, indeed, that opinion becomes less volatile, we shall not know what weight to assign to either point of view.

Continuismo cannot be regarded as a problem in and by itself. To detach it from its environment is to consider the image in a mirror as unrelated to the object which causes it. *Continuismo* is simply a reflection, a symptom, and a result of the larger problem of dictatorship.

CHAPTER 10

—— Legislatures ——
versus
Executives

No. 30
The Role and Organization
of Legislative Assemblies
in Latin America

by ASHER N. CHRISTENSEN

*T*HE formulation of public policy is, in the United States, a function that primarily pertains to the elected representatives of the people or the legislature. It is the Congress or the state legislature which is mainly concerned with what laws are to be approved, and what their content is to be. The executive, of course, has powers — both constitutional and extra-constitutional — in the field of legislation, but in general he does not dominate and control legislative decisions. He may influence but he cannot command.

As was noted earlier, our presidential system of government, based upon the theory of separation of powers, was widely copied in Latin America. Yet there the center of political gravity is found not in the national legislature but in the office and person of the president. One might justly raise the question, therefore, " What is the role of legislative assemblies in Latin America, and how is the legislative branch of the government organized? "

A national Congress in a Latin American republic resembles our own in its structure and internal organization, but certainly not in the place it occupies in the national political life. Its functioning as a body to decide upon questions of public policy is narrowly limited by the dominance of the President. Having already seen *why* executives control policy in Latin America, we now may turn to the more specific details of *how* that control is expressed.

In the first place, since the constitutional powers of the executive in the area of legislation are much more broadly stated, the scope of congressional authority is inevitably diminished. Many of the constitutions permit the executive to introduce bills into the Congress, and in a few countries *only* the President may initiate legislation on certain matters, such as the military forces, the civil service, and the budget. In some of the republics the presidential powers have been so interpreted that the approval of the Congress is assumed if it does not reject measures initiated by the President. Like our President, the Presidents of several Latin American states may veto the acts of the legislature, but unlike him they may also veto *items* of proposed legislation and accept the parts of which they approve. Hence the American practice of attempting to control the executive through " riders " to measures is almost unknown in Latin America.

In most of the nations the Congress is in session for a relatively short time each year, and it may be called into special session usually only on presidential summons. Many of the Presidents of Latin America have a power over special sessions which our President does not have, although a few of our state governors do. They may limit the subject matter of legislation to topics indicated in the calling of a special session. In the United States the Congress meets as long as it wishes to in annual sessions. The actions of the President can be theoretically subjected to legislative scrutiny 365 days a year, and in recent years we have approached that figure. Even though the Congresses of Latin America had powers commensurate with ours, the fact that they are in session for short periods limits their effectiveness as checks upon the executive.

The Latin American President has another constitutionally conferred power that greatly enhances his legislative authority. This is the power to promulgate what are known as " decree-laws." Our executives have a similar authority in their right to issue executive orders. But in the United States these can be, and frequently are, checked by the courts. Court decisions have held that these orders may supplement and implement legislative action, but they cannot add new substantive material. The President cannot *legislate;* he can only fill in details in matters of policy decided upon previously by the Congress. In almost all of the Latin American states " decree-laws " may and do incorporate new substantive material, or may even decide upon policy when the Congress has indicated no general policy whatever. The lawyer from the United States could not, in many instances, determine from the subject matter of a " decree-law," nor from its clauses, whether it was an act of an executive or a Congress. He would have little difficulty in reaching a decision were he examining a *statute* and an *executive order* in the United States.

In addition to broad constitutional powers, the authority of the President is increased by his political powers and position. It is well known that our party system is one in which a member of Congress may oppose the President on every main issue even though both are members of the same political group. The President has — for a wide variety of reasons — little or no control over the nomination and election of members of Congress. The article by Professor Tannenbaum in an earlier chapter indicated that in Mexico no person may become a candidate for Congress unless he is " satisfactory " to the President. The Mexican practice is widespread in all of Latin America. It is little wonder, therefore, that the legislatures of that region do not show the independence of ours, nor the same predilection to oppose and attack the President.

There are, finally, conditioning factors that for want of a better name we might call " socio-cultural." It must be recalled that we in the United States, with the legacy of English political institutions, have had several centuries of experience with parliamentary techniques and practices. As a result we expect that legislative bodies will conduct themselves with order and decorum, that minorities will, if defeated, continue to " play the game," that differences will be ironed out by give and take, by compromise. Many Americans are puzzled by the greater noise and confusion of a Latin American legislature in session, by the lack of procedures to effect compromises, and especially by the tactics of a defeated minority which often absents itself in a huff from the legislative chambers. It is such a feature that James Bryce probably had in mind when he spoke of the greater political maturity of the Anglo-American.

Perhaps, too, the dependence of the Latin American upon direction from above influences the acts of legislative assemblies in Latin America. For example, the Argentine Constitution, like our own, charges the President with the responsibility of informing the Congress on " the state of the nation." Although the constitutional clauses are identical, the practice is not. In Argentina the Congress will not begin its work until the President has given the " state of the nation " address. This, coupled with the fact that the Congress may meet only from May to September, means that the President can limit the length of this short session, and several have. One cannot imagine the Congress of the United States refusing to assemble and begin its legislative work merely because the President had not completed the message he must send to them.

The above-mentioned basic factors are in part the explanation of the weakness of the legislature and the legislative place in the scheme of things in Latin America. But before concluding this general statement it is worth while to note some of the general features of organization and procedure of the congresses. While they in most instances closely parallel those of this country, there are some important and interesting differences.

Of the twenty congresses, fourteen are bicameral in organization and six unicameral. Five of these six are in Central America; Paraguay also has a unicameral legislature. In a half dozen of the countries the bicameral form is related to the question of federalism, past or present. One of the houses represents the political subdivisions of the federal union, the other the people. The model of the United States was copied, and the same reasons theoretically explain bicameralism there as here. In the remainder, however, one sees no *federal* reason for two-housed legislatures; in fact, one can find in several instances no reason for the existence of two houses in the Congress other than the fact that our federal Constitution was copied. The same might be said concerning the existence of bicameral state legislatures in the United States.

The terms of members of Congress in Latin America are frequently longer than those in the United States. In the bicameral assemblies the terms of members of the upper house (usually known as the Senate) range from four to nine years, with eight countries establishing a term of six years or longer. The terms of members of the lower house (most commonly called the Chamber of Deputies) range from two to six years. Four of the countries follow our practice of staggering the terms of the upper house so that it is impossible to elect an entirely new Senate at one election. In addition, three others stagger the terms of members in the lower house, two of them being countries which also stagger elections in the Senate. Of the six unicameral assemblies, the terms range from one year to six, and in two of them the terms are also staggered. One of the unicameral nations, Guatemala, and one of the bicameral, Mexico, absolutely prohibit the re-election of any member of the Congress to the next succeeding session.

The election of members of Congress in Latin America resembles our own system. Thirteen of the fourteen Senates are chosen by direct popular vote. The fourteenth — that of Argentina — is chosen by following our original method of election: the provincial (state) legislatures make the choice. In the federal systems, representation in the Senate is equal for each of the states or provinces. In some of the nonfederal governments the Senate also equally represents the major *administrative* subdivisions of the nation; in others Senators are apportioned on the basis of population. There are several unusual features of the composition of the Senates. In all Senates, including countries having a federal form of government, the capital city and the Federal District are represented. The residents of Mexico City or Rio de Janeiro have a voice in the Senate — and also the house — which, of course, the residents of Washington and the District of Columbia do not. Two of the federal governments now, and others in the past, allow the territories some representation, constitutionally, in the lower house of Congress. In the United States there is a restricted kind of representation for territories, but it is based on congressional action. In Ecuador, in addition to the politically elected Senators, there are eleven " functional " Senators who represent economic groups such as labor unions, manufacturing associations, farm organizations, and who are chosen by them respectively. In Nicaragua ex-presidents become members of the Senate — an idea that former Governor Alfred E. Smith once proposed as a " novel " experiment. Finally, in Venezuela, there are four at-large Senators chosen from minority parties in proportion to their strength, in order to give voice to groups that would otherwise be unrepresented.

The lower chambers in all of the bicameral assemblies and the six unicameral legislatures are chosen by direct popular vote. Several of the republics have experimented, at one time or another, with some kind of proportional representation for the lower house.

A curious feature of the election of members of the congresses of Latin America is the fact that in a few countries alternates or substitutes for the members are chosen at the same election. In two countries this is done in connection with the selection of Senators and in five for members of the house. It is the expectation that by this system the costs and perhaps turbulence of another election would be avoided should the incumbent, for any reason, be unable to occupy his seat in the Congress.

As in the United States, the two chambers of the bicameral legislatures are equal and coordinate in matters of general legislation. Likewise, each of the houses has special functions. Bills referring to revenue measures and the armed forces frequently must arise in the lower house. The upper chambers usually have the power to approve or reject presidential appointments although it is generally true that the President alone may fill a large number of high judicial, diplomatic, and administrative posts without senatorial confirmation. In such instances the power of the legislative branch to check the executive is significantly reduced.

In bicameral assemblies the problem of compromising the often-expressed differences between the two houses is an important one. In the United States such disagreements are settled, if they are, by conference committees in which each of the two houses is equally represented. Long experience with parliamentary problems has indicated this to be a practical method of compromising differences of opinion.

Many of the bicameral legislatures of Latin America have arrived at the same method of agreement between the two houses. Some others, however, still have unique and unusual mechanisms indicating a lack of legislative experience. In Argentina and Chile the chamber which changes a measure received from the other house may, by an extraordinary vote, force the other body to accept its modifications unless the latter can vote it down by another extraordinary vote. In three other countries these disagreements are voted upon finally in a joint session. This gives the larger house an advantage unless, as in Uruguay, the vote must be by a two-thirds majority.

The legislative articles of the Latin American constitutions resemble those of our state constitutions when referring to the sessions of the legislature. Although most of the constitution writers in the former region have been keenly aware of executive domination and have hoped to counteract this by strengthening the legislative arm of government, they nevertheless have almost always been reluctant to allow the Congress to meet freely and with no limits placed on the length of the session. Sixteen of the 20 republics specify one session per year which may run from 60 days to 270. But 14 of the 16 permit a session of 6 months or less, and 11 allow a maximum of 4 months or less. Four of the constitutions authorize 2 sessions a year.

Limited sessions raise the problem of special meetings and the related question of who may summon the legislature into a special session. In 9 of the countries only the President may convoke a special session, and in 5 of these the Congress is limited, in the special meeting, to the consideration of only those matters mentioned in the executive convocation. Several authorize the President to call a special meeting if requested to do so by a certain percentage of the membership of one or both houses.

A final feature worthy of note is the establishment in five of the republics of a Permanent Committee of the Congress. Three theoretical bases for such committees exist, two of which are applicable to legislatures in the United States — especially at the state government level — and one which is not. In the first place, inasmuch as the Latin American legislatures meet but for short periods in each year, some mechanism is needed to take care of that urgent legislative business, such as treaty approval or confirmation of appointments, which arises after adjournment.

Secondly, these committees constitute a sort of interim legislature, and in Uruguay, for example, they work on the agenda of the next session, conduct investigations and research relating to legislative matters, and so forth. In the performance of this function these committees resemble the legislative councils of several American states. Like them they are made up of a certain number of representatives from each of the houses of the legislature.

The third, and unique, function of the permanent committees is to act as a legislative watchdog, to see that the executive stays behind the limits of his authority, broad as they may be. If acts of the President require congressional approval when the Congress is in session, the same acts must go before the permanent committee if it is not.

As an illustration of this special place of the Permanent Committee the power of the President over intervention may be cited. In both Argentina and Mexico the President has broad powers to order interventions. In both countries the Congress is theoretically empowered to approve or reject presidential intervention decrees. But, as Professor Gomez indicated in his article, most of the interventions in Argentina are ordered between September and May, when the Congress is not in session. There is no Permanent Committee in the Argentine Congress! In Mexico, however, the Permanent Committee has authority to act for the Senate when the Congress is not meeting.

The Permanent Committees, like many other of the interesting legislative mechanisms encountered in Latin America, are and can be effective only if the parent body, the Congress itself, is really independent and really can oppose the president. This level of political experience, of political maturity, is not as yet common in those twenty republics.

No. 31 [The parliamentary form of government fuses executive and legislative authority, and in theory it makes the executive and his department heads or ministers responsible to the legislature. In this form of political organization it is theoretically impossible for the executive to dominate the political scene. Actually, the party structure of a nation which has a parliamentary system may alter or even reverse the relationships that should exist between the leader and the led, between parliament and the first or prime minister.

The parliamentary form of government has not been popular in Latin America. It is not strange that political units whose history has shown, almost without interruption, the tendency of the executive to control the government and politics of the colony or nation should reject this plan of political organization. A few of the countries, however, have ventured into the parliamentary area, some with surprising and unexpected results. The origins of the parliamentary system in Latin America, why it was established in a few republics, and how it has functioned politically are the subjects of Professor Stokes' article.]

Parliamentary Government in Latin America*

by WILLIAM S. STOKES

DEMOCRATIC Caesarism," whether by military *caudillo* or *doctor en filosofía,* had discouraged administrative efficiency and contributed to political disorganization in Latin America. Concentration of executive authority without responsibility has given free rein to the worst administrative practices of poor presidents without demanding the best from competent chief executives; and, with minority

* William S. Stokes, " Parliamentary Government in Latin America," *The American Political Science Review* (June, 1945), Vol. XXXIX, No. 3, pp. 522–536. Reprinted by permission of *The American Political Science Review.* The footnotes in the original version are omitted here.

groups in congress dominated by a rubber-stamp majority — the entire legislature gasping in the shade of strong executive government — active groups have turned to revolution as an outlet for political and administrative expression. Poor organization of power and authority constitutes one of the most important problems of government in Latin American countries, and a dovetailing of a series of approaches probably is necessary for complete solution — better preparation of leaders, elimination of *caudillismo,* reform of codes and laws to conform with the spirit of the democratic constitutions, reorganization of parties along doctrinal lines rather than those of *personalismo,* and development of public opinion and participation in politics by the masses through education and increasing the standard of living.

A number of Latin American countries, however, have experimented with parliamentary and semiparliamentary government in the hope that by extending to the legislature the prerogative of simple question, interpellation, and vote of censure or lack of confidence, the following objectives might be realized: Parliamentary government might (1) constitute a needed balance against irresponsible, strong executive leadership; (2) serve as an institutional device to absorb party passions and eliminate the necessity for revolution; (3) make for responsible government by majority, with acceptance of the idea of a loyal opposition; and (4) increase interest and participation in government, with clearer definition of rights and duties and greater respect for law.

The experience of the Latin American republics with parliamentary government must be approached in terms of past working attempts and contemporary established systems. The parliamentary and semiparliamentary forms once employed by Chile, Brazil, and Bolivia, and to a lesser extent by Haiti and Honduras, must not be entirely subordinated to the working systems of cabinet government and ministerial responsibility in Uruguay, Cuba, and, perhaps, Peru. In addition, however, it must be noted that separation of powers has been modified toward cabinet government in Costa Rica, Chile, Haiti, Mexico, and Panama by permitting ministers to attend the sessions of the legislature and debate but not vote, and in Argentina,

Bolivia, Colombia, Ecuador, Guatemala, Honduras, Nicaragua, El Salvador, and Venezuela by permitting the legislature to force ministers to appear and be subjected to questioning.

The most clear-cut working example of a parliamentary system among countries no longer using the form is Chile. The idea of ministerial responsibility is rooted deep in Chile's early independent experience, and the country operated under a complete system of cabinet government from 1891 to 1925. The constitutions of Chile down to the document of 1814 justifying Carrera's dictatorship tended to restrain executive authority in favor of congressional dominance. The documents from 1818 to 1823 were plainly autocratic, and the 1826 and 1828 federal and semifederal constitutions restated the doctrine of executive omnipotence. On the other hand, the organic law of 1833 balanced the executive and legislative powers so evenly as to encourage each to seek superiority over the other. In Articles 26, 76–92, the basis for cabinet government was set up in that all presidential orders had to be signed by the minister of the appropriate department; each minister was personally and collectively responsible for acts signed by himself and the cabinet; ministers were required to transmit administrative reports to the legislature at the opening of its sessions; cabinet members could be selected from the Senate or Chamber; ministers could attend Congress, debate but not vote, and the Chamber could charge ministers with misfeasance and malfeasance in office, to be tried before the Senate for violation of their responsibility. The President, however, could initiate legislation by message, and his executive powers were broadly expressed, including the right to " appoint and remove cabinet ministers at will."

Diego Portales directed government under the Constitution of 1833 into strong executive channels, however, and the impetus of this trend gained momentum in the middle of the nineteenth century as conservative presidents, supported by a social and political aristocracy accustomed to relying upon executive power for their privileged status, administered the country honestly and efficiently, and thus did not shake the uninformed masses out of their apathy. The fact that executive leadership characterized government did not preclude the parallel development of the idea of responsibility, and the legislature came increasingly to demand the right to check and criticize the government. Indeed, the beginnings of responsibility have an earlier origin than 1833. In the face of repeated frustrations at the first national Congress of July 4, 1811, the *Exaltados,* who wanted ". . . to transform the colony into a country master of its destinies . . . ," resigned and returned to face their constituencies in a new election. When the moderates later lost their majority and could no longer carry out the program under which they were elected, they too resigned. Some prominent scholars argue that the parliamentary system began with the Constitution of 1833, but although simple question appears to have taken place almost from the beginning (and on August 31, 1840, and July 20, 1846, the Senate and Chamber established the conditions under which ministers could debate), the first interpellations did not occur until the administration of Bulnes in 1843. Although the first vote of censure against a ministry, that of Domingo Santa María in 1849, was withdrawn after a long debate, the ministry fell anyway as a result of ". . . the force of opinion." Congress censured the ministry headed by José Joaquín Pérez in 1849, that of Amunátegui in 1870, of Altamirano in 1875, and of Vicente Reyes in 1878. By constitutional amendment in 1874, cabinet ministers were definitely made responsible to Congress for their acts, and the brilliant Chilean scholar Huneeus could write in 1879: " The power of the Houses to vote acts of censure against the Ministers of State . . . is unquestionable."

By the time Balmaceda was elected President in 1886, therefore, he was confronted with the fact of cabinet government. In addition, the powers of the President had gradually been whittled away. In 1871, the President's term was limited to five years, without immediate re-election; in 1874, his authority to employ the *estado de sitio* without congressional approval was strictly regulated and his power to appoint the Council of State was taken away by the legislature; by laws of 1874, 1875, and 1880, the judiciary was made more independent; the power of executive-appointed *intendentes* was reduced, the secret ballot introduced, and the suffrage extended to all literate males in 1884; laws of 1874, 1880, and 1884 disqualified congressmen from running for office if they already held a position to which they had been appointed by the President; the cumulative vote was introduced in laws in 1874 and 1884; and Congress was given power to check the executive's administration of the budget through laws of 1883 and 1884. Thus, when Balmaceda's refusal to appoint a ministry acceptable to the majority in Congress led to military victory for congressional forces in the battle of Placilla on August 28, 1891, the idea that no President should govern without a parliamentary majority had become a fixed part of Chilean governmental organization and procedure.

Government under the " parliamentary republic " in Chile from 1891 to 1925 is often criticized for the ministerial instability it produced, and many opponents attribute to it the declining quality of representatives, the logrolling on appropriation measures, the subservience of congressmen to local pressure group interests, and the prevalence of bribery in elections. The Constitution of 1925, drafted under the guidance of Arturo Alessandri, " the Lion of Tarapacá," re-established the presidential system, although ministers were still allowed to appear before Congress. The 1925 document, however, did not wipe the political slate clean. The idea of responsibility is neither dead nor moribund, and presidents since 1925 have not been able to restore the *caudillismo* of the 1830's nor the executive aristocracy of the 1850's. Congress has continued to exercise a vociferous and frequently compelling voice in formulating policy and checking administration. Although the form of the parliamentary system is gone, ministries continue to change frequently when the President and his cabinet cannot command the respect and confidence of the legislature.

The parliamentary experience of Brazil under the 1824 Constitution has had less effect on the political institutions of that country. The reasons perhaps are twofold: On the one hand, the parliamentary system was more nominal than real, and on the other, it represented part of the trappings of the monarchy to be swept away in the path of the democratic republic. The Constitution of 1891 and subsequent documents show slight trace of the 1824–89 parliamentary experience. Bolivia, Haiti, and Honduras have made paper and real attempts to install the parliamentary system, with the result that some responsibility has been enforced on the executive, although the prevailing norm still is, if not *caudillismo,* at least very strong executive government.

The right of ministers to appear before Congress has been incorporated in most of the fourteen constitutions of Bolivia. The document of 1931, however, made attendance compulsory upon request of the legislature and established responsibility of the cabinet through interpellation and vote of censure. The fact that political parties were accustomed to the idea of cabinet ministers acting as a cushion between the executive and legislative branches might have pointed to at least a modified success of the parliamentary system. From 1931 to the formation of the 1938 organic law destroying the parliamentary system, however, Bolivia was governed by executives who tolerated little interference from the legislature. The Constitution of 1938 maintains the traditional doctrine of voluntary and compulsory attendance of ministers, who are subject to interpellation and censure. A vote of censure or lack of confidence, however, no longer makes resignation obligatory. The legislature's actions are purely recommendatory. Nevertheless, the legislature of Bolivia has on a few occasions, at least, indulged in the form and procedure of the parliamentary system, even though power in substance has been controlled by the executive. The devices of question, interpellation, and censure are accepted mechanisms in the machinery of government, and it is possible that a modified parliamentary system might evolve. The Peñaranda government (1940–43), for example, was at least indirectly influenced by legislative criticism of its administration. Victor Paz Estenssoro, leader of the *Movimiento Nacionalista Revolucionario* and one of the President's bitter enemies, attacked the government viciously on August 24, 1943. The entire cabinet of nine resigned three days later. On September 15 a vote of censure was averted by 48–47 in the Chamber. Again there was a cabinet change (two days later), although the executive was not forced to consider congressional opposition.

The evidence of parliamentary government in Haiti is ephemeral at best. The provisions establishing ministerial responsibility in the constitutions of 1806 and 1843 were never enforced, and the attempts made to impose the system on the executive in 1859 and 1867 were miserable failures. The more serious conflict over cabinet government in 1874 — in which the legislature censured two of the President's ministers — resulted not only in the refusal of the President to dismiss the men, but in the dissolution of the legislature as well.

The experience of Honduras with parliamentary government from 1925 through 1931 is more important. The chaos precipitated by the elections of 1923 and the subsequent revolution in 1924 severely weakened executive control of government. The Congress accepted this opportunity to increase its power by providing the new Constitution of 1924 that on a vote of censure a minister or the entire cabinet was obligated to resign. Where ministers formerly sent their *memorias* to Congress by messenger, beginning in 1925 they appeared personally to read the report and answer questions. Following several investigations, including frequent interpellations, the Congress voted censure against the Minister of Finance late in 1925 and forced his resignation. In the same year, the Congress questioned cabinet ministers on budget requests, and refused to approve the executive acts in the departments of *fomento* and government for designated periods in 1924. In 1927, a vote of lack of confidence forced the Minister of Finance to resign, and in March, 1931, the Ministers of Government, War, and Finance were obligated to give up their posts. From 1925 through 1931, Congress challenged the executive on policy, appointments, and administration, and did so through the pattern of parliamentary government. The newly born *" parlamentarismo "* came to an early death in 1932, however, with the election to the presidency of Dr. Tiburcio Carías, who re-established the old lines of authority running from the *Casa Presidencial* to the Congress. The final step was taken in the Constitution of 1936, which denied the right of Congress to censure the actions of any executive officer.

Of the contemporary parliamentary systems of Latin America, that of Peru has acted as a façade behind which the executive has pursued a policy of governmental control without responsibility. Constitutionally, the organic law of June 10, 1834, extended ministers the privilege of attending either chamber without a vote; the document of November 13, 1860, allowed a " permanent committee " of seven senators and eight deputies to take action against ministers in the President's failure to act (repealed August 31, 1874); and the Constitution of 1920 provided that ministers must resign on vote of censure in either chamber. The extant Constitution, that of 1933, authorizes the legislature to force attendance of ministers, subject them to interpellation, and effect their resignation through vote of censure. Strong executive control of government during the twentieth century, however, has relegated these provisions to a position of secondary importance. The difference between law and practice (*el derecho y el hecho*) has been great. The statement made by Professor Stuart in reference to government under the Constitution of 1920 that ". . . in spite of the implications in the new constitution that Peru is tending toward the parliamentary system, in reality the government is carried on under a system which is in the highest degree presidential," is equally valid in describing government under the Constitution of 1933. It is worth noting, however, that the form of the parliamentary system has been maintained for decades in Peruvian government, and that the incumbent President Prado has occasionally taken cognizance of the apparent will of the badly organized political groups in the legislature. Available evidence points to the probability that the parliamentary form will remain and gradually narrow the discretionary authority of the President.

The formula theory of Uruguayan constitutional development — that extreme presidential government under the Constitution of 1830 was matched by extreme congressional government under the Constitution of 1917, with the 1934 organic law producing a synthesis in the form of a parliamentary system — fails to evaluate correctly practical experience in ministerial responsibility under each of the constitutions. As a matter of fact, " When the constituents [of the constitutional convention drafting the 1830 document] began their work, ministerial responsibility had already become a necessary element in our governmental customs." During the colonial period, the *cabildos* constantly made inquiries of the *Gobernadores,* who frequently answered these requests for information personally and submitted to questioning and criticism. Thus, when the *Junta de Representantes* acted as the legislative body from 1825 to 1827, it felt free to call in ministers regularly for questioning. The provision in the *Reglamento* of the *Junta* allowing questioning of ministers was probably influenced in wording by Article 30 of the Constitution of 1819 of Argentina. It is not surprising, therefore, that Article 53 of the 1830 document granting interpellation passed the convention without discussion, although the idea of ministerial responsibility was analyzed intelligently. Article 53 did not concede to the legislature the power to censure ministers and force their resignation, but an early struggle with the executive over control of finances led to that development. The Permanent Committee represented the interests of the legislature when not in session, and by 1832 was demanding the appearance of ministers for questioning. In 1848, when civil war prevented the election of a new legislature and the president appointed an " Assembly of Notables " to perform the legislative functions, that body immediately began to hold the executive and his ministers responsible. By 1852, the language of the legislature included such terms as " cabinet," " prime minister," " ministerial confidence," " declaration of censure," and majority and minority " leaders "; and lack of confidence in the executive's cabinet was voted in 1853, 1864, 1873, and 1874, with interpellation common from 1888. During the nineteenth century, the legislature repeatedly analyzed important economic, social, and political problems, checked the administration of government carefully, and occasionally challenged the executive on policy. It is true, however, that late in the 1890's the power and prestige of the executive increased markedly, to result, by about 1908, in strong presidential government within the parliamentary form. It was this executive discretion that the great Uruguayan statesman, José Batlle y Ordóñez, ably opposed in arguing for the Constitution of 1917.

The Constitution of 1917 divided the executive branch between a President elected directly, with important powers in the domestic and foreign fields, and a nine-man national Council of Administration elected directly by proportional representation, with important powers in finance, education, public works, labor, and manufacturing. Congress retained the power of interpellation through Article 50. The division of executive power reduced the authority of that branch, while increasing that of the legislature. Under the Constitution of 1917, ministers were subjected to unwarranted interpellation and vote of censure on a number of occasions. In addition, on appropriation bills and financial administration, the legislature from time to time was guilty of delay and obstruction. Dr. Gabriel Terra, who became President in 1931, had always opposed the division of the executive power, and in addition he was almost immediately hampered in his task of administration by a hostile Congress, which subjected his cabinet to incessant interpellation. He had, however, consistently defended ministerial responsibility. Thus, when he led the *coup d'état* of March 31, 1933, against the Congress and National

Council, his views on governmental organization were well known. President Terra called a constituent assembly, which, convening on June 25, 1933, to draft a new constitution, demonstrated a desire to retain the parliamentary system with modifications in the executive branch.

Under Uruguay's Constitution of 1934, the President may select his nine-man cabinet from either chamber, giving five or six seats to the majority, and at least three to the minority, party. The bicameral legislature sitting in general assembly may freely interpeilate ministers and force their resignation through vote of lack of confidence. If the vote on the President's cabinet is less than two-thirds against the President, he may dissolve the legislature and call for elections. The new General Assembly is obligated to consider the vote of disapproval that forced the resignations and election, and on sustaining it, the President himself, along with his ministers, is forced to resign. Confidence in the successful operation of the parliamentary system in Uruguay is predicated on the valid assumption that it constitutes a time-tested mechanism of utility in harmonizing executive-legislative relations and relating authority and responsibility in government.

The semiparliamentary system inaugurated by Cuba under the Constitution of 1940 finds some legal basis in the constitutions of the monarchy and the revolutionary constitutions of the nineteenth century. The Spanish Constitution of 1812, for example, established a type of modified ministerial responsibility, and the *Constitución Autonómica* of 1897 permitted ministers to be selected from the legislature and to attend its sessions. The revolutionary Constitution of Guáimaro of April 10, 1869, however, created a government of legislative supremacy in which the executive officers were selected by the legislature and held responsible. The document was probably modeled on the English system. During the first three decades of the twentieth century, academic circles debated the presidential-parliamentary issue, with most of the pros and cons, aired in the constituent assembly which met from June 20, 1927, to May 11, 1928. A number of men prominent in public life advocated the parliamentary system from the beginning of the republic, and one scholar argued that the Constitution of 1901 contained provisions which could be construed as the beginning of parliamentary government in Cuba. The man who labored longer and with most conviction, however, was Dr. José Manuel Cortina, who served as president of the constitution committee which drafted the organic law of 1940.

In the decade from 1930 to 1940, the demand for a parliamentary system to harmonize the executive and legislative branches, improve administration, and decrease the possibility of revolution increased. The constitutional reforms of 1935 (never put into effect) established a parliamentary system in which the President would govern with a cabinet selected from the majority parties in a bicameral legislature, with the ministers liable to interpellation and forced resignation through censure. Dr. Gutiérrez' draft of a proposed constitution submitted in 1936 made presidential ministers responsible to a unicameral legislature through interpellation and censure. The constitution completed by Dr. Sánchez Ocejo in December, 1938, went even further and permitted the executive to dissolve the legislature on vote of lack of confidence. On the other hand, of fifteen political parties outlining their platforms prior to the 1940 constituent convention, only two — *Partido Revolucionario Cubano (Auténtico)* and *Partido Social Demócrata* — called for a parliamentary system. Of these two parties, the first was of considerable importance at the convention, as forty-four out of eighty-one delegates were in the opposition *bloc* led by Dr. Grau San Martín of the *Partido Revolucionario Cubano*. Those magazines reflecting economic and political interests likely to be affected by a parliamentary system did not join the controversy or discussion. Nevertheless, after a number of lively and a few brilliant speeches, the convention accepted the articles necessary to the new system without amendment.

The formal organization of the parliamentary system is clear, and the provisions elastic enough to permit growth and development through custom and usage. The President may select his ministers from either of the two houses of the legislature. The cabinet — or Council of Ministers as it is called — has legal status, and the President is instructed to report through it to Congress. Acting as liaison agents between the President and legislature, the ministers are expected to attend the sessions and may be summoned for questioning. Interpellation may be begun through a written motion signed by one third of the members of either house and concurred in by an absolute majority of all the members within eight days. Disapproval may be total — when the prime minister or more than three ministers are challenged — or partial, and if the legislature votes lack of confidence, resignation is obligatory within forty-eight hours. The legislature can deny confidence, however, only after the minister has held office for at least six months, a question of confidence cannot be raised in the final six months of a presidential period, and an issue of confidence that has been voted down cannot be raised again for a year. The President is denied the power to appoint the same minister to the same portfolio after a vote of censure.

The form of the parliamentary system was adhered to almost immediately, but the motions did not begin to have practical effect until May 1942. The constitution went into effect on October 10, 1940, and President Batista appointed Senator Carlos Saladrigas prime minister. He announced in his acceptance speech that he intended to make the parliamentary system work. The cabinet began functioning as a body with the prime minister or President presiding over the regularly scheduled meetings. Congress convened in November, and the *líderes* of the various parties organized into majority and minority *blocs*. From the beginning, however, Congress showed little inclination to check actively the administrative policy of the Council of Ministers. In February 1941 Representative Almagro proposed the first interpellation, but the House did not approve his action. Prime Minister Saladrigas appeared for the first time before the Chamber on February 10 to outline government policy and to advise the majority party group on legislative priority. When Saladrigas appeared again on February 12, Representative Ichaso of the opposition asked him a few questions. On March 18, the prime minister conferred at length with opposition members to achieve their support of the government's sugar and financial program. Despite these favorable beginnings, however, by July, 1941, it appeared that serious cleavages between the ministers and opposition leaders in Congress had developed. The bitterness was readily apparent, yet the solution was not approached through the parliamentary pattern. Congressmen brought pressure on the President outside the legislature, and on July 9 it was announced that President Batista had conferred with the prime minister and leaders in Congress to discuss possible resignations. The entire cabinet resigned on July

16, and only five out of the seventeen ministers were reappointed.

During the remainder of 1941, tension between the executive and legislative branches mounted, but the legislature did not take advantage of its prerogatives to clarify the sources of friction. Senator Manuel Capestany called for the interpellation of the Minister of Communications in August, but his request was denied. Indeed, the Senate during most of the year was little more than a rubber stamp for the President and a debating forum for the airing of party and personal grievances. The Senate approved all the presidential and cabinet decrees without extended debate, and did not push its right to receive information from the executive branch. In both the Chamber and Senate, opposition leaders prevented a quorum by remaining away from the legislature. Dr. Gustavo Gutiérrez, a strong advocate of the parliamentary system, resigned as president of the Chamber in October, 1941, for that reason. Toward the end of 1941, however, the issue of a $25,000,000 Export-Import Bank loan encouraged executive and legislature to work within the parliamentary framework. The Prime Minister and Ministers of State and Treasury met with house leaders in November to plan strategy for achieving approval of the lower house, and when the issue was considered the prime minister and three other ministers defended the government's request to consummate the loan.

The year 1942 saw the first decisive step toward the crystallization of the parliamentary system. In May, the parliamentary committee of the *Partido Revolucionario Cubano (Auténtico)* revealed that it had met under the chairmanship of Dr. Grau San Martín to decide whether to introduce a bill in the Senate to investigate the executive's activity under the war emergency legislation. Dr. Grau and his committee also met with the Council of Ministers; but as the conversations were unsatisfactory, the opposition group drafted a *cuestionario* to be answered by the council. At this point, the government urged that the opposition content itself with a petition for written data. Under the capable leadership of the *P.R.C.,* however, the Senate voted to submit the Prime Minister and Ministers of Commerce, State, Treasury, Public Works, Defense, and Government to interpellation. The many carefully drafted, intelligent questions put to the ministers related to price ceilings on consumers' goods, the black market, immigration, use of public tractors for political purposes, sale of scrap iron, and national defense. Prime Minister Salad-rigas defended the government ably, each minister read a prepared answer to the formal questions, and then met all oral challenges. This was the first interpellation, and the maintenance of decorum and restraint characterized it as successful from the procedural standpoint. On May 29, the Senate voted approval of the ministers and stated officially that the parliamentary system had begun. As an anticlimax, the entire cabinet resigned on June 18, and the President accepted the resignations of seven, although one remained in the government as minister without portfolio.

The first crisis in the operation of the parliamentary system was successfully, if modestly, met. Both the executive and legislative branches demonstrated an ability to work within the new relation-ships, and even though no minister or cabinet had been driven from power by vote of censure by the middle of 1944, it appeared that the parliamentary system had at least an even chance for survival.

From this survey of past and contemporary parliamentary systems in Latin America, the conclusion is evident that even in the more advanced countries the results have not squared with the hopes of the proponents of the system. Perhaps, however, the fact of failure in some cases and only moderate success in others is not the most important conclusion that can be drawn. What does appear to be significant is that political and academic leaders have concluded that separation of powers into water-tight compartments has en-couraged irresponsible and undesirable executive omnipotence. In adopting cabinet government, they argue from the assumption that responsibility of the executive and his cabinet to the representatives of the people may increase the likelihood of efficient, democratic government and decrease the possibilities of revolution arising out of political frustration. It is yet too early to attempt to measure with finality, or even comparative precision, the degree to which parlia-mentary government may contribute to the achievement of these goals. Enough positive progress has been made in countries like Chile and Uruguay, however, to warrant encouragement in the ex-periment of cabinet government; and as a device susceptible of molding to variable governmental environments, it shows promise of being instrumental in furthering progress of the Latin American countries toward the political maturity which they seek.

CHAPTER 11

The Courts;
Public Administration;
Municipal Government

No. 32
Strong Governments and Weak Courts

by *ASHER N. CHRISTENSEN*

*T*HE judicial articles of Latin American constitutions and the organization of the courts in almost all of the countries bear many resemblances to American theory and practice. Constitutional borrowing has been almost as prevalent in judicial matters as it has been in those dealing with federal systems or the structure of the national legislature. Judicial procedures, however, and more especially the relationships existing between the courts and the other main branches of government, differ sharply in the governmental areas.

One of the most significant contributions made by the United States to the political institutions of the world is judicial review. While arguments still persist over the intention of the framers of our Constitution concerning this power of the courts, it is quite clear that the exercise of the power to review, to check, and to block executive or legislative action is a part of our *constitutional* system. We have long and strenuously debated the desirability and results of judicial review, but the majority of its most bitter opponents will admit that a change can be realized only by changing the constitutional bases of our government. Constitutionally, therefore, if the executive exceeds his authority his action can be halted by the courts. Constitutionally, the Supreme Court may nullify a policy agreed upon by the Congress and approved by the President.

The Latin American courts theoretically occupy the same position in the governmental framework as ours do. They form an independent and coordinate third branch or department of the political structure. American influence is seen not only in the general role of the courts but even in judicial organization. Why is it, then, that the courts of Latin America have been even less effective than the legislatures in limiting the authority of strong presidents?

With but the possible exception of Chile it can be asserted that the courts occupy a very minor position in the political life of the several republics. One almost never encounters any judicial veto, or even restriction, of a presidential decree or legislative enactment. Decisions like those that our Supreme Court handed down in 1934 and 1935 are not — and many would say could not be — pronounced by Latin American jurists. Power struggles between the executive and the courts, or the congress and the judiciary, like those which took place in the United States in 1936–37 or 1866–68, are unknown.

Many commentators have discussed the divergence between the power of the courts in the two Americas. Although they differ as to the causes of the distinction they are almost in unanimous agreement concerning the end result. Some emphasize the institutional history of Latin America and stress the importance of the political institutions of the mother country as a basic conditioning factor. No judicial body in Spain could challenge the prerogatives of the Crown. For over three centuries in Latin America no courts existed which could oppose the political actions of viceroys or governors. The *audiencias* and the *residencias* exercised what appeared to be judicial functions, but they were branches of the executive arm of the home government. The mere act of signing a declaration of independence, or of drafting and promulgating a constitution, did not — and could not — change long-established and deep-rooted patterns of political behavior. The writers of this view note that the courts of England had to struggle to win their position of relative independence, and that those of the United States, despite their rich English heritage, were not strong and independent in the early years of the republic.

Other historical analysts maintain that the institution of the *caudillo* is a determining factor of utmost importance. Judicial decisions and orders meant as little to the man on horseback, assuming that any court would dare to block the *caudillo,* as the resolutions of a legislative assembly. But no court dared to check a Rosas, a López, or a Gómez. Much of the nineteenth century was dominated by the *caudillo* in almost all of the Latin American countries, and one of the many political heritages of this era is judicial temerity. One of my Venezuelan students once asked me, "If the United States had experienced the " age of the *caudillos,*" if President Jefferson could have had Chief Justice Marshall summarily shot after his decision in *Marbury v. Madison,* might this not have retarded the emergence of a strong and independent judiciary? " The question is, admittedly, an " iffy " one, but it does highlight the social and political environment in which courts operated in nineteenth-century United States and in Latin America.

Another group of investigators base their interpretation upon socio-cultural data. Some would argue, as the Argentine writer and statesman Sarmiento did, that the wild and free frontier spirit of independence with its bitter opposition to restraints, legal or otherwise, made it extremely difficult to establish what might be called the " rule of law." This frontier character has still not disappeared in Latin America; there are no monographs noting, and perhaps lamenting, the passing of the " last frontier." Still others hold that the rural and agricultural base of the economy is an influence. Law, and the rule of law, they would maintain, is more an expression of an urban than a rural culture. In the United States, the " law west of the Pecos " and its exponent, " Judge " Bean, were rural and frontier institutions.

A third " school " bases its reasoning on the widely differing sources of the legal systems of the United States and of Latin America. Latin American law traces its ancestry back through Spanish and French law to the codes of ancient Rome. The " law " in Latin America is primarily a body of formally prepared, adopted, and promulgated rules. It is not a statement of legal principles based upon the reasoning and opinions of judges. There is no common law, as we understand the term, in Latin America. Judge-made rules, judicial interpretations, applications and modifications of the formal or written law are much less significant. The emphasis is on the *code* and not on the *case*.

This of course influences the training of lawyers, of those who later become judges. In England and in the United States legal education emphasizes the importance of the jurist in the determination of the principle of law to be applied to a particular case, and gives first place to the judge's opinion, and his legal logic. Most of the time of the law student is spent reading cases, not collections or codifications of law. Judicial review is related not only to the kind of law we have but also to the kind of legal training we practice. Latin America's law and its system of law training are not as conducive to strong and independent judges and courts.

Some explain the timidity or reluctance of the courts to limit the power of executives on political grounds. Presidents manipulate the whole of the political process, including that part which relates to the selection or supervision of courts. Brought up in the tradition of personal control they select judges who come from the same background and tradition, who will accept that control. If, as is provided in some of the constitutions, the President has been deprived of the power to name the judges and if, as usually is the case, this power is then lodged in the legislature, there is still no guarantee of a stronger judiciary. We have already seen that legislative bodies too, in Latin America, are generally subservient to presidents.

One final point can be mentioned. One of the factors that has enhanced the power and prestige of our courts is the important function they have of umpiring federal-state conflicts. Our federal system is real as well as constitutional. Conflicts between federal and state powers or policies constantly arise, and *they are submitted to the courts for adjudication*. This augments both the work and the political importance of the bench.

Federalism in Latin America is, at best, a weak political institution. Conflicts between central and local authorities are not resolved, to the same degree, by recourse to judicial processes. The conflicts do not arise as often, and if they do intervention frequently takes the place of judicial resolution. Argentina's federal system is perhaps most like ours. Its Supreme Court has so stated, and that court often cites United States cases. But there are few cases in which the Argentine Supreme Court has upheld the rights of the provinces as against the authority of the central government.

The constitutions of Latin America reflect in many instances the concern of their planners and framers over executive domination. In the judicial articles one finds many clauses that were included to bulwark the power and independence of the courts. In some of the countries the authority to name the judges has been denied to the executive and it has been given to the Congress. In others, where the President appoints the justices, he may appoint only those whose names appear on a list or panel. This panel is prepared by incumbent judges or by "outside" commissions of supposedly disinterested and nonpolitical members.

To increase the court's power as a check upon the other branches of the government six of the constitutions specifically state that the courts have the power of judicial review. These six are Chile, Colombia, Cuba, Ecuador, Uruguay, and Venezuela. In one of these, Ecuador, it is a limited power, however; it may be exercised only if the President and the Congress disagree as to the constitutionality of proposed action. In a seventh country, Argentina, the Congress has "recognized" the power of judicial review as belonging to the Supreme Court even though the constitution is silent on the point. The Cuban constitution furthermore permits any twenty-five interested persons to challenge the constitutionality of an act of Congress even though they have no direct interest in the law or its application. In the United States, the written Constitution does not directly authorize the courts to declare executive or legislative action unconstitutional; the Congress has never directly and openly "recognized" the power as one belonging to the courts.

Despite these constitutional or statutory authorizations or recognitions in seven republics, it cannot be said that judicial review as a political and real institution is any more important there than it is in the other thirteen whose constitutions are silent on the subject. It certainly can be stated, however, that in comparison with the United States, all twenty of the nations are characterized by the failure of judicial review to be an important factor in political life.

The constitutional provisions establishing the judicial departments of Latin American governments detail many common and several unique features. In most of the republics the highest tribunal is known as a Supreme Court. It ranges in size from three members to twenty-one, compared with our nine. In general, constitutions fix the size of the highest court in Latin America; in the United States this is done by act of Congress. In nine republics the justices of the high court are appointed by the Congress, a practice that probably reflects the desire to remove the bench from presidential influence or control. Four other constitutions provide for the method of selection we use: nomination by the chief executive with the approval of the upper chamber of the legislature. In one country, however, the President may name the justices without legislative approval. The remaining methods of selection are: the lower house chooses from a panel prepared by the upper; one half of the judges are chosen by the lower house and one half by the upper; or the selection is made by the upper chamber of the legislature on its own initiative and without limits on its discretion.

The practice of preparing panels of lists from which appointments must be made, regardless of the final location of the appointing power, is common. It is frequently stipulated that the names of ranking or senior lower court justices must be on all panels. This means that lower court justices reach the Supreme Court more frequently than they do in the United States. Another unusual and praiseworthy feature of judicial appointment in Latin America is that the Supreme Court itself frequently appoints the justices of the lower courts. Election of judges, a common American practice at the state level, is unknown in Latin America. It might be added that it is a feature of American government that puzzles the Latin Americans. They fail to see, and perhaps they are not alone, why judges should be made to campaign for votes, and they quite rightly wonder if this does not influence the decisions they make.

Most of the larger nations have a court organization that resembles ours. In the federal systems separate and distinct national and state or provincial courts exist, the latter usually organized as the state or provincial constitution disposes. At the national level one usually finds an intermediate court, principally of appellate jurisdiction, and similar in function to our Circuit Court of Appeal. The lowest level of the court hierarchy is composed of courts of first instance, with original criminal and civil jurisdiction analogous to the District Courts of the United States. In a few of the countries, courts of limited civil and criminal competence resembling our justice of the peace courts are found.

In only five of the nations do the judges of the highest court enjoy a life tenure, a factor of great importance in the establishment of a really independent judiciary. In the other fifteen constitutions the tenure of the justices of the Supreme Court ranges from two to ten years. Uruguay furnishes the curious example of a life term for judges of the lower courts but not for Supreme Court judges. Guatemala and Costa Rica, which both provide for a brief four-year term for judges of the high court, also stipulate that judges may not be reappointed for the succeeding term. In several of the republics the term of the judges is coterminous with that of the President or the Congress, which fact is, of course, significant in explaining the weakness of the judiciary.

A few of the constitutions contain clauses that concern or regulate the removal of justices from their offices. The process of impeachment is common in all of Latin America and it can be used against judges as it can be in the United States. As is the case here, it is rarely employed. Argentina, however, recently and for the first time in its history impeached and removed members of the Supreme Court. In Mexico a judge may be removed if charges are preferred against him by the President and if these charges are approved by a majority vote in each house of the Congress! Chile, however, shows the other extreme; judges may be removed from their posts only by a two-thirds vote of the Supreme Court. As we have seen, Chile is the one nation of Latin America in which the President cannot enforce his will against the opposition of the Supreme Court. In several nations removal by the President has occurred even though the constitutions do not authorize such action. The practice of justices conferring with the executive in order to obtain his views before reaching a decision is not unknown.

The Supreme Courts of Latin America commonly exercise a function that has long been recommended in the United States, and which our national Supreme Court, and the highest courts in a few states, perform in a limited manner. This is the task of administrative supervision over the judicial business and procedure of the entire court system. Latin American high tribunals are much more administrative agencies than their North American counterparts. In Peru, for example, the Supreme Court not only administers the work of all of the courts, but it also recommends legislation referring to civil and criminal matters and judicial organization and procedure to the national Congress.

Many varieties of special courts and special judicial functions, not usually found in the United States, are commonly found as a part of Latin American judicial establishments. As one might expect, the European antecedents of Latin American law have resulted in the creation of special administrative courts with jurisdiction over the general administrative acts of government departments, cases in which citizens seek compensation for injury resulting from governmental action, and the whole broad field of what we call administrative law. Colombia now has the most completely developed system of administrative courts which closely resembles the French administrative court organization.

Judicial relationships with budgetary and fiscal matters, and especially with the accounting or auditing of public funds, is fairly common. Brazil, in its new constitution, established a number of highly specialized tribunals dealing with fiscal, military, labor, and electoral matters. The Electoral Tribunals of that country represent a new and different attempt to limit the President's control over elections by giving this special court jurisdiction over all cases involving the application of the election laws, disputed elections, and similar litigation.

Many of the Latin American courts follow a procedure that has been the subject of discussion in this country. Some of the Supreme Courts, usually the larger ones, are divided into chambers or sections. One such chamber hears criminal cases, another civil, a third administrative and so on. It is the expectation that by so assigning the justices to specialized sections each of them will become more expert in one of the many branches of the law.

One final note concerns judicial procedures. Latin American constitutions do not prescribe the large number of procedural rights for the protection of those accused of violation of law that is listed in our bills of rights. The burden of proof as to innocence is generally placed on the accused, rather than, as our Constitution and laws provide, putting on the state the obligation of proving the accused guilty beyond all doubt. We tend to think of juries as an indispensible part of judicial procedure — a reflection of our English legal heritage. Juries are the exception and not the rule in Latin America. Only five of the countries use juries in deciding criminal cases; in one of them only lawyers may be on the jury panels. Mexico and Cuba formerly used the jury system in criminal cases; but the practice has been abandoned in Cuba, and it is retained in Mexico only in cases relating to the freedom of the press. The Argentine Constitution provides for the use of juries in criminal cases, but the congress has never enacted the necessary enabling legislation. Given the different sources of Latin American law the absence of the jury is not to be regarded as unique. Many other countries which base their law on Roman law do not make use of the jury. The jury in England and the United States is, in fact, much more than a part of judicial procedure. In its early history and development it was a part of the democratic movement, and it now is a part of the democratic tradition.

No. 33   [The work of government, its ability to undertake and perform functions and services, is dependent in large measure upon the organization and personnel of its administrative agencies. Unless government departments, divisions, and bureaus are logically organized and well-integrated and coordinated, unless they are manned by capable civil servants, governmental performance falls below even minimum standards. This is true whether the political structure is autocratic or subjected to democratic controls and responsibilities, whether it is federal or unitary in form.

The science of public administration and the political movements to re-examine and overhaul the administrative machinery of government are relatively new in the United States. They are of even much more recent development in Latin America. Professor Ebenstein examines the progress of administrative thinking and action in Mexico, the obstacles that confront the administrative planner, and what administrative reform portends for the future of democratic government in that republic.]

Public Administration in Mexico*

by WILLIAM EBENSTEIN

POLITICAL science, as the term is understood in Great Britain and the United States, does not exist as yet in Latin America. As in continental Europe, constitutional law, public law, and, more recently, administrative law are the only three fields in the organized study of government. This limitation is partly due to the traditional predominance of French and, to a lesser degree, Spanish scholarship in Latin America with the consequent emphasis on legal structure rather than on political processes. The pressure of government policies in Latin America, ranging in the different countries from subtle suggestion to imprisonment or assassination, has also proved to be a serious obstacle in the development of a real *ciencia política* south of the Rio Grande; there can be a science of politics only to the extent that freedom of inquiry and expression is guaranteed by law and protected by society. (This is, of course, also true north of the Rio Grande.)

What is characteristic of political science in Latin America is even more characteristic of the art and science of public administration. Political instability in some parts of Latin America, the emphasis on personal loyalties and services in a historical environment dominated by the *caudillo* (boss, chief, leader), and the survival of extra-governmental organizations of considerable scope or authority, such as the Church, are some of the factors that have so far impeded the growth of a coherent body of public administration and its systematic study and instruction. Only recently, some major Latin American universities have established chairs in administrative *law*. The gradual industrialization of Latin America and the ensuing growth of business enterprises has fostered more interest in problems of administration on a large scale. In highly industrialized nations like England

* William Ebenstein, "Public Administration in Mexico," *Public Administration Review* (Spring, 1945), Vol. V, No. 2, pp. 102–112. Reprinted by permission of *Public Administration Review*. The footnotes in the original version are omitted here.

or the United States big business has often had to face administrative and managerial problems similar to those of the government, the biggest business in operation. There has been in such technologically advanced countries a continual give-and-take between private and public large-scale organizations. In Latin America, on the other hand, the Church has been until recently the only organization other than government operating on a large scale and servicing millions of people.

As yet we have no account, in English or in Spanish, of the major political institutions in Latin America. There are competent discussions of particular aspects of politics in this or that country, usually confined to a relatively short period; but we have not been given so far a comparative study of such Latin American political institutions as the presidency, the party system, the press, the civil service, and the military. In the field of public administration there is an even slighter literature. It is therefore a real event in Latin American studies that we now have at our disposal a study of public administration in Mexico, written by Professor Lucio Mendieta y Núñez and published in Mexico City in 1943. Professor Mendieta y Núñez is one of the leading social scientists of Mexico, who, as director of the Institute of Social Investigations of the University of Mexico and as the author of authoritative works on Mexican agrarian and indigenous problems, has done a great deal in bringing orderly methods into the investigation of some of the fundamental problems of Mexican contemporary life. His book on public administration in Mexico is the first of its kind, not only in Mexico but anywhere in Latin America. His method of analysis may appear somewhat unorthodox with its mixture of political, economic, sociological, anthropological, and legal data, but the resulting richness and color perhaps compensate for the methodological eccentricities.

HISTORICAL BACKGROUND

In the United States there has been a tendency of long standing to interpret our political institutions in strictly American terms. According to that school of thought, inspired by patriotic motives, our political institutions began in 1776, and the period preceding that date is of interest only to the student of colonial history. Similarly, since the achievement of independence in Mexico in 1821, there has been a tendency to forget, deny, or attack the Spanish basis of Mexico's political habits and administrative techniques and procedures. Now, however, in Mexico as in this country, we are beginning to find a more balanced appraisal of the pre-independence political and administrative heritage. Without falling into the pitfalls of *Hispanidad*, Professor Mendieta y Nuñez stresses the significance of the colonial experience in Mexico.

Further, Mexico offers the fascinating example of an American nation in which the study of pre-colonial political and administrative ideas and institutions is of the greatest interest. In pre-conquest Mexico the Aztec king headed public administration, and he was assisted by the nobility, the clergy, and the military class; it is obvious that the subsequent Spanish theory and practice of government, before and after Mexican independence, did not constitute a marked deviation from the preceding Mexican (Indian) pattern. This situation is in contrast with that in English-speaking North America, where the gulf between the Indians and the English settlers with their religious and political experience of self-rule was so wide as to be practically unbridgeable. In some parts of Mexico, where Spanish is neither spoken nor understood and where the social and political institutions of pre-conquest days are well preserved, the weight of tradition is particularly evident. In such areas, personal loyalty to the *jefe* (chief) of the local group or tribe still constitutes the main administrative vehicle through which political decisions and measures of a central or regional character are transmitted. The more impersonal, standardized procedures and agencies of modern public administation are absent in such communities.

This fact explains one of the greatest obstacles in Mexican public administration. The tendency in modern government, with its multitude of activities and agencies, is to create uniform standards for efficiency and economy. The difficulty in Mexico, from the days of the Spanish conquest, has always been to devise varying standards of political control and operation necessitating divergent administrative techniques and methods. In the old days, the lines of distinction were drawn in terms of Spaniards, *criollos* (sons of Spaniards born in Mexico), mestizos (persons of mixed Spanish and Indian blood), and Indians. All these differences have been swept away in law and, to a great extent, in custom. Nevertheless, even the recent Mexican administrations, inspired as they have been by the highest sense of justice and equality, have realized that several millions of Mexicans present special political and administrative problems because they have not been integrated as yet into the national Mexican civilization.

If it is true that some elements of pre-conquest political organization linger on in contemporary Mexico, it is even more true of post-conquest colonial institutions. The great administrative conceptions and institutions introduced by imperial Spain into Mexico, the New Spain, have retained much of their vitality to this day. Administrative decentralization is a strong tradition in the United States because even before 1776 there was no one governor or viceroy of the Crown in North America. Each colony was set up by a charter of its own and led its own political life and had its own administrative procedures. When independence was won, this decentralization had become so strongly entrenched that federalism was the only practical solution. In Mexico, the situation was exactly the opposite. Political and administrative centralization of Mexico under the Crown of Spain, represented by the Viceroy in Mexico City, established a tradition of administrative hierarchy that is as strong today as ever. The President of the republic is not only the political head of the nation but also the administrative chief in a sense which is not known in this country.

Again, as in colonial Mexico, the only real elements of administrative decentralization in modern Mexico are to be found in whatever autonomous life exists in municipal government. In colonial Mexico, the *ayuntamientos* were the only institutions in which elements of local administration, self-government, and elections of officials were countenanced. This tradition is still alive and could form the starting-point for a new revival of local and regional self-government.

The administrative machinery of Mexico differs greatly from that of the colonial period in one respect: the position of the Roman Catholic Church. In colonial Mexico, the Church was not only a religious and economic body of the first order but also an important administrative organization. The fields of education, intellectual life, and social welfare were almost completely in its hands. Even purely technical education, the spreading of more advanced arts and crafts, was very largely its domain. In the rugged conditions of Mexican life after the Conquest, the Church was charged with many functions which it did not have in Spain itself. The State used the Church for many of these tasks not only because it approved of the general attitudes which it taught (obedience to Spanish rule, social discipline, promise of future happiness in the world beyond), but also because the Church was the only organization in Spain that had adequate personnel trained in the administration of vast territories and large numbers of people.

In contemporary Mexico the scope of public administration has been enlarged so that all former functions of the Church, with the exception of religion, have been taken over by public agencies, federal or local. Much of the struggle between Church and State in Mexico in the last ninety years is due to the historical root of the extensive administrative scope of the Church in the colonial period. The borderline between administrative function and political influence is not very easy to draw. Where the Church has insisted on its right to render services and perform functions of a purely technical and administrative nature, the State has seen the desire to maintain a position of real political authority. As in other countries, the struggle for political power has been carried on in Mexico behind the cover of administrative and functional divergencies.

ADMINISTRATIVE CONTROL AND PLANNING

Because the Mexican legislative body, the Congress, has little effective authority, the scope and power of the highest government departments is inevitably very considerable. Under the presidential system, so typical of the political tradition in the Americas, the President's authority is broad in any case. In the Mexican system, which has a legislature, but one which cannot be quite compared with the British parliament or our Congress, the highest administrative officers command enormous authority. As all members of the Mexican Congress normally belong to one party, the official government party, the President finds little difficulty in persuading Congress to pass laws submitted by him for its approval. In addition, the Constitution confers upon the President ample powers of issuing decrees and regulations that, for all practical purposes, are the law of the land. The whole problem of delegated legislation presents, in Mexico, relatively few political and judicial issues because of the high degree of concentration of judicial, legislative, and executive powers in the presidential office. Whereas delegated legislation is a political problem full of tension and discord in Britain and the United States, it is but a technical issue in the operation of the Mexican system of government.

The President's term is six years. This enables a President to make fairly long-term plans and to build up political and administrative machinery of his own. However, he cannot be re-elected, so that in practice his tenure is not so extended as that of a President of the United States who, as occasionally happens, serves more than one four-year term.

In selecting the highest administrative officers — the heads of the ministries and high government agencies, the *departamentos* — the President of Mexico is not completely free. Where the President of the United States has to consider claims in his own party, claims of various regions and interests, and, negatively at least, the sentiments of the opposition party, the President of Mexico has to take into account the claims of deserving leaders of the official government party, the only party that really counts (now called Party of the Mexican Revolution). Also, although the small opposition parties are not represented in Congress, they still have a legal existence and have to be appeased, directly or indirectly. In one sense, the position of the President of Mexico as the head of the administrative hierarchy is different, say, from that of our President: in Mexico, it is not customary to attack publicly the person of the President by the printed or spoken word. If criticisms of administrative officers of the highest rank are made, it is usually emphasized that deficiencies are not due to presidential shortcomings.

Seven years before the outbreak of the Russian revolutions in 1917, Mexico embarked upon a great revolutionary career of far-reaching social and economic changes which have by no means been completed. One of the central concepts of the Mexican Revolution is the idea that the nation, through the political organization of the state, is responsible for the achievement of progressive social objectives for the benefit of all citizens. This adherence to the philosophy of the positive state does not necessarily imply the adoption of socialism as the eventual goal of national policy. In any case, however, the Mexican Revolution was born in protest against the laissez-faire ideology of the Díaz régime, to which the misery and degradation of the masses were attributed. State intervention in social and economic affairs has therefore been the watchword of the new régime from its inception. The large-scale expropriations of landed estates, owned by Mexicans or foreigners, the nationalization of the oil industry against the bitter opposition of British and American financial interests, and a series of legislative measures affecting the social welfare of the individual citizen have all proved that Mexico is fully aware that her pressing political, social, and economic problems cannot be solved without a substantial amount of planning. It is therefore rather remarkable that, so far at least, little attention has been given in Mexico to planning as a management tool in public administration. Public administration is essentially conceived of in terms of operation, and as yet there has not been an adequate grasp of the intricate administrative aspects of planning, integration, and coordination.

Likewise, the whole conception of financial management as a focal point of public administration is relatively new in Mexico. The struggle for the control and allocation of public finances was one of the chief origins of representative government in England many centuries ago, and much of the history of British politics can be written around the issue of the control of public finance. The Treasury in Britain and the Treasury and the Bureau of the Budget in the United States have always been planning agencies of the first order, even at a time when the term " planning " was loaded with unpopular and disreputable connotations. Lacking the historical background of the struggle for the control of public finance, Mexico has not developed, so far, the conception of financial management as a key tool of the effective coordination of administrative functions and authorities. The Mexican Treasury has, it is true, a separate section for the study and investigation of long-term economic and financial problems, but this section has in no way the character of what could be fairly described as a central planning agency for the whole machinery of government. At best, it is engaged in research, or finding out and interpreting the facts, rather than in planning, or making policy.

In the context of Mexican politics there can be only one place in the administrative organization in which the practical difficulties caused by inadequate planning and coordination can be solved: the office of the President of the republic. According to the law, the office of the personal secretary to the President does not possess the administrative authority of a ministry or high government department. But what the law has failed to provide for, the facts of administrative life have made inevitable. In a strictly extralegal manner the personal secretary of the President has become a sort of minister without portfolio. The President gives, through this office, a certain amount of unity and direction to the conflicting tendencies of different ministries and government departments, and the department of studies within this office provides a channel through which the planning, control, and criticism of governmental activities can be carried on from an over-all point of view. In the United States, too, some of the administrative assistants of the President have gained, despite their genuine passion for anonymity, a position of influence which is by no means clearly defined in legal or constitutional terms.

There are two drawbacks to the office of personal secretary to the President, in Mexico. First, there is no continuity of incumbency or administrative practice. By the very definition of this office, each President makes his appointments from among his closest and most trustworthy friends. As Mexican Presidents can never be re-elected, six years is the longest period during which an appointee can hold this office. Thus, the office of the personal secretary of the President cannot build up the permanent staff and administrative tradition of, say, the Bureau of the Budget in the United States. The second drawback is the fact that the office of the personal secretary of the President is essentially an operating agency, engaged in the daily routine activities of practical politics and immediate issues. If it has become the chief agency for planning, criticizing, controlling, and coordinating administrative authorities, it has developed that function by sheer necessity rather than as a result of deliberate planning.

This union of planning and operating functions in the office of the personal secretary of the President clearly indicates the failure to appreciate the fundamental differences between these two types of activity.

The failure to do adequate planning is undoubtedly also due in part to the state of economic organization in Mexico. Speaking of the urgent need for more governmental and administrative planning in Great Britain, the London *Observer* (November 21, 1943) commented that " what is happening in government, under pressure and only half-consciously, is precisely what has happened, deliberately, in Big Business itself." If this statement accurately describes the situation in Britain, with her advanced industrial administrative and managerial standards, it also helps to explain the situation in Mexico, where economic organization is much less advanced.

THE CIVIL SERVICE

Legislation on matters pertaining to the civil service is very recent in Mexico because, as Professor Mendieta y Nuñez points out, the Mexican governments from national independence onward were continually involved in internal disputes and in civil wars, and were therefore so unstable that they could not occupy themselves with the regulation of the civil service. Since the victory of the Revolution that began in 1910, however, Mexico has gradually gained in stability, which culminated in the great reforms of President Cárdenas, a master organizer and administrator. Soon after he came into office in 1934, President Cárdenas initiated the " Juridical Statute of the Workers in the Service of the Powers of the Union," which was subsequently modified by a similar statute of April 4, 1941, under the present administration of President Avila Camacho.

One of the most interesting features of Mexican legislation on civil service is the idea that public servants do not possess any mystical quality that raises them above the level of so-called ordinary workers and employees. The language of the law expresses this revolutionary attitude of the new Mexico by referring to public servants as " workers in the service of the Union " and by trying to apply the general principles of workers' legislation to public workers. Article 123 of the Mexican Constitution establishes the right of labor to strike. This is, in itself, quite remarkable. What is even more remarkable is that the same article also establishes the right of public employees to strike, provided the procedures of arbitration, set up by law, have failed. Employees of the Ministry of National Defense and members of the armed forces are deprived of the right to strike, and in case of war, strikes of any public employees are outlawed.

Although Mexican legislation started out with the ideological conception of the equality of public and private employees, the very nature of some of the work that public employees are called upon to perform has forced the legislators to recognize differences between public employees in terms of the more or less essential character of their particular functions. The Mexican civil service legislation distinguishes between " workers of confidence " (*trabajadores de confianza*) and " ordinary workers " in public employment. Nowhere is there a clear definition of the public " workers of confidence," and the definition that all those employees whose appointment has to be approved by presidential decree are " workers of confidence " is purely formal. In general, what is called the administrative class in other countries makes up the " workers of confidence " in the Mexican civil service. It is interesting that while we think of the highest administrative class in this country or in England in terms of the policy-framing authority that it possesses, in Mexico the element of personal relationship between ministerial and departmental heads and their immediate subordinates is the decisive criterion in legally defining this top group in the bureaucracy. This is but one of the many ways in which the personal nature of Mexican, as indeed most Latin American, government and administration expresses itself. It reflects surviving elements of the old feudal Spanish order in which personal trust and confidence were the determining factor in governmental relationships.

One of the main purposes of introducing the concept of the " workers of confidence " into legislation was to deny them the rights of unionization and the strike which were granted to the other groups of public employees. It was realized that there could be no stability of public authority if the highest government officials or members of the armed forces could combine in order to strike and thus coerce and negate the very governments of which they were instruments.

The question of trade unions among public employees has caused a good deal of discussion and, in some cases, legislation. Since 1927 Great Britain has had special legislation, under the Trade Disputes and Trade Unions Act, forbidding associations of civil servants to be affiliated with political or labor organizations which admit members outside the civil service. In this country there is freedom of trade unionization among public employees not as a matter of specific authorization but because there is no legal rule against it. The right of public employees to strike has not been definitely settled, but so far our government has denied its existence.

In Mexico the civil service statute specifically deals with this whole problem. Public employees are explicitly authorized to form trade unions for the purpose of studying, improving, and defending their common interests. However, only one trade union in each "bureaucratic entity" is legally recognized — the trade union that represents the majority of the workers. In general, each ministry, autonomous agency, or bureau represents one entity which forms the basis of trade union organization. "Workers of confidence," or members of the administrative class, are excluded from such trade unions, on the ground that high officials will probably tend to side with the government as an employer rather than with the employees of the lower brackets.

One of the most remarkable legal provisions of the Mexican civil service statute is the rule that once a public employee has become a member of a trade union of his "entity" he cannot voluntarily resign his membership. He is obliged to continue his membership, unless he is expelled from the union. Needless to say, this confers a very real authority on the leadership of such trade unions. Actually, the civil service statute declares expressly that the closed-shop principle cannot be recognized by the government in any case. However, since the law recognizes the principle "once a trade union member, always a member" for public employees, one of the main efforts of such organizations consists in selling employees the idea of membership. The trade union principle is much more practiced in Mexico than in most other nations, and if the trade unions of public employees do not possess the fullfledged monopoly of the closed shop, they have something which is very similar to it.

The trade unions of public employees are under the legal obligation to register with the Arbitration Tribunal, which examines their constitution, their membership, and their claim that they represent more employees than any other trade union in a particular "bureaucratic entity."

The Arbitration Tribunal is made up of three members: one representative of the government, one of the employees, and a third member chosen by the two. Its main function is to settle disputes between public employees, individually or collectively, and the government. The Arbitration Tribunal also settles the important question of who represents, legally, a given category of public employees. Despite the name of this board, its decisions have legal force, and it is actually more nearly a court than an arbitration tribunal. In some of the cases it decides, as in those between the government and its employees, it has more nearly the character of an arbitration tribunal because both parties to the dispute are represented on the board. This is not the case, however, when it decides intra-union conflicts.

Another important function of the Arbitration Tribunal is the certification that a strike of public employees is legal. The right of public employees to strike is not absolute. Thus, employees of institutions of public health and safety are expressly exempted from the categories of public workers who have the right to strike. Otherwise, this right depends on the interpretation of the Arbitration Tribunal. If it decides that the projected strike is illegal and the workers proceed to strike, the law provides that they must be immediately dismissed. If the Tribunal decides that the strike is justified, the government will ordinarily give in. Much depends on the political situation. On several occasions, the unions have insisted on striking in order to maintain their prestige among their members and the public at large, although they could probably have won their demands peacefully. On the other hand, there is no question that in other instances political pressure of the government has operated through the Arbitration Tribunal and has led to solutions which the government wishes at the moment. The relations between the trade unions of private or public employees and the government are of a much more intimate character than in this country or in Great Britain. And this intimacy is described by some observers of Mexican affairs as a relationship of domination of the trade unions by the government.

The great problems of the civil service in Mexico are the relative failure to recognize the merit system in appointments and promotions and the relatively high prevalence of personal gain through public employment. As to the first evil, it is only fair to point out that England had institutions of political self-government for centuries before it introduced, less than a century ago, a real merit system into its public service. In the United States, the merit system is of even more recent origin and still has to face the hostility of those who are unwilling to give up the sweet uses of patronage for the benefit of political, and personal, friends. It is therefore not surprising that in Mexico the merit system for appointments and promotions, although provided by law, has so far been very largely a dead letter of the statute. The practical application of the merit principle in Mexico is delayed in part by the failure to establish a national civil service commission on the British or American model. Following the example of most continental European countries, Mexico does not know the institution of a national civil service commission that tackles the whole problem of the civil service — methods of classification, standards of attainment for entry into and promotion within the civil service, salaries, and all the other administrative issues upon which the efficient management of public service depends. Instead, each government department in Mexico (as in Europe) solves its own problems of personnel as well (or as poorly) as it can, and there is no institutional safeguard or device to prevent overstaffing in one place and understaffing in another, or unevenness of standards among departments.

The present political régime of the " Mexican Revolution " is of recent origin, and the leaders of that régime know that latent enmity still exists among members of the privileged groups who are unwilling to accept the new state of affairs. As long as that relative insecurity exists, it is hardly to be expected that technical merit will replace political trust and reliability as a guiding criterion in making appointments and promotions. Mexico is on the road toward democracy. In a generation or two, the present social and economic democracy will result in greater political democracy. This change will be accompanied, no doubt, by an increasing application of the merit system.

Political instability throughout the history of Mexico since the achievement of independence has also resulted in the evil of militarism in government and administration. With few exceptions, the presidents of Mexico have been army leaders. The apostle and first leader of the Mexican Revolution, Francisco I. Madero, issued in 1908 his clarion call for civilian, democratic government which galvanized Mexican public opinion against the militaristic despotism of General Díaz. Government by civilians was Madero's foremost demand for a new Mexico. Madero became the first President after the triumph of the revolution in 1911, but in 1913 he was assassinated by General Huerta. The civil war which ensued lasted for over seven years. War and revolution filled the decade from 1910 to 1920, and continued sporadically in the next decade. A host of generals were made in the turbulent period and, paradoxically, the end of the Mexican Revolution saw more influence of the military than had the beginning. Since that time, army men have considered high posts of a political, financial, or diplomatic character as a domain of their own. Only if Mexico continues on the road of stability will the prestige of the generals and colonels decline.

The poverty of Mexico also obstructs the introduction of the merit principle. It is a common experience in all poor countries that a career in public service or the army is considered very desirable when other economic opportunities are scarce. Many a Mexican thinks that a career in the public service or the army is the only one open to him, because much of the business, mining, banking, and other types of private economic activity is controlled by American or other foreign interests. Also, since Mexican standards of living are low, public employment assures at least a minimum of economic security as well as a certain amount of social prestige.

The second great problem of the Mexican civil service is often referred to as " administrative irregularity." It may interest students of political psychology and artistic expression that there are in Mexico fifteen terms to denote graft. Professor Mendieta y Nuñez writes as follows: " The immorality of the bureaucracy which is in direct contact with the public or which exercises any sort of function which affects private interests is beyond any doubt. . . . But it is clear that this judgment, which is not ours but a general one, admits of exceptions. The immorality of those who manage the material interests of the State is no less evident." But, Professor Mendieta y Nuñez explains, this phenomenon is partly due to the fact that the people themselves look upon a public figure who does not acquire wealth while holding office as an imbecile: "For the thief who fails, jail and ignominy; for the thief who triumphs, all the goods of the world. This is the social law of our country, at least for the time being."

According to the "Law of the Responsibilities of Federal Officials, Employees and High Officials of the States" of December 30, 1939, all public officials and employees, on assuming public office, must declare before the Attorney General of Mexico the real estate and cash deposits in their name. Obviously, it requires little ingenuity to circumvent this provision. Proceedings against malefactors in office are discouraged by the provision that charges of alleged takings of bribes must be made openly and not anonymously and that they must be preferred not later than one year after leaving office.

As a good patriot Professor Mendieta y Nuñez is rightly indignant about the widespread political and bureaucratic corruption in his country; but the picture is perhaps not so unique and black as it seems to him. It might be said with some justice that the main difference between corruption in the United States and in Mexico is that in this country fewer individuals are in the habit of obtaining illicit revenue and that the amounts involved are usually larger. In Mexico the idea seems to prevail that illegal extra income from bribery should be fairly equitably distributed among all levels of the administrative hierarchy. Some claim that this method of corruption, while admittedly demoralizing more employees, is at least more democratic!

If Mexico develops a truly functioning party system, the problem of integrity in the public service will be easier to solve, because the existence of two or more parties is a protection against the plundering of the public.

Another way of helping to meet this problem would be to raise the salaries of public employees. While the wages and salaries of Mexican workers in private enterprise have been adjusted in the last ten years to rising living costs, the salaries of public employees have been raised very little, if at all. One reason why the Mexican public takes small-scale bribery of minor officials for granted is that everyone knows that official salaries are not high enough, even for Mexican standards. There is a vicious circle involved at this point. The government claims that it does not have enough funds to pay higher salaries; yet one of the reasons why revenues are low is that they flow partly into the pockets of the officials rather than into the public treasury. The official who accepts bribes may think that he is merely getting the additional salary he ought to receive from the government in the first place. Clearly, such a system puts a premium on attitudes and abilities which are not conducive to the highest standards of equity and efficiency.

CONCLUSION

Public administration in Mexico and its problems and difficulties can be understood only against the background of Mexican society and politics. The objectives of the triumphant Mexican Revolution require a large, well-trained administrative staff to carry out the long-term social, educational, and economic reforms. The high rate of illiteracy (about 40 percent), the relatively moderate degree of industrial and managerial experience and skill in private business, the feudal elements of the political structure — all combine to make the administrative realization of these long-term policies difficult.

Despite these grave obstacles the progress made so far is remarkable. Time after time, in Mexico and abroad, it has been predicted that lack of administrative personnel and experience would prevent achievement of the objectives of the major Mexican reforms in the fields of education, agriculture, and labor legislation. Yet in each case the record shows that the reforms have been carried out, on the whole, quite satisfactorily. Mexico is still in an era in which professional politicians and army leaders who participated in the Revolution have a great deal of influence and authority. As in Soviet Russia, however, the expert in ideological manipulation is increasingly being replaced by the expert in managerial and administrative skill. Mexico, like other Latin American nations, is sending more and more young men and women abroad to acquire those skills at a speedy rate. A new generation of leaders is growing up that rebels against those elements in Mexican government and politics that pervert and defile the objectives of the Mexican Revolution. President Cárdenas will go down in Mexican history as a great president not only because of his fearless struggle for popular rights and achievements, but also for his record as a first-class administrator who has given more stability to Mexico than any president who preceded him. In the present administration of President Avila Camacho, himself a man of no exceptional administrative talent or energy, there are men like Jesús Silva Herzog, Ramón Beteta, and others who have shown themselves to be administrators of the highest ability and integrity. The younger generation in Mexico looks to these men as the representatives of a new type of governmental leader in their country. Lastly, the fact that the first treatise on Mexican public administration has recently been published — the fact that a man of the great intellectual and scholarly achievements of Professor Mendieta y Nuñez puts the problems of public administration in Mexico before his countrymen — augurs well for a brighter future.

In the last thirty years Mexico has been, in many ways, the leading Latin American nation, in terms of political, cultural, and social reforms. It is not impossible that the high degree of energy and genius displayed in those reforms will also soon translate itself into administrative progress of a far-reaching character.

No. 34 [As is indicated in the following article, the study of municipal and local government is almost an unknown and unexplored field in Latin America. Even Latin American writers have done comparatively little research and publication on local government organization, structure, and activities in their respective countries.

Superficially this is puzzling. In most of the nations urbanization characterizes the population distribution, and in some to a very high degree. Some of the largest cities in America are found in Argentina, Brazil, and Mexico. Furthermore, even in those countries that are predominantly rural, there is a pronounced urban economic, cultural, and political influence. Historically, it was in the colonial cities that the only evidences of self-government appeared, and in the early nineteenth century the polity of the whole nation was often dominated by the city. One would expect that these factors would emphasize the political importance of the municipality.

The explanation may be in the centralist tendencies which are so common in the governments of all Latin American countries. Local government is a concern of the national administration — of presidents and congresses, and not of mayors and councilmen. If the several lines of inquiry suggested by Professor Fitzgibbon are initiated and followed, we may in the future be able to discuss the role of cities in the government and politics of Latin America with greater precision.]

*Our Municipal Neighbors to the South**

by RUSSELL H. FITZGIBBON

MANY years ago county government in the United States was described as the dark continent of American politics. The characterization was apt, and the phrase itself may have been in part responsible for the considerable illumination which has been given that particular governmental area in recent decades.

If a view of the politics of the whole hemisphere be taken, the figure of speech might well be transferred to Latin American municipal government. For the politics and administration of the cities of Latin America are still in large measure unexplored — certainly unpublicized — aspects of the whole picture of government in the New World. The average person in the United States is uninformed about some of the most elementary features of governmental forms and trends in the cities of "the other America." About national governments, yes, in part; but scarcely at all in regard to the political life of the municipalities.

This is the more unfortunate because so much of the political motivation and activity of the score of Latin American republics is city-bred. That rural areas are frequently tributary — economically, culturally, politically, and in other ways — to the urban population nuclei which they surround is a well-recognized phenomenon; but

* Russell H. Fitzgibbon, " Our Municipal Neighbors to the South," *National Municipal Review* (February, 1941), Vol. XXX, No. 2, pp. 80–84, 103. Reprinted by permission of the *National Municipal Review*.

so obvious is that relationship in many of the Latin American countries that one sometimes encounters a situation in which the metropolis seems virtually to have swallowed the remainder of the country. In some of the smaller countries — Uruguay, for instance — the picture begins to approximate, roughly, that of the old Greek city-state in which the surrounding country was technically a part of the city.

Even in some of the larger countries, such as Argentina, the same relationship is present, though perhaps in less exaggerated form. If the general dominance of New York City plus the political leadership of Washington were rolled into one, with the features of preeminence of perhaps Pittsburgh and Chicago and Los Angeles and a few other cities thrown in for good measure, we should have something of the relationship between Buenos Aires and the rest of Argentina. Further exposition would be beside the point; the net result is that the industrial, literary, artistic, religious, and many other centers of gravity, in addition to the political, rest in urban centers in Latin America to a much greater degree than anything with which we are familiar in the United States.

Thus far, such serious study as has been given to Latin American governments has all but completely been concentrated on the topmost levels. This is natural, if not logical, in view of the historic and very general tendency of the centralized and executive-dominated national governments to extend their control into all other levels and all geographic areas of the various countries. For one thing, all but four of the Latin American republics have unitary rather than federal governments. Even in the remaining four — Mexico, Venezuela, Argentina, and Brazil — the centralizing tendency has generally been so strong, both politically and administratively, throughout most of the more than a century of independence, as to make the national governments partly unitary on a *de facto* if not on a *de jure* basis. Needless to say, there has been little formal obstacle to such a trend in those countries organized upon a constitutionally unitary basis, but even in the nominally federal countries the tendency has been so marked as to lead one writer some years ago (before the Vargas *coup* of 1937) to label a book he had written, *His Majesty, the President of Brazil*. The almost universal acceptance in Latin America of presidential rather than parliamentary government is another factor which has facilitated executive control of the national government.

This does not justify the conclusion that political consciousness and activity exist only in the national arenas and around the national capitals. Regional politics in various Latin American countries is well organized and highly articulate. In Mexico, it may be a Michoacán clique, centering around the leaders of Morelia, the state capital, competing for political control against, say, the political bosses of Sonora or Chihuahua in the north. In Brazil, the picture revolves around the time-honored political rivalries of the states of São Paulo and Minas Geraes and, latterly, Rio Grande do Sul.

In Argentina, the dominant issue of the first half century and more of independence was the contest for control between the *Porteños* (the inhabitants of Buenos Aires) and the hinterland provinces. In Nicaragua, it was a traditional battle between the Conservatives of Granada and the Liberals of León.

CITY VERSUS CITY

In any case, it has usually been *city* against *city,* with the political leaders of one city or another temporarily lifting themselves by their bootstraps, as it were, into roles on the national stage. With some exceptions, though, they remained in spirit city bosses instead of becoming national figures.

Almost the whole tradition of the Iberian veneer of government in Latin America emphasized control from above. Municipal autonomy and democracy which, in thirteenth- and fourteenth-century Spain had reached a high and prominent peak of development, had very largely atrophied by the end of the fifteenth century. The governmental institutions of the two mother countries were transferred with great faithfulness to their colonies. Hence, the early colonial *cabildos* and *ayuntamientos* mirrored the corresponding municipal institutions in Spain and Portugal.

Enough of the memory of vigorous municipal life in an earlier century in the peninsula still persisted to make the early colonial municipalities almost the only seat of self-government in the vast new world which Spain and Portugal conquered. This modicum of political self-assertiveness quickly withered, however, and for some two centuries after about the middle of the sixteenth, municipal autonomy in Latin America was almost a fiction. In the latter part of the eighteenth century, because of complicated factors associated with the nascent independence movement, municipal consciousness and activity began to revive, although in the field of politics the movement was somewhat artificial.

Another aspect of municipal life and organization which must be taken into consideration in accounting for what exists in that area today, is the aboriginal elements which persisted. It has been remarked that the implanting of Hispanic civilization involved the imposing of institutions from above. This led in some instances to the overlaying of a solid and tenacious core of native institutions with a more or less superficial veneer of Spanish or Portuguese practice. Native literatures — where they existed — were rooted out because they were so obviously " profane " in contrast to the orthodox Catholic writings which were supported by the State. Native languages, however, were not rooted out. They persist today in many areas, and some of them — Guaraní, Quechuan, Mayan derivatives — came to be historically important. The Catholic religion, closely allied with the government as it was, could obviously tolerate no open rivals, but oftentimes the forms of the Church were merely superimposed on the continuing paganism of the native. The natives also strenuously resisted Spanish efforts to win them away from a subsistence economy to the sale-for-profit economy of the invaders.

NATIVE GOVERNMENTS PERSIST

So it was in the field of government. In certain areas, native populations of considerable density and great development had already established well-organized political institutions. This was notably true in parts of Mexico, in Guatemala and other portions of Central America, in Peru, and elsewhere in the Andean highlands. So far as " national " governments developed by the natives were concerned — the Inca empire in Peru, the Aztec federation in Mexico, perhaps the Chibcha organization in northern South America — the Spanish quickly wiped them out by means of the substitution of their own large-unit forms. The local units persisted, however, and even now, in direct proportion to the retention of native culture-patterns in one area or another, reflect a good deal of vitality. In the more primitive regions of highland Guatemala, for example, one sees almost a dual scheme of local government, the *intendente* being the agent of national authority while the *alcalde auxiliar* is chosen by and represents a tenacious nativist democracy.

The native contributions to Latin American political institutions have thus been made chiefly on a horizontal plane and on the lower levels. The interaction of the native and alien elements in the evolution of modern municipal institutions has been most interesting and significant.

MUNICIPAL STUDY NEEDED

Several studies of the governmental structures and operation of particular Latin American countries have been made within recent years. These, for the most part, have been vertical in character, i.e., studies of the governments of single countries. Relatively little emphasis has been placed on municipal government and politics, important as those aspects are. No adequate study of any Latin American political institutions among horizontal lines has yet appeared, although the importance of this, in view of our new consciousness of, and mushrooming interest in, Latin America as a whole, would seem to be obvious.

One badly needed study, for instance, would deal with organized municipal life and activity in Latin America. If limited in scope to the field of politics and government it might logically fall to the lot of political scientists. On the other hand, if such a survey were to view the municipal life of Latin America more broadly, there obviously would be the necessity for cooperation by the economist, the sociologist, the historian, the geographer, the ethnologist, and probably other social scientists. Even if the objective of the research were primarily to trace the lines of political activity, much use would need to be made of the cognate social sciences.

An investigation of the political life of the municipalities of Latin America might be made on the basis of a considerable expansion of some such outline as the following:

Historical. What — in detail — has been the course of the growth of Latin American urban life and its political machinery? After a general survey, a sufficient " breakdown " should be made to account for the various differences of development encountered in the several parts of Spanish America, Brazil, and Haiti.

1. What municipal political inheritances are historically traceable to the Spanish, Portuguese, and French?

2. What has been transmitted to the present generation from pre-Columbian native political life?

3. What royal instructions were issued to the conquistadores in regard to the founding of cities?

4. What was the relationship of Latin American municipalities to the governments of the mother countries during the colonial period?

5. Careful study of various *Actas de Cabildos* is needed.

Ethnic. What population factors contribute to the present political life and governmental organization of Latin American cities? The supposition that particular racial groups have a "genius" for political activity should be examined with regard to Latin America and either substantiated or refuted.

1. How does the urban ethnic composition of various parts of Latin America differ from the rural composition of the same countries, if at all, and how does this affect the problem of government? What peculiar racial problems confront municipalities?

2. Are particular types of political life and governmental institutions "naturally" suited to specific racial combinations?

Geographic. How have geographical factors impinged on municipal political developments?

1. What has been the relationship of waterways, land resources, altitude, rainfall, and other climatic factors?

2. What geographical factors have contributed to the founding and growth of particular cities, especially those in the tropics in contrast to those in mid latitudes?

Economic. How are political institutions conditioned by economic aspects?

1. The problem of land utilization of tributary areas needs intensive study. How dependent is urban life and its governmental development on that factor?

2. What is the scheme of taxation and the basis of the tax structure of Latin American cities?

3. What sources of revenue other than taxation have been used and what have been their political purposes and consequences?

4. What has been the borrowing record of urban governments? What has borrowed money been used for?

Political. To what extent does a general pattern of governmental organization emerge for Latin American cities, and where (and why) do differences appear?

1. How politically conscious are the urban inhabitants of Latin America? What is the discernible trend, if any, in that regard?

a. What municipal suffrage qualifications prevail and how are they changing, if at all?

2. What forms of party organization and activity characterize Latin American cities? Is there anything distinctive about this in contrast to such phenomena for the respective countries as a whole?

a. To what extent is municipal politics — and administration — dominated by *personalismo* (i.e., " bossism ")?

3. What political and administrative subdivisions of cities are there? What examples of functional devolution?

4. What functions, strictly and quasi-governmental, have the municipalities undertaken?

a. What has been done, for example, in regard to municipal ownership and operation of utilities?

b. How have education and other cultural activities been handled and what has been the relationship at such points between municipal and national governments?

c. What is the record of public health work of the cities?

5. What — in detail — is the political and/or governmental relationship existing between cities and their respective national governments?

a. To what extent is national authority limited in the cities, and in what degree and ways do the national governments limit the natural governmental activity of the cities?

b. Precisely what is the status of municipal units in regard to the question of autonomy? In regard to the problem of territorial relationship to other units of government?

c. Where — and why, for how long, in what form — do we find a peculiar political organization for the national capital?

Interest in Latin America seems now at flood tide but there is no evidence that the crest has yet been reached. It would seem desirable, consequently, that every effort be made to encourage the scientific and sober study of various aspects of the Latin American scene.

CHAPTER 12

The
Political Party Pattern

No. 35
The General Nature of Political Parties in Latin America

by ASHER N. CHRISTENSEN

A MONG the many factors which determine the existence and smooth operation of popular self-government is the political party. It is difficult to conceive of the processes of popular election of officers, the organization and work of legislative assemblies, and the responsibility of the governors to the governed without the institution of the party.

A real party system implies much more than the fact that political parties are allowed to exist. In a larger and more important sense it rests upon what we might call a " climate " of political party government. This climate includes, among many other features: a wide franchise; an electorate that has access to political information; social institutions that enable that electorate to express its opinions freely; systems of balloting and election administration which assure that this opinion, freely expressed, is also effectively stated; political parties that are, themselves, subject to some restraining influences on the power of the inner group, oligarchy, or machine; a sense of fair play in party campaigns; and a readiness to accept the voters' verdict on election day. It will aid us in the understanding of Latin American government if we turn our attention to the political party system of Latin America with these factors especially in mind.

Constitutionally, the suffrage appears to be broadly based in Latin America, at least for males. Twelve of the 20 republics grant the right to vote to men only, 6 to men and women equally, 3 to women in municipal elections only, and 2 to women if they meet special qualifications. In Guatemala all men over 18 may vote but only literate women have that right. (There is no evidence that the women of Guatemala object to the placid assumption that an illiterate man is as civically competent as a literate woman.) In El Salvador men may vote at 18 but women who have had less than 3 year's schooling must be 25 and those who have finished high school must be 21 or over!

The age qualification for voting is generally lower than it is in the United States. Seven countries establish it at 18; two, at 18 if the would-be voter is literate, otherwise it is 21; one, at 18 for men and at 21 or 25 for women; two, at 20 (in one of these the age is reduced to 18 if the person is married, owns property, or is a professor!), and two, at 18 if married and 21 if not. In 6 of the republics the age qualification is 21, which is the qualifying age in 47 of our 48 states.

The second postulate was that voters have a readily available means of informing themselves on political issues. When we examine the constitutional and social institutions of Latin America which bear on this point we see that the right to vote, and therefore the right to form active and vigorous political parties, is seriously limited. A literacy requirement for voting is stipulated in the constitutions of 6 countries although it is not rigorously enforced in 2 of them. Two other states place the qualifying age higher for illiterates than for literates; in 12 of the republics the constitution is silent on the question of literacy. Americans would not regard a literacy test as discriminatory or onerous, but it must be recalled that illiteracy in Latin America runs as high as 80 percent of the total population in one country and is over 35 percent in several. Consequently, a literacy requirement disenfranchises a significant portion of the potential voters, and, it should be added, it denies the vote to that group of the population which is most in need of programs of economic, social, and political reform. It is not strange that land reform looms large as an issue in many of the countries of Latin America, or that so little has been done in this field. The landless, the poor, and the illiterate have no voice in government.

Even the literate are handicapped in the expression of their political views if they cannot easily obtain political information through schools, the newspapers, the radio, and the other media of public information. But authoritarian governments throughout history have restricted freedom of press and speech, and they continue to do so in Latin America. The usual accompaniment of the *caudillo* is a rigid control over newspapers and radio stations, a prohibition of political meetings (as communist or subversive, of course), and a lessening of governmental support for public education. Even the college graduates are denied the channels of information, and this, in turn, limits the expression of their free political views.

In the third place, the socio-economic pattern commonly found in Latin America is a further restriction on political and voting freedom. Several of the earlier chapters have emphasized the dependency of the bulk of the population on the land owner or *patrón*. If the *patrón* intimates that the sharecropper should not take time off to go to the polling place, the sharecropper does not go. Or, if he suggests that the peon should support a particular candidate or political party, the *patrón's* view virtually controls the peon's vote. The mere fact that the constitution states that all men may vote does not mean that they can and do vote. (Social controls over the political views and votes of people are not unknown in the United States where the constitution and the laws appear to establish universal suffrage.)

Effective voting and effective parties also depend upon election systems that facilitate the free expression of the political views of those who do start for, and arrive at, the polls. Generally speaking, the Latin American election systems are woefully deficient in this respect. Since the 1880's in the United States we have used the so-called Australian ballot. The ballots used at an election are prepared and printed by the state, and the state administers the election. In Latin America, the practice that we abandoned in the latter part of the nineteenth century is still widely followed. There, in fifteen of the twenty nations, the parties print the ballots. They, of course, do what our parties formerly did when they had this freedom. Each of the parties uses a differently colored or shaped ballot so that it is easy to check on voter behavior if that is desired. Thus, a sanction is added to the social control of voting just mentioned. It is true that in nine of these fifteen nations the government does furnish an official envelope in which the voter places his ballots before depositing them in the ballot boxes, but it is still possible, without much difficulty, to ascertain how Juan Pueblo voted. Only five countries, Cuba, El Salvador, Mexico, Nicaragua, and Venezuela use the Australian ballot system.

The currently used voting procedures are complicated in many of the Latin American nations, which is a factor of greater importance if the electorate is poorly informed. In several it is extremely difficult to vote a split ticket and in three it is legally impossible. These general election voting devices resemble those we use in this country in closed primaries. The voter is forced to make a choice between all of the candidates of one party and all of those of another. Political independence is discouraged and with it the rise of independent parties.

Election administration is poorly organized on the whole. Although fraudulent voting has long been known in the United States, and especially in municipal politics, it is much less common here than in Latin America. One of the common political jokes in Latin America refers to the fact that the results of an election are known *before* it is held; our intricate system of public opinion polls and voting devices and mechanisms has been " improved " upon.

Election administration is not only poorly planned but it is also commonly under the control of the national administration and the president. A strong president can influence the polling in a precinct hundreds of miles from the national capital. Two examples suffice to reveal the problem of sound election administration. In Mexico, until recently, the first person to arrive at a polling booth on election day was to administer the election in that precinct. The results of this system were, to say the least, surprising and exuberant. When Venezuela attempted to control " repeating " three years ago by marking the hand of each voter with an ink that would not wear off for two or three days, the solicitous party leaders were quick to raise the objection that this was an unwarranted regimentation.

The political parties and party systems of contemporary Latin America resemble our own of seventy-five years ago. The literature of American political history is full of indictments of the boss, machine, or oligarchy, and its control over our parties in the period following the Civil War. Parties were under no regulation concerning how they were organized, the systems of nomination they used, and how they planned or financed campaigns. The unregulated nominating convention meant that candidates could be and were hand-picked. Slowly we began to control the party by legal means, first attempting to regulate the nominating convention, and eventually, at the state level, we gave to the voter the power to nominate party candidates through the direct primary. The unregulated convention is the rule today in Latin America. Candidates can be and usually are hand-picked. In governments characterized by " strong " presidents it requires little imagination to determine whose hand it is that selects the candidates of the " in " party.

Similarly, party organization is under the almost complete jurisdiction of the party itself. The party chairmanship, the number and selection of party committees, and similar matters are controlled by the inner group. Party finance is subject to very little public regulation. If the ruling group can depend on 90 percent of the potential campaign funds, if no limits are placed on where and how it can raise money, or for what purposes such money may be spent, it is little wonder that its ability to win elections is increased.

It is not suggested that the solution to these problems is to be found in a legal regulation of political parties such as we have in the United States. Government regulation in governments dominated by presidents would certainly not produce the same results in Latin America as it has in the United States. Basic economic, social, and cultural changes have to come first. Until they do come, Latin American political parties will continue to be irresponsible — irresponsible in the sense that the inner ring is not and cannot be held accountable to the rank and file of the party membership.

The success of party government is also dependent upon the willingness of all parties to accept the voters' verdict. No one expected, in this country in 1948, when all the public opinion surveys showed the incumbent president was going to be soundly defeated at the polls, that Mr. Truman would use his powers as commander-in-chief of the armed forces to stay on in power. After the votes were counted no person believed that Mr. Dewey should claim fraud and violence and attempt to take over the presidency by force. The whole idea is happily foreign to our way of political life. In Latin America one can hardly count the number of instances in which a defeated administration refused to give up the reins of office and used its control over the armed forces of the state to stay in power. In a like manner, defeated candidates have often raised the cry of fraud and violence, and have attempted to take power. Perhaps the best illustration of our willingness to accept election results is that afforded by the disputed presidential election of 1876. The nation accepted the verdict, even though many felt that Tilden had won but had been counted out. In how many Latin American nations would a similar decision be accepted by candidates, parties, and people?

The difference in the political climate of the two Americas is evidenced in campaign techniques. Professor Tannenbaum earlier referred to campaign slogans in Mexico such as " Long Live X " and " Death to Y." This is partly hyperbole of expression, but it is also partly an evidence of the intensity of political propaganda. If campaigns emphasize such irreconcilable views as the above, it is not surprising that X does not wish to give way to Y should he win the election.

The merit system is fairly well established in the United States and our laws insulate the civil servant from the heat of party campaigns. We have gone so far as to prohibit civil servants in many jurisdictions from taking an active part in such political activity. Tradition, if not law, prohibits the use of public property for campaign purposes. One does not expect to see placards on the Capitol, the White House, or the Washington Monument urging the voters to support the Republican or Democratic ticket. State highways are not painted by state highway employees with signs exhorting the motorist to vote for the party in power. Municipal trucks do not carry signs urging the re-election of the incumbent mayor. In Latin America it is common to see such political advertising on public buildings and public property.

There are even highly developed and refined uses of public enterprises so as to help the party in power and to defeat the opposition.

A government-owned light plant may fail on the evening that the opposition party has scheduled a rally in a public park or building. "Owing to technical difficulties" a state-owned radio station or chain is forced to leave the air just when the candidate of the opposition has started to speak. Repairs are usually quickly made, and the government party finds all in working order when its turn comes round to use these facilities. These techniques, it must be repeated, are known in the United States, but their employment is much less frequent.

Comparing the general party picture with our own one notes several differences. The two-party system characterizes our politics whereas that of Latin America is much more commonly based on a multi-party organization. Even in the multi-party countries two groups usually dominate, the Liberals and the Conservatives. However, owing to the existence of several parties, it frequently happens that no one of them gets a majority in the legislature so that coalition governments are common. The instability of coalition governments is well known, and Latin America is no exception to the general political principle. The politics of Chile in the last three decades well illustrates this point.

The two major parties generally represent different social and economic groups, the Conservatives relying on the landowners, the Church, and the military for their support, and the Liberals on the industrialists and the middle classes. However, there is a considerable agreement between these two parties. Liberal parties may differ with the conservatives on tariff policy or Church-State relationships, but they do not necessarily assume an entirely different stand on social legislation or labor laws. Colonel Perón, in his campaign for the presidency of Argentina, constantly asserted that neither the Conservatives nor the Radicals (the liberal party) had done anything for the common man.

The minor parties are based upon a wide variety of social groups or issues. Some have arisen because of religious questions, others are parties of strong leaders. Some are loose confederations of vague nationalistic groups, others are cohesive and highly disciplined parties representing the organized workers, the farmers, and, in a few instances, even the Church.

In some of the nations, parties are allowed to organize and campaign freely, even though against hopeless odds. In Mexico, for example, a two-party or even a multi-party system exists in theory, but one party, and the same one, always wins the elections. Other countries have outlawed certain political groups, such as the Anarchist, the Socialist, or the Communist, and in still others no party except that of the administration may legally exist.

In the last three decades two highly important party changes have taken place. One of these is the emergence of political groups based upon the rapidly growing labor union movement, and the other is the development of indigenously nationalistic parties whose interest is focused on basic national economic problems. These parties are now competing for power with the much older, stronger, and more firmly entrenched liberal and conservative groups. In the thinking of many observers, these new political groupings may cause a change in the pattern of political party activity in Latin America. One can be sure that such a basic change will be opposed by the more conservative party groups, and in their opposition the latter will take recourse not only to political but also more direct and perhaps more violent action. The recent *coup* in Venezuela is a case in point.

No. 36   [The following article is much more than an analysis of the trade union movement in Latin America. Professor Alexander is concerned with both the economic and political effects of the movement. As the number of organized workers becomes larger, one naturally expects an increasing sense of political as well as economic power among the workers of the several Latin American nations. Will this power be used within the older traditional parties of these countries, or will it seek expression in new ways? To what extent will the Communist party try to capitalize on the new situation? What methods of counteracting communist influence are being tried? Finally, what does the increasing political significance of labor in Latin America mean in terms of its general political structure and institutions? These are the questions to which the author addresses himself.]

Labor Movements in
Latin America*

by ROBERT J. ALEXANDER

FROM MUTUAL ASSISTANCE TO TRADE UNIONS

*T*HE outstanding fact about Latin America today is the continent-wide feeling of unrest and revolt. This revolt is not a phenomenon which is confined to the New World by any means, but is rather part of the world-wide awakening of peoples in backward areas. It expresses itself in an exaggerated nationalism, and in social ferment within the frontiers of each country. It is in the light of this awakening that the labor movements of Latin America must be seen.

The labor movements of the Latin American countries have been profoundly influenced by the geographical, political, economic, and social surroundings from which they have sprung. Perhaps the first point to be noticed by a European or North American is that the labor movements in each of the twenty republics of Latin America have developed independently and in their own particular manner. We are too apt to lump "Latin America" or "South America" together as one more or less unified though incoherent country. This is far from the truth. Each of the Latin American countries has a distinct personality, a distinct history, tradition, and way of looking at things. The racial make-up, the stage of economic development, and many other factors have determined that the history of each of these countries — and certainly of their labor movements — will be distinctive.

Nevertheless, there have been certain lines of development characteristic of all the labor movements in Latin America. The progression from mutual benefit societies and anarcho-syndicalist societies of resistance, to a more or less organized and stable labor movement is a pattern which one can find in most of these nations. There have been some labor movements which have greatly influenced develop-

* Robert J. Alexander, *Labour Movements in Latin America* (London: Fabian Publications Ltd., and Victor Gollancz Ltd., 1947). Reprinted by permission of The Fabian Society.

ments in neighboring countries, principally the pioneer Argentine labor movement, whose influence has been felt throughout South America.

These movements started with mutual benefit societies, and the first anarcho-syndicalist *"uniones de resistencia."* After the First World War there was usually a struggle for influence between these older tendencies and new socialist and communist political ideologies. But during this early period the labor movement still remained a small-scale affair and included only a comparatively small proportion of the organizable workers. By the middle 1930's, the anarcho-syndicalist influence had been supplanted by some brand of Marxist ideology. The last step, which has taken place in many of these countries during the last ten years, has been that of the vast and rapid expansion of the labor movement, accompanied by the rapid growth of one or another political party making a special appeal to the working class, often with the participation of this party in political power; the result has been the almost complete unionization of industrial, transport, and even commercial workers. There are variations in this pattern from country to country, and in any given nation it is sometimes difficult to say when one phase finished and another began. Some countries like Colombia and Venezuela had practically no anarcho-syndicalist phase; others like Uruguay have not yet reached the last part of the cycle. In Brazil, the near-fascist corporate-state régime of Vargas has warped normal developments. Mexico went through the first phase and then as a result of the Revolution jumped into the last much earlier than most of these countries. But as a general pattern of development for the Latin American labor movements, that outlined here is a valid one.

The stage of economic development reached in each country has determined the speed at which the labor movements have grown. Industrial development in Latin America received its first great stimulus during World War I, and took giant strides during World War II. During both wars they were cut off from their normal sources of supply for industrial products, Europe and the United States and were forced to provide for themselves many of the things which they had previously bought abroad. There is now growing up in many of these countries a considerable light industry and the beginnings of heavy industrial development.

Twenty or twenty-five years ago the typical "industrial" establishment was a small workshop with its "maestro" and his two or three assistants. Today in Brazil, Argentina, Chile, Mexico, and some other countries there are factories, employing two or three thousand workers, principally in the textile trades. But, according to a questionnaire which this writer sent to most of the important industrial establishments of Chile, the typical industry in that country employs less than 500 workers. With the exception of mining enterprises, there are only two or three Chilean factories which employ more than 2,000 workers, and they are all textile plants. There are no more than half a dozen to a dozen establishments which employ between 500 and 2,000 workers. There are probably not more than 200 industrial establishments in all of Chile which employ more than 100 workers. The large plants are confined to textiles, railway workshops, foundries and small metallurgical works, chemical industries, breweries, one or two clothing manufacturers, and printing establishments. Although there are bigger industries and more of them in Brazil, Argentina, and Mexico, Chile is a good example of a comparatively industrialized Latin American country.

This late industrial development determined the type of labor movement which could exist. Until 1914, the only large groups of workers who could be classed as industrial were railway workers, maritime workers, miners, and small groups of textile workers. The rest of the working class was made up of artisans rather than industrial laborers. For the artisan, the characteristic type of organization was the mutual benefit society and not the trade union, since he was his own employer or worked in a shop where there were only one or two wage earners. His income was small and ceased immediately if he were taken ill or experienced some other misfortune, so it was necessary for him to band together with his fellows to try in a communal fashion to fend off the disastrous consequences which came from sickness and death. The result was the formation of mutual benefit societies. But these societies were a good deal more than just insurance groups. They usually had a headquarters which served as a social center for members. Usually, too, the societies were organized on the basis of trades — the shoemakers, tailors, etc., organizing in their individual groups — so that these mutual benefit organizations could serve when necessary as defenders of the interest of the trade. More often than not the societies served a cultural purpose too, having a library, and frequently having a school where the sons of the members — or the members themselves — could learn their alphabet. To this day the leading workers' society in Guayaquil, Ecuador, runs a night school which has some 1,700 pupils.

These early mutual benefit societies also included groups of workers who were not artisans. For instance, the first organizations of railwaymen in Chile and in Argentina and of textile workers in Peru were mutual benefit societies. Even the dock workers in Chile, who later became among the most militant trade unionists, first formed mutual benefit organizations.

The mutual benefit societies continue in existence in all of these countries to the present day. But their importance in most of the countries has waned with the growth of a strictly trade union movement. In many cases, the trade union movement developed under the wing of the mutual benefit societies, but went on to displace those societies as the center of the labor movement. Generally the mutual benefit societies were much less political than the later unions, and have remained much more conservative in their outlook. In countries where industry is comparatively advanced the mutual benefit societies have a distinctly secondary position in the labor movement. In countries like Ecuador where there are even now only relatively small industries, the mutual benefit societies continue to play a leading part: the trade unions and mutual benefit societies are both affiliated to the central labor organization, the *Confederación de Trabajadores del Ecuador,* and to its local branches. In Peru, though there is considerable industrial development, the labor movement has until the last couple of years been seriously hampered by a succession of dictatorships. As a result, the mutual benefit societies, which were considered less "dangerous," maintained a leading position in the labor movement because of the hostility of the government to strictly trade union organization. With the advent of a more democratic régime in Peru, the position of the mutual benefit societies is rapidly becoming less important in the general labor picture. In Chile, on the other hand, there has for many years been a sharp distinction between purely mutual benefit societies and the trade unions. The former have their *Confederación Mutualista de Chile* which is quite distinct from the trade union *Confederación de*

Trabajadores de Chile. Many Chilean unions, however, have mutual benefit features.

This early period is also marked by the preponderant influence of anarcho-syndicalism. The small artisan was an extreme individualist and he was a true believer in the axiom of Thomas Jefferson that "that government is best which governs least." Hence the philosophy of anarchism suited him better than any other. It was among the artisan class that the anarcho-syndicalists had their strongest supporters, and it is among this group today that there still exists in many countries a remnant of anarchist influence — among shoemakers, printing-trades workers, and bakers, for instance.

The first purely trade union organization came in the fields of transport and textiles where large groups of workers were grouped together under one employer. For instance, in Argentina and Chile, organizations of the engineers and firemen of the railways which date from the middle 1880's share with the printing-trades workers and the bakers the honor of having the longest continuous history. In Cuba the first strong trade union organizations were the tobacco workers and the railway and port laborers. In a series of countries — Argentina, Chile, Cuba — the maritime workers took a leading part in a great wave of strikes which greeted the end of World War I. In Argentina the port workers tied up Buenos Aires for several weeks, and nearly brought down the government of the time. In Peru the maritime workers of the port of Callao organized in 1913 the first general movement in favor of the eight-hour day, and six years later the textile workers of the capital city of Lima led the way in another general strike which finally succeeded in achieving legislation providing for the eight-hour day.

In some countries the mining and oil workers were among the first to be organized. This was the case in Chile, where the nitrate workers were forming *mancomunales* as they called their early organizations, in the early 1900's when there were few other organized labor groups in the country. In Mexico the miners and the oil workers were among the earliest organized and strongest of the labor groups. In Venezuela, after the death of dictator Juan Vicente Gómez, the petroleum workers were among the first laborers in the country to try to form trade unions. In Peru the workers of the Cerro de Pasco Copper Mining Company tried to organize as early as 1917, though they were not effectively organized until 1945.

With the growth of industry during the last few years, trade union organization has spread further afield in all of these countries. In Chile, Peru, Argentina, Mexico, and Cuba practically all of the urban workers who could be organized have joined unions in recent years. Even in such industries as the packing houses in Argentina and Uruguay, where the employers have always fought the establishment of unions with all the measures at their command, the workers have finally succeeded in organizing.

The various governments have been reluctant to allow their own employees to organize. In almost all countries where there are labor codes the government workers are forbidden to organize under those codes. However, although these workers are generally forbidden to form "labor organizations" as defined under the labor laws of the various countries, and are not allowed to use the conciliation and arbitration procedures established under those codes, they are usually permitted to form regular "civil societies" with the same legal status as a charitable organization or a ladies' sewing club which might seek incorporation. So for all practical purposes, the government workers in the various Latin countries have organizations, and in many instances they function as unions, though they do not have this legal status.

For instance, in Chile there have been a number of strikes of municipal employees, and in most of the important cities of the country the municipal workers present lists of grievances and demands for wage increases about as often as do the unions in private industry.

Generally the law forbids public employees the right to strike. In most cases this prohibition is extended to cover the public service industries, and the government is almost always given special powers to deal with walkouts in these vital industries.

One question which arises with regard to the organization of government employees is the definition of a government employee. In countries where the railways and other public utilities are government-owned, the regulations concerning regular government workers are extended to include these categories. In Chile, for instance, the workers on the state railways are forbidden to form *sindicatos* (trade unions) under the labor code, but the employees of the various retirement funds administered by the government and other such semiautonomous government agencies are allowed union rights under the code, on the plea that they are "semigovernment employees." Though the railway workers are ostensibly not supposed to organize unions, their workers' federation is probably the strongest in the country and they are protected by the best labor legislation in the nation.

The agricultural workers remain the most important single group which is for the most part still outside the scope of organized labor. The organization of agricultural labor touches the heart of the most critical problem of Latin America, the problem of land distribution. So far no country in Latin America, with the exception of Mexico, has had the courage to face the problem involved in the concentration of the ownership of the arable land in the hands of a small group of "oligarchs." This problem plagues Cuba, Chile, Brazil, Peru, and Argentina. Even the all-powerful Perón government has not done anything to change the situation — in spite of considerable oratory which has been expended on the question by Señor Perón and his friends. Generally, the land worth owning in most of these countries is owned by a small group which uses only so much of the land as is convenient, pays miserable wages to its farm workers, and lives as an absentee landlord class. This group is the most powerful influence in politics, in the armed forces, in the Church, and in most other important fields and has prevented any large-scale attack on the landlord problem in any of the Latin American countries except Mexico, and perhaps Venezuela.

Because the organization of agricultural workers would be a real threat to this landlord class, it has not been allowed by the governments of the Latin American countries until the present. For instance, an ostensibly democratic and liberal government of Bolivia arrests most of the leaders of the agricultural workers' unions as "subversive"; the extremely liberal Chilean President Pedro Aguirre Cerda issued a special order in 1939 prohibiting rural union organization. However slowly but surely, the labor movement is moving into the countryside. In Chile during the last year the organization of rural workers has been greatly encouraged by the revocation of President Aguirre Cerda's edict: in Peru the *Aprista* movement is working its way into the most isolated Indian villages with its gospel of social reform and education and with trade union organization to boot. Even in backward Ecuador there is a strong agricultural labor organization along the coast. In Argentina one of the positive achievements of the *Peronista* régime has been to permit and actually stimulate the organization of the workers on the sugar plantations in the province of Tucumán. Finally, during the last two years there has been a veritable rash of agricultural union organization in Venezuela under the revolutionary government in power in that country. The spreading of trade union organization among the agricultural workers on a really large scale in Latin America will bring a social revolution in almost all of these countries.

It is, of course, difficult to say just how many workers there actually are in these labor movements. The Latin American statistics-gathering machinery leaves much to be desired, and estimates are usually colored by one or another bias. For instance, in Argentina we received estimates varying from 250,000 to 1,000,000 for the strength of the Peronista *Confederación General del Trabajo,* and recent *CGT* publications have mentioned 3,000,000 as the goal towards which the *CGT* membership is driving.

A reasonable estimate of the membership of the labor movements of Latin America, in comparison with the total population of each of the countries, is as follows:

Country	Union Membership	Population
Argentina	500,000	16,000,000
Bolivia	70,000	3,500,000
Brazil	500,000	45,000,000
Chile	350,000	5,000,000
Colombia	150,000	10,000,000
Costa Rica	30,000	750,000
Cuba	300,000	5,000,000
Dominican Republic	25,000	2,000,000
Ecuador	75,000	3,000,000
Guatemala	50,000	3,500,000
Haiti	15,000	3,000,000
Mexico	1,000,000	20,000,000
Nicaragua	25,000	1,000,000
Panama	25,000	750,000
Paraguay	25,000	1,000,000
Peru	350,000	7,000,000
Uruguay	75,000	2,250,000
Venezuela	200,000	4,000,000

It can be said that for all practical purposes there is no labor movement in Salvador and Honduras because the dictatorships there will not permit one. The labor movement of the Dominican Republic is little more than a tool for the dictatorship of Generalissimo Trujillo.

The relative strength of the Latin American labor movements can be judged when one notes that in the United States there are 15,000,000 trade unionists in a total population of something more than 140,000,000. Similar figures for Great Britain indicate an even higher percentage of trade unionists in the total.

FOREIGN INFLUENCES

Foreign influence and immigration have played an important part in the development and history of the Latin American labor groups. In Argentina the organized labor movement received its first great impulse from a visit to that country in the 1880's of the famous Italian anarchist, Enrico Malatesta, and several years later Malatesta, and another Italian anarchist, Pietro Gori, helped to found the first important central labor organization there, the *Federación Obrera Regional Argentina*. The organization of the unions of railway engineers and firemen in Argentina and Chile — *La Fraternidad* and *Federación Santiago Watt* (James Watt) respectively — was stimulated by a visiting delegation from the railway labor unions of the United States in 1885–86. In Bolivia one of the first moves towards labor and socialist organization, which in 1913 brought about the formation of a Socialist party and a number of trade unions in the city of Oruro, came after the importation into that country of a number of Spanish books on socialism, a series of propaganda publications of the Spanish Socialist party. In Cuba and Puerto Rico the labor movement started through direct stimulation from Spain when those two countries were still Spanish colonies.

In Argentina the influence of immigration and of intellectual currents from Europe was particularly important in the early days of the labor movement. During the first thirty years of the twentieth century the working class of Argentina was largely made up of immigrants, principally from Spain and Italy. These immigrants brought with them the ideas of anarchism, syndicalism, and socialism which were then current in their native lands, and transplanted them to the New World in the form of labor organizations and political parties. It is to this influence more than anything else that the absolute predominance of the ideas of anarchism, syndicalism, socialism, and communism in the Argentine labor movement up until the revolution of 1943 can be traced.

The same can be said, to a somewhat lesser degree, of Uruguay where the influence of Italian and Spanish immigrants was of fundamental importance in giving ideological direction to the labor movement — and of Brazil, where the Portuguese and Italian anarchist immigrants were to a large degree responsible for the anarcho-syndicalist influence which controlled the labor movement of that country until the advent of Getulio Vargas.

There have been frequent organizational contacts between the trade union and political labor movements of the New World and those of Europe, more so in the past than at the present time. The Socialist party of Argentina was affiliated to the Second International from the foundation of the party. The anarcho-syndicalist organizations of the continent were among the founders of the International Workingmen's Association after the First World War. The Communists of Latin America have always maintained the closest relations with the European and particularly the Russian Communist parties, and a number of the leaders of New World Communist parties have spent some time being schooled in Moscow.

The central labor organization of Brazil sent a delegate to the conference which reorganized the International Federation of Trade Unions after World War I, while the Argentine *CGT*, the Mexican *Confederación de Trabajadores de Mexico*, and the Chilean *CTCh* were affiliated to the International Federation of Trade Unions in the days before the last war. A number of the Latin American central labor groups are at the present time affiliated to the World Federation of Trade Unions.

However, it is interesting to note that there is considerable discontent among the Latin American labor and socialist people with the attitude which their European comrades adopt toward them. There is a general feeling that the labor and socialist people of Europe don't give enough weight to the position of the Latin American labor movements. For instance, the leader of one of the New World Socialist parties told this writer that his group was not affiliated to any international organization because they were not in complete agreement with the principles of the groups now in existence — but that the most important reason why they were not affiliated was that the Europeans didn't want them, that the Europeans felt that the Latin American movements didn't count. This is a point of view which is held very widely in Latin America and is perhaps something of which the leaders of the European socialist and labor movements ought to be aware, and attempt to rectify. The labor and socialist organizations of the New World are of considerable importance in the world situation today and it is high time that this importance be recognized.

The Communists, of course, do not overlook their Latin American affiliates; they make sure that these are invited to and attend WFTU meetings and they build such figures as Vicente Lombardo Toledano into much more impressive figures than they really are.

The Latin American labor movements have a strong tradition of nationalism and anti-imperialism. The heyday of the anti-imperialist phase of the labor movements was the 1920's and early 1930's. At that time the incipient labor movements were the strongest opponents of foreign capitalist enterprises in the Latin American countries. For instance, the Nicaraguan Agusto Sandino — be he patriot or bandit — was strongly anti-imperialist, anti-United States, and had strong connections with what little labor movement there was in Nicaragua and with the labor movements of Mexico and other neighboring countries.

The labor organizations among the banana workers of the United Fruit Company in Costa Rica and Colombia were the strongest enemies of that firm. More recently, the attitude of the labor unions in the oil fields of Mexico had a great deal to do with the decision of the Mexican government in 1938 to expropriate the foreign-owned wells. Labor organizations in such industries as the Chilean copper and nitrate mines, the Uruguayan and Argentine meat-packing houses, foreign-owned railroads in Chile, Peru, and Uruguay have maintained an attitude of opposition to those companies not only as employer, but because they are at the same time foreign-owned. There is still much talk about " foreign imperialism " among these workers though in at least a few cases, such as the nitrate and copper miners of Chile, the workers live in better circumstances with more pay and better living conditions than the vast majority of their fellow workers in that country.

This early anti-imperialism of the Latin American union groups did not prevent some cooperation between these labor movements and that of the United States. The American Federation of Labor and the Mexican *Confederación Regional Obrera Mexicana* jointly protested against General Pershing's invasion of Mexico in 1916 and were at least in part responsible for the withdrawal of that " punitive expedition." Later, at the end of 1917, President Gompers of the AFL went to Cuba personally to persuade some American railwaymen imported there to break a Cuban railway workers' strike to return home. From 1917 until the early 1930's there existed a Pan American Federation of Labor, the most important members of which were the AFL and the Mexican *CROM*.

It was in the early period that the *Aprista* movement gained continent-wide, and perhaps world-wide, fame with its theory that the incipient working class must join with the native capitalist class and the peasantry to fight the imperialists and their allies, the big landowners. And the theme of "national unity" has continued down to the present day, appropriated when it was convenient by the Communists — though they were the staunchest opponents of the doctrine when Haya de la Torre and other *Apristas* first enunciated it in 1924–28. This idea that the native promoters of industry and the workers both had a common enemy in the great foreign companies which operated within the boundaries of the Latin American countries has led to a kind of class collaboration which has been endorsed by all but the most extreme revolutionaries in Latin America's labor movements. The anarcho-syndicalists are probably the only ones who have not approved of the doctrine. The outstanding example of this kind of class collaboration is the industry-labor pact signed in Mexico in 1945, providing for cooperation between the leading industrialists and the *Confederación de Trabajadores de Mexico,* then the leading labor organization in the country. It was designed to stimulate the further industrialization of the country and to avoid labor conflicts which might be prejudicial to the development of native-owned Mexican industry.

In recent years this policy of class collaboration has fitted in very well with the international Communist slogan of national unity, and particularly with the Communist attempts to line up everyone possible against the United States and Great Britain. Since the principal foreign enterprises in the Latin countries are British and American, the Communists, through the labor organizations which they controlled, could hit more or less directly at the United States and Britain themselves by adopting this class collaboration policy aimed against all big foreign corporations.

There has been a change in the anti-imperialist position of many of the Socialist and allied organizations in Latin America in recent years. Although they have not dropped their opposition to imperialism, they have tended to soft-pedal the attacks against the United States and Britain. There are various reasons for this. First of all, these countries are feeling their own strength, and though they may walk with considerable caution in front of the governments of the United States and Britain, they no longer have the exaggerated fear and respect which they once had for the foreign corporations working within their frontiers. The government of Chile, for instance, doesn't hesitate to force the foreign-owned mining companies there to give their workers a wage raise. Nor does it hesitate to put discriminatory taxation on the big foreign-owned mining companies — both notions which twenty-five years ago would probably have been unthinkable.

The Socialists have also come to realize that if these countries are to be industrialized within any reasonable space of time, it will be necessary to have foreign capital and that this capital must come principally from the United States and perhaps from Britain. Therefore, they have turned their attention not to an open onslaught on all foreign capital within their nations' frontiers, but rather towards evolving methods by which this capital can enter and develop the industries needed there, gaining a reasonable profit, but not coming to dominate the countries politically and economically.

In the third place, there has been a fundamental change in the policy of the United States with regard to the Latin American countries since the 1920's. In the time of Theodore Roosevelt, who counselled his friends to " tread lightly and carry a big stick," and of his immediate successors, the Colossus of the North thought nothing of sending marines or army troops to "settle" a strike or thwart a revolution in any of the Central American countries and particularly those which rim the Caribbean. During the first three decades of the present century this threat of outright military and political intervention hung heavy over the heads of the Latin American countries.

With the advent of the Good Neighbor policy of Theodore's distant cousin, Franklin D. Roosevelt, this situation changed fundamentally. The United States no longer sends troops into the Latin American countries to clean up their internal squabbles. In fact the policy of the United States has been criticized in recent years for abstaining too much from interference in the affairs of these countries, and therefore permitting the existence of dictatorships such as those of Benavides and Prado in Peru. This change in policy, marked also by such minor but significant things as changing the name of relations among the American countries from "Pan American" to "Inter-American," and by consultations among all of the American republics upon the occasion of any untoward events in any one of them, has had a profound effect on the labor and socialist movements of these countries.

Finally, as one of the leaders of the *Aprista* movement of Peru said to this writer, in the 1920's when the *APRA* launched its great anti-American-imperialism campaigns, the chief menace to the welfare and security of the countries of Latin America was the United States. Since that time, there has arisen a greater menace, that of totalitarianism, in all of its various manifestations.

The result of these events has been that the Socialist and allied groups in Chile, Argentina, Uruguay, Cuba, Peru, Brazil, and to a lesser extent in Ecuador and Venezuela, have drifted away from their extremely belligerent attitude toward the United States and now have taken up a more friendly position. In the case of the Panamanian Socialist party, which suffers from the racial distinctions which unfortunately many Americans have brought with them to the Canal Zone, the attitude toward the United States and American imperialism hasn't been modified quite so much. Nor has it among certain Colombian groups, who still are galled by the *coup* which Theodore engineered with his Big Stick in Panama more than a generation ago.

The course of the Communists' attitude toward imperialism and American imperialism in particular has varied more in accordance with the changes in the foreign policy of Russia and the consequent line of the Comintern than with any developments in the New World. Thus Roosevelt was an "imperialist war-monger" from 1939 to 41, the Communists welcomed the establishment of United States military bases in Latin countries from 1941 to 45, and now the United States has replaced the Nazis in the Communist chamber of horrors.

POLITICAL INFLUENCES IN THE LABOR MOVEMENTS

One cannot separate the labor movements of Latin America from the politics of those countries. Since its inception the trade union movement has been highly political and remains so to this day. The political colors of the labor movements of different countries vary, and within a single country the shade differs from time to time, but there is no labor movement in Latin America which can truly be called apolitical in the sense of the American labor movement.

The Anarchists. In the early years of this century the predominant political thinkers in the labor movement were the "antipolitical" anarchists. They controlled the pioneer labor organizations of Argentina for the decade from 1901 to 1911 almost without competition, and they continued to be a force there for many years. At the same time the labor groups of Uruguay, Peru, Chile, and Mexico were deeply influenced by the followers of Bakunin and Malatesta. There was scarcely a country in the continent that didn't have its anarchist publications.

The labor movement in those days took the form of spontaneous, sporadic, sometimes bloody revolts of the workers, rather than a highly organized, consistent labor movement. The form of organization was the *Sociedad de Resistencia* or Resistance Society, which had no permanent officers, in which everyone was free to speak his piece though it might take all night to conduct a meeting, in which there was little or no preparation for strike action — no strike fund and no strike delegates. Often a union which would appear as a result of strike action would disappear soon afterwards. One of the hottest issues during this anarchist phase was the question whether the unions should have paid officials. Most of the anarchist-controlled organizations, even the central labor organization itself with thousands of members, did not have any full-time or even part-time paid officials. The union activities were all conducted after working hours and on week ends. This, of course, did not lend strength to the organizations.

The governments of all of these countries were brutal in combatting the anarchists and the labor movements which they controlled. The great massacre of nitrate workers in Iquique in 1907 when hundreds were killed is still remembered by the workers of Chile. The old Argentine anarchist leaders who remember the way they were jailed, held incommunicado without food and water, tortured, and generally persecuted by the governments of that country in the early years of the present century do not feel that the *Peronista* government is profoundly different in this sense from its predecessors. The Mexican textile strikes of the same period, inspired and led by the anarchist brothers, Flores Magón, were equally brutally suppressed by the dictatorship of Porfirio Díaz which governed that country in the early 1900's.

In spite of their antipolitical philosophy, the anarchists in their heyday were as political in their control of the unions as the Marxists ever were. For instance, the complete unification of the Argentine movement was thwarted several times by the insistence of the anarchist leaders that the unified trade union federation include in its declaration of principles a statement in favor of anarcho-communism. And the anarchists in most of these countries had organized "societies" which acted within the unions in roughly the same way which the political parties were to do later. That this was true is indicated by a meeting of the *Confederación General de Trabajadores,* the present-day anarcho-syndicalist organization in Chile which this writer attended, where almost a whole morning was devoted to a discussion of the part which the strictly anarchist elements should play in that labor movement.

The Syndicalists. A syndicalist group also developed as a deviation from this anarchist trend. The syndicalists, who took their thinking and organization from the pre-1914 *Confédération Générale du Travail* in France, came as near to being an apolitical group as any that has appeared on the stage of the Latin American labor movement. Their stronghold was also in the Argentine, where first the so-called *Federación Obrera Regional Argentina* of the Ninth Congress and later its successor, the *Unión Sindical Argentina,* were relatively strong organizations. This syndicalist group evolved out of the left wing of the Socialist trade unionists and the more moderate wing of the anarchists, both of which were tired of the constant bickering between the anarchists and Socialists in the unions and aspired to found a labor movement which would be free from the meddling of both of these political groups. The *FORA* of the Ninth Congress was founded in 1915 when a group split away from the orthodox anarchist *Federación Obrera Regional Argentina* (henceforth called " of the Fifth Congress ") because they objected to pledging allegiance to anarchist communism. It was for seven or eight years the principal labor organization in the country, and in 1922 was converted into the *Unión Sindical Argentina* or *USA* which continued to be a force down to the advent of Perón, though a definitely secondary force. Similar groups appeared in Uruguay, Chile, and one or two other countries.

The Socialists. In the early days of this century the chief rivals of the anarchists in the labor movements of Latin America were the Socialists. The Socialist party of Argentina is the oldest organization of its kind in South America, dating from 1896, but even before this, as far back as the 1870's, there were conflicts between the followers of Bakunin and the followers of Marx in Argentina, Uruguay, and Brazil.

In Argentina the first central labor organization, the *Federación Obrera de la República Argentina,* was founded by the Socialists in 1899, but was taken over and renamed the *Federación Obrera Regional Argentina* by the anarchists in 1901. During the next two decades the Socialists controlled successively the *Unión General de Trabajadores* from 1902–05, the *Confederación Obrera Regional Argentina* from 1909 (though here they lost control to the syndicalists), the *Confederación Obrera Argentina* from 1926 to 30, and the *Confederación General de Trabajadores* from 1903 until 1943.

With the rise of Perón, the Socialists lost control of the labor movement almost completely and now are left only with a small group of relatively ineffectual unions. In their time, the *COA* and the *CGT* under Socialist control were the majority groups in the country's labor movement.

In Chile first the *Partido Democrático,* which was a mildly socialist group with some contact with the Second International, and then the *Partido Socialista Obrero* were the chief rivals of the anarchists in the labor movement. In Peru the Socialist groups developed rather late, after the First World War, and never had much influence except among the oil workers of the northern part of the country. In Mexico groups which called themselves Socialist arose during the Mexican Revolution, while in some other countries there were Socialist orientated groups.

After the First World War some of these Socialist parties, notably those of Chile and Uruguay, went over to the Communist International and it was some years before new Socialist organizations arose. However, during the last fifteen years Socialist groups have been founded in Chile, Peru, Ecuador, Colombia, Panama, Cuba, and most recently in Brazil. In Uruguay, Chile, Ecuador, Brazil, Panama, and Cuba these parties have considerable force in the labor movement though only in Ecuador do they control the majority of the workers' economic organizations.

There has been some contact among these various Socialist groups. As early as 1919 there was held an All American Socialist Congress in Buenos Aires; and in 1940 and 1946 conferences were held in which the Socialist and *Aprista* groups cooperated. Another such conference is planned for the near future.

The Communists. The Communists have been active in the labor movement since the First World War. Communist parties were formed relatively early in Argentina, Chile, Mexico, Uruguay, and Brazil. In Argentina the party developed from a left-wing split-off from the Socialist party. In Uruguay and Chile the Socialist party itself went over to the Comintern. In Brazil the Communist party was founded by a group of ex-anarchists.

By 1930 there were Communist groups or parties in most of the Latin American countries, and in 1929 two congresses were held, one of labor organizations controlled by the Communists, and the other of the Communist parties themselves, in Montevideo and Buenos Aires respectively.

In the 1920's the only labor organizations of any importance which the Communists controlled or influenced very much were those of Chile, where they controlled the *Federación Obrera de Chile,* the principal labor group of the time, Cuba, where in the late 1920's they got control of the *Confederación Nacional de Obreros de Cuba,* and Brazil where they disputed control of the unions with the anarchists. In Mexico the *Confederación Regional Obrera Mexicana* under Luis Morones for some time played coyly with the Profintern, but never actually affiliated to this Red International of Trade Unions. During the famous Third Period of the Comintern, when the Communists all over the world adopted an extremely sectarian position, they founded a series of more or less fictitious central labor organizations in most of the Latin American countries where they had any influence at all.

However, it was in the late 1930's and the 1940's, with the great rise in the powers of the labor movements themselves, and with the control which they exercised over the *Confederación de Trabajadores de America Latina* (the *CTAL*), that the Communists really became the important factor they now are. At the present time they control majority groups in the labor movements of Chile, Colombia, Guatemala, Panama, and Uruguay; are elements of importance in Bolivia, Cuba, Ecuador, Venezuela, Brazil, and Paraguay. They have lost practically all of their influence in Argentina, where in 1943 before the rise of the *Peronistas* they were fighting with the Socialists for supremacy in that country's labor movement; and in Mexico where they had considerable force in the *Confederación de Trabajadores de Mexico* (*CTM*) which was for some time the majority labor group, but which now has been reduced to one of seven or eight labor groups with more or less equal power. The Communists have lost ground since 1945 in other countries such as Venezuela, Ecuador, Peru, and Cuba, principally due to the rapid rise of other political groups, the *Acción Democrática* in Venezuela, the Socialists in Ecuador, and the *Apristas* in Peru.

Nevertheless, the Communists still maintain a more or less fictitious front as the controlling element in the labor movement of Latin America as a whole, through their domination of the *Confederación de Trabajadores de America Latina*. Although the president of this organization, Vicente Lombardo Toledano, claims not to be a Communist, he has faithfully followed the Comintern's rapid changes of policy for ten or a dozen years, and it is certain that a large majority of the executive council of the *CTAL* are Communists, though many of them represent no one in the labor movements of their respective countries. Thus the Argentine is represented in the council of the *CTAL* by Rubén Iscaro and Francisco Pérez Leiros, the first a Communist and the second a Socialist, neither of whom are now members of labor organizations in their own country and are certainly not leaders of any unions.

The Peruvian representative on the *CTAL* is Communist Juan P. Luna, who now holds no office in a trade union and is back to driving his taxicab. In the case of Ecuador, the labor organization of that country is represented in the *CTAL* by Pedro Saad, a Communist, though the Communists have lost control of that central labor organization. The *CTAL*, although it began in 1938 as a real central organization of Latin American labor, with practically all of the important union organizations of the continent represented, is now reduced to little more than a sounding board for Communist oratory and high-sounding *pronunciamentos*.

There are some elements opposed to the Communists who hope to be able to capture control of and reform that organization. Their possibilities of success seem small since the Communists have for some time ably manipulated the delegates of such comparatively insignificant labor organizations as those of the Dominican Republic, Honduras, and Nicaragua, where there are dictatorships which don't allow much real labor organization.

The Peronistas. In recent years a group of parties which we can for convenience call *Peronistas* has had considerable influence in the labor movements of Latin America. The three principal parties in this class are the *Partido Peronista* of President Perón in Argentina, the *Partido Trabalhista* of ex-president Vargas in Brazil, and the *Movimiento Nacionalista Revolucionario* in Bolivia. It is a characteristic of each of these parties that their wide working class support represents a more or less blind response from elements in the population which have until recently been unorganized or only scantily organized. Perón's real power is based on the hundreds of thousands of workers whom he has attracted to the labor movement for the first time and on the undoubted gains which he obtained during his period as Secretary of Labor for such groups of workers as those in the packing houses and the sugar plantations of northern Argentina.

Vargas' party in Brazil and the labor unions which it controls are made up to a large degree of elements which were not in the labor movement before Vargas' destruction of the free labor movement in the middle 1930's, and who believe sincerely but mistakenly that the labor movement in Brazil began with Getulio Vargas. Finally, in Bolivia the most powerful element in the working class support of the *MNR* is the miners' group, which was never effectively organized before the *MNR*-dominated government of Colonel Villarroel (1943-46), and which did win some improvements and changes during that régime, and which now believes that the Bolivian trade union movement began with Colonel Villarroel.

It is characteristic of these parties that they are more in the fascist current than anything else, though this writer believes it is unrealistic merely to label them " fascist." Like the *Aprista* group of parties which have many affinities with the Socialist parties, the *Peronista* group of parties, which have affinities with the fascists, are an eminently American group of organizations, arising from essentially American conditions, and the arousing of the masses to political, economic, and social activities. They cannot be explained away, destroyed, or even effectively combatted if one confines oneself to labelling them fascist.

There are certainly fascist overtones in the *Peronista* régime — one need but mention the ex-adviser of Primo de Rivera and friend of Mussolini, the Spanish economist José Figuerola; the son of a prominent nazi and private secretary to Perón, Señor Freude; and the pro-German ex-chief of Perón's Federal Police Force, General Filomeno Velasco, to realize the fascist-minded nature of the *Peronistas* and their régime. But it is not simply that; and unlike the fascist régimes of Europe which were more movements of desperation than of hope, there is a strong element of hope and first awakening which gives great motive power to these movements, particularly those of Perón and the *MNR*.

The Apristas. Another political force in the labor movements which is distinctly American, and from this writer's point of view more helpful, is that group of parties which we shall call *Apristas*. They include the *Partido del Pueblo,* or *Aprista* party of Peru; the *Partido Febrerista* of Paraguay, the *Partido Acción Democrática* of Venezuela, and the *Partido Auténtico* of Cuba. Each of these movements is a democratic political force, with a Socialist orientation, but which rejects the idea of blindly applying Marxism to the countries of America. These parties consciously try to ally the working class, the middle class, and the agrarian working class in a united front against the semifeudal landowning oligarchy which has so long controlled their respective countries, and to bring about in those countries a social transformation which will raise the standard of living and level out some of the vast inequalities which exist in those nations.

Each of these parties has wide working class support and in Peru and Venezuela they have almost unquestioned hegemony over the labor movement, while in Paraguay and Cuba they are one of the two most important elements. These parties are strong supporters of political democracy and seek, as far as possible, to bring about basic social transformations through democratic processes. The *Aprista* parties, too, represent a phase of this blind social awakening which has already been mentioned, but in these cases this awakening is being directed into much saner and happier channels. They have aroused in the masses of their respective countries profound hopes and one can only wish that these hopes will not be betrayed.

Catholic Influences. Finally, mention should be made of Catholic influences in the labor movements of Latin America. Although it cannot be labelled exactly " political," Catholic influence is certainly of the same genre as that of the Socialists, Communists, and *Peronistas*.

The Catholic Church's intervention in the labor movement has spread over a considerable period of time. *Círculos Obreros* or " Workers' Circles " were organized in many countries during the early years of the present century and even before. These were half mutual benefit societies, half religious organizations. The actual launching of Catholic trade unions is of more recent origin. In Brazil the Confederation of Catholic Workers was launched in 1932, but was more or less snuffed out by the corporative trade union set-up established by Vargas in the middle 1930's, and Catholic activity in that country returned to the *Círculo Obrero* stage.

In Argentina there has been a very significant trade union movement among women white-collar workers led by Monseñor De Andrea, which has gained considerable benefits for its members and has perhaps twenty-five to thirty thousand workers organized. There is another more general Catholic trade union movement in Argentina, but it has been more or less obliterated by the rise of *Peronismo*. In Chile from time to time the Church or elements of the Church have tried to organize trade union movements, but without much success. There exists today an avowedly Catholic labor group, the *Federación Obrera de Chile,* which is very poor materially and spiritually. More interesting in Chile is the Catholic-Social political party, the *Falange Nacional* (founded some years before the Spanish Falange of Franco and having nothing at all to do with that organization), which is led by a brilliant group of young intellectuals and has some support among the working class, principally in unions which are under the general control of the Communists.

In Ecuador there is a Catholic labor movement of some importance headed by the *Confederación Nacional de Trabajadores Católicos* and the *Confederación Ecuatoriano de Obreros Católicos.* This group has perhaps 15 to 20 percent of the organized labor groups of the country within its ranks.

In Colombia there is a new and fast-growing Catholic labor movement, headed by the *Unión de Trabajadores Colombianos* and directed and inspired by the Jesuits. It dates only from 1946, but has acquired proportions which will soon make it a real challenge to the Communist and Liberal controlled *Confederación de Trabajadores de Colombia.* Those directing this organization are exceedingly intelligent, and the movement has the good will of a number of employer groups which are opposed to the " Red " *CTC* and hope that this new organization will be less militant and perhaps more malleable by the employers. On the other hand, the continued control of the *CTC* which the Communists exercise, due to a " deal " with one faction of the Liberal party, gives the Catholic *UTC* a very good talking point which the Catholics are not loathe to use. This is certainly the Catholic labor movement in Latin America with most promise for the future.

Finally, mention should be made of the *Confederación de Trabajadores " Rerum Novarum "* of Costa Rica, which is one of the oldest of the American Catholic labor groups. It is under the direction of Padre Nuñez, an able and intelligent Catholic priest of considerable prestige, and there are a number of other clergymen, many of them comparatively young, who are interested in this movement. It represents a powerful balance to the completely Communist-controlled *Confederación de Trabajadores de Costa Rica.*

EFFECTS OF POLITICAL INFLUENCE

Opinion is no doubt divided on whether or not the extreme political control of the labor movements of Latin America has been a good thing for those movements and for the workers themselves. It is certainly true that the help of friendly governments has been a crucial factor in the rapid growth of the labor movements of Argentina, Chile, Peru, Venezuela, and Cuba in the last few years. The political consciousness of the labor movements of various of these countries has also been decisive in gaining advanced codes of labor legislation, and in resolving immediate labor conflicts in favor of the workers. Also it might be noted that the existence of strong labor movements in Peru and Venezuela, for instance, is doing much to defend the political democracy which those countries are enjoying at the moment.

But there are serious disabilities involved in the extremely political nature of the Latin American labor movements. First of all, there is the tendency for them to become nothing more than the organs of the government. This trend is accentuated in Argentina, where the *CGT* has become so much the creature of the Perón government that it is even aiding the pro-Franco policy of the Perón government by sending a message of greeting to the Spanish dictator upon the occasion of the visit of Señora de Perón to Spain. The same trend could be noted in Chile during the period in which the Communists were in the government, early in 1947.

In all of the countries where the party which has a majority in the labor movement is in power, or where that party is cooperating with the government, the labor movements' freedom of action is seriously hampered, and the relations between employers and workers tend to become confused with what is good for the political future of the government. This was true in Peru, for instance, when the Communists were the majority group in the labor movement and were cooperating with the Prado dictatorship; it has perhaps been true in Cuba under the *Auténtico* régime and in Venezuela under the *Acción Democrática* government.

Another great inconvenience has been revealed in recent months in Colombia. There the labor movement was controlled by the Liberal party which had been in the government during sixteen years, and under whose wing the movement had grown, and the Communist party. In the presidential election of 1946 the Liberals lost control of the government, and in the congressional elections of 1947 the Communists were virtually eliminated from the national political scene, with the result that the *Confederación de Trabajadores de Colombia* is going through a period of decline and serious internal crisis.

Finally, the danger of splitting along political lines is a very real one. For instance, in series of countries — Chile, Guatemala, Uruguay, Peru, Colombia — there have from time to time been splits not over any questions concerning the labor organizations themselves, but rather as a result of differences of opinion over political issues or attempts by one or another political group to seize complete control of the unions, or to upset a rival group which had that control. But it is worth noting that the labor leaders of Latin America with whom this writer has talked — some four hundred in all — have been all but unanimous in saying that though the other fellow may take political considerations into account when dealing with strictly union problems he, the speaker, never did this. This statement was made whether or not the speaker was willing to admit that he was a member of a political party — and most of them were members of one or another.

CONTINENTAL FEDERATIONS

At various times during the last forty years there have been more or less successful attempts to form a central organization covering unions throughout the Latin American continent. Before the First World War there were frequent contacts among the anarcho-syndicalist movements, and a loose organization was established among them.

In 1916–17 the Pan American Federation of Labor came into existence. At that time the United States had sent General Pershing on a " punitive expedition " to chase Pancho Villa back into Mexico and " castigate " him for alleged trespasses on United States territory. At about the same time, President Wilson sent American troops to Vera Cruz. The Mexican labor organizations protested vigorously against these policies and asked for aid in combatting them from the American Federation of Labor. Contact was made between the two labor groups and a founding meeting of the Pan American Federation of Labor was held early in 1917 in Texas. The headquarters of the PAFL were established in Washington, and Carlos Loviera, a Cuban long resident in the United States, was put in charge of its activities.

Near the end of 1917 as a result of the PAFL's and Samuel Gompers' personal intervention in the Camaguey railway strike, the PAFL won adherents in Cuba. During the next ten years labor organizations in ten or a dozen different countries, principally around the rim of the Caribbean, affiliated to the Pan American Federation of Labor. But the American Federation of Labor and the *Confederación Regional Obrera Mexicana* of Mexico remained the two principal organizations within the Federation. Santiago Iglesias, secretary of the Free Federation of Labor of Puerto Rico (affiliated to the American Federation of Labor) was for many years the Secretary of the PAFL and its chief figure.

Controversy has not ceased to rage around the Pan American Federation of Labor. Communists and other leftists accused the Pan American Federation of Labor of being a tool of the AFL which, according to the Communists, was playing the game of the United States State Department in relation to the Latin American countries. Charges were also made that some members of the PAFL, such as the Venezuelan member, represented fictitious organizations, sponsored by the various Latin American dictatorships.

On the other hand, the supporters of the Pan American Federation maintain that it served a very useful purpose in bringing together many of the principal labor organizations of the continent at that time. They also point to various instances in which the PAFL protested vigorously against Dollar Diplomacy and the tyrannies of local dictators. For instance, the Cuban ex-members of the PAFL cite various instances when that organization intervened to defend its Cuban affiliates against the persecutions of the Machado dictatorship. In the case of Mexico, too, the PAFL defended the Mexican régime when it was under serious fire from elements in the United States.

In sum, it can probably be said that the record of the Pan American Federation of Labor, though perhaps not spotless, was fairly satisfactory. It was the first serious attempt to bring together some of the principal labor organizations of the continent into a central body. It served a useful purpose in protesting against actions of the United States government at a time when that government had never heard of a Good Neighbor policy. It was not a radical organization, but it cannot justly be said that it was a reactionary one.

In 1929 a conference of all the Communist trade union organizations of Latin America was held at Montevideo and the *Confederación Sindical de America Latina* was formed. Most of the unions belonging to this confederation were fictitious or nearly so. This was during the famous " Third Period " of the Comintern when it was Communist policy to launch their own central trade union organizations even though they had little or no trade union strength. By 1929 even the once-powerful organizations which were affiliated to the *CSAL* were much reduced in membership and strength, for instance, the *Federación Obrera de Chile* and the *Confederación Nacional Obrera de Cuba,* which were suffering severely from the dictatorships of Carlos Ibañez and General Machado respectively. This Communist confederation continued until the middle 1930's when it lapsed at the time of the " Popular Front " policy of the Comintern. So far as this writer knows, no further congress of the organization was held after the 1929 meeting.

The anarcho-syndicalist organizations of the continent have been represented on the *Asociación Continental Americana de Trabajadores* since a few years after the First World War. However, the *ACAT* never was of first-rate importance and since 1919 the numerical strength and relative importance of the anarcho-syndicalist trade unions has been steadily declining.

There is no organization uniting the various national Catholic trade union movements, and so far as this writer knows, none of the American Catholic trade union groups was ever affiliated to the Christian Federation of Workers between the wars. There have been several " seminars " of the Catholic Social Action, where Catholic labor leaders have been present from most of the American countries, including the United States and Canada. There has also been at least one conference — in Montevideo in 1946 — of the Catholic Social political parties of the Western Hemisphere, at which several of the Catholic trade union groups were also represented.

THE CONFEDERACION DE TRABAJADORES DE AMERICA LATINA

The most recent central labor organization among the Latin American trade union groups is the *Confederación de Trabajadores de America Latina,* the famous *CTAL.* The *CTAL* was founded in a well-publicized congress held in Mexico in the summer of 1938. This congress was attended by delegates from Argentina, Chile, Colombia, Ecuador, Peru, Venezuela, Cuba, and Mexico as well as fraternal representatives from the American CIO (John L. Lewis), the French *Confédération Générale du Travail* (Leon Jouhaux), the International Federation of Trade Unions, the Indian trade unions, and the International Labor Organization. At the time of its foundation the *CTAL* was a truly representative organization, having within its ranks practically all of the important national labor organizations in Latin America. However, as the years passed, the *CTAL* came more and more under Communist influence. This was to a very great degree due to the influence of the president of the *CTAL,* Vicente Lombardo Toledano.

Lombardo Toledano was until 1940 secretary-general of the *Confederación de Trabajadores de Mexico,* and was at that time forced out, reportedly because he was considered by the incoming Avila Camacho government as too friendly to the Communists. However,

Lombardo continued as president of the *CTAL*, and made of that organization his vehicle. He has followed the Communist line through all of its twistings and turnings during the last ten years. Though it is likely that he is not a member of the Communist party, he had certainly worked much more closely with the Communists in the *CTAL* than with their opponents.

Communist influence in the *CTAL* also increased greatly during the war because they made giant strides in the separate Latin American labor movements. The Communists were rapidly gaining force in the Argentine labor movement before the military dictatorship was established in 1943. They were by 1943 or 1944 the majority group in the Chilean labor movement; they and their sympathizers were of great importance in the Mexican labor movement; they dominated the Cuban *CTC* more or less completely; they dominated the Colombian *CTC* with facility though actually a small minority in that organization; they dominated the Peruvian *CTP* so long as the dictatorship was in power in that country, and they worked with it. As a result of all this, the Communists gained representation from these various national organizations on the council of the *Confederación de Trabajadores de America Latina*.

Finally, Communist influence in the *CTAL* has been strengthened by the fact that some of the principal noncommunist or anticommunist organizations in the *Confederación* have either withdrawn or have become inactive in the *CTAL*. Thus after the split in the Chilean labor movement, the *CTC* controlled by Bernardo Ibañez withdrew from the *CTAL;* the Peruvian *CTP* suspended, though did not break entirely, its relations with the *CTAL* after the *Apristas* got control of the Peruvian national organization; the *CTM* in Mexico was divided several times, leaving little more than a Communist-controlled rump in the organization which still adhered to the *CTAL*.

All of these factors led to the more or less complete capture of the *Confederación de Trabajadores de America Latina* by the Communists. To counter this tendency a fairly well-organized movement has grown up throughout Latin America in opposition to the Communists. A group of independent organizations of various political tendencies exists in Uruguay. There were splits in the Chilean, Cuban, and Colombian central labor groups — the last of these being patched up, but somewhat precariously so. And within the *CTAL* the control of the Peruvian *Confederación de Trabajadores del Peru* changed from the Communists to the *Apristas,* the *Confederación de Trabajadores del Ecuador* was captured by the Socialists, while in Venezuela, though there is no confederation, the vast majority of the unions are under anticommunist influence.

Observing these developments, and perhaps aiding them in some degree, has been the American Federation of Labor. The AFL's policy has been that of avowedly fighting whatever Communist influence there is in the labor movements to the south, and fighting the *CTAL* in particular as a Communist-controlled organization. No doubt in part the American Federation of Labor's dislike of the *CTAL* stems from the close relations which the *Confederación* has had in the past with the CIO, the AFL's domestic rival.

The American Federation apparently favors the foundation of a new confederation which would rival the *CTAL*. They argue correctly that it is no longer true that the Communists have a majority of the labor organizations of Latin America under their control. Working from this premise, they say that it is logical to organize a new confederation on the basis of the anticommunist majority in the unions of the continent. There has been some talk of making the new organization inter-American, as was the Pan American Federation of Labor, rather than strictly Latin American.

However, there is a strong desire among the anticommunist union leaders of Latin America to try to conquer the *CTAL*, oust Lombardo Toledano and take over the organization. The supporters of this tactic point out that the *Confederación de Trabajadores de America Latina* has established a reputation, that its representatives are accepted as the spokesmen for Latin American labor, and that it is more advantageous to capture a going concern than to create a new one. And they point out that it is distinctly possible that such a conquest could be achieved. They cite the fact that Peru, Ecuador, Venezuela, perhaps a majority of Cuba, as well as one or two of the smaller groups are now in the anticommunist camp and that if they work in a concerted, organized manner they might well be able to dislodge the Communists. If this proves impossible, these elements believe it will then be time enough to discuss the formation of a new confederation.

LATIN AMERICAN LABOR CODES

Both a cause and a result of the rapid growth of the labor movements of Latin American countries during the last dozen years or so has been the creation of labor codes in almost all of these nations. Even in cases where there is no avowed labor code, the labor legislation of each of these countries is fairly complete. In fact labor legislation is becoming so important in the structure of Latin American law that in some countries it is now treated as a separate division of the law, distinct from criminal law and civil law.

The codes have two purposes: they are intended to guarantee to the workers certain rights of organization and collective bargaining, and they are intended to give the government control not only over the collective bargaining procedures, but over the organizations themselves.

Before the institution of codes of labor law in most of these countries, the position of the workers was very poor. There still persists in Spanish America the subconscious belief that those who work with their hands are beyond the pale, a psychological hangover from the days of slavery and the impressment of the Indians by the *conquistadores*. In addition there was the experience, not confined to Latin America, that nascent industrialism produces deplorable working conditions for those workers who are first brought into it. This was the experience of Great Britain at the beginning of the industrial revolution — an experience which stimulated the work and works of Robert Owen, Charles Kingsley, and Charles Dickens, to mention but three. It was the experience of the United States as well, in the early days of the textile trade and of coal mining. So it is not unnatural that the beginnings of industrialization should bring exceedingly bad labor conditions to these Latin American countries.

The importance of this motive in the establishment of labor codes is shown by the case of Chile, where ex-President Arturo Alessandri, who was chiefly responsible for the labor code in that country even before there was much industry there, said that his principle motive in pushing through the labor code proposal was to correct a ferociously one-sided situation then existing in employer-worker relations. President Alessandri was deeply influenced by the charter of the International Labor Organization, and it was in a large degree the desire to live up to this document and subsequent conventions of the ILO which inspired the Chilean labor code.

The second motive for the establishment of labor codes in Latin America was the desire on the part of the governments to control the labor movements of their countries. The codes generally provide for minute regulation of the affairs of the unions such as is virtually unknown in Europe and North America except in fascist or Communist controlled countries. In Chile the labor code states that all unions must be recognized by the government. In order to gain government recognition the unions must meet certain requirements. They must have not less than twenty-five members, they must be organized in a meeting at which a government inspector of labor is present and bears official witness to the act of constitution. The minutes of this first meeting, with the provisional list of officers, must be submitted to the scrutiny of the government. Qualifications for the officers of unions are established: minimum age, number of years in the company, complete lack of any criminal record.

Once recognition is obtained, the minutest activity of the unions is subject to supervision. Meetings for the election of officers must be attended by a government inspector of labor; so must meetings at which a strike vote is taken. The list of newly elected officers must be submitted to the government, which can throw them out if they in some manner contravene the provisions of the labor code. The annual budgets of the unions must be submitted to the *Dirección General del Trabajo* for the government's approval, and if there is too much divergence between the proposed budget and the way in which the money is actually spent, the union must ask for permission for this divergence. The use of union funds for certain things is forbidden: the employment of full-time union officials, political activity, and the investment of union funds in such things as cooperatives, union headquarters, and building projects, are subject to strict supervision.

In most labor codes of Latin America a detailed procedure is provided for the settlement of collective disputes. In most cases there are procedures for conciliation and arbitration, and usually it is mandatory for the two sides to appear before the government conciliation boards, but is optional whether or not they accept arbitration. " Legal " strikes or lockouts can only be declared under these labor codes if all of the process provided in the codes is gone through.

Any walkouts or closings before the completion of these government procedures is illegal and subject to punitive measures on the part of the government.

It should be noted that in Chile as in most of the other countries of Latin America, the labor code is not fully enforced. For instance, the government control over the internal affairs of the unions in Chile is much lighter than might be the case under the actual provisions of the law. The enforcement or nonenforcement of the control features of the labor codes depends to a large degree on the political situation in the respective countries. When a government in which the labor parties have much influence is in power, the labor code is likely to be strictly enforced for the employers and less strongly enforced in its provisions for the control of the unions. On the other hand, when a conservative régime comes to power, it usually uses the labor code to the utmost as a weapon for weakening its opponents. Cases of these two contrasting attitudes on the part of governments towards their labor laws are provided by the Chilean leftist governments since 1938, on the one hand, and the conservative régime which has been in power in Colombia since the middle of 1946.

This close control of the labor organizations by their governments through the medium of the labor codes can be exceedingly dangerous to the trade unions. For it can be used as a political weapon. This fact is best brought out in Argentina, where the legal mechanism established by Perón — in a country which previously had had but little formal labor legislation — has been one of the prime methods used by the government to make the unions subservient to the government's policies and politics. It is virtually impossible in present-day Argentina for a union which is led by those not in sympathy with the régime to obtain government recognition. Although the law specifies that the majority union in each industry or profession must be recognized by the government, a number of instances are well known in which the *Peronista* government recognized unions which were very small minority organizations but were *Peronista,* instead of recognizing old-line majority but anti-*Peronista* organizations. The result is that the anti-*Peronista* unions have virtually disappeared because it is practically impossible for such a union to function. For instance, it is now necessary for all collective bargaining negotiations to be channeled through the Secretariat of Labor and the Secretariat will, of course, not recognize the right of any union which does not have the so-called *personeria gremial* granted by the government to participate in such negotiations.

CONCLUSION

To sum up, the labor movements of Latin America are of increasing importance in the life of the twenty republics of that part of the world. During the last decade or more they have experienced an astoundingly rapid growth in size and importance. They are one of the most important expressions of a continent-wide awakening of " backward " peoples and " oppressed " classes there, which unrest is the most important factor in the social and political picture of that part of the New World.

The labor movements of Latin America are political in their leadership and policies. They are almost all controlled by politicians of one or another camp, five such groups being most important: Socialist, Communist, *Peronista, Aprista,* and Catholic, though in the past the anarchists and syndicalists played a very important role. This political control of the labor movements has in some ways aided their development through favorable treatment from sympathetic governments, labor codes defending the rights of the workers, and other means. On the other hand, the political influences in the labor movements of Latin America have tended to split the trade unions, and the labor codes themselves have imposed definite restrictions on the unions.

The labor unions of the New World have had several continental organizations, ranging from the " antipolitical " anarcho-syndicalist *ACAT* to the comparatively conservative Pan American Federation of Labor. At the present time the *Confederación de Trabajadores de America Latina* is the principal international labor group. Having originated as a real united front of the labor movements of the continent, it has in recent years become a spokesman for the Communists, and is now under a great deal of pressure both from within and without, from anticommunist elements.

With nearly 4,000,000 organized workers in Latin America, the trade union movement of that part of the world is bound to play an increasingly larger part in the affairs not only of its own region, but of the international labor movement as well. It is time that the democratic workers' organizations of the other parts of the world, and particularly of Europe, paid more attention to the labor movements of Latin America.

No. 37 [The masses in Latin America, largely denied a political voice in the old liberal-conservative alignment, are today playing an increasingly important role in Latin American government. One reason for this is the emergence of organized labor as a political force. A second explanation is the appearance, in some of the nations of Latin America, of political groups that seek to enlarge the political horizons of agricultural workers, of the Indian population, and of the economically insecure generally.

These so-called *Aprista* parties are indigenous; they reflect the economic problems of specific countries. The author of the following essay believes they are forerunners of new political alignments.]

The Latin American Aprista Parties*

by ROBERT J. ALEXANDER

*I*N recent years the masses have begun to play an increasingly active part in the political life of the Latin American countries. As a result, the traditional Conservative and Liberal parties, with their quarrels over the status of the Church, have in most countries become less important. In their stead have come groups with different appeals and programs, directed more toward the working class, peasants, industrial middle class, and intellectuals.

* Robert J. Alexander, "The Latin American *Aprista* Parties," *The Political Quarterly* (July–September, 1949), Vol. 20, No. 3, pp. 236–247. Reprinted by permission of *The Political Quarterly*.

Some of these parties are patterned on European models — socialists, communists, radicals. Others, however, are indigenous. Such are the *Peronista* and *Aprista* groups of parties. The first of these, which takes its name from Argentina's President Juan D. Perón, would perhaps be labelled " fascist " by the less sophisticated, but it is fascism with a difference, which draws most of its support from the trade unions and the working class in general, and is bitterly opposed by both the landlord and capitalist classes.

The *Aprista* parties, which are the subject of this article, form a group made up of parties which have grown up independently in their respective countries, which have had relatively little contact with one another, at least in their formative period, yet which have developed in a parallel way, due to the force of circumstances which are common at the present time to most of the Latin American countries.

The name for this conglomeration of parties comes from the senior member, the *Partido Aprista Peruano,* or People's Party of Peru. It has been formally organized as a political party since 1931, but its origins go back to the period following the 1914–18 war. The other *Aprista* parties are of more recent origin. They include the *Partido Revolucionario Cubano (Auténtico)*, generally called the *Auténtico* party, of Cuba, which was organized in the middle 1930's by Dr. Ramón Grau San Martín; the *Partido Acción Democrática* (Democratic Action party) of Venezuela, which was established in its present form in 1941, though its origins can be traced back to 1937, and which ruled Venezuela from October, 1945, until November, 1948.

Other *Aprista* parties are the *Partido Social Demócrata* of Costa Rica, established since the Second World War and the dominant factor in the revolutionary junta now governing that country; the *Partido Febrerista* of Paraguay, which was organized in the middle of the 1940's; and the *Mouvement Ouvrier et Paysan* of Haiti, headed by Dr. Daniel Fignolé, and established after the revolution of January, 1946. The Popular Democratic party of Puerto Rico, headed by the island's governor, Luis Muñoz Marín, should probably be included in this group, although it is not operating in an independent country.

The general principles of the *Aprista* parties are similar, though adapted in each case to the situation existing in the specific nation.

It must be emphasized, however, that the programs of the individual parties have grown up as the result of specifically local conditions, and that there is no central " brains trust." or directing authority. The similarity of approach on the part of the different groups results from the fact that in their individual countries, the parties have to face the same kinds of problems, and experience has taught them what they believe to be the correct approach to these problems.

The *Aprista* parties are young and have not developed political philosophers, with the exception of Victor Raúl Haya de la Torre, the great leader of the Peruvian People's Party. Therefore, there is no fount of given doctrine, and the remarks which follow concerning the programs of the *Aprista* parties are derived from many discussions which this writer has had with leaders and rank and file members of the various *Aprista* parties, and from the actions of the parties themselves.

The programs of the *Aprista* parties can probably be summed up in nine major points. Political democracy, agrarian reform, over-all economic planning, industrialization, socialization of industry, social security, education, nationalism, and inter-Americanism are the principles for which these parties stand.

The *Apristas* are among the principal exponents of political democracy in Latin America. Of course, in the world today it is virtually inconceivable for any political group openly to come out in opposition to the principle of democracy. Opposition is expressed through " interpretation." The *Apristas* do not try to interpret democracy out of existence. For instance, Haya de la Torre and Rómulo Betancourt, leader of the Venezuelan *Acción Democrática* party, have taken a strong position against the outlawing of any political party, even a totalitarian one. They justify their position on several grounds. In the first place, as believers in political democracy, they think that it is wrong in principle to outlaw any political group. They believe that suppression does not solve the problems which give rise to the growth of totalitarianism. Judging from the experience of his own party, Haya de la Torre feels that suppression is likely to make the totalitarians stronger by creating martyrs of them. Finally, they feel that the ideas of the communists and any other totalitarian group can be met and worsted in the field of argument, and if argument is backed up by effective action to end the conditions which give them a sounding board, the totalitarians need be no danger.

In actual practice, the *Aprista* parties have been almost unanimously democratic when they have had an opportunity to act otherwise. When the Peruvian People's Party won an election in 1945 and had an administration which, though not made up of *Apristas,* was friendly toward them, the party took no move whatsoever to persecute its defeated enemies, in spite of the fact that for fifteen years those enemies had kept the *Aprista* party illegal and had hounded its leaders and members unmercifully.

The Democratic Action party of Venezuela, which came to power in a *coup d'état* in October 1945, carried through reforms which brought real political democracy to Venezuela for the first time in its history. A new constitution was written, which for the first time adopted the principle of universal adult suffrage with the secret ballot.

Both the *Acción Democrática* régime in Venezuela and the pro-*Aprista* government in Peru were notable for the liberty which the average citizen enjoyed during them. For example, the trade union movement in both countries had been severely restricted previously, with frequent police intervention in the meetings of the labor organizations. Indeed, in Peru under the pre-1945 dictatorship it was impossible for a union to hold a meeting without a police officer present. All of this changed with the advent of the *Apristas* to power or the fringes of power. For the first time in their histories the labor movements of Venezuela and Peru were able to function freely without any interference from the police.

The same general picture can be obtained from the experience of the *Auténtico* government which has ruled Cuba since 1944. Although that government in many ways has not lived up to the hopes which were placed in it, the régime has steadfastly rejected all suggestions that it suppress civil liberties, and it has maintained the freedom of expression for all, from the communists to the reactionaries.

The only serious breach of democratic procedure by an *Aprista* party was committed by the *Partido Social Demócrata* in Costa Rica, which, after it came to power in a civil war early in 1948, outlawed the Communist party, which had been one of the principal supports of the defeated opposition. This writer was in Costa Rica about the time this decree was issued, and talked with leaders of the Social Democratic party and of the government, and in spite of the arguments put forward by these people, he feels that a mistake was made in taking this action — for much the same reasons put forward by Haya de la Torre and Betancourt.

Political democracy — defined as a régime in which there is freedom of press, speech, thought, and organization, in which rights of the parties opposed to the government are protected as well as those of the government supporters, and in which government is through duly elected representatives of the citizenry of the country — is, then, the first plank in the platform of the *Aprista* parties.

Perhaps the most revolutionary stand of the *Apristas* is their advocacy of agrarian reform. This problem is of varying importance in each country, but is most pressing in Peru. Most of the land is in the hands of large landowners, and from time immemorial they have had a running struggle with the ancient Indian communities which existed before the arrival of the white man. For the Indians it has been a losing battle.

The *Apristas* have sought to reverse this trend, to restore to the Indians the titles to their ancient lands, and then to help them adapt their age-old communal system of agriculture to modern agrarian techniques. At the same time, the *Apristas* have sought to push forward a great system of irrigation along the hot, dry coastal areas, which, indeed, under the ancient Incas were rich agricultural areas.

During the short period of legality of the *Aprista* party from 1945–48, it carried on a vigorous campaign on the behalf of the Indian communities. Indians would walk into Lima from as far as a thousand miles away to present their problems to the *Aprista* party, and the party carried their case before the proper governmental authorities. It was also pushing through parliament a general measure to allow confiscations in the case of land which was unused, or where the Indians were being brutally exploited. Their pushing of these measures probably had more to do with the *Aprista* party's being outlawed once again, after a *coup* in October 1948, than anything else in their program.

One of the most notable agrarian reform programs of an *Aprista* party is that of the Popular Democratic party of Puerto Rico. This group, when it came to power in 1940, found that there was on the statute books an old law passed by the United States Congress in 1900 and reiterated in 1917, according to which the amount of land which could be held by corporations was limited. This law had never been enforced. However, the Popular Democratic régime, under Senator Luis Muñoz Marín (now governor of the island), set out to enforce the law, and to give small plots of land to the " jíbaros " or agricultural workers. Of course, Muñoz Marín and his friends realize that there is not enough land on the island to go round, and they are therefore advocating industrialization and other measures, but the agrarian reform program is one of the keystones of the party's policy.

In Venezuela, too, the *Acción Democrática* régime has carried out interesting experiments in agrarian reform. The government already owned a great deal of land, which had been confiscated from the estates of defunct dictator Juan Vicente Gómez. On these and other government-held lands the *Acción Democrática* régime began experimenting with various kinds of settlements. Some of these were cocoperatives, where the land was owned by individuals, but farmed jointly. There were some cases in which land was given outright to individual farmers. There were yet others which were real collective farms. Also, the government experimented with settling some of the immigrants, whom they were attracting to the country, on these farms. In most cases, foreigners were mixed with native Venezuelans.

The *Apristas* are generally in favor of over-all government economic planning. They are not dogmatic in this regard, and have no specific means of achieving this planning upon which they all insist. And the degree to which the *Apristas* advocate general planning of the economy differs with the various parties. It is probably true that the *Auténtico* party has pushed this aspect of its program less than almost any other of the *Aprista* parties. On the other hand, the Peruvian People's Party has the most all-encompassing outline for economic planning of any of the *Aprista* groups.

Under the leadership of Haya de la Torre and of Carlos Manuel Cox, the Peruvian *Aprista* party's economics expert, the party has worked out a program for an economic congress, to be the principal element in the planning of the country's economy. This is to consist of representatives of the principal functional groups in society — the manual workers, the white-collar workers, the armed forces, the native industrialists, the foreign industrialists, the foreign and domestic mining interests, and various others.

It will be the duty of this economic congress continually to study the economic situation, and to draw up plans and programs for the economic development of the nation, which will be submitted to the political congress, which will continue to be based on universal adult suffrage exercised on a geographical basis, and will remain the legislative branch of the government.

The Venezuelan Democratic Action government got a chance to put into operation its ideas concerning general over-all planning of the economy. It organized the Venezuelan Development Corporation, which invested in a great many agricultural and manufacturing enterprises. Its work was coordinated with that of other government enterprises, such as the Agricultural and Grazing Bank, the Institute of Immigration and Colonization, and to direct the economy along the lines adopted by the government. The *Acción Democrática* government frankly adopted the policy of " sowing petroleum." The country is now experiencing a great boom based on the exploitation of its petroleum wealth. It is realized, however, that this wealth will not last for ever, and the *Acción Democrática* government decided that it would make the greatest possible use of this wealth to develop agricultural and manufacturing resources which would give the country a balanced economy when the petroleum is all gone.

Other *Aprista* parties also favor over-all guidance of their countries' economic life. The Social Democratic government of Costa Rica, for instance, took immediate steps to give the government powers of general direction of the economic system, by nationalizing the banks, and laying the groundwork for the establishment of a National Development Corporation.

Even the *Auténticos* have followed a policy of having the government direct the general lines of economic policy. Traditionally, they have sought to stabilize the price of sugar, the country's main product, while at the same time developing other industries which can reduce the exaggerated dependence of the island on its principal crop.

The *Aprista* parties have all supported the principle of industrialization. For the most part they have thought of it in terms of their own particular nations. However, Haya de la Torre has had wider visions of developing industrialization on regional lines. Thus as part of his program for inter-Americanism, he has advocated the planned development of manufacturing industries, and particularly of heavy industries among the South American countries, so as not to have duplication and to make the best possible use of the available resources and capital. The principle of stimulating industrialization through the mechanism of a development corporation has won the approval of all of the *Aprista* groups.

As an ultimate objective, the *Aprista* parties are generally in favor of socialization of industry. However, they are far from doctrinaire about the matter. Haya de la Torre has probably done more thinking on the subject than most of the other *Aprista* leaders, and his position is that though the party will probably one day ultimately want to socialize industry, that is not at the moment a pressing problem. As he explains, " We are not now faced with the problem of dividing the wealth, but with that of creating it."

The countries of Latin America, though possessing considerable wealth in natural resources, are poor in so far as actual factories, transportation facilities, and profitable agricultural establishments are concerned. And the *Apristas* feel that the immediate task is to develop the resources of the region and gain for its inhabitants a standard of living commensurate with Latin America's possibilities.

In line with this, the *Apristas* are anxious to get investments of all sorts. They realize that there is not enough capital in Latin American countries to push forward industrialization at the rate which they would like to see it develop, and that much of the capital already in Latin America shows a tendency to remain in comparatively unproductive types of agriculture or to go into commerce and urban real estate. Therefore, the *Apristas* recognize the need for the introduction of foreign capital into their countries. This matter will be discussed in another connection further on.

Although not pressing nationalization of industry at the present time, the *Apristas* will not refuse to socialize any industry on principle. They judge each case of nationalization on its merits. In practice, the problem more frequently arises as to whether the government shall take the initiative in launching a new enterprise. However, as instanced in the case of the nationalization of the banks by the Social Democratic party government of Costa Rica, the parties will nationalize if they think necessary.

As popular parties, appealing especially to the urban workers, the *Aprista* parties are strong backers of social security. Thus the Venezuelan *Acción Democrática* government pushed the development of a social security system, establishing it first in Caracas, having as its objective the extension of the system throughout the nation. In Peru, the *Apristas* drew up a project for a cradle-to-grave social security scheme, which they would have put into practice, if they could have stayed legal long enough. In Puerto Rico the Muñoz Marín régime has cooperated with the United States federal government in establishing a social security system in the island.

One of the cornerstones of the *Aprista* program is a crusading belief in the education of the masses. The original *Aprista* movement in Peru began right after the First World War as a move on the part of a group of students in Lima's San Marcos University to carry out an adult education program among the workers of Lima and Callao. When the government interfered with this, the students and their working-class allies turned to political action, and the *Aprista* movement was born. Ever since those days the Peruvian *Aprista* movement has been founded on an alliance of part of the country's intellectuals with working-class elements and the People's Party has taken a lead in conducting adult education work itself. During its period of legality from 1945 to 1948, the *Aprista* party established throughout the country a series of "popular universities" where workers could take a great variety of courses from reading and writing through advanced economics, history, and foreign languages. Each *Aprista* member who was able to do so was required to devote at least some time to instructing in these "popular universities." Those who needed to take the courses had that as part of their party duties.

In Venezuela, the *Acción Democrática* government's educational program during its three-year period in office was the most spectacular part of its entire administration. Attendance at the country's schools was doubled, the student body in the normal schools increased three- or four-fold, new school buildings went up, the educational system was extended into the countryside, which had been virtually without schools hitherto. Vast adult education programs also were carried out.

In Haiti, the new *Mouvement Ouvrier Paysan* of Professor Daniel

Fignolé lays great emphasis on worker education. Part of the head-quarters of the movement is used as a school, the organization has established smaller adult education centers in the countryside. Fig-nolé himself is a teacher, and was for a short while Minister of Edu-cation after the 1946 revolution.

Traditionally the *Aprista* parties are nationalist. The original *Aprista* party of Peru started in part as a movement to resist "Yan-kee imperialism," and the Cuban *Auténtico* party was founded on a similar basis. Although the direction of their attack has been some-what modified in recent years, the *Aprista* parties are still nationalist. However, they are not usually jingoistic.

Instead of pushing — as in times past — for the expulsion of for-eign capitalists from their countries, the *Aprista* groups now express their nationalist sentiments in seeing to it that these companies live up to the social laws of their respective countries. And the *Apristas* are interested in finding new ways in which the investment of for-eign capital in their nations can be intensified without the usual risks to the national sovereignty. In this connection, the *Acción De-mocrática* government of Venezuela worked out a very interesting arrangement with Nelson Rockefeller for the establishment of com-panies with participation by Rockefeller and the Venezuelan De-velopment Corporation, and with the proviso that the Venezuelans would have full stock control of the new enterprises within ten years.

The nationalism of the *Aprista* parties is much more akin to the universalist feeling of Mazzini and his friends in the nineteenth cen-tury than that sword-rattling jingoism of Hitler and his associates in the twentieth. It is not isolationism. One of the five fundamental propositions upon which the Peruvian *Aprista* movement was first launched was unity of the Latin American nations. Years later, in 1941, Haya de la Torre published a program for the Americans in which he advocated the immediate establishment of a customs union among the Latin American nations with a unified currency, customs regulations, etc., and then the formation of a continent-wide eco-nomic unit, including both Latin America and the United States and Canada. At the same time, he advocated the establishment of an inter-American mechanism for the maintenance of democracy within the republics of the hemisphere.

In practice, the *Aprista* parties have carried out their belief in inter-

Americanism. It was the Betancourt government in Venezuela which proposed the establishment of a customs union among Venezuela, Colombia, Ecuador, and Panama, a project which was finally agreed to at a conference in Quito, Ecuador, in the middle of 1948. In Costa Rica, the Social Democratic government has advocated the establishment of a Central American customs union, and also sent an observer to the Quito conference.

The broad outlines of the programs of the *Aprista* parties are similar. Likewise, the groups to which they make special appeal are broadly the same. First of all, they have a large following among the intellectuals in virtually every country in which they operate. The principal leaders of the *Aprista* parties are themselves intellectuals.

Their appeal is also to the urban working class. In every country where they are allowed to function freely, the *Aprista* parties either control the organized labor movement or are one of the two groups fighting for control. In recent years the *Apristas* won out over the communists in the labor movements of Peru, Cuba, Venezuela, and Costa Rica. In Paraguay, the *Febreristas* and communists are the two principal forces in the labor movement. In Puerto Rico, the Popular Democrats have a large following in the unions.

The *Aprista* parties make an appeal to the agricultural workers. During the 1945–48 period, the Peruvian People's Party laid special emphasis on helping the Indians and on recruiting among them. In Venezuela, the *Acción Democrática* people organized the first agricultural workers' federation in the country's history in 1947. In Cuba, the *Auténticos* have always had considerable support among the agrarian workers, support which was shown in the 1948 elections to have increased.

Finally, in some regions the manufacturing employers tend to be friendly toward the *Apristas*. This seemed to be true in Venezuela, during the *Acción Democrática* régime there. However, it probably should not be said that the majority of the members of this class are pro-*Aprista*.

The chief enemies of the *Apristas* are the landlords, and their political allies and spokesmen. The merchants also tend to be anti-*Aprista,* because the classical Latin American merchant importer does not particularly want to see industrialization. Nor is he favorable to a pro-working class outlook such as that of the *Apristas —*

which means lower prices and mass production rather than selling a
little bit at a high price.

The question arises as to whether or not the *Apristas* can be
equated with any world grouping of political parties. This writer
believes that the *Apristas* generally fall into the category of socialist
parties. They are certainly socialists with their own peculiarities, but
that is the most logical category in which to classify them.

The *Aprista* parties in their programs parallel very closely the
older type of socialist party. The principal items of programmatic
agreement among socialist parties are: social ownership and control
of the principal means of production and distribution, over-all economic planning, cradle-to-grave social security, and political democracy. On all of these points the *Aprista* programs are in agreement with the socialists, though sometimes with a difference in
emphasis.

Furthermore, the *Apristas* in many instances recognize their kin-
ship to the European socialists. They all tend to look with hope to
the British Labour party. In many cases, the *Apristas* use the word
" socialist " as synonymous with themselves. Thus in Venezuela, this
writer heard trade union leaders, both inside and outside the *Acción
Democrática* party, refer to members of that party as " the socialists,"
though this practice is not too widespread. In Peru, the principal
trade union leader of the *Aprista* party assured me that the People's
Party was really that country's socialist party (though there is a group
in Peru which calls itself *Partido Socialista*). In Cuba, one of the
principal leaders of the *Auténtico* trade union movement told me
that the best definition for the *Auténticos* was socialist nationalists.

Finally, the principal *Aprista* parties are united with the leading
socialist parties of the American continent in a very loosely organized
union of democratic and allied parties. This grouping, which has had
several plenary meetings and trade union conferences, includes the
socialist parties of Uruguay, Argentina, Chile, Ecuador, and Panama, and the *Aprista* party of Peru, *Acción Democrática* party of
Venezuela, and *Febrerista* party of Paraguay. Whether or not they
be socialist, the *Aprista* parties of Latin America are a leading element in the political picture of Latin America, and to a great degree
the future of political democracy and social progress in the continent
is tied up with these parties.

PART FIVE

Facing Contemporary Problems

CHAPTER 13

Dealing with the Land Problem

No. 38 [Many of the economists, sociologists, historians, and students of government who have written earlier articles in this book have emphasized the importance of land and systems of landownership in the economy, the society, and the government in Latin America. How the land is owned and worked is one of the basic conditioning factors of government there.

A land problem common to many Latin American countries is the large estate or *latifundio* system. The prevalence of the *latifundio* and the many questionable economic and political institutions that flow from it make it evident that social and political reform must be based on land reform. One may properly ask why the governments of Latin America do not take steps to broaden the base of landownership. Many of them have tried to do this, but only a few have succeeded.

The difficulties in the way of land redistribution are enormous. Politically, any step in this direction arouses the immediate and bitter opposition of the landed oligarchy which, as we have seen, has so long controlled the politics of the Latin American republics. The landowners, to protect their own property and social interests, have continually sought the aid and support of the Church (itself a large landholder in several countries) and the army in order to block land reform. A systematic study of the causes of revolution in Latin America would reveal that a high percentage of these political upheavals have been touched off either by a program of land redistribution or by an opposition to such action.

Most students of the problem would probably agree that Mexico is the Latin American state in which land reform has been most vigorously advocated through public policy, and in which, in fact, the most extensive acreage of land has actually been redistributed. Although opinions, in and out of Mexico, are still violently divided as to the soundness and wisdom of the kind of land policy that has been followed by the Mexican government, the fact remains that thousands upon thousands of former *peons* are now farming land which in most cases they communally own, land which was formerly the property of a few owners.

The author of the following article indicates the social and political theories that underlie Mexican agrarian reform, the action that has been taken, and how this program has affected the former landowners, the new class of small farmers, and the Mexican nation as a whole.]

Land for Peons — Agrarian Reform in Mexico*

by CHARLES A. THOMSON

I T is one of the paradoxes of modern history that alongside these United States, the world's leading capitalistic nation, there has developed what is probably the world's most socialistic country with the exception of Soviet Russia. Certainly, Mexico's large-scale program of peaceful socialization is not paralleled elsewhere in Latin America. While in recent years most of the other nations to the south have moved to the right, Mexico has shifted to the left. It is engaged in an active effort to lift the economic and social level of its working masses and to gain for Mexicans, as opposed to foreigners, a larger share of the national wealth.

But when we talk of Mexican socialism, the accent must be on the

* Charles A. Thomson, " Land for Peons . . . Agrarian Reform in Mexico," *The Southwest Review* (January, 1938), Vol. XXIII, No. 2, pp. 148–166. Reprinted by permission of *The Southwest Review*.

adjective Mexican. For socialism in Mexico is *sui generis*. It is distinctly different from the Russian brand. Mexico's revolution, starting in 1910, had a seven years' start over the Russian movement, and has developed in substantial independence of the Soviet experiment. Nationalism, the desire to remake Mexico for the Mexicans, has been a far more important influence than Marxism. The labor movement is dominated by Marxist leaders, but in other social activities, Mexican socialism is something much more vague, much less dogmatic than the teachings of *Das Kapital*. Some years ago when I asked one of Mexico's most brilliant younger leaders to define Mexican socialism, he smiled, hesitated, at first declared that it could not be done, and finally said that it meant substantially bettering the lot of the common man.

The Mexican Revolution was the result, not of propaganda from the outside, but of conditions inside Mexico. It sprang fundamentally out of the people, out of the soil. It was anonymous, as Tannenbaum has said. Seven years of turbulent and confusing struggle passed before its principles found conscious expression in the Constitution of 1917. It has thrown up its leaders from the masses; and when these latter have played their followers false, the revolution has devoured them. Calles was the last of a long line who have been overturned or pushed to the side as the Revolution has moved onward.

The Mexican Revolution found a new focus for its forces in the person of President Lázaro Cárdenas, who entered office on November 30, 1934. In contrast to the reactionary trend which had set in under Calles, Cárdenas brought a revival of energy and enthusiasm to Mexico's quarter-century campaign for social revolution. Under him new stimulus has been given to the drives toward greater nationalism, more effective political democracy, land reform, labor organization, popular education, and limitation of the powers of the Church.

This simple and democratic president of Mexico is to my mind one of the most remarkable figures of the present-day world. In part a Tarascan Indian, from the southwestern state of Michoacán, he left school at the age of thirteen, to be the chief breadwinner for his widowed mother and seven brothers and sisters. Five years later he joined the armies fighting for the revolution, and rose rapidly until at the age of twenty-four he was made a general. Later he was elected governor of his native state of Michoacán. In his administration he mingled devotion to such solid virtues as economy and a balanced budget with energetic application of social reforms — distribution of lands to the Indians, construction of schools, roads, and railways, and enforcement of the anti-Church laws.

Cárdenas now rules Mexico as a paternalistic dictator, but among dictators he is probably unique. Not so much, perhaps, in his tremendous energy, although that is remarkable. He works from early morning to midnight and after, and easily tires out his most devoted collaborators. He has a rare degree of personal courage — for him no armored motorcars or escorts flourishing submachine guns such as many Latin American rulers employ. He is said never to carry a weapon, and on his frequent trips through the country, his personal bodyguard is often left far behind as the president mingles in large crowds. More exceptional probably, his personal honesty is admitted by his most bitter opponents. He is somewhat of a puritan in his personal habits, and does not smoke or drink. He is genuinely modest, and happily free from that eager appetite for adulation so common among dictators in Latin America and elsewhere.

While his government is not one " by the people," its popular support and its aims make it to a considerable degree a government " of the people and for the people." He has moved to refashion the official National Revolutionary party, and to give the workers and peasants greater representation in its membership, which had previously been confined to government employees and officeholders. Much of his time he has spent in extended trips through the country, interviewing officials and local leaders, but also spending hours in patient attention to the pleas of humble farmers and artisans. Asked why he did not try to save his strength he replied: " *Por Dios,* these people need so much. At least, patience I have to give them." Through these trips he not only keeps close to the people, but he cuts bureaucratic red tape, and builds for himself a political machine which rests directly on the support of the masses.

President Cárdenas has been called both a communist and a fascist. In fact, he is neither. He is a man of action rather than an intellectual. His thinking is guided not by a fixed body of doctrine, but by a few fundamental convictions. His associates say he reads widely, but his ideas have been shaped far less by books than by the conditions of life in Mexico which he finds and sees and touches. If he has what could be termed a philosophy, it is to help the ordinary and common man. He naturally aligns himself with the worker as against the employer, with the land-hungry peasant as against the great *hacendado*. He sees his goals clearly, but he picks his way to them step by step, by whatever gradual, winding, opportunistic way may open up. Probably the most important goal in Cárdenas' mind is the return of the land to the people. Agrarian reform is the primary plank in his platform. That was the fundamental demand of the revolution. It must be satisfied, he believes, if Mexico is to have social peace. But it is necessary for other reasons, too. When asked why he considered this program so urgent, Cárdenas answered: " Because a peon cannot be a citizen. No one can be a citizen unless he walks on something that is his own." In his view, if Mexico is to have self-respecting citizens, they must be free men, economically as well as politically.

But historically Mexico has been a country of vast estates. Land monopoly by the few has gone hand in hand with landlessness for the many. The *hacienda* has steadily encroached upon and swallowed up the *ejidos,* the communal lands of the villages. In 1910 from 95 to 99 percent of rural families in most of the states owned no land. Agrarian reform got under way in 1915, but at best it advanced at a halting pace. After fifteen years, the agricultural census of 1930 revealed that more than 80 percent of all the land in privately owned farms was still in plantations of 2,500 acres and over. At the same time, some 2,500,000 persons working in agriculture were landless; that is, seven tenths of the agricultural population were condemned to the role of a rural proletariat, dependent for their livelihood on day wages or such a meager income as they could gain from share-cropping or tenant-farming. If you want more facts of this character, read Eyler N. Simpson's *The Ejido: Mexico's Way Out,* a masterly study of the agrarian problem, and the most important book on Mexico published in recent years.

It would be incorrect, of course, to assume that all Mexico's agricultural problems would be solved if its lands were divided more fairly. There are other difficulties in the picture. Mountains make much of Mexico a country on end, and less than half of its area can

be classified as level. Likewise less than half of the republic, it is estimated, has enough rainfall for efficient agriculture. Of the 485,000,-
000 acres which make up Mexico's territory, only 7.4 percent is listed
as crop land, 33.8 percent as pasture, and 13.2 as forest — in all, some
280,000,000 acres of what might be called *agricultural* land. The balance of 45.6 per cent is in large part uncultivable. In contrast to Mexico's 7.4 percent of crop land, the proportion in most European countries runs between 20 and 40 percent. But to these natural handicaps,
the *hacienda* system added further barriers to progress. It often prevented the most efficient use of land, retarded agricultural development, and by its economic inequalities made social and political advance almost impossible.

Before we go farther in this discussion of Mexico's land reform,
we must understand the meaning of the word *ejido*. It is a descend-
ant of the Latin verb *exire,* " to go out." In Spain the term was applied originally to the uncultivated lands lying on the outskirts (on
the way out) of a rural village; these lands were held collectively. In
present-day Mexico the word is used in connection with lands
granted to villages under the agrarian reform, and is sometimes extended to the village itself. The communal lands held in the *ejido* are
to be clearly distinguished from the small, privately owned farms.
Title to the former is held not by the individual, but by the village.
The fertile part of these common lands is divided into small plots
of approximately equal size, which are given out to the heads of the
families living in the village. These persons are called *ejidatarios*.
The *ejidatario* holds his land as long as he lives, and can pass it on
to his heir. But he must farm it steadily, and loses his rights if he
fails to do so two years in succession. Nor can he sell, mortgage, or
rent the plot.

By the middle of 1933 a sharp division of opinion had developed
between two groups of Mexican leaders, as to the program and goals
of agrarian reform. Simpson calls these groups respectively *veteranos*
and *agraristas*. The former, led by ex-President Calles, held that the
program of land distribution had substantially failed to achieve the
results desired. The *ejido* had not lived up to expectations. As a system of collective or communal holding, it was declared to be economically inefficient. The plots assigned had been too small for cultivation by modern methods. This group argued that the *ejido* should

be regarded as a transitory form of agricultural organization, to give way eventually to a system of small properties, whose size, however, should be sufficient to " encourage and stimulate men of ambition." They declared that the program of distribution had already extended over too much time, so that the confidence of landowners had been undermined and production seriously diminished. The *veteranos* held consequently that *ejido* distribution should be wound up as speedily as possible, and that major emphasis in the future should be placed on the creation of a large number of middle-class independent farmers.

The *agraristas* yielded no whit to the *veteranos* in criticism of agrarian policies followed in the past. But they differed profoundly from their opponents on the future direction of the movement. They demanded that complete socialization of the land should be the goal. The *ejido* should be recognized not as a transitory but as a permanent feature of the country's agricultural system. In fact, if Mexico were to be saved " from a new cycle of concentration of rural property," the *ejido* should become the fundamental unit in a new social and economic organization of agricultural life. With this goal in view, the program of distribution would have to continue for an indefinite period, since the establishment of *ejidos,* in relation to the total need, had really only begun.

How far had the agrarian program advanced when President Cárdenas took office? Some 20,250,000 acres had been distributed to peasant communities, which included 806,000 heads of families. Yet the needs of 1,200,000 heads of families, entitled under existing legislation to receive lands, were still unmet; and an additional 1,000,000 persons engaged in agriculture — principally plantation laborers and residents of small villages — were also unsatisfied. Thus, in comparison with the 800,000 farmers supplied with plots, some 2,200,000 were still landless. Progress had also been slow in breaking up the *haciendas* or large plantations. Approximately two thirds of the big holdings had been left undisturbed.

The Six-Year Plan, which was in effect the party platform for the Cárdenas administration, called for aggressive advance on agrarian reform. It pledged lands and water to " all centers of population " lacking them. But at the same time the document declared for respect of small private properties, thus straddling on the point at issue between the *veteranos* and the *agraristas*.

President Cárdenas on entering office lost no time in casting his lot substantially with the *agraristas*. While he has not been unfriendly to the small farmer class, his major influence has been directed toward rapid expansion of the land reform and an increased emphasis on the *ejido*. In a speech delivered at Torreón on November 30, 1936, he stressed its importance in the following terms:

In the early stages of the Revolution there may possibly have been some people in whose mind the *ejido* was but a mere supplement to the wage-earning system and insufficient in itself to guarantee the land laborer the economic independence that is the foundation of every civil liberty. But this view exerts no influence whatsoever on the fulfillment of the duties of the Government today. Groups of peasants were in the past given worthless bits of land, and lacked farming implements, equipment, credit, and organization. . . . But the nation's conception of the *ejido* has been in reality far other. . . . As an institution [the *ejido*] shoulders a double responsibility: as a social system it must make the country worker free from the exploitation to which he was subject under the feudal as well as under the individualistic system; and as a system of agricultural production it must render such a yield as to provide the country at large with food. . . .

The Constitution further guarantees the permanence and the stability of the *ejido* institution, preventing its absorption by large estates as well as its degeneration into individual holdings so small as to defeat the ends desired of it.

Effective as was this statement, the actions of President Cárdenas have been even more eloquent. During the first 3 years of his administration, almost 29,000,000 acres of land were distributed to 663,000 peasants, an area nearly 50 percent greater than the total amount of land allotted during the preceding 20 years. Altogether, between 1915 and 1938, some 49,000,000 acres have been divided — almost one fifth of Mexico's estimated 280,000,000 acres of *agricultural* land.

But Mexico has come to realize that it is not enough to give a prospective farmer a piece of land. If he is to secure implements, seed, work animals, and to keep himself and his family alive until harvest time, he must have credit. He must also belong to a community where he can feel at home. Consequently, the government program has been threefold in character, complementing the division of land with the extension of agricultural credit and the organization of *ejido* or village communities, including the establishment of producers' and consumers' cooperatives. President Cárdenas reorganized the system of rural credit. A National Bank of Agricultural Credit had been set up as early as 1926, but most of its funds had been absorbed by large landowners. Reorganizations effected in 1931 and 1934 included provisions for loans to small farmers and also to *ejidatarios* or communal farmers. But this type of loan was to be made only to local cooperative societies, grants of credit to individuals being prohibited. The cooperatives in turn were to extend advances to their individual members, and in addition were to furnish them with seed, fertilizers, and farming implements, and to organize the production and marketing of crops.

At the end of 1935 facilities for the financing of communal farmers were further improved by the establishment of a new and separate bank, the National Bank of *Ejido* Credit, which was to concentrate solely on the needs of this class. It was founded with an authorized capital of 120,000,000 pesos, which the federal government pledged itself to cover in full before the end of the Six-Year Plan. During 1936 this new bank, in addition to advances of about 9,000,000 pesos for the Laguna region alone, granted loans amounting to 26,400,000 pesos. These went to some 3,400 local cooperative societies, representing 300,000 communal farmers or about one fourth of the total number of *ejidatarios* in the country. The 26,400,000 pesos were divided as follows: 17,000,000, or approximately two thirds, for living expenses to the communal farmers and their families (to take the place of the wages they formerly received as farm hands); 7,500,000, or most of the remaining one third, for seeds, animals, and implements; 400,000 for improvements on lands and buildings; and 1,000,000 in commercial credits. At the end of the year, 14,000,000 pesos had been repaid to the bank — 10,000,000 in cash and 4,000,000 in produce.

In theory this plan was directed toward ultimate control of the bank by the communal farmers. Their local credit societies were to purchase its stock, in accordance with a program which would give them ownership in twenty-five years. But actually the process at present represents an extension of state socialism. Almost despotic powers are concentrated in the hands of the bank. It controls overseers in the villages who keep account of the hours worked by each farmer. A peso and a half are advanced for each eight-hour day. At harvest time, after the bank has been reimbursed for its short-term loans, any profits remaining are to be divided among the communal farmers in proportion to the number of working days each individual has put in. Critics have pointed out that it is the bank which organizes the local credit societies, decides what crops are to be cultivated, furnishes the money for expenses, names the foreman, pays wages, collects and sells the harvests, carries the accounts, and finally has the say as to who can work. From this point of view, the peon has only changed masters and substituted for the landowner the more impersonal overlordship of the bank.

The most significant feature of the agrarian program under the Cárdenas administration has been the attempt to reorganize the economic and social foundations, not merely of single villages but of entire regions. The first experiment in this field was begun in the Laguna region in October, 1936. This area, lying in the north-central section of the country, might be called Mexico's Egypt, since its soil consists of alluvial deposits laid down by two rivers — the Nazas and Aguanaval which, incidentally, have no outlet. These rivers are irregular in their floods, and artesian wells are used for supplementary irrigation. By 1920 the Laguna had become the most important agricultural zone in Mexico, with the possible exception of Yucatán. Its principal crops, cotton and wheat, were in great part raised on big plantations, many of which were owned by British and Spanish citizens. Irrigation works and large-scale cultivation had called for extensive capital investments.

Until President Cárdenas entered office, the landholders in the region had succeeded in avoiding partition of their estates. But a strike of farm hands in August, 1936, led to an appeal to the President, and a decision on his part to begin distribution of land in the area. He issued a decree ordering the allotment of communal lands to all needy villagers and farm hands. Existing owners were allowed to keep a maximum of 370 acres of irrigated land.

President Cárdenas himself spent a good part of November and December in the region, supervising the land division and the organization of the *ejido* villages. Large amounts of agricultural machinery were shipped in. New schools were established. Housewives were organized in village groups to work for pure water, better housing, more adequate sanitation, consumers' cooperatives, and to campaign against drunkenness and vice. One observer reported:

The peasants spent the day and even the night in visits to their *tierritas* [little lands], counted on their fingers, gathered at sunset and exchanged impressions like partners in a business, whose prosperity left them perplexed. . . . They worked in the *ejidos* even at night, by the light of lamps carried by the tractors.

Some 600,000 acres were distributed to approximately 30,000 peasants. It was estimated that the area divided represented about two thirds of the cultivable portion of the region; the other third remained in the hands of the former owners. But since members of this group had been permitted to select the lands they would keep, the result was that their third was reported to contain about two thirds of the artesian wells. It is well to keep in mind, therefore, that the Laguna region represents not a completely collectivized system of agriculture, but a mixed system, in which both *ejidos* and individual properties are operating side by side.

Following this effort to remake the Laguna region, the government focused its attention in August, 1937, on the rich henequen-producing area in Yucatán, Mexico's southeastern peninsula. Here, according to the estimate of one government agent, 40 individuals controlled the production of 50 percent of the fiber. During 1937, 250,000 acres were reported distributed to 8,000 peasant families living in 42 villages. The same general procedure was followed as in the Laguna region. Large holdings were broken up, the owner being left with a maximum of 370 acres of fiber-producing land and a corresponding area of uncultivated land. The territories expropriated were distributed among small farmers in parcels of about 10 acres. These *ejidatarios* were to be assisted financially through the National Bank of *Ejido* Credit. A state-sponsored organization was also to regulate the production of the fiber, and to control its sale and that of products manufactured from it, principally binder twine. The entire henequen zone in the state of Yucatán has been estimated to cover some 2,400,000 acres. But only 400,000 acres, approximately, is planted to henequen; and of this cultivated acreage, about two fifths is producing fiber, the remainder containing henequen plants in various stages of growth. It has recently been reported that some of the cooperative farms set up by the agrarian reform have been placed under the supervision of former henequen planters, as employees of the *ejidatarios,* and are being successfully operated. As a third large-scale move, the Cárdenas administration toward the close of 1937 took over some 52,000 acres, principally from 40 American citizens, situated in the Yaqui Valley of the northwestern state of Sonora.

In the Laguna region, the majority of lands taken were British-owned; Mexican landholders were principally affected in Yucatán; but in the case of the Yaqui Valley, Americans were the chief sufferers. What has been Mexico's policy about compensating property owners for lands seized? The legal basis for the agrarian reform was laid down in Article 27 of the 1917 constitution. This article sought to substitute for the individualistic theory of private property what has been called the theory of " social use." The latter theory recognizes the right of private property, but argues that group interests inevitably take precedence over the interests of the individual; and individual interests must at times be sacrificed to forward group interests.

The constitution, while recognizing the right of private property, declared that " the ownership of lands and waters comprised within the limits of the national territory is vested originally in the Nation." The state was asserted to " have at all times the right to impose on private property such limitations as the public interest may demand. . . . For this purpose necessary measures shall be taken to divide large landed estates; to develop small landed holdings; to establish new centers of rural population with such lands and waters as may be indispensable to them." Article 27 also prescribed that " private property shall not be expropriated except for reasons of public utility and by means of (*mediante*) indemnification "; and provided that payment for property taken was to be made on the basis of the declared value of the holding for taxation, plus 10 percent. Landholders were offered 20-year, 5-percent bonds in payment. In most cases they have refused to accept payment in this form. They have argued that the real value of their lands is far greater than the declared value for taxation, and have demanded immediate payment in cash rather than delayed compensation through bonds. Moreover, service on the bonds issued has not been kept up, so that within recent years they have been quoted at about one tenth of their face value. Although the total agrarian debt of the government has been estimated at somewhere between 660,000,000 and 950,000,000 pesos, only 24,000,000 pesos' worth of bonds have been delivered to landowners.

United States citizens, who before the agrarian reform got under way owned approximately one tenth of the private lands in Mexico, have suffered from land seizures along with other foreigners and with Mexicans. For almost twenty years the United States and Mexico have been engaged in recurring controversy over compensation for lands seized. At first the Washington government attempted to uphold the individualistic theory of private property, and argued that land could not be taken except for a public purpose, and then only on payment of " actual, fair, and full compensation." But by 1923 the dispute had narrowed down to a discussion of the adequacy of the payment offered for lands which citizens of the United States had owned when the Mexican constitution went into effect in 1917. There was, apparently, tacit recognition of the fact that owners who had acquired lands after that date had done so with a knowledge of the existing agrarian legislation and of the risks they were running. The so-called Bucareli conferences of 1923 achieved a temporary measure of agreement, which, however, Mexico soon after refused to recognize. Ambassador Morrow was not able to make any substantial change in the situation, except to use his influence to slow up the program of agrarian reform. A General Claims Commission was set up in 1924 to consider claims for damages against both the United States and Mexico, but agrarian claims were later excluded from its jurisdiction. At present no international machinery exists for the settlement of controversies over land seizures, and the State Department at Washington relies solely on diplomatic negotiations.

When any seizure now affects an American citizen, the Department urges the Mexican government to make a satisfactory adjustment with the owner. Such representations have led to promises of compensation, but apparently no substantial indemnification. Mexico's position is that it wishes to pay, and will provide compensation when it is financially able to do so. But at the moment it can take no further steps. Since 1933, in fact, Mexico has suspended both the issuance of new agrarian bonds and service on existing bonds. The most tangible recent move on the part of the Mexican government was the proposal made to United States citizens who lost lands in the Yaqui Valley. They were offered compensation in the form of other lands, of inferior quality, at the ratio of one and one-half acres of new lands for every acre of good land taken.

As yet it is too early to pass judgment on the results of President Cárdenas' major experiments in the Laguna and Yucatán. But on the Laguna region at least, data are available to bring our story fairly up to date. Production of the two principal crops suffered to some degree during the first year. Some 120,000 bales of cotton were harvested (of which 80,000 to 90,000 bales were produced on *ejido* lands), as compared to 157,000 for the previous year, during which, it is reported, conditions were exceptionally favorable. Wheat acreage was reduced from 100,000 to 20,000 acres for 1937, but increased in 1938 to 75,000 or 80,000. Moreover, the National Bank of *Ejido* Credit, which had been delayed in selling the cotton of the 1937 harvest, was pinched for funds, and consequently not in position to make advances desired by the communal farmers to prepare the fields for the next crop and carry on other slack-time work. Unrest developed and by February 1938 the situation threatened to become acute. From one third to one half of the 30,000 peasant farmers in the region were declared to be without work, and the remainder were working only three or four days a week. In a public protest meeting at Torreón, a resolution to President Cárdenas was approved, demanding extension of immediate aid, authorization of credit, reforms in the bank, and an amendment permitting the institution to loan more than 70 percent of the probable value of the crops.

It may fairly be argued, of course, that the results of the first year alone do not provide an accurate index for any large-scale experiment. Extensive unemployment during the early months of the year has been a recurring phenomenon in the Laguna area. Some degree of disorganization inevitably resulted from such an economic and social revolution. The *Ejido* Bank also was apparently guilty of some administrative mistakes. Moreover, nature was accused of not cooperating with the government.

But regardless of adverse factors, it may be expected that agrarian reform will be actively pushed in Mexico, as long as President Cár-

denas is in office. Before his term is out in 1940, he apparently hopes
to come close to breaking up all the *haciendas*. His aim is to make
Mexico a country of small holdings. Although he prefers the communal system of the *ejido*, he is not likely to take hostile action
against existing privately owned farms of moderate size. The speed
at which this program can advance, with its demands for extensive
agricultural credit, will naturally depend in large degree on the nation's finances. If the present petroleum controversy leads to curtailment of Mexico's all-important oil and silver exports, government
revenues will be sharply cut, a political overturn may be threatened,
the country will have to pull in its belt, and the land program will
suffer along with other plans of the administration.

Irrespective of these immediate possibilities, Mexico's agrarian reform has now gone far enough to reveal the tremendous difficulties
barring the way toward ultimate success. The *ejido* program, as
President Cárdenas has indicated, seeks two goals: first, as a social
system, to free the rural worker from the exploitation he suffered
under the feudal as well as the capitalistic system; and second, as an
economic system, to produce the food which Mexico needs. Can the
political boss in the local *ejido* be prevented from becoming a worse
tyrant than the former landowner? To date, graft, corruption, and
violence have been all too prevalent in many communal villages.
Can the extension of agricultural credit by the central government
be so controlled that national credit agencies will not become organs
of absentee domination, exploiting the peasants to the advantage of
the reigning political group at the capital? There is the further question whether all the rural landless can be provided with plots without extensive redistribution of the population, a problem complicated all the more by the Mexican's fervent devotion to the spot
where he was born. And what of the *ejido* as a production unit?
The *hacienda* is conceded by most students to have been economically inefficient. But can the *ejido* overcome the tendency of the
Mexican peasant to grow only enough food for his own needs, thus
failing to produce the necessary surplus for distribution to the rest
of the people in the country? Government supporters quote statistics
to prove that *ejido* plots are more intensively farmed than privately
owned land. It is generally admitted that the peasant is better fed
and better off than formerly. But Mexico still imports corn and

wheat; and if agricultural production has not decreased, it has shown no marked increase.

If agrarian reform is to bring lasting benefit to Mexico, her leaders are faced with the necessity of supplementing the program of land distribution and credit extension with a fundamental re-education of the peasant masses. Happily the Cárdenas régime is giving major attention to this task; for only if Mexico's peasants learn to work their land more efficiently, and to work together more constructively, will the *ejido* prove to be " Mexico's Way Out " toward a better life.

No. 39 [Land redistribution alone will not improve the social, economic, and political position of the Latin American peon. The *latifundio* system, despite its many disadvantages, did make it possible to accumulate the capital needed for the purchase of modern equipment and the utilization of the latest technological advances in agriculture. If a large estate *is* broken up and redistributed among the many peons who formerly worked the land for the owner, these newly "independent" farmers would be immediately confronted with the problem of financing the purchase of seed, machinery, fertilizers, and insecticides. It must be recalled that the peon is penniless and has no savings, credit, or other financial resources to help him work and manage his farm. Unless some means are found to provide working capital for the new owners and to enable them to take advantage of the most improved and efficient agricultural techniques, land redistribution might result in a lowering of farm production. This has occurred in more than one instance.

Part of the preceding article discussed the question of making working capital available to the new owners. In the following article the emphasis is on a governmental program that has as its objective bringing to the farmer, at a cost that he *can* pay, the results and the advantages of the most recent technological developments in the science of farming.

Programs similar to that of *SCIPA* are now found in several of the Latin American states. There is every indication that this approach to the problems of land utilization will increase in significance within the next few years. It might be noted that our Point Four Program could be of the greatest importance in the Latin American land and agricultural changes that are to come.]

SCIPA *Means Food**

by ROBERT K. SHELLABY

I was standing at the edge of an *hacienda* in one of Peru's rare fertile coastal valleys that bridge the gap between Andean foothills and the sea. Across the dusty road I saw fields being tilled by the primitive wooden plow pulled by an ox. On my side of the road, I watched a United States-built tractor cultivating in a matter of hours what it was taking days to do by oxen a few feet away.

The contrast was one of Peru with and without modern techniques. The tractor came from a machinery pool that is part of the Peruvian-United States cooperative food-growing program.

During the five years this scheme has been under way, Peru has enormously increased production of high-nourishment foods, and has helped feed United States troops stationed there for defense of the Panama Canal. Unselfishly, the United States has helped finance the undertaking as part of its Good Neighbor policy. Selfishly, it has done more than procure food and friendship for its troops: it has developed a trade partner, whose purchases of farm machinery, insecticides, and other supplies are steadily rising. One recent order surpassed in value all the money the United States is now spending on the plan.

In Peru the program is known as "*SCIPA*," from the initials of *Servicio Cooperativo Interamericano de Producción de Alimentos.* It operates as a special executive agency of the Ministry of Agriculture. Originally, equal funds came from both countries. Now Peru contributes at least three dollars to every one coming from the world-pressed taxpayer in the States.

Through February of this year, the five-year program had received $1,249,000 from the United States. Peru had agreed to match this amount with $1,536,000, but exceeded its share by $701,000. Thus Peru has shouldered about two thirds of the cost, with its percentage still growing.

* Robert K. Shellaby, "SCIPA Means Food," *Américas* (May, 1949), Vol. 1, No. 3, pp. 15–19. Reprinted by permission of *Américas,* a monthly magazine published by the Pan American Union in English, Spanish, and Portuguese.

Because of the Peruvian project's success, President Truman pointed to it as a model in asking Congress to extend for five years the Institute of Inter-American Affairs, which sets the cooperative machinery in motion for these programs. Until Mr. Truman's 1949 request, the Institute had been limping along on a year-to-year basis, at the mercy of Congress, causing embarrassing uncertainty in Peru. But the work has proved so effective that Mr. Truman also mortared it into his famous " Point Four " proposal in his inaugural speech, calling for a world-wide program of technical aid for undeveloped countries.

Peru's cooperative plan has weathered the severest tests. Only those who know the country first-hand can appreciate its almost air-tight division geographically and climatically. Its four distinct regions are also isolated as far as economic development and communication are concerned.

The 1,500-mile-long coastal shelf, largely desert, fronts a country as large as the three United States Pacific Coast states plus Arizona. Hardly 5 percent is under cultivation, while most of the 52 rivers are useless or almost so. Peruvian-United States teams are teaching water conservation and hope to work out means of irrigating the desert.

Next up the hill from the sea is the *sierra,* or forbidding Andean ranges. The three to five parallel ranges have peaks up to 22,000 feet, half again as high as anything in the mainland United States. Yet the high plains and valleys above 10,000 feet can be irrigated by conserving seasonal rainfall. Already 3,500,000 acres are under cultivation, three times the coastal cultivated area. But miserable roads frustrate exports.

Beyond lies the *montaña,* fertile slopes east of the continental ridges, where rivers and rainfall are abundant. But here impenetrable forests have kept cultivation down to barely half that on the coast. A meager population plus wretched communications check development of cash crops for export to less favored regions.

Finally, there is the *selva,* the forest covering 40 percent of Peru. Here population and cultivation are the smallest of all four areas, but by no means potentially the smallest.

Aviation is making valiant efforts to knit the regions together, but nothing like mass transportation has been developed. Astride this defiant terrain, Peruvian-United States teamwork is driving toward better food for Peruvians, more diversified products for their " money " or export crops, and a general lifting of their living standards.

Nature's challenge along the coast was seared into my memory by the 93-mile drive north from Lima along the ocean to visit the typical extension station near Huacho. The arid Pacific Southwest in the United States is a rose garden compared to the mountainous, empty sand hills of this Peruvian Sahara. Dropping over a verdureless lip of sand into the valley housing Huacho was like coming upon an oasis. Although it is a main coastal community, Huacho is detached and far enough from Lima to be untouched by tourism or the more baneful effects of modern civilization. In microcosm, it was struggling, deserving Peru.

Huacho is one of the thirty *SCIPA* country stations, something like the familiar county agricultural agent in the United States. Here the staff was Peruvian, except for visiting experts, one an Englishman, the other a North American. All were fighting shoulder to shoulder in the battle for Peru's economic independence.

Cotton was being cultivated into a major product, as an edible oil and as a cash crop. Irrigable land stretched for miles away from the broad valley mouth. If only leading landowners could be persuaded to use scientific weapons, innumerable smaller farmers would be sure to imitate. The success so far encouraged further hope.

I saw both small farmers and *hacienda* operators reaping benefits from machinery pools like the one at the Huacho station. That one was organized under Ernesto Morante, *SCIPA's* capable rural agent. Señor Morante is one of those hardy combinations of experienced farmer and articulate adviser who have meant so much to the program. " The tractor pools have been a big help to the small farmers who have five acres or less," he pointed out. " Plowing by a yoke of oxen costs them at least 200 soles (then about eighteen to the dollar) per *fanegada,* or about one-and-a-half acres. With a *SCIPA* tractor, the cost is about half."

Señor Morante's principal aides are Toribio Velarde, office manager, and Augusto Bohórquez, field chief. They figured that in one year 3,219 hectares had been plowed by their pool. Operations included clearing, plowing, harrowing, furrowing, seeding, and leveling, to cultivate beans, corn, rice, cotton, yucca, and other food products. The 7,136 hours of work in surrounding valleys helped 16 *haciendas* plus 30 other landowners.

"We're banking on continuation of the project," Morante told me. "It's a decisive factor now because of the scarcity of farm machinery." Five staff members and I toured the plowing areas, then headed for the insecticide "sales" demonstration up the sand-wreathed valley.

On the whole, the *hacienda* appeared to be heading for renewed prosperity. The farm hands' pay was rising. More food was being grown to supplement their pay. However, while the manor house looked comfortable enough for a hard-pressed venture in an unfriendly climate, the field hands' housing was distressingly primitive. Still, as one member of our party remarked: "We are starting at the right place. If we get the fields to produce more and keep the crops well sprayed, then better housing will follow."

Perhaps the most gratifying aspect of the work is the training of Peruvians to direct it. They headed practically all main divisions at the time I visited *SCIPA* installations. This is considered a remarkable achievement in five years for a country trying to change from oxen to tractor in one leap.

John R. Neale, *SCIPA's* tireless roving director, and his assistant, William J. Green, are quick to praise the capable Peruvian staff. In fact, the *norteamericanos* do not look upon their agency as permanent. They are anxious to get able nationals with vision and enthusiasm to carry on the work. Already many Peruvian trainees have come to the United States on travel grants to absorb "know-how."

Leading Peruvian enthusiasts have been Godofredo A. Labarthe and Colonel Armando Zamudio, Ministers of Agriculture during critical stages of *SCIPA* development. On the *SCIPA* staff, Manuel de Mendiburu has had the job of coordinating all phases of the work as Secretary-General.

SCIPA is dedicated to the principle that complete food self-sufficiency for this variegated country is possible even if not as yet economically sound. It hopes to return to the day when Peru under the Incas maintained a population as large as today's 7,000,000 on its own produce. Efficiency must offset the trend that has added more mouths to the cities and substracted hands from the farms.

SCIPA's main problem is to make better use of existing cultivated land and to expand wherever possible. *SCIPA* found that most of the 5,000,000 acres under cultivation produce food for home consumption. Yet agriculture accounted for 67 percent of the $135,000,000 Peru got for all its exports in the latest year for which figures are available (1947).

Peru would have been much better off if it had not had to take $40,000,000 from export sales to buy foodstuffs abroad. *SCIPA* seeks to reduce that $40,000,000. Peru may produce all it wants of rice, 120,000 tons a year. But it runs a deficit of 120,000 tons of wheat. With proper help, some sections could easily produce an excess for less favorable sections. So *SCIPA* is flying wheat seeds from Arequipa to Cuzco.

SCIPA has found that enough bread grain could be produced if the Peruvian government would finance and supervise a program of experimentation, education, and agricultural credit supply. Machines, fertilizers, seeds are also needed. Such a program would still permit expansion of cotton and sugar, principal cash crops, for export.

SCIPA's success depends on effective wage, price, and tax policies. Exorbitant land rents, for example, perpetuate poverty-stricken share croppers.

Meanwhile, *SCIPA's* program bears directly on Peru's basic economy, including food, education, health, and sanitation. But it prefers to remain a special executive agency rather than a " normal " component of any ministry so that it will be free to pioneer new patterns. Nine general projects and some 65 subordinate units are being sponsored, among them economic studies and analyses, engineering and land use, agricultural extension, nutrition and dietetics, home gardens, even fishery development.

Much has already been done. But the problem remains vast. As Mr. Green told me, back in *SCIPA* headquarters in Lima, " The problem is enormous, but not as critical as the one I found when working for UNRRA in China."

Many of the program's benefits cannot be reduced to dollars and cents. And much that could be would cost too much to compile. For instance, the wartime victory-garden phase for urban dwellers has turned into a major perennial home-garden project. Somewhere between five and ten thousand tons of vegetables have been grown under *SCIPA's* aegis — vegetables that probably otherwise would never have been grown. Lack of seeds alone would have prevented unaided development of this important adjunct to the nation's table.

One of the project's most spectacular results was the salvage of the 1948 potato crop. Peru's native potato, classically misnamed " Irish," is a staple food, all-important to many regions. Blight threatened. By persuading big and little farmers in critical areas to use insecticides and scientific methods, *SCIPA* was responsible for saving two thirds of the crop in Lima's main valley and 90 percent of the crop in another part of the country. Since there are only about half a dozen really fertile valleys crossing the desert coastal plain, this was a vital achievement in terms of total food supply.

Peru has yet to reach the minimum decent food standards set by the Food and Agriculture Organization conference during the war at Hot Springs, West Virginia. Lima is consuming less than three quarters of this minimum, with the percentage in rural areas dropping to 42 percent for Huánuco, bringing the national average down to about 50 percent.

For example, Lima, far above the national average, consumed only 31 percent of the minimum quantity of milk fixed at Hot Springs. So the *SCIPA* program imports milk cows and fosters better care of cattle. Although Lima compensates for the present milk lack by showing favorable quantities of grains, meats, and sugar, it compares unfavorably in fruits, garden produce, and fats.

To bring the national average up, Peru must produce 263,000 additional tons of grain, 111,000 more tons of vegetables, 277,000 tons of fruit, 180,000 tons of meat, 69,000 tons of fats, and 277,000 tons of milk. Peruvians still average 50 centavos a day for food, with the sol more than 10 to the dollar. Many spend as little as 10 centavos, now far less than one cent in U.S.

This is the challenge to all Peruvians and to United States *SCIPA* workers. It may be some time before they produce the additional 1,800,000 metric tons of food needed to reach the Hot Springs minimum. But at least they know a vigorous start has been made.

CHAPTER 14

Government and the Development of Industry

No. 40 [One of the truly amazing economic developments of the contemporary period is the rapidity with which industrialization is taking place in Latin America. This basic change in the economy will, without doubt, be accompanied by changes in other social institutions.

If this industrialization results in an escape from the "monoculture" that has characterized Latin American economy in the past, if it raises the terribly low standards of living of the masses, if it creates larger and politically more conscious and vocal middle and working classes, the government and politics of Latin America will soon react to these changes.

Professor Wythe, in commenting on this industrialization, notes that in the process itself governments are very much involved. In many of the nations the stimulus to industrialize has come from government, and government credit or development agencies play a highly significant part in the planning, building, and operation of new industrial establishments.]

Progress in Industrialization of Latin America*

by GEORGE WYTHE

ONLY a decade ago the subject of industrialization of Latin America was all but ignored by United States scholars and businessmen. During the intervening ten years it has become a favorite theme for popular writers and speakers as well as academic investigators. This period has also witnessed significant developments in the industrialization of the countries to the south. Perhaps the time has arrived for a new appraisal of the subject.

For years there have been some substantial manufacturing industries in Latin America. Brazil had nearly three million cotton spindles before the Second World War, and that country, as well as several others, supplied the major portion of their requirements of such articles as cotton and woolen textiles, rayon yarn and manufactures, shoes, hats, beverages, glassware, tires, furniture, and other types of consumer goods, as well as of cement, construction materials, and other capital goods. Some important assembly operations had grown up, and secondary metalworking operations were expanding constantly. Most important of all were the industries producing manufactured foodstuffs and semimanufactures, such as sugar, meats, and copper bars.

WARTIME EXPANSION

During the war, industry expanded on a broad front. Practically every branch of industry shared in the advance. Quantitatively, the enlarged output of manufactures came about chiefly through the expansion of facilities by established enterprises. For example, cotton spinning, weaving, and knitting mills operated on three eight-hour shifts daily. In this field and in other industrial branches, the en-

* George Wythe, "Progress in Industrialization of Latin America," *The Annals of the American Academy of Political and Social Science* (January, 1948), Vol. 255, pp. 48–57. Reprinted by permission of *The Annals of the Academy of Political and Social Science*. The footnotes in the original version are omitted here.

largement of capacity was financed out of lush profits. Shortages of machinery, fuel, and raw materials placed a limit on expansion in many lines, but on the whole the Latin American countries fared fairly well under the wartime allocations of scarce goods and materials.

The years since 1939 have also witnessed the establishment of many new industries. A large proportion of these may be considered to be strictly local enterprises, but many of the larger and more important plants have been undertaken with United States financial and technical participation. Examples of the latter are the Volta Redonda steel works in Brazil; a rayon and nylon factory in Argentina; tire factories in Chile, Peru, Colombia, Cuba, Uruguay, and Venezuela (tire factories existed in Argentina, Brazil, and Mexico before the war); glass and refractory plants in several countries; and establishments producing rayon, electrical equipment, containers, agricultural implements, and paper in Mexico. New assembly plants for motor vehicles and radio receivers have been erected in several countries, and numerous branches of chemical and pharmaceutical manufacturers have been established. Not all of these are as yet in operation, but most of them have sufficient financial, technical, and official support to ensure a fair degree of success.

At the same time, some governmentally supported, as well as a few privately sponsored, ventures proved to be overambitious and have had to be abandoned. One example is the national motor factory erected about twenty-two miles from Rio de Janeiro in the Serra do Mar foothills. In 1943 this company signed a contract with a United States firm providing for the assembly and eventual manufacture of airplane motors. A number of Brazilian engineers were sent to Paterson, New Jersey, for training, and some motors were produced. By the end of 1945, however, the Brazilian government decided to abandon the undertaking. The company was reorganized with a view to the production of tractors for agricultural use. The plan is to arrange with foreign manufacturers for the assembly of tractor parts until such time as the factory is prepared to undertake complete manufacture.

This project is of considerable interest, furthermore, because the Brazilian government is using this plant as a nucleus for an interesting experiment in community planning. Two experts from the United States were engaged to plan a model industrial city for 25,000 inhabitants. The plans provide for drainage, road construction, and agricultural development as part of the general scheme.

In addition to these more substantial enterprises, there sprang up during the war a number of improvised operations, working with secondhand or locally contrived equipment, and at times using poor-quality or substitute materials. During the period of scarcity these companies were able to sell inferior articles at high prices, and some of them made profits large enough to enable the promoters to amortize their investments after a year or two of operation. Some of these " war babies " have already folded up, but others are trying to get sufficient protection to enable them to continue operations.

Many of the new enterprises are tucked away in back patios of old colonial-type residences, but not a few are housed in fine, modern structures, well-lighted and ventilated, and representing advanced ideas of factory layout. A fair idea of the variety and the extent of recent industrial developments may be obtained by a ride through the suburbs of such cities as Mexico, D.F., Buenos Aires, and São Paulo. Not long ago there was a saying in Mexico, " fuera de Mexico, todo es Cuautitlán "; that is, outside the capital everything is rural like Cuautitlán, a sleepy, dusty pueblo surrounded by agave and cornfields. But within recent years Cuautitlán and the adjacent villages of Tlalnepantla, San Bartolo Naucalpan, and Ecatepec have come to comprise an industrial agglomeration containing more than 700 factories with an initial capital investment exceeding 600,000,000 pesos ($125,000,000) — not impressive by the United States scale of things, but striking enough in comparison with the same area a decade ago. These communities lie within a radius of fifteen miles northwest of Mexico, D.F. on land bordering trunk railway lines and asphalted highways.

A few established industries have moved to this region to take advantage of cheap sites and to gain exemption from state and municipal taxes for periods ranging from eight to twenty years; but most are new enterprises, including plants producing (or preparing to produce) electric equipment, cement, brick and refractories, chinaware, glassware, bottles, tools, soap, flour, wire, leather, asbestos products, woolen goods, cigarette paper, chemicals, tires, aluminum articles, preserved foods, containers, ink, and varnishes. There are also an automobile assembly plant, foundries, and metalworking establishments. This list includes only those plants representing an investment of $20,000 or more. The largest single investment runs to between fifteen and twenty million dollars.

IRON AND STEEL INDUSTRIES

The possibilities of the iron and steel industries have attracted considerable attention. Before the war Mexico and Brazil were the only countries producing pig iron regularly on a significant scale, although there was intermittent production by a government-owned plant at Corral in Chile. In addition, there was some production of steel ingots from scrap in these three countries and in Argentina.

Mexico and Brazil. The Monterrey iron and steel works, in northern Mexico, is the oldest and most successful iron and steel producer in Latin America. During the war it installed a new blast furnace, more than doubling its pig iron capacity, and also enlarged its ingot and mill capacity. Its principal products consist of rails, structural sections, bars and wire rods, and miscellaneous items for the use of the railways and the mining industry. A second Mexican primary producer began operations in 1944 at Monclova, state of Coahuila, northwest of Monterrey. It produces pig iron, hot plate and strip, and cast-iron pipe, but its cold mill is still in the experimental stage. There are still various kinks to overcome: coke is scarce, the equipment is secondhand, and Mexican industries consuming plate and sheets complain of the high cost and low quality of the local product. Mexico's annual iron and steel requirements are around 450,000 metric tons, of which about 300,000 tons are now being supplied by national producers.

Prior to the inauguration of the National Steel Works at Volta Redonda in 1946, Brazil had twenty-five or more charcoal-burning blast furnaces producing somewhat in excess of 200,000 metric tons of pig annually, of which half was accounted for by the Belgo-Mineira works in the state of Minas Geraes. The growing scarcity and increasing cost of wood within convenient reach of the ore bodies or the markets imposed definite limitations on these operations. At times Brazil has exported small amounts of pig iron to Argentina, to Europe, and to the United States, but there has not been much surplus in recent years. Concrete reinforcing bars account for a large part of the output of the steel mills, along with some production of light shapes and wire and wire rods. In 1943 the Belgo-Mineira company began production of light rails, and it is also installing a pipe mill.

The national steel company has completed most of its installations. It has purchased coal fields in the state of Santa Catharina, where it has constructed a power plant and a washing plant, and has made considerable investment in roads, workers' houses, and other facilities. It has also acquired iron-ore properties and limestone deposits in the state of Minas Geraes. The production of pig and ingots got under way in June 1946, following the inauguration of the coke plant. Recent reports indicate that the plant is producing about 700 tons of pig iron and about 475 tons of ingots daily. Output has been limited by the insufficient supply and poor quality of domestic coal, and the difficulty of obtaining imported coal. The rolling mills produce plate and rails principally. It is expected that the hot strip mill and the cold strip mill will be in operation before the end of 1947.

Chile and Peru. Chile has long aspired to have a basic steel industry. There has been intermittent production of pig iron, as has been mentioned, at Corral since about 1910. In 1934 the Chilean government bought into that company and provided funds to install a new furnace and a rolling mill. The total production of this company, together with the output of other establishments working with scrap, amounts to around 30,000 metric tons of rolled steel. Chile's normal annual requirements are in the neighborhood of 100,000 tons.

After considerable discussion and investigation the Chilean government decided to proceed with plans for a new iron and steel works to be located at a site known as Huachipato on San Vicente Bay, a few miles west of Concepción and the port of Talcahuano. The site is close to the principal coal mines and to ample hydroelectric power, but at considerable distance from deposits of iron ore, limestone, and other necessary raw materials. In November 1945 the Export-Import Bank of Washington authorized a line of credit of $28,000,000 to finance the purchase of the United States equipment, materials, and services required in connection with the construction of the Concepción plant by a new company known as the *Compañia de Acero del Pacífico* (the Pacific Steel Works), and also several millions of additional credit to provide electric power for the plant. The rest of the capital was to be raised in Chile. This was originally estimated at $25,000,000, but it is likely that a considerably larger amount will be required. According to the latest available information, this project still has some hurdles to make, financial, technical, and commercial. Technically, the chief problem lies in the poor coking qualities of the Chilean coal and in the fact that the present supply is barely adequate for the country's needs.

Peru is studying the possibility of a steel industry in the Santa River valley, which is rapidly undergoing an economic transformation. This region produces anthracite coal, which is exported through the port of Chimbote. Although the domestic steel market consumes only about 40,000 tons annually, Peru is in some respects the best equipped of the South American countries to produce high-grade and special steels, since it has coal, iron ore, vanadium, molybdenum, and other required minerals. Obviously, it will not be easy to make a success of a technically complicated venture in a locality with such limited industrial antecedents.

Argentina and Colombia. Argentina has the largest steel consumption (about 700,000 tons before the war) of any of the Latin American republics. Some iron ore is found in the foothills of the Andes, but it is low grade and inconveniently located. Furthermore, Argentina is almost entirely deficient in native coal, although some coal and asphalite were produced during the period of most critical fuel shortage. For some years the Argentine Military Factories Administration has been investigating mineral deposits. A small blast furnace was erected at Palpala, in the northwestern province Jujuy, over a thousand miles from Buenos Aires, and in October 1945 it began producing pig iron. It is understood that a second blast furnace has been erected, raising Argentina's pig iron capacity to about 45,000 tons a year. Considerable scrap is available. Argentina normally imports some pig iron from Brazil, and is now negotiating for supplies of iron ore from Chile and other countries. There are a number of companies producing steel ingots and mill and foundry products. Annual production is 150,000 tons. In 1944 the Administration of the Military Factories called for bids for the formation of a " mixed company " to establish an iron and steel industry. Recently it was announced that tentative arrangements, subject to congressional approval, had been made with a United States company to establish facilities on the Plata River, near Rosario, for a secondary steel operation.

Colombia has gone into the question of an iron and steel plant at Pas del Rio, department of Boyacá. In fact, a steel industry has become psychologically a *sine qua non* of every industrially conscious nation. All the countries are still under the psychological influence of the wartime shortages, although, in practice, the Latin American republics probably fared relatively better than any other part of the world, since they were able to carry out a large amount of public and private construction which has transformed the skylines of the capitals and chief cities. There would definitely appear to be a place for some development of secondary steelworking operations, and possibly for blast furnaces in a few countries. But some of the best-informed observers feel that undue emphasis at this stage upon heavy industry will prove to be unfortunate, since in most cases these small iron and steel works are high-cost producers that are bound to be a serious drain on the national treasuries as well as a handicap to other industrial enterprises, which will have to bear the cost of expensive basic materials.

CHEMICAL INDUSTRIES

In the chemical field, the most conspicuous developments have been in connection with pharmaceutical specialties, toiletries, paints and lacquers, and similar locally compounded preparations which rely heavily on imported raw materials; but there is also substantial output of basic industrial chemicals such as acids, industrial alcohol, and by-products of coal and wood distillation.

During the war all the countries have felt keenly the scarcity of caustic soda and soda ash, which are used in large quantities in the manufacture of soap, paper, glass, rayon, textiles, and chemical pulp. In each of the four or five principal republics there is now some production of alkalies, and plans have matured for the construction of a number of government-sponsored plants. Brazil, for example, has obtained a $7,500,000 credit from the Export-Import Bank to finance the establishment of an alkali industry at Cabo Frio, state of Rio de Janeiro, and the Argentine Five-Year Plan calls for an output of 40,000 tons of caustic soda annually. In Mexico, the *Nacional Financiera* has made arrangements with an American chemical engineering firm to construct an alkali plant which will utilize the brines of the old Texcoco Lake. Colombia is anxious to industrialize the famous salt deposits at Zipaquirá.

Rayon yarn plants had been established in several Latin American countries before the war. These rely heavily on imported raw materials and therefore have been forced to curtail operations during recent years. At the same time, several new factories have been launched. In Mexico the new plant of Celanese Mexicana, S.A. was inaugurated at Ocotlán, Jalisco, on April 12, 1947. Cellulose acetate is imported from the United States. In Chile, a rayon yarn mill was completed in 1941. In Cuba, work is progressing on a mill at Matanzas, which will have sufficient capacity to supply not only Cuba's needs but also a substantial surplus for export. In Argentina, a new rayon and nylon plant was recently completed.

In considering the chemical industries it is necessary to keep in mind the complex interrelationship among chemical products. The manufacture of one product frequently involves various by-products, with a resulting loss unless there is a ready market for these by-products. The absence of adequate markets in some of the Latin American countries may make the price of the finished items considerably above the cost of imported products.

In view of the extensive use of chemicals in practically all manufacturing operations, healthy industrial development may easily be hampered if plants are required to use high-cost, nonstandardized local chemicals. For example, the leather industry may be discouraged from adopting improved methods, as the result of unfavorable customs tariffs on necessary chemical products. Some industries have also been penalized by the obligation to use local fuels.

It is clear that some branches of the chemical field will continue to expand, but there are serious handicaps to the rapid development of the heavy chemical industry. In addition to the restricted market, there are the virtual absence of research and the shortage of trained personnel, which make it difficult to produce articles of standard high quality.

COMMERCIAL POLICY CONSIDERATIONS

The industrializing trend in Latin America is, of course, a matter of great interest to the United States. It is evident from numerous pronouncements of high officials of this government that the United States views with sympathy all efforts to enlarge and improve the economies and well-being of the other American republics. Nor has this sympathy remained on the purely platonic level. Substantial financial assistance has been extended several countries in establishing new industries. Technical assistance has been provided. Facilities and financial aid have been granted to enable a large number of Latin Americans to obtain training in the United States. Except for the emergency restrictions imposed as a result of wartime shortages, no restraints have been placed on the export of machinery, information, or skills. On the contrary, special consideration has been given to all requests for assistance.

It is also of interest that this point of view has met with widespread acceptance among American industrialists and businessmen, although some manufacturers and exporters are bound to suffer from the loss of traditional markets. Many concerns, large and small, have opened their doors and cooperated in providing training to hundreds of Latin Americans.

At the same time, there have been some misgivings that the more extreme demands for protection voiced by some elements in Latin America might have serious repercussions upon our efforts to moderate protection and to keep down to a minimum other and more vexatious forms of restraint on international trade, such as exchange controls, quotas, and licensing arrangements. This question has come in for considerable discussion at Geneva in connection with the meeting of the Preparatory Committee of the United Nations Conference on Trade and Employment. The draft charter which was before the Conference contained a special chapter (Chapter IV) on " Economic Development," and gave specific endorsement to developmental programs, including industrialization, in the following words:

The Members recognize that the industrial and general economic development of all countries, and particularly of those in which resources are as yet relatively underdeveloped, will improve opportunities for employment, enhance the prosperity of labor, increase the demand for goods and services, contribute ultimately to economic stability, expand international trade, and raise levels of real income, thus strengthening the ties of international understanding and accord.

The draft charter also sanctioned what may be called " reasonable protection " to industries, as follows:

The Members recognize that special governmental assistance may be required in order to promote the establishment or reconstruction of particular industries and that such assistance may take the form of protective measures. At the same time they recognize that an unwise use of such measures would impose undue burdens on their own economies, unwarranted restrictions on international trade, and might increase immensely the difficulties of adjustment for the economies of other countries.

Latin American View. Within recent months, as some types of goods have become more abundant in the United States and certain European countries, Latin American imports have soared to unprecedented heights. There is still a large backlog of demand and there are also considerable reserves of purchasing power; but many of the republics have used up their exchange reserves, with the result that the volume of imports will have to be adjusted to current exchange availabilities — including, of course, receipts for loans, investments, and " invisibles," as well as exchange derived from exports.

By far the larger part of the imports consists of machinery, transportation equipment, fuel, and essential foodstuffs and raw materials; but war-stimulated prosperity has engendered a big demand for luxuries and for better-quality consumer goods than are produced locally. Some of the new industries are unable to meet this competition and have raised the cry of " dumping." In some countries the manufacturers' associations have received strong support from labor organizations. It is quite possible that protection will be given to some ventures of dubious economic benefit. At the same time, there is ample evidence that many of the higher officials recognize the dangers of protection *à outrance* and intend to proceed cautiously with measures that might injure the long-run interests of their respective nations. For example, President Miguel Aleman of Mexico, in his inaugural address on December 1, 1946, stated:

Our national industries shall enjoy a wise tariff protection to guard them from a ruinous alien competition, not by imposing prohibitive tariffs on the products of other lands — which would isolate us commercially — but by looking to the general benefit of the nation and providing for international cooperation.

In some countries merchants' associations and chambers of commerce have taken a strong stand against a policy of excessive protection to inefficient industries, and insist that government assistance should be limited to those enterprises that are operated with reasonable efficiency and are able to produce goods of satisfactory quality and in quantities sufficient to meet a substantial proportion of local needs. There are also some differences between the point of view of the new enterprises that produce only for the locally protectd market, and that of some of the older industries that are anxious to reduce production costs to the point where they can continue to compete in export markets in which they gained a foothold during the war years. In the latter case, steps are being taken to modernize equipment and production methods and increase labor efficiency. There are other handicaps that remain to be overcome, such as high interest rates, high costs of fuel and transportation, and the fact that investors are accustomed to much larger profits than are usual in the older industrialized countries.

GOVERNMENT-SPONSORED DEVELOPMENT CORPORATIONS

The efforts of the larger republics to develop the heavy industries emphasize the importance of state intervention in the industrialization of Latin America. In several countries the stellar role has been given to government-controlled corporations, such as the development corporations in Chile and Venezuela, the *Santa* corporation in

Peru, and the *Nacional Financiera* in Mexico. In Argentina the Central Bank is the directing force, and considerable use has been made of the " mixed company," in which private capital participates but control resides in the government.

The *Corporación de Fomento de la Producción,* in Chile, is perhaps the archetype of this form of organization. Its far-flung interests extend to upwards of a hundred corporations in many fields of activity. It is carrying out the extensive net of hydroelectric power development, and it has had a hand in practically every important industrial enterprise established since the Corporation's organization in 1939. It is the organizer and promoter of the new steel company.

The *Santa* corporation (*Corporación Peruana del Santa*) was created by the Peruvian government in 1943 to administer the development of the resources of the Santa River, the country's largest river on the Pacific slope. It took over the work already started toward the construction of a hydroelectric plant at Cañon del Pato. Railway and highway transportation are also being improved, and sanitary and water facilities are being provided. About 25,000 tons of anthracite coal are now being exported annually through Chimbote. Studies are being made of the possibilities of steel and chemical production.

The *Nacional Financiera* in Mexico is nominally an independent institution, but the government owns 51 percent of the subscribed stock and guides its policy. It was founded in 1934, but was reorganized in 1941 to act as an investment board. In addition to its paid-in capital of 12,000,000 pesos at the end of 1946, it has raised funds by selling about 45,000,000 pesos of its own bonds, and has sold so-called certificates of participation (which bear fixed rates of interest) aggregating 256,000,000 pesos.

The *Nacional Financiera* has invested in practically all the larger industries established in Mexico in recent years. At the end of 1945 it held 50 percent or more of the stock in the *Altos Hornos de México* (the new steel plant at Monclova), in *Guanos y Fertilizantes de México* (a company organized to exploit guano deposits and to manufacture fertilizer), and in several companies in the cement and packing fields. It had smaller stock participation in other corporations manufacturing cement, sugar, paper, glass, rubber goods, cop-

per products, and electrical equipment. It also held a large proportion of the bond issues of several of these enterprises. The *Nacional
Financiera* also makes loans (principally short-term) to industrial
concerns.

Although official action stands out conspicuously in some countries
and in some industries, private initiative has not been lacking, and
has, indeed, been the principal factor in Argentina, Brazil, Cuba,
Colombia, and other countries. In these countries and in Chile and
Mexico, the older industries, such as the textile, leather, paper, and
glass, have used their profits to expand, modernize, or branch out
into new lines. In some instances established firms have solicited
and obtained the technical and financial collaboration of United
States firms to introduce new processes or to put their operations on
a sounder basis.

The major portion of private foreign capital entering Latin America in recent years has been in connection with petroleum, other
minerals, and transportation, particularly aviation; but substantial
investments have also been made in branch plants or through participation with local groups. It appears likely that substantial
amounts of private foreign capital will continue to enter Latin
America. In fact, some observers feel that the flow may become
larger than is strictly desirable. For one thing, excessive reliance on
foreign financing may tend to postpone measures necessary to tap
local savings. While the amount of local industrial capital has increased both absolutely and relatively during the last decade, most
investors still prefer real estate and mortgages to industrial stocks
and bonds, and the banks usually accommodate only the larger established enterprises that are represented on their boards. Even the
special credit institutions authorized for the specific purpose of
originating and financing industry have, in practice, found it more
profitable to finance trade, or commodity and real estate speculation,
than to work in their intended fields. On the other hand, a significant change has taken place in both official and private attitudes, and
the number of nationals having a stake in industry is steadily increasing.

SUMMARY AND CONCLUSION

In conclusion, it may be pointed out that the economic and social changes of recent years have affected the prospects of certain types of industries. The growth of literacy and of national consciousness has stimulated the printing and publicity industries. Buenos Aires is now the most important publishing center of the Spanish-speaking world. Mexico, Chile, and Brazil also have important publishing industries. These developments have, in turn, stimulated paper manufacture, commercial art, and other lines. The growth of cities and new sanitary regulations also give rise to new activities, such as the packaging of foodstuffs, cosmetics, and pharmaceuticals.

The weakening of the ties of the patriarchal family and the growing urbanization of life are reflected in the erection of modern apartment houses and of small but well-equipped homes. The middle class has expanded relatively and numerically, and a growing proportion of manual laborers are able to purchase household utensils and appliances, radios, phonographs, and motor cars. Women are finding a larger place in offices, factories, service industries, and professional occupations; they, like their sisters of other nationalities, give priority in their purchases to nice clothes, jewelry, and beauty preparations. Back in the 1920's and 1930's, when I lived in Mexico, it was very difficult to obtain the many useful utensils and gadgets that fill our five-and-ten-cent and department stores, but many of these items are now manufactured in Mexico and in several other Latin American countries; and local varieties of the five-and-ten-cent store, as well as branches of United States firms, have been very successful in this line of merchandising.

Most of the Latin American manufacturing development has been in connection with consumer goods, but heavy industry has made a beginning. Both Argentina and southern Brazil are now producing many kinds of machines and tools of a type not requiring great power or very advanced engineering skills.

One dilemma that faces all industrializing countries is the conflict of interests between the producers of raw materials and fuel, and the finished-goods manufacturers who need to buy materials and fuels in the cheapest and most dependable market. Inadequate and high-cost transportation remains a bottleneck.

The size of the market imposes a basic limitation in certain directions. Consciousness of this limitation has brought about renewed discussion of the possibility of economic or even political union among some of the countries.

The last decade has been a significant period in the economic upsurge of the Latin American republics. The industrial sector has been expanded and consolidated. Not least in importance has been the change in attitudes which has accompanied and facilitated the evolution.

There is obviously room for further industrial development as population and wealth increase, and there are also abundant opportunities for the modernization and technical improvement of many existing operations. Sound industrial progress should go forward hand in hand with the concurrent evolution of other sectors of the economy.

No. 41 [Governments and political leaders in Latin America have long recognized the consequences that flow from the one-sided nature of the economy of the area. For a half century or more they have discussed the necessity of expanding industrial activity. However, rebuilding the economy involves so many technical and financial problems that it has been extremely difficult to formulate policies which were within the capabilities of the individual nations. Lack of public funds for higher education, especially in highly specialized and technical fields, has resulted in a shortage of experts and technicians. Shortage of capital has made it almost impossible to finance new industrial enterprises and has raised these questions: Where could the nation, acting by itself, secure the economists, engineers, and other technical advisers? Where could it obtain funds not only to finance new industries but to make those studies which might indicate *what* new industries ought to be encouraged and undertaken?

The postwar international agencies in the fields of technical assistance and credit have, in part, furnished the answer. This feature of international organization and government can make a real contribution to the economic development of Latin America. How some of these agencies cooperated with the government of Colombia, and how the blueprint for future governmental action was drawn, is discussed in " Colombian Blueprint."]

Colombian Blueprint*

by LAUCHLIN CURRIE

THE war brought forcibly to people's attention the fact that the world has suddenly grown very small, that it is no longer safe or even possible to ignore political, social, and economic developments in other countries.

As a consequence of this growing awareness, the United States sponsored creation of international organizations to preserve peace and bring about a greater measure of economic well-being throughout the world. One of these agencies was the International Bank for Reconstruction and Development. Born in the reconstruction period, it naturally directed its earlier activities more toward reconstruction than toward development of its member countries. But with war damage partly repaired and the emergence of the ECA program to carry on this work, the bank was free to study what will constitute its major continuing activity — helping underdeveloped areas.

Colombia offered itself as a test case for a new method of approach. It invited the Bank to organize a mission to make a comprehensive survey of the country's whole economy for the purpose of recommending, on the basis of its findings, a sound program of over-all development in which Colombia, foreign private capital, and foreign-government and intergovernmental lending agencies could play their appropriate roles. Early in May 1949, I was invited to organize and head the proposed mission.

In extending help to underdeveloped areas, the International Bank finds itself in a largely uncharted sea. The ideal formula or formulae have admittedly not yet been found. Following centuries-old lending precedent, the Bank has heretofore emphasized chiefly the economic soundness and productivity of specific projects presented to it. On the other hand, President Truman's Point Four Program emphasizes — at least to start with — technical assistance wherever it is needed.

* Lauchlin Currie, " Colombian Blueprint," *Américas* (January, 1950), Vol. 2, No. 1, pp. 16–19. Reprinted by permission of *Américas,* a monthly magazine published by the Pan American Union in English, Spanish, and Portuguese.

In my opinion both approaches have their merits and drawbacks. Unquestionably, underdeveloped areas need technical assistance of all kinds. But it is not always easy to translate advice into practice. The record in this respect, to put it kindly, is spotty. It may be that to bear fruit, advice must be coupled with positive incentives.

Specific project loans, on the other hand, are subject to different limitations. Their immediate aim is to finance one particular worthwhile project — one that serves a definite purpose and, other things being equal, will add to a country's total production. But other things are rarely equal. While theoretically a loan is earmarked for a specific project, actually it is a loan to a country which adds to the supply of available foreign exchange. To put it another way, it releases for different purposes exchange that might otherwise have financed the project in question. The net effect on the country's total productivity therefore ultimately depends upon the wisdom with which the total currently accruing capital resources, foreign and domestic, are put to work. For instance, it is perfectly conceivable that, because of policies pursued by the borrower, a substantial volume of foreign lending may result in little perceptible increase in over-all production or in the people's standard of living. Moreover, when a lending agency acts on specific loan requests, it cannot always be sure that the borrowing country's most urgent or most productive capital requirements are being met.

The Colombian mission was conceived against a background of these considerations. The approach was frankly experimental and, of course, no advance commitments were entered into by either Colombia or the Bank. It was agreed that responsibility for the mission's organization and report would be the International Bank's, although Colombia agreed to underwrite part of the expense and to provide all necessary facilities and technical assistance to the mission.

Another innovation was the formula worked out to further the cooperation of various international agencies. While, for efficiency's sake, responsibility for the mission was centered in one agency, the International Bank requested the Pan American Sanitary Bureau, the Food and Agriculture Organization, and the Monetary Fund to nominate acceptable experts in their own fields.

Partly because of the interest aroused by this new approach, we were fortunate in securing the services of an outstanding group of technicians in a wide variety of fields. The Bank contributed three from its own staff who, besides making valuable contributions to the report, will be a continuing source of informed advice on Colombia to the Bank management. Altogether there were for varying periods of time fourteen members of the mission, assisted by about the same number of Colombian experts, who, however, take no responsibility for the findings or recommendations of the report.

We arrived in Bogotá July 11 [1949] and the last of the mission departed on November 4. We covered the whole country from the Ecuadorean border to the Caribbean Sea, from the Pacific to the headwaters of the Amazon, by every known means of transport, conducting hundreds of hours of interviews from the President on down to *colonos,* the colonists in remote areas. During this time, the mission made the most intensive and extensive economic survey of Colombia every undertaken.

In the preparatory work carried out before we left by the Bank's economic department — which greatly expedited our work — it was found that many statistics were available, but they had not been revised or worked up in a form suitable for planning purposes. Consequently, a good bit of our time was spent in developing data as bases for recommendations. For the first time, for example, we constructed series on national income and capital formation, balance of payments, sources of money supply, highway and air traffic flows, together with basic data on health and sanitation, housing and municipal services — all information vital to intelligent planning. Economists from the *Banco de la República,* our host in Colombia, were a great help in much of this work. It is to be hoped that they and other government economists will improve upon the series and keep them up to date.

Colombia proved to be a fascinating country to study. The enthusiasm of the members of the mission ran high because of the great economic possibilities they found and the whole-hearted cooperation they received at every hand. We came to have a high regard for the country's beauty and resources, for the intelligence and hospitality of its citizens. While the Colombians take pride in their history and achievements, they welcome constructive criticism.

Indeed, in many cases, they are more critical of their shortcomings than foreigners.

But Colombia is also a difficult country to study. In addition to the lack of basic statistics, we had difficulty in grasping in a short time, in a strange country and — for many of us — in an unknown language, the rather bewildering complex of laws and administrative practices. Finally, because of many factors, including the peculiar topography of the country, we found an unbelievable diversity of agricultural and industrial production, modes of living, and peoples. Therefore, generalizing became unusually hazardous.

All this would not have been so serious if our purpose had been only to present a number of qualitative suggestions. Our basic aim, however, was much more ambitious. What we were attempting was to work out an actual quantitative and specific plan — a blueprint showing how to spend so many pesos and so many dollars, to increase production by so much. This growth in production was designed not only to look after the requirements of a population increasing at the rate of 2 percent every year, but to bring about an actual rise in their standard of living within a period of, say, five years. An appraisal of our success in developing such a plan must await completion and publication of the report, which will take some months. However, we left Colombia convinced that the physical and manpower resources were at hand to provide a much higher standard for Colombians in terms of health, education, and general economic well-being.

These resources include sufficient arable land to provide, if properly used, a balanced diet for the people, substantial dollar-earning exports, and many agricultural raw materials for domestic fabrication. In fuel and power — the other most essential physical resources — Colombia is peculiarly rich, with substantial amounts of both coal and oil plus a great hydroelectric potential. In addition, a valuable asset for the future lies in the immense tracts of tropical forests, at present almost untouched.

Much has already been accomplished. Despite incredible difficulties, a network of rail, road, and air transport has been built up, linking hitherto almost completely isolated sections of the country. A considerable expansion of agricultural and livestock production has substantially met the food calory requirements of a growing population. In the past twenty-five years, some half billion barrels of oil have been produced, and the country supplies its own needs in important items like cotton textiles, shoes, cement, beer, cigarettes, and bagging. Capital has grown rapidly, and a new middle class has been created in the cities. All this was made possible chiefly by the development of a large export market in coffee and to a lesser extent in oil and gold. This provided foreign exchange for machinery and vehicles as well as raw materials and consumption goods.

Despite this gratifying progress and growth, however, one cannot escape the conclusion that with better organization and planning, Colombia could have done much more. The living standards of the bulk of the people are deplorably low, not only in material things but in the more important intangibles of health and education. Their diet is unbalanced. Birth and mortality rates are very high; consequently, the life expectancy at birth is low. Housing is most inadequate and, in general, fundamental requirements such as enough pure water are lacking.

In too many fields there is evidence of inadequate analysis. Too often direct controls have been substituted for planning, and in most cases the administrative machinery is not equal to its burdens.

These shortcomings are known and deplored by thoughtful Colombians. But it has proved difficult to secure agreement on a mode of attack. Perhaps this is where a foreign technical mission can make its greatest contribution. It can provide an objective approach, divorced from political and sectional considerations, that is hard for local experts to attain. It can bring to bear a wealth of experience from more technically developed economies, arising from past successful *and* unsuccessful attacks on similar problems.

It is too early to assess the success of the mission or to speculate upon the possible impact of its forthcoming report upon Colombian economic policy. However, every member of the mission came away with the firm conviction that, regardless of the help afforded by additional foreign financial assistance, Colombia could do a great deal in every field to raise the standard of living of its people through better use of its own rich resources. To realize its truly great potentialities, the main responsibility must be born by Colombia itself.

No. 42   [The blueprint for action is but the first step in the economic reconstruction of a nation. It will indicate the directions toward which the economy ought to be pointed and, more specifically, what new industrial or commercial activities ought to be encouraged and developed. But these, in turn, cannot be undertaken without funds to finance their establishment and operation.

In Latin America the financial backing of many new — and old — economic enterprises has come from the government. As is indicated in the following article, the so-called *fomento* corporation is not unique to Chile. Similar government agencies are to be found in a half-dozen Latin American countries and, it might be added, in our own island possession, Puerto Rico. These corporations for economic redevelopment are now among the most important of the functions of government in Latin America.]

Bootstrap Economy*

by SERGIO CARVALLO

Stretching to the southernmost tip of South America, along the lofty range of the Andes, lies a narrow band of earth lashed by the Pacific's waves, cut by roaring rivers, and studded with mountain peaks, that bears the name of Chile. It's a peculiar land, reaching from the tropics to the pole, squeezed between mountains and ocean. And the five and a half million souls who live there make up an unusual people, racially and socially homogeneous.

Under the burning rays of the tropic sun, the torrid, dry expanse of the northern desert bears rich and inexhaustible deposits of nitrates and copper that are the living sap of the nation's economy and make ours a mining country. It is a zone of effort and privation. The climate, the way of living, the vicissitudes of fortune, the very nature of the exhausting work are harsh and demanding. In this environment our copper, iron, nitrate, sulphur, silver, gold, and

* Sergio Carvallo, " Bootstrap Economy," *Américas* (April, 1950), Vol. 2, No. 4, pp. 6–8, 41–43. Reprinted by permission of *Américas,* a monthly magazine published by the Pan American Union in English, Spanish, and Portuguese.

manganese are produced, while borax lies waiting for human hands to tap its rich beds.

Farther south, the rivers grow larger. They no longer lose themselves in the hot desert sands, but flow on to the sea. Along their routes flourishing green valleys offer sweet-smelling fruit. Then we come to the torrential stream of the Aconcagua, which marks the beginning of the true agricultural zone. In this region, wheat and vineyards, truck gardens, rice, tobacco, hemp, forage, medicinal and industrial plants like poppies and sunflowers prosper in close-pressed confusion. Here cattle graze on rolling fields hemmed about by hills and mountains and cut now and again by the singing waters of a cold, fast river.

This lovely panorama obscures the hum of the region's drudgery and harshness. Irrigation is difficult, for water must be carried great distances by costly engineering works. In winter the full rivers wash away whatever lies in their path. Erosion is an endemic evil plaguing the land, and the undependable rainfall may suddenly destroy the most promising prospects. While the soil is rich and yields well, this land will give its reward only for hard work and ceaseless energy.

The beating of the waves proves victorious in Chacao, where the continent is ground up, to break out in thousands of picturesque islands scattered through the southern sea. Here the temperature falls and the landscape turns gray. A little to the north, just past the magnificent River Bío-Bío, immense forests begin to cover the long valley with their dense shade, opening only to let through the deep emerald waters of another peaceful river — the Calle-Calle, the Bueno, or the Maullín. And while the forests provide man with a wealth of wood, the oil zone releases its potent black spurts, bearing new promise, and rich marine life accumulates along the 2,400 miles of coast line.

Effort is the basic characteristic of the Chilean. For everything there requires energy and struggle, whether travel on its winding mountain roads, digging mineral wealth in the rigorous climate of the northern pampas, or cultivating those rich fields that demand constant battle with nature to obtain water and prevent erosion.

All this has molded a virile, energetic people, with great endurance, enterprising, particularly suited to industrialization. Still more, the country's isolated position, with an extensive open coast on the Pacific, points toward a natural maritime and industrial calling.

The realistic Chileans became aware of this some time ago. During the First World War the country took its first big steps toward industrialization, although some industries of importance had existed since the middle of the nineteenth century — shipyards, for example, which built vessels of medium draft, all sorts of textile plants, and pottery works.

In the last twenty years, industrialization has taken on a much faster tempo. The basic tool has been an organization known as the *Corporación de Fomento de la Producción* (Corporation for the Development of Production), which went into action in April 1939. The idea behind it was to rebuild Chile's economy, stressing the development and national use of the country's resources to improve living conditions. This was a genuinely native idea, and the Development Corporation is a truly national product, not modeled on any foreign example. In ten years of successful activity, it has become the principal agency for carrying out the government's economic policy.

Originally the Development Corporation was financed by a series of special taxes turned over directly to it. These included payments in Chilean currency, for investment within the country, and in foreign exchange, for the service of foreign debts. But since 1948 a total quota for the organization, worked out according to its needs, has been included in the general national budget. Similarly, the annual national foreign exchange budget provides the necessary foreign funds. In addition to these government contributions, the Corporation has considerable income of its own, made up of profits on investments, interest, amortization, and repayment of loans, plus commission fees for services to private individuals.

The Corporation is directed by a Board made up of representatives of public and private organizations concerned with encouraging production, with the Minister of Economy and Commerce as chairman. Executive officers are responsible for daily administration. The staff is organized on a technical basis, in five departments corresponding to the major fields of activity: mining, agriculture, industry, fuel and energy, commerce and transportation.

Corporation action for industrial development may take several forms. Sometimes it goes into the production field itself, forming an autonomous affiliate, with capital subscribed by both the Corporation and private individuals or concerns, but with the Corporation keeping supervisory powers over the new company. This has been done, for example, with the *Compañía de Acero del Pacífico* to exploit the Huachipato iron and steel works and the *ENDESA (Empresa Nacional de Electricidad, S.A.)* to carry out the electrification plan. In other cases, where existing companies are already carrying on work that is to be strengthened, the Corporation may give them technical assistance and lend them money to expand their activities, improve production, or increase their capital. In this case, the Corporation becomes in effect a partner in the business for the term of the loan or other assistance. Finally, it can make direct loans, with ordinary collateral, to individual producers or small businesses. In special cases, it is free to adopt other means for effective action. But all of its aid must go toward new development, not for regular day-to-day commercial financing.

In the field of mining, the Development Corporation has aimed principally at the production of refined metals, both for industrial use within the country and to offer products that can be more profitably exported than crude ores. At the same time, it has encouraged production of metallic gold, for use in direct international payments.

Under this program, it undertook to establish a foundry for gold and copper and to develop mines to supply it. The plant was planned to handle 142,000 tons of ores, concentrates, and flux a year, to give an annual production of 7,200 tons of copper, 2,600 kilograms of gold, and 4,500 kilograms of silver. It is now nearing completion at Copiapó. As a natural complement to this foundry and the one in Chagres, construction has begun on an electrolytic copper refinery, with an annual capacity of fifteen to twenty thousand tons of refined copper. Also under way is an electrolytic zinc refinery, planned and financed by the Corporation, which within two years should produce 2,000 tons of metallic zinc and, as a by-product, some 3,600 tons of sulphuric acid.

Along with these large-scale projects some smaller jobs have been launched, among them a lead foundry, two plants for concentrating copper ore, with daily capacities respectively of 200 and 400 tons of ore, and a cyaniding plant for gold ore, which to date has produced 1,400 kilograms of metallic gold.

The total investment in mining activities runs to 213,000,000 pesos. So far, 103,000,000 of this has been repaid, leaving a net investment of 110,000,000 pesos. Since a large part of the funds went into works that are still under construction, the return on those in operation is thus extremely high.

The agricultural program began with the so-called "Immediate Action Plans," more or less experimental, on two-year schedules, up to 1946. Investments were mainly devoted to the development of fruit-growing in the northern and central zones, introduction of breeding stock of pedigreed milk and beef cattle, encouragement of industrial crops — flax, hemp, and particularly oil-bearing plants — increasing tree stands, and establishing a liberal credit policy for the improvement of agriculture in general.

Initial success in these directions led to an expanded agricultural program, begun in 1946 and now well under way, with the dual aims of progressive mechanization and development of mechanical irrigation. Agricultural machinery has been imported and distributed, after careful study to determine the best types of equipment for the various zones, types of farm, soil characteristics, and crops. Up to 1949, 3,275 tractors and 1,348 harvesters had been brought in, with the necessary plowing and cultivating implements. This machinery represented a 449,047,439 peso investment and benefited more than 5,000 farmers. Figuring 370 acres per tractor, an immediate result of the mechanization plan thus has been tractor equipment capable of cultivating around 1,200,000 acres.

In 1946 a "Mechanized Agricultural Team Service" was started, with an initial capital of 50,000,000 pesos for importing new machinery. Its principal functions are to make the new mechanical equipment available for use wherever it is needed, to introduce new types to help diversify cultivation systems, and to train technical personnel in the operation and maintenance of the machinery. This service finances itself from fees charged the farmers it serves, which cover the costs of administration and maintenance on a strictly business basis.

The Corporation has gone into mechanical irrigation on a large scale, taking advantage of both surface and subterranean waters.

Surface streams are used, through mechanical equipment, in regions where gravity irrigation is economically unfeasible, and underground waters are brought to the surface and put to work in the fields. In either case, cheap electric energy is provided by the Corporation's electrical affiliate, with electric power abundant in spring and winter when irrigation is needed. This program is carried out through loans to the owners of the land to be irrigated. The debt thus incurred can be met by the beneficiaries through the increased production on the irrigated land. Underground waters are captured with the Corporation's own equipment, including pumps and motors especially imported for the purpose, and the new irrigation systems are left in full operating condition. Through loans amounting to 25,697,330 pesos, some 50,000 new acres have been irrigated, and the water system has been improved on another 180,000.

Finally, experimental plantings of sugar beets have been made in various areas, in the hope of establishing a beet sugar industry, and the cattle program has been tackled on the three fronts of forage, animal health, and increased production of both milk and meat.

On the industrial side, Corporation activities first aimed at expanding existing factories and creating new industrial plants for products which formerly were imported at high places or in quantities insufficient to meet the demand. Investments were directed toward increasing production in iron, metallurgical, chemical, textile, food, manufactured copper, electrical, cement, tire, wood, and other industries. Later plans called for development of vital heavy industry, using the country's own raw materials.

The iron and steel industry was considered basic in this new program. It was approached in two directions: one, by enlarging and modernizing the Corral plant to increase production, improve machinery, and reduce costs; the other, by creating a new siderurgical plant with sufficient capacity to meet national needs and compete in foreign markets.

The first project has already been successfully carried out. The *Compañía Electro-Siderúrgica e Industrial de Valdivia* was given an initial capitalization of 48,000,000 pesos and its financing was completed with authorization of loans up to 37,000,000 pesos. With normal stable production, it is estimated that this company can save the national economy around $4,000,000 a year.

With the aid of the United States Export-Import Bank, the second phase is being carried out now through the establishment of a great iron and steel center in the province of Concepción. A corporation was created, with capital subscribed by the Development Corporation, other state agencies, and private sources, to produce pig iron and rolled steel from Chilean ores. Construction began on the San Vicente Steel Plant, better known as Huachipato, in 1947, and two years later it went into partial production. Full operation is scheduled for the end of this year. Plans called for an original capacity of 203,000 tons of blast-furnace pig iron a year, with the plant so designed that it can easily be expanded to three times this capacity. It will use 350,000 tons a year of iron ore from the El Tofo mines in Coquimbo, and the El Tofo and Romeral mines alone assure adequate ore for at least 30 years' operation. To start with, 327,000 tons of Chilean coal will be needed annually for coke, with 91,000 tons of limy rock from Guarello Island as a flux.

It is interesting to note that the annual Chilean consumption of iron, steel, and by-products that can be provided by this plant represents some $35,000,000 worth. National production of these important materials will mean a saving of $14,000,000 in foreign exchange. The effects are already being felt.

A parallel electrification plan started in 1943 to provide electricity throughout the country and help stimulate industry. First, it will develop seven separate regional generating and transmission systems, determined by geographical considerations and availability of water power. By 1960, it will be possible to undertake interconnection of the regional systems, to facilitate transmission of excess energy from one zone to another. A final third stage will call for a unified command to operate the whole network on the most efficient and economical basis.

For the greatest flexibility and best commercial application of the complex hydroelectric development work, the autonomous *ENDESA* corporation was created, with a present capital of a billion pesos. So far *ENDESA* investments amount to around a billion and a half pesos — 90 percent of this from Corporation subscriptions. Some 256,000,000 pesos have gone for purchases abroad.

To take advantage of Chile's enormous hydroelectric resources, estimated at over 12,000,000 horsepower in the areas already studied, six great generating centers have been planned with a total capacity of 8,200,000 horsepower. The first was inaugurated at Pilmaiquén in 1944, with a capacity that will reach 24,000 kilowatts, to serve the area between Valdivia and Puerto Montt in the South. Two others are already in operation: " Abanico," opened in 1947 with total capacity of 129,000 kilowatts, near Concepción, where all the industries connected with the Huachipato enterprise will be located; and " Sauzal," a 76,200 kilowatt plant in the central zone. " Los Molles " in the North will open as a 16,000 kilowatt plant this year. Later additions will be " Cipreses," near Talca, with 108,000 kilowatts, and " Calafquén," near Osorno, with 73,600.

Despite the visible evidence of petroleum deposits in Chile, commercial exploitation was never undertaken until 1941, when extensive exploration was begun by the Development Corporation. Nearly 100,000,000 pesos were invested in soundings and geological and geophysical studies. By 1949 twenty wells had been drilled, averaging 300 meters apart. Twelve proved to be gushers, five yielded natural gas, and three were dry. These positive results proved the existence of commercially important quantities of petroleum in Tierra del Fuego, and the high quality of the product induced the Corporation to plot a broad plan of development of the whole industry, covering not only prospecting and production of crude oil but also refining and transportation of finished products to consuming centers.

Studies are being carried out; the explored fields are already in production — aiming at a 13,000-barrel daily capacity — and construction has begun on a 43-mile pipeline to storage tanks and docks. A refinery is being built near Valparaíso. Last year saw the first export to Uruguay of Chilean petroleum.

Aside from these large basic undertakings, the Corporation has offered its assistance in a great variety of fields, including such industries as fishing, lumber, meat-packing, transportation, tourism, marketing, importing, and exporting. It has also made financial, economic, and technical studies, publishing works on national income and other subjects.

On several occasions, particularly in connection with large-scale projects, the Corporation has made use of foreign credits, drawing on direct loans, guaranteed by the Chilean government, from the Export-Import Bank in Washington. The Corporation was the recipient of the first development loans granted by the International Bank for Reconstruction and Development in Latin America. A loan of 13,500,000 United States dollars went toward the work of the electrification plan, and $2,500,000 was granted for importing agricultural machinery. The Corporation's high credit rating abroad is due to its careful, detailed planning of all its projects, the country's solvency, and regular attention to debt service.

So this organization boldly faces Chile's future, lifting the industrial level to win greater economic independence and better use of natural resources. In its ten brief years, the Corporation has amassed a record of concrete achievements that has brought it international prestige. Similar agencies in other countries — Venezuela, Costa Rica, Guatemala — have used it as a model. And in Chile the Corporation's work has just begun.

CHAPTER 15

Government
and
Social Security

No. 43 [Governments in Latin America have been engaged in one field of governmental activity, that of labor legislation and more particularly social security through public welfare programs and the social insurances, for a much longer period than has the government of the United States. With us social security is a relatively new idea and a new political program. Some of the social security legislation of Latin America dates back thirty years or more. We are still debating the advisability of certain new programs of social insurance which have long been in operation in the nations to the south of us.

Professor Jordan, in his contribution to this book, surveys the general development of labor and social security legislation in Latin America. Although the benefit standards of social protection there are much lower than they are in the United States, there is a much wider acceptance of the view that government has a responsibility for social welfare. Government in the area has tried to live up to this obligation with a notable sincerity and success.

The author also comments on the remarkable degree to which Latin America has cooperated with inter-American and international agencies in attempting to establish broad programs of labor protection and social welfare. The region stands out as one in which this kind of political action is needed, has been sought, and *is* working.]

Labor and Social Security in Latin America*

by HENRY P. JORDAN

ALL too frequently North Americans — political analysts, business-men " with an eye to the future," and even men of good will — look at the Latin countries of our hemisphere with almost exclusive re-gard to their potentialities of technical and commercial development. There can be no doubt that these potentialities are great and chal-lenging. Nor does that attitude imply that the intensified exploration and exploitation of those opportunities would of necessity be de-signed to gratify merely one-sided interests, as so often in the past, or to serve the ends of streamlined power politics through the medium of economic " collaboration." In fact, the activities of inter-American agencies set up under resolutions of the various confer-ences of late years, from Lima to Rio de Janeiro, have tended to prove that genuine cooperation toward mutually agreed aims is sought.

But there is a strong feeling on the part of Latin Americans, espe-cially those not directly concerned with commercial enterprise, that the human factor in the hemisphere equation is taken too lightly in the United States, and that there is too much superficial faith in a solution of Latin American problems through technical means, such as aviation, and the mechanical offspring of our gadget civilization. They insist that more attention should be paid to the welfare of the masses through simple improvements in general living standards attainable by all, and that the labor factor demands more serious consideration and a deepened study by all who wish to contribute to the future happiness of the Americas. In Latin America, the mush-room growth of modern luxury trades, transportation and commu-nications, superimposed upon semifeudal social relationships and primitive living standards of the laboring masses and the lower

* Henry P. Jordan, "Labor and Social Security in Latin America," *International Postwar Problems* (January, 1945), Vol. II, pp. 107–125. Reprinted by permission of the American Labor Conference on International Affairs. The footnotes in the original version are omitted here.

middle class, has already resulted in bewilderment and some resentment. Such a state of mind lends itself easily to the enticing siren songs of a romanticizing fascism almost at any time and anywhere.

Recent manifestations of a greater awareness of the role labor is destined to play in the development of Latin America are therefore of signal importance. A milestone in inter-American labor relations was reached when at the Conference of Commissions of Inter-American Development, held in May, 1944, in New York, United States labor brought forth a demand for increased participation by organized labor in postwar economic planning and development throughout the Western Hemisphere. The demand was justified by the desire to protect wage and living standards in the United States against competition from manufactured goods produced by low-wage countries. At the same time, however, adherence to the program of Latin American industrialization was stressed by the United States labor representatives who declared themselves concerned mainly with the question " whether such industrialization will be carried out on the basis of standards which will strengthen our American way of life and extend it as effectively as possible to the rest of the Americas." They advocated the creation of an inter-American production and planning council in which the labor organizations of all the American republics would be represented. For the efforts directed toward the establishment of better trade relations among the American countries would have to be supported by an increase in the purchasing power, or ability to consume, of 130,000,000 Latin Americans, most of whom are " workers " in the sense of accepted theory.

It is further significant that the labor demand was in substance taken up by the Committee on Economic Development of the Conference, which recommended the establishment of machinery for protecting the rights of labor, including inspection and employment services, minimum wages, maximum hours, prohibition of child labor, and social security — besides government aid for the vocational and technical training of workers and the improvement of health and nutrition standards. This recommendation was ratified later, at a plenary session of the Conference. But most decisive was the success of the labor representatives when the Conference adopted a resolution calling for the addition of labor members to the national commissions, and another by which the Conference went on record as favoring the extension of the collective-bargaining principle to all participating countries. Thus the demand for full recognition of labor rights and labor's interest in the hemisphere development program was officially, if tentatively, implemented.

Even before this Conference Latin American labor had laid far-reaching plans for its future. At a meeting of the executive council of the *CTAL* (Confederation of Latin American Workers), convened in Montevideo in February, 1944, the ideas advanced at the New York Conference of Development Commissions were discussed at length. Moreover, collaboration with the labor movement of the United States was established through the participation of a " fraternal delegate " of the Congress of Industrial Organizations, Martin Kyne, who represented the CIO Committee on Latin American Affairs.

In previous statements the *CTAL* had expressed its basic belief that labor throughout the world must take a more active part in political affairs; and, further, that this applies especially to the labor movement of Latin America, where the answers to all questions concerning conditions of work and human welfare " are, by the very fact of economic under-development, predicated upon the solution of political problems."

II

In appraising the present-day situation of Latin American labor one has to bear in mind that the laboring masses are to a considerable extent inarticulate. The background of an economy that has all the earmarks of feudalism covers wide areas of all Latin American countries. Even where, as in Argentina, Mexico, and Chile, important sectors of the working population are organized, there are enough outside the pale of organized, or even regulated, labor to justify the statement that what we read and know about labor conditions in Latin America reflects the real picture only in part. In Chile, for instance, the first effort to organize farm workers was launched as late as 1939. In Mexico, the membership of workers' organizations under federal jurisdiction was 335,492 persons in 1941.

And while it is true that there are "a great many" organizations which have never registered, even the cumulative report of all major labor organizations, including agricultural, reached a grand total of only 1,805,000 workers out of a population of almost 20,000,000. These and other facts tend to show that in speaking of Latin American labor certain qualifications have to be made. Although a number of them are applicable also to other countries in and outside the Western Hemisphere, they require special attention when the subject of discussion is Latin America as a whole.

This fundamental fact about Latin American labor is not surprising if the historical development of the Latin American economy is considered. Briefly, what is still at the base of contemporary Latin American life is the colonial economic system of the former Hispanic (Spanish and Portuguese) rulers. Divested of its political drag toward Europe, that system was continued in essential respects under the more "liberal" governments of the republican régimes. The break with European sovereigns meant in the first place that the political, social, and economic domination by Spanish and Portuguese governors was replaced by that of "native" elements. But these were with few exceptions of the same European stock and background as the former. The feudal colonial economy they have carried down to this generation was tempered only in spots with the free-enterprise spirit of pioneer capitalism when the modern mining interest in metals other than gold and silver, in transportation, rubber, and other forest industries and, finally, oil brought about a partial integration of the southern continent with the world economy. At any rate, the role of the laboring masses was hardly affected by that development. The *estanciero,* or *hacendado,* or *fazendeiro,* was in complete control of the indigenous population who had to make their living in that system, but had not yet tasted of the accomplishments and liberties of Western civilization.

The transition to a freer and more industrialized economy and to a new view of labor's place in society was slow and, on the whole, gradual. True, waves of European immigration toward the end of the nineteenth century, and in the first decades of the twentieth, brought in some elements of disturbance, such as the early attempts at organizing certain labor groups in Argentina, where syndicalist ideas had been " imported " by immigrants from Italy and Spain, as well as thoughts of labor rights and social security engendered mostly by Germans reminiscing of the Bismarckian social legislation in the Fatherland. But these influences were no real menace to the vested interests. The latter succeeded in holding and maintaining political and economic control over the supply of labor to the extent that until shortly before the First World War there was no possibility anywhere for labor to assert collective power. This condition was buttressed by the state of peonage which was the traditional mode of existence for the bulk of the all-important class of agricultural laborers. Even where peonage was legally abolished, as it was in Peru (1915), the social situation remained largely unchanged as long as the Indian was bound to the land.

However, European influence, through immigration, example, and thought, began to bear fruit in the years immediately preceding and following the First World War. This development was helped by incipient industrialization in Latin America, with its attendant transformation of the old personal relationship between *patrón* and employee into that of impersonal management, and the drawing together of large numbers of workers in urban communities where organizing activities could be carried out more easily. The impact of the rising tide of immigration can be gathered from the fact that, significantly, in Uruguay it made up about one quarter (509,400) of the total population (2,123,000) in the years between 1900 and 1937, and more than one quarter in Cuba, in approximately the same period, and similarly contributed to social change in other countries.

Labor legislation dealing with wage and hour standards, collective bargaining, labor contracts, workmen's compensation, child labor, and other matters was passed on a great scale during those years in all the major countries of Latin America. Likewise public health services and other auxiliary machinery were instituted by governments and by the labor organizations themselves. Almost hand in hand with this came the installation of social-insurance systems covering many different hazards of social insecurity. The formal — legal — structure of this legislation is usually very good, and in a number of countries the regulatory and administrative setup for carrying it into effect is equally so. But the real problems and difficulties arise in connection with the enforcement of legislation in the wide areas of unevenly developed economies. Difficulties are due also to the lack of funds for the maintenance of adequate machinery and the payment of benefits, and to the lack of properly trained public-service personnel. The chief problems, however, are supplied by the tremendous expanse of territory, the scarcity of transportation, and the inadequate development of governmental machinery in remote parts of the republics.

It seems certain that many of these handicaps will disappear as the process of industrialization goes on. Standards of enforcement are relatively high even now in Uruguay, Chile, and Mexico. But difficulties founded in natural conditions can be overcome only with time. A general warning seems to be justified that enthusiasm over up-to-date and forward-looking legislation on the statute books of any country is gratuitous unless the object of such legislation is implemented by administrative practice reaching the masses of citizens for whom the laws are intended.

Moreover, in all this a distinction must, of course, be made between Latin American countries where there is a free labor movement acting in its own interest according to its own wishes and policies, and those where dictatorial governments are keeping a strong hand on the unions or, without allowing for union organization at all, maintain strict State control over labor affairs, limit or abolish the right to strike and withhold other privileges essential to the growth of a free labor movement. Enlightened dictatorship, to be sure, has seen fit in many instances to make considerable concessions to the interests of labor — especially in the field of social insurance — so as to appease possible opposition from this quarter. Thus less than a year ago the Argentine government issued a decree setting up a " Secretariat of Labor and Social Security " which is not only to regulate relations between capital and labor, but to " strengthen national unity by securing greater social and distributive justice " and to bring about " an early and effective improvement of the standard of living." General Juan D. Perón, War Minister and leader of the Axis-inspired *GOU,* is the head of the new department. Similarly in Brazil, despite its firm alliance with the United States and measures taken against Axis nationals, the Fascist example has been emulated in the treatment of labor unions generally as well as by the recent creation of a National Council of Industrial and Commercial Policy. Among the duties assigned to this Council is " the coordination of union activities in industrial development and the elevation of the standard of living," but labor as such has no voice in its deliberations.

The tragic plight of labor in Bolivia was highlighted by the strike of the tin miners of Catavi in December, 1942. That strike provided a long-awaited opportunity for study and report on conditions in that revolution-ridden country. A commission of experts from the United States was sent to Bolivia at the request of the Bolivian ambassador in Washington. The inclusion of labor officials in the commission caused satisfaction in United States labor circles and was, at the same time, a significant portent for the future participation of organized labor in the conduct of inter-American relations. The commission found that, although the Bolivian Constitution of 1938 — recognizing the principle of collective bargaining and the right to strike — and the labor code of 1942 and other legislation meet legitimate demands for progressive social legislation, the actual living conditions of the workers are deplorable. For little of that legislation has so far been put into effect. Collective bargaining, for instance, seems hardly to exist. The reasons for this and other shortcomings are to be found at least in part in the economic and political power of the mining companies, who have often dangerously rocked the boat of the republic. Analogous situations exist naturally in all countries where dictatorial government and the influence of powerful private corporations or individual producers have vitiated progressive constitutional enactments or special legislation.

III

The provisions for labor and social security on the national level as well as the record of Latin American governments regarding international teamwork in these matters are remarkable indeed. It is not too much to say that in several aspects of labor legislation Latin America is more advanced than the United States and a number of European countries even in the pre-Fascist era. This may seem paradoxical, given the difficulties of enforcing the pertaining legislation. But the Latin American peoples and governments have shown determination and persistence in finding ways to broaden the application of their laws by adjusting them to reality through appropriate revisions and often enough by drawing upon the experience and advice of outside agencies.

The sweeping stipulations covering the rights of labor contained in national constitutions and legislative acts of most Latin American countries are known or can be checked easily. Besides assuring the right to association and organization, to collective bargaining, to the eight-hour day and minimum wages, laws have also been made for the protection of women and children, workmen's compensation, annual vacations, dismissal wages, and company housing of employees. "In the matter of the eight-hour day Latin America has led the world." The principle of the eight-hour working day had found recognition in Latin America long before it was made law elsewhere (for public works in Chile since 1908; generally in Uruguay since 1915). The principle of a dismissal compensation (severance pay) has been adopted in various countries (in Peru, for example, for commercial employees as early as 1924). Minimum-wage legislation — frequently in conjunction with price-control laws called for by the war emergency — has made considerable progress in recent years (in Brazil, Chile, Mexico, Haiti, Paraguay, Guatemala, Uruguay, etc.). As for the protection of women, the laws of Mexico, Argentina, and Brazil have set the pace for those of other countries dealing with working and wage conditions for women, job maintenance and compensation during pregnancy, and the like. The principle of nondiscrimination in pay between men and women is generally accepted. Indeed, in some respects Latin American women may be called better off than many women employed in United States industry.

An interesting feature is contained in the Uruguayan law of November 12, 1943, setting up minimum wage boards. This law establishes also a system of family allowances for dependent children of workers whose wages or salary do not exceed 200 pesos per month. The allowances are automatically payable to the person responsible for support, for each child up to fourteen years of age, and up to sixteen where the child is still in school. The plan is to be financed by compulsory contributions from the employers. The introduction of this item — long accepted in various European countries — into official social-security programs on this continent may yet turn out to be of far-reaching consequence.

All the South American and several Central American republics have compulsory insurance systems that cover varying risks of the working people. Home workers and domestic workers as well as agricultural laborers are usually not covered in the beginning, but are included later (as in Uruguay, Chile, Peru). The insurance systems have generally developed in stages, at first comprising specified categories of employees and workers within relatively easy reach of administrative authority (bank employees, maritime workers, railway and streetcar employees — Bolivia, Colombia; coffee warehousemen — Brazil; journalists — Argentina, Bolivia, Cuba, Chile, etc.), but may finally be applied even to small merchants — as in Chile — or independent farmers — as in Uruguay. As far as the range of risks covered is concerned, there are no great differences from the system of the United States, except that unemployment insurance has been instituted so far only in a few countries and that some risks are included in some Latin American countries which are not covered here; among the latter are funeral expenses and sickness and maternity care on a remarkably broad scale, with cash benefits in several cases. Probably the most far-reaching coverage exists in Chile, whose system of socialized medicine has been extended to preventive medicine by the Preventive Medicine Act of 1938, and where later regulations have provided for medical aid to mothers from the first prenatal examination until the child is at least two years old.

The costs of the several systems are usually divided between employers and the employees, in varying ratios; but in some instances the national government makes contributions as a third party interested in the system, or backs it up with a guarantee fund. The rates of contributions by individuals are usually between 3 and 6 percent of the wages, which is higher than in the United States. In practically all systems the compulsory feature is limited to income groups up to a maximum defined by law; but provision for voluntary participation of higher-paid employees is frequently made. The retirement age at which benefits can be claimed is often lower than in the United States system. This is due in part to differences in climate and average life expectancy, but also to the fact that the possibility of retirement at the discretion of the insured, eventually with small benefits, is held to be a desirable social goal as much as old-age insurance proper.

IV

For the most part Latin American labor and social-security legislation has been enacted since the foundation of the International Labor Organization, under the direct inspiration of the standards laid down by the International Labor Conferences, and in many cases after consultation with the technical services of the International Labor Office. The countries of Latin America have collectively ratified over two hundred conventions adopted by the International Labor Conferences. Notwithstanding the difficulties of enforcement, the influence of the International Labor Organization in bringing about a widespread improvement in standards of labor protection has been nowhere as great as in Latin America. This is particularly true of the forty-eight-hour week, the prohibition of nightwork in industry for women and minors, and factory inspection. Numerous missions were dispatched from the International Labor Office (ILO) to South America to supply technical information or to advise governments in drafting or revising social legislation. In the field of social insurance, this form of collaboration on the spot was initiated by a visit which M. Adrien Tixier, then chief of the Social Insurance Section of the ILO, paid in 1934 to Argentina, Brazil, Chile, and Uruguay. The original suggestion for this mission had been made by the Brazilian government. Other missions led by other officials of the ILO followed, among them one to Venezuela, in 1938, and another to Bolivia, in 1940, proved to be of major consequence for the shaping of general labor and social-security (insurance) legislation in those countries. In the case of Bolivia, attention was also given to the prevention of occupational diseases in the mining centers; and a delegate of the ILO, D. H. Blelloch, assisted in the revision of the Bolivian labor act of 1939 (Busch Labor Code), which was enacted into law in December, 1942.

Supplementing their participation in International Labor Conferences and the collaboration with the ILO, the American republics have developed a system of labor conferences and regional agencies of their own. These arrangements and activities can be considered a distinct success for the idea of regionalism in nonpolitical international organization. Indeed, long before this tendency became as strong as it now is, the International Labor Organization had initiated regional activities, and projected the extension of such activities to new areas, within a broad framework of general international cooperation. The most successful experiment in regional action made thus far by the International Labor Organization has been the holding of the First and Second Labor Conferences of American States which are members of the International Labor Organization, in Santiago, Chile (1936), and Havana (1939).

These conferences gave the American countries a most valuable opportunity of bringing the urgent needs of their social development forcibly to the attention of the Organization, and of focusing attention upon the special problems with which geography, the mingling of races, and the nature of their economies have confronted them. They have exercised a far-reaching influence on the development of the general work of the Organization itself by directing attention to American conditions and needs. Out of them has grown the First Inter-American Conference on Social Security, held at Santiago in September, 1942, which provided the hemisphere with new directions for the further collaboration of all its member states as regards social insurance and the problems of social security. It was a logical result of these efforts that at the latter conference a Permanent Inter-American Committee on Social Security was formed, which is to conduct its labors in cooperation with the ILO and the Pan American Union.

The First Inter-American Labor Conference (Santiago, 1936) studied, among other things, the difficulties encountered by individual American states in the application of advanced social legislation. Furthermore, a social insurance committee was set up to examine trends and methods of promoting social security through governmental action in the Americas. Special consideration was given to the prospects of further investigations to be focused upon agricultural problems and their implications for social security; but some of these plans will presumably have to wait until after the war.

The delegates to the Havana Conference (1939) gave much

thought to various aspects of the American economy. The single-crop systems of some of our Southern neighbors were discussed, and proposals considered to extend to agricultural workers all the social protection gained by industrial workers; in this connection the needs of the Indian population were emphasized. The Conference reaffirmed the Santiago resolution that social insurance should apply to all persons regardless of occupation; that there should be equality of treatment for native and foreign workers; and that insurance provisions for maternity benefits and compulsory unemployment insurance were desirable. Moreover, the problem of immigration came up for consideration; its importance for the American future and the need for the Western Hemisphere to be prepared for the reception of more immigrants from Europe were stressed, and the setting up of machinery to handle this problem was advocated. Finally, in the Declaration of Havana the faith of the participating nations in international cooperation was restated, and further support of the International Labor Organization pledged. Similarly, at the Conference for Social Security (Santiago, 1942), agreement was established that all categories of workers should be covered by compulsory social-insurance programs, including agricultural, domestic, and white-collar workers, and the self-employed; further, that insurance should be provided against occupational diseases; and that in accordance with the position taken by the International Labor Organization both workers and employers should have a part in the administration of institutions serving social security.

The comprehensive program of social insurance and public assistance adopted at these conferences has received moral support by the recommendation of the Inter-American Juridical Committee, set up by the Third Meeting of American Foreign Ministers at Rio de Janeiro in January, 1942, that the work of the ILO in the Americas should be continued. The Committee paid tribute to the important function of the ILO in fostering social justice as a basis of world peace and good relations in this hemisphere. This is precisely what the International Labor Organization has come to mean for many Latin Americans, namely, an international agency that is capable of aiding them in the solution of some of their most pressing regional problems.

At the Havana Conference it was contemplated that a Third Labor Conference of American States would be held after an appropriate interval, and an invitation to hold that conference in Mexico City was extended by the Mexican delegation. The course of the war, the holding on the American continent of the 1941 and 1944 Conferences of the International Labor Organization, and the meeting of the First Inter-American Social Security Conference have caused the lapse of a longer interval than was intended at the time of the Havana Conference. Since the creation of the Inter-American Conference on Social Security as a continuous institution provides specialized machinery for the further consideration of the problems of social security, a third labor conference could initiate regional consideration of other questions of social policy especially interesting to the Americas. Among them may be mentioned: the modalities of the application of labor legislation to rural workers; the development of vocational training; health, safety, and welfare standards in large-scale industrial and agricultural undertakings; the improvement of labor inspection; methods of wage payment and wage regulation; procedures for the settlement of industrial disputes; and the composition and procedure of labor courts.

In some instances the International Labor Organization could no doubt make valuable contributions to even more limited, but useful, regional action in parts of America where groups of states have created their own agencies for research, coordination, and administration. Thus the convention establishing the River Plate Regional Office of Economic Information and Studies, concluded at a conference of the La Plata states (Argentina, Bolivia, Brazil, Paraguay, and Uruguay) in 1941, provides for the coordination of studies made by that office with those undertaken by the ILO. The International Labor Conference held in New York, 1941, adopted a resolution envisaging collaboration with the River Plate office. Further, since that New York conference the United States and British governments have created the Anglo-American Caribbean Commission to encourage and strengthen social and economic cooperation in the Caribbean and to deal " primarily with matters pertaining to labor, agriculture, housing, health, education, social welfare, finance, economics, and related subjects " concerning their territories in that area. More recently they have instituted " a regular system of West Indian conferences . . . to discuss matters of common interest and especially of social and economic significance to the Caribbean countries." The first of these conferences took place in March, 1944; it was attended by representatives of the British and American (Puerto Rico, Virgin Islands) Caribbean possessions and has opened an era of promising collaboration between the governments and peoples concerned. The arrangements for the West Indian conference leave open the possibility of participation by other countries interested in the development of the Caribbean region. As the scope of the work done by the Anglo-American Caribbean Commission and its affiliates broadens, there will be increased opportunities for the ILO to assist in reforms of labor organization and in the development of institutions ministering to the social-security needs of the islanders and inhabitants of the states surrounding the Caribbean Sea. We have the word of a staff member of the Pan American Union for the alarming fact that thus far Cuban labor has formed about the only link between the United States and Caribbean labor, and that there is much despondency among the working population of the Caribbean, due to the apparent lack of a plan for meeting their elemental needs. Obviously much can be done.

V

It must be recognized that Latin America has its special problems awaiting solution by regional action and coordination on the supraregional level. Of these, the conditions of life and work of the indigenous inhabitants in relation to general agrarian policy — the so-called Indian problem — and that of immigration as a factor in the labor situation of Latin America stand out most immediately.

As for the Indian problem, here too the approach on the (regional) basis of hemisphere cooperation has proved to be of positive value. Without the First Inter-American Congress on Indian Life at Patzcuaro (Mexico), in 1940, the answering of questions that affect mainly the bulk of the population in the " Indian " States — Mexico, Guatemala, Ecuador, Peru, Bolivia — would probably have been left forever to the more or less successful reform attempts made (or not made) by the respective national governments. Under the leadership of Mexico an exchange of ideas and experience has been initiated which is now institutionalized through the offices of the Inter-American Indian Institute operating from Mexico City. It has given impetus to new legislative and administrative measures in several countries that will stimulate everywhere movements for the restoration of lands to the Indian peasantry, for the end of all forms of peonage, and for a spread of rural education and modern hygiene. One of the developments that has a generally hopeful portent, even in the countries now under dictatorial rule, is the great and rapid increase of the cooperative movement by which landless Indian laborers are benefiting in many ways. South American governments have begun to recognize the value of the Indian tradition of collectivism and are trying to adapt it to the modern forms of producer, consumer, and credit cooperatives in agriculture and small industries (handicrafts). All this, however, should not obscure the fact that at the root of the Indians' present-day existence are the monocultural (single-crop) economic system prevalent in a large part of Latin America and the social evil of *latifundismo*. Both constitute problems that can be brought to solution only through the means of an enlightened economic and social policy, integrated with the whole political course of the individual nations and the hemisphere.

This holds equally true for policies and measures dealing with questions of labor supply, of which immigration is one with incisive international implications. Again, a third labor conference of American states would also afford an opportunity for giving further consideration to this problem as it affects the Americas. Such a procedure would seem appropriate, especially in view of the requests made to the International Labor Organization by the Santiago Conference on Social Security and the First Inter-American Conference on Population Problems (Mexico, 1943), that it should develop this side of its work; and considering the fact that the matter was eschewed by the latest International Labor Conference. It seems certain that immigration will be of increasing importance in connection with the advancing industrialization of Latin America. But uncontrolled immigration might cause economic dislocations and resentment that would frustrate long-term prospects. Therefore comprehensive planning with due consideration to the financial problems involved is definitely called for. Meanwhile, the several governments have been developing their own immigration policies, yielding to momentary anxieties and pressures. After 1935, there was not a country in Latin America which did not enact restrictive legislation regulating and limiting the number and type of foreigners to be admitted. The trend is now, on the whole, nationalistic in the narrow sense and, accordingly, not conducive to a constructive solution of the migration problems with which Latin America will be faced after the war.

Whatever official policies may be, it is clear that well-intentioned governments and international organizations cannot do the job alone. The labor and social security problem of Latin America has to be seen in relation to the economy of Latin America as a whole, and to its future. That means that it is closely tied in with the problems of an economy characterized by large exportable surpluses of agricultural and mining products that await their absorption by a reconstructed world-trade system.

Moreover, diversification of production and a higher degree of industrialization in almost all Latin American countries have been recognized as necessary here and in the southern continent. But much depends on how those objectives are achieved. From the economic viewpoint, the equalization of purchasing power is no doubt the most urgent problem of inter-American relations. The very process of industrialization, however, will carry in its wake new social contingencies and requirements. The danger may arise, for example, that even a temporary — almost unavoidable — differential between wages and standards of living in newly industrialized countries, on the one hand, and those with established industries, on the other, would have a detrimental effect on labor in the latter. Resentment and a reinforcement of isolationist tendencies, with restrictive foreign policies, might follow. The net result would thus be the opposite of what was intended.

In that evolution, therefore, the attitude of outside groups is all-important. This does not concern only the United States government and technical experts, traders and investors, but also American labor. It augurs well for the realization of the part United States labor will have to assume, that its leaders have been engaged for some time in creating a better understanding of Latin American issues among their followers, and that they have formulated concrete proposals for the overcoming of some of the obstacles that will be found in the way to a fruitful solution of the hemisphere problem. In this connection the " resolution concerning economic and financial cooperation between the nations of the American continent," submitted by James B. Carey at the Havana Conference, 1939, would still seem a landmark of positive thought. In that resolution a demand, among others, was put forward that in all credit agreements concluded between American nations provision should be made for the effective endorsement of fair labor standards in all work financed by virtue of such agreements. Now the United States government and its agencies have made it a practice to insert a " labor clause " in their procurement contracts with Latin American republics. But these clauses relate to the war situation only. Their continuation and technical perfection in peacetime credit arrangements, including those of private institutions and investors, with extension to all matters in which American labor has a legitimate concern, remains to be desired and should be insisted upon. United States labor might even suggest — in its own interest as well as for the general improvement of hemisphere relations — that the Latin American nations pass uniform legislation making the insertion of such clauses in all foreign investment contracts mandatory. Some assurance would thus be had that industrialization in Latin America will be carried out in a way which will mutually strengthen efforts to preserve acceptable working conditions and living standards, or to improve them wherever necessary.

The possibilities of effective hemisphere cooperation in the labor field depend lastly on decisions on a broader plane. Good Neighbor policy, by all tokens to be continued after the war, cannot rest on interdependence gained through economic and military strategy in that war. Nor will asseverations of friendship and peaceful intentions do in the long-run future. On all sides there must be the will to supplement that " political " policy by economic and social statesmanship which will fulfill the promise of America for a richer life in terms of freedom, justice, and material well-being for unsung millions of men. Restrictive policies of all kinds, social, economic, or political, will frustrate the attainment of that goal. The remaining problems are therefore, above all, a change in social relationships that have become callous or stagnant, and the reversal of nationalism — embodiment of suspicion, fear, envy, and vanity. Only an international security system and a United States over-all policy that would insure our Latin neighbors against ourselves can provide an adequate basis for social security in Latin America.

CHAPTER 16

—— *Governmental* ——
Educational
Programs

No. 44 [Americans are apt to think of public education in terms of well-constructed buildings, well-trained teachers, and a wide curricular offering of academic and "practical" subjects. We regard our schools as being outside of the realm of political, social, and economic issues, and we assume that their function is not to espouse a particular social or political doctrine.

Most of us would be surprised, and many shocked, on our first visit to a Mexican village school. The adobe building which houses it was probably built as a cooperative project by the pupils and the teacher. The teacher, in all probability, has had little formal teacher-training; he might be the local carpenter. It would be hard to guess the "grade" of the class by observing the students, for there would be children of eight and men or women of eighty present in the classroom. The courses would also seem strange; most of them would be based on some local or community problem such as increasing the corn crop or installing the most primitive of sanitary facilities for the village. Running throughout all the instruction is an openly stated social or political objective, for the Mexican school program has a conscious political direction. To reach their revolutionary goal the schools employ new and radical educational techniques and teaching methods.

Professor Sánchez discusses the contemporary educational program of Mexico in the following selection. Although this program has been widely attacked as "radical," the author holds that its basic philosophy is built upon the traditions of the past, and that in its curriculum and methods it is related to Mexican life and culture.]

*Education**

by GEORGE I. SANCHEZ

Mᴇxɪᴄᴏ in revolution lends itself to varied evaluations. Two-score years of hectic activity in the search for national reforms that will compensate for the neglect of centuries has resulted in many changes in the social and economic processes of that nation. The pressure of time and of revolutionary enthusiasms has led to the inauguration of programs and the use of methods that to some may seem unwise and that in many instances are at least unconventional. Because these changes are both a product and a part of a social revolution, they take on the nature of controversies and are subject to conflicting interpretations.

PROGRAM APPROVED ABROAD

It is inevitable that, because of their revolutionary character, some of these changes may be regarded as precipitate. Some may be considered as unprecedented, and, as a consequence, they will be deemed unsound or unwarranted by conservatives. Others of these changes, though not open to criticism on these grounds, have been subject to abuses. All in all, it is understandable that Mexican events of the recent past should evoke contradictory opinions from observers. It is all the more significant, therefore, that the nation's program of education has been well received by all competent students of Mexican affairs.

Inman, commenting on Mexican education, states:

Whatever have been the abuses of the revolution, it is unanimously admitted that the rural school movement has bestowed untold blessings upon a class of people who previously had been almost completely neglected.

Tannenbaum expresses a similar view when he states:

---

* George I. Sánchez, " Education," *The Annals of the American Academy of Political and Social Science* (March, 1940), Vol. 208, pp. 144–152. Reprinted by permission of *The Annals of the American Academy of Political and Social Science*. The footnotes in the original version are omitted here.

No outcome of the Mexican Revolution is more significant than the rural educational movement that has grown from it. . . . It is the most modern, yet the most delicate and sensitive, large-scale movement of cultural stimulus and social awakening that can be recorded in America, and perhaps in the world.

The almost universal acclaim that has been accorded this phase of the revolutionary program is evidence that Mexico is proceeding along educational paths that educators elsewhere deem worthy. However, those who have visited schools throughout the republic know that this acclaim is not based upon those features which elsewhere constitute measures of educational excellence. The school buildings are, as a general rule, inferior to those of the United States. The teachers are not highly trained. Academic achievement by the students is comparatively low, and relatively little emphasis is placed on that educational goal. Administrative and financial aspects leave much to be desired. Generally speaking, then, the technical phases of the " science of education " do not constitute criteria to which Mexican education responds favorably. Interestingly enough, though, this lack of technical excellence has not been considered important enough to detract from the evaluations that have been made of the program.

A SOCIAL PHILOSOPHY OF EDUCATION

It is apparent that Mexico's educational efforts transcend the spheres which are subject to objective measurement. The Mexican school, poor as it is from a material standpoint, is symbolic of a theory of education that is in itself a social philosophy. Rafael Ramírez, one of Mexico's truly great schoolmen, is insistent that " we are more interested that [our] population should be cultured, taking the word in its precise acceptance, than that it should be learned," and that " we will continue to sustain and support this school which we have created and which cultivates culture." In this stress upon acculturation lies the essence of the new education in Mexico, and it is in that direction that we must look to discover its values.

The Mexican social philosophy of education has its roots in the complex origins of the Mexican nation. This philosophy harks back to the trials and tribulations of a people in the making. In order to understand and appreciate the educational viewpoint now being expressed, it is imperative that one be familiar with the antecedents which this viewpoint reflects. For — and this cannot be overemphasized — the schools of the Revolution are but the expression of a mass reaction to conditions experienced over more than four centuries of contact with Western civilization and, before that, during the pre-Columbian era.

From prehistoric times, the peoples of Mexico have been intimately associated with the land. Mexican economy is and always has been an agrarian economy. The use and management of land has been the axis around which Mexican culture has revolved and from which it has derived its sustenance and its inspiration. The search for arable land and the struggle to hold it has been the motive force which has impelled the growth and development of the peoples of Mexico — whether reference be made to the Aztec, the Maya, the Tarascan, the mestizo, or any other important social group or culture in that country. This identification of land and its problems with Mexican culture must not be overlooked in any attempt that is made to understand the social events which are products of that culture. It certainly must be recognized as an important factor in the development of the Mexican social philosophy of education.

EARLY RECOGNITION OF MEXICO'S NEEDS

The first European educators who came to Mexico seem to have sensed immediately the true character of the problem of education in the new lands. Instead of insisting upon European standards of academic achievement through rote learning, these men set out to adapt their techniques to the new milieu — a milieu in which utility and reality played dominant roles. Fray Pedro de Gante, in the first school established in the New World (1523), created a true " school of action." At Texcoco and later (1526) in Mexico City, " two hundred years before Pestalozzi, three hundred years before Froebel, and almost four hundred years before John Dewey, he had an activity school, a school based on current life." Others, like Fray Pedro, were similarly impressed by the need for a new approach to cultural development and to social organization. Early in the sixteenth century, Bishop Vasco de Quiroga busied himself in establishing " foundling hospitals " and schools for the Indians and in organizing their village life. He planned a community school of a special kind, in which the social and economic affairs of an entire village were intimately blended in a sort of agrarian and patriarchal communalism.

This responsiveness of Mexico's great educators to the agrarian folk culture of her peoples constitutes the outstanding contribution of the nation to the theory of education. It is significant to note that this contribution is not of recent date, but that it formed the basic principle upon which the earliest cultural programs inaugurated after the Conquest were founded. It should be stressed, again, that the schools of the Revolution are simply reiterating an educational viewpoint that was first expressed in sixteenth-century New Spain. This viewpoint, though not put into general practice, and long ignored by governments, has served as a guiding principle to social reformers through the centuries. The desire and hope to develop an " integral education " — an education adapted to the total cultural situation — has long motivated the efforts of many of Mexico's humanitarian leaders, even though it has been given a clear-cut expression only recently.

THE MESTIZO

The birth of a mestizo class is probably the most significant single factor in Mexican sociology. The rise of this mixed-blood group of the population marks the unfolding of Mexican nationality — a nationality that embodies both European and indigenous cultures but that is distinct from either in many respects. Unhampered by European standards and traditions, and being native to the land, the mestizo identified himself with native patterns. Being Spanish as well as Indian, he would not accept the limitations inherent in Indian life or those imposed on the Indian by the Spaniard. Here, indeed, was a class that was destined by nature to create nationality out of the conflicting and irreconcilable forces represented by conquering Spaniard and conquered Indian. As Justo Sierra has aptly stated, the mestizo, or half-caste, was " the future owner of the country, the future revolutionary, the future author of nationality."

The educational crusaders of the sixteenth century soon recognized the problem of the mestizo. Fray Pedro de Gante attempted to enroll mestizo children in his school for Indians. Archbishop Zumárraga and Viceroy Mendoza in 1547 brought about the founding of the famous school of San Juan de Letrán for mestizo boys. Shortly thereafter the school of Our Lady of Charity was founded for the education of mestizo girls. These efforts took place before any provision was made for the education of Spanish children, and were continued and expanded, for both Indians and mestizos, by later officials and religious orders.

From the very beginning, the education of the mestizo was regarded as a problem distinct from that of the Indian. It is to be noted also that education for Spanish children was regarded as distinct from both Indian and mestizo education. Schools for Spanish children sought to approximate European curricula and standards. Mestizo and Indian schools attempted to modify those standards in the light of the social and economic factors peculiar to the condition of these sectors of the population. This effort to achieve fidelity to real life in the education of these classes marks the beginnings of a typically Mexican approach to education. The stress of economic exploitation of the resources of New Spain and the political complications incident to the decline of Spain as a world power soon relegated educational efforts in behalf of the Indians and the mestizos to the background. However, here and there over the land a religious order or a parish priest persisted along the paths laid out by Fray Pedro, by Bishop Quiroga, and by those other early educators who had envisioned an "integral education." Furthermore, those who had known the early schools at first hand carried on the memory of that realistic approach to Mexican cultural problems and passed it on to tradition. The cultural neglect of the masses during the later colonial period contrasted with the humanitarian attitude taken before, and tended to perpetuate that tradition. The denial of education to the underprivileged classes only served to instill into them a yearning for the institutions whose fruits they had once tasted.

INFLUENCE OF THE EARLY SCHOOLS

The Mexican masses, particularly the mestizos, who in time rose to numerical preponderance, carried on the memory of those early schools. That was the only education they knew. And, significantly enough, that education fitted their situation. In that educational approach, labor was dignified. Arts and crafts were indispensable phases of the curriculum. Native resources and native ways, language, and techniques, were part and parcel of the system. It gave due regard to the rurality of the common people and sought to respond to their agrarian economy.

It should not be inferred that the "socialistic" doctrine of education was set forth in its entirety as long ago as the sixteenth and seventeenth centuries. It should be recognized, however, that the groundwork for such a doctrine was laid through the activities of those colonial schoolmen who sought to attune the educative process to the rhythm of the Mexican environment.

Through the years, under the pressure of subjugation and exploitation, the peasant class longed for a way out — for redemption. They and their champions embellished the earlier educational viewpoint, incorporating in it elements from each new experience. The common people suffered the loss of their lands, were cast into peonage, were stepchildren in their own home. Mexican customs were belittled and foreign patterns were exalted by the ruling class. Nativism was unfashionable, social welfare was classed as radicalism.

It is no wonder that these experiences should have made a lasting impression upon the populace — a populace that knew only its own traditions and that was a class apart from the dominant culture. It is not surprising that these experiences should affect the hopes and aspirations of the proletariat with respect to government, labor, land, and education. It is particularly easy to understand how these experiences should have served to intensify the desire for schools that were schools of the people, where the Mexican and his life were dignified.

The mestizo, because his position was the most uncertain in all these events, came to symbolize the neglect of the common man. Precariously situated between the two races, he reacted to the impulses of both. His affinity to the Indian and the land allied him to native culture. His relation to the Spaniard placed him closer to the ruling class than was the Indian. Circumstances, then, made him a cultural nationalist. His experience as a social and economic outcast instilled into him a lasting resentment against the existing order. To compensate for his miserable condition, he slowly and unconsciously developed a viewpoint which in essence was a negation of the forces of exploitation — peonage, foreign domination, clericalism. To the mestizo, the land question, nativism, liberty, and education were inseparable phases of the one issue — the right of Mexicans to Mexican nationality.

SOCIALISTIC EDUCATION

The problem faced by the reformers of the Revolution that began in 1910 was, in essence, that of meeting the deficiencies of the Mexican scene through programs which were in accord with popular sentiment. The masses, emerging victorious from a bloody struggle with their oppressors, demanded the fruits of their victory — land, liberty, education, effective suffrage. At long last, the common people had come into their own and were in a position to insist that Mexican affairs be conducted in a Mexican way for Mexicans. Their leaders must needs heed the voice of the populace and seek, in a new government, the answer to these demands.

It required no meticulous researches to point out the needs of the people. Illiteracy had reached staggering proportions. Disease was rampant. The people were hungry — for food and for the land that produced it. They lacked the training and the tools to perform the common and technical tasks of production. The worker's status was undefined. The Mexican, in victory, emerged upon a prostrate and exhausted nation. He was confronted with the task of building a new Mexican nationality from the ground up.

It is absurd to attribute the inspiration for Mexico's revolutionary undertakings to foreign auspices. Communalism is native to Mexico. Nativism is a product of the obscurity into which the Indian and the mestizo, constituting today more than three fourths of the population, were relegated in the past. Agrarianism is inherent in the Mexican economy and has been established as the fundamental way of life in Mexico from pre-Columbian times, through three hundred years of colonial régime, through the nineteenth century, to the present. It is not surprising, then, that the Mexican educational viewpoint should reflect these basic factors of Mexican culture, particularly in view of the fact that the only educational experiences which the common man had were those in which these factors had played important roles.

The Revolution gave expression to these latent social impulses. In the process, it became increasingly evident that education must assume far-reaching responsibilities in the total revolutionary program. Social and economic reforms required a program of enlightenment for the masses. It was inevitable that the schools should take an active part in land and labor questions, in the conflict between the State and the clergy, in promulgating the doctrines of the Revolution. Education expanded into new spheres. It passed on from the instruction of the individual to community education. The school relegated reading and writing to a secondary position and took on the task of social welfare — health, agriculture, village organization, recreation, and homemaking. A long tradition and the Revolution made the Mexican school " The House of the People," the " School of Action," the " Socialistic School."

Lack of financial and technical resources proved a blessing in disguise. Schoolhouses were built by the peasants not only because the *campesino* was fired by the zeal of a new day and not only because he was stimulated by the missionary teacher, but also because funds and a planned program of school construction were lacking. Recourse was taken to inspired villagers for teachers because trained ones were not available. The usual materials of instruction were wanting, so the teacher resorted to native materials. Unconsciously and of necessity, a premium was placed on creativeness, on Mexican ingenuity. Lack of precedents and of material resources gave Mexico's educational leaders an opportunity to put into practice their social philosophy of education. Because it depended on native resources and native creativeness, the program of education became a truly Mexican program that fitted Mexican needs and conditions.

Socialistic education is a program of Mexican ideas and ideals. It has grown out of Mexican soil and has been nurtured on native resources. It stresses the real life problems of the common people through methods and materials that are within their reach and understanding. In addition, education is not divorced from the other salient phases of current Mexican life. The school program seeks to become an integral part of community life — of farming and marketing, of health and sanitation, of homemaking and social organization. It is a phase of the total program of revolutionary reforms and is intended to operate in intimate relationship to that larger program.

SCHOOLS FOR THE PEOPLE

Before the Revolution, schools were virtually unknown to the rural population. That group constitutes more than two thirds of the total population. The peasant is the typical Mexican, and rural life is typical of Mexican life. Furthermore, this forgotten major fraction had fought and won the Revolution. It followed that, in education as in economic reforms, first consideration had to be given to rural areas. The organization of a system of rural schools was seriously undertaken shortly after 1920 and has progressed apace since that time. It is in the development of that program that Mexico has made its greatest contribution to educational theory and practice. In meeting the problem of education for the rural masses, the " men of the Revolution " have shown a creativeness and a sense of fitness that has received the acclaim of the world.

This contribution of Mexican education is illustrated clearly in four of its phases: the rural school, the school for Indians, the rural normal school, and, above all, the Cultural Mission. These agencies reflect most clearly the educational philosophy which has been referred to above. It is here that the Mexican social doctrine of acculturation is most vividly expressed.

RURAL SCHOOLS

The rural school is a humble structure. The building was built or improvised from the community's resources through popular subscription and effort. A blackboard; some rustic benches or tables; and, among the fortunate ones, a few books; a map; and some pamphlets, make up the equipment and instructional material. The teacher may have attended a teachers' institute or two for a few days, or he may be among the lucky ones who is a *normalista* — one who has gone to a normal school. More often, the teacher is an ambitious boy or girl from the village with very little formal education, but who has impressed the federal supervisor with his enthusiasm and zeal. The national government pays the salary of the teacher (usually less than one dollar per day) and may occasionally furnish a few materials (pamphlets, window glass, tools).

The curriculum of the rural school is undefined. Through pamphlets and bulletins, teachers' meetings, and the like, the teacher has been drilled in the theory of Mexican education — in the social doctrines of the day. The supervisor has suggested activities that are in keeping with these ideas and has pointed out that the school is for adults as well as for children, and that community affairs are within the scope of action of the school, the teacher, and the pupils.

The details of the program are left to the teacher. Impressed by the spirit of reform, he turns to meeting environmental deficiencies. Literacy, national language, recreation, health and sanitation, agriculture, and marketing are fields of action for the schools — subjects of the curriculum. The public market, the village plaza, the fields and gardens, have become school laboratories. Local fiestas and other community affairs are avenues of expression to the rural school. All these activities furnish the inspiration for the classroom phase of the school's work.

NORMAL SCHOOLS

The normal schools have recognized the significance of this community type of education and are seeking to promote it through teacher education. In the first place, these normal schools have been placed in rural areas which are typical of the regions to be served by their graduates. These teacher-education institutions, like the rural schools, are adjusted to their setting. Agricultural activities suited to the area form a basic part of the training course. As a matter of fact, during the first two years the course does not differentiate between those students who are to be graduated in agriculture and those who are to become teachers.

The students serve apprenticeships in real rural schools. They go into the surrounding territory on campaigns of various sorts — health, agriculture, literacy, and adult education in general. These pupils are taught to take advantage of native resources — materials and culture. As the institution is a partially self-supporting boarding school, the students are given varied experiences in such activities as self-government, homemaking, construction, small industries, and marketing. Thus prospective teachers carry out under competent guidance what the rural teacher in the past has had to improvise.

The stress given to action in the field of community education has its influence in the academic courses. While the usual education courses — psychology, methods, and the like — form a part of the curriculum, they are as yet rudimentary and undeveloped. Much better work is done in subjects considered of more vital importance: agriculture, health, general science, history. All in all, the striking feature of the normal schools lies in that they are in reality field laboratories in rural reconstruction. The fact that they are established in rural areas for rural students from those areas who are given real life experience in meeting regional social and economic problems is the significant aspect of this contribution to the theory of teacher education. The immaturity of their academic work can be solved in time. The salient feature of the Mexican rural normal school is that it is grounded upon what appears to be a very sound principle of acculturation.

INDIAN SCHOOLS

Indian schools reflect this same approach to education. They are elementary coeducational boarding schools located in regions with a large Indian population. The children perform all the tasks of the school and the school farm through a division of labor organized by student government. They make their food, their clothes, and their classroom and dormitory furniture. More often than not they construct the school plant, adapting an old government building, a church, or a ruined *hacienda* to this purpose. The teachers oftentimes are Indians who have attended a normal school. The institution is partly self-supporting, the federal government paying teachers' salaries and a small monthly food and clothing allowance per pupil.

Like the normal schools, the Indian schools serve not only the enrolled students but the people in the surrounding territory as well. The schools and their activities are kept at a level only slightly above the situation of the people of the area, and every effort is made to keep standards of achievement — in health, agriculture, homemaking, and other lines — at points that are within the reach of the community. The guiding principle of the program is the aim to prepare the children to live progressive lives in their communities by acquainting them with practices and ideas which fit their milieu but which are calculated to improve it. This acquaintance is brought about not only through the usual academic school subjects but also by related real life activities.

THE CULTURAL MISSION

The Cultural Mission is Mexico's pre-eminent teacher-education agency. It is also the one agency that is most representative of the ideas and ideals which motivate Mexican education, and of the practice thereof. It is understandable that this should be the case, for the Cultural Mission is an outgrowth of the first exploratory steps that were taken in the field of rural education. Originally, the *misionero* was the individual sent out (1921) by the central government to establish the first rural schools in a region and to act as the spearhead of the newly inaugurated school movement. These missioners founded " The House of the People " — the first of the new rural schools. In time the task of founding schools, selecting teachers, supervising them, and stimulating the movement became too large for one individual. The Cultural Mission was created to meet this exigency.

The missions are, in effect, traveling normal schools. In fact, the program of the rural normal schools is patterned largely after that of the missions, and these schools may be thought of as stationary or permanent cultural missions. The personnel of a cultural mission usually consists of an agricultural worker, a nurse, an educator, a music teacher, a physical education and recreation director, a manual arts instructor, and a social welfare worker. These agents undertake school and community education and seek to link the rural schools with the vital problems of the districts served by those schools.

Through teachers' institutes, through field activities in the communities, through recreational programs, and through field and classroom demonstrations, the mission seeks to orient community life and to guide the program of the rural school.

The Cultural Mission is not only an agency for teacher education, but it is also a center of propaganda and stimulus for the rural communities. In this latter capacity each mission tries to guide rural people in such matters as housing, cooperative marketing, health, and farming. The mission remains in each community of its circuit for about eight weeks. In time it returns to former centers of operations to renew its efforts. In all these activities the assembled teachers of the surrounding area are utilized as understudies to the missioners. In the institute classes the missioners try to get the teachers to relate this experience to the instructional programs for both children and adults. The idea is to get the teacher to act as an individual cultural mission in his classroom and community work.

This method of combining public field-service activities with teacher education and classroom instruction *in situ* has proved a valuable one. In addition to the contribution rendered in the fields of supervision and in-service education, this program keeps rural education in close tune with rural life. It is this desire to establish a harmonious blending of the " science of education " with a people's culture that symbolizes the Mexican social philosophy of education. The Cultural Mission illustrates this ideal in practice.

Special application of this approach to Mexico's educational problems are to be observed in various fields. Arts and crafts schools, day and night schools for workers and out-of-school youth, technical secondary schools, kindergartens, and other special schools are being established to reach various sectors of the population in a program of cultural rehabilitation. It is significant to note that urban schools, once of a formal and strictly academic (preparatory) type, are responding to the new viewpoint with courses, activities, and methods which reflect the influence of what is taking place in rural education. It must be emphasized, however, that Mexico's contribution to education is coming from her unique approach to mass education, and that mass education in Mexico is primarily rural education.

THE PROSPECT

The realities of the Mexican scene are still such that only a tentative success can be attributed to the nation's program of cultural rehabilitation. It remains for the future to determine whether the revolutionary ideal — "To Educate Is To Redeem" — is attained. From this distance, however, it appears that in education, Mexico has placed her faith in a sound philosophy. Cultural nationalism, agrarianism, and the identification of social welfare with pedagogy in an action program involving the entire human and material resources of the community combine into a promising social philosophy of education. The adaptations to this philosophy that have already been made in professional techniques — in supervision, in teacher education, in classroom instruction — evidence the administrative resourcefulness of the nation. The creativeness that produced the "House of the People" and the Cultural Mission is worthy of confidence. Future educationists and future administrations have a well-defined and laudable pattern to follow. Twenty years of the new education, though a relatively brief experience, has constituted an effective demonstration of a way out for the hitherto forgotten masses. Mexico's educational undertaking is proceeding along lines which should lead to success and bring the blessings of cultural well-being to her people.

No. 45 [The social importance of a school in a society in which illiteracy is common and schooling for the masses almost unknown is emphasized again in the following article. Such a school is indeed a community center, and its influence upon the community has a deep social significance.

"More Than ABC's" is of interest not only because of its educational implications, but also because it exemplifies another instance of inter-American cooperation. This kind of joint enterprise in cultural fields, even though it be restricted to technical or professional matters, is of paramount importance in the development of a real Pan American sentiment and unity.]

More than ABC's*

by WILLFRED MAUCK

THE brown road, lying straight as a measuring stick across the endless, rock-strewn fields of the *altiplano,* was dotted irregularly with moving bits of color. It was Corpus Christi time, and all along our route from La Paz to Achacachi, groups of Aymarás made their way, brilliant with festival costumes in every hue of the rainbow, flourishing long poles decked with gaily colored streamers. Some were swirling in a dance as they went along, the women's black skirts billowing out above petticoats of orange, blue, red, yellow, and green. Most of the pilgrims greeted us as we passed. They did not know us; but they are a courteous people. Besides, although they might not be able to read the Spanish legend on our car — *" Servicio Cooperativo Interamericano de Educación "* — many of them knew the *Servicio's* emblem.

On our left, the rock-walled fields, surrounding scattered adobe homes, sloped gently upward to the low hills that screened Lake Titicaca from our view. Far to the right, against a clear blue sky, the peaks of the Cordillera Real kept pace with us. A banner of white cloud floated from the white cone of Iliampu. Peaked-capped boys, whirling their slingshots, chased their herds of llamas and alpacas out of our path.

It was my first glimpse of rural Bolivia, and I asked endless questions of my companions, to whom the scene was a familiar one. For nearly three years they had been living in rarefied highlands of the *altiplano,* working day by day and month by month in a cooperative program with Bolivian teachers and officials.

Like other Latin American republics, Bolivia is engaged in a reorganization and reorientation of her rural education system. And like several of her neighbors, Bolivia invited the United States government, through the Institute of Inter-American Affairs, to collaborate with her in the program. Each country pays the salaries and expenses of its own technicians and specialists. Each also contributes its

---

* Willfred Mauck, " More Than ABC's," *Américas* (October, 1949), Vol. 1, No. 8, pp. 12–15, 46. Reprinted by permission of *Américas,* a monthly magazine published by the Pan American Union in English, Spanish, and Portuguese.

share of the funds for direct expenditures on project activities. When the program started in September 1944, Bolivia was paying about four dollars to every five coming from the United States, and today she is providing about three quarters of the project funds. Now the chief of the Institute's field staff, Ernest Maes, and one of his specialists, Lloyd Tireman, were pointing out to me, as a representative of the Institute's Washington Office, what was being done.

Before long, we would be driving along the shores of Titicaca to the rural normal school at Santiago de Huata. A narrow road branched off to our left, toward a village. " That is the *comunidad* of Batallas, over there," said Ernest, as we passed the road junction. " One of our central schools is there."

" I should like to see it, if there is time," I said.

We turned the car around and took the road to Batallas. It was just an unscheduled deviation from our plans for the day; but it turned out to be one of the most interesting experiences of a long trip through several countries. Ever since then, Batallas has been to me a symbol both of international collaboration and of a rural community's sturdy march of progress.

" Before we get to Batallas," said Ernest, " I want to explain what it was like before we and our Bolivian colleagues started work here, for the school has brought about many changes in the last few months. The schoolhouse was too small to accommodate the students. You see, children came here from many kilometers' distance, walking all the way, frequently without breakfast, to join with the children of the village itself. The school was dark and uncomfortable, with almost no furniture. There was not even a blackboard to help the teacher in her work. The curriculum was the same as in the city schools of La Paz, with no bearing upon the daily lives of the children and their parents. The method of instruction was memorization — the teacher read or recited to the children their lessons in anatomy, in geography, in arithmetic. The pupils copied faithfully in their notebooks what the teacher read to them; then they learned it all by heart.

" Of course, many children of the *comunidad* did not come to school at all, in spite of the compulsory education laws. There was not room for them, for one thing. But even if there had been, one can scarcely blame their parents for feeling that since the youngsters were learning little that could be useful to them in later life, they might better be at home learning the tasks of farming and home-making. The teachers are hard-working, and they were doing their best . . . but here we are at the school."

The cluster of school buildings stood in a walled compound at the near edge of the village. As we approached the gate, a group of men came toward us. We were pleasantly surprised to see that one of them was Señor Raúl Bravo, Bolivian Director of Rural Education in the Ministry of Education, who was working closely with us in the cooperative program. He promptly took charge of our visit and acted as our interpreter, in Spanish, with the Aymará-speaking villagers.

Before we entered the compound, I noticed a ring of armed men, irregularly spaced in a circle around the walls of the school grounds. "What are they doing?" I asked Señor Bravo. He smiled grimly.

"That is an interesting story," he replied. "You see, the laborers on the nearby *haciendas* have taken to arms against the landowners. In other days when such disturbances occurred, the villagers were accustomed to make common cause with the laborers. But this year the men of Batallas kept aloof because, they said, men from La Paz were transforming their school, and the school was transforming the *comunidad,* and all that would be lost if Batallas were to join in the uprising. When the laborers threatened to destroy the school, the villagers set up this cordon of guards. Batallas is safe."

We looked thoughtfully for a moment past the silent line of guards toward a distant eucalyptus grove on a hillside, where Discontent was ruling. Then we turned in to the school grounds.

My first impression was that the whole community had gathered at the school. There were dozens of children in all parts of the grounds. But there were also many adults, some mingling with the children, others gathered in a group before the main building. As we approached, we could hear the voices of students and teacher, discussing the lesson. "They are studying nutrition just now," said Señor Bravo, "finding out what they should eat each day to keep them well."

"But what are the adults doing, standing by the door and windows?" I asked.

"They are learning, too," replied Señor Bravo with a smile. "You usually find several parents here every day. What the children are learning is of great importance in the home. These are intelligent people, and they are not wasting an opportunity which lies at their very doors."

The parents made way for us, and we entered the school. Instantly all the pupils rose in greeting. We were introduced to the teacher and gave her our special congratulations, as this was *Día de los Maestros* (Teachers' Day). Proudly the teacher — a graduate of the rural normal school at Santiago de Huata — showed us the classroom and the handiwork of her students decorating the neatly whitewashed adobe walls.

"A few months ago," she explained, "this was the school's only building. There were no windows — only the door for light and ventilation. The walls were unpainted and undecorated. The pupils sat on the earthen floor, or on stones they brought from the fields. Now the children and I have worked together, with some help from the parents, to make the windows, paint the walls, build adobe benches and desks. They may not look as comfortable to you as wooden furniture, but there is no wood here, and this is much better than anything the children have had before. And, see, we have even made a blackboard! The men and women of the *Servicio Cooperativo* showed us how to make a smooth surface on the adobe walls and cover it with lampblack and eggwhite. It is wonderful to be able to work with a blackboard!"

"Now," said Señor Bravo, "I want to show you that this lesson in nutrition the children are studying is not mere theory." He led us outside through an archway into a courtyard between two new buildings. The aroma of food drifted from an open doorway. Inside, over a simple but effective adobe stove, the school lunch was being prepared by two teachers and a group of children. "The children no longer come hungry to school, and go home hungry," continued Bravo. "Their diet, based on foods available in this locality, is carefully planned in accordance with the principles they are learning at this moment."

"Who supplies the food?" I asked. (My part of the conversation at Batallas always ended with a question mark.)

" We must buy a little, and the children bring in some of it. As for the rest — follow me."

He led the way around the buildings to the rear of the school. Here more children and a sprinkling of adults were cultivating an extensive garden divided into neat patches, each the particular responsibility of a group of children. Some of the produce, Señor Bravo explained, was used in the school lunches. The rest was taken home by the children or sold for the benefit of the school. The children had been organized into school agricultural clubs (*Clubes Escolares Campesinos*), and the work in the gardens was part of both their school instruction and their club activities. " The club members," said Bravo, " make it part of their duty — and pleasure — to learn how to improve their tools and cultivation methods. Then, in cooperation with the organized parents' association, they carry their new methods to their own farms."

At one corner of the garden, a small group was working busily with shovels, adobe bricks, and a mixing trough. " Those boys and the two men who are helping them with the heavy work are building an inexpensive but effective row of latrines for the school. Until the cooperative program entered Batallas, neither the latrine nor the necessity for it was known here. Now the instruction in sanitation and hygiene is showing results."

" But we are aiming also at community education," I pointed out. " If that instruction is put into effect only at the school, will it really have any permanent effect as far as the children are concerned? "

" Ah," said Ernest Maes, " we shall have to *show* you the answer to that."

We made our way once more to the compound gate and walked toward the village. I was doing some thinking. " But Ernest," I said, " we think of a school primarily as a place where one learns reading, writing, and arithmetic. From what I have seen so far, this school teaches only agriculture, health, and — "

Señor Bravo broke in. " No, no! Our children must be taught to read and to figure, of course. And you should see how interested they are in it! For they are taught to read about things that are familiar to them — their fields, their school activities, their homes. They work out arithmetic problems which deal with the measurements of their fields, the census of their farm animals, the weight of their produce, the prices in the market place at Achacachi. It has meaning for them, and that kind of learning is not a burden."

Four or five villagers were approaching us at a dignified and formal pace. At their head walked a man carrying an impressive-looking staff. His wife was beside him. "Here is the *alcalde* of Batallas," whispered Bravo. "He has been informed of your visit and has come to welcome you."

The *alcalde*, or mayor, and his following stopped before us, making gentle gestures of greeting. Señor Bravo stepped forward and explained to him in Aymará who we were and why we had come. First the *alcalde*, then his wife, advanced and gave each of us a dignified but friendly embrace. Then the *alcalde* made a brief speech in Aymará. "He says," translated Señor Bravo, "that it is a fortunate omen that brings you to Batallas on the *Día de los Maestros,* for it gives him the opportunity he has long desired to express to you and to the *Servicio Cooperativo* the sincere appreciation of his people for the work that has been started here. He says the *Servicio* has made every day a *Día de los Maestros* in Batallas. He asks you to accept the hospitality of his people and to permit him to show you the changes which are taking place among them under the cooperative program. He adds," Bravo continued with a grin, "that he must make a confession. He accepted the cooperative program with reluctance at the beginning, because it seemed dangerous to meddle with the ancient ways of doing things. But now he wishes to be considered a colleague in the program."

My brief reply was less eloquent, for the *alcalde* had a natural gift of oratory, but it was no less sincere. Our two groups joined, and we proceeded toward the nearest houses. On the way Señor Bravo explained that the school children had formed teams, to each of which one or two members of the parents' auxiliary was attached. The teams moved from one household to another in the *comunidad,* helping the owners to improve their homes and fields and teaching them how to maintain them as pleasanter, more comfortable, and more healthful places to live in. The *alcalde* had decided to take us first to two homes not yet reached by the school, and then to two or three which had been "transformed," as Bravo translated it.

As we approached the first house, a woman who was standing in the low doorway twirling the inevitable spindle of wool stepped forward shyly to greet us. The *alcalde* apparently explained the nature of our visit and asked permission to enter. Bravo translated her reply under his breath. " She says we are welcome, and asks the *alcalde* when the children will come to her home, for she wishes it to be like that of some of her neighbors."

Tireman, Maes, and I stooped to follow the *alcalde* into the one-room house. After the bright sunlight, it was several moments before we could see. The doorway, which we could not help blocking for lack of standing room, was the only opening. I was startled by the sudden rush past my legs of two chickens, which apparently resented our intrusion and slipped past me, squawking, into the farmyard. By that time, the room began to take shape in the darkness. At one end, three stones supported a blackened pot. This was the kitchen. The walls and roof were blackened by smoke, and some of the acrid fumes that had not yet found their way through the roof made our eyes smart. At the other end of the room, a pile of thick blankets on the earthen floor marked the family bedroom. Between the " bedroom " and " kitchen," much of the tiny floor space was taken up with neat little piles of food — one of meat, another of potatoes, and so forth. A few earthen dishes leaned against the farther wall. Two cords strung from one side of the room to the other bore a few articles of clothing. We stepped again into the sunlight, with some difficulty as a sheep chose that moment to try to enter the house, and the doorway was not wide enough for two-way traffic. We thanked our hostess and promised that the children would come soon. Her smile would have done credit to a diplomat's lady.

At the next house, the woman was courteous but not cordial. She explained that we were welcome but that she hoped the school would not interfere with her home. " Old ways are best," she said — or the equivalent adage in Aymará. Except for the difference in greeting, this house was much like the first. Then the *alcalde* smiled. " Now I show you the new day," Bravo translated.

Our third visit showed a startling difference. This house had been whitewashed, inside and out. The next thing I noticed was two windows cut through the adobe and flanking the doorway. Inside, I got the impression of spaciousness, in contrast to the two interiors we had visited. This was no doubt partly due to the whitewash and the light; then I noticed that there was no " kitchen." The pile of blankets occupied one end of the room — but they rested on a neat platform of adobe, some twenty inches above the floor level. Next I realized that none of the floor space was used for food storage. A series of niches had been cut into the back wall. Here the food was stored, the few dishes were neatly stacked, and some clothing was folded into piles. The floor was of bare earth, but carefully swept, and there was no evidence of farm animals or fowls. We stepped outside, and the *alcalde* led us to one end of the house to a lean-to shed. Here was the transplanted kitchen, from which the smoke could not enter the house. Yet the fire gave some warmth to the sleeping quarters on the other side of the wall. Behind the lean-to were several small pens, separated by adobe walls, where the farm animals were kept. And beyond was a new, sanitary latrine, exactly like those at the school. The master of the house explained proudly that he himself had helped the children build it.

Twice more the *alcalde* led us to homes where the school had been at work. The last was his own, with the added dignity of an attractive adobe wall, neatly whitewashed, surrounding home and field.

It was time for us to go, and the *alcalde* walked with us back toward the school and our waiting car. I was silent, thinking of what these people were doing for their own benefit, and happy that in some measure the people of my country, through the Institute of Inter-American Affairs, had had an opportunity to work with Bolivians through their schools. I was thinking of the teachers who had done their work well, of the parents who had worked so hard beside their children and who were not afraid to try something new, of the children themselves, who were already proving themselves in citizenship.

At the school we stopped, while the *alcalde* cleared his throat and made another brief, easy address. He repeated his appreciation and emphasized once more his change of attitude — from tolerance to active support for the cooperative program. Near the end he smiled, and an almost mischievous look came into his eyes as he spoke his last sentences. Bravo roared with laughter. " He says, ' I was born in an evil time, as you can see! When I was young, I had to keep silent and listen to my elders, and I longed for the day when I should be grown and able to speak with all authority. Now I am old, and lo! I must be silent and listen to my children! ' "

CHAPTER 17

—— *Public Policy* ——
in Health
and Housing

No. 46 [Earlier articles in this book have emphasized the influence of economic factors upon the political organization of society
in Latin America. We have seen how the low living standards in
several of the Latin American nations have made it difficult for their
people to play a vigorous and hence a determining part in political
affairs. It has been indicated that one of the causes of low living
standards is the inability of the millions in Latin America to work
efficiently. In part, this is due to an *economic* cause, the lack of capital. Lacking capital, Latin American industrialists find it difficult to
introduce modern technological improvements.

The economic productivity and prosperity of Latin America is
also seriously impaired by the terrible toll that illness takes each
year. The vital statistics, when available, graphically portray the
costs of disease in terms of lives lost or damaged, but they probably
can never indicate the costs in terms of lost economic production.
And unless production can be increased and diversified, standards
of living will remain low.

Most of the republics of Latin America cannot finance programs
of public health broad enough in scope to " make America healthy."
However, through cooperative plans and policies, with inter-
American administration, much can be done. The author of the following selection concludes that " in no field of international activity
has collaboration been so successful as in that of health."]

To Make America Healthy*

by ALVARO PEREZ

DURING the recent earthquake that destroyed Central Ecuador, a doctor and a sanitary engineer joined the voluntary workers and members of the government already at the scene to undertake the difficult and noble task of saving what was left. The newcomers, representatives of the Pan American Sanitary Bureau, were fulfilling a mission entrusted to them half a century before. Their job was to guarantee the life of the survivors by warding off diseases that generally follow in the wake of such catastrophes.

Laying waste entire cities, the earthquake had swallowed up thousands of people. Survivors found refuge in half-destroyed houses or crowded into tents, without food, water, or proper ventilation. The Pan American Sanitary Bureau in Washington sent a special plane loaded with drugs, chemical products to purify water, insecticides, and medicines, giving its representatives the weapons they needed to fight pestilence and typhoid and to prevent dangerous contagion.

Forty-seven years earlier, in December 1902, a group of medical men from all over the hemisphere met in Washington, D.C., to start an international agency to make America healthy. They realized that germs disregard frontiers, that human pain does not respond to political treaties. To these men it seemed only logical for the countries to pool their resources to guard the people's health and give them a better life. So the Pan American Sanitary Bureau was born.

In those days, public health work like that carried out in Ambato, in Pelileo, in Píllaro — or, rather, in what was left of these towns on the Ecuadorean plateau — was only a dream. The years between have been an inspiring epoch in man's fight against disease in America, a battle no longer isolated, local, patchy, but carefully planned through a single, continental system.

* Alvaro Pérez, " To Make America Healthy," Américas (January, 1950), Vol. 2, No. 1, pp. 20–23. Reprinted by permission of Américas, a monthly magazine published by the Pan American Union in English, Spanish, and Portuguese.

For the Pan American Sanitary Bureau has now become a vast network of public health activities, operating through permanent sectional offices in El Paso, Texas, Guatemala City, and Lima, Peru. Through them the Bureau can intervene quickly in case of epidemics, and can serve as consultant for hygiene authorities in diverse areas. It has at its fingertips the latest scientific developments in medicine and sanitation, which it channels through all the countries.

The Pan American Sanitary Bureau was born at a time when people feared each other. Every government had established preventive health measures that heightened already-existing barriers between the countries. Quarantine was a continual nuisance to travelers. Relations between people, trade, any kind of interchange, found an inevitable obstacle in the provisions each government established to protect its population.

In these circumstances, the Second International Conference of American States met in Mexico in 1901 and agreed that a mission made up of at least five members would be established in Washington. Later, in October 1905, the first Pan American Health Code was signed in Washington. Following the lead of Guatemala on April 27, 1906, all the governments quickly ratified it, with Chile the last to deliver on July 15, 1907. The countries of America were eager to put in force a charter that would set forth fundamental measures of defense against contagious diseases.

With the creation of the new body, it was a question of coordinating preventive measures. The United States delegation to the first conference described the existing situation like this: " The aim of this conference is to make sanitation take the place of quarantine. When the idea we envisage crystallizes, the sanitation of Western Hemisphere cities will be so perfect that propagation of contagious diseases will be impossible, and quarantine measures that impede travel and trade, with their annoying delays and high cost, will no longer be necessary."

But this time has not yet arrived. Quarantine measures are still necessary in some ports, where the familiar chains with brass discs are still visible to remind us that man's fight against plague has not yet ended. Joint international action to prevent rats from traveling across the ocean, carrying the insect that harbors nefarious disease germs, continues as a basic precaution. Modern air transport, while drawing our countries closer, increases the danger of contagion. A mosquito carrier of yellow fever can travel very comfortably aboard luxury air liners from the Brazilian backlands to New York skyscrapers. Therefore fumigation is necessary in airports, which sometimes surprises and annoys the passengers, even though in many cases it has kept them from carrying a hidden enemy.

The first Pan American health conferences were of a speculative nature, consisting largely of conversation and interchange of information. Like islands in a scattered archipelago, flimsily connected by diplomatic relations, our nations did not really function as a continental whole. The sanitation pioneers found a wide gap between their brilliant ideas and the actual isolation in which our people lived. But while they waited for the opportunity modern communications have made possible, they laid the base for subsequent operations that saved many of our urban and rural groups and helped prevent unforeseen disasters.

Take what happened in San Miguel, El Salvador, for example. The scene could have been any one of the tropical corners of our continent. Tenacious heat, sticky humidity; a group of sick country people, children without shoes, people without a future. Malaria threatens. Ground planted during the dry season becomes marshy valleys during the rainy season. Pedro and Luz Rodríguez live off the land on their small coffee farm. Pedro dies of malaria, leaving his family without support. The children are not old enough to work, but they have already become victims of a common enemy. Malaria reigns. The Sanitary Bureau comes to the rescue, looks for and finds the breeding-place of the anopheles mosquito, and sets out to exterminate it. It cleans up the land, digs drainage ditches, and a better soil emerges from a stagnant pool. Months later, the malaria is under control, and the Rodríguez family and their neighbors are incorporated into a better society.

Science has demonstrated that in the case of malaria, it costs less to cure it than to suffer from it. The economic, effective use of DDT has made this possible. Thus malaria has become as expensive as a luxury item, and no nation can afford it. This very practical consideration is the basis for the Pan American Sanitary Bureau's antimalarial campaigns, which cover most of the affected zones of the continent.

Around 1935, the Sanitary Bureau again had an opportunity to put its system of international cooperation to good use. A plague epidemic broke out in Asunción, Paraguay, traveled south to the Strait of Magellan and north along the Pacific coast. Most of the ports became infected, a calamity for navigation, trade, and travel. Like an oil stain, the disease spread inland to the cordillera. As local doctors were fighting a losing battle, an S.O.S. was sent to the Pan American Sanitary Bureau.

A mission of specialists arrived in Ecuador. Dr. John R. Murdock, now Assistant Director of the Bureau, led the dramatic campaign that began to take shape. Most cases were concentrated in the Guayaquil area. Isolated cases cropped up along the rivers and rail centers, starting with Durán, across the river from Guayaquil. The Sanitary Bureau scientists segregated the stricken and organized other control measures. When the region appeared free of common plague, pneumonic plague, an even deadlier disease, suddenly struck in Riobamba. The first victims were the Sisters of Charity in the local convent. In a few weeks, fifteen of the eighteen nuns and the doctor who treated them had died. Panic gripped the country. When Dr. Murdock went to Quito to urge a more drastic course on the Ecuadorean government, he called on the United States Ambassador, who received him at one end of a huge salon, with a peremptory warning not to come close.

The medical specialists of the Pan American Sanitary Bureau had gone to Ecuador to save the population from catastrophe. Nevertheless, popular imagination, feverish from the epidemic, did not understand their purpose and feared their presence to the point of violence. The automobile in which the doctors traveled was stoned, their presence in the towns caused mass terror.

Finally, the government declared a state of siege; only then could the sanitary authorities, backed up by the army, cope with the situation. The people had abandoned the region in a panic. They were as terrified of the doctors as if they were the plague itself. But with tenacity, with admirable devotion, the sanitation doctors succeeded in isolating the cases and established the origin of the epidemic.

With singular patience and energy, they pursued their task until they had rid Ecuador of the disease. The campaign continued, and since then not a single case has appeared in an American port.

One of the fondest hopes of our most progressive statesmen has been the Pan American Highway, a road linking north and south. When it began to take form, it was discovered that the projected highway, intended to make way for the exchange of products and ideas, was also used by pernicious germs to menace the health of neighboring peoples.

Investigations conducted by the Sanitary Bureau revealed that *onchocerciasis,* a disease from an African parasite that causes blindness, existed from southern Mexico to Northern Guatemala. These initial findings sparked an active campaign to eradicate the disease.

Two years ago a case demonstrated how cooperative measures can be by-passed unless controls are reinforced by action. A traveler came to New York from Mexico. And he brought smallpox. New York authorities, whose health services have been developed to the highest point, recognized the awful menace to the city. Only drastic action and efficient cooperation between the health services of the two countries — promoted by the Pan American Sanitary Bureau — prevented an epidemic from acquiring major proportions.

World health authorities meeting in New York in 1946 to establish the World Health Organization submitted the work of the forty-four-year-old Pan American Sanitary Bureau to world-wide scrutiny. At the Twelfth Pan American Sanitary Conference in Caracas in January, 1947, it was decided to enlarge the services of the office. The World Health Organization agreed that the Pan American Sanitary Bureau should act as regional office in the Americas for the world organization, and its activities were incorporated into the W.H.O.

The work of the various specialists sent out by the Sanitary Bureau through its divisions on Hospital Administration, Public Health, Tuberculosis, Venereal Disease, and Veterinary Public Health is extensive. The hospitals section, for example, tries to standardize hospital systems of the continent and acts as a consultative authority for carrying out projects, securing equipment, and preparing personnel. An active division on nursing keeps its fingers on the pulse of nurses' groups throughout the hemisphere, coordinating their work, helping to develop their programs, broadening their horizons, and reducing to a common continental denominator the problems of the nursing profession.

So that the experience and methods of the Pan American Sanitary Bureau can be used by sanitation authorities in other countries, the Washington office publishes a monthly bulletin of specialized information. Thus the findings of a laboratory worker in Colombia can serve an investigation in Paraguay, and scientific discoveries in Uruguay are known and applied in Honduras. The Bureau also puts out weekly and monthly epidemic bulletins, and is in radiotelephone communication with stations throughout the continent, in Europe, and in Asia, to warn of epidemics and other dangers confronting public health.

But the Sanitary Bureau does not limit its activities to work done by highly specialized personnel. It has also organized a system of scholarships to prepare specialists in the field of public health to carry on work in their respective countries. In Maracay, Venezuela, students on Sanitary Bureau scholarships are studying malaria and tropical diseases. A few weeks ago, a group of Mexican students headed by the Director of the Institute of Tropical Diseases in Mexico, Dr. Gerardo Varela, came to Atlanta, Georgia, to study the latest systems of rabies control and to make microscopic examination of specific cases. They were helping to coordinate an international system of control between the United States and Mexico.

Last year health problems focused the Bureau's attention on the Caribbean area. In Havana a case of smallpox broke out. The Bureau stepped in, isolated the case, and took strong precautionary measures to keep the disease from spreading. In the Panama Canal Zone, specialists from the Bureau anticipated an outbreak of yellow fever. Thanks to the Bureau's fast action, in two months 500,000 of Panama City's 650,000 people were vaccinated; 60 percent of the region's affected houses were fumigated; and 50 percent of the country's total population was vaccinated.

The same year a case of encephalitis appeared in animals in the Dominican Republic. The Bureau turned to its veterinary section. As a result, the epidemic was blocked, and valuable experience was acquired in the process.

After half a century of action, new horizons are opening up for the Pan American Sanitary Bureau. Its Director, Dr. Fred L. Soper, speaks from many years of successful experience in the field of public health when he says: " Technical collaboration provides a frictionless tool in developing good relations between nations and produces results of international significance because they are applicable in many countries. In no field of international activity has collaboration been so successful as in that of health."

No. 47 [The greatest health hazard in many of the republics of Latin America has been malaria. If the war against this disease can be won not only will millions be relieved of its physical costs but it also may be possible to put into useful productivity millions of acres of land which are now closed because they lie in malaria-infested country. DDT, a principal weapon in the war against malaria is, as Mr. Weyl indicates, a factor in public health, in economic betterment, and in social and political progress.]

Man against Malaria*

by NATHANIEL WEYL

MAN's battle against malaria, the tropics' number one health hazard, has reached and passed its turning point. For the first time in history, the swift elimination of this disease from the Americas is definitely in sight. Chief new factor in the struggle is DDT, aided by a group of lesser known insecticides.

The stakes of this silent, undramatic war are of major importance

* Nathaniel Weyl, " Man Against Malaria," *Américas* (September, 1949), Vol. 1, No. 7, pp. 4–7, 28–29. Reprinted by permission of *Américas,* a monthly magazine published by the Pan American Union in English, Spanish, and Portuguese.

to Latin America. Malariologists estimate that there are 15,000,000 sufferers there — roughly 10 percent of the population. Death statistics underrate the menace. As Dr. George Giglioli, one of the world's greatest hunters of the *anopheles darlingi* mosquito, points out, they ignore the much larger toll of masked malaria deaths from anemia, nephritis, prematurity, and other ailments.

In 1938 alone, malaria took a toll of a million lives in India. In the Americas it causes millions of broken lives, is a barrier to educational progress, a drag on economic development. Chronic illness causes low productivity.

Malaria is also a major road block to opening up millions of acres of tropical land. At a time when the world's population is increasing by about 20,000,000 a year — approximately the present population of Mexico — the creation of new land resources is of paramount importance both to the Americas and to the world at large. Rapid scientific progress within the past decade has made it possible to synthesize proteins and fats from sugars and carbohydrates far more efficiently than through animal husbandry. As these developments become economically feasible, the importance of man's tropical feeding grounds — lands of abundant moisture, maximum solar radiance, and greatest photosynthetic efficiency — should increase.

The malaria map of the world . . . shows that all of Latin America, with the exception of the Andean Cordillera and the three southernmost countries, is subject to significant infection. Uruguay is the only country naturally free of infection south of Canada. But both Argentina and Chile, which have had malaria problems, have successfully controlled the disease. Anopheles mosquitoes have been found at altitudes above 10,000 feet, but, as a general rule, the dividing line between heavy and light malaria incidence is the 3,000-foot contour.

Malaria is an extremely ancient, ubiquitous disease. Three demons in Chinese mythology, one with a hammer, another with a pail of cold water, a third with a stove, represented the familiar malaria symptoms of headaches, chills, and fevers. Four centuries before Christ, Plato was able to distinguish between continual, quotidian, tertian, and quartan fevers. Around 50 B.C., the Latin writer Varro theorized about swamps where " certain minute animals are bred . . . and borne by the air . . . and cause diseases which are difficult to be rid of." The Romans knew enough not to build their houses near swamps and to drain them where possible.

For the next 1,700 years, man's knowledge of malaria shrank like a skull in the hands of the Ecuadorean *Jíbaros*. Meanwhile, the small, upside-down-sleeping anopheles mosquito quietly made history. According to some historians, it knocked out the golden age of Greek civilization in the fourth century B.C. Arnold Toynbee's eloquent plea for the acquittal of anopheles — hailed before the bar of history for the assassination of Ceylonese civilization — is well known to readers of the unabridged *Study of History*.

The first great step toward malaria control in the Christian era was the use of quinine in the seventeenth century. There is a romantic story of its discovery that tells how Countess Chinchona, the lady of the Viceroy of Peru, was saved from death by malaria through the application of this mysterious Indian remedy. Unfortunately, there is not a word of truth in it. The facts show that the discovery grew out of a swindle. Demand for a medicinal bark and febrifuge known as *quinua-quinua* reached such proportions in Europe that Latin American suppliers smuggled in a bark that looked like it but did not affect the temperature of the human body. Then somebody found out that the ersatz product was an effective remedy for recurrent malaria attacks. This was the beginning of the medicinal use of quinine, made from cinchona bark.

The Continental Congress ordered three hundred pounds of cinchona for the American troops fighting the British " bloody backs " in the Revolutionary War's southern campaigns. In 1807, a Baltimore physician named Crawford proposed the extravagant theory that malaria was caused by mosquitoes. But the world knew better. It was caused, as its name indicated, by miasmas and impure air arising from swamp waters. The first reference to the disease by its modern name in the English tongue apparently derives from Sir Horace Walpole, who in 1740 wrote of " a horrid thing called mal'aria that comes to Rome every summer and kills one."

President Jefferson had to abandon the mud-and-frame village of Washington during " the sickly season " for the cool breezes of Monticello, and malaria reached into the North and caused massive casualties while the Erie Canal was being dug; but its cause remained hidden. Then in 1898 a young Scottish doctor, Ronald Ross, proved conclusively after several years of research that the disease was due to a parasite with a peculiar and complicated evolution, moving from the anopheles mosquito to man and back again. His epoch-making find, which earned him the Nobel Prize, came twenty years after the less spectacular discovery of DDT, which was to become such a powerful antimalaria weapon.

A year or so after the discovery that the anopheles mosquito was the villain in the malaria story, William Crawford Gorgas descended on Havana, which had just been taken by United States expeditionary forces. This energetic army medical officer knocked down a malaria rate of 909 per thousand to 19.

When Theodore Roosevelt decided to go ahead with the Panama Canal project, Gorgas was given complete control over sanitation. It was a thankless job. In eight years French engineers trying to build the canal had thrown away 50,000 lives and $200,000,000. Gorgas found the Canal Zone a wilderness of ponds, marshes, swamps, standing water — all places where the anopheles thrived. Organizing an efficient corps of sanitary inspectors, he smashed yellow fever in the course of two years with hardly less spectacular results against malaria. In mid-1906, malaria incidence was computed at 1,263 cases per 1000 men. Seven years later, hospitalizations of canal workers for malaria were down to 76 per 1000. It is calculated that Gorgas' work saved 71,000 lives, 39,500,000 man-days of illness, and $80,000,000. " There is nothing to match the work of Gorgas in the history of human achievement," wrote the eminent medical historian, Sir William Osler.

Gorgas set the pattern. For the next forty years, the malaria campaign was to move along several not always effective fronts. Permanent malaria control consisted of smashing up the mosquitoes' breeding places. Sluggish rivers were rechannelled; swamps were filled; wherever water was lethargic, it was made to move fast.

This type of malaria control has been used recently in Managua, Nicaragua (1942), and Chimbote, Peru (1944). The Managua project gives some idea of the tremendous engineering and earth-moving job involved. The main malaria hazard was the intermontane Lake Managua. After eleven years of hard work based on international cooperation, the lake's exposed beach was drained. Two miles of sub-surface, open-jointed drains were run into paved canals for groundwater drainage. On the other side of the lake, two miles of channel were regraded with three rubble-masonry drops. Another malaria-breeding problem was solved by building a 13,800 foot trapezoidal ditch to drain storm waters into Lake Managua from an even worse source of pestilence.

In certain types of terrain, these challenging engineering projects may be the ideal solution. They are permanent unless, of course, the new channels silt up. They may bring as a by-product fertile land reclaimed from swamp. But in many regions they are economically impossible. The seasonally inundated areas of the Amazon Basin can never be drained; irrigated agriculture on reclaimed land requires slow-moving channels of sweet water. There are regions in which the cost of drainage is utterly disproportionate to potential productivity.

Sometimes the mosquito population can be kept down by weekly spraying of breeding areas with Paris green and other chemicals. The other pre-DDT approach was to drug the people and forget about the mosquito larvae. Until very recently, this was simply a matter of quinine therapy. But World War II stepped up chemical research on antimalarials. German laboratories prepared for war-autarchy; then, after the Japanese sweep into the great cinchona-producing Dutch East Indian possessions, England and the United States entered the race for new synthetic drugs that would enable desert and jungle fighters to stay in combat in malarial areas.

After its discovery by a Strasbourg chemist called Zeidler in 1874, DDT was promptly ignored. Then, under the impetus of World War II, it was used extensively in the armed forces as a bug killer. By 1946, supplies of DDT began to percolate down to civilian projects. From the outset, the results in the fight against malaria were spectacular.

Obviously a mature anopheles on the wing represents one of the hardest conceivable targets for any marksman, even when armed with the DDT bullet. But the malarial mosquito rests and feeds. Although the habits of the different species vary, the preponderant behavior pattern of the more dangerous varieties is to gorge on human blood in the shade and comparative cool of house interiors.

This is the time and place for the kill. While DDT is sometimes used to destroy breeding areas, more often it is sprayed on the interior walls of buildings. If all potential anopheles mothers are destroyed, sooner or later there will be no larvae. The DDT cure, therefore, can be permanent. If all houses are sprayed, all man-eating anopheles must die, except for the minority which feeds out-of-doors. To survive, the parasite must move endlessly from mosquito to man and back again. Thus the chain of infection can be broken.

DDT preparation has demonstrated unique potency as a mosquito killer when applied as a clinging wet spray. In Italy, for example, one yearly application has proved to be sufficient protection, even though mosquitoes breed nine months out of the year.

Dr. Carlos Alberto Alvarado, director of Argentina's battle against malaria and other tropical diseases, points out that DDT has revolutionized the strategy of the campaign. Instead of the gigantic task of destroying all potential mosquito breeding grounds, the emphasis has been narrowed to killing infected adults as they enter houses to strike. The costs of a malaria program used to depend on terrain and topography. It was a question of the amount of spraying and drainage needed to put all stagnant water within the mosquito flight-radius of the human population into motion, or destroy it as a larval culture medium. Interior use of DDT means not only lower, but uniform costs — so much per head of population. Of course there are variables: texture of wall surfaces, dwelling area per person, cost of training spray crews, cost of transporting equipment to the theater of action. But these are inconsequential. The important thing is that today there is no place in the world about which we can complacently say that the inhabitants are doomed to suffer from malaria because a war against it would cost too much.

In the fall of 1947, Dr. Alvarado's organization took steps to wipe out the malaria menace in the endemic area of Argentina's northeast, where there were 300,000 malaria sufferers in a population of 1,000,000. Nine months later, the first phase of the campaign had been completed and the anopheles had been purged from 40 percent of the region. Dr. Alvarado hopes to be able to announce this year conclusion of the second phase and a permanent 95 percent reduction in the malaria rate. Meanwhile, the excellent Argentine control measures remain in effect. New malaria cases must report immediately; they must submit to blood tests. Any autochthonous case brings the health authorities into the area with DDT spray crews.

The anopheles mosquito is sovereign over most of the unexploited subcontinent in the Amazon Basin. A century ago, Alfred Russell Wallace, codiscoverer with Darwin of the evolutionary theory, observed that, when traveling on the Amazon system, one is more or less safe from malaria on black water, but not on white. Wallace did not know the reason, but we know it today. Black waters are humus-laden; they are highly acid, and this acidity kills off mosquito larvae.

After Pearl Harbor, it became necessary to expand wild rubber gathering within the Amazonian wilderness of marsh, plains, and jungle. Listless people could not produce. Accordingly, on July 17, 1942, the United States and Brazil agreed to conduct a joint Amazonian health and sanitation program.

By 1945, 22,074 cases were registered in the health posts constructed and maintained by *SESP*, the Brazilian organization created under the joint agreement. Almost 1,000,000 atabrine tablets were distributed. Three hospitals were set up and 27 health posts established. Some 387 doctors, engineers, nurses, aides, and inspectors — most of them locally trained — dedicated themselves to the battle against malaria and other Amazon diseases. Several engineering projects were undertaken, the most important being the Belem Dike, which prevented the flooding of low-lying lands adjacent to this city of 200,000 inhabitants.

In May 1945, the town of Breves at the mouth of the Amazon, where 20 percent of the population showed malarial infection in blood smears, was chosen for a key experiment in DDT control. All houses were sprayed. Simultaneously, other antimalarial control measures — larviciding and intensive medication — were dropped. Within a year, the population of *anopheles darlingi* had shrunk to such meager proportions that it was " not possible to measure it with the methods we have available." As for the darlingi larvae, they had disappeared. Since malaria remained prevalent and endemic in neighboring communities that had not been given DDT, the Breves experiment was regarded as conclusive.

The villages up the river heard the news. Impoverished communities raised funds by voluntary subscription so that they could be given DDT treatment. By May 1948, 27 localities had been placed under control, and the malaria incidence in these areas had already declined by 56.7 percent.

The Brazilians are approaching the problem of malaria control with thoroughness and energy. In the mineral-rich state of Minas Geraes, a major campaign is under way. After extensive preliminary surveys, a decision was taken to DDT 310,000 houses, containing 77,500,000 square meters of wall surface. This will require 40 tons of spray, 900 sprayers, 31 trucks and jeeps.

In southern Brazil, the elusive outdoor feeder *anopheles kerteszia* constitutes a problem. It breeds in the water cups of the bromeliads — vines and lianas that festoon themselves around the straight boles of the great trees. The Brazilians send spray crews by helicopter to kill the kerteszia larvae by DDTing the forest cover. In another area, all trees harboring bromeliads within the critical flight radius of the infected villages were recently cut down. One hopes that the cost in soil erosion will not be greater than the gain in health.

All over the sprawling continent-and-a-half of Latin America, the fight against malaria is taking on new life. Chile began a vigorous drive in 1937 against endemic malaria in low-lying intermontane valleys. Every weapon in the arsenal was used: dosage of the inhabitants, drainage of stagnant lakes, cleaning up of pond margins, spreading of oil film on stagnant water surfaces, introduction of Gambusia fish that eat mosquito larvae. In 1944, DDT was applied to house interiors on a six months recurrent basis. " Since April 1945," Dr. A. Neghme reported, " not a single autochthonous malaria case has been diagnosed." Chile has banished the anopheles.

A nationwide DDT campaign has been launched in Venezuela and the health authorities in that country hope that it will soon have the honor of becoming " the first tropical country to eliminate malaria." In 1948, Venezuela reported that 175 communities with 55,000 inhabitants were receiving DDT treatment.

To vary the plot, take a Haitian town that was resurrected without benefit of DDT. " Death is no stranger to Léogâne — but last week it was no longer the mayor," the Latin American edition of *Time* commented in reporting this battle of human muscle against endemic disease. The town of Léogâne epitomized on a small scale the impact of civilization on malaria — and of malaria on civilization. In the seventeenth century, it was a thriving entrepôt and hideout for buccaneers. Later, these pirates settled down and became planters and the city prospered. During the Haitian revolution under Toussaint Louverture, Léogâne was burned. The town was abandoned; the drainage ditches choked up with silt; running water spilled over its channels to form fresh water lagoons in which anopheles bred. Agriculture decayed, the population sickened, and for a century and a half the mosquito was sovereign.

In 1944, the Haitian government and the American Sanitary Mission started to bring this town back to life. The task: to build a 1,000-meter canal with masonry lining and heavy conrete inverts to carry a maximum flow of 1,750 cubic feet of water per second from the swollen and sluggish Rouillonne River to the sea. Since it was wartime, no mechanical equipment was available. Eight hundred Haitians worked on this back-breaking job of earth-moving until the river ran swiftly again. In a brief period, the malaria rate declined from 71.6 percent to 22.7 percent. Land worth $10 a hectare before the drainage program sold for $180 after completion.

The miracle at Léogâne will doubtless be repeated elsewhere in Haiti. This densely populated republic has a considerably higher malaria rate than its West Indian neighbors, the chief reasons being poverty and the individualized irrigation of small peasant proprietors.

There are endless episodes in this continental campaign against malaria. But the lesson is always the same: the job can be done quickly and effectively; the cost is far less than the gain in human lives and productivity.

DDT is the critical new factor, but it is not necessarily the complete answer to the malaria problem. First, there are the species of anopheles that feed out-of-doors. To try to shoot them down with the DDT bullet is difficult, sometimes hopeless. Fortunately, these varieties are not important.

There is another disturbing thought. The house fly has already countered the DDT menace to the survival of his species by developing resistant strains. Will the anopheles accomplish the same triumph of swift environmental adaptation? There are no signs of this as yet. As matters now stand, the prospects are that man will succeed in eliminating malaria from the Americas as a major disease hazard and that he will achieve this within a few years.

No. 48 [Public housing programs have evoked wide discussion in the United States in the last two decades. As a result, the American public is well-informed on the economic, social, and even political consequences of the urban slum.

One would expect that societies in which the standard of living is much lower than ours, and in which urbanization is an important demographic factor, would also be faced with the problem of the slum and what to do about it. The manner in which many of the Latin American governments have begun to cope with the problem is through public housing programs, many of which antedate our own. These housing plans do not compare with ours in scope because no government in Latin America has as large a resource in public revenues as has the United States. It is, however, important to compare Latin American public policy in this field with that of this country. This general survey of housing progress is made in the essay which follows.]

Housing Progress in South America*

by JACOB CRANE

Early this year I visited a number of countries in South America, to talk with officials in housing and urbanism and to explore the possibilities for international cooperation in these fields. The trip was made under the auspices of the State Department and by invitation of these countries. The principal stopping points were in Brazil, Uruguay, Chile, Peru, Ecuador, and Colombia. On the way home, I also visited Panama.

In each country there was evidence of an enormous interest in housing, an interest by no means confined to officials and professionals. As elsewhere in the world, critical shortages and bad housing conditions have grown worse during the past six years. The

* Jacob Crane, "Housing Progress in South America," *Bulletin of the Pan American Union* (May, 1946), Vol. LXXX, No. 5, pp. 241–248. Reprinted by permission of the *Bulletin of the Pan American Union.*

problem has become a major public issue — a cause for concern almost as great as inflation and the rising cost of living. Then, too, the postwar home figures in the dreams and plans of the average South American as of the North American. The people of these countries share the universal hope for improved living conditions.

In these countries, as elsewhere, government authorities have become increasingly aware of their responsibilities in meeting the housing crisis. I found officials and technicians eager to learn from the experience of other countries and anxious to take whatever steps are necessary to relieve the situation. In the countries visited the interest of governments is principally in workers' housing and this is the aspect to which my trip was mainly devoted.

Discussion and observation this time confirmed my belief, held from previous visits, that the housing problems of these countries are more or less similar; and fundamentally, they are similar to our problems in the United States. We all have things to learn from one another.

I visited all types of housing, from the most up-to-date to the most wretched. I found that once the problem of slums is faced as a universal evil, barriers to free discussion are soon overcome. In these countries officials are only too well aware that for every worker's family benefited by decent housing, there are thousands still to be reached. They see the flowering of expensive new villas within and on the borders of their cities, knowing that this is matched by a continuing growth of slums. They know that, in many instances, they are still unable to prevent the formation of new colonies of miserable shacks on the less desirable land. Adequate provisions of water, sewerage, and other facilities are major problems. High urban land costs, shortages of materials and trained labor, high construction costs, and limited economic resources present in some cases almost insurmountable difficulties.

Despite the handicaps in several of these countries the workers' housing programs sponsored by the governments are relatively as far advanced as in the United States. Some have had longer experience in this field than we have, notably Chile. All of them are very much interested in United States experience. Many are eager to get materials and equipment again, and they even hope to get houses, or components of houses. Several desire loans from the United States, capital being a critical need. They are also anxious to explore and develop more fully their own sources of materials, and to modernize their building industries. They seek machinery and techniques for this purpose. Each one wishes to exchange professional people and, in several cases, students also.

As in the United States, one central problem is to reduce the initial cost and the annual cost of workers' housing. In many cases housing projects have raised the living standards of moderate-income workers, but have not reached the poorer families where the need is greatest. For reducing costs, several alternatives are open, and exchange of experience is extremely important on this fundamental point.

The most prevalent method of financing workers' housing in these countries is through the use of social security reserve funds. The experience of Brazil in this respect is extraordinarily interesting, and in projects such as Realengo near Rio de Janeiro the results are outstanding. The national social security agencies are semiautonomous, with representation of the government and with a degree of responsibility to the Reinsurance Institute and to the Ministry of Labor. There are many of these social security institutes, among the most important being the Institute of Industrial Workers, the Institute of Commercial Workers, and the Institute of Government Employees. These social security agencies have built up very large reserves, and they use these reserves both for investment purposes and for various social welfare purposes. Housing is considered good both as an investment and as a means of raising the standard of living of the workers. They have very large programs coming on, utilizing the experience of the past; and their work is undoubtedly destined to be among the most important. In Brazil I was also impressed by the good concrete engineering and the ingenuity of design.

Although the results differed widely, financing of housing with social-security funds seemed well accepted. The only qualification I found was the belief that it is better for the agency to own workers' housing than to lend for workers' housing, since ownership is a hedge against inflation, and, of course, inflation is one of the great difficulties.

In Chile and Uruguay the social aspects of housing have been very thoughtfully considered and developed. We can learn from their housing management methods, as we can from the engineering in Brazil. Uruguay's present workers' housing projects are small in size and number. But here, as in Chile, the effort is to provide not only homes but an education in living. Individual gardens are encouraged, and libraries are a popular feature, as well as the more usual services, such as clinics and recreational areas for the children.

In Uruguay, as in many places, rural rehabilitation is also a major problem. On a trip to Canelones, in the beautiful country outside of Montevideo, I had a glimpse of some of the difficulties. At the edge of this town is a community of people living in mud huts, without water or sanitary facilities of any kind. Close by, new housing has been constructed — modest structures, but immeasurably better than the neighboring huts. In a resettlement program undertaken in cooperation with the government's National Housing Institute, it is proposed to offer these new dwellings to the neighboring inhabitants, without cost at the outset. But in some quarters I found that the prospect of moving was viewed with indifference, if not downright distaste. One old *campesino* was adamant. " After all," he told me, " the things which really count in life are *maté* [a kind of South American tea], good conversation, roast meat, and good books."

Despite this rural philosopher, the increased self-respect and productiveness of workers who move from slums to new housing is very remarkable indeed. It should be recognized in any program of international cooperation which seeks to build up production and purchasing power.

Chile still leads in the relative extent and scope of its workers' housing program, which now has projects throughout the country, from Punta Arenas, the southernmost city, to the northern desert. Yet in spite of the great efforts made to combat it, Chile still has a tremendous slum problem. Efforts are now being made to modernize and expedite building methods. Labor arrangements on some projects offer special incentives for work done well and rapidly. In Chile, I was particularly impressed by the degree of representation of the tenants in the councils and operation of the *Caja de la Habitación,* the country's national housing agency.

Just coming into existence was Peru's new National Housing

Corporation, which has a big program in prospect. Preliminary work has begun on a site which I visited just outside of Lima. Here neighborhood planning for a large-scale workers' housing project is progressive and extensive.

In Colombia the major part of the work is carried out by the country's principal housing agency — the *Instituto de Crédito Territorial*. It is concerned with both urban and rural housing. In addition to providing homes throughout Colombia, this organization now contemplates a supplementary program for agricultural and social education.

In Ecuador, the *Cajas* (social security funds) for workers in all categories have provided money for housing, and in many cases the houses are built and owned by the *Cajas*. Here, in even greater degree than in some of the other countries, a major problem is to secure facilities, such as water supply and sewerage connections, from the municipalities.

Tradition tends to hold back new methods in housing in Latin America, as it does nearly everywhere else. In organization and planning, however, it seemed to me that advances had been made since my previous visit in 1941. Among new projects now in prospect is Panama's program for twin houses for workers' families to be built this year outside of Panama City, with social security funds loaned to the *Banco de Urbanización*. Venezuela's *Banco Obrero* contemplates construction of 40,000 new workers' dwellings to be built within the next decade.

In almost all these countries, there is still no over-all national housing agency and no over-all national housing program. The experience of the United States in this respect may be valuable to them.

In conversation with workers and their families, it developed that in general they seemed to desire homes of types resembling those of the well-to-do in their communities. The desire for home ownership is strong, although the concept of " home security " is gradually becoming accepted.

I saw many instances of enterprise and ingenuity displayed by workers who had constructed and decorated their homes themselves. This leads me to believe that schemes based on provision of materials and facilities and of instruction and technical aid have not been sufficiently explored. The principle of " land and utilities housing," developed in Puerto Rico and in Venezuela, for example, is probably susceptible of wide adaptation and use. The principle referred to is based on the proposition that the land and utilities (water supply, sewerage, etc.) are provided by a public agency at a very low rental to insure the workers complete security in the occupancy and use of a piece of land and to provide them with that primary essential, sanitary facilities. Then the individual family is permitted to build its own house on the plot of ground, and, under certain regulations, to improve the house from time to time as it is found possible to do so. Assistance may be given in the way of materials and technical advice. This arrangement is particularly useful in tropical climates, where the land and the sanitation are the most important elements for satisfactory dwellings and where the character of the house itself is somewhat less important and may in fact be quite primitive. There are many variations of this principle. Similar schemes have been developed in Sweden and in the British West Indies.

Another point which struck me is that the importance of community facilities in large-scale housing projects is more firmly established in Latin America than in the United States. In fact, the experience of some of these countries in this respect should be useful the world over.

In every country I visited I found strong spontaneous interest in the possibility of a world organization for housing and urbanism, through which the exchange of information and experience, and of resources, both technical and material, could be facilitated. In the countries with problems peculiar to tropical housing I found keen interest in the prospect of an institute for special study of these problems. Correspondence with this in view is now going on among officials and professionals in these countries and with an interested group in Puerto Rico. There was also concern that arrangements be carried out for continuance of inter-American conferences on housing and urbanism. It was the consensus that there was need for an inter-American publication in this field, and for an exchange of exhibitions as well as publications.

In conclusion, it seems to me clear that it is in the interest of all of us to develop cooperation in housing and urbanism among the countries of America to the fullest extent possible. I am confident that their desire to effect arrangements for these purposes is very strong and that they are prepared to carry their share of the cost of such cooperation. Beyond the utilitarian and humanitarian aspects, cooperation in this field constitutes an excellent means of strengthening international ties, particularly during these years of housing crisis throughout the world.

No. 49 [From a general discussion of South American housing programs we turn to a specific contemporary example of government housing activity. The author of " Neighborhood No. 3 " is as much concerned with the social and political values that will flow from this Peruvian housing development as he is with the fact that it will make it possible for many more of his countrymen to live in decent homes.]

Neighborhood No. 3*

by FERNANDO BELAUNDE–TERRY

ANCIENT seat of empire and viceroyalty, Peru has always clung to tradition and been reluctant to accept innovations: " This is not acceptable in our medium. . . ." " That would do very well somewhere else, but not in Lima. . . ." " We have to keep in mind the peculiarities of our way of life. . . ." Anyone wanting to change the old pattern in any way must listen with saintly patience to objections like these.

* Fernando Belaúnde-Terry, " Neighborhood No. 3," *Américas* (November, 1950), Vol. 2, No. 11, pp. 19–22. Reprinted by permission of *Américas,* a monthly magazine published by the Pan American Union in English, Spanish, and Portuguese.

Nearly all the political, social, and economic evils of the Peruvian people have their origin in the alley and the *ranchería* — in human urban and rural slums. Born in the sick brain of some speculator tricked out as an architect, they are a constant invitation to discord and vice. " We model our houses," says Winston Churchill, " and then our houses model us." In the spirit of this great truth, we Peruvian architects have wanted to supply houses that will mold a citizenry capable of getting ahead, enjoying an equality so far denied them. The truth is that the sky, spread out generously above the garden of a mansion, in the slum is cut up by courtyards into niggardly patches. Grass, trees, space, are a long way from these teeming neighborhoods. Water itself becomes an extravagant luxury in these unnatural dwellings. The " essential joys " vigorously demanded by Le Corbusier are refused the man of meager resources who has the misfortune to live in the hovel, a foretaste of the grave and a bulwark of misery.

Lima's Neighborhood Unit No. 3, built by the government National Housing Corporation, is simply a sincere effort to stretch out a hand to these people, to give them justice without " charity " or demagogy. Eliminating all superfluous ornament, all needless luxury, it still puts its residents on a par with the highly privileged in the matter of close contact with nature. It even gives them an advantage: while the mansions of Lima are short of water in summer, the pipes in our brand-new community can barely hold up under the pressure of a liquid that for once is germ-free.

The 1,112 dwellings of Neighborhood Unit No. 3 are far from being exotic palaces. They are simple apartments with no wasted space or costly fittings, where life can be lived without severe hardship. Since planning problems and economy ruled out individual houses, two types of multifamily buildings were adopted, of two and four stories, with the larger families in the former. Each family has its own bath, living room, and a kitchen with dining area, plus from one to four bedrooms depending on its needs. The buildings are uniformly oriented for sunshine and spaced to let in air and light. Apartment entrances are grouped to avoid annoyances and friction.

Rents on the different units vary according to the size of the family and its ability to pay, and are never allowed to exceed a quarter of the monthly income. For example, an apartment suitable for a married couple costs between 106 and 138 soles (a sol is worth about six cents U.S.); a family with two or three children would need a place renting for 142 to 178 soles. These rents cover interest and long-term amortization of the capital investment, a total of 6 percent; public services like water and sewers; and social services, including nurseries, playgrounds, parks, and community center. Despite careful screening, eligible occupants far outnumber the available dwellings. Inhabitants of existing slums receive preference, and families with incomes greater than seven times the rent are rejected.

When private capital was first called upon to underwrite the bonds to finance a large part of the work, many people thought those who were proposing such a plan were ignorant or out of their senses. I had the pleasure of winning a bet by personally obtaining a large sum from managers of industries in the neighborhood during a single morning's voluntary experimental work — in the course of which be it said in passing, I did not shove a revolver in anybody's chest. As it turned out, 82 percent of the investment was obtained from private sources, a remarkable achievement. The point is that together with the monetary dividend, these bonds pay a moral dividend. It is now a proved fact that private capital can and should participate in the financing of economic housing.

An urban development limited by the capacity of two good public elementary schools and by the radius of action of a pair of legs means a population no greater than six thousand and an area no larger than seventy-four acres. In Neighborhood Unit No. 3 no child of school age need go without the inestimable benefit of education; no trip to or from home is more than an easy five- or ten-minute walk, free of traffic dangers.

The city planner with his pencil poised over his drawing board is the first great traffic director. And whenever the accident rate goes up disproportionately, he should also be the first to shoulder the blame. In the first quarter of this century city planning was nothing but unconditional surrender of man to the automobile. Now the pedestrian is beginning to come back into his own; the community spirit is being reborn, and the automobile is tending to assume its proper place in the hierarchy of values as a useful tool in the service of man.

Its speed, its usefulness, its power, ought not to continue as a public danger — I say this remembering bitterly young lives cut short. The pedestrian, in turn, ought no longer to be an obstacle in the way of rapid transit where an express highway calls for it. To the shattered formula " automobile versus man " we must oppose the triumphant " man plus automobile." This theory, widespread in books, has been applied sparingly in practice. By carefully separating vehicular and pedestrian traffic, following the shining example of Radburn, New Jersey, the unit in Lima has incorporated it successfully.

Locating the project in a desirable section and near a shopping district would have meant paying a price out of reach of the future occupants' purses. It was necessary to leap the economic barriers that encircle the modern city: in this case a jump of two and a half miles, equivalent to the one taken earlier by industry, was enough to find land of moderate price and convenient location between Lima and Callao. In housing also, union makes strength. A dozen isolated dwellings could not conquer isolation in the middle of nowhere. But 1,112 family houses, with all their complementary buildings, are like a mechanized army division with its supplies and its stores, capable of imposing its own law.

The presence of schools, church, shops, and a market, a civic center, sports and recreational facilities, cancels out the charge of " distance " made against any attempt at a satellite development. The most important consideration is that the wage earner should not have to commute too far to work, that family travel expenses be reduced or abolished. A self-sufficient project solves this problem; moreover, the complementary buildings are sources of additional income. While construction was in progress, an observer who went through it pronounced the inclusion of a movie theater to be demogogic, claiming it would have been better to use the same materials to build more houses. Thus he sought, no doubt without being aware of it, to rupture the harmony among the urban functions of housing, *recreation,* employment, and circulation. Today we could show this man that the advantageous terms under which the theater is rented make possible a lower rate of interest on the houses.

Nothing is more satisfactory than proving in practice the validity of ideas conceived theoretically. I have often visited the unit accompanied by my children, who range in age from three to seven. Because there is no mind healthier and freer of prejudice than a child's, his opinion is valuable. Every time we have spent an afternoon there, my youngsters have resisted returning home, and more than once have pleaded with me: " Why don't we come and live here? " Here is conclusive proof that the unit has nothing basic to envy our spacious and comfortable residential neighborhood.

In talking with the fathers and mothers there, I have heard an interesting " complaint " from the housewives. Lima children, especially in the crowded zones, suffer from lack of appetite; pallor is one of their characteristics. But here the mothers attribute to their children such voracity — stimulated beyond doubt by exercise in the open air — that the greater expense for food throws the already precarious family budget off balance.

Another gratifying and useful experience is proving the psychological effects of the traffic-separation system, which go beyond the important safety aspect. In the old working-class neighborhoods the motorist very rarely finds a friendly atmosphere. His show of wealth is resented, and he is considered, sometimes with reason, a threat to passers-by. In such circumstances, it is not unusual for the motorist to hear unpleasant remarks or for the car — " capitalism on wheels " — to be damaged. How different it is at Neighborhood Unit No. 3! One day I came to the parking lot there, and made a stab at driving my car along the wide paths to a place where a statue was being put up. At once a group of children surrounded me and, with an almost protective attitude, explained that I could come in only on foot. Pretending I did not know the place, I asked these improvised and captivating guides to show me through it. Their clothing immediately betrayed their modest circumstances, but in their healthy faces and friendly manner could be seen the real results of the flourishing new community.

Only yesterday I attended the distribution of prizes for an athletic competition. Seventeen soccer teams in their playing uniforms stepped up to receive trophies. Basketball is popular too, and the girls are prominent in the Lima volleyball picture. As I looked at the smallest and happiest *calichines* in their bright-colored shirts, I suddenly saw the champions of the future.

No opinion is worth more to the city planner than a doctor's, since both professions deal in terms of human life. One of the most enthusiastic comments on the project came from Social Security's Dr. Pedro Martínez, whose daily visits to sick workers have taken him to the most remote residential areas. He reports that nowhere in Lima do families of limited means live better than in Neighborhood Unit No. 3. "There is a chasm," he says, "between the new achievement and everything that has gone before."

But we who are trying to solve the housing problem do not want to hear only flattering reactions. It has been said that, for some, "experience is like the stern lights of a ship, lighting only the route that has already been traveled." We, on the other hand, would like it to illuminate the road ahead as well. So we are always ready to listen to criticism.

We have learned, for example, that we have to give up the plan of a single room for cooking and eating. *Limeños,* even those in modest circumstances, like to maintain certain formalities in their way of life. They prefer the social and service functions to be distinct, and occupants have changed their apartments around to conform to this idea. In newer units built by the Corporation, living room and dining room are combined, but the kitchen is separate.

For recreational activities, we have come to see the necessity for not one community center, but several. Different groups always spring up on the basis of age and customs, even when all have a common economic background. Providing these facilities in future projects would avoid a lot of argument.

A few changes are also called for in the shopping center. Some stores need more room than others. In several cases, space for a workshop ought to be included. A bakery as well as a store, for example, so bread can be sold hot first thing in the morning and not have to be brought from a distance.

Fortunately, these are minor modifications. The fundamental plan is well worth repeating. But it is a good idea always to be ready for improvement, whenever there is a place for it, because "those who do not correct themselves, love themselves more than the truth."

When a project leaves the architect's drawing board and takes shape, it is only a body without a soul. The human being who comes to live there gives it the breath of life. We have had the satisfaction of proving the efficiency of this unit, with more than a thousand families — out of 12,500 who applied — enjoying all its benefits every day of the week. We have seen it smiling at dawn, when the men leave for work. We have watched the forming of an intense community spirit and the spontaneous and vigorous creation of social and sporting organizations. We have seen its team colors victorious and its sporting fields filled with players on holidays. The value of leaving 88 percent of the area open has been confirmed. We have been entertained by the children at play, climbing about on the grotesque cement animals in the playground; flying imaginary airplanes and sailing concrete ships; playing Indian or balanced on the see-saws. Above all, we have seen an inspiring vision of the new generations that will come forth.

Generations of strong, worthy, and simple people. Generations of good citizens, in every sense of the word, capable of living democratically, for, as a great Peruvian said: " Without citizens, there is no Republic."

CHAPTER 18

— Latin America — in American and World Affairs

No. 50 [The enthusiastic advocate of international government frequently cites the political organization of the American states to prove his point that sovereign nations *can* establish an international society which is really effective in solving their political differences and disagreements. The skeptic will reply that peace has been kept in America not because of the political influence or authority of a regional international organization but because one of the twenty-two American states is by far the wealthiest and the strongest. America, unlike Europe, they argue, is not a political society in which one finds several powerful contending political rivals, but it is a family in which one brother overshadows the other twenty-one.

This factor has been one which has long concerned the Latin American states, and *because* of it they were reluctant, for decades, to devolve any real *political* authority upon their common international agency. Despite this, this organization has grown from a small Bureau which was, in its early years, only a clearing house for commercial information to an agency which is a significant factor in inter-American politics and a real moral force in the American community. The reasons for this increase in prestige and power are many and varied. Part of the explanation is undoubtedly found in the effectiveness which the Pan American Union displayed in disposing of problems which were within its limited authority. Its work in the field of inter-American problems in health, housing, education, etc., was commented on in earlier chapters.

No student of inter-American affairs can deny the enormous contribution of the Pan American Union to that essential intangible of
international organization: a sense of political community. It is this
contribution which interests the author of the following article.]

The First 60 Years*

by HERNANE TAVARES DE SA

Simón Bolívar was the first to express forcefully the concept of an
inter-American organization and take action to form one. He
called the first inter-American congress, which met in Panama in
1826; the delegates of Central and South American countries there
signed the "Treaty of Perpetual Union, League, and Confederation." But the treaty was never ratified and Bolívar was to die an
embittered man, seeing his dream fall short of fulfillment.

Throughout the nineteenth century the idea persisted and came
in for desultory discussion in several conferences of Latin American
nations. But until 1889 no concrete steps were taken. In the fall of
that year eighteen countries attended the First International Conference of American States, which met in Washington on the initiative of United States Secretary of State James G. Blaine. This first
of the large-scale gatherings of the nations of the Hemisphere —
which were to become habitual — gave no indication then that it
would have far-reaching effects.

Washington was then a quiet, provincial town, devoted to un-
pretentious living. Manuel Elguera, attaché to the Peruvian delegation at the Conference, reminisced about the meeting in a charming
letter which the *Bulletin of the Pan American Union* requested of
him for its fiftieth-anniversary issue in 1940: ". . . The social life

* Hernane Tavares de Sá, "The First 60 Years," *Américas* (March, 1950), Vol.
2, No. 3, pp. 2–6, 41–42. Reprinted by permission of *Américas*, a monthly magazine
published by the Pan American Union in English, Spanish, and Portuguese.

was most agreeable; the delegates were overwhelmed with official and unofficial attentions. Everything was very simple, for embassies were not yet in fashion. Any morning President Harrison could be seen out driving in a small carriage with his wife, holding the reins himself. On the streetcars one might meet the Vice President, Mr. Morton, or Alexander Graham Bell, or other outstanding individuals. There was not the slightest difficulty in visiting public offices. I spent many days in watching with interest the casting of great cannon, and it never occurred to anyone to ask who I was or what I wanted at the Navy Yard."

In regard to the Conference itself, Mr. Elguera wrote: " As for matters related to the working of the congress, I must confess frankly that I found the sessions very dull. There was much discussion over matters that did not seem to be of great importance. . . ."

This opinion was not shared by all contemporary observers. As a matter of fact, clashes of personalities and modes of behavior often made the sessions very lively. It was the first time that Anglo-Saxons and Latins met around a conference table.

Matías Romero, Mexico's Minister of Foreign Affairs, who headed his country's delegation, speaks of ". . . interchanges of the liveliest type, frequently very personal "; then, too, " because of the difficulty of obtaining correct translations, some of the delegates, endowed with the highest degree of arrogance and frequently not understanding any of the ideas expressed in the original discourse, got a wrong impression about these, sometimes to the extent that they considered them insulting and gave responses which provoked further animated remarks, thus endangering not only the harmony of the assembly but also the success of the work of the Conference. . . ."

But, on the whole, wiser counsel prevailed and the Conference closed on a note of cordiality, though not of high accomplishment. One United States newspaper reflected the prevailing opinion when it announced that " the Pan American Conference is pronounced a failure by those most concerned." The *Revue Sud Américaine,* published in Brussels, wrote that the Conference had achieved only " wholly platonic recommendations which even then encountered a good deal of dissent. All the main proposals were aborted there in the balance-sheet of the Pan American Congress."

There was, however, one far-reaching achievement — almost ignored at the time. On April 14, 1890, the Conference accepted unanimously, with a minimum of discussion, a proposal to create an
International Union of American Republics " for the prompt collection and distribution of commercial information " which was to be
represented by a " Commercial Bureau " with headquarters in Washington. This was to dole out information of special interest to merchants and shippers.

The infant Bureau, which was to become the Pan American
Union, would be maintained to the tune of $36,000 a year by contri-
butions from 18 countries on the basis of population. The United
States, which then had half of the Hemisphere's inhabitants — 50,-
000,000 — was to contribute half the sum. The two countries with
the smallest populations had to contribute less than $100 each, and
only four gave more than $1,000.

Establishment of the Bureau was considered relatively so unimportant that no ratification was expected from the eighteen nations.
The payment of their quotas was considered in itself a sufficient expression of acquiescence.

But the Bureau's usefulness was quickly recognized. By November
7 of the same year it had started operations by sending a circular note
requesting information of a commercial nature from all the Latin
American countries. In its first four months, 700 inquiries were received from merchants and manufacturers. During the first year
there were 38,000 requests for the Bureau's bulletin from the United
States alone, while an almost equal number of requests came from
Latin America.

Though its practical usefulness became apparent almost immediately, the inner contradictions inherent in the nature of the Bureau
were to engender severe crises. In theory an international organization, the Bureau operated in practice as an adjunct of the United
States government, staffed almost exclusively by United States citizens. All the Latin American nations resented this. Two of them —
Mexico and Argentina — carried their resentment to the point of
suspending payment of their quotas for a time.

But then came the Second Pan American Conference in Mexico
City in 1901, followed in 1906 by the Third in Rio de Janeiro.
In Mexico City the so-called " Guatemala Plan," presented by Gua-

temala's chief delegate, proposed two important innovations for
the Bureau — that it begin to operate outside the purely commercial sphere and that it become truly international. Thus the
Governing Board, forefather of the OAS Council, came into
being.

In Rio de Janeiro the Bureau was given a really ample scope. Two
of its most important new functions were to "act as a Permanent
Committee of the International American Conferences, recommending topics to be included in the programme of the next Conference
. . . [and] to keep the records of the International American Conferences." By then, the necessity of meeting periodically was being
impressed upon the governments.

When the Fourth Conference met in Buenos Aires in 1910, the
Bureau was no longer a controversial issue. The Buenos Aires Conference further enlarged the Bureau's functions and changed its
cumbersome name to Pan American Union. That same year, the
institution also acquired solid and attractive headquarters. Andrew
Carnegie had made a grant of $750,000 to build a marble palace on
the corner of Constitution Avenue (then B Street) and 17th Street.
The governments put up the other $250,000 needed. The building
was to become a Washington landmark and a tourist mecca.

With this new home, the Pan American Union became the tangible permanent symbol of inter-American relationships. Its days of
uncertainty were over. The cozy cloak of respectability descended
upon it, and a certain solemn ponderousness was acquired. Even the
procession of Directors General slowed down to a more dignified
pace. During the first seventeen years six Directors had flitted
through, holding the position for an average of three years; after
that John Barrett stayed on for thirteen years and Dr. Leo S. Rowe
for twice as many. On retiring in 1920, Director General Barrett
wrote in his final report to the Governing Board of the changes that
had taken place during his tenure. A staff of 20 and a $56,000 budget
had grown to 75 employees and a budget of $200,000. The Columbus
Memorial Library, which had only about 5,000 books in 1906,
counted 45,000 by 1920 (today it has upwards of 150,000 books, and is
easily the world's best collection on the Western Hemisphere).

These years had also seen Hemisphere trade reach impressive proportions. It amounted to less than $450,000,000 when Mr. Barrett

took office, and he had been called in the press an "irresponsible enthusiast" for predicting that it would reach the billion mark in 1920. As a matter of fact, in that year the figures showed exchanges of over three billions.

Meanwhile, for the first time United States public opinion was awakening to the existence of Latin America. In his last year in office, Mr. Barrett reached some 100,000 people through public addresses, and was able to accept only a fifth of his invitations from chambers of commerce, civic associations, and the like.

During these first decades of the twentieth century the Pan American Union was submitted to searching, if affectionate, criticism. Actually, most of the criticism failed to take into account that the Union was merely a reflection of the times. Its shortcomings were those of the inter-American system itself as it evolved, slowly shedding limitations and inequities.

For it must be remembered that none of the fundamental issues of international life in the Hemisphere had yet been squarely faced. The principle of nonintervention was not accepted by the United States until 1933 at the Montevideo Conference and a few more years passed before it became firmly established. Meanwhile, the Latin American nations were reluctant to delegate very much power and influence to the Union, which they considered overshadowed by the Washington government.

After the hard years of intervention had run their course, but before the good-neighbor honeymoon was launched, there was an interregnum of a few years, marked by the Fifth Conference at Havana in 1928 and the Sixth at Montevideo in 1933. This was a period of transition for the inter-American system. Under the powerful pressure of an aroused and conscience-stricken United States public opinion and the combined efforts of Latin American diplomacy, the suspicion and fear of years were being swept away. The solid foundation of Pan Americanism was being laid.

During those years, the punctilious courtesy and warm affection that Dr. Leo S. Rowe harbored for all the nations of the Hemisphere was a much-needed balm. Director General from 1920 to 1946, he was the living antithesis of all the "Colossus of the North" had been and a reassuring indication of what it was to become.

Of slight physique, mild-mannered, with a ready smile, deeply engrossed in the everyday life of the Latin American countries, the Director General stood for a homely, man-in-the-street concept of Pan Americanism. Dr. Rowe's daily routine was centered around this personal approach to Latin America. Every morning at nine, he walked across the gardens between the Director General's residence and the Pan American Union carrying a metal suitcase. This relic of his southward trips contained the reading material he took home every evening, including not only official papers but also newspapers from several of the countries, which he read regularly.

He would spend most of his morning seeing people. Any Latin American passing through Washington had ready and prompt access to the office of the Director General. Dr. Rowe not only practiced an old-fashioned courtesy which fully matched that of any of his southern visitors, but he was also always ready to render service, in an official or a personal capacity.

Dr. Rowe's attitude toward the American nations stemmed from deep convictions and a sincere respect and appreciation for other cultures and other ways of life. In his book *The United States and Puerto Rico*, published in 1904, sixteen years before he became the Pan American Union's Director General, he wrote: " In Puerto Rico we have come into the midst of a people foreign to us in manner of thought and distinctly European in their institutional life. . . .

" To the mass of Americans resident in the island — and this is particularly true of the lawyers — the entire system of law and government, of domestic and public institutions, was bad simply because it was different from our own. Everything that did not conform to our system was not only un-American but anti-American. . . . The only way to make Americans of the Puerto Ricans, it was argued, was to give them, without delay, the system of law of one of our states. ' This is the way we do it in the States' was regarded as an argument sufficient to bring conviction to the mind of every native. . . .

" The significant and important fact which our contact with the Spanish-American civilization in the West Indies illustrates, is the necessity of a greater elasticity of ideas, a broader sympathy, and a readiness. or at least a willingness, to understand the point of view of people whose training, traditions, and system of law are essentially different from our own. . . ."

By the time of the Second World War, it was possible to look back and take stock of the services the Pan American Union had rendered. An independent observer, Olive Holmes (now specialist on Latin America for the Foreign Policy Association), prepared a thesis for Columbia University on the Union in which she said:

" The difficulty of finding a formula satisfactory to all the members of this international institution had first to be surmounted; this was the task of years. There was the fear of the small Latin American states, jealous of their rights, that the Bureau would be a veiled means of domination by the ' Colossus of the North.' Again, there was the apprehension in the United States that it would have to support the Bureau single-handed. The indifference to the purposes of the Bureau at first manifested by certain Republics, the inertia of diplomatic conferences, the lack of expert advice and guidance in the problems of international organization, political and economic difficulties of the Member States — these, too, were obstacles that had to be overcome before the Bureau (or the Pan American Union, as it is known today) could attain its present proud position.

" It is difficult to say just when the American countries began to realize the value of the conferences, or when the need of an international secretariat to consolidate and further the work begun by the conferences became apparent. It is likely that this realization was a gradual process, in the course of which the Bureau was given more and more functions as its usefulness as an agency of inter-American cooperation in all its manifestations became increasingly apparent."

Meanwhile a new phase began and ended for inter-American relations. It comprised roughly a decade, from the enunciation of the Good Neighbor policy by President Roosevelt in 1933 to the closing months of the Second World War. A strange combination of circumstances, most of them originating outside of the Hemisphere under the aegis of a man named Adolf Hitler, created a sudden and passionate interest in Latin America among the people of the United States. Everything about that part of the world became almost overnight both fashionable and absorbing. Demands for information and orientation on every aspect of life south of the border poured in from all corners of the United States. Universities, women's clubs, chambers of commerce, civic associations wanted to know about Latin America and know fast.

It was suddenly realized that Latin America had a culture, and the knowledge was transmitted to the United States public at a breathtaking pace. Painters, architects, and musicians below the Rio Grande were proclaimed excellent or even unexcelled. The writers had profound and thrilling things to say. Unfortunately, they said them only in Spanish and Portuguese. No matter: United States publishing houses threw themselves into the breach and a somewhat haphazard group of novels was translated. Meanwhile, representatives from Latin America were asked to come and take a good look at the United States — something they were more than willing to do. Thousands of them left their offices, studios, drawing boards, classrooms, and surgery wards, and for a hectic few weeks were rushed over the length and breadth of the United States. There was hardly time for them to meet the people — the country's greatest asset — but it was assumed that a quick look at Detroit's assembly lines, Pittsburgh's blast furnaces, and Manhattan's skyscrapers would win them over. The Great Honeymoon was on.

More prosaic and tangible matters were also attended to. There were raw materials that had to be gotten from Latin America. Tin, rubber, quartz, mica, manganese, all were desperately needed as the war clouds gathered in Europe and the Far East.

United States embassies throughout Latin America, until then somnolent backwaters of diplomatic *douceur de vivre,* were inconvenienced by a steady stream of bright, tweedy experts fresh out of Harvard or Princeton, with a tender addiction to pipes and a voracious appetite for statistics. The statistics were mainly nonexistent, and the tweeds clashed with the climate, but they kept coming. In one large South American country, a hard-working commercial attaché had previously held the fort for United States trade against the enterprise and guile of British and Germans, so adept at wooing the native with culture-sprinkled sales talk. Now two dozen commodity experts, financial analysts, and trade advisers were considered hardly enough.

Trade relations between the United States and Latin America, which had been at the root of the First Inter-American Conference and were the sole concern of the Pan American Union in its beginnings, had finally come of age, with a strange godfather in the person of a German ex-corporal. During the confusion and urgency of these years, economic relations of great scope were established. They developed amid war's inevitable waste and lack of perspective, with jarring disruption and suffering for backward, slow-moving economies. But on the whole the phenomenon was hopeful. Never again would economic relations between the two continents sink to their prewar level of primitive, exploitative give-and-take of raw materials and manufactured goods. Powerful, complex economic interests had been shaken into action; for better or for worse, they would keep going through the postwar years.

And today? As it completes sixty years of existence, the Pan American Union finds itself in an ancillary but key position within an inter-American system that has reached maturity under the name of Organization of American States. The Union still holds the limelight for the same reasons that have been valid ever since its first marble building was dedicated in 1910. It stands as a solid, visible symbol of the inter-American system, today at the threshold of a new phase.

In truth this system, which during most of these sixty years had grown steadily but slowly, even lackadaisically at times, has picked up speed. Faced since 1945 with the challenge of finding their place within the world system, the Americas in four years crystallized into a formal structure concepts and aspirations that had been evolving for half a century. Intervention has been eliminated from the American scene. The rights and dignity of the small republics have been fully and graciously acknowledged by the United States, which has consequently grown in moral stature.

A system of law and a machinery for peace is now operating in the Hemisphere in a climate of international morality. They have not yet been put to a truly severe test, but situations that only a few years ago would have meant deep unrest and definite danger of war have been met peacefully.

In a larger sense, the great pride and hope of the OAS does not reside merely in its charter, which after all is but a structure, sturdy and well-proportioned as it may be. To give life and significance to inter-American relationships, there must be willingness and ability to face real problems and help find answers to them. There are signs that this is beginning to be done; a survey of the tasks now being tackled in the Americas shows that the emphasis is shifting to what is useful and needed.

The OAS and the United States government called a conference in Denver in 1948, where for the first time conservation was studied in terms of future human needs by relating resources to population trends, and where the creeping menace of erosion was spelled out. In cooperation with Brazil and UNESCO, the OAS sponsored a seminar on literacy and adult education at Rio de Janeiro. Out of this seminar came a vast program, which the Pan American Union is now beginning to carry out through a considerable expansion of its educational services. The Inter-American Statistical Institute, later to become one of the specialized organizations under the OAS, started the ball rolling for the 1950 Census of the Americas. Now in a few months' time every nation in the Hemisphere will strive to write out in facts and figures fundamental realities — population, housing, trade, industry. Without such knowledge one cannot even begin to plan; the effort acquires its true meaning when it is recalled that some of these nations had never had a census, others had not had one for several decades. Seminars on social problems, discussing issues close to the lives of people everywhere, such as low-cost housing, are being organized. The first meets in Quito next May [1950].

Hardheaded, practical initiatives like these seem to indicate that a new spirit of service today animates the inter-American system. At the center of all these programs stands the Pan American Union, in whose technical offices the work will be done. The Union can be either a springboard for achievement or a bureaucratic morass. Which it will be depends, in the final analysis, upon the 289 men and women who constitute its working staff. They have today certain assets in common that justify reasonable optimism.

For the first time in its long history, the Pan American Union personnel tends to be truly representative. A roll call today is sprinkled with Spanish and Portuguese names. Many of the people are fresh from their countries, bringing to the Union as precious

working capital an intimate first-hand acquaintance with the throb-
bing realities of Latin America — malnutrition, illiteracy, poverty,
but also a first-hand knowledge of what is being accomplished
against tremendous odds; of the drive and will that is found in the
young generation; of the unsung exploits of engineers, doctors, and
pioneers everywhere.

The newcomers are working as a team with the veterans of the
lean years, whose experience, devotion, and intimate personal knowledge of the day-to-day mechanics of inter-American dealings is a
treasured and irreplaceable asset. The United States contingent in
the Union is continually being reinforced with technicians of the
highest caliber, who had already acquired a solid reputation working
for the United States government or for private institutions.

Most of the staff has now moved to the new administration building, whose interiors are austerely designed for work, and work only.
But they have not lost their sentimental attachment for the "old
building" across the street, which is more than just a handsome
structure with noble halls and exotic touches.

President Theodore Roosevelt, who stopped by frequently on his
daily horseback ride to survey the progress of the works, was fond of
calling it "the capital of the Western Hemisphere in the capital of
the United States."

The words of Joaquim Nabuco, first Brazilian ambassador to
Washington, one of the driving forces behind Pan Americanism during its formative years, sound today as pertinent as when he said
them at the laying of the cornerstone of the building, in 1908:

"There has never been a parallel for the sight which this ceremony presents — that of twenty-one nations of different languages,
building together a house for their common deliberations. The more
striking is the scene as these countries, with all possible differences
between them in size and population, have established their Union
on the basis of the most absolute equality. Here the vote of the
smallest balances the vote of the greatest. So many sovereign states
would not have been drawn together so spontaneously if there did
not exist throughout them, at the bottom or at the top of each
national conscience, the feeling of a destiny common to all America."

No. 51 [The inter-American political community is no longer expressed in an organization which is limited in its powers to minor matters, and which serves only as a clearing house for inter-American information. In the six decades that have transpired since the " Commercial Bureau " was first organized, the world has witnessed the emergence and development of a truly remarkable international political society. In 1948, at Bogotá, the American republics formally launched the Organization of American States which, although based upon the politically weaker organization that preceded it, has an infinitely larger political responsibility and authority.

Many people ask, particularly after observing the clashes which occur in United Nations meetings: How can an international political organization really function? Who speaks for the member nations? How are agreements reached? What prevents personality and political clashes? To these and many similar questions, " International Isle " gives a partial but a highly significant answer.]

International Isle*

PARADOXICALLY, Washington, D.C., has hundreds of thousands of United States citizens who pay taxes but cannot vote. And in the heart of the national capital there is a small international island whose people cannot vote but neither do they pay taxes. What's more, they enjoy immunity from the laws of the land. Not even the police can cross the island's undefended borders without permission of insular authorities. For this territory belongs to the Organization of American States.

Like asphalt rivers, 18th Street and Virginia Avenue split the islet in two. But when the new OAS administration building opens in August [1949], international immunity will extend from the Pan

* ———, " International Isle," *Américas* (June, 1949), Vol. 1, No. 4, pp. 2–5, 35. Reprinted by permission of *Américas,* a monthly magazine published by the Pan American Union in English, Spanish, and Portuguese.

American Union through the connecting tunnel beneath the feet of unsuspecting United States citizens who converge every morning on the Navy Department building across Constitution Avenue.

Most of the OAS island's seven and a half acres are covered with vivid green lawns shaded by sycamores, poplars, evergreens, and flowering trees. The rest is white marble from Georgia and Italy. Two palaces shine through the thick foliage with a brilliance that in winter carries the snowline to the rooftops. Between these main buildings, a whitewashed house in sober Spanish renaissance style opens through a loggia that is a reproduction of an Aztec temple into formal, almost academic gardens. There, delicate water lilies from the American tropics, Egypt, and India float on a glazed tile pool presided over by Xochipilli, Aztec god of flowers. The tip of the Washington monument is mirrored among the enormous rimmed pads of the Victoria Regina of Brazil and in the spring mingles with the shimmering reflections of pink and white magnolia blossoms.

Young couples wander up and down the neat gravel paths, unaware that they have left their country and for the moment are under the protection of not one, but twenty-one flags. Ruffled by the soft Potomac breezes, the gay banners fly from the Pan American Union's front terrace, only a short stroll from the White House.

Nor is this " inter-nation " restricted to a single language. It has four. As one steps into the Pan American Union vestibule, he enters an atmosphere that vibrates with staccato Spanish r's, soft Portuguese cadences, French nuances, and the southern drawl. Unlike the " foreigners " outside, citizens of this international territory are not divided into only two colors. Here one finds many different shades of skin, eyes, and hair, from the New England blond and Irish redhead to the blue-black hair of the Yucatán or Cuzco Indian. A few paces farther, a miniature tropical jungle reaches up toward the movable glass roof of the patio. Aloof from seasonal changes outside, coffee, rubber, cinchona, and banana trees grow around a fountain decorated with Indian motifs.

Some two to three hundred thousand tourists, without a visa or any other border-crossing formalities, invade the island's territory every year. Most are North Americans. They pile out of buses to swarm into the buildings and grounds, chattering and laughing with youthful gaiety at the guides' witticisms. They try to strike up a conversation with the green parrot and ancient macaws, make bets on the nationality of the various flags, examine the shields of the member states, and pay their respects to the twenty-one marble busts in the Hall of Heroes, a silent council in endless session. But when they have the chance, they prefer to peer from the vast Hall of the Americas at the more human spectacle of an OAS Council session in the adjoining room.

There they see the twenty-one Council members at work around a huge oval table of highly polished Dominican mahogany, seated in high-backed chairs crowned with the seals of their respective countries. At each place a little microphone records the minutes of the meeting. Much of the discussion is in Spanish, the native tongue of eighteen members. But the meeting is conducted in all four OAS official languages — without interpreters. This is what impresses the tourists most — more than the United Nations' simultaneous interpretation equipment. For the modern mind easily accepts a translation machine. But here is a phenomenon: twenty-one men seated around a table, speaking in four different languages, debating and persuading, reaching amicable conclusions. If this can work, the observer reflects, probably the Tower of Babel difficulty was only a case of slight misunderstanding.

All this is only on the surface. The really remarkable feat, given much less consideration by the tourists, is the fact that these men from all over the hemisphere understand each other's aims and ideologies — plus the fact that this has been going on in one way or another for sixty years.

The Council is a kind of parliament of the Americas meeting in this island's neutral territory. Each of the gentlemen around the mahogany oval represents a nation: the oldest, the United States; the youngest, Panama; the largest, Brazil; the smallest, El Salvador. Yet, whether born in 1776 or 1903, whether they have 3,286,170 square miles or 13,176, all are equal and each representative is entitled to just one vote in every Council decision. Eleven votes usually decide the issue; in a few cases it takes fourteen, or two thirds. Theoretically, the parliament is in session all year, but when the torrid Washington sun and the humidity of the Potomac basin interfere with the exercise of deliberative faculties, it may decree a summer recess.

The Council has heavy responsibilities. Nevertheless, its functions have been carefully limited by the Inter-American Conferences, for there was a long-standing prejudice against it. When it was known as the Governing Board of the Pan American Union, the United States Secretary of State was automatically its chairman, and the other members were the ambassadors of the various countries to the United States. Its powers, like those of the Union as a whole, were small. Above all, it was forbidden to deal with political questions. It met once a month. The agenda was slight, almost always innocuous. Proposals were drawn up in advance. Although the Secretary of State called for it, there was rarely any discussion. The sessions were brief. For the most part they were protocol meetings to receive distinguished guests.

Then came what might be called the Chapultepec Revolution. The first change introduced by the 1945 Conference made the chairmanship elective and banned re-election for the term following. The second, which did not last, stipulated that the members should be separate, special delegates to the Board, instead of the ambassadors to Washington. Last year at Bogotá this provision was altered to allow the governments freedom to name either special *ad hoc* representatives or the chiefs of their diplomatic missions in Washington.

In practice, the Chapultepec Revolution has triumphed. Partly because of these changes, partly because of new functions assigned to the Council, the group's entire character was radically altered in less than a year. It undertook intensive preparatory work for the Rio de Janeiro and Bogotá Conferences. Committees met morning and afternoon, and complex legal discussions lasted for hours. Reams of reports, studies, and drafts were turned out. The ambassadors kept up exhaustive correspondence with their governments, asking for instructions, presenting their own ideas, reporting the latest developments. For all practical purposes, the Rio treaty was drawn up in the Council. The same was true of the extensive documents presented at Bogotá. In all fairness, the success of the two Conferences was due basically to the Council's labors.

At Rio one more task was assigned to the Council: to act as provisional organ of consultation pending the meeting of Foreign

Ministers. In this capacity, the Council takes on all the powers of the meeting of Foreign Ministers, even to applying sanctions to an aggressor. It recently undertook this role with brilliant success in the conflict between Costa Rica and Nicaragua.

The Council holds two open meetings a month. The audience is small. So is the meeting hall, with room for only forty visitors in a single row of chairs around the damask-hung walls. But the reporters for the international news agencies and sometimes special correspondents are there. The journalists must be quadrilingual too. Sometimes they need clarification of a point, willingly supplied by an ambassador or some other official. The atmosphere is serious but not gloomy. Debates are rare, not because there is always agreement, but because the open meeting climaxes a serious of previous agreements reached in committee. A less formal atmosphere prevails in the committees, which meet almost daily, sometimes two or three a day. It is not unusual for the discussion to be carried on in the affectionate Spanish " *tu,*" even with the North Americans who never master this verb form, or with the Brazilians, who are addicted to the third person formality of " *o senhor.*"

Council members who represent their countries as ambassadors to the United States at present include the delegates of Costa Rica, Chile, El Salvador, Guatemala, Haiti, Honduras, Nicaragua, Panama, and Paraguay. The others also have the rank of ambassador, granted by the OAS Charter to avoid inequality. Unlike ambassadors to the White House, OAS diplomats do not appear in the State Department's monthly blue book, which Washington hostesses scan scrupulously for cosmopolitan adornments for their tables. A law has been proposed to grant the *ad hoc* Council members all the privileges and immunities of the ambassadors to the United States. But until their status is defined, they will continue to give butlers nightmares at seating time. Where should they be placed in relation to regular ambassadors? Does a Chargé d'Affaires outrank his country's Ambassador to the OAS? These problems raise eyebrows in the State Department protocol office, but until Congress expresses itself, the officials leave the question for the hostesses to solve in their own way.

Social Washington has already found a practical answer. Anyone over forty, with a foreign accent, is an ambassador. Every army uniform in the same age group automatically belongs to a general, or, in the naval ranks, to an admiral. The diplomats' wives in turn have established a charming generalization that makes a senator of every bald or gray-headed North American. All of which makes receptions easier, happier, and much more important.

Another difference between White House ambassadors and the *ad hoc* Council representatives is sartorial. The first generally dress more formally than the second. Since they may have to attend two or more receptions, cocktail parties, or ceremonies of various sorts, they sometimes start the day with the neutral striped-pants costume that meets every situation up to dinner time. The *ad hoc* representatives more often appear in gray flannels and sweater. Several go hatless. Some drive their own automobiles. They live in rented houses in the bourgeois residential districts. Almost all have large families.

In a city where most of the population is made up of white-collar workers, the OAS ambassadors lead an existence much like high federal government officials. For social functions, they rely on the salons of the large hotels. The Argentine delegate and Chairman of the Council took over the old house of ex-President Hoover on S Street, with ample halls that rival any of the embassies. But Señor Corominas shares the simple tastes of his colleagues.

The Council's heavy work schedule takes up too much time for the members to keep up with Washington's exhausting social life. Occasionally they can be found among the city crowds in art galleries or movie theaters. Sometimes they flee to New York to catch up on the theater, for the political capital of the world has no legitimate stage.

After one hundred and fifty years, Washington is still a provincial city. Its gushing artificial stream of diplomatic cocktail parties has imperiled the Senate quorum on several occasions, provoking debate in the Chamber. But for anyone who does not belong to this set, there is little to do but work.

In the Pan American Union, Council members have both their office and their club. Soon after assuming their posts, they slip into the easy air of solid comradeship that prevails in the Council. Some are very old friends. They met fifteen or twenty years ago at inter-

American meetings in Montevideo, Buenos Aires, or Lima. Usually they belong to the group of experts in inter-American affairs that has been working for years on continental problems. Some have been active in the work of preserving peace in the Hemisphere since Chaco War days. But they are not all career diplomats. Many have been politicians, journalists, bankers, farmers. Drawing from their own experience, they bring to the problem under study a practical, human point of view.

Through frank and sincere conversations, the ambassadors soon become well acquainted with the political, economic, and social situation in the twenty-one countries, and they discuss these things with complete freedom. As they learn, their interest in other countries grows. They begin to compare notes on their problems and the methods of solving them. They exchange newspapers, pamphlets, books. Basically, the atmosphere is that of a cosmopolitan university rather than of a diplomatic corps. When they take up a problem, they acquire within a few days a remarkably deep understanding of it. And their interest in solving it is not merely the cold diplomatic desire to avoid difficulties, but a lively, generous interest stemming from a genuine continental patriotism.

No. 52 [Formal political documents, be they national constitutions or international covenants, usually establish intricate machinery for the resolution of political disagreement or open conflict. The basic question is, however, does this mechanism work or is it but an expression of a pious hope? The League of Nations was powerless to stop the aggression of Japan, Germany, or Italy; the United Nations in 1951 had certainly not convinced a majority — here or elsewhere — that the charter agencies and instrumentalities would settle the contemporary international conflict. (It should be noted, however, that in both theory and practice the United Nations has gone much farther towards the goal of international government than did the old and abandoned League.)

Turning to the Americas, one may similarly ask if the Organization of American States is an effective instrument of inter-American peace. It is true that the political problems confronting it are tiny in comparison with, let us say, the United States-Russian conflict. Nevertheless, we must not lose sight of the fact that disagreements between the politically much weaker American republics may be just as deep and just as charged with international danger as those which exist between the great powers. If unresolved they might blaze into wars involving not only the two original protagonists but also their immediate or remote neighbors. In attempting to resolve them OAS encounters, as does UN, national interests and rivalries, national fears and jealousies, and national patriotic feelings. It is consequently of great interest and importance to ascertain what the record discloses. " The Secret of Peace " subjects the record to such an examination.]

The Secret of Peace*

by ALBERTO LLERAS

E VER since the discovery of America, there has been more peace here than in any other part of the globe. Nevertheless, hardly any American nation has always been at peace with all its neighbors. In addition to actual wars, the foreign relations of each country have been spiced with border incidents, clashes, and interventions.

The gradual development of the inter-American system has closely corresponded with a notable lessening of these frictions. The evolution of standards of law to proscribe war culminated in the Inter-American Treaty of Reciprocal Assistance, signed in Rio de Janeiro in 1947, two years after its basic principles were established in the Act of Chapultepec. Since the approval of that Act at the Mexico City Conference just before the first meeting of the United Nations, the peace of America has not been disturbed.

But it has not been completely out of danger. A series of incidents

* Alberto Lleras, " The Secret of Peace," Américas (June, 1950), Vol. 2, No. 6, pp. 9–11, 42, 44. Reprinted by permission of Américas, a monthly magazine published by the Pan American Union in English, Spanish, and Portuguese.

occurred during the last few years in the Caribbean region. Although some of these incidents could technically be considered as internal disturbances, the fact is that each one was followed by an angry protest from the affected government, claiming that it was the victim of an international plot. A year and a half ago, one of these incidents led to the first application of the Treaty of Reciprocal Assistance, on the request of Costa Rica, which charged that Nicaragua gave protection to invading revolutionary forces. Months later, Haiti asked for application of the treaty, charging intervention by the Dominican government against the Haitian government. Venezuela made public accusations against the Dominican Republic, and the latter on various occasions accused Costa Rica, Cuba, Guatemala, and Venezuela of organizing movements directed against the Dominican régime. Altogether and at various times seven American states, or one third of the Organization's twenty-one members, were involved in this Caribbean agitation.

International tension in the affected area became very great. The interruption of relations between some of these republics made the application of normal diplomatic procedures more difficult. The Inter-American Peace Committee studied the cases brought before it and achieved excellent results in some of them, despite the fact that it lacked any compulsory force, its action being limited to the recommendation of methods for resolving disputes. The OAS Council's first application of the Rio treaty was surprisingly effective. The difficulties between the two republics involved in the dispute disappeared, and neither of them subsequently figured in the incidents that continued to upset the region.

There was, then, a serious danger of a disturbance of the peace of the Hemisphere right up to the time when Haiti, on the one hand, and the Dominican Republic, on the other, brought the situation before the Council of the Organization, both requesting application of the Treaty of Reciprocal Assistance. This happened January 6, 1950. Haiti charged the Dominican Republic with permitting Haitian exiles Alfred Viau and ex-Colonel Astrel Roland to make provocative broadcasts against the Haitian government over a Dominican radio station, and accused Rafael Oscar de Moya, First Secretary of the Dominican Embassy in Port-au-Prince, of involvement with John Dupuy and others who were plotting assassinations and arson. The

Dominican Republic denied these charges and in turn reiterated its accusations against Cuba, Guatemala, and the former government of Venezuela, based on the frustrated plan of a force gathered at Cayo Confites, Cuba, in 1947, to invade Dominican soil, and the equally unsuccessful invasion by air, from Guatemala, which ended at the Dominican port of Luperón, on June 19, 1949.

On January 11, the Organ of Consultation provided in the Treaty — the Meeting of Ministers of Foreign Affairs — was convoked. The Council was already acting provisionally as an Organ of Consultation, and had established an investigating committee, which presented its report on March 13. During this interval, the threats to the peace were dissipated. The Council, at its April 8 meeting, took a series of decisions based on the report and conclusions of the investigating committee.

Without mentioning specific incidents, the Council held that facts verified by the investigating committee, from among those charged against the Dominican Republic, were contrary to norms contained in several American conventions and the OAS Charter. It noted the repeal of the Dominican Republic's special war powers as evidence of an intention to maintain peace and avoid a repetition of such incidents. It called on the Dominican government to take measures to prevent government officials from tolerating or encouraging subversive or seditious movements against other governments, and asked both the Dominican Republic and Haiti to avoid the continuation of any hostile propaganda, urging them to strengthen their relations with each other.

The Council then found that officials of the Cuban and Guatemalan governments in some cases lent aid to the anti-Dominican forces gathered on the territory of the two countries, and again declared that principles set forth in inter-American agreements had been violated. It recognized declarations made by the chief executives of these states as guaranteeing there would be no recurrence of such acts. It requested the Cuban and Guatemalan governments to adopt adequate measures so as not to permit the existence in their territories of groups organized on a military basis with the deliberate purpose of conspiring against the security of other countries, to control war materials that may be or may have been in the possession of the revolutionary groups, and to prevent illegal traffic in arms.

The Council called on all the governments involved in the whole situation to ensure absolute respect for the principle of nonintervention, and to avoid hostile propaganda, and urged Cuba and the Dominican Republic to settle the controversy remaining between them.

Clearly, its action as Organ of Consultation had been sufficiently effective to dissolve the dangers that had been so ominously accumulating over this part of the Western Hemisphere.

Why? In what did the effectiveness of the Council lie? What are the formulas that achieve such far-reaching remedies for situations that, in any other part of the world, would lead to war? This, and not the anecdotal detail of the facts that produced the state of insecurity in the Caribbean region, is what is important to examine. Certainly there could have been an international war in the Caribbean; disturbances of the peace have been produced with less inflammable material, not only in other parts of the world but right here in America. It is also certain that the danger has disappeared. And that no one in the Hemisphere — neither the chancelleries nor public opinion as expressed in the press and on the radio — fails to attribute the good result to the Organization of American States. And in this we can include the public opinion and chancelleries even of the countries affected.

Evidently this effectiveness does not lie, as some suppose, in the machinery created by the American countries to settle their conflicts. It lies in the good faith with which the American states have created that machinery, use it honestly, and give collective respect to its action, both when it favors their individual interests and when it runs against them. There are no " better " or " worse " international organizations, nor can the failures of an organization always be attributed to its technical defects. When the American states established theirs, they accepted its principles in good faith. All were resolved never again to resort to war as a legitimate instrument of inter-American policy. The American peace machinery operates with disconcerting ease. All the states cooperate to make it function well. Peace is their collective interest. But the states are aware that war is a constant threat, even sometimes against the will of the parties. For this reason, they endow their organization — which is the sum of all of them — with sufficient powers to contain war, or extinguish it, or nullify its effects. And they pledge themselves, knowing what they do, to respect their organization.

But that is not all. The American states, as they have demonstrated this time, have an international policy marked by courage and responsibility. They have the courage to call things by their right names. They have the courage and sense of responsibility to hear these things said when they are adverse to themselves. The committee's report points out facts that imply violations of inter-American obligations. None of the states affected by the report's statements tried to evade its responsibility. This is an impressive example of international frankness and loyalty. We can say that it is without precedent in the history of international associations. It is impossible to say which of these two instances was the more important: when five representatives of states — not five commissioners or five men, but five states — expressed their opinion of the causes and remedies for the situation, without any reticence; or when, one after the other, the states cited in the report and conclusions praised the impartiality and probity of the committee members and refrained from creating the sort of incident we are used to seeing in international meetings whenever anyone must point out that the policy of a certain country is at fault.

But in both cases the Organization, that is, the American states, demonstrated a maturity of conduct that indicates that the sixty years since they took the first steps to associate themselves honorably in a policy of peace and cooperation have not passed in vain. In these two instances (of the presentation of the report and its discussion in the Council) the tension of the Caribbean area was dissolved, almost automatically. States with such a profound sense of international responsibility and of their obligations within the Organization could not be, never will be, a danger to peace.

In the juridical field, this second application of the Treaty of Reciprocal Assistance reveals new and very important points. The Council, acting as Provisional Organ of Consultation, has taken a step in the definition of the concept of aggression that has been sharply debated since the already remote days of the League of Nations. Examining the events that occurred and the intervention by foreign governments in domestic revolutionary situations in certain countries, the Council declared that " Even though the said facts fortunately did not result in the violation of international peace, they did very seriously weaken American solidarity; and if they were to persist or recur, they would give occasion for the application of the procedures of the Inter-American Treaty of Reciprocal Assistance in order to protect the principle of nonintervention and to ensure the inviolability or the integrity of the territory or the sovereignty or the political independence of any American state against aggression on the part of any state or group of states." Actually, this affirmation creates nothing more nor less than the teeth that were missing in the inter-American treaties and conventions which, in the committee's judgment, were violated in the cases it investigated. It is almost the same as saying that intervention, as condemned in those treaties and conventions, is one of the acts of aggression that give occasion for applying the measures contemplated by the Treaty of Reciprocal Assistance. No future meeting of the organ of consultation, in similar cases, could fail to be guided by this criterion if there should be any doubt as to the application of the Rio de Janeiro Treaty, or if it should be necessary to define the aggressor in the circumstances covered by Articles 6, 7, and 9 of that treaty. Indeed, the Council was acting under the power of Article 9, which authorizes it to characterize acts other than armed attack and invasion as acts of aggression.

Another result of this meeting of the council, acting as organ of consultation, was a basic clarification of the supposed conflict between the principle of non-intervention and the principle of democracy. Within the limits of the most rigorous juridical concept, and in defense of the best interests of the American community, the Council once more made it clear that no government or group of governments can feel authorized, in the name of democratic principles, to violate the principle of nonintervention. It recommended that a study be undertaken of the possibilities of stimulating and developing the effective exercise of representative democracy, set forth in Article 5 (d) of the Charter, as well as in Article XX of the American Declaration of the Rights and Duties of Man. The relevant section of Article 5 of the OAS Charter says that " The solidarity of the American States and the high aims which are sought through it require the political organization of those States on the basis of the effective exercise of representative democracy." And Article XX of the Declaration says that "Every person having legal capacity is entitled to participate in the government of his country, directly or through his representatives, and to take part in popular elections, which shall be by secret ballot, and shall be honest, periodic and free." The American states have evidently acquired an obligation to proceed in conformity with these principles. But even if that obligation went still further and there were some compulsory force to compel its execution, this power would never be given to individual states, for each to put into operation according to its own conception against other governments. We cannot tell whether some day there may be machinery in the Organization to give effect to those principles. But violation of the principle of nonintervention can never be justified as a legitimate individual means of carrying them out.

Another principle that comes out of this meeting reinforced by the approval given to a concept expressed by the investigating committee is that no American government may resort to the threat or use of force, even in the name of legitimate self-defense, in any manner inconsistent with the provisions of the UN Charter, the Rio de Janeiro Treaty, and the OAS Charter. Legitimate self-defense implies a previous offensive act. Therefore, it is obvious that if it is made into a threat it is not legitimate, nor is it defense. Of course a state can defend itself, if it is attacked, without violating any international commitment. But this right must not be converted into a provocation. Still less when all the resources of collective self-defense are at hand, as they are in the Treaty of Reciprocal Assistance.

The same delegates who made up the investigating committee, the representatives of Uruguay (who served as chairman), Bolivia, Colombia, Ecuador, and the United States, remain charged with overseeing the manner in which the recommendations of the Council are carried out. But their task, which was originally a tremendous one and executed with courage and responsibility, is now much easier. The difficult thing was, at the same time, to dissipate the tension in the affected area and strengthen the authority of the Organization. Both objectives were achieved. For many years people will study this episode as an admirable precedent. And thus they will see still more clearly that the secret of peace lies not in the machinery of international organizations, but rather in the conduct of the states that compose them.

No. 53 [The international relations of Latin America are closely tied to those of the United States for many reasons. Geographical proximity alone would magnify the influence of the northernmost American republic even if other economic and strategic factors were absent. Latin America is brought to a more real and a more direct relationship with the rest of the world through its inevitable ties with the United States.

The Point Four policy has, therefore, a double significance for the area. As has been noted in several of the immediately preceding articles, Latin America can obtain assistance (and is doing so) from the United States in undertaking to solve its basic economic and social problems through the " technical " assistance contemplated by President Truman when he first stated his now famous fourth point. In this manner, the foreign policy of the United States becomes important in the social and economic development of the other American republics.

But Point Four is not an inter-American policy; it is international. Through participation in it the nations of Latin America will be drawn into a much closer and a much more direct relationship not only with the United States but also with the United Nations and other international political and administrative agencies.]

Preface to Point Four*

by CLARENCE PIERCE

ON April 10, 1950, anyone pushing his way through the crowded corridors of the Pan American Union would have heard phrases like " Point Four " and " Technical Assistance " coming from groups of distinguished-looking gentlemen in earnest conversation. The gentlemen in question were government delegates to the first extraordinary session of the Organization of American States' Inter-American Economic and Social Council, which on that date was

* Clarence Pierce, " Preface to Point Four," *Américas* (June, 1950), Vol. 2, No. 6, pp. 28–29, 32. Reprinted by permission of *Américas,* a monthly magazine published by the Pan American Union in English, Spanish, and Portuguese.

completing three weeks of hard work. The phrases referred to a resolution to establish an OAS technical cooperation program on which they were about to vote. This program and the possibilities of its development held the center of the stage at the Council session.

It was not the only item on the agenda. There were three others, important ones; but they were problems of great complexity which no one expected would be solved at the session. So there was not the ready optimism about them that prevailed about the program of technical cooperation. This was something specific and tangible.

In voting for the resolution, the representatives assembled in the great Hall of the Americas hoped to give life to the glorious picture painted by Harry S. Truman in his inaugural address in January 1949. As most people know by now, Point Four comes from the fourth point in the international program enunciated by the President of the United States in that speech. He said:

We must embark on a bold new program for making the benefits of our scientific advances and industrial progress available for the improvement and growth of underdeveloped areas. . . . This should be a cooperative enterprise in which all nations work together through the United Nations and its specialized agencies. . . .

Immediately after its announcement as a United States policy, international organizations took up the challenge and began considering expanded programs of technical cooperation. The Inter-American Economic and Social Council invited the delegate of the United States to explain the policy more fully. On March 3, 1949, delegate Willard L. Thorp explained that the United States wished to work through all international organizations that had the technical resources and the experience on which to build a program. Mr. Thorp pointed out that the Pan American Union and several inter-American specialized agencies met these qualifications — that the United States would be happy to see technical-assistance activities developed within the Organization of American States.

This was a green light for the Inter-American Economic and Social Council. The Secretariat of the Council was directed to study and report on the possibilities. Several reports were considered by the Council in regular sessions, and final documents were developed for consideration in the extraordinary session. These included a draft resolution and examples of types of augmented technical assistance that could be carried on by the Pan American Union and the Inter-American Institute of Agricultural Sciences at Turrialba, Costa Rica.

So that the Council might benefit from their advice in a general OAS program of technical cooperation, six inter-American specialized agencies with considerable experience in providing technical assistance were invited to attend the Council's extraordinary session. These were the Pan American Sanitary Bureau with nearly fifty years of inter-American service, the American International Institute for the Protection of Childhood with almost twenty-five, the Pan American Institute of Geography and History with nearly twenty years, the Inter-American Indian Institute and the Inter-American Statistical Institute with ten years each, and the five-year-old Inter-American Institute of Agricultural Sciences. Observers from the UN, its Economic Commission for Latin America, and the FAO also attended.

The resolution adopted by the Council at its last plenary session on April 10 represents a very high level of inter-American cooperation. According to its provisions, an annual program of technical assistance projects will be developed and conducted by the Inter-American Economic and Social Council. This is as it should be; for, under the charter and in accordance with the Economic Agreement of Bogotá, this Council has the responsibility of fostering such a program. It will be drawn up by a Coordinating Committee on Technical Assistance composed of a representative of the Pan American Union and of each of the cooperating inter-American agencies, with the OAS Secretary General as chairman. After careful consideration of projects proposed by the cooperating agencies, the Committee will develop them into a program for presentation to the Council. The Committee will have its own secretariat.

After the Council approves the content of each year's program, the governments will be invited to contribute to its cost by making deposits in a special account for this purpose. As far as possible, such deposits will be in convertible currencies, but they may be made partly in local currencies, or partly by an evaluation of materials and services to be used for the common benefit. Allocations to cooperating agencies from the special account will be made by the Committee, as funds are available, for projects approved by the

Council and in accord with priorities determined by the Council.

In giving technical assistance, inter-American agencies will call upon those countries with technical resources and knowledge to share them — through the agencies — with the countries requiring such techniques or knowledge. For example, in some areas of Latin America, food production is insufficient because of disease and eroded land. This problem could be tackled on a regional basis, with the Institute of Agricultural Sciences assuming the initiative and consulting with those agencies that could collaborate on it, such as the Pan American Sanitary Bureau, the Food and Agriculture Organization, and the Pan American Union's Division of Education. This last unit would be helpful in advising on media to instruct the people affected, many of whom are illiterate.

The agencies would assay what technical resources and personnel could be brought to bear on the problem from all twenty-one participating countries; then, if the project seemed feasible and the governments of the area concerned displayed an interest in it, the agencies could agree to sponsor it jointly.

Obviously, such a project would have to compete with many other worthy proposals. And funds are limited. Ultimately, the member governments would decide, through the Council, what technical assistance should be given and how much it would cost.

So far, the Council has not dealt specifically with another, related aspect of economic development — the flow of investment capital. It has been concerned only with the question of providing technical assistance, the sharing of " know-how."

Even if nothing had been accomplished but the notable achievement of inaugurating a technical-cooperation program, the special meeting of the Council would have been amply justified — as Dr. Ramón Cereijo, chairman of the extraordinary session, pointed out in his closing speech. Yet, though it represented perhaps the most immediate and tangible benefit, technical cooperation was by no means the only substantial development.

Dr. Cereijo, Argentina's Minister of Finance, reflected accurately the sentiments of most delegates that the session had proved more successful than expected. The Inter-American Economic and Social Council is a permanent agency of the Organization of American States, meeting regularly in Washington. The annual extraordinary sessions, with specially appointed delegates if possible, are designed to deal with some of the more outstanding and troublesome economic and social problems of its members. Therefore, some of the items on the agenda of this session were long-standing problems.

The first item — preparations for the Economic Conference of Buenos Aires — received careful consideration and the decision was to let the Council's next extraordinary session set the date after reviewing the studies and reports of regular Council sessions. This long-awaited conference has been postponed many times. Speaking for the host country, Dr. Cereijo renewed the warm invitation of his government. United States Assistant Secretary of State Edward G. Miller, in his closing speech, paid particular attention to this point on the agenda. He said he wished to make it clear that the United States would participate in any conference anywhere, at any time, provided there was good reason for the conference and fair chance of reaching an agreement.

Another item was the very difficult question of reservations to the Economic Agreement of Bogotá. When this pact was negotiated, so many important reservations were imposed by governments that general ratification of the agreement was made difficult, if not impossible. At the Council's extraordinary session, it was agreed to eliminate many of these reservations, but the general feeling was that enough remained to interfere with ratification. The Council asked the governments to put into effect themselves, or through bilateral or multilateral agreements, the provisions on which agreement had been reached. The Council, in turn, was to continue studying the provisions on which major reservations remained. The Council also requested the Inter-American Juridical Committee to study the legal effects of reservations to multilateral instruments.

The last item on the agenda — the economic effects of recent currency devaluations — represented the first concerted attempt on the part of any international organization to study this question. Generally, it was agreed that not enough time had yet elapsed to judge accurately the repercussions on the economies of the American republics. Only in the case of Bolivia, as a result of the accompanying drop in the price of tin, could a substantial adverse effect be traced. Countries with markets in the dollar area did not expect serious trouble. General concern was expressed about the possible future effects of devaluation on the competitive position of colonial dependencies of European states in the export of raw materials also sold abroad by American countries. The Council was asked to consider this problem in connection with the technical-assistance programs.

The magnificent Hall of the Americas in the Pan American Union has witnessed many historic occasions. This first extraordinary session of the Inter-American Economic and Social Council was the latest in a long series of events resulting from sixty years of inter-American cooperation. It is inherent in the nature of economic and social problems that they are not susceptible of quick or easy solution. The fact that twenty-one American republics met in Washington from March 20 to April 10, 1950, dealt with difficult mutual problems, made progress on some of them, and inaugurated one new program of major importance, is a very good augury for the future.

No. 54 [The idea, or ideal, of a regional and international political organization has long interested the political leaders of Latin America. One of the questions constantly in the mind of Simón Bolívar was the possibility of an inter-American organization of states through which the independent nations of North, Central, and South America could and would act together in working out their regional or hemispheric problems.

Although the idea was received with both understanding and enthusiasm in Latin America in the decades that followed the attainment of independence, the interest in an inter-American organization began to wane in the late nineteenth and early twentieth centuries, *after* the Pan American Union was established.

Following World War I there was a definite schism in the political thought of Latin America with reference to any world government. Many writers felt that Latin American adherence to the League of Nations would enable the republics of the area to maintain their economic and political independence as against the " colossus of the north " and frankly advocated a policy of full acceptance of the League idea as a means of counterbalancing the influence of the United States in America. Others, however, felt that the great powers would dominate any world organization, and that the United States, being one of this select group, would be able to exert an even greater influence in the politics of the Americas through the League. The recognition of "regional understandings" in the Covenant of the League reinforced their objections to this plan of world government, and influenced Latin American states to move slowly and cautiously with reference to the League of Nations.

The end of World War II once again raised these basic questions. Would the Latin American states view the new United Nations as a political organization in which they were regarded as the political equals of the other members, or would it, too, be an instrument for the strengthening of the hegemony of the United States in America?

The role of Latin America in international politics and world government is discussed in the article which follows. It is important to note that the article was written before the Charter of the United Nations was drafted at San Francisco in 1945. The author, therefore, limits himself to a consideration of those factors that are the basic influences in shaping Latin America's attitude toward international political machinery. Those who are familiar with post-1945 developments in inter-American or international union will be impressed by the insight evidenced in Professor Whitaker's analysis.]

The Role of Latin America in Relation to Current Trends in International Organization*

by ARTHUR P. WHITAKER

II

. . . AMONG the factors that play an important part in determining the international role of Latin America, the following seem particularly pertinent to the present discussion.

* Arthur P. Whitaker, "The Role of Latin America in Relation to Current Trends in International Organization," *The American Political Science Review* (June, 1945), Vol. XXXIX, No. 3, pp. 503–511. Reprinted by permission of *The American Political Science Review*. The first section of the text and the footnotes in the original version are omitted here.

1. **Political Fragmentation.** Politically speaking, there is no such thing as Latin America; there are only the twenty independent, highly variegated states south of the Rio Grande to which we give a specious unity by calling them all "Latin American." To be sure, there are many ties and points of similarity among them, some of which will be noted below; but they also differ greatly from one another in other respects — such as language, area, population, and climate — and the obstacles to unity have increased in recent years, mainly because many of them have experienced a rise of rather exaggerated nationalism. Two conspicuous illustrations of this lack of unity have recently been given by Argentina and Brazil. For the past three years, Argentina has been following a policy toward the present war which is not only independent of, but contrary to, that of the rest of Latin America; and it is a matter of common knowledge that Brazil has been seeking to obtain for itself a position of pre-eminence over the rest of Latin America in the projected general international organization. These facts are well known, but they need to be emphasized here because of their pertinence to the question under consideration. They make it highly unlikely that the Latin American states will act as a bloc in dealing with the important international problems of the present or the visible future.

2. **Economic Colonialism.** Though in varying degrees, all the Latin American nations are economically colonial, and their dependence is mainly upon the United States, Great Britain, and (in "normal" times) Western Europe. Consequently, all of them (even those of the Pacific coast) are economically an integral part of the Atlantic world, but their position in it is one of inferiority. Their leaders not only admit these facts, but insist upon them and make them a basis of national policy — a policy designed to gain what they call economic independence for their respective nations. Since they believe that the two main causes of their economic colonialism are, first, that Latin American economies are based mainly upon the production of foodstuffs and raw materials for export, and, second, that a large part of the means of production and distribution in Latin America is owned by foreign investors, the two principal devices by which they seek to gain their independence are industrialization and the establishment of controls over (or the expropriation of) foreign holdings.

Between World Wars I and II, various Latin American governments pursued one or both of these objectives with considerable
vigor and some success. Since 1939, however, wartime conditions
have checked this movement, and in some respects Latin America
seems likely to emerge from the war in an even greater degree of
" colonial " dependence than before the war. The war has made it
difficult or impossible to obtain equipment for expanding — in some
cases even for maintaining — Latin American industry. At the same
time, it has put a high premium on the production of raw materials,
thus stimulating this " colonial " type of economic activity. It has
also led to a general (and, in some countries, an extremely steep) rise
in prices.

In these and other ways, the war has created complex and difficult
problems of postwar readjustment which the Latin American governments will not be able to solve without foreign aid. For example,
although several of them have accumulated large dollar and sterling
balances, these will not be adequate to their postwar needs, and extensive foreign credits will be required. In such a situation, the governments will be less free than formerly to extend controls over foreign investments. It is this prospect that has led most of them to
favor strongly the establishment of an international fund of the kind
proposed at Bretton Woods, since they hope that this would enable
them to obtain the desired financial assistance without exposing
themselves to the dangers of imperialism inherent in loans obtained
on a national basis. Whether this hope is well grounded remains to
be seen.

From present indications, they are more likely to have to depend
upon bilateral relations with one or more of the greater states. Some
of them — notably Argentina — may swing back to their former
position in the British orbit. Others such as Chile and Mexico, hope
that the increasing interest that the Soviet Union has recently been
displaying in Latin America will yield them new and important
economic benefits. Yet it is difficult to believe that any country except the United States has the combination of political interest and
economic strength necessary to provide Latin America at large with
the continuing economic assistance it will need in the long period
of postwar readjustment that lies ahead. Consequently, many Latin
Americans (among them the Mexican Foreign Minister, Ezequiel

Padilla) have urged the establishment of an at least partially closed regional system supported by the United States and including what may be called a " hemispheric " protective tariff system — not permanently, but at least for a long transitional period. This is an issue that is likely to be pushed more strongly as the tapering off of wartime purchases in Latin America intensifies the already serious economic difficulties facing that area.

3. **Military Weakness.** Although there are great inequalities among the Latin American states in point of both actual military power and war potential, when compared with the Great Powers they all fall into the same category in this respect. This has always been true throughout their history and is likely to continue to be true for a long time to come. It is true even of Brazil, which has recently become the leading military power in Latin America, partly through its own efforts and partly because it has received more than half of all the Lend-Lease aid given by the United States to Latin America. Brazil is the only Latin American country that has sent an expeditionary force to any of the battle-fronts — although at last reports this force (which was in Italy) consisted of only two divisions. This is not said with any intention of reflecting on the war effort of Brazil or Latin America at large, for most of our Southern neighbors have contributed to this effort loyally and effectively. The purpose is merely to emphasize the fact that a great discrepancy in military strength still exists between the Great Powers of the world and all the nations of Latin America. This discrepancy has been increasing throughout the past half-century as a result of the growing mechanization of warfare and the failure of Latin America to keep pace with the Great Powers in the development of the industries that produce modern machines. When the veil of military secrecy is lifted at the end of this war, it will probably be seen that, in comparison with the Great Powers, Latin America is weaker than it has ever been before.

Recent developments in plans for postwar organization have given a new significance to the inferiority of the Latin American nations in this respect. Their weakness has always made them vulnerable to aggression. If present plans are carried out, it will also limit their participation, in common with that of all other small states, in the most important body in the new international organization, the Security Council. Most Latin Americans recognize, however, that this differentiation between large and small powers is necessary and reasonable; and while it gives them a certain community of interest with the other nations of the small-power category in other parts of the world, this interest is not likely to become strong enough to draw them away from their regional association with the United States.

III

The special political and military relationship of the Latin American states to the United States is so important a factor in shaping their international relations at large that it calls for more extended discussion. It is difficult to give a precise and authoritative definition of this relationship, which is an intricate web composed of both the older bilateral relations as well as the newer multilateral relations, and which has found formal expression chiefly in hemispheric pronouncements that conceal as much as they reveal of the realities of the situation. Even if a satisfactory definition could be found, it would probably be less useful for the present purpose than a description of the principal functional elements in the relationship. In the chronological order of their appearance, these are: (1) the Monroe Doctrine, (2) the inter-American system, and (3) the increasing preponderance of power of the United States in the Western Hemisphere. Limitations of space require extreme brevity in pointing out the significance of each of these elements in relation to the subject of this paper.

The significance of the Monroe Doctrine has long been a subject of controversy, and in recent years the problem has been further complicated as a result of the so-called Pan Americanization, or continentalization, of the Doctrine. Ever and anon since 1936 we have been assured that some new inter-American instrument has Pan Americanized or supplanted the Monroe Doctrine; the statement was made again very recently in connection with the Declaration of Chapultepec adopted by the Inter-American Conference at Mexico City. This may be so in a technical sense and yet if we look at the realities of the situation, we may come to a different conclusion. Official Washington has done little to clarify the problem. It has not made any definitive pronouncement on the subject in recent years, though it has fostered the belief that the Doctrine has in fact been Pan Americanized, in the sense that the objectives of the Doctrine are now pursued through cooperative inter-American action and not, as formerly, through unilateral action by the United States. Nevertheless, though the Doctrine is never paraded in public these days, the sound view seems to be that the Pan Americanized version has not superseded the unilateral Doctrine, but has merely been superimposed upon it.

In this connection, two observations are pertinent. The first is that (as explained more fully below in connection with the inter-American system) inter-American policy and action are determined largely by the United States, particularly in the more important cases, such as those involving hemisphere defense, so that as regards decisions leading to action, the distinction between the original Doctrine and the Pan Americanized version of it is largely verbal. The second observation is that unilateral action by any of the American states (including the United States) for the main purpose of the Doctrine, the defense of the Western Hemisphere against external aggression, was specifically authorized by one of the inter-American instruments adopted by the Meeting of American Foreign Ministers at Havana in 1940. It should also be noted that the unilateral Doctrine has never been explicitly abrogated or disavowed by our government. It has been changed only in that the excrescences which had grown up on it before 1930 have been lopped off and that the other American nations have obligated themselves to join in supporting its main objective.

At any rate, whether or not one wishes to use the term " Monroe Doctrine," the essential features of the system contemplated by it still exist. The United States still determines whether or not the hemisphere is to be defended; it can still take unilateral action to this end; and it still bears the main burden of the defense. The chief difference is that it is far better able to bear this burden now than ever before. This situation is well understood by the Latin American nations, and they know that it affords them a greater degree of protection against external aggression, and at lower cost to themselves, than is enjoyed by any other group of small powers in the world.

This consideration, together with their need of the economic aid and cooperation of the United States in the postwar period, explains why most of them wish to maintain, and even strengthen, their regional relationship to the United States in the postwar period — a relationship to which in many other respects they are indifferent if not antagonistic.

How this situation will be affected by the establishment of the general international organization remains to be seen. Present indications are that no substantial change will be made. To be sure, we have no reason to expect that the League Covenant's oracular pronouncement respecting the Monroe Doctrine as a " regional understanding " will be repeated in the charter of the new organization. On the other hand, any material interference with the decisive role that the United States actually plays in this respect seems unlikely, in view of the fact that this country will be a senior partner in both of the international organizations (the general organization and the inter-American system) that will have jurisdiction over American security questions under the new dispensation. In one respect — the protection of the American republics from aggression by one of their own number — the security functions of the United States in this hemisphere may actually be augmented as a result of the agreement on this subject entered into by the Chapultepec Conference; but this is a question that never lay within the scope of the Monroe Doctrine.

IV

The inter-American system is a much more important factor in Latin American affairs today than it was a decade or more ago, largely because it has been considerably strengthened in recent years and has begun to assume the character of a genuine regional system. In 1943 and 1944, it suffered from internal dissension over a number of questions (especially the Argentine problem) and from neglect by the United States, whose attention seemed to be largely absorbed by the war and by negotiations with the other Great Powers. In the closing months of 1944, however, our government addressed itself to the urgent inter-American problem with a zeal and vigor that indicated a determination to make up for lost time. The results to date appear to have been very satisfactory, especially as regards the Chapultepec Conference (the first consultative meeting of the American republics since January, 1942).

As already noted, that Conference adopted a number of highly important measures designed to strengthen the inter-American system within the framework of the general international organization. It also placed the thorny Argentine problem in the way of settlement (though this was obviously done under pressure from a number of the Latin American republics that sympathized with Argentina, and at the cost of a retreat from the high ground taken by most of the American governments only a few months earlier). The Conference gave a general endorsement to the projected general international organization. In this connection, however, a rift appeared between the United States and the Latin American republics. The latter insisted upon drawing up several amendments to the Dumbarton Oaks proposals for presentation at the San Francisco Conference, with a view to improving the position of the small powers, placing the reign of international law on a firmer footing, increasing the autonomy of the inter-American system in regard to inter-American disputes, and for other purposes. The United States opposed any inter-American action of this kind and refused to sponsor the amendments at San Francisco, although all of them were supported by a majority of the Latin American delegations, and some unanimously.

It should be noted, however, that this question, which was not strictly an inter-American one, was the only important question for which the Conference failed to find a generally acceptable solution. There was also wide disagreement on the Argentine problem in the early stages of the Conference, but it was finally overcome by a formula. On the whole, the meeting was a distinct success. It appears not only to have arrested the serious deterioration in inter-American relations that had been going on since the summer of 1943, but also to have opened a new phase of development which promised to be the most important in the history of the system.

From the point of view of the Latin American states, the inter-American system as it has so far functioned has had one great advantage and one serious, though less weighty, disadvantage. On the one hand, this system has regularized, and has enabled them to

ts**:

derive extensive benefits from, the special relationship to the United States in which geography has placed them, and in which they would stand even if there were no inter-American system. It has made it easier for them to obtain the aid and cooperation of the United States in economic, technical, and other matters of considerable moment to themselves; to induce the United States to accept their views on important political questions (for example, to accept the principle of absolute nonintervention, adopted at the Buenos Aires Conference of 1936); and to give a measure of reciprocity to the military protection that they receive from the United States — a change which has probably increased their security and has certainly pleased their national pride.

On the other hand, the system has had the disadvantage of limiting the freedom of action of the Latin American states by bringing them closer into the orbit of the United States. To be sure, the latter has for a number of years shown scrupulous respect for the basic inter-American principle of juridical equality within the proper sphere of that principle, which is legal. But in the realm of policy the crucial inter-American decisions have usually (though not invariably) been made in Washington. Thus, when the United States followed a policy of rigorous neutrality and so-called " isolation " from 1935 to the fall of France, inter-American policy, too, was one of neutrality and what may equally well be called isolationism on a continental scale. When after the fall of France the United States shifted to nonbelligerency and intervention, inter-American neutrality became meaningless; and when the United States entered the war, inter-American policy was changed again and was thenceforth directed toward promoting the war effort. To give another example even more germane to the subject of this paper, so long as the United States was unwilling to have the problem of general international organization discussed on a regional American basis, no such discussion was held. When the United States gave the green light (as it did only after the Dumbarton Oaks meeting), the Inter-American Conference at Mexico City was promptly called and this subject, in its inter-American aspects, was made the first item on the agenda.

It is this sort of thing that has given rise to the long-standing

Latin American complaint that the Pan American Union lies in the shadow of the Washington Monument and is in effect a branch of the State Department. From present indications, there is little if any likelihood that this ground of complaint will be removed in the post-war period, whether by the establishment of the projected general international organization or otherwise. Indeed, at the present writing, the inter-American system seems likely to become more than ever before an instrument of United States policy. Without venturing into the field of conjecture, we may point out certain established facts which point in this direction: first, that the United States possesses a greater preponderance of military and economic power in the Western Hemisphere than ever before; and second, that the present plans for a general organization have established a pattern of Great-Power ascendancy which can hardly fail to affect the inter-American system, especially since this system is to be fitted into the framework of the general organization.

In the latter respect, the new organization differs materially from the League of Nations; for the latter had no organic relation to the inter-American system. The two were entirely separate and distinct entities, and while there was some cooperation between them, there was also a certain degree of rivalry. For these reasons, the League was attractive to many Latin Americans, who welcomed it as an alternative or counterpoise to the hemispheric system. The new plan contains no such feature: regional organizations and arrangements are encouraged, but they are to exist, not outside the world organization, but within its framework. Moreover, as small nations, the Latin American states will find the general organization less attractive than they found the League. As some of their writers have already pointed out, the ancillary social and economic organizations of the new order appear to be developing along lines that are more " democratic," and therefore more to the taste of the small states; but the central organization, with its dominant Great-Power pattern, seems to have no great charms for them.

These considerations increase the probability that in the postwar world most of the Latin American states will willingly associate themselves with the United States even more closely than before in a regional system which is apparently entering upon a new period of growth and of increasing activity for the promotion of the defense and general welfare of its members. If the crucial decisions leading to this development were not made in the Latin American capitals, and if the relationship bids fair to be one of continued and perhaps increasing tutelage, most of the nations of that area may nevertheless be expected to give greater weight to the juridical equality, the security, and the other advantages they derive from the inter-American system, and to cooperate in the new phase of its development now opening.

No. 55 [Two factors emerge as primary influences when we examine the place of Latin America in contemporary international politics. One is that the several governments urgently need technical help and financial assistance in order to cope with the many varied and complex social and economic problems that have delayed the arrival of a working and a workable democratic political society. The second is the primacy of the United States in the entire region: the influence which it can wield for political progress, the *status quo,* or a backward step.

In the past we have evidenced impatience, irritation, annoyance, and even open opposition to political events and changes in the countries to the south of us. At times our policy toward the Latin American republics has not furthered the development of political democracy; in other instances it has aroused deep suspicion and even animosity.

The international events of the past decade have given to the United States a new leadership in America and in the world. Acting through inter-American and international organizations, we have a new power — and a new opportunity — to shape the political organizations of other nations. If this opportunity is accepted and exercised with care, patience, and understanding, it will enable us to further the cause of democracy in America. If, on the other hand, in taking this opportunity we fail to consider the basic conditioning factors of life and society in Latin America, our potential as a political and moral leader is accordingly diminished or dispersed. The author of the final article in this book believes that history has afforded us " a clean field for a positive policy based on good will and an inspired purpose."]

On a Certain Impatience with Latin America*

by "Y"

" Democracy even under a tyranny continued to advance."
— Edith Hamilton, " The Greek Way "

PUBLIC opinion in the United States has shown a sporadic impatience at the failure of many Latin American republics to achieve a greater degree of political democracy. The persistence of dictatorships in our midst throughout a war fought for democracy was a moral embarrassment. The establishment of new dictatorships after victory has seemed to some like a rejection of what we fought to achieve. While we were still fighting we put the best face on the business, just as we did with respect to our Soviet ally. The war over, opinion in this country has sometimes tended to react in the manner of a stern father in the privacy of his home after his children have publicly embarrassed him.

But is the relationship of the United States to the Latin American nations in fact paternal? Or is it fraternal? The distinction is fundamental to the question of what the United States ought to do about the state of democracy in Latin America.

The traditional political orientation of the twenty-one American republics is democratic. For Americans south as well as north, the ideal state is a free association of individuals who exercise their freedom under laws of their own making, enforced by officers of their own choice. This ideal gives a common direction to the political development for which all Americans strive; north and south, all are agreed on where they want to go.

The position of the United States within this community is distinct in several important respects, however. We had already achieved, by the time of our independence in 1776, a political sophistication that the others are, for the most part, still on their way to achieving. The fact is that we gained our national independence

* " Y," "On a Certain Impatience with Latin America," *Foreign Affairs* (July, 1950), Vol. 28, No. 4, pp. 565–580. Reprinted by permission of *Foreign Affairs*.

from the mother country because we had come of age and were ready for it. The other Americans gained theirs because the mother country was struck down. When, in the first quarter of the nineteenth century, the Spanish empire fell apart under the impact of Napoleon, most of its American members were able to shake themselves free, along with Brazil and Haiti. But they were quite unready to assume the responsibility of self-government. The result was a sordid chaos out of which Latin America has still not finally emerged.

The political independence of the Latin American republics survived under the protection of British seapower, which supported our Monroe Doctrine, although that independence was at one time threatened by the British themselves in the River Plate and, at another, temporarily subverted by the Hapsburg dynasty in Mexico. But colonialism continued of necessity in the economic affairs of Latin America. Foreign interests teamed up with the governing élite to maintain the old design for exploitation of raw materials from the primitive American countries in the markets of the developed countries overseas. Foreigners built and managed the public services and transportation systems of the Latin American republics, controlled their agricultural and industrial enterprises, and in return reaped profits that were largely spent abroad. Economically, there was less difference between India and South America than there was politically, and it is not certain that the political advantage was entirely on the side of the South Americans.

Like colonial dependencies the world around in the nineteenth century, however, the Latin American countries were getting ready for democratic self-government. The situation today cannot be accurately appraised unless it is seen in perspective. Over the past century and a half, to take a generous span, there has been a steady, marked improvement in the economic and social welfare of the Latin American peoples, and a growth in responsible political behavior. Chaos and tyranny have been on the wane. Nowhere today will you find government exercised as blindly and as brutally as it was by the Emperor Christophe in Haiti. Nowhere will you find chaos such as confronted John L. Stephens when he arrived in Guatemala City on a diplomatic mission from President Van Buren and had to search for a government to which he could present his credentials. The political picture today, moreover, compares favorably with the picture only twenty years ago, when Machado ruled in Cuba, Gómez in Venezuela, Ibañez in Chile, and Leguía in Peru. It does not compare unfavorably with the picture a dozen years ago, when Vargas was dictator in Brazil, Ubico in Guatemala, Martínez in El Salvador, Carías in Honduras, Benavides in Peru, Busch in Bolivia, and Terra in Uruguay.

Moreover, the masses are today acquiring a political consciousness of which they showed few signs or none a generation ago. Labor is organizing, and labor organizations are moving in the direction of responsible maturity. The proof of this popular emancipation is in the increasing degree to which political leaders present themselves as men of the people and make their appeal, whether demagogic or not, to popular sentiment. Even Generalissimo Trujillo, " benefactor " of the Dominican people and master of their destinies, advertises himself in every village of his land as the friend of the laboring man. There can be little doubt that there has been and continues to be a steady growth over the decades in individual freedom and respect for human rights. Not only are dictatorships fewer than they used to be, the outcry against those that do exist is greater. Honest elections are more common than they were. In the alternation that so many countries experience between elective and arbitrary governments, the periods of the former appear to be growing longer, those of the latter shorter.

The historical path of progress is upward by ups and downs, perhaps in obedience to something like the Hegelian principle of action, reaction, and synthesis. Latin America's progress toward greater democracy has suffered repeated setbacks that have not, however, affected the underlying trend. One such setback occurred at the end of the 1920's and in the early 1930's, but was followed by the steady, continuing gravitation toward the ideal of democracy. A lesser setback appeared to be occurring in the late 1940's, but its manifestations were relatively isolated. The reactionary *coups* that took place in 1948 and 1949 in Peru, Venezuela, and Panama, and the degeneration of the political situation in Colombia, gave rise to a wave of editorial alarm and pessimism in the United States (and throughout the hemisphere), where to some it seemed that all the gains of democracy were being wiped out by a landslide of reaction. But at the same time that democracy was suffering a setback in these four of the twenty-one republics, Costa Rica was returning to constitutional democratic government after a chaotic civil conflict, Honduras was enjoying the relatively liberal administration of an elected president after years of dictatorship, and Bolivia had a degree of democracy, shaky as it was, that observers a few years before thought could not possibly be realized in a country afflicted with such dire economic and social problems. Toward the end of 1949, Venezuela was restoring some constitutional guarantees and Peru was preparing for an election.

The relapses in individual countries during the late 1940's, it should be noted, were not unrelated to world economic conditions, any more than those of twenty years earlier had been unrelated to the economic collapse of those times. Nevertheless, they gave occasion to the critics who think all is lost whenever they see evidence that all is not won.

II

Implicit in what has been said above is the view that democracy is achieved by evolution rather than revolution. Those whose prime animus is against dictatorships have propagated a common delusion that democracy is the absence of dictators. They have thoughtlessly given dictatorship the positive and democracy the negative position; and on that basis they have assumed that democracy could be attained by the revolutionary overthrow of dictators. That, in a schoolboy's misconception of our history, is the meaning of 1776. The crusading spirit finds it easier to be against the infidel than for the faith.

Democracy is not an absolute condition, to be assumed by a people as one puts on an overcoat. It is political maturity. Like all maturity, it is various in its degrees and manifestations, and it is produced by the slow process of maturation. You cannot impose it by force, you cannot acquire it by decree or legislative enactment, you cannot produce it out of a hat by exhortation. It must be cultivated lovingly, tirelessly over the generations. It must be cultivated with perseverance and the stamina that comes from an assured faith in the possibilities of human nature. It must be built up, as Woodrow Wilson said, " by slow habit."

Democratic government is the outward and visible sign of this inward and spiritual grace. The overthrow of dictators, as we have so often seen, may result only in the chaos that leads to renewed dictatorship. By getting rid of its dictator a nation gains nothing but the opportunity which it may not be prepared to exploit. Self-government has an inward as well as an outward sense, and the inward comes first. The enjoyment of freedom, among peoples as well as individuals, demands an acquired capacity for responsible behavior. This capacity is the mark of maturity, which in mortal men is the final product of slow growth from helpless and irresponsible infancy.

Maturity is not guaranteed by lapse of time. In this imperfect world not all individuals and not all peoples, however long they live, achieve it. The opportunity is denied the majority. It is denied them by poverty and the sordid necessities of their circumstances; it is denied them by the lack of means for education; it is denied them by the want of inspiring leadership; it is denied them by the absence of a tradition based on such leadership and nourished by it. Consequently, the realistic approach to the promotion of democracy, regarded as something positive, must endeavor to provide the opportunity and the inspiration for growth. That done, it is still necessary to maintain patience with the slowness of the process.

The obstacles to the growth of democracy in Latin America, specifically, have been and continue to be: (1) poverty, which limits the enjoyment of political freedom by imposing its own kind of bondage; (2) illiteracy, which goes with poverty and perpetuates it; (3) social insecurity, which makes for desperation and focuses men's attention on more practical immediate objectives than those of political democracy; and (4) a tradition of political behavior marked by intemperance, intransigence, flamboyance, and the worship of strong men.

A detailed discussion of the economic and social problems of the other American republics is outside the scope of this article. The political behavior, however, calls for special comment. Go into some Latin American countries where free speech is allowed, and, if an election campaign is in progress, note the campaign language painted

on the walls of the towns: *Viva Rodriguez! Que muere Gonzales!*
(Long live Rodriguez! Death to Gonzales!). The Gonzalistas, in
turn, announce that when they get into power they will hang the
Rodriguistas. Imagine an election campaign conducted in the United
States or England in such terms! Imagine placards crying " Death to
Dewey! " and " We are going to hang Truman! " These terms of
life-and-death provoke desperate measures and countermeasures in
election campaigns, to the subversion of democratic scruples. The
important point here, however, is that this is not the behavior of
mature men and women. It resembles, rather, the conduct of schoolboy gangs. Carried far enough, in the name of freedom, it leads to
chaos and the suppression of freedom.

Worship of the " man on horseback " (through self-identification)
is another manifestation of immaturity. It is characteristic of ado-
lescence, this admiration for the ruthless hero who tramples down
all opposition, makes himself superior to law, and is irresistible to
passionate women who serve his pleasure in droves.

The twenty-one American republics vary widely in the degree of
their development as in most other characteristics. Each has its own
politics, its own aspects of democracy, its own failings. It is a popular misconception that you can divide them, as they stand today,
between those that are immaculate democracies and those that are
black dictatorships. All of them are shades of gray. Two of them,
the United States and Uruguay, are among the few outstanding democracies of the world; but a part of the colored population of the
former is effectively disenfranchised. The nearest approaches to a
truly stifling dictatorship are to be found in the Dominican Republic
and Nicaragua, where the governments have a personal rather than
an ideological base and the ideals of democracy are accorded lip-
service. (It is never wise to underestimate the significance of lip-
service.) All the American peoples enjoy areas of freedom more or
less wide in their political lives; all of them are subject to restrictions
more or less great. Some have ostensible freedom severely qualified
in practice by the prevalence of governmental corruption: individuals must pay for the privileges of citizenship or can buy exemptions
from rule. Other peoples are in effect denied the power to choose
their governments but are ruled with a light hand (like those of our

District of Columbia). Under such circumstances, no clear line can be drawn, for purposes of policy, between the sheep and the goats.

The special position of the United States, however, still holds. It is the oldest and the most mature as well as the most powerful of the twenty-one republics. Few would deny that this imposes a special responsibility upon it. The differences of opinion concern the nature of the responsibility and how it should be discharged.

III

The question whether the backward countries of Latin America were to be regarded as responsible adults or as irresponsible children was first answered by us in the early years of the twentieth century. With the construction of the Panama Canal we felt that we could no longer tolerate disorder and the lack of responsible government when such conditions invited and seemed to justify European intervention in an area that had become vital to our security. We therefore took it upon ourselves to exercise a paternalistic police power in the Caribbean. Theodore Roosevelt's " corollary " to the Monroe Doctrine told the Europeans, in effect, that we would be responsible for keeping order among the children in our own yard. The assumption, which was not without validity at the time, was that these republics had not reached the stage of development at which they could be responsible for their actions. Consequently, when chaos threatened our interests and those of other mature nations, we did not scruple to land armed forces and establish military governments of our own in the Dominican Republic, Haiti, and Nicaragua.

There are several reasons why public opinion in the United States today tends to be more impatient than it used to be with Latin American failures in democracy. One primary reason is that today we have formally accepted the other American republics as adults and our equals in dignity. We measure them, accordingly, by a new and more rigorous standard of political behavior.

The turning point in our attitude came between 1928 and 1936, with our abandonment of intervention and our adoption of the Good Neighbor policy. It may in fact be said that at the Montevideo and Buenos Aires Conferences of 1933 and 1936 we joined with the Latin Americans in formally declaring them to be of age. The evolution that reached this conclusion was more in themselves than in us. They had arrived at the stage, with respect to us, that we had arrived at with respect to England in the 1770's. Unlike the England of George III, however, we had sense enough to join them in their declaration of independence, which we had resisted at Havana in 1928. More than that, having taken the new direction from them, we proceeded to put ourselves in the lead. It was an act of statesmanship such as has rarely been displayed by any world power. The era of good feeling that followed was its reward.

We should remind ourselves constantly of this, because our initiative in proclaiming the Good Neighbor policy was an expression of our best and truest instinct, upon which our country was founded and by which it has grown great. In the Philippines yesterday and in Puerto Rico today we see the salutary working of that same instinct. It teaches a lesson that the British learned partly from us in our revolt, and that has enabled them to transmute their old empire into the present Commonwealth of Nations. The two traditional associations of states that exist today, different as they are in certain fundamentals, exist simply by virtue of such self-denial. If Athens had exercised it in the fifth century B.C. she need not have fallen at the height of her glory before the Peloponnesian coalition.

The acceptance of equal status is the essence of our Good Neighbor policy, which is not, as some think, a policy of philanthropic largesse. It is, in the words of Franklin D. Roosevelt's original proclamation, the policy of " the neighbor who resolutely respects himself and, because he does so, respects the rights of others." These words in themselves have no sanctity. They do not even have a precise meaning. They were not limited in their application to the inter-American community, although that was where, in 1933, they were bound to have their chief significance. They are quoted here simply because they presuppose a world of adults in which all have equal rights. They might have been rhetoric; but the good faith with which they were spoken was demonstrated when, in the subsequent inter-American conferences, we joined the other American republics in accepting the juridical equality of all, and, consequently, abjuring intervention in the affairs of any.

In international affairs, as elsewhere, matters which are in fact the product of a slow and continuing evolution are often formalized at a particular instant. The difference between twenty and twenty-one years of age is not as great as our laws make it seem. The United States formally proclaimed its independence in 1776, but whether we could make it good by establishing ourselves firmly as a nation remained a question for almost three generations. Is it any wonder that the ability of all the Latin American republics to make good their claim to adult equality should still be questioned today, so short a time after they have, so to speak, turned twenty-one?

The maturity of nations is generally less than the maturity of men, in the sense that the most mature nation will be childish in its behavior by comparison with the most mature man. As the very existence of national governments indicates the incapacity of men for perfect self-government, so the immaturity and irresponsibility of nations warns of the dangers of international anarchy. In the absence of any other international regulation, this universal immaturity virtually requires the development of a system in which the strong nation lords it over the weak. At a time when we considered that at least some of the other American republics were excessively immature and irresponsible, we did not scruple ourselves to exercise certain powers of government over them. With the advent of the Good Neighbor policy we abandoned the use of such powers on the theory that all the members of our community were of age and had achieved a capacity for responsible conduct that allowed us to risk the anarchy which, in default of any superior authority, must reign among sovereign equals. That was the situation in the latter 1930's, when the rising menace of fascist imperialism overseas promoted an exceptional measure of self-discipline in the relations among the American republics, and thus contributed to the justification of our risk.

The implications of such a situation as confronted us in 1933 may be brought out by a comparison. Relations among the American republics at the beginning of the century were like the political relations among the pioneers on our Western frontier a century ago. On the frontier there was, as yet, no organized community, with police and judiciary, to protect the rights of the individual. Consequently, everyone carried arms and undertook, himself, to make good his own rights. If he was injured he did not call in the police but set out on his own to obtain retribution. In actual practice, however, the definition and the procurement of justice became privileges of the strong, who indulged in "intervention" against those whose weakness compelled them to submit. The development of effective community organization doomed such interventionism. The community as a whole, through administrative instruments created for the purpose, gave protection to the rights of each member alike, and it could not tolerate the usurpation of its functions by individuals. The practice of government by the strong succumbed, accordingly, to the principle of equality under law.

The United States in the 1930's seems to have been unusually forehanded in renouncing intervention and accepting the principle of equality under the law before there was any provision for law-enforcement by the community. This was certainly an act of faith on its part. It is no coincidence, however, that at Buenos Aires in 1936 the same inter-American conference that adopted the treaty commitment on nonintervention also adopted the principle of formal consultation among the American republics for the purpose of dealing by concerted action with situations of common concern. This was followed, in successive inter-American conferences, by the creation of the necessary instruments. The establishment of the Consultative Meetings of Foreign Ministers at Lima in 1938 was the first step in that direction. Today we have, in the Treaty of Reciprocal Assistance which was signed at Rio de Janeiro in 1947, a provision for action by the community as a whole to meet any armed attack against any of its members, whether from outside or inside the community. Thus our inter-American community has now assumed active responsibility for protecting the rights of its member states, and if such situations as jeopardized the order of the Caribbean at the turn of the century should recur, the United States would now have no right to deal with them on its own. It would have to look to the community for regulatory action.

The official inter-American system, now formalized in the Organization of American States and other agencies, has undertaken, like the United Nations, to define the rights of individuals as well as the rights of states. However, while it has made some provision for community enforcement of the latter rights, it has thus far confined itself to proclaiming human rights. Thus a government that is restricted by the community in its foreign undertakings is secure from community sanctions in the treatment it accords its own people, for this is a domestic matter in which an unqualified sovereignty is still the rule. The community has formulated applicable standards but has not provided for enforcing them. We in the United States may appreciate the difficulty of making any such provision when we consider the reluctance with which we ourselves would, for example, view the interposition of the American republics for the enfranchisement of the citizens of the District of Columbia.

This jealous protection of sovereign freedom in the domestic field is illustrated by the disposition that the American republics have shown in recent years to join together in withholding official recognition from a revolutionary government as long as there is a reasonable and unresolved suspicion that it has had the assistance of another state in its advent to power. This represents, not a qualification of sovereignty in the country concerned, but its protection. No American state can today be brought before any official tribunal on grounds of not practicing democracy at home.

IV

The development of a wise foreign policy can take place only in terms of the historical perspective. The historical view shows us a group of twenty-one separate nations striving for democratic self-realization, and also working for the development of a community to regulate their affairs. One may reasonably speculate on the possibility of a day when the international community is capable of guaranteeing the democratic rights of the individual within each nation. More than that, a constructive foreign policy might well promote the evolution of basic conditions which would increase this possibility. Under any circumstances, it will continue to be a question how far international community can make itself effective in any particular case or at any particular time. Our own attitude toward our own sovereignty must necessarily enter into a determination of our position on such a question.

The fact is that today the Organization of American States, like the United Nations, is unable to do more than formulate standards and develop general resolutions for the guidance of such governments as are willing to heed them. It can promote democracy through the expression of moral purpose — by focusing international opinion in general terms. This is important and provides an opportunity for United States leadership, but most of us would feel it frustrating if our policy had to rely on this exclusively for the promotion of democracy in the hemisphere.

A more direct and immediate opportunity arises from the fact that the American republics, as nations or peoples if not as governments, are striving to rise above their submerged pasts into the daylight of democracy. If the ideal and the will to realize it were lacking, it is hard to see what the United States could do. It would find itself in the position of a gardener who waters a dead shoot. Our actual position, however, is that of seeking to help a vital and growing process.

We recognize that extreme economic and social misery, and inadequate education, are obstacles to the growth of democracy. All the American republics are committed by their policies to reduce these obstacles. They are committed as well, by their policies and by acts of inter-American conferences, to cooperate for this purpose. The capacity of the United States to contribute to the achievement of this community goal is so much greater than that of any other country that the concept of cooperation often becomes a matter more of spirit than of substance: it is as if John D. Rockefeller and the average reader of this article had pooled their wealth. The concept is, however, essential in a community of juridically equal and self-respecting states. It is invaluable not only for moral but for practical reasons; in no other context could the assistance of the United States be effective.

Active cooperation for economic development is, then, one of the prime policies by which the United States exercises leadership and makes its practical contribution to the growth of democracy. In response to requests from the other American republics, based on their own plans and their own efforts, our government finances development projects and furnishes technical knowledge and skills for their realization. This is the policy behind our Export-Import Bank and the International Bank for Reconstruction and Development, in which we are the principal stockholder. It is the policy behind our Institute of Inter-American Affairs, a government agency under the Secretary of State which, since 1942, has been cooperating with government agencies in the other American republics to develop their agriculture, their public health, and their basic education. It is, finally, the policy expressed by President Truman in Point Four of his Inaugural Address last year, the policy of promoting economic development by disseminating techniques and stimulating the productive investment of capital.

In a large sense, however, our increasingly varied and comprehensive activities in the field of economic development represent the most direct practical expression of the moral leadership that our position and our policy require of us. This is brought out by looking at the context of our technical and financial cooperation.

Those who come bearing such gifts must, first of all, be trusted. When our government sends an agricultural technician to a foreign country, the effectiveness of his mission depends on his being accepted at face value. If it were thought that he was a secret agent of the United States, if it were thought that his real purpose was to spy or to develop markets for the United States by inhibiting competing production, his advice would be distrusted and his assistance rejected. If he used his position to meddle in local politics, he would lose his usefulness. The policy of technical assistance, therefore, can be successful only where the moral credit of the United States prevails. That is why our State Department has opposed all proposals that we make our assistance contingent on the granting of special concessions, or acquiescence in demands that we may be pressing in other connections. The accepted purity of our motives is more important, in the long run, than any particular advantages that might be gained by compromising them.

The agricultural technician, if his mission is a success, justifies himself by more than his technical contribution. He is in himself a living sales-demonstration of our democracy: its honesty, its high purpose, its competence, and its energy. In backward countries where people have grown cynical under the oppression of venal and futile officials, his example and his accomplishment recreate hope and reinforce the democratic ideal. The moral influence that we can achieve in this way is a priceless asset in the conduct of our diplomacy and the promotion of our democracy. It is based on a very simple cornerstone of our foreign policy. We must be trusted. To be trusted we must be trustworthy.

When it comes to moral leadership, our example is necessarily more important than our precept. The fact that in this country we hold orderly elections, accept their results, and change our administrations without force has an incalculable influence throughout Latin America. Our forbearance in not using our power to gain imperialistic ends gives us a moral authority that represents a welcome alternative to the rule of force. Courage and coolness in the face of difficulties, self-discipline, our efficiency, our ability to solve problems and get things done are persuasive arguments in favor of our way of life. They keep the ideal alive among peoples who might otherwise give themselves up in despair to totalitarian rule.

The danger of precept is self-righteousness, which assumes that the ideal is already sufficiently exemplified in the preceptor. It will do us no harm to recognize that this is a national weakness in ourselves which makes us intolerant of the shortcomings of other nations, even when we share them. This is the typical expression of the xenophobia that is widespread in this country, as it is in others. It is found in the belief that other countries think only of their own selfish interests, while we simply look out for our rights. It is found in the indignation at political corruption abroad that assumes the absence of anything comparable at home. It is found in our impatience with discriminatory trade and employment practices in other countries and indifference to discriminatory legislation at home.

This moral danger is directly relevant to the problem of our Latin American policy; it is the basis of the paternalistic school. Almost invariably, national self-righteousness is dominant in the breasts of the interventionists or quasi-interventionists who advocate forcing the Latin Americans to live up to our concept of political democracy. It is outspoken among those who would have us turn our backs on the other American republics because they are unworthy of us.

Given the good example, given the perception that the example will not support self-righteousness, given the tolerance that must follow from such a perception, moral leadership still requires the inspiration of the word. Abraham Lincoln and Franklin D. Roosevelt gave this inspiration. Their leadership was exercised, not in the attempt to reform others and not in moral denunciation of others, but in the eloquent definition of a common ideal for the strengthening of a common purpose. Such leadership expresses itself as what " we " (nations or peoples) must do, not as what " you " must do. That is one reason why Lincoln was a greater moral leader than Carrie Nation.

It is easy to say that our policy is that of giving moral leadership. The translation of that policy into action depends on intangibles. It depends on the maintenance of our own inspiration and the clarity of our purpose. We must cultivate these things in ourselves, and to the extent that we have them we must speak of them. It is on this sort of thing, as well as on technical assistance, that our contribution to the continued growth of Latin American democracy depends. Democracy will tend to be strong there as it is robust, positive, and vivid here.

V

The other American republics are younger and less mature than the United States. Their historic drive is in the direction of the orderly practice of political democracy. They have made progress since the days when Bolívar, on his deathbed, is reported to have said that America was ungovernable. They govern themselves today more or less badly, more or less well. The ferment of new ideas — ideas of economic and social democracy, ideas emanating from the United States among other sources — contributes to their instability, as it also does to their progress. The achievement of greater maturity depends on their experience in exercising, for themselves, the responsibility of adult nations. There is no evidence that our assumption of such responsibility on behalf of Haiti, the Dominican Republic, and Nicaragua brought them nearer maturity.

The United States should, therefore, encourage the Latin American states to participate responsibly in the councils of the world. We should, as occasion allows, take them into our confidence and seek their advice as equals. We should cultivate close working relations with their statesmen in dealing with world affairs. Nothing is so conducive to the achievement of adult stature as to be treated like an adult, nothing so stultifying to development as to be treated like a child. Nations are the same as individuals in this. The man who writes a letter to the newspaper advocating a national policy of one kind or another would expend more forethought on his proposal if he knew it might be adopted simply because he made it. The fact that what he says is not likely to exert a determining influence leaves him free to indulge in irresponsibility. History shows that when we have asked the advice of Latin Americans and shown a disposition to be guided by it, they have behaved in more statesmanlike fashion than when we have undertaken to tell them what they must do for their own good. We can best promote responsible attitudes and actions among the other American republics by encouraging them to partake of responsibility.

We must continue to cooperate with the other American republics as friends for the common objectives of improving human life and securing human freedom in the hemisphere, and not for motives that would discredit our cooperation. The very fact that these nations are, in so many respects, younger than we, and much weaker, should persuade us to maintain an attitude of *noblesse oblige*. We North Americans, by our nature, feel better when we are conducting ourselves in a broad and generous way than when our behavior in the world is mean, quarrelsome, and niggardly. That is our natural instinct. But we have a mortal fear of being " suckers " that impels us constantly to throttle our instinct. In the case of the other American republics we can afford by virtue of our preponderant strength to fulfill our capacity for greatness.

Latin America, free of iron curtains, dedicated to the attainment of democracy, striving for human betterment, offers us a clean field for a positive policy based on good will and an inspired purpose. Such a policy must be for democracy rather than merely against dictators; it must be cooperative rather than self-righteous and denunciatory; it must be candid rather than conspiratorial; and it must seek its own realization by developing the moral credit that supports it. In no other way shall we contribute to realizing the kind of democratic hemisphere that all of us, paternalists and fraternalists alike, seek to achieve.

Biographical Summary

(Numbers in parentheses refer to articles in the book.)

ALEXANDER, ROBERT J. (36,37). Born, 1918. Undergraduate and graduate work in economics at Columbia University. With the Office of Inter-American Affairs, 1945–46. On the faculty of the Department of Economics, Rutgers University. Author of several articles on Latin American labor problems.

EDITORIAL STAFF: *Américas* (51). *Américas* is a monthly magazine published in English, Spanish, and Portuguese by the Pan American Union.

ARCINIEGAS, GERMÁN (19). Born, 1900. Colombian writer, government official, and educator. Graduate of the Faculty of Law, University of Bogotá. Visiting professor at Columbia University, the University of Chicago, and the University of California. Member of the Colombian diplomatic corps, 1931–33; member of Colombian Congress, 1933–34. Twice Minister of Education. Director of the newspaper *El Tiempo* of Bogotá. Author of *The Knight of El Dorado* and editor of *Green Continent.*

ARNADE, COLONEL KURT C. (21). Former member of the German General Staff who left Germany because of his opposition to the Nazis. Military Adviser to Chiang Kai-Shek, 1935. Later Military Adviser to the Bolivian government and professor of Military History and Tactics at the Bolivian *Escuela Militar* (West Point).

BELAÚNDE, VÍCTOR ANDRÉS (6). Born, 1883. Peruvian professor, diplomat, lawyer, and writer. Graduate of the Universities of Arequipa and Lima. Member of Peruvian diplomatic corps for many years. Founder and director of the review *Mercurio Peruano.* Has been visiting professor at Columbia University and the University of Virginia. Author of many novels and historical works, among them *Bolívar and the Political Thought of the Spanish American Revolutions.*

BELAÚNDE-TERRY, FERNANDO (49). Born, 1912. Peruvian architect. Graduate of the University of Texas. Practiced architecture in Mexico, 1935–36, and in Lima since 1937. Former member of Peruvian Congress. Founder and director of *El Arquitecto Peruano*. Professor of Architecture at the Universities of Lima and San Marcos.

CARVALLO, SERGIO (42). Educated in Chile and at the University of Buenos Aires. Practiced law in Chile and also contributed to newspapers and periodicals. Has published articles on Chilean industrialization problems. Now a staff member of the Cooperatives Section of the Pan American Union.

CHAPMAN, CHARLES E. (5). Born, 1880; died, 1941. Graduate of Tufts College; Ph.D. at the University of California. Professor of Latin American History at the University of California until his death. Was a member of several Latin American academic and learned societies. Author of *A History of Spain* and *Republican Hispanic America — A History*.

CHRISTENSEN, ASHER N. (3,4,30,32,35). Born, 1903. Graduate of University of Minnesota; graduate work at the University of Chicago and the University of Madrid. Cultural Attaché, United States Embassy, Buenos Aires, 1942–45. Visiting professor or lecturer at universities in Argentina, Venezuela, Paraguay, Honduras, and Guatemala. Professor of Political Science, University of Minnesota.

COMPTON, GEORGE C. (10). Roosevelt Fellow to Chile, 1942–43. Translator for Bogotá Inter-American Conference, 1948. Now editorial staff member of *Américas*.

CRANE, JACOB (48). Born, 1892. Graduate of the University of Michigan, College of Engineering. Municipal engineer and city planner. Assistant Administrator, United States Housing Authority, 1938–40. Housing consultant to the governments of Great Britain and Panama, and to the United Nations.

CRAWFORD, W. REX (7). Born, 1898. B.A. and Ph.D. at the University of Pennsylvania. Exchange professor in Chile, 1941. Cultural Relations Attaché, United States Embassy, Rio de Janeiro, 1942–45. Professor of Sociology and Director of Inter-American Activities, University of Pennsylvania. Author of *A Century of Latin American Thought*.

CURRIE, LAUCHLIN (41). Born, 1902. Graduate of London School of Economics and Politics; Ph.D. at Harvard. Professor of International Economics, Fletcher Graduate School of Law and Diplomacy. Administrative Assistant to President Roosevelt, 1939–45. Sent on several special diplomatic missions. Consultant to the International Bank for Reconstruction and Development. Now financial adviser to the Colombian Government.

DAVIS, KINGSLEY (9,16). Born, 1908. Graduate of the University of Texas; Ph.D. at Harvard. Now professor in the Department of Economic and Social Institutions, Princeton University. Author of several studies on class structure, social organization, and population problems.

DOZER, DONALD M. (20). Born, 1905. Graduate of Wooster College; Ph.D. at Harvard. One time professor at Boston University and the University of Maryland. Foreign trade analyst, Foreign Economic Administration, 1944. Acting Chief, Division of Research for American Republics, State Department, since 1947. Author of several articles on Latin American affairs.

EBENSTEIN, WILLIAM (33). Born, 1910. Doctor of Laws, University of Vienna. Professor of Political Science, Princeton University. Spent 1940–42 in Mexico on research project dealing with Mexican political parties. Contributor to *Journal of Politics; Public Administration Review; Encyclopædia Britannica.*

EFRON, DAVID (13,14). Born, 1904. Educated in Argentina; Ph.D. at the University of Buenos Aires and at Columbia University, N.Y.C. Fellowship to the Sorbonne and the Friedrich Wilhelm University at Berlin, 1929–31. Member of the faculty of Sarah Lawrence College. Executive Secretary and Research Director of the Council for Pan American Democracy.

FITZGIBBON, RUSSELL H. (15,18,27,29,34). Born, 1902. Graduate of Hanover College; Ph.D. at the University of Wisconsin. With the Office of the Coordinator of Inter-American Affairs, 1944–45. Professor of Political Science, University of California, Los Angeles. Author of *Cuba and the United States; The Constitutions of the Americas;* and many articles dealing with Latin American government.

GAMIO, MANUEL (8). Born, 1883. Mexican anthropologist. Ph.D. at
Columbia University. Delegate to many inter-American and international scientific congresses. Has lectured in several universities in the United States. Director of the Department of Demography, Ministry of Interior, Mexico. Author of many books and
articles on Mexican population problems and immigration.

GOMEZ, ROSENDO A. (26). Born, 1916. Graduate of the University of
Vermont; Ph.D. at the University of Minnesota. Now on the
faculty of the University of Arizona.

HARING, C. H. (23). Born, 1885. B.A. and Ph.D. at Harvard. Professor of Latin American History at Harvard since 1923. Delegate or adviser to many inter-American conferences. Member
of several Latin American academic societies. Author of *South
America Looks at the United States; Argentina and the United
States; The Spanish Empire in America.*

HUMPHREYS, ROBIN A. (22). Born, 1907. Undergraduate work at
Cambridge University; graduate work at the University of
Michigan. Now professor of Latin American History, Univer-
sity of London. Author of *The Evolution of Modern Latin
America.*

JORDAN, HENRY P. (43). Born, 1897. Ph.D. at the University of Berlin.
German diplomatic service (during Weimar republic) in Latin
America. Visiting professor, University of Puerto Rico, 1943.
Professor of Political Science, New York University. Author of
the section on " Latin American Government " of *Foreign Gov-
ernments,* edited by F. M. Marx.

LLERAS, ALBERTO (52). Born, 1906. Undergraduate work at universities in Colombia; LL.D. at the University of California. Journalist; Representative and Senator, Colombian Congress; President
of Colombia, 1945–46. Now Director General, The Pan American Union.

MARTIN, PERCY ALVIN (24). Born, 1879; died, 1942. Graduate of Stan-
ford University; Ph.D. at Harvard. Professor of Latin American
History at Stanford, 1923 until his death. Member of many Latin
American learned societies. Author of *The Republics of Latin
America* (with H. G. James); *Simon Bolivar, The Liberator*
(with J. F. Rippy and I. J. Cox); and *Argentina, Brazil, and
Chile.*

MAUCK, WILLFRED (45). Born, 1891. Graduate studies at Columbia University, London School of Economics, University of Geneva. Adviser on Student Exchange, Coordinator of Inter-American Affairs, 1942–43. Acting President, Institute of Inter-American Affairs.

MECHAM, J. LLOYD (11,25). Born, 1893. B.A. and Ph.D. at the University of California. Visiting professor, University of Mexico, 1943–44. Member of several Latin American academic societies. Author of many studies of Latin American government and *Church and State in Latin America*.

MOSK, SANFORD A. (12). Born, 1904. B.S. and Ph.D. at the University of California. Member of the faculty of Department of Economics, University of California.

MURKLAND, HARRY B. (1). Born, 1902. Newspaper and periodical work with the *Newark News* and *The Christian Advocate*. Assistant to the editor of *Foreign Affairs*. With the office of Coordinator of Inter-American Affairs, 1943–44. Pan American editor of *Newsweek* since 1944.

NESS, NORMAN T. (13,14). Born, 1903. Undergraduate work at Carleton College; Ph.D. at Harvard. Director, Office of Financial and Development Policy, State Department, 1946–48. Adviser, Inter-American Conference on Problems of War and Peace, Mexico City, 1945. Now a business executive.

PÉREZ, ALVARO (46). Colombian journalist; free-lance writer for *El Tiempo* of Bogotá. Student at Columbia University School of Journalism. Three years on Latin American desk of Associated Press. Now Public Information Officer, Pan American Sanitary Bureau.

PIERCE, CLARENCE (53). Graduate of New York School of Social Work, Columbia University. Chief, Pan American Union Section of Labor, Social Security, and Migration. Now working on development of technical assistance program of the Organization of American States.

SANCHEZ, GEORGE I. (44). Born, 1906. Ed.D. at the University of California. Technical Advisor, Venezuelan Ministry of Education, 1937–38. Director of *Instituto Pedagógico Nacional* at Caracas. Professor of Latin American Education, University of Texas. Author of *Mexico — A Revolution by Education*.

SCHURZ, WILLIAM L. (2). Historian, journalist, State Department officer. Has been economic adviser to Latin American governments. Author of *Latin America*. Now President, The American Institute for Foreign Trade.

SHELLABY, ROBERT K. (39). Journalist. Latin American editor of the *Christian Science Monitor*. Has traveled widely in Latin America and as a newspaper correspondent has reported many inter-American conferences.

SOULE, GEORGE (13,14). Born, 1887. A.B. at Yale. Journalist and writer, formerly editor of *The New Republic*. Author of *A Planned Society; An Economic Constitution for Democracy*.

STOKES, WILLIAM S. (31). Born, 1906. A.B. and Ph.D at the University of California, Los Angeles. Professor of Political Science, University of Wisconsin. Research work in Honduras, contributor to *Foro Hondureño; American Political Science Review; Encyclopaedia America*. Author of *Honduras*.

TANNENBAUM, FRANK (28). Born, 1893. Ph.D. at the Brookings Institution. Newspaper correspondent in Mexico, 1922–24. Professor of History, Columbia University. Visiting professor at São Paulo and Lima. Author of *The Mexican Agrarian Revolution; Whither Latin America*, and many articles on the government and politics of Latin America.

THOMSON, CHARLES A. (38). Born, 1893. Graduate work at the University of Mexico and the University of Chicago. Research Specialist in Latin American Affairs, Foreign Policy Association. Chief, Division of Cultural Relations, State Department, 1940–44. Adviser, Office of International Education and Cultural Affairs. Delegate to UNESCO. Author of *La Revolución Social Mexicana*.

TAVARES DE SÁ, HERNANE (50). Staff member, Pan American Union. Contributor to *Holiday; Life; Saturday Evening Post; Saturday Review of Literature*. Author of *The Brazilians — People of Tomorrow*.

WEYL, NATHANIEL (47). Has been associated with the Federal Reserve Board, Board of Economic Warfare, and other government agencies as a Latin American Consultant. Author (with wife) of *The Reconquest of Mexico*.

WHITAKER, ARTHUR P. (17,54). Born, 1895. B.A. at the University of Tennessee; Ph.D. at Harvard. Rhodes Scholar. Professor of Latin American History, University of Pennsylvania, since 1936. Visiting professor in Peru and Colombia. Head, Latin American Unit, Department of State, 1943–45. Author of *The United States and the Independence of Latin America; The United States and South America: The Northern Republics,* and many articles on Latin American history.

WYTHE, GEORGE (40). Born, 1893. B.A. at the University of Texas; Ph.D. at George Washington University. Spent fifteen years in U.S. Foreign Commercial Service. Chief, American Republics Division, Office of International Trade, U.S. Department of Commerce. Author of *Industry in Latin America; Outline of Latin American Economic Development.*

" Y " (55). Anonymous contributor to *Foreign Affairs.*